Black's New Testament Commentaries

General Editor: Morna D. Hooker

COLOSSIANS

BLACK'S NEW TESTAMENT COMMENTARIES

THE GOSPEL ACCORDING TO ST. MATTHEW
Floyd V. Filson

THE GOSPEL ACCORDING TO ST. MARK
Morna D. Hooker

THE GOSPEL ACCORDING TO ST. LUKE
A.R.C. Leaney

THE GOSPEL ACCORDING TO ST. JOHN
Andrew Lincoln

THE ACTS OF THE APOSTLES
C.S.C. Williams

THE EPISTLE TO THE ROMANS
C.K. Barrett

THE FIRST EPISTLE TO THE CORINTHIANS
C.K. Barrett

THE SECOND EPISTLE TO THE CORINTHIANS
C.K. Barrett

THE EPISTLE TO THE PHILIPPANS
Markus Bockmuehl

THE FIRST AND SECOND EPISTLES TO THE THESSALONIANS
Ernest Best

THE PASTORAL EPISTLES
J.N.D. Kelly

THE EPISTLE TO THE HEBREWS
H.W. Montefiore

THE EPISTLES OF PETER AND OF JUDE
J.N.D. Kelly

THE REVELATION OF ST. JOHN THE DIVINE
Ian Boxall

COMPANION VOL. I
THE BIRTH OF THE NEW TESTAMENT
C.F.D. Moule

COLOSSIANS

Paul Foster

Bloomsbury T&T Clark
An imprint of Bloomsbury Publishing Plc

B L O O M S B U R Y
LONDON · OXFORD · NEW YORK · NEW DELHI · SYDNEY

Bloomsbury T&T Clark

An imprint of Bloomsbury Publishing Plc

Imprint previously known as T&T Clark

50 Bedford Square	1385 Broadway
London	New York
WC1B 3DP	NY 10018
UK	USA

www.bloomsbury.com

BLOOMSBURY, T&T CLARK and the Diana logo are trademarks of Bloomsbury Publishing Plc

First published 2016

© Paul Foster, 2016

Paul Foster has asserted his right under the Copyright, Designs and Patents Act, 1988, to be identified as Author of this work.

British Library Cataloguing-in-Publication Data
A catalogue record for this book is available from the British Library.

ISBN:	HB:	978-1-62356-712-5
	PB:	978-1-62356-579-4
	ePUB:	978-0-56766-966-7
	ePDF:	978-0-56766-965-0

Library of Congress Cataloging-in-Publication Data
A catalogue record for this book is available from the British Library.

Typeset by Forthcoming Publications (www.forthpub.com)
Printed and bound in India

CONTENTS

ABBREVIATIONS

AB	Anchor Bible
ABD	D. N. Freedman (ed.), *The Anchor Bible Dictionary*, 6 vols. (New York: Doubleday, 1992)
ABR	*Australian Biblical Review*
ABRL	Anchor Bible Reference Library
ACCS	Ancient Christian Commentary on Scripture
AF	M. W. Holmes (ed.), *The Apostolic Fathers: Greek Texts and English Translations*, 3rd ed. (Grand Rapids, MI: Baker, 2007)
AnBib	Analecta biblica
ANRW	*Aufstieg und Niedergang der römischen Welt.*
ANTC	Abingdon New Testament Commentaries
ASNU	Acta seminarii neotestamentici upsaliensis
AUSS	*Andrews University Seminary Studies*
BDAG	F. W. Danker (ed.), *A Greek Lexicon of the New Testament and Other Early Christian Literature*, 3rd ed. (Chicago: Chicago University Press, 2000)
BDF	F. Blass and A. Debrunner (eds), *A Greek Grammar of the New Testament and Other Early Christian Literature*, trans. R. W. Funk (Cambridge: Cambridge University Press; Chicago: Chicago University Press, 1961)
BHGNT	Baylor Handbook on the Greek New Testament
Bib	*Biblica*
BNTC	Black's New Testament Commentaries
BR	*Biblical Research*
BSac	*Bibliotheca sacra*
BZ	*Biblische Zeitschrift*
BZNW	Beihefte zur Zeitschrift für die neutestamentliche Wissenschaft
CBQ	*Catholic Bible Quarterly*
CNT	Commentaire du Nouveau Testament
CTJ	*Calvin Theological Journal*
CTM	*Concordia Theological Monthly*
CurTM	*Currents in Theology and Mission*
EA	*Epigraphica Anatolica*
ÉB	Études bibliques

EDNT	H. Balz and G. Schneider (eds), *Exegetical Dictionary of the New Testament*, 3 vols. (Grand Rapids, MI: Eerdmans, 1990–93)
EKKNT	Evangelisch-katholischer Kommentar zum Neuen Testament
ESV	English Standard Version
ETL	*Ephemerides theologicae lovanienses*
EvQ	*Evangelical Quarterly*
EvT	*Evangelische Theologie*
ExpTim	*Expository Times*
EzNT	Erläuterungen zum Neuen Testament
FB	Forschung zur Bibel
FRLANT	Forschungen zur Religion und Literatur des Alten und Neuen Testaments
FTS	*Freiburger Theologische Studien*
GNB	Good News Bible
GNS	Good New Studies
HKNT	Handkommentar zum Neuen Testament
HNT	Handbuch zum Neuen Testament
HTKNT	Herders theologischer Kommentar zum Neuen Testament
IBC	Interpretation: A Bible Commentary for Teaching and Preaching
ICC	International Critical Commentary
Int	*Interpretation*
IVPNTC	The IVP New Testament Commentary Series
JBL	*Journal of Biblical Literature*
JETS	*Journal of the Evangelical Theological Society*
JHS	*Journal of Hellenic Studies*
JRGS	*Journal of the Royal Geographical Society of London*
LSJ	H. G. Liddell and R. Scott (eds), *A Greek–English Lexicon*, rev. H. S. Jones, 9th ed. with new supplement (Oxford: Clarendon, 1996)
JSNT	*Journal for the Study of the New Testament*
JSNTSup	Journal for the Study of the New Testament: Supplement Series
JPTh	*Jahrbuch for protestantische Theologie*
JSPL	*Journal for the Study of Paul and His Letters*
JTS	*Journal of Theological Studies*
JTSA	*Journal of Theology for Southern Africa*
KEK	Kritisch-exegetischer Kommentar über das Neue Testament (Meyer-Kommentar)
KJV	King James Version
KNT	Kommentar zyn Neuen Testament

LASBF	*Liber annuus, Studium biblicum franciscanum*
LD	Lectio divina
LNTS	Library of New Testament Studies
LTQ	*Lexington Theological Quarterly*
MAMA	Monumenta Asiae Minoris Antiqua
MNTC	Moffatt New Testament Commentary
NA²⁸	*Nestle–Aland: Novum Testamentum Graece*, 28th ed., edited by the Institut für Neutestamentliche Textforschung, under the direction of Holger Strutwolf (Stuttgart: Deutsche Bibelgesellschaft, 2012)
NAB^(1/2)	New American Bible (1st and 2nd ed.)
NAC	New American Commentary
NAV	New American Version
NCB	New Clarendon Bible
NCBC	New Century Bible Commentary
NDIEC	S. R. Llewelyn and J. R. Harrison (eds), *New Documents Illustrating Early Christianity*, 10 vols. (Grand Rapids, MI: Eerdmans, 2012)
NEB	New English Bible
Neot	*Neotestamentica*
NET	New English Translation
NICNT	New International Commentary on the New Testament
NIGTC	New International Greek Testament Commentary
NIV	New International Version
NIVAC	NIV Application Commentary
NLT	New Living Translation
NovT	*Novum Testamentum*
NovTSup	Novum Testamentum Supplements
NRSV	New Revised Standard Version
NTD	Das Neue Testament Deutsch
NTL	New Testament Library
NTOA	Novum Testamentum et Orbis Antiquus
NTS	*New Testament Studies*
NTTSD	New Testament Tools, Studies, and Documents
ÖTK	Ökumenischer Taschenbuch-Kommentar
PAST	Pauline Studies
PNTC	Pelican New Testament Commentaries
Rahlfs	A. Rahlfs (ed.), *Septuaginta*, Duo volumina in uno (Stuttgart: Deutsche Bibelgesellschaft, 1979 [1935])
RB	*Revue biblique*
REB	Revised English Bible
RevExp	*Review and Expositor*

RevQ	*Revue de Qumran*
RevScRel	*Revue des sciences religieuses*
RHPR	*Revue d'histoire et de philosophie religieuses*
RNT	Regensburger Neues Testament
RRef	*La revue réformée*
RSV	Revised Standard Version
RTR	*Reformed Theological Review*
SBLMS	Society of Biblical Literature Monograph Series
SEÅ	*Svensk exegetisk årsbok*
SNT	Studien zum Neuen Testament
SNTSMS	Society for New Testament Studies Monograph Series
SNTSU	*Studien zum Neuen Testament und seiner Umwelt*
ST	*Studia theologica*
SUNT	Studien zur Umwelt des Neuen Testaments
SVTQ	*St. Vladimir's Theological Quarterly*
TCGNT	B. M. Metzger, *A Textual Commentary on the Greek New Testament*, 2nd ed. (Stuttgart: Deutsche Bibelgesellschaft; New York: United Bible Societies, 1998 [1994])
TENT	Texts and Editions for New Testament Study
THKNT	Theologischer Handkommentar zum Neuen Testament
TNTC	Tyndale New Testament Commentaries
TU	Texte und Untersuchungen
TWNT	G. Kittel and G. Friedrich (eds), *Theological Dictionary of the New Testament*, 10 vols. (Grand Rapids, MI: Eerdmans, 1964–74)
TynBul	*Tyndale Bulletin*
TZ	*Theologische Zeitschrift*
UNT	Untersuchungen zum Neuen Testament
VE	*Vox evangelica*
WBC	Word Biblical Commentary
WD	*Wort and Dienst*
WMANT	Wissenschaftliche Monographien zum Alten und Neuen Testament
WTJ	*Westminster Theological Journal*
WUNT	Wissenschaftliche Untersuchungen zum Neuen Testament
ZBK	Zürcher Bibelkommentare
ZNW	*Zeitschrift für die neutestamentliche Wissenschaft und die Kunde der älteren Kirche*
ZTK	*Zeitschrift für Theologie und Kirche*

PREFACE

Colossians is small, but beautifully formed. Its theological richness is disproportionate to its size. While the lyrical Christological themes expressed in the poetic section of Col. 1:15–20 are well known, the theological perspectives the letter presents are far more wide ranging. For those interested in the development of the early Jesus movement, especially in its Pauline ambit, Colossians offers significant insights. The epistle provides evidence for the spread of the Pauline mission into areas the apostle had not personally visited, it reveals the use or co-opting of trusty lieutenants who propagated Paul's understanding of the gospel in the inland area of Phrygia, and it attests the existence of a circle of Pauline associates actively engaged in the spread of the Christian message. Theologically, the letter presents a highly Christocentric vision for the community's beliefs, commitments, and shared practices. Phrases such as 'in Christ', 'in him', or 'in whom', ring out like a refrain throughout the letter. This understanding that believers now find the totality of their existence in union with Christ not only shapes a theoretical understanding of their new mode of existence as those who have 'put on the new self' (Col. 3:10), but being 'in Christ' is seen as transforming their ethical behaviour, and renewing the way in which the Colossians are to conceptualize social relationships especially in the household setting.

These rich and evocative theological perspectives, which are inextricably linked to the ethical vision for believers enjoying a new mode of existence in union with Christ, provide much of the enduring value of this letter for Christian thought and life in the subsequent generations. This absolute recognition of the fulness of life in Christ also results in an exclusivist view in regard to the value of any other religious rites or practices. Therefore, the theological vision espoused in the letter can brook no rivals. Improving upon or supplementing the quality of life in Christ is an impossibility from the author's viewpoint. In fact, it is worse than that – it debases the new mode of existence in which believers now partake. It is for that reason that any other form of teaching or philosophy is described as 'vain deceit according to the traditions of men' (Col. 2:8), and moreover it explains why the author reacts so stridently against any person, actual or potential, who casts aspersions on the spirituality enjoyed through the new life in Christ by those attempting to require further religious disciplines. Such teachers are accused of abusing the Colossians (Col. 2:18) through enticing them to acts of self-centred or self-delighting worship (Col. 2:23). Furthermore, the letter sees those who adopt such supplementary practices as surrendering the completeness of the transformed lives they have received in Christ. This tension is probably reflective of the common cultural outlook, which adopted a syncretistic approach to various religious cults in the Eastern Mediterranean world. According to Colossians, this is not possible for those who 'have been raised with Christ' (Col. 3:1).

Therefore, in Colossians, one finds a multifaceted reflection on what life in Christ means for believers in terms of their religious practices, their ethical behaviours, and their social interactions. This presentation of a vision of the impact of being in Christ for praxis, ethics, and societal relations is a complex undertaking. That this is attempted with such depth of thought and sophistication of theological reflection in so short a compass attests to the acuteness of the mind behind this letter. While it remains the constant task of Christian thinkers to tease out the interplay between theology, anthropology, ethics, praxis, and civil society, the author of Colossians has presented an enduring model of how that vital and vibrant theological work might be undertaken in every generation while remaining fully committed to life in Christ.

The act of writing a commentary on a biblical text is a privilege, it requires both time and dedication, and it demands a humble acknowledgement of the indebtedness to previous commentators. There are a number of contested issues in relation to Colossians. Where I have differed with the views of fellow commentators, that has been done with respect; where I have agreed with them, I am conscious of the debt I owe them. In all cases I have learnt much, been guided well, and admired their scholarship. I hope my contribution will be adjudged worthy to be counted among that great cloud of witnesses. Debts of various sorts are accrued when writing a major scholarly work. First, I would like to thank my colleagues in the School of Divinity, at the University Edinburgh. Their encouragement has been unfailing. Secondly, I would like to thank various classes of students who have taken the exegetical courses I have offered on Colossians. Thirdly, I would like to thank staff at the Vose Seminary in Perth, Australia, who permitted me to use their library freely in July and August 2013, during which period much progress was made on completing the commentary section of this book.

My hope is that readers will find the discussion of Colossians offered here balanced and yet also providing some new ideas and perspectives not found in existing commentaries. Above all, I hope it stimulates closer study of the letter itself, and spurs others to write about and reflect upon this rich theological jewel in the Pauline corpus of writings.

Paul Foster
All Saints' Day
1 November 2015

INTRODUCTION

1. *Colossae the City*

The site of Colossae is located in Asia Minor, modern Turkey, 106 miles (170 km) east of Ephesus (the major city in Asia Minor in the first century). In the Byzantine period the settlement in the area was known as Chonai (Chonae), and the small town is now known as Honaz (urban population in 2012 was 10,859). There has been some debate as to whether the settlements of Colossae and Chonai are successive names for the same urban site, or whether geographically these are closely proximate, but not identical sites (see below).

Colossae was located on the banks of the Lycus River, which is a significant tributary of the Maeander (now called the Büyük Menderes). The Maeander river-system facilitated trade and social interaction among the human communities located along its extent. This resulted in a broadly integrated society with similar social, political, and religious systems. Life in the area was typical of ancient inland areas in the Eastern Mediterranean world, with scattered urban centres of varying sizes and an extensive rural hinterland. Thonemann, in his study of Maeander valley during antiquity and the Byzantine period, represents the presence of the inhabitants in the following manner:

> The cities of Maeander valley possessed theatres, public buildings, magistrates and a water-supply, and were conquered from time to time by Hellenistic kings; the rural population cultivated wheat, vines and olives, and concealed as much of their livestock as they could from tax-assessors. (Thonemann 2011: xv)

The Maeander emptied into a large bay on the western coast of Asia Minor. In the Roman period three of the twelve traditional cities of the Ionian league stood on this bay, although by the Roman period Priene and Myus had already lost their harbours due to an accumulation of silt. In the first century Miletus was still active as a port city (cf. Acts 20:17–38), but it too lost its harbour due to silt build-up during the early Christian period.

The Lycus River joined the Maeander approximately 100 miles (60 km) west-north-west of the river mouth at Miletus, and continued to its source in a south-easterly direction. Ancient Colossae was approximately 20 miles (12.5 km) away from the confluence of the two rivers. The Lycus Valley was extremely fertile, due to the deposits of river sediment. This allowed for the wider region to be self-sufficient to a large degree due to agricultural production, and the surplus of food production was able to support the urban populations in the area. In the first half of the first century the Lycus Valley had three major urban population settlements, Hierapolis on the northern side of the Lycus River and Laodicea on the southern bank. These cities were 'a few miles [approx. 10 miles (6 km)] from the junction with the Meander, six miles apart from each other and within sight of each other across the intervening plain, and Colossae about ten miles upstream [from Laodicea] on the southern bank of the Lycus' (Dunn 1996: 20).

The location of Colossae has been much debated in the modern period, with eighteenth- and nineteenth-century cartographers locating the city in various places on their maps (Cadwallader and Trainor 2011: 9–47). One of the major confusions was equating the town of Honaz (known as Chonai during the Byzantine period) with Colossae. William Hamilton is typically credited with recognizing that Honaz and Colossae were not identical sites (Hamilton 1837). Although in reality William Ramsay presented the decisive case for viewing Colossae and modern Honaz as distinctive sites (Ramsay 1890: 134–35). The present site of modern Honaz is three kilometres south of the mound on which ancient Colossae was located. The latter was therefore closer to the Lycus river than the modern urban centre. While the tell, or mound, of the site of ancient Colossae has not been excavated, a number of archaeological remains and inscriptions have been discovered. The remains of two columns are still visible in a field adjacent to the mound, and there is evidence of an ancient Odeon (a building for musical or literary performances). The presence of these features 'suggest an *agora* or market place of considerable expanse where conceivably a number of civic buildings, temples and statuary could be found' (Canavan 2012: 15). Together with the remains of a large necropolis with multiple styles of graves, these archaeological features suggest an ancient urban centre of significant size. It appears that by the beginning of the ninth century CE the site of Colossae had been abandoned. The remaining inhabitants dispersed, probably with several relocating to Chonae, approximately three kilometres further south. The reason for this population movement is uncertain. Perhaps the settlement had shrunk to such a degree that Colossae became unsustainable as an urban centre, or perhaps the move further inland occurred to avoid flooding from the Lycus River.

During the first century, however, it appears, in comparison with the two other nearby urban settlements of Laodicea and Hierapolis, that Colossae was the smallest of the three. The first of these, Laodicea, was probably founded on the site of a previous settlement. Antiochus II renamed the city of Laodicea in honour of his wife Laodike, and a major building programme commenced around 261 BCE. By the first century CE Laodicea had become the largest urban centre in the Lycus Valley, with Strabo (c. 63 BCE–c. 23 CE) noting 'Laodiceia, though formerly small, grew large in our time and in that of our fathers' (Strabo, *Geog.* 12.8.16). In fact, the rise of Laodicea may have been a contributing factor to the relative decline of Colossae.

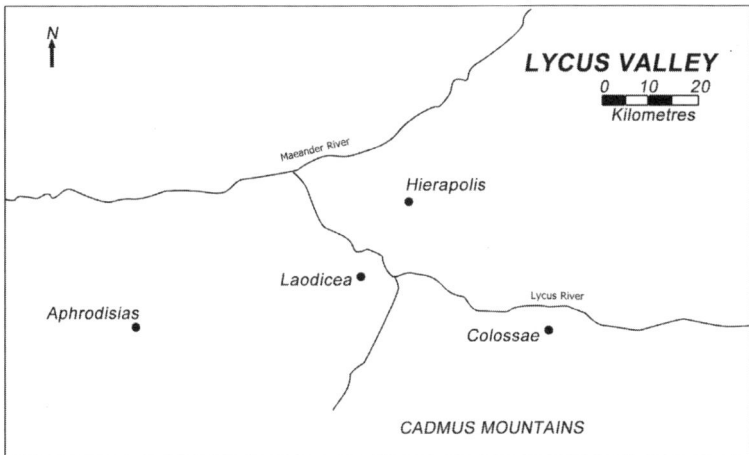

Map 1: The Lycus Valley

A major earthquake struck the Lycus Valley around 61–62 CE. On the basis of this event it has become standard in the literature to speak of the devastation of the city of Colossae, and to infer the almost immediate abandonment of the city as a population centre. This understanding of the destruction of the city has been a major factor in

3

seeking to determine the dating of the letter. Thus Dunn states, 'the likelihood that Colossae was seriously affected by the earthquake in 60–61 would point to a date [of composition] not long prior to the earthquake' (Dunn 1996: 39 n. 10). The commentators are unanimous in their assessment of the impact of the earthquake. Lightfoot, in a convoluted but careful discussion, states, 'a great catastrophe overtook the cities of the Lycus Valley', and offers his opinion that 'it is far from improbable that...the catastrophe was subsequent to the writing of these letters [both Colossians and Philemon]' (Lightfoot 1886: 38, 39, 40). Similarly, Abbott mentions 'the absence from Col. of any reference to the earthquake which visited the cities of the Lycus' and consequently infers that 'the Epistle was written from Rome around A.D. 63' (Abbott 1987: lix).

Tacitus is the earliest writer to mention an earthquake striking the Lycus Valley during the Neronian period. In his *Annals*, the event is dated to 60 CE, although later sources place the event three or four years later. Tacitus writes:

> Eodem anno ex inlustribus Asiae urbibus Laodicea tremor terrae prolapse, nullo a nobis remedio propriis opibus revaluit.

> In this year, Laodicea, one of the illustrious cities of Asia, was destroyed by an earthquake and rebuilt itself through its own resources, without help on our part. (Tacitus, *Ann.* 14.27.1)

The next surviving reference to this earthquake in the Lycus Valley is found in Eusebius' *Chronicon*, which although no longer extant at the relevant point in the Greek original survives in the Armenian translation, where it is stated that the three cities of Laodicea, Hierapolis, and Colossae were destroyed by earthquake. However, the event is dated to 63 CE. Jerome reproduces the same tradition in his Latin translation of Eusebius' work, but 'dates the earthquake in 64 CE, thus synchronizing it with the catastrophic fire that consumed Rome in the same year' (Huttner 2013: 101). This evidence suggests that there was a noteworthy and destructive earthquake in the region at some point between 60 and 64 CE. It is known that the population centres of Laodicea and Hierapolis continued after this date. However, the case for the abandonment of Colossae has recently been shown to be questionable.

Alan Cadwallader has published an inscription found on a 1.2 metre high white marble cylindrical bomos, which appears to have functioned as the base for a small statue or bust. The bomos came from a field close to the mound of Colossae, although it was removed from that site and was discovered on Mount Honaz. The inscription is damaged, but honours the person responsible for the repair of the baths in Colossae. It is dated to 'the latter part of the first century, possibly early second century' (Cadwallader 2012a: 111). The dating is based both on the pattern of the naming formula and the type of script. This monument in honour of the repairer of the baths lists the names of the donors and the cost of the bomos: 'on the bomos from their own resources 1050 denarii' (line 5). While the inscription is broken in several places, the meaning is clear. Principally it lists the names of the donors who set up this public monument. It commences in the following manner:

> For good fortune.
> For Korymbos the patriot …
> […]
> … for the repair of the baths … and for the water channel …
> … of the Colossian people … on the bomos from their own

The consequence of this inscription for the hypothesis that Colossae became an abandoned and uninhabited site after the earthquake of the 60s is obvious. Cadwallader notes that:

> There is an almost axiomatic status among New Testament commentators upon the Epistle to the Colossians on the demise or rapid decline of Colossae following the 61/2 CE earthquake that severely impacted the Lycus Valley. The authority derives from J.B. Lightfoot and W.M. Ramsay. This inscription suggests that the axiom must be revised … Comparison is usually made with Laodikeia, the nearest city to Colossae (18 km away). The Roman historian, Tacitus, noted that Laodikeia lifted itself from the ruinous effects of the earthquake (*Annals* 14.27). Because no mention is made of Colossae by Tacitus, it had been assumed that Colossae disappeared or virtually so. (Cadwallader 2012a: 112)

Fig. 1: The 1.2 metre high marble bomos, with inscription in honour of Korymbos, the repairer of the baths at Colossae. Thanks to Alan Cadwallader for permission to use this picture, which appeared in *Antichthon* 46 (2012b)

It is likely the case that Tacitus does not mention Colossae because it was a less significant urban centre than Laodicea (he does not mention Hierapolis either). The inscription reveals an active population in the late first century. Whether the restoration work to the baths and water channel was the repair of earthquake damage cannot be established with certainty, although the dating to the second half of the first century is suggestive. If that were the case, then the inscription reflects an urban population rebuilding some of the important civic infrastructure of the town. Hence it appears that Colossae continued as a settlement throughout the second half of the first century and beyond. This then opens up the possibility of the letter being written after the mid-60s, and more importantly it could still have been addressed to Colossian believers in that later period.

The inscription on the bomos also presents other important information of an ethnographic character. The names on the inscription are 'overwhelmingly Greek' (Cadwallader 2012a: 111). This suggests that Hellenistic identity was prized, and while the population may not have been Greek in origin their *polis* and social structures reflected Greek influence and perhaps aspirations to be viewed as a cultured society, as that would have been judged by Hellenistic norms. The presence of so many donors reflects a wealthy elite in the city. The named repairer of the baths and water channel, Korymbus, may have been more affluent, or perhaps more public-minded, than the named individuals on the bomos. Cadwallader suggests that the name Korymbos might 'bear theophoric associations with the cult of Dionysios (and its bunches of flowers and fruit – the *coyrmboi*)' (Cadwallader 2012a: 113). If this supposition is correct, this then provides further evidence for the synthesis between Greco-Roman religion and culture, in combination with adherence to local cultic practices.

Cadwallader has also published a second, less extensive inscription (Cadwallader 2007). This is also dated to the late first century, and is found on a pedestal of local limestone. It refers to the civic officer Markos, who held the position of chief interpreter and translator. The reference to a 'chief' translator suggests the presence of more than one person undertaking this work, which may reflect a sizable urban population. The inscription reads:

Μάρκωι Μάρκου Κολοσσηνῶν ἀρχερμηνεῖ καὶ ἐξηγητῇ

To Markos son of Markos, chief interpreter and translator for the Colossians

The need for multiple translators and interpreters in Colossae during the late first century, among whom Markos was chief, may attest to a linguistically diverse community, or to the fact that being located on a significant trade route the ability to communicate between different language groups was essential. The claim in the letter that for believers ethnic distinctions no longer held significance (Col. 3:11), might reflect the cultural diversity that is suggested by this inscription.

Therefore, Colossae continued as an urban centre throughout the first century and beyond. Two larger neighbours, Laodicea and Hierapolis, overshadowed Colossae in size and commercial importance. Colossae, however, remained a significant population centre, situated on the trade route along the Lycus River. It possessed a number of civic structures and institutions typically commensurate with urban population centres of the late antique period, such as a water channel and public baths, an agora, and an Odeon. The site requires excavation to establish a fuller knowledge of the buildings that might have existed in the town. However, like its larger neighbours, there appears to have been significant rebuilding after the earthquake in the mid-first century, and continued inhabitation after that.

2. *The Religious Environment of First-Century Colossae*

In common with most cities in the eastern Mediterranean during the first century, Colossae had a multitude of religious cults and practices. Such pluralism did not create rigidly drawn boundaries between religions. Those engaged in various cults often adopted a syncretistic attitude, as they engaged in the cultic worship of multiple deities and performed rites at a number of different shrines. In the eastern Empire urban settlements that were not specific Roman colonies (such as Philippi) frequently maintained their own systems of traditional religion. However, the innovation of veneration of the emperor, typically in the form of the worship of the semi-deified living Augustus, was often introduced alongside, and without replacement of, the traditional cults. The political stability of the Augustan age was much admired. There was also a widespread belief that power had coalesced in the person of the emperor. The desire to define and understand this imperial power resulted in it being regarded by contemporaries as 'the epiphany of a divine power in the hands of a mortal' (Scheid 2003: 165). At Colossae there was an imperial altar, and hence a cult venerating the emperor (Price 1984: xii, xxv). However, since the site has not been excavated it is not possible to give extensive details based on archaeological data concerning the imperial worship, or in regard to the presence of other temples or altars in Colossae.

2.1. *Local Cults and Imperial Worship*
Notwithstanding this, the similarity of socio-cultural structures in the urban communities throughout the Lycus and Maeander Valleys (and further afield) permits inferences to be drawn based on the surviving remains of ancient cults and information contained in texts and epigraphical sources. Maier has used the excavated and well-preserved city of Aphrodisias as a helpful comparison, the site of which is located approximately 25 miles west of Colossae (Maier 2013: 94–99). The city was named after Aphrodite, the Greek goddess of love, equated with the Roman goddess Venus. The statuary remains show that 'Aphrodite represents the cosmic force that integrates imperial power with the power of the local elites' (Edwards 1994: 711). This collocation of divine, imperial, and local power is apparent from the iconography from the site. The inscription on the Sebastion at Aprodisias states that the building was jointly dedicated 'to Aphrodite, the Divine Augusti and the People'. Moreover, given that the Julio-Claudian dynasty based its legitimacy on the claim of divine descent from Venus, the incorporation of the worship of the emperor within a shrine jointly dedicated to the equivalent Greek goddess continued the syncretistic practice of religion for the purpose of legitimizing the dynastic imperial line.

Fig. 2: The Sebasteion at Aphrodisias – combining veneration of Augustus and Aphrodite. Photo by William Neuheisel, https://www.flickr.com/photos/wneuheisel/7471669758/ (accessed 24 June 2014), and is free to use for private or commercial purposes: https://creativecommons.org/licenses/by/2.0/deed.en_GB

Religion in Phrygia, and more widely in western Asia Minor, prior to imperial influence, synthesized the veneration of the deities of the Greek pantheon with worship and participation in the traditional local mystery cults.

2.2. *Jews in Phrygia in Antiquity*

Was there a Jewish community in Colossae, or were there even individual Jews in the city at the time the epistle was written? Despite some highly confident assertions that the deviant teaching to which the author was responding was the result of Judaizing influences (see Dunn 1995; esp. Wright 1986: 23–33 ['Paul's polemic in Colossians makes sense as a warning against Judaism', p. 29]), the honest answer is that there is no conclusive evidence either for the presence or absence of Jews in Colossae during the mid- to late first century. One of the reasons for this is the lack of an archaeological excavation of the site. Based more on textual evidence for the wider area, Dunn asserts that,

> Colossae, and the other Lycus Valley cities, probably had substantial Jewish ethnic minorities. This implies the presence of (probably) several synagogues in Colossae, bearing in mind that just as almost all churches at this time were house churches (see on Col. 4:15), so many Jewish gatherings for prayer must have been in private houses. (Dunn 1996: 29).

This inferential argument lacks the solid support of any material evidence from Colossae. The text of the letter does, however, have a number of fleeting references to Jews (Col. 3:11), or to Jewish customs such as Sabbath observance (Col. 2:16). These two statements may be generalized comments, rather than specifically reflecting the socio-religious make-up of the Colossian community. Alongside these references to Jews or Sabbath practice, the author describes his addressees as 'formerly alienated and hostile in mind' (Col. 1:21). Moreover, he describes his ministry as that of making known God's 'mystery among the gentiles' (Col. 1:27), and he reminds his readers that they have been 'circumcised with a circumcision made without hands' (Col. 2:11). None of this proves the presence or absence of a Jewish community in Colossae, although it can be observed that in contrast to several of the other Pauline letters there is a relative lack of interest in Jewish matters in Colossians. Therefore, in order to attempt to answer the question of the presence of Jews in Colossae it is necessary to consider wider historical, archaeological, and inscriptional evidence from the surrounding region of the Lycus Valley, and more widely in Phrygia (see Map 2).

Perhaps the earliest possible reference to the presence of Jews in the wider region is to be found in the brief writing attributed to the prophet Obadiah. This contains a description of 'the exiles of Jerusalem who are in Sepharad' (Obad. 20). The city of Sepharad is the Hebrew name for the capital of Lydia, better known as Sardis. Around 620 BCE the Lydian empire expanded its frontier eastwards, and incorporated the western part of the Phrygian kingdom. The eastern area of Phrygia fell to the Assyrians. Around 540 BCE, the Persian Emperor Cyrus conquered Lydia, and with it the region of Phrygia. The specific date of Obadiah is contested, and is made more complicated by arguments concerning the composite nature of the text. However, it is typically dated to either the sixth or fifth century BCE. As such, the dislocation of Jewish exiles to Sardis is either the result of the Babylonian conquest of Jerusalem in 587 BCE, or part of the policy of Cyrus and his successors in the late sixth or early fifth century BCE.

Firmer evidence for the presence of Jews in Phrygia is found in the aftermath of the conquest of Alexander. With the division of the empire between his successors (οἱ Διάδοχοι, the *diadochoi*), the region of Phrygia oscillated between the control of various factions, but was most frequently under the rule of the Seleucids based in Syria. Under Seleucus I (312–281 BCE), Josephus states that Jews were granted full civic rights in the cities he founded (Josephus, *Ant.* 12.119). However, it is unclear what these civic rights might have entailed. Later, Antiochus II (261–246 BCE) is reported to have planted Jewish colonies on the western coast of Asia Minor, in the region of Ionia (Josephus, *Ant.* 12.125). The first secure reference to Jews in the region of Phrygia is to be dated to the period 212–205/4 BCE, during the reign of Antiochus III. As a result of his territorial gains to the east of his empire, he recaptured land that was part of Babylonia in the sixth century BCE. He translocated two thousand Jewish families then resident in Babylonia, and resettled then in the Anatolian regions of Phrygia and Lydia. Moreover, Josephus cites a piece of correspondence, generally assumed to be genuine in its major details (Williams 2013: 364), from Antiochus III to his satrap in Lydia that reflects the ruler's positive disposition towards Jews.

King Antiochus to Zeuxis his father, sending greeting.
If you are in health, it is well. I also am in health. Having been informed
that a sedition is arisen in Lydia and Phrygia, I thought that matter
required great care; and upon advising with my friends what was fit to
be done, it has been thought proper to remove two thousand families
of Jews, with their effects, out of Mesopotamia and Babylon, unto the
castles and places that lie most convenient; for I am persuaded that
they will be well-disposed guardians of our possessions, because of
their piety towards God, and because I know that my predecessors
have borne witness to them, that they are faithful, and with alacrity do
what they are desired to do. I desire, therefore, though it be a laborious
work, that you remove these Jews, under a promise, that they shall be
permitted to use their own laws. And when you shall have brought
them to the places forementioned, you shall give everyone of their
families a place for building their houses, and a portion of the land
for their husbandry, and for the plantation of their vines; and you shall
discharge them from paying taxes of the fruits of the earth for ten years;
and let them have a proper quantity of wheat for the maintenance of
their servants, until they receive breadcorn out of the earth; also let a
sufficient share be given to such as minister to them in the necessaries
of life, that by enjoying the effects of our humanity, they may show
themselves the more willing and ready about our affairs. Take care
likewise of that nation, as far as you are able, that they may not have
any disturbance given them by any one. (Josephus, *Ant.* 12.148–53)

No doubt there is, at least at some points, an ideological bias contained in this reported piece of correspondence (see Trebilco 1991:
5–6). However, the opening decision that two thousand families be
relocated to Lydia and Phrygia to strengthen the political grip of
Antiochus III on the region is typically understood as having a historical basis. Such acts of resettlement accord with a general policy
of establishing colonies to safeguard frontier zones and trade routes,
as well as being a means of suppressing rebellion. The authenticity of
the number of families mentioned cannot be independently verified,
but there is perhaps no need to doubt it as an approximately accurate
figure. On this basis Trebilco estimates that 'the total number of
people probably exceeded 10,000' (Trebilco 1991: 6). Nothing is
known beyond this concerning the distribution of such a significant
population throughout the sizeable area of Lydia and Phrygia.

Seleucid influence in Phrygia came to an end when the Attalid
dynasty, centred on the city of Pergamum under the leadership of
Eumenes II (197–158 BCE), allied with Rome. As a reward for their
part in the military campaigns against the Seleucids the Attalids

were given control of the former Seleucid territory in Asia Minor, including Phrygia. The Attalid dynasty came to an end in 133 BCE when the last ruler died without an heir, and the city of Pergamum and its territories came under Roman rule. Josephus records a decree from the people of Pergamum upholding Jewish rights, which was issued in support of the Roman Senate's ruling in favour of Hyrcanus (133–104 BCE). Upon receiving a letter from the Senate supporting Hyrcanus, the document from Pergamum states, 'we laid up the epistle in our public records; and made a decree ourselves, that since we also are in confederacy with the Romans, we would do everything we could for the Jews, according to the senate's decree' (Josephus, *Ant.* 14.253). Therefore, during the late second century it appears that the rights of the Jews in Asia Minor, including the region of Phrygia, which the Seleucids had established, were upheld.

The next piece of documentary evidence of note that relates to the Jewish inhabitants of Phrygia concerns Lucius Valerius Flaccus' confiscation of the Temple tax, collected from diaspora Jews in the region and sent to Jerusalem. Writing in the 60s BCE, Cicero confirms the existence of two sizeable Phrygian Jewish communities. The incident in question related to significant sums of gold coinage that had been collected in two cities of Phrygia, Laodicea and Apamea. The Roman governor of Asia, Flaccus, confiscated the money destined for the Temple on the basis that it contravened the laws concerning the export of gold.

> For I do not suppose that the religion of the Jews, our enemies, was any obstacle to that most illustrious general, but that he was hindered by his own modesty. Where then is the guilt? Since you nowhere impute any theft to us, since you approve of the edict, and confess that it was passed in due form, and did not deny that the gold was openly sought for and produced the facts of the case themselves show that the business was executed by the instrumentality of men of the highest character. There was a hundredweight of gold, more or less openly seized at Apamea, and weighed out in the forum at the feet of the praetor, by Sextus Caesius, a Roman knight, a most excellent and upright man; twenty pounds weight or a little more were seized at Laodicea, by Lucius Peducaeus, who is here in court, one of our judges; some was seized also at Adramyttium, by Cnaeus Domitius, the lieutenant, and a small quantity at Pergamum. The amount of the gold is known; the gold is in the treasury; no theft is imputed to him; but it is attempted to render him unpopular. (Cicero, *Pro Flacco*, 68–69)

On the basis of the levy being the annual half-shekel tax, and using the Pompeian standard of 36 aurei (gold denarii) to the gold pound, Bruce has estimated that 45,000 half-shekels (*didrachma*) were collected at Apamea and 9,000 at Laodicea. While the cities were collection centres, and hence this would not represent the number of Jewish males in the urban locations, this is seen as implying the presence of at least 54,000 Jewish males throughout the two regions (Bruce 1984a: 5–6). However, one must take three factors into account. First, the tendency to inflate figures; second, the reliability of the conversion rates used for translating the given weights to their shekel equivalents; and, third, the possibility that wealthy individuals may have made larger donations. While this creates the possibility of a significant margin of error, nevertheless there would have been a sizeable Jewish population in the two areas. The city of Apamea located in Phrygia, was a centre of Seleucid power, and it seems likely that many of the Jews who were resettled by Antiochus III made their home in the city. The city is mentioned in the Talmud (*Ber.* 62a; *Nid.* 30b), which attests to its importance as a centre for diaspora Judaism. The city is located approximately 55 miles (90 km) east-north-east of Colossae. Hence, the concentration of Jewish population and wealth at Apamea is unlikely to be representative of the whole region of Phrygia (Ramsay 1895–97: II, 667). For this reason the figures concerning Laodicea give a better sense of the demographic of the Jewish population in the region of the Lycus Valley.

Therefore, if, although unlikely, the figures were not subject to inflation, then the amount of gold collected at Laodicea would reflect at most a population of 9,000 Jewish males throughout an indeterminate region of Asia Minor. However, it is more likely that the correct population estimate should be significantly lower than this (at least in relation to the number of Jews who were willing to engage actively in the custom of paying Temple tax). Moreover, it is unlikely that the Jewish population was distributed evenly throughout the region. Thus, while there is no basis to doubt the presence of Jews in Asia Minor, or even specifically in Laodicea, it is impossible in the absence of hard artefactual or textual evidence to extrapolate from this to conclude that there must have been Jews in Colossae. There may have been Jews in the city, but while Jews were found in many locations in Asia Minor this does not mean there were synagogues and Jewish communities in every urban centre or settlement.

The ongoing presence of Jews in the region is attested a few decades later, after the composition of the letter to the Colossians. Writing to the believers resident in Magnesia on the Maeander, Ignatius provides a series of warnings against the threat of Judaism (Ignatius, *Magn.* 8.1–10.3). A similar, cautionary message is also found in his letter to the Philadelphians (Ignatius, *Phld.* 6.1–2), located further north in Asia Minor. However, in writing to believers in Ephesus, Tralles, and Smyrna no explicit reference is made to Jewish opponents. The presence of Jews in Ephesus (Acts 19:8) and Smyrna (Rev. 2:9) is attested by New Testament writings. While less is known about Tralles, an inscription dated to the third century CE might record a donation made by a wealthy female adherent on what might have been the wall of a synagogue (Trebilco 1991: 157–58). However, the inscription is also open to alternative interpretations. Notwithstanding this, in larger population centres the presence of Jewish communities was not uncommon, but this is not invariably necessarily the case. The size of such communities varied considerably dependent on several factors. Therefore, in the face of no extant evidence from Colossae, all that can be said is that there is no conclusive evidence for the existence of Jews in the city. Furthermore, the letter does not betray any significant interest in Jewish matters. However, if archaeological exploration were to unearth artefacts or inscriptions of a Jewish character in Colossae this would not necessarily be surprising, although it would not automatically imply that the deviant teaching that the author was confronting arose from Jewish mystical ideas concerning angels as intermediary beings.

While certain Jewish communities enjoyed a long history in certain urban centres in Phrygia, by the late antique period or the early medieval period at the latest these Jewish groups disappear from the surviving record. Ramsay comments on the eventual disappearance of a distinctive Jewish population in the region of Phrygia. Due to loss of connection with Palestinian Judaism and lack of preservation of Semitic language, it is suggested that over the course of several centuries the descendants of these transported Jews assimilated to the prevailing culture (Ramsay 1895–97: II, 674–76). Inscriptional evidence from the first century CE from Akmonia suggests that Jews in that location did not maintain an exclusive adherence to Judaism, but accommodated the imperial cult within their religious practices. The worship of empress Poppaea Sabina as Sebaste Eubosia appears to have formed part of the devotional practices of certain Jews (see Ramsay 1895–97: II, 637–40, inscr. 530 = CIG 3858). As supporters of the Roman state and participants in the Imperial cult, many of the Jews in the region appear to have adopted the Greco-Roman culture of the region.

This would align with the syncretistic tendencies that the author of Colossians is attempting to combat among believers in Christ in that city. Ramsay therefore comes to the conclusion based upon an existing tendency of loyalty towards the Roman state that eventually the majority of Jews in the region were Christianized. He states that the Phrygian Jews, 'were probably to a larger extent Christianized at an early period; and even those who had taken the Imperial side, and conformed to State worship, were likely in the fourth century to continue the same conformity when Christianity had become the State religion. Thus the Phrygian Jews melted into the general Chr. Population' (Ramsay 1895–97: II, 675–76). While that description might be too absolute, and motivated by a desire to depict the 'triumph' of Christianity, it is true that the Jews disappear largely from the historical evidence preserved for Phrygia by the third and fourth centuries. The process of assimilation to the wider culture is undoubtedly a key factor in this disappearance, although it might be better to think of Jews assimilating to the dominant majority Hellenistic culture with its syncretism of local, Greek, and Roman cultic practices, rather than seeing the majority of Jews becoming Christianized. Such a process appears to be already underway by the first century, with certain Jews willing to accommodate participation in the Imperial cult alongside their Jewish religion. It therefore appears that the spirit of religious pluralism that was predominant in the Greco-Roman culture of Phrygia had also had some impact on several Jewish communities in the region. The consequence of this was, in some areas, a loss of strong Jewish identity and a lack of concern about separation from the wider culture.

3. *Believers in Jesus in the Lycus Valley and Phrygia*

The Phrygian region was not immune from cultural and religious interchange. The settlement of Colossae was located on the south bank of the Lycus River, approximately 20 miles (32 km) east of the

INTRODUCTION

point of confluence with the larger river, the Maeander. The Lycus Valley is not mentioned by name in the New Testament, but was located in the western region of the ancient kingdom, and subsequent Roman province of Phrygia. Inscriptional evidence reveals that the earliest recoverable form of language was part of the Indo-European family, with various items of vocabulary similar to Classical Greek (see Brixhe 2008: 72).

In the New Testament, Phrygia is mentioned three times in the book of Acts, and once in the subscript that is appended to certain manuscripts of 1 Timothy. In Acts, on the Day of Pentecost, the miraculous gift of speaking in various languages enables Phrygian visitors to Jerusalem to hear the gospel proclaimed in their own language (Acts 2:10). However, it is probably not the case that one can infer from this the presence of believers in Jesus residing in Phrygia from the early 30s, directly as the result of the Pentecost preaching. According to the descriptions of Paul's missionary journeys in the narrative of Acts, as part of the second missionary journey (Acts 15:16–18:22), starting in Iconium Paul and his associates travelled in Asia Minor journeying west through the eastern region of Phrygia before turning north to Galatia: 'they went through the Phrygian and Galatian region' (Acts 16:6). Based on the sequence of the regions listed this suggests, 'a broad arc along the eastern border of the province of Asia, so that contact with the Lycus Valley is also ruled out during the secondary missionary journey' (Huttner 2013: 82). According to the chronology of Acts, perhaps sometime around 52–54 CE, during the third missionary journey, having left Antioch Paul 'passed successively through all the Galatian region and Phrygia' (Acts 18:23), then 'having passed through the upper country came to Ephesus' (Acts 19:1). If the sequence is correct, this might suggest a more northerly route from Antioch, travelling east to west across the Anatolian high plateau before moving south into Phrygia, and then recommencing the westward progression towards Ephesus. Details are scant, so it is impossible to tell whether a more northerly route through Phrygia is envisaged, perhaps through Philomelium and Sardis, or a more southerly route through Apamea, perhaps visiting Laodicea, and following the Maeander to Ephesus. Either way, if the fleeting details of this part of the journey as described in Acts are historical, then Paul and his companions had some familiarity with certain areas of Phrygia, although he had not visited Colossae in the Lycus Valley. Huttner entertains the possibility that during his extended stay in Ephesus Paul might have made various trips into the interior regions (Huttner 2013: 83). However, while this is not impossible, there is no textual or artefactual evidence to lend weight to this supposition.

Map 2. Phrygia and Significant Cities in the Region and Neighbouring Areas

The epistle to the Colossians describes Epaphras as being responsible for bringing the gospel to Colossae (Col. 1:7). He is claimed, or perhaps co-opted, as part of the Pauline circle. Hence the author's purpose might be to bring the first generation of believers at Colossae, whom Paul had not converted, more directly under the ambit of the Pauline mission. The cities of the Lycus Valley, Hierapolis, Laodicea, and Colossae are described as having communities of believers in Christ at the time when the letter was written.

Moreover, Epaphras is portrayed in the letter addressed to the Colossians as being 'one of you' (Col. 4:12). Therefore, it appears that Epaphras, an inhabitant of Colossae, learnt the message of Christ in another unknown location, before bringing it back to the town where he lived. The scope of Epaphras' missionary work was larger than being restricted to his hometown, since he was also active among believers in Laodicea and Hierapolis (Col. 4:13). It is uncertain, however, whether Epaphras was himself instrumental in establishing Christian communities in Laodicea and Hierapolis, or whether, given his role in Colossae, he became a prominent figure in the neighbouring towns where there already existed groups of believers in Jesus. Certain subscripts to 2 Timothy add the detail that the letter was, 'The first to Timothy written from Laodicea' (Codex Alexandrinus, fifth century), while other later manuscripts continue the description with 'which is the foremost city of Phrygia Pacatiana' (1739^c 1881). It was under the reign of Diocletian that Phrygia was divided into two provinces, the eastern portion of the former unified Phrygian region became known as Phrygia Saluraris (Phrygia I), the western portion was Phrygia Pacatiana, with Laodicea as its capital city. These later subscripts are of limited value. While they refer to Laodicea, they cast no light on the establishment of communities of believers in Jesus in the Lycus Valley. It is difficult to infer anything further from the Pauline epistles or Acts concerning the establishment of Christianity in Colossae, or the other cities of the Lycus Valley, or within the region of Phrygia more widely.

The city of Laodicea is also mentioned twice in the Apocalypse of John. The first time it occurs is in a listing of the seven churches to which the vision is addressed (Rev. 1:11). It may, however, be the case that the sequence in the listing envisages a circuit, initially moving northwards on a coastal route from Ephesus first to Smyrna and then Pergamum, before looping back southwards on an interior route through Thyatira, Sardis, and Philadelphia, before entering Phrygia with Laodicea being the last city in the list. It is conceivable that such a circuit could be concluded by returning along the route of the Maeander. The second reference to Laodicea occurs at the beginning of the section addressed to the church in that city (Rev. 3:14–22). It contains the withering accusation that the Laodiceans are 'lukewarm' (Rev. 3:16) in nature, and trust in their material assets (Rev. 3:17–18). In comparison, the five references to Laodicea or Laodiceans in Colossians (Col. 2:1; 4:13, 15, 16 [twice]) are all neutral. While, as has already been mentioned, the letter of Cicero to Flaccus provides documentary evidence for the presence of a Jewish community in Laodicea, the author of Revelation does not reference the presence of Jews or a synagogue, as is the case in some of the other letters to the churches (cf. Smyrna, Rev. 2:9; Philadelphia, Rev. 3:9). The details in the Apocalypse provide no insight into how the community of believers was established in Laodicea. It appears to be the case that those addressed in Revelation are in some way associated with a Johannine circle of communities (Aune 1997: liv–lvi). However, it is not necessarily the case that such Johannine believers addressed in Laodicea were distinct from, or mutually exclusive, of the Pauline group of believers in the same location who had received support from Epaphras (Col. 4:13).

In the century after the New Testament period, there are references to believers in Phrygia and the Lycus Valley, but these are relatively sparse. Among the Apostolic Fathers, the shadowy figure of Papias, bishop of Hierapolis only partially emerges. He is described by Irenaeus as 'a hearer of John and a companion of Polycarp' (Irenaeus, *Ad. Haer.* 5.33). Dating Papias' period in office as a Christian leader is notoriously contested. The narrower range of dates encompassing the 120s or 130s is the typical consensus position (for instance, see Hengel 1993: 77; Hill 2004: 383–84). For those who do not embrace the narrow range, nearly all would agree on a date in the wider range of 100–140. Papias' knowledge of the gospel tradition shows that Hierapolis was not isolated from developments in wider Christianity during the first half of the second century. While Hierapolis is also described in the sources as being devastated by an earthquake in the 60s, this was not the end of habitation. The urban centre of Hierapolis recovered and thrived in the ensuing decades. Moreover, Christianity appears to have become the dominant religion by the fourth century. By the sixth century, in 531, Justinian raised the rank of the bishop of Hierapolis to metropolitan status, thereby showing the ecclesial importance of the city.

Similarly, there are references to second-century church leaders in Laodicea. Perhaps most prominent was the Quartodeciman bishop of Laodicea, Sargaris, who was martyred on the 6th of October, around the year 166. Again this provides evidence of a continuing Christian presence in the Lycus Valley in the century following the composition of Colossians. While the preservation of the names of Christian leaders reflects the presence of believers in the region, it reveals little about the life and practices of believers in Phrygia.

Perhaps the most productive insight into the existence of early Christians in Phrygia after the New Testament documents were written is to be found in the evidence of a large number of Christian inscriptions, often in funerary contexts, that date to the period before the reign of Constantine. Commenting on the wealth of pre-Constantinian evidence from Phrygia, in comparison to other areas of the Roman Empire, Chiricat has made the following assessment. He states, 'the Phrygian evidence is of capital importance in our understanding of the origins and development of the Church in the ancient Mediterranean world' (Chiricat 2013: 198). A number of these inscriptions can be dated to the second as well as the third century, thus providing a window into the social status of both individual believers and Christian communities in the period. In general, pre-Constantinian Christian inscriptions are hard to distinguish from those of pagan funerary monuments (Chiricat 2013: 199). However, in several cases key phrases or terms betray the Christian nature of the epitaph or iconography. In relation to the two earliest identifiable Christian monuments from Kadoi in the upper Hermos Valley (dated to 157/8 CE and 179/80 CE respectively), it is the images employed that reflect the Christian character. As Chiricat describes the images:

> The reliefs of these two monuments show individuals holding a circular object incised with a cross (possibly a depiction of the eucharist bread), and a bunch of grapes whose stalk in the later example ends with a *tau*-shaped cross. These two dated monuments form part of a group of second- or third-century Christian epitaphs from the region of Kadoi, Synaos and Ankyra Sidera, many of them distinguished by the same 'cross-in-circle' or 'cross-in-wreath' motif. (Chiricat 2013: 200)

Later, around the later third or early fourth century, various funerary inscriptions from the region of Appia survive. These state that they were erected 'by Christians for Christians'. This epigraphical evidence attests to the continued presence of Christian communities throughout Phrygia in the second to fourth centuries. Moreover, while the social status of those erecting the monuments was not particularly high, nevertheless, in line with members of the wider society, the early Christians of Phrygia often set up lavish funerary monuments.

Two of the most explicitly Christian funerary inscriptions, probably dating to the second half of the third century and first half of the fourth century respectively, are provided below. The first was set up by a female Christian, Aurelia Procula, to be the burial place for herself and her family:

> Ramsay 1883: 339–400, no. 17; Ramsay 1895–97: II, 529, no. 374; *MAMA*: IV 359. Ancient Eumeneia
>
> Aur(elia) Procula
> constructed
> the tomb for herself and
> her husband and her
> children Philippos
> and Paulina, in
> memoriam; and if
> anyone tries
> to inter another,
> he shall have to reckon with
> the living God.

This inscription reflects its likely Christian provenance in two ways. First, unlike curse formulae on similar tombs in the region, the names of pagan gods are not invoked. Second, the description of 'the *living* God' is highly suggestive of the Christian origin of Aurelia Procula and her family.

The second example is even more clearly identifiable as a Christian epigraph, which reflects the Christian faith of Dionysios who had the tomb erected.

> Ramsay 1895–97: II, 719, no. 654. Macil (near ancient Stektorion, in Phrygian Pentapolis):
>
> Aur(elius) Dionysios,
> presbyter,
> while still living
> constructed
> the resting place.
> Peace to all
> the brothers.

The self-identifying term, 'presbyter', is 'undoubtedly referring to his status as a member of the Christian clergy' (Chiricat 2013: 204). The term 'resting place' is distinctively Christian (very occasionally

Jewish) terminology denoting a place of rest until the resurrection. The final sentence praying for peace for 'all the brothers' reflects the fraternal language of early Christian communities.

While the letter to the Colossians offers the earliest insights into one early Christian community in the region of Phrygia, other literary, documentary, and epigraphical evidence from the late first century through to the beginning of the fourth century reflects a continued and an increasing Christian presence in the region. It would be incorrect to take each individual example of the presence of Christianity as reflecting uniform practice across the region. As Mitchell has noted there was a 'cellular organization' of Phrygian society (Mitchell 1993: II, 41). It is likely during this earliest phase of Christianity in Phrygia and the Lycus Valley that Christian communities tended to exist for most of the time as separate entities. Perhaps practice was only shared or unified through the activities of travelling teachers, such as Epaphras. It is only in the fourth century, with the imperial adoption of Christianity, that translocal ecclesial structures brought systematic oversight and uniformity to a far greater degree. However, in the second half of the first century, the community of believers in Colossae was likely to have viewed itself as a relatively autonomous, voluntary religious association.

In contrast, and perhaps as a challenge to that prevailing mentality, the letter, addressed to Colossian believers, encourages them to consider the universal nature of the church. The group is urged to see itself as being linked to fellow believers in Hierapolis and Laodicea, and more widely to Pauline Christianity, and even to a universal church under the headship of Christ (Col. 1:18). This was a radical departure from the typical outlook of Phrygian society where people identified with their own city, and where the horizons of small communities rarely extended beyond their local urban settlement and hinterlands. In this sense one key goal of the letter might be to bring the Colossian community more closely into the fold of early Pauline groups of believers in the region and to make it part of a network of communities of early believers in Christ (cf. Trebilco 2011: 184). Therefore, the vision of the letter appears to have had significant social implications in terms of the way Christian believers in Colossae were encouraged to conceive of their identity. Not only were they to consider the unity and common life of fellow believers in the same location, alongside this they were to understand that they had been called to something on a fundamentally different scale – the universal body of Christ. This was a significant development of the Pauline understanding of the church. However, according to the author of the letter, such an ecclesiology enabled believers to transcend all national and social barriers (Col. 3:11).

4. *The Theology of Colossians*

The author of Colossians promotes a system of belief in a divine being, God. However, knowledge of God, as well as reconciliation to the deity, and relation with that divine being are seen as only possible through Christ. In this sense the author's christological affirmations and his teachings about God are not just interwoven, they are inextricably interdependent upon each other. To become part of God's kingdom one must promote the message of Christ (Col. 4:11). Yet these categories are almost reversible, for the letter also states that the only way to be 'transferred into the kingdom of the son' (Col. 1:13) is to be rescued by God. Furthermore, the sole way, according to the author, to know the mystery of God is to know Christ (Col. 2:2). In fact, it is upon the core teaching of the centrality, uniqueness, and supremacy of Christ that all the theological themes of the letter are constructed. For instance, the emphasis on the enjoyment of the blessing of a new type of existence is predicated on unity with Christ in his death and resurrection (Col. 2:20; 3:1–3).

In this overview of the author's theology several key aspects of the belief system of the letter will be discussed. The term 'belief system' is chosen intentionally, since the author does not provide a discourse on individual aspects of doctrine, and the letter certainly does not offer a systematic treatment of the newly established faith. Instead there is a selective appeal to certain aspects of an inter-locking system of belief in Christ. This web of relationships between individual ideas becomes the epistemological key for understanding how the author conceives the constituent parts as forming a unified system of faith. Topics that will be considered as contributing to that system of belief include the author's understanding of God or the Father, the central role of Christ as the focal point of the author's theological scheme, and alongside this the lack of interest in the Spirit (or pneumatology to use the technical term). Further aspects to be considered will include the author's ecclesiology, eschatology, and the understanding of the gospel as the communicative message of God's redemptive work through Christ. Colossians is a particularly rich and developed articulation of those aspects of theology that are considered pertinent to its argument. However, the letter does not seek to present a theological treatise in glorious isolation from the realities of the lives of believers in the first-century setting of Colossae in Phrygia. Therefore, the theology of the letter must be seen for what it is, a situationally focused response to problems that the author perceived as requiring robust and radical correction. This means that its theological statements are not exhaustive, but arise from specific concerns, and address only those topics where the author considered that remedy was necessary, or reminder would be helpful.

4.1. *The Understanding of God*

The term God, θεός, is used 22 times in the letter (23 if the variant reading 'the word of God' were accepted in preference to 'the word of Christ' in Col. 3:16). The term 'father', πατήρ, is less common, occurring five times and on one occasion it denotes earthly fathers who are not to provoke their children (Col. 3:21). On three of the remaining four occasions the term 'father' is coordinated with the noun 'God' (Col. 1:2, 3; 3:17) and in fact on the other occasion when the term 'father' is used (Col. 1:12) two of the surviving manuscripts also introduce the term 'God' (365 ‭א‬), thus speaking of 'God the Father'. Therefore, the paternal role of God is a dominant feature in Colossians. However, that paternity has a dual aspect. God is denoted as the father in relation to Christ, 'God the Father of our Lord Jesus Christ' (Col. 1:3), but just prior to that affirmation the author reminds his audience that God stands in a paternal relationship to believers, 'God our Father' (Col. 1:2). The basis of this dual paternity is not explained, although it may be warranted to speculate that from the perspective of Colossians the portrayal of God in a parental relationship with believers comes about through their union with Christ, since in him they share all the blessings of the age to come.

God is the one to whom believers are encouraged to render devotion. Thus the author declares that corporately 'we give thanks to God' (Col. 1:3), but such an act of thanksgiving to God is to be mediated through Christ, since the Colossians are to 'give thanks to God through him' (Col. 3:17). Furthermore, God is the focus of the group's worship since they are instructed to be 'singing in your hearts to God' (Col. 3:16) with an attitude of gratitude.

The concept of 'the will of God' is also important to the author of Colossians. He makes reference to this idea on three occasions, Col. 1:1, 27 (less directly); and 4:12. The first occurrence is a declaration of the legitimacy of Paul's apostleship: 'Paul and apostle of Christ Jesus through the will of God' (Col. 1:1). Hence while the apostleship of Paul means that he is an envoy of Christ, it accords with the divine purpose that he should fulfill that role. Here there is a close linkage between serving Christ and being aligned with the divine will. This expression finds exact parallels in 2 Cor. 1:1; Eph. 1:1; and 2 Tim. 1:1, and as such reflects a central understanding that Paul's apostleship is divinely intended. The idea of being commissioned by God also comes to the fore when the author speaks of 'the stewardship of God that was given to me' (Col. 1:25). The second reference to God's will concerns his desire to reveal Christ to gentile believers such as the Colossians (Col. 1:27). The third instance in the letter of the expression 'the will of God' occurs in a description of Epaphras' work on behalf of the Colossians. He is said to intercede for them in order that they might be 'fully convinced in all the will of God' (Col. 4:12). The immediate context does not make explicit the nature of the conviction that the Colossians should hold in order that they might be fully aligned with the divine purpose. However, the wider thrust of the letter, and its response to the deviant teaching, suggests that Epaphras' prayer is that the Colossians might recognize the sufficiency of Christ as God's means to establish salvation. The desire that they become fully convinced of God's will suggests that the will of God has already been established. However, it appears to be the case that the Colossians need to recognize that the divine purpose has been realized and it is not in need of any further supplement. In particular, it does not require augmentation with the type of teaching promoted by those who promise ecstatic and visionary teachings (Sumney 2008: 275).

Believers have a new status in relation to God. They are the chosen ones or the 'elect of God' (Col. 3:12). Moreover, while the believers' new mode of existence is said to be through union with Christ, that union is understood to be in the divine realm: 'your life is hidden with Christ in God' (Col. 3:3). The Colossians are also informed that they have gifts or attributes from God that allow them to progress in their faith. Through the gospel, they have been given a 'hope laid up in heaven' (Col. 1:5) and an understanding of the grace of God (Col. 1:6), they are to increase in their knowledge of God (Col. 1:10), it is the Father qualified to share in the inheritance of the holy ones (Col. 1:12), and God has willed to make known to the Colossians the hope of glory, which is Christ (Col. 1:27). This disclosure is the only revelatory event the Colossians require, and it is described as 'the knowledge of the mystery of God' (Col. 2:2), and if the Colossians hold fast to this mystery without deviation caused by other teachings they will 'grow with the growth of God' (Col. 2:19), which he supplies.

While several of the references to God are constructed in terms that characterize his relationship with the Colossians on one hand, another group of references depicts the unique relationship between Christ and God. Principally he is 'God, father of the Lord Jesus Christ' (Col. 1:3). This filial relationship places Christ in a unique position as one who makes the father known. While God is not perceptible to human sight, Christ 'is the image of the invisible God' (Col. 1:15). The development of this description of Christ as 'icon', or image of the deity, is one of the most theologically ground-breaking ideas in the epistle, although it does have an antecedent in the Pauline writings (2 Cor. 4:4). This idea conveys the notion that Christ's role is revelatory and unique since, as God's true image, he discloses God's nature and will (Pao 2012: 95). Christ has a permanent place of honour in relation to God since he is 'seated at the right hand of God' (Col. 3:1). Christ is also the means by which believers are given access to the divine realm and the one through whom they have new life in that sphere: 'your life has been hidden with Christ in God' (Col. 3:3).

The portrayal of God in Colossians is multifaceted, and yet for the author of this letter it is only possible to make such statements because God has revealed the divine mysteries in Christ (Col. 1:27; 2:2), who is himself the visible representation of the invisible God (1:15). God and Christ share a unique familial relationship as father and son. Believers are said to have participated in Christ's death (2:20) and resurrection (3:1). This union with Christ creates a filial relationship between believers and God, so that he can be called 'God our father' (1:2). Thus both Christ's role in the divine plan and his own nature as the image of the invisible God, mean the God of Colossians becomes visible and knowable through self-disclosure of himself in Christ.

4.2. *Christology*

Beyond any doubt, the central concern of the letter is to provide believers with a better understanding of what is presented as the unique significance of Christ. The author describes this instructional task as a struggle on behalf of the Colossians (Col. 2:1), in order that they might come to an understanding that will provide deeper perception of the purposes of God achieved in Christ (2:2). The author assures readers of the benefits they already possess in him, and the futility of trying to supplement their new life in Christ with any other religious practices or beliefs. It is therefore unsurprising to see the prevalence of references to Christ in the epistle, and that the author's arguments focus upon the uniqueness of Christ in God's plan of salvation.

The letter presents Christ as the visual representation of God that can be perceived by humans (Col. 1:15). Moreover, the only way to enjoy divine blessing is to exist in the kingdom of the son (1:13). Humans can only come to completeness in Christ, and one can only know God by knowing Christ who is the mystery of God (2:2). Existence in Christ requires a changed way of life. Those who have faith in Christ (2:5) are to 'walk in him' (2:6). Union with Christ requires putting to death earthly passions (3:5, 8–9). Concomitant with stripping away these former practices is the need to put on a new mode of existence (3:10), which is reflective of life in Christ who 'is all and in all' (3:11). Societal relationships and responsibilities are reformulated for those who now exist in Christ. Earthly relationships are subsumed under a deeper reality that understands household obligations as being actions carried out for Christ, rather than for the apparent power-brokers of husbands, parents, or masters (3:18–4:1). This Christ-centred transformation of believers' lives can only take place when they allow Christ's word to dwell in them (3:16). Moreover, as Christ's peace rules in their hearts, both individually and collectively, they become one body (3:15). Furthermore, the Colossians are to recognize that as a consequence of dying and rising with Christ they must seek the things above (3:1). However, ultimately it is only when the enthroned Christ is revealed, that the new life that believers are already said to possess will be recognized by those who cannot see that status in the present. Hence while believers can be described as experiencing resurrection with Christ, it is only when he is revealed that they will enter into his glory with him (3:3). The wealth and abundance of this glorious new mode of existence is the mystery that God discloses to gentiles, such as the Colossians. However, according to the author, it is not the case that Christ is simply the revealer of the content of the divine mystery. Even more fundamentally it is declared that Christ, who dwells in believers, is in fact the mysterious revelation of God. Hence, it is through union with Christ that the hope of participating in his glory is realized (1:27).

In this way the whole argument of Colossians is dependent on a correct understanding of the identity of Christ. The motivation for a change in individual moral practices and the way in which one behaves in societal relationships stem from this new life in Christ. In Colossians, Christ alone is the basis for a transformed mode of life, he is the ground or the basis to which the Colossian believers are now to hold fast, and he is their hope for a glorious future with God. In effect Christ is presented as the centre and totality for ethics, experience of religious life, and eschatological hope – he 'is all and in all' (Col. 3:11).

Leaving aside the author's argument and flow of thought in the letter that is developed in relation to Christ, the sheer numerical volume of references to Christ in such short compass is astounding. In the 95 verses that comprise Colossians, the term 'Christ', Χριστός, occurs 26 times. The term Jesus, Ἰησοῦς, occurs six times (Col. 1:1, 3, 4; 2:6; 3:17; 4:12; however, note that there is among these a reference to a certain 'Jesus Justus', Col. 4:12). In Colossians the name Jesus is never used independently of either or both of the terms 'Christ' and 'Lord'. This is not surprising, since the singular usage of the term 'Jesus' is rare in the Pauline corpus. It sometimes occurs on its own when the 'name' of 'Jesus' is being stressed in a particular way, 'at the name of Jesus' (Phil 2:10); or unusually to speak of 'faith in Jesus' (Rom. 3:26); to describe the resurrection by the one 'who raised Jesus from the dead' (Rom. 8:11); as a negative citation attributed to others, 'Jesus is accursed' (1 Cor. 12:3); and in a few further instances (2 Cor. 4:10; 11:4; Gal. 6:7; Eph. 4:21; 1 Thess. 1:10; 4:14). Hence, the fact that in Colossians the name 'Jesus' is always combined with a christological title, or perhaps better as an honorific (see Novenson 2012: 87–97), simply reflects the standard Pauline pattern, as well as typical early Christian usage.

The term 'Lord', κύριος, occurs sixteen times in Colossians (twice in the plural form referring to earthly masters). Of the fourteen usages of the singular form, four refer unambiguously to Christ since they are used in combination with 'Christ', or 'Jesus', or both of those terms (Col. 1:3; 2:6; 3:17, 24). However, it is argued that the other ten occurrences refer to Christ, rather than God. Nine of these usages of 'Lord', κύριος, occur in close succession in the so-called household code, including the two plural forms (Col. 3:18, 20, 22 [twice], 23, 24 [twice]; 4:1 [twice]). Potentially the most ambiguous use of the term occurs at the end of Col. 3:22, where slaves are told they should carry out their duties 'fearing the Lord'. Some manuscripts, including 𝔓⁴⁶ ℵ² D² K 104 630 𝔐, replace 'Lord' at this point with 'God'. This, however, is not necessarily decisive for determining the correct meaning of 'Lord', κύριος, in this context. At the end of the instructions to the slaves, the author provides the summary statement 'it is the Lord Christ whom you serve' (Col. 3:24b). Hence the most obvious and consistent way to understand the earlier references to the 'Lord' (in the singular form) in the household code is as denoting Christ, since this explicit reference to the 'Lord Christ' clarifies that sense intended throughout Col. 3:18–4:1.

Similarly, when the term 'Lord', κύριος, is used in the description of Tychicus as 'a fellow slave in the Lord' (Col. 4:7), and in the command to Archippus to pay attention to 'the ministry you received in the Lord' (Col. 4:17), it is highly likely that in both these cases the reference is to Christ as Lord. The author understands Paul to be called as 'an apostle of Jesus Christ' (Col. 1:1), and his co-workers are understood as serving the same Lord. Hence their servitude or ministry is work on behalf of Christ who is typically described as Lord. This usage aligns with the reminder given to earthly slaves earlier in the letter that they serve the Lord Christ (Col. 3:24). Similarly, the mild rebuke to Archippus that he should fulfil the ministry (διακονία) he received in the Lord is an encouragement to commit to the work of service that has been given to him as one who is part of the body of Christ. As Moo notes, in the Pauline letters, the term διακονία 'usually refers…to service of the risen Lord and his people' (Moo 2008: 352). Here too then the term refers to Christ as 'Lord'.

There are two remaining usages of the term 'Lord' that have occasioned more debate as to whether their referent is Christ or God. The first is the instruction to walk in a manner worthy of the Lord… and increasing in the knowledge of God' (Col. 1:10). The syntax of the sentences suggests that one conducts one's life worthily of a figure called 'the Lord', and the result is a growth in the knowledge of God, with the 'Lord' and 'God' best understood in this context as distinct figures. Moreover, similar behavioural imperatives in Colossians are stated in relation to Christ: 'let the peace of Christ rule in your hearts' (Col. 3:15); 'let the word of Christ dwell in you richly' (Col. 3:16). This makes it likely that the command to walk in the Lord is a behavioural instruction incumbent on those who live in union with Christ. The passage that has caused the most debate concerning the referent of 'Lord' is the instruction to forgive one another 'just as the Lord forgave you' (Col. 3:13). The notion of Christ forgiving sins has been seen as uncharacteristic of the Pauline epistles (Dunn 1996: 231). However, the author's point when taken with the following imperatives that refer to the actions of Christ, is that the Colossian believers are to demonstrate the same pattern of behaviour, including forgiveness, which they have seen in and received from Christ (see the discussion of Col. 3:13 for supporting evidence). Therefore, it appears that the author is consistent in using the term 'Lord', κύριος, to designate Christ alone. This application of the title 'Lord' to Christ is a reflection of the author's elevated christology, which places Christ in a unique redemptive role and attributed to him a place in creation that cannot be matched. It is for this reason that the letter is so strident in refuting any challenge to the uniqueness and supremacy of Christ in terms of his relation to God and his salvific role.

The so-called Christological Hymn (Col. 1:15–20) is frequently seen as one of the richest and most highly condensed expressions of the author's views on the ontological, soteriological, ecclesial, and cosmic significance of Christ. While many see this material as being a pre-formed unit (at least at some level) that has been incorporated into the letter, it needs to be noted that the language of nearly every phrase in this poetic section is taken up somewhere else in the letter. This would suggest that the author had digested the contents of this statement to such an extent that it shaped his entire theological outlook. Moreover, in his detailed study of this unit, Stettler has convincingly demonstrated the coherence of Col. 1:15–20. This renders it unlikely that this material originated in a pre-Christian setting, only later undergoing heavy reworking to make it suit a Christian purpose (Stettler 2000: 75–103). Therefore, the content of the hymn makes it more likely that it originated as a Christian composition. Furthermore, given the way the ideas and phraseology of this poetic section are reused at various points throughout Colossians it is certainly not unimaginable that the author of the letter was also directly responsible for the composition of this unit. If, however, it was an earlier Christian piece, its poetic devotion and praise of Christ made it particularly suitable to the overall argument of the letter. If the writing of this poetic section does not belong to the author of Colossians, he has made it his own by tightly linking it with the wider thematic concerns of the letter. Since here it is considered more likely that the author of the letter also composed this unit, there will be no attempt to reconstruct an earlier version of this hymn. Furthermore, one might suggest that the failure of scholars to come to any strong consensus concerning the form of the supposed original hymn may at least give pause to consider whether that hypothesis might be flawed. Often scholars have attempted to produce such a pre-Christian form by stripping away all references to Christ, the church, and the cross, thereby creating a hymn in praise of wisdom.

More relevant for this discussion is the content of this poetic section, which is best seen as having a lyrical quality rather than conforming to a strict poetic form. The first part of the section (Col. 1:15–17) celebrates Christ as the firstborn of creation (Col. 1:15), and attributes to him agency in the creation of all things (Col. 1:16). This part of the hymn comes to a climax by asserting Christ's chronological and ontological priority in relation to the entire created order (Col. 1:17). The second half focuses on Christ's redemptive work and his priority as head of the church. Hence, by emphasizing Christ's unique relationship both to creation and to the church, the author is employing this doxological language to gain the audience's assent to the theological statements contained in the hymn. The concern the author has in relation to a defective understanding of christology at Colossae has not been raised at this point, since the author first seeks to establish common christological ground. However, it is likely that the problems that will be addressed later in the letter are in the author's mind as this christological affirmation is formulated. The aim is to gain a shared affirmation of these lofty theological statements contained in the hymn, prior to challenging the Colossians by informing them that the ideas of those proclaiming a different philosophy (Col. 2:8) actually deny the sufficiency of Christ. Hurtado has recognized the power of the language that is used here. He sees the author drawing upon the traditional language of devotion to produce 'a fresh and memorable declaration of Christ's glorious status. Those who first heard this celebration of Jesus probably recognized basically familiar convictions expressed freshly and eloquently' (Hurtado 2003: 508). While there is much to agree with in this statement, it is likely the case that the poetic material is serving the overall argument of the letter in a more focused manner, by acting as a corrective to teaching that challenged the uniquely glorious status of Christ. In particular, the statements in this section that announce Christ's superiority over the cosmic powers (Col. 1:16) – and the fact that only through Christ are earthly or heavenly things reconciled – preview the perspectives later in the letter that through the cross Christ triumphed over such forces (Col. 2:14–15). As Moo has observed, '[t]he false teachers, it appears, argued from cosmology to spirituality: because the universe was filled with spiritual powers of various sorts, ultimate spiritual "fullness" could be achieved only be taking them all into consideration' (Moo 2008: 111). Therefore the material in Col. 1:15–20 in the form it is presented must be treated as an integral part of the argument of the letter. To reduce it simply to a pre-Pauline source or an authorial digression misses its function in the overall argument of the letter. Since the earliest stage of usage of the poetic material that can be known with any degree of certainty is its occurrence in Colossians, and given the tight fit between the content of Col. 1:15–20 and the rest of the letter, it is plausible to see this as the context in which the poetic unit originated. Even if this material drew on wider devotional affirmations that had precedent in Pauline and early Christian circles of believers, Col. 1:15–20 has been so heavily reworked to fit the themes and argument of the letter that it is probably better to speak of earlier influences, rather than of dependence upon or incorporation of a literary source.

One of the striking claims of the author of Colossians is that believers have a new mode of existence that is brought about through union with Christ. Such participatory language is frequently, but not exclusively, based upon the Pauline prepositional phrase 'in Christ', ἐν Χριστῷ (Col. 1:2, 4, 28; 2:5). The same idea is expressed when the noun 'Christ' is replaced by the pronoun 'him', ἐν αὐτῷ (Col. 2:6, 7, 10, 11). Although less frequent, this metaphor can be inverted. So instead of declaring that believers exist in Christ, it can be claimed that Christ dwells in believers (Col. 1:27). This idea also finds expression in other Pauline letters, where the indwelling presence of Christ means that the sinful body is dead, but the Spirit enlivens believers (Rom. 8:10). At various points the letter seems to understand 'in Christ'/'in him' primarily in spatial terms. The instruction to the Colossians to 'walk in him' requires a new mode of conduct commensurate to the new sphere of existence in which believers now dwell (Col. 2:6). This spatial sense is developed in a more explicit sense in the following verse where the agricultural and architectural images of being 'rooted and built up in him' (Col. 2:7) reflect growth and maturation within a spiritual sphere. This spatial understanding may derive, at least in part, from the concept of transference relating to those who have become believers being transferred out the domain of darkness 'into the kingdom of the son of his love' (Col. 1:13). Hence the preposition 'in' appears to be used in a locative sense 'to denote the reality in which one participates' (Macaskill 2013: 239).

The cosmic dimension of the christology of Colossians is not only present in the poetic material where it is stated that 'in him were created all things' (Col. 1:16). This statement portrays the understanding of Christ as the originating agent of the entire created order (Fee 2007: 332). However, this claim is balanced with an equally breath-taking assertion that Christ is also the teleological goal for the entire cosmos. The 'renewal in knowledge' (Col. 3:10) for the transformed person is not limited to individuals, but encompasses a renewal of the cosmic order where 'Christ is all and in all' (Col. 3:11).

Therefore, in a very real sense the overarching theological theme of Colossians is that of teaching a correct christology. The author asserts that Christ is the pre-temporal agent of creation, thereby demonstrating that the cosmic powers derive their existence from him. He is also uniquely the reconciler and redeemer of the entire cosmic order. Not only does this result in the defeat of malevolent cosmic 'rulers and authorities' (Col. 2:15), it frees the Colossian believers from any requirement to appease or show deference to such forces. Since believers are already 'in Christ', participating in him both by having been buried with him in baptism and though being raised with him (2:12; 3:1), this christological understanding leads to new ethical demands. Believers are to 'put off' (3:8) behaviours that characterized their previous mode of existence and instead 'put on' a form of conduct that befits life in Christ (3:10). This clothing metaphor is used to construct a new identity for the Colossians as those dressed with the ethical practices that align with life in Christ. Hence, the ethical imperatives are predicated on the claim of new existence in Christ, and thus community members are urged 'to construct their own identity in Christ' (Canavan 2012: 190). Ultimately the letter demonstrates the uniqueness and supremacy of Christ in creation and redemption. Attempts to supplement faith in Christ with other religious commitments or experiences reflect a fundamental failure to perceive the preeminence of Christ in all things, and to recognize that believers already exist in him, having been raised with him and transferred into his kingdom.

4.3. *The Missing Spirit*

When one considers the frequency of use of the term 'spirit', πνεῦμα, in the various writings of the Pauline corpus the following figures emerge (see below). For each writing of the Pauline corpus the table below lists in the second column the total words in the epistle,[1] the second column gives the total number of times the word 'spirit', πνεῦμα, occurs, and the third column figure records the number of times the reference is to the Holy Spirit. In certain cases it is debatable whether or not the use of 'spirit', πνεῦμα, is indeed a reference to the Holy Spirit: for instance, does 'the spirit of holiness' in Rom. 1:4 refer to the Holy Spirit? The answer is probably yes, however the point here is not to discuss each case in the Pauline corpus but to show how the profile of the individual letters aligns or differs in relation to their use of the term 'spirit'. The final column calculates the ratio of words in each letter to the number of times a reference to the 'Holy Spirit'. The higher the number, the less frequent are references to the 'Holy Spirit'.

---

[1] http://catholic-resources.org/Bible/NT-Statistics-Greek.htm (accessed 22 July 2014). Word counts vary depending on determinations about different words in various textual variants. However, the comparison would remain broadly the same even if this were to be taken into account.

Letter	Words in each letter	Occurrences of πνεῦμα	Reference to Holy Spirit	Words/Holy Spirit
Romans	7111	34	26[2]	273.5
1 Corinthians	6829	40	22[3]	310.41
2 Corinthians	4477	17	11[4]	407
Galatians	2230	17	15[5]	148.67
Ephesians	2422	14	11[6]	220.18
Philippians	1629	5	3[7]	543
Colossians	1582	2	1[8]	1582
1 Thessalonians	1481	5	4[9]	370.25
2 Thessalonians	823	3	1[10]	823
1 Timothy	1591	3	2[11]	795.5
2 Timothy	1238	3	1[12]	1238
Titus	659	1	1[13]	659
Philemon	335	1	0[14]	undefined

The letter with the highest frequency of references to the 'Holy Spirit' is Galatians. Rounding to the nearest whole number in that letter there is a reference to the 'Holy Spirit' every 149 words. After this in descending order is: Ephesians (every 220 words); Romans (274 words); 2 Corinthians (310 words); 1 Thessalonians (370 words); 2 Corinthians (407 words); Philippians (543 words); Titus (659 words); 1 Timothy (796 words); 2 Thessalonians (823 words);

---

2 Rom. 1:4; 2:29; 5:5; 7:6; 8:2, 4, 5 [×2], 6, 9 [×3], 11, 13, 14, 16, 23, 26 [×2], 27; 9:1; 14:7; 15:13, 16, 19, 30.
3 1 Cor. 2:4, 10 [×2], 11, 12, 13, 14; 3:16; 6:11, 19; 7:40, 12:3 [×2], 4, 7, 8 [×2], 9 [×2] 11, 13 [×2].
4 2 Cor. 1:22; 3:3, 6 [×2], 8, 17 [×2], 18; 5:5; 6:6; 13:13.
5 Gal. 3:2, 3, 5, 14; 4:16, 29; 5:5, 16, 17 [×2], 18, 22, 25 [×2]; 6:8.
6 Eph. 1:13; 2:18, 22; 3:5, 16; 4:3, 4, 30; 5:18; 6:17, 18.
7 Phil. 1:19; 2:1; 3:3.
8 Col. 1:8.
9 1 Thess. 1:5, 6; 4:8; 5:19.
10 2 Thess 2:13.
11 1 Tim. 3:16; 4:1.
12 2 Tim. 1:14.
13 Tit. 3:5.
14 Phlm. 25.

2 Timothy (1238 words); Colossians (1582 words); and Philemon (no references to the 'Holy Spirit').

It is perhaps unsurprising to find in the brief personal note, Philemon, that there are no references to the Holy Spirit. Similarly, given the routinization of the charisma that appears to be at play in the Pastoral Epistles, where a more institutionalized form of church leadership and governance is being advocated, it may in fact be surprising to see any references to the Spirit. There is only one reference to the Spirit in 2 Thessalonians, which is the same as Colossians, but the letter is about half the length (823 words compared to 1582 words).

Therefore on the spectrum of references to the Holy Spirit in Pauline letters (with the exception of Philemon), Colossians has the lowest volume of such references. In fact, even the sole text that is understood here as referring to the Holy Spirit has been understood by some commentators not as a reference to the Spirit, but as having some type of adjectival function. Thus Schweizer states in relation to the phrase τὴν ὑμῶν ἀγάπην ἐν πνεύματι that, 'this love is further described as spiritual love', and again, 'it is rightly translated by "spiritual love"' (Schweizer 1982: 37–38, 38 n. 18; cf. Moule 1957: 52). This, however, does not appear to be the most natural way to read the expression, and it is preferable to understand it as describing the corporate love that exists among believers as a result of their shared mode of existence in the Spirit. Nonetheless, it is worth remembering that even this sole reference to the Spirit in Colossians is somewhat ambiguous.

It is appropriate to ask about the cause of this disproportionate level of reference to the Holy Spirit in Colossians, especially in comparison with most of the Pauline letters typically deemed authentic by most scholars. It may be the case that the circumstances behind Colossians led the author to downplay references to the Holy Spirit. Perhaps the false teaching, with its emphasis on worship of the angels and ecstatic visions (Col. 2:18), caused the author not to mention experiential aspects of life in the Spirit. This may have been to avoid a debate with those teaching a different philosophy, who may have claimed that their religion offered greater spiritual experiences. When one considers that the eschatology of Colossians concentrates on the blessings that believers already enjoy in union of Christ, it is all the more remarkable that in this letter the Holy Spirit is not mentioned as a primary example of those already-realized blessings (Sumney 2008: 42). Alternatively, it is possible that the neglect of the role of the Spirit in Colossians reflects a different author, who has such a strong emphasis on union with Christ and participation in the divine life through Christ alone, that there is little room in his theological understanding for the Holy Spirit. Perhaps what some have described as the 'binitarian' pattern of Christian worship, whereby Christ is treated as a recipient of cultic worship alongside God (Hurtado 2003: 134–35), has for the author of Colossians evolved into a binitarian theology to the extent that it is difficult to integrate the Holy Spirit into this schema. Christ has been presented as the totality of believers' experience and faith, thereby making a role for the Spirit virtually superfluous.

4.4. *Ecclesiology*

Here the discussion focuses on the topic of ecclesiology, rather than the church at Colossae as is common in those commentaries that touch this topic (cf. O'Brien 1982: xxvii–xxx; Barth and Blanke 1994: 17–20). The reason for this is that the author provides little information about the physical community of believers at Colossae, but instead offers a still-partial yet fuller reflection on what the church is in relation to Christ. Hence the author provides an embryonic theology of church, or an ecclesiology, rather than offering a description of the local church in Colossae. This no doubt reflects the statement that the author had not met the Colossians (Col. 2:1). It is also interesting that the typical Pauline epistolary greeting to nascent communities of believers includes addressing them as a 'church', ἐκκλησία, in a certain location (cf. 1 Cor. 1:2; 2 Cor. 1:1; Gal. 1:2; 1 Thess. 1:1; 2 Thess. 1:1). By contrast, when addressing the Romans and the Colossians, two communities that Paul is said not to have visited in person, he addresses believers in different terms (Rom. 1:7; Col. 1:2; but cf. Phil. 1:1).

The term ἐκκλησία, 'church', occurs four times in Colossians (Col. 1:18, 24; 4:15, 16). However, the importance that is given to this topic in Colossians cannot be gauged solely in terms of the number of occurrences of the term. The author's ecclesiology, or understanding of the corporate gathering and life of believers, permeates many of the instructions, teachings, and ideas given in the letter. The ἐκκλησία is conceived as an organic entity, the body of Christ of which Christ is the head (Col. 1:18). Thus, the author's christological understanding is closely tied to the way in which the community of believers is defined. Believers only constitute the 'church' through their relationship to Christ, who welds believers into a single corporate entity in relationship to him and under his headship.

While it has been noted that the author speaks in more detail in abstract terms about the church, there are some insights given about local church structure. In this way the author follows the typical Pauline pattern of referring to smaller localized groupings using the term 'church'. Yet strikingly, there is perhaps more detail provided about the local church in Laodicea, rather than the church in Colossae to which the epistle is addressed. In relation to the church of Laodicea, the author notes that at least one group meeting takes place in Nympha's house (Col. 4:15). She appears to have been a Laodicean convert who lived in a domestic dwelling space that was sufficiently spacious that it could accommodate a group meeting of Christ-followers in Laodicea. However, there is not sufficient detail given to tell whether this was the only meeting place for the church in Laodicea, and whether the space was large enough for all Laodicean believers to meet simultaneously in this single location. If there were multiple gatherings in Laodicea it is not necessarily the case that these would have all met in the homes of wealthy patrons (Adams 2013: 19). The only activity of the Laodicean meeting that is described is that group members are to listen to the reading of letters sent in Paul's name (Col. 4:16). By contrast, no information is given concerning the meeting place of Colossian believers. Thus it is unclear whether they met in a domestic space or in some other convenient location. Perhaps given the contents of the household code, with its disproportionate amount of space given to addressing slaves and the fact it addresses wives, children, and slaves first in each of the three pairings respectively (Col. 3:18–4:1), one could infer that the social make-up of the community was predominantly slaves, perhaps with some free women and their children. However, that remains an inference.

While neither the ideas of the 'church' as the body of Christ, or as a term that describes the unity of believers translocally is without precedent in the authentic Pauline writings, the universal view of the church that is presented in Colossians (and Ephesians) is more developed than what is found in the earlier letters. Moreover, when the author presents his theoretical understanding of the nature of the 'church', ἐκκλησία, it is apparent that those ideas are fundamentally tied to the christological perspectives in the letter. Christ is viewed having priority both over the cosmic forces (Col. 1:16) and also over the church (Col. 1:18). In Col. 1:18 the author deploys the Pauline metaphor of 'the body', τό σῶμα, to describe the church. This metaphor is well-known in other Pauline letters, being most fully developed in 1 Corinthians (1 Cor. 12:12–31). In that context, employing an extended metaphor, Paul discusses various body parts, 'the hand', 'the ear', 'the eye', and sees them as reflecting the different functions various believers must carry out. However, organically they form the whole body which is the church. In Colossians the metaphor is compressed. Instead the only body part that is explicitly mentioned is 'the head', and it is Christ who is described as the 'head of the body, the church' (Col. 1:18). The emphasis falls heavy upon Christ's primacy over the church, which is a corporate entity constituted of Christ-followers.

This image of the organic body of believers that exists under the headship of Christ is used on two further occasions in the letter. In the enigmatic statement concerning Paul's sufferings filling up what is lacking in Christ's afflications, it is stated that such sufferings are 'on behalf of his body, which is the church' (Col. 1:24). However, in this context there is no reference to Christ's role as head of the church, as was the case in Col. 1:18. A significant development is that whereas Paul had used the body metaphor to describe local gatherings of believers (1 Cor. 12:12, 27; cf. Rom. 12:4), here the perspective is universal. Paul's sufferings are on behalf of all believers, and collectively those believers in all locations constitute Christ's body. The thought is not developed in this context, but in some sense apostolic sufferings serve and sustain the church (Moule 1957: 80).

The final place in Colossians where the author uses the head and body image is found after the rebuttal of those accused of delighting in acts of self-humility and the worship of angels (Col. 2:18). The root cause of this deviance is because such people are 'not holding to the head, from whom all the body through the joints and the ligaments, being supplied and held together, increases with the increase of God' (Col 2:19). While the body is not here explicitly identified as the church, both earlier statements in the epistle and the corporate image make it clear that this is still the referent of the term 'body'. Once again, the author offers a very flattened metaphor that speaks simply of the head and the body. Drawing on Col. 1:18, readers of the epistle see that Christ as head sustains and enables growth to occur in the body. No further source of sustenance is required. This perspective aligns with the christology of the letter, which repeatedly emphasizes that everything that believers require for their spiritual existence is to be found in Christ without any need of supplement. Therefore, it appears that the author's understanding of the headship of Christ in relation to the church conveys a range of ideas. First, it speaks of primacy and authority, since as head he is to 'be first in all things' (Col. 1:18). Yet alongside this, the headship of Christ is a way of describing his empowerment and provision for the body, which is the church. Therefore, whereas the body metaphor was present in other Pauline letters, the image occurs in a different form in Colossians. Most striking is the way Christ is presented as the head of the body. As a corollary of this focus on Christ's headship, other aspects of the metaphor as it had been used elsewhere are not preserved. The extended descriptions of the functions and necessity of various body parts are dropped. This is because the author does not use the body image to correct defective intra-group relationships. Instead the image is pressed into the service of the author's overarching christology. It is because Christ is the ultimate source and the full sustainer of the church that the Colossians are to resist teaching that called upon them to supplement such Christ-centred faith.

Relationships between members of the church are discussed in Colossians, but not by using the body metaphor (cf. 1 Cor. 12:12–31). Instead this is achieved more indirectly as part of the general ethical teaching of the letter. Believers who have a new mode of existence 'in Christ' are to reform their behaviour in light of that renewal. While there is a focus on moral transformation throughout much of Col. 3:1–17, at a few points the author articulates some basic corporate ethics. According to the ecclesiology expressed in the letter, followers of Christ are held to a higher moral standard than that which operated in their former lives. Hence they are told, 'do not lie to one another', and the basis for such an action is that since their life is now hidden with Christ (Col. 3:3) they should live as those who have 'stripped off the old man with his practices' (Col. 3:9). The author therefore calls for a new ethic between group members that is edifying and sustaining of the group in the same manner that Christ's headship builds up the church. Furthermore, alongside instructions to abstain from certain activities within the group, such as lying, the author calls on group members to display certain behaviours as part of their corporate life. Therefore, as a collective body, they should be 'bearing with one another and forgiving each other if any one of you has a complaint against the other' (Col. 3:13). Again the author provides a christological basis for this call for inner-group tolerance and forgiveness, since believers are reminded that such actions are a reflection of the forgiveness that they received from Christ (Col. 3:13). Thus, the ecclesiology of the letter emerges from its christological understandings. As Moo observes, 'Christ establishes not only the pattern but the possibility of forgiveness' (Moo 2008: 280). This observation could be extended by noting that for the author the new life in Christ that believers now enjoy becomes the pattern and basis for the way in which they are to live collectively as the body of Christ.

The activities that characterize the corporate life of believers are also briefly mentioned in Colossians. The author affirms that the Colossians, 'were called in one body' (Col. 3:15). In this relational unity believers are instructed to be engaged in mutual instruction, moral encouragement, and communal acts of worship: 'in all wisdom teaching and admonishing each other, with psalms, hymns, spiritual songs in gratitude singing in your hearts to God' (Col. 3:16). Therefore, collectively, followers of Christ are to worship God, thanking him in the name of Christ (Col. 3:17) for the new heavenly life in which they now participate (Col. 3:1–4). This idealized description of corporate life follows on from the imperative 'to let the word of Christ dwell in you richly' (Col. 3:16a). Therefore, connection with Christ should not produce individualism, or a focus on one's own spiritual experience. Instead it should result in a mutuality that seeks the growth and spiritual development of other believers in the ἐκκλησία, 'church'. These activities are seen as an extension of the apostolic calling, where the author states that Paul and his associates are actively engaged in 'admonishing every man and teaching every man in all wisdom' (Col. 1:28). Thus it is possible to envisage that believers came together for collective meetings and that the church's activities included corporate teaching and correction, with both of these modes of instruction designed to produce conformity to the central values of the group. While there may not have been fixed offices or leadership roles at this stage, it is not unlikely that the tasks of teaching and admonishing fellow believers might have been undertaken by a subset of the larger community of believers in Colossae.

The church is also to be a worshipping community that directs its thankfulness to God through corporate acts of singing. The use of psalms is probably illustrative of the possibility the early church took over some forms of Jewish musical worship, although knowledge of synagogue worship is itself extremely limited for the first century. However, the *Songs of the Sabbath Sacrifice* (4Q400–407, 11Q17, along with another fragmentary copy found at Masada) suggest that songs or poetic forms were used in Second Temple Judaism as part of Sabbath day worship. These songs purport to describe the worship offered to God by angels standing around his throne. Thus, human worshippers could understand their own worship to be joined with that of angelic beings in the praise of the deity (cf. Col. 2:18). Such a practice was not unique to Jewish religion. In Dionysian Mysteries, the deity who was viewed as the god of music and poetry was worshipped using these media. In addition to the secret initiation rites, in Athens a public festival was conducted with dramatic, musical, and poetic elements. The paraphernalia of the cult included the *salpinx*, a long straight trumpet, the *tympanon*, which was a combination of bells and drums, and the pan-pipes. Among the Orphic hymns was one that contained an extended invocation to Dionysus:

> I call upon loud-roaring and revelling Dionysus,
> primeval, double-natured, thrice-born, Bacchic lord,
> wild, ineffable, secretive, two-horned and two-shaped.
> Ivy-covered, bull-faced, warlike, howling, pure,
> You take raw flesh, you have feasts, wrapt in foliage, decked with grape clusters.
> Resourceful Eubouleus, immortal god sired by Zeus
> When he mated with Persephone in unspeakable union.
> Hearken to my voice, O blessed one,
> and with your fair-girdled nymphs breathe on me in a spirit of perfect agape.

Therefore, the use of music and song in a worship context would not have been unfamiliar for the new community of Christ-believers in Colossae. This would have been a standard mode of worshipping divine beings, regardless of whether the Colossian believers had previously been part of a Jewish or Hellenistic religious context.

Hence in summary, the key development that the author of Colossians presents for early Christian understandings of ecclesiology is that of representing Christ as the 'head of the body, the church' (Col. 1:18), where the church is understood in a universal sense. In Colossians this metaphor of the church as body is developed from the formulation given in the authentic Pauline letters. However, rather than being presented as a physiological image of corporate life and relationships, it depicts the organic relationship between all believers as they are incorporated into a single entity and enjoy life through their linkage with the head, Christ. The image of Christ as head not only incorporates ideas of priority and leadership (Col. 1:18), but also of sustenance (Col. 2:19). Hence growth of the body is only possible in relationship with Christ (Moo 2008: 67). Therefore, the ecclesiology of Colossians is subservient to the author's overarching christology. The cosmic Christ, who is the first born of all creation (Col. 1:15) and in whom all things hold together (Col. 1:17) has his priority and headship recognized first in the church where he is head and where he is seen to have 'first place in all things' (Col. 1:18). Christ, who holds the cosmos together, is therefore also seen as the head also holds together the entire body. This 'entire body' is the universal church, ἐκκλησία (Col. 2:19). However, insights concerning local churches come to the fore in the discussion concerning the ethical behaviours required between group members (Col. 3:9, 13), in descriptions of corporate instruction and worship (Col. 3:16), and in relation to Laodicean believers who worship in the house of a patronness called Nympha (Col. 4:15). The Laodicean believers are to gain further Christian instruction through the reading of Pauline epistles. Therefore, while the theology of a universal church is more prominent in Colossians than in earlier Pauline letters, it has not totally subsumed the local understanding of the church and the need to provide instructions on how to regulate the collective life of believers. However, it is in respect to a universal perspective on the church, regarded as Christ's body over which he acts as head, that the author enlarges early Christian thinking on the nature and significance of the church.

4.5. *Eschatology*

For the author of Colossians, the significance of Christ does not affect believers only on an individual or even corporate level. Rather, it has implications for the total renewal of creation. Peace is established through the cross, and as a result all things are reconciled to Christ, 'whether things on earth or things in heaven' (Col. 1:20; cf. Rom. 8:18–25, where creation still eagerly awaits its renewal). Therefore, the reconciling work of Christ is seen as having brought about a new order of peace. Potentially this is a claim that might stand in subversive tension with Roman ideology, with its claim that the *Pax Romana* had been established through the benevolent semi-divine emperorship of Augustus and his successors. Given the prominence of the proclamation of imperial peace under the Julio-Claudian emperors, it is likely that the claim of peace through the cross and the reconciliation of all things in Christ would have been heard as a counterclaim in the face of the rhetoric of stability and peace established by Roman rule.

This renewal is described as creating a new mode of existence for believers in their current state. Thus believers are told that through their baptism they have already been 'raised up with him through faith' (Col. 2:12). While believers were formerly dead they have now been made alive through Christ (Col. 2:13), and through the cross the 'debt' against believers now is cancelled (Col. 2:14). Furthermore, followers of Christ have been raised with Christ, and their life is now to be found in the heavenly sphere with God, rather than on earth (Col. 3:1–3). Thus they are already participating in the new mode of existence that life in Christ brings. The author does not describe such blessings as part of a hoped-for future, but as the reality for those who already belong to Christ.

However, the future aspect of Christian hope is not entirely muted in the epistle. Perhaps the most obvious place depicting a future dimension to the blessings received in Christ is immediately after those statements concerning the experience of new life that has already been received. Initially, the author declares that believers have been raised with Christ (Col. 3:1), and that their life is hidden with Christ in God (Col. 3:3). Yet immediately following on from these affirmations indicative of a realized eschatology, a future expectation is related: 'when Christ is revealed, who is your life, then also you with him will be revealed in glory' (Col. 3:4). It appears that the author did not perceive any tension between the belief that believers had been already raised with Christ, and the claim that their new life in Christ still awaited manifestation in the future. In various of the letters generally considered to be authentically Pauline there is a difference in emphasis between realized aspects of eschatology and the future eschatological hopes for believers. The result is that tension between future and present eschatological expectations are typically constructed in a different way. The eschatological expectations that have been experienced are those realized by Christ, whom God has already raised from the dead and who has become the first-fruits of God's transformative work in defeating death (Rom. 6:9; 1 Cor 15:20; 1 Thess. 1:10). However, what remains is for believers to experience the same eschatological transformation. Primarily in earlier Pauline theology such blessings will be received at the parousia (1 Cor. 15:23; 1 Thess. 2:19; 3:13; 4:15; 5:23), although at times a process of transformation is already envisaged as taking place (2 Cor. 3:18). Moreover, even in some of the authentic letters Paul focuses on the implication of the present reality of living with the risen Christ. Hence Paul can tell the Corinthians that believers carry the death of Christ with them 'so that the life of Jesus may be displayed in our body' (2 Cor. 4:11). Notwithstanding this perspective, a few verses later Paul declares that resurrection is a future event for the Corinthians: 'he who raised Jesus will raise us with Jesus in our turn' (2 Cor. 4:14). There is a discernible shift in emphasis in Colossians, with the experience of resurrection for believers not being delayed until the coming of Christ. Rather, the co-resurrection of believers with Christ is clearly announced as having taken place (Col. 3:1). However, the tension that arises comes about because those who are not believers are unable to see the new heavenly life experienced by the Colossian believers. Therefore, it is the visible manifestation of what the letter portrays as the present but invisible reality of resurrected believers that requires future disclosure.

While some have rejected the idea that there is any development in the eschatological hopes expressed in the corpus of thirteen Pauline letters (Dunn 1998: 313),[15] more commonly scholars have

---

[15] While Dunn sees Paul using a range of imagery that cannot be forced into a single unified or consistent picture, he does maintain that the Pauline eschatological expectations are remarkably constant. He states, 'Paul's conviction

seen the highly charged statements concerning the parousia becoming softened with the passage of time. Instead these are replaced with a more realized version of eschatology that understands believers as already participating to some extent in resurrection life, and hence experiencing some level of transformation that brings them closer to the vision of divine life. While any schematization of the data can flatten some of the subtle differences, Charles' proposal of four stages of eschatological development in Pauline thought remains useful for mapping some of the broad contours across the letters. Charles excludes the pastoral epistles from his framework (Charles 1913: 437–63), which may be summarized as follows:

Stage 1:   1 and 2 Thessalonians
             Salient features: (a) Prior apostasy and coming of Antichrist;
             (b) in response, the parousia and final judgment; (c) followed
             by resurrection and blessed consummation for believers.
Stage 2:   1 Corinthians
             Salient features: (a) The parousia and final judgment; (b) the
             resurrection organically connected with that of Christ; (c)
             final consummation and perfected kingdom where God has
             become all in all.
Stage 3:   2 Corinthians and Romans
             Salient features: (a) Universal spread of Christ's kingdom
             on earth; (b) the parousia and final judgment; (c) the resur-
             rection and immediate sequel of departure from this life.
Stage 4:   Philippians, Colossians, and Ephesians
             Salient features: (a) Everlasting duration of the kingdom of
             Christ; (b) the extension of Christ's redemption to the world
             of spiritual beings.

Charles sees Colossians as representative of the fourth stage of this development in Pauline eschatological thinking. No doubt the establishment of the kingdom of Christ is to be seen in claims that the realm in which believers have their new existence is 'the kingdom of the son of his love' (Col. 1:13). This idea may be expressed more clearly in Ephesians, where the teleological goal of the universe is to partake 'in the kingdom of Christ and of God' (Eph. 5:5). Similarly, the claim that Christ's redemptive work has a cosmic reach is seen

---

that the parousia was imminent and becoming ever closer also seems to have remained remarkably untroubled by the progress of events and passing of time' (Dunn 1998: 313).

in the christological hymn where all the powers both visible and invisible are said to have been created by Christ (Col. 1:16; cf. 3:11). Moreover, through the cross peace is restored with all things both on earth and in heaven, and through Christ's redemptive work there is a cosmic reconciliation. Again these ideas may find further development in Ephesians, where the dispensation or stewardship that will characterize the fulness of time is to be 'the summing up of all things in Christ, the things in heaven and the things in earth in him' (Eph. 1:10).

It appears that there is sufficient textual support to accept the broad outline of Charles' proposal – although Ephesians may represents a more fully developed phase of thought than Colossians (and it is difficult to see where Philippians actually fits in). Hence Colossians can be understood as being located towards the latter stages of the development of Pauline eschatological thought. While it retains a belief in future blessings for believers when their life in Christ is made manifest, those blessing are already said to belong to them in the present. However, this future dimension contains no explicit reference to the second coming of Christ, and instead of parousia language the author prefers the language of manifestation or revelation, φανερόω (Col. 3:4).

The question that remains is whether this degree of development is possible within the thought of the same person. Perhaps it should be noted that for a person who underwent the shift of religious allegiance that Paul had experienced (cf. Phil. 3:4–7), this change in eschatology may not have represented such a significant paradigm shift. However, this change in perspective does appear to reflect a regularization of Christian life and a social conservatism that is not representative of wider Pauline theology. The same social routinization is observable elsewhere in the epistle. While it can maintain the inclusive and emancipatory Pauline charter that abolishes social distinctions (Col. 3:11), it almost immediately qualifies that radical outlook with the household code that advocates maintenance of societal norms (Col. 3:18–4:1). The eschatological emphasis in Colossians centres upon a realized experience of Christian hope, and this forms a marked contrast with the earlier Pauline letters. However, Colossians has not domesticated Paul's fervent eschatology to the degree that it has lost all of its future orientation. Therefore, what Colossians presents is an eschatology that is in broad continuity with Pauline theology, since it also sees all heavenly blessings coming through life in Christ. Yet, while stemming from that stream of thought, the radical apocalyptic vision of a triumphant second coming and accompanying judgment has been lost. Instead, the focus falls upon living a transformed life in the present on the basis of the belief that Colossian believers now live in a new existential realm, although those around them cannot see the transformation which they have undergone (cf. Punt 2011: 299–300).

4.6. *The Gospel*
The teaching concerning the message of Christ, which Epaphras announced to the Colossians (Col. 1:7), is described using the umbrella term 'the gospel'. The term itself only occurs twice in the letter (Col. 1:5, 23). However, there are a number of near synonyms such as 'the word of truth' (Col. 1:5) that stand in apposition to the term 'the gospel'. Other near synonyms include, 'the word of God' (Col. 1:25), 'the word of Christ' (Col. 3:16), and simply 'the word' (Col. 4:3). It is possible to trace a dual background for the term 'the gospel'. It is used in a verbal form in the Septuagint, where it can refer to the proclamation made by a herald announcing salvation: 'how lovely on the mountains are the feet of him who brings good news (εὐαγγελιζομένου), who announces peace and brings good news (εὐαγγελιζόμενος) of happiness, who announces salvation...' (LXX Isa. 52:7). In this context the participial form of the term is used to denote the proclamation of good news. It is interesting to see it used in a context where there is also an emphasis on the announcement of peace. In Colossians part of the message is that cosmic peace has been established through the blood of the cross (Col. 1:20). The second context in which the term was used in the first half of the first century was in imperial edicts celebrating the regnal years or birth dates of emperors. The so-called Priene inscription was a text set up to declare the magnificence and the beneficence of the emperor Augustus. The inscription has been found in multiple locations in Asia Minor, with thirteen fragments being found in five different cities including Apamea in Phrygia. The noun 'gospel' occurs in a genitive plural form, εὐαγγελίων, and it is likely that the term is used a second time at another place in a damaged line of the text (Stanton 2004: 31). The relevant portion of the inscription reads as follows, with reconstructed words in brackets:

49

> And Caesar [when he was manifest], transcended the expectations of [all who had anticipated the good news (εὐαγγελία)], not only by surpassing the benefits conferred by his predecessors but by leaving no expectation of surpassing him to those who would come after him, with the result that the birthday of our god signaled the beginning of the good news (εὐαγγελίων) for the world because of him. (lines 37–41)

Both in this section and in the larger inscription it is hard not to be struck by the similarity of some of the claims made for Augustus and those that early Christians such as Paul made on behalf of Christ. Augustus had been made manifest, he surpassed the expectations of those who awaited the good news, he could be addressed as 'our god', and his birth was 'the beginning of the good news for the world'. In an earlier section of the inscription, Augustus is said to be filled with divine power for the benefit of humanity, and a reconstructed section of a partially defective line might refer to him as 'a saviour'. Thus there are clear cosmic and soteriological consequences linked to the figure of Augustus.

Read against this background Pauline statements about the gospel and the significance of Christ could easily be heard as subversive counterclaims that undermined Roman religious and political ideology. For the early believers in Jesus the good news of peace, reconciliation, and salvation were to be found in the proclamation of the risen Christ, and not in the figure of the emperor.

While the term 'gospel' may have had wider resonances, it is also used in Colossians to represent an assured body of teaching or a message that proclaims the sufficiency and efficacy of Christ's work. As such, adherence to the gospel proclaimed by Epaphras and Paul is a corrective and bulwark against what others are teaching – namely that faith in Christ needed to be supplemented with ecstatic religious practices that were likely to have been imported from some of the local mystery cults. In the context in which the term 'the gospel' is first used in the letter it is an act of communication, which informs hearers of events that have soteriological import since the gospel message passes on knowledge of heavenly hope (Col. 1:5). Reception of the gospel is also described as an auditory event since people hear the gospel. Moreover, the content of the message is portrayed as reliable, since the gospel is also described as 'the word of truth' (Col. 1:5). This truth claim undergirds the message of the letter. Since the gospel is a divine word of truth, believers require no further teaching to give them access to divine hope.

The second and final explicit use of the term 'gospel' in the letter makes these claims even more stridently. Believers are to continue in the faith by not being 'moved away from the hope of the gospel that you have heard' (Col. 1:23). Again the reception of the gospel is represented as an auditory event, and its content is the message of hope. Paul is portrayed as a minister of the gospel. This instantiates his own trustworthiness as one who can proclaim the gospel, and also as one who can adjudge the claims being made by those instructing the Colossians to supplement their faith. In the material that follows, Paul is presented as declaring that he has a stewardship given to him that is to fulfil 'the word of God' (Col. 1:25). This is to be understood as proclamation of the gospel, which is understood as communicating 'the mystery that has been hidden away from the ages and from the generations – but now was made manifest to his holy ones' (Col. 1:26). Thus the proclamation of the gospel is an apocalyptic act, in so far as it is the revelation of previously undisclosed divine mysteries.

In the remainder of the letter, although the term 'gospel' is not present, the author continues to use near synonyms. Providing teaching concerning the corporate life of the community, the author instructs believers to 'let the word of Christ dwell in you richly' (Col. 3:16). It is apparent that the message of the gospel is not just the introductory or initiatory stage of Paul's or Epaphras' proclamation – it remains the content of teaching and believers are told to reflect on the gospel corporately and let it permeate their being as it dwells within them. The depiction of Paul as one actively called to proclaim the gospel is reinforced at the end of the letter, where he requests prayer on his behalf by the Colossians in order that 'God might open for us a door for the word, to speak the mystery of Christ' (Col. 4:3). Here 'the word' is the briefest of near synonyms used in the letter for the 'gospel'. Hence, it is also stated that Paul is suffering imprisonment because of his commitment to proclaiming the gospel.

Although only explicitly used twice in the letter, 'the gospel' is an important concept for the author. It denotes the true and reliable message concerning Christ, which requires no further supplement or expansive teaching. The Christian message is described using the term 'gospel' and near synonyms using the term 'word'. Part of the corporate life of believers is a pattern of reflection on 'the word of Christ'. This is seen as strengthening the community, and by implication guarding against divergent teaching. Paul is presented in the letter as an exemplary steward of the gospel (Col. 1:23, 25), and it is because of his unwavering commitment to proclaiming the gospel that he is now incarcerated. Thus Paul is presented to the Colossians as the example *par excellence* of the necessity of remaining focused to the gospel without any deviation, such as that being suggested by those trying to have the Colossian believers engage in other religious practices. Therefore, the gospel announces the previously hidden heavenly hope and it makes clear that Christ is the totality of the divine mystery made known through proclamation of the Pauline message.

5. *The Missing Old Testament in Colossians*

The bare facts are that the Jewish scriptures are never directly cited in Colossians, there is only one echo or allusion that is widely recognized by commentators, which is the intertextual link with LXX Gen. 1:26–27 in Col. 3:10, and in addition to this there are a few places where biblical language may have shaped formulations used in the letter, i.e. LXX Prov. 8:23–27 in Col. 1:17, and LXX Sir. 1:24, Isa. 45:3, Prov. 2:3 in Col. 2:3. However, the verbal parallels in these two examples are so fleeting that it is impossible to tell whether there is an intentional echoing of specific biblical texts, or if the biblical phraseology has permeated the religious language of the author of Colossians to such an extent that the phrases have become his normal mode of expression, or whether the slight similarities are due simply to coincidence.

Recently, especially under the influence of the work of Richard Hays,[16] scholars have found a greater range of intertextual links between the New Testament and the Jewish scriptures even in cases where the verbal parallels are slight. Hays laid out seven criteria for determining the plausibility of a proposed 'echo' or 'allusion':

---

[16] Two of Hays' books have proved particularly important, the first being foundational for subsequent studies: R. B. Hays, *Echoes of Scripture in the Letters of Paul* (1989); and *The Conversion of the Imagination: Paul as Interpreter of Israel's Scriptures* (2005).

1. **Availability**: Was the proposed source of the allusion/echo available to the author and/or original hearers?
2. **Volume**: What is the degree of explicit repetition of words or syntactical patterns?
3. **Recurrence**: How often does Paul elsewhere cite or allude to the same scriptural passage?
4. **Thematic Coherence**: How well does the alleged echo fit into the line of argument that Paul is developing?
5. **Historical Plausibility**: Could Paul have intended the alleged meaning effect?
6. **History of Interpretation**: Have other readers, both critical and pre-critical, heard the same echoes?
7. **Satisfaction**: Does the proposed reading make sense?

These criteria are useful, although they have not always been given close attention in subsequent work. The result has been the proliferation of proposed echoes or allusions, even when they defy the majority of Hays' criteria.

In relation to Colossians there have been three recent studies on the use of the Jewish scriptures as a whole in the letter, and several other studies that have looked at the use of individual texts by the author of Colossians. The first major study in this area in the post-Hays era was a chapter written by Gordon Fee in a Festschrift for Earle Ellis (Fee 2006). The next two studies were related, but undertaken independently. In the *Commentary on the New Testament Use of the Old Testament*, Greg Beale contributed an extensive treatment of the Jewish scriptures in Colossians (Beale and Carson 2007: 841–70). To date the only monograph length treatment on the topic has been Christopher Beetham's published PhD thesis. The thesis was completed in 2005 under the supervision of Beale, but published three years later (Beetham 2008). While there is considerable overlap in these three works, it is also noteworthy that the level of disagreement is significant between these three scholars who are basically using the same method. In total Fee detects ten echoes. Beale prefers the term 'allusion', which he sees as reflecting intentionality on the part of Paul (whereas an echo is seen as more loosely defined, sometimes 'as unconscious and unintentional sometimes as conscious and intentional' Beale 2007: 841). He argues for seventeen allusions to the Jewish scriptures in Colossians. By contrast, Beetham classifies the intertextual links as either being stronger allusions or weaker echoes. In total he finds eleven intertextual relationships, two allusions and nine echoes. Strikingly, even one of his stronger allusions is rejected by Fee. The proposed allusions and echoes detected by these three scholars can be presented in the following table. As a helpful comparison, the table also lists the passages from Colossians contained in the NA[28] appendix IV: *Loci Citati vel Allegati, A. Ex Vetere Testamento*:

	Passage in Colossians	Intertext from OT	NA[28]	Fee	Beale	Beetham
1	1:6, 10	Gen. 1:28			A	E
2	1:9–10	Exod. 31:3; 35:31–32; Isa. 11:2		E (Isa. 11:2)	A	E (Isa. 11:2, 9)
3	1:12–14	Exodus motif		E	A	E
4	1:13	2 Sam. 7:12–16		E (2 Sam. 7:14, 18)	A	E (2 Sam. 7:12–18)
5	1:15	Gen. 1:26, 28		E		
6	1:15	Gen. 1:27			A	
7	1:15	Ps. 89:27 [LXX 88:28]		E	A	
8	1:15–17	Wisdom theme			A (poss.)	
9	1:15–20	Prov. 8:22–31				A
10	1:17	Prov. 8:23–27	A			
11	1:18	Gen. 1:1		E		
12	1:19	Ps. 68:17 [LXX 67:17]			A	E
13	1:26–27	Dan. 2			A	
14	2:2–3	Dan. 2; Prov. 2:3–6			A	
15	2:3	Sir. 1:24–25; 1 En. 46:3; Isa. 45:3; Prov. 2:3–4	A			

16	2:11	Deut. 30:6			A	E
17	2:13	Gen. 17:10–27			A	E
18	2:22	Isa. 29:13	A	E	A	E
19	3:1	Ps. 110:1	A	E	A	E
20	3:9–10	Gen. 3:7–21			A	
21	3:9–10	Gen. 1:26, 28		E		
22	3:10	Gen. 1:26–27	A		A	A
23	3:12	Deut. 7:6–8		E		
24	4:1	Lev. 25:43–53; Eccl. 5:7	A			
25	4:5	Dan. 2:8			A	
	Total:		6	10	17	11

Here A = allusion, and E = echo, as defined by the scholar in question. Some entries in the table occur as variations of each other, such as the fifth and sixth rows, the fourteenth and fifteenth, and the twenty-first and twenty-second. However in these cases it was important to reflect the differing formulations of the intertextual link as presented by each scholar.

It is immediately apparent that only three examples have the support in all four lists (taking rows twenty-one and twenty-two together). These are the echo or allusion of Isa. 29:13 in Col. 2:22; Ps. 110:1 [LXX 109:1] in Col. 3:1; and Gen. 1:26–27 in Col. 3.[9]–10. Taking these three examples in turn, the following textual parallels occur in the Greek text (English translation supplied):

LXX Isa. 29:13   καὶ εἶπεν κύριος ἐγγίζει μοι ὁ λαὸς οὗτος τοῖς χείλεσιν αὐτῶν τιμῶσίν με ἡ δὲ καρδία αὐτῶν πόρρω ἀπέχει ἀπ᾽ ἐμοῦ μάτην δὲ σέβονταί με διδάσκοντες ἐντάλματα ἀνθρώπων καὶ διδασκαλίας

And the Lord has said, This people draw near to me, with their lips they honour me, but their heart is far from me: but in vain do they worship me, teaching the precepts and doctrines of men.

Col. 2:22   ἅ ἐστιν πάντα εἰς φθορὰν τῇ ἀποχρήσει, κατὰ τὰ ἐντάλματα καὶ διδασκαλίας τῶν ἀνθρώπων

referring to things which all perish as they are used, according to the precepts and doctrines of men?

The key phrase is to be found at the end of both verses: ἐντάλματα ἀνθρώπων καὶ διδασκαλίας (Isa. 29:13b) and τὰ ἐντάλματα καὶ διδασκαλίας τῶν ἀνθρώπων (Col. 2:22b). There are four shared words (if one includes the conjunction καί, 'and'). There are, however, differences in the two constructions: literally 'precepts of men and doctrines' in LXX Isa. 29:13, and 'precepts and doctrines of the men' in Col. 2:22. There may be some connection here, but the verbal correspondence of only four words (one of which is a conjunction) with differences in ordering does not necessarily establish that the text of Isa. 29:13 is being used either directly or intentionally. It is possible that the phrase 'the precepts and doctrines of men' had become a stock phrase used to denote human instruction, and circulated independently of its original context.

LXX Ps. 109:1 εἶπεν ὁ κύριος τῷ κυρίῳ μου κάθου ἐκ δεξιῶν μου ἕως ἂν θῶ τοὺς ἐχθρούς σου ὑποπόδιον τῶν ποδῶν σου
The Lord said to my Lord, Sit on my right, until I make your enemies a footstool for your feet.

Col. 3:1 Εἰ οὖν συνηγέρθητε τῷ Χριστῷ, τὰ ἄνω ζητεῖτε, οὗ ὁ Χριστός ἐστιν ἐν δεξιᾷ τοῦ θεοῦ καθήμενος
If then you have been raised up with Christ, keep seeking the things above, where Christ is, seated at the right hand of God.

The key phrases here are εἶπεν ὁ κύριος τῷ κυρίῳ μου κάθου ἐκ δεξιῶν (LXX Ps. 109:1a) and οὗ ὁ Χριστός ἐστιν ἐν δεξιᾷ τοῦ θεοῦ καθήμενος (Col. 3:1b). In the passage from the Psalm it is the Lord who invites 'my Lord' to 'sit on my right'. Therefore the passage conveys the imperative command for one known as 'my Lord' to sit on the right of the deity. In Col. 3:1, the text literally states that 'Christ is at the right of God seated'. Here the verb is not an imperative instructing one to take a sitting position, but a participle (probably with stative aspect) denoting that Christ has already taken his position at the right hand of God. Although the idea of sitting at the right of a potentate was ubiquitous in the ancient world, the prominence of Ps. 110:1 [LXX 109:1] is well known. This makes it likely that Ps. 110:1 stands behind Col. 3:1 at some level, but also given the wide circulation of that text in early Christian circles and the fact that it is not quoted directly here (only the idea of sitting at the right is employed) it may well be the case that this is an indirect or mediated use not of the text of Ps. 110:1, but of an idea that might have stemmed from that text.

LXX Gen. 1:27   καὶ ἐποίησεν ὁ θεὸς τὸν ἄνθρωπον κατ' εἰκόνα θεοῦ ἐποίησεν
                  αὐτόν ἄρσεν καὶ θῆλυ ἐποίησεν αὐτούς
                  And God made man, according to the image of God he made
                  him, male and female he made them.

Col. 3:10   καὶ ἐνδυσάμενοι τὸν νέον τὸν ἀνακαινούμενον εἰς ἐπίγνωσιν
                  κατ' εἰκόνα τοῦ κτίσαντος αὐτόν
                  and have put on the new self who is being renewed to a true
                  knowledge according to the image of the one who created
                  him.

The key parallel phrases here are κατ' εἰκόνα θεοῦ ἐποίησεν αὐτόν
(LXX Gen. 1:27) and κατ' εἰκόνα τοῦ κτίσαντος αὐτόν (Col. 3:10).
The key differences are that the genitive noun, θεοῦ, 'God' contained
in LXX Gen. 1:27 is replaced by the substantivized participle τοῦ
κτίσαντος in Col. 3:10, and secondly that this makes the verb ἐποίησεν
redundant and hence it is not present in Col. 3:10. The use of the
participle could be due either to a desire to use a circumlocution, or in
order to emphasize the creative role of God. Beetham classes this as
an allusion (Beetham 2008: 267). However, it is not justified to read
into Col. 3:10, in the manner that Beetham does, a fully developed
Adam christology. In relation to Col. 3:10 Beetham states, '[t]he last
Adam Messiah Jesus, *is* the image of God and serves as the head and
prototype of the new humanity of the new creation' (Beetham 2008:
244). Here the christological ideas of Rom. 5:12–21 are being read
into Colossians on the basis of what is at best a snippet of the creation
story from Genesis, even though the intertext contains no reference to
Adam. Instead it focuses on the role of the creator. In part, Beetham's
argument is based on the assumption that the author of Colossians
had knowledge of Paul's Adam christology. This would of course
be the case if the author were Paul himself (assuming Colossians
to be later than Romans). However, Beetham claims to eschew the
idea that his study has implications for the question of authorship:
'there is possibly little here that furthers the debate concerning the
authorship of Colossians' (Beetham 2008: 263). Yet the allusion only
becomes plausible on the basis of Pauline authorship, or at the very
least on the assumption that the author had a detailed knowledge of
the letter to the Romans, which cannot be established on the basis
of the text of Colossians. The conclusion Aageson advances appears
more balanced, '[w]hile the allusion to Gen. 1:26–27 is unmistakable,
a developed Adam/Christ Christology is not and at most may be only

implicit' (Aageson 2012: 128). Moreover, one must bear in mind the widespread circulation of the story in contexts independent of the text of Genesis, hence 'the well-known character of [Gen. 1:26] makes the assumption of a direct allusion less likely and certainly not necessary' (Moritz 2004: 181 n. 4).

A further significant piece of evidence comes from Ephesians. Here it is assumed that Ephesians (in some way) is dependent on Colossians. While that position is not held universally, it is perhaps the most common explanation of the textual relationship of the two letters (see Mitton 1951: 68–74; Lincoln 1990: xlvii–lviii; Hoehner 2002: 33; for an alternative view see Best 1997). It then becomes instructive to briefly consider the way Ephesians uses scriptural texts in passages where it parallels Colossians. Replicating a table constructed by Moritz, it becomes clear that in several instances Ephesians develops traditions that appear to have been derived from Colossians through the addition of quotations drawn from the Jewish scriptures (Moritz 2004: 183).

Colossians		*Ephesians*	
Parallel from Colossians	*Verses with Old Testament material*	*Parallel from Ephesians*	*Verses with Old Testament material*
Col. 1:13	–	1:15–23	1:20, 22
Col. 1:3–27; 2:9–14	–	2:11–18	2:13, 17
Col. 2:15	–	4:8–10	4:8
Col. 3:5–12	3:10	4:25–5:2	*4:25f.*, 30; 5:2
Col. 3:16	–	5:13–20	5:14, 18
Col. 3:18f.	–	6:1–4	6:2

There is a clear pattern whereby the author of Ephesians supplies a citation from the Jewish scriptures into a section of text with a parallel in Colossians, even though the parallel section of Colossians does not (in all but one case) allude to the Old Testament.

There are several reasons why this may be the case. First, using Hays criterion of 'availability', the two authors of these epistles may have had different mental repositories of scriptural knowledge. Second, again using the notion of 'availability', it may be the case that the author of Colossians was sensitive to the background knowledge of his readers, and presupposed a lack of knowledge of the Jewish scriptures beyond a rudimentary level. Third, in terms of the criterion of 'satisfaction', to establish the case being argued in Colossians it could also be the case that the author wished to construct an argument built upon uniqueness of Christ without reference to any supporting scriptural authorization. These are suppositions, and the reason for the lack of scriptural material in Colossians cannot be known with certainty. The phenomenon of the lack of citations or allusions drawn from the Jewish scriptures does, however, remain striking.

This absence of biblical quotations is even more striking (although not without parallel) when comparisons are made with the other letters in the Pauline corpus. The preponderance of biblical quotations in Romans is well known, with many passages containing citation formulae (cf. Rom. 9:25–33). Likewise, 1 Corinthians contains numerous quotations from Jewish scriptures, some with citation formulae (1 Cor. 1:19, 31; 2:9; 3:19–20; 6:16; 14:21) and other passages without an introductory formula (1 Cor. 2:16; 5:13). The number of quotations is not as numerous in 2 Corinthians as is the case in either Romans or 1 Corinthians, but there are nonetheless a significant number of examples, such as 2 Cor. 4:13; 6:2, 16–18; 8:15, to name a few. The same pattern is in evidence in Galatians, with numerous citations present with or without introductory formula (Gal. 3:6, 10, 11, 12, 13, 16; 4:27, 30). Although not as replete, the Jewish scriptures are used in the Pastoral Epistles, being either cited explicitly (1 Tim. 5:18–19; 2 Tim. 2:19), or through more integrated but nonetheless obvious use of the Old Testament (Tit. 2:14). The lack of Old Testament quotations in Philemon is perhaps unsurprising given its length and personal nature. More surprising is the lack of explicit citations in Philippians and 1 and 2 Thessalonians. At least two of these letters, if not all three, are genuine letters of Paul (on the authorship of 2 Thessalonians, see Foster 2012). This lack of quotations from the Jewish scriptures may be due to the gentile character of the audience addressed. In fairness, knowledge of the ethnic composition of the communities to which the Pauline letters are addressed is scant. The overwhelming gentile character of the community addressed in 1 Thessalonians is more or less stated explicitly, with the comment that the addressees had 'turned to God from idols to serve a true and living God' (1 Thess. 1:9). While the ethnic composition of the community in Philippi is not as explicit, the warning, 'beware the mutilation [false circumcision], for we are the circumcision' (Phil. 3:2–3), suggests that Paul was addressing an audience who could at best only claim to be the circumcision in a metaphorical sense. It cannot be proven that the recipients of Romans, the Corinthian correspondence, or Galatians would have been more familiar with the Jewish scriptures than the recipients in Thessalonica or Philippi. Hence the use of scriptural citations may reflect more about the author than it does about the audience.

So what is one to make of the lack of use of the Jewish scriptures in Colossians? There are a number of factors to consider. First, the letter could be addressed to a context were the recipients were gentiles and hence did not have knowledge of Jewish scriptures. Thus it could be inferred that it was redundant to use such texts since they were not part of the shared intertextual repertoire between author and audience. This appears to explain the lack of scriptural citations in the Thessalonian correspondence, and that may be the case here. Second, the circumstances of the author might have meant that he did not have direct access to the written texts of the Jewish scriptures. It is interesting that among the so-called prison epistles, Philippians, Philemon, and Colossians all lack explicit Old Testament quotations. However, against this observation, Ephesians, which is purportedly also written from a prison context (Eph. 6:20), does contain several extensive citations from the Jewish scriptures. Third, the absence of quotations of the Jewish scriptures in Colossians may be due to a lack of 'availability' of scriptural material to the author. This may be not just in terms of lack of physical access to written copies of these writings, but if we are dealing with an author different from Paul it may be the case that that person was not well versed in those scriptural texts. This might explain the manner in which the author of Ephesians introduces scriptural citations into parallel contexts.

None of these suggestions can be fully supported given the limited evidence, but the absence of quotations from the Jewish scriptures in Colossians is a fascinating phenomenon. If the letter is written by Paul, this could be due either to his recognition that his audience would not recognize such material, or that his imprisonment meant that he had no access to the necessary texts. If the epistle is written by another author, the lack of scriptural citation could still be due to the audience's lack of knowledge of the Jewish biblical texts, or it could reflect the author's own lack of familiarity with such writings.

6. *Authorship, Date, and Place of Writing*

These three issues are intrinsically intertwined. Taking them in the order listed, the answer to each in turn impacts on the possible answers that can be given to the other questions. As the letter presents itself, it is written by Paul and Timothy to the believers who form the fledgling Jesus community in Colossae. While the letter commences addressing its audience in the first person plural in the opening thanksgiving (Col. 1:3), the plural quickly gives way to the first person singular with Paul speaking of his proclamation of the gospel: 'of which I, Paul, became a servant' (Col. 1:23). This first-person form of address remains explicit throughout the section from Col. 1:23 to Col. 2:5. In the final chapter, the first person plural is briefly taken up again with a request for prayer 'for us' that 'God might open a door for us' (Col. 4:3). However, the plural form is immediately dropped and throughout the rest of the chapter the first person singular form is used with a reference to Paul's imprisonment following on from the plural form: 'because of which also I am bound' (Col. 4:3b). It is apparent from the final verse of the letter that Paul is not the physical scribe of the letter since it is only at this point that he takes up the pen: 'The greeting of Paul in my hand' (Col. 4:18a). Nonetheless, throughout the letter he is presented as the principal author.

6.1. *On the Assumption of Pauline Authorship*

If this information is taken at face value, then Colossians is written by Paul and Timothy, with Paul being the principal author and an unknown figure (perhaps Timothy, but equally perhaps not) being the physical writer of the letter. In turn this would mean that the letter would then have been written during Paul's lifetime at a time when he was incarcerated, and hence he could implore the Colossians to 'remember my bonds' (Col. 4:18; cf. Col. 4:3). Many commentators do adopt this reconstruction, and consequently consider both the places were Paul is known to have been imprisoned for a significant time, along with other possible locations where he might have been jailed. Locations of very brief periods of imprisonment, such as the overnight incarceration in Philippi narrated in Acts, have not been considered as likely places for the composition of the letter. This is because they are of implausibly short duration, and in the case of Philippi it would have been physically difficult for Paul or his associates to write the letter with feet in stocks (Acts 16:23–24). Hence there are commonly considered three viable places of imprisonment from whence the letter might have originated if Paul is taken to be the author. Taking these in chronological order, the three commonly proposed locations from where Paul may have written the letter, with the typical proposed dates, are:

Ephesus	52–54 or 55–57
Caesarea	58–59
Rome	60–63

Each of these solutions has both attractive and problematic features. It is helpful to consider the relative merits of each of these proposals in turn.

6.1.1. *Ephesus*
The major difficultly with the proposal that Ephesus is the place from which Colossians was written is that while there are references to Paul spending time in Ephesus, there is no description of him being imprisoned in the city. Therefore, a period of imprisonment in Ephesus is an academic hypothesis, based upon the lengthy duration in Ephesus ('two years', Acts 19:10) and the description in Acts of Paul and his associates causing a civic disturbance and with the threat of being brought before the civil authorities (Acts 19:38–40). While the idea of an Ephesian imprisonment is hypothetical, it is plausible and has various attractive features in relation to the location for the writing of the letter to the Colossians. The greatest advantage of an Ephesian location is the geographical proximity to Colossae and the Lycus Valley. The various trips that are mentioned in Colossians and Philemon become more difficult (but not impossible) to envisage as the distance between the letter's origin and destination increases. There are various trips of Paul's associates mentioned or implied to and from Colossae. These include the trip made by Epaphras coming from Colossae and sharing with Paul news of the growth in the community of believers in that city (Col. 1:7–8); the journey of the runaway slave Onesimus to Paul – although perhaps greater distance is an advantage in this case (Phlm. 8–12); and the return trip of Tychicus and Onesimus back to Colossae (Col. 4:7–7; Phlm. 12). Apart from the distance of travel to be undertaken on these journeys being lessened if Paul was based in Ephesus, one must also take

into account Paul's stated plan to visit Philemon (Phlm. 22), who is typically understood to be part of the Colossian community. Later in his missionary career Paul seems to have been focused on travel west to Spain (Rom. 15:14–33). Hence the proposed visit to Colossae might be more readily understood at an earlier stage in Paul's career. However, Paul's travel plans were subject to modification, and he was capable of stating more than one planned itinerary. On balance, Ephesus is attractive because of its geographical proximity to Colossae, but less persuasive because of the hypothetical nature of an Ephesian imprisonment.

6.1.2. *Caesarea*
Considering the possibilities in chronological order, the next option is that Paul wrote Colossians during the period of imprisonment in Caesarea. According to Acts, the Roman governor Felix kept Paul in custody in Caesarea, albeit with some freedom (Acts 24:23), for a period of two years until Felix was replaced by Porcius Festus (Acts 24:27). Antonius Felix was the Roman procurator of the province of Judaea between 52–58/59 CE. According to Acts, Paul remained in prison after Felix returned to Rome (Acts 24:27). When Porcius Festus succeeded Felix, at the beginning of his period in office, he sought to win favour with the Jews by handing Paul over to them (Acts 25:9). In order to avoid this eventuality, Paul declared his right to be tried before Caesar's tribunal (Acts 25:11–12). Therefore, this period of imprisonment in Caesarea coincides with the end of the procuratorship of Felix and the commencement of Festus' time in office, that is 58–59.

Despite the textual evidence in support of a period of imprisonment in Caesarea, this option for the location of the composition of Colossians has gained far less support than that of the letter being written either during a hypothetical imprisonment in Ephesus or from Rome. However, like all of the proposals, the evidential basis is slender, apart from the fact that Acts records a period of imprisonment in Caesarea. After problematizing the possibility of an Ephesian imprisonment as 'pure imagination', one of the staunchest proponents of a Caesarean origin for Colossians, Bo Reicke presents one textual argument for the letter being written during this period of captivity. He states, '[i]t was only at Caesarea that he [Paul] was able to announce that he was "now also a prisoner of Christ Jesus"

(Phm. 9)' (Reicke 1973: 435). The argument here is that Philemon and Colossians were written at the same time. The 'now' in Phlm. 9 shows that this is the first time Paul had been a prisoner (in any extended sense). Since there is no basis for an Ephesian imprisonment, this means the first period of extended captivity that would have permitted the language of 'now' having become a prisoner was the first known incarceration, which was in Caesarea in 59. Hence just as Philemon was written from Caesarea, the same must be the case for Colossians. Therefore, Reicke states, '[a] necessary conclusion is that Philemon and Colossians were sent from Caesarea to Colossae ca. A.D. 59' (Reicke 1973: 435). The second inferential piece of evidence that is used to support a Caesarean origin for the letter is that several of the same associates named in Col. 1:7; 4:7–14; and Phlm. 23–24 were present with Paul during the Caesarean captivity. It is noted that Felix not only permitted Paul a degree of liberty but also commanded the centurion that he should not prevent any of Paul's acquaintances from ministering to him (Acts 24:23). While none of the associates is named here, four chapters earlier a group of associates is named: 'he [Paul] was accompanied by Sopater of Berea, the son of Pyrrhus; and by Aristarchus and Secundus of the Thessalonians; and Gaius of Derbe, and Timothy; and Tychicus and Trophimus of Asia' (Acts 20:4). However, the reality is that the only names that this passage from Acts shares with the associates named in Colossians or Philemon are Timothy, Aristarchus and Tychicus. This is not the strongest evidence for asserting the provenance of the letter being Caesarea, especially as these three are not specifically named in connection with Paul's imprisonment in Caesarea.

The strongest piece of evidence in favour of the identification of Caesarea as the place where Colossians was composed is that Acts records an extended period of imprisonment in that location. However, the other arguments that have been put forward are much weaker and do not make the case any more compelling. To base so much on Paul's statement that now he was a prisoner of Christ Jesus (Phlm. 9) loads far too much interpretative weight on this verse. The overlap between the named figures in Colossians and Acts is not as significant as is suggested, and none of the associates are actually named as being at Caesarea. Again, this argument appears tenuous. The evidence for Caesarea being the place of composition is slight, and definitely far from compelling.

6.1.3. *Rome*

By far the most popular suggestion among those who hold to the view that Paul wrote Colossians is that it was composed in Rome. The identification of Rome as the place of composition is based upon the tradition at the end of the book of Acts that Paul was under house-arrest in the imperial capital. Two statements describe Paul's custody. First, it is stated that 'Paul was allowed to stay by himself, with the soldier who was guarding him' (Acts 28:16). Second, that 'he stayed two full years in his own rented quarters, and was welcoming all who came to him' (Acts 28:30). It is often overlooked, but these descriptions appear to represent a situation that is markedly different to that described in Colossians, where the author calls upon the audience to 'remember my chains' (Col. 4:18). It is possible that Colossians was written at a later stage of Paul's custody in Rome, when perhaps the initial relative freedom had been revoked, and he had become subject to harsher conditions.

The other piece of ancient evidence in favour of a Roman setting is to be found in some subscripts appended at the end of manuscripts of Colossians. A variety of colophons, which are found in manuscripts as early as the fourth or fifth centuries, state that the letter was 'to the Colossians written from Rome'. While the manuscripts may date to the fourth or fifth centuries it is not necessarily the case that the subscripts were composed during this period. The earliest manuscript to reference Rome as the place of composition is the fourth-century Codex Vaticanus, B 02. However, it appears that the first corrector (B^1) added the subscript around the sixth century. The fifth-century manuscript, Codex Alexandrinus, contains the subscript 'to the Colossians from Rome' (f.110r). Here it is difficult to date the subscripts, but the script looks similar to that of the main text, which is typically dated to the fifth century. Regardless of the exact dates of these subscripts, they have a pedigree that dates back to some time in the late antique period. Therefore, the antiquity of the view that Paul wrote Colossians during the period of his Roman imprisonment can be established.

Despite the positive points in favour of the composition of Colossians in Rome, the hypothesis is not without difficulty. One of the major problems, as was the case with the identification of Caesarea as the place of origin, is the distance between Rome and Colossae, which is approximately 1,200 miles (1,920 km) as the crow flies.

This stands in comparison to the distances between Caesarea and Colossae of 480 miles (775 km), and Ephesus and Caesarea of 106 miles (170 km). While the distance between Rome and Colossae is significantly greater than that between Caesarea and Rome, it must be remembered that Rome and Ephesus were major cities in the Empire, and that consequently there must have been frequent journeys made by travellers between these two locations, typically by sea. So, despite the distance, the journey was not impossible. It would, however, have lengthened the period for communication, especially in comparison to the theory that Colossians was written in Ephesus.

Therefore, if Paul was the author of the letter, then there are three possible places that are commonly considered as locations where the letter may have been written. Perhaps the least likely is Caesarea. The positive arguments in favour of this location are weak, with the strongest being the fact that Acts attests an extended period of imprisonment in Caesarea. Deciding between Ephesus and Rome is difficult. In favour of the former is its proximity to Colossae and other cities of the Lycus Valley. Against this identification is the fact that an Ephesian imprisonment is a scholarly inference, with no decisive textual evidence to support this hypothesis. By contrast, a Roman imprisonment is documented in the book of Acts, Rome is by tradition the place of Paul's execution, and certain manuscripts of Colossians state that the letter was written from Rome (although that detail may have been added to colophons on the basis of information in Acts). Against Rome as the place of composition of the letter is the distance between Rome and Colossae, and the fact that the circumstances of Paul's custody in Rome as described at the end of the book of Acts do not align with the more exacting restraint alluded to in Colossians.

On balance, for those who hold to the Pauline authorship of Colossians, the theory that the letter was written from Rome around 60–61 may be the more plausible hypothesis. Not only does this place the letter in a location of known incarceration, but dating it to the later period would perhaps allow more time for some of the theological developments that appear in the letter. However, the most problematic aspect of this scenario is the distance between Rome and Colossae.

6.2. *The Case against Pauline Authorship*

In 1996, in relation to the authorship of Colossians, Raymond Brown wrote '[a]t the present moment about 60 percent of critical scholarship holds that Paul did not write the letter' (Brown 1997: 610). More recently in a survey of attendees at the British New Testament Conference in 2011, responses were gathered from 109 people concerning their opinions on the authorship of the Pauline epistles. Of these 56 were of the opinion Paul was the author of Colossians, 17 were against Pauline authorship, and 36 were undecided (Foster 2012: 171). Those attending the conference included New Testament scholars both in post and retired, PhD students, and some people with a general interest in New Testament scholarship. While a slight majority of 51.4% were in favour of Pauline authorship, it was perhaps surprising to see only 15.6% were decisively against Pauline authorship. By contrast, 33% saw the evidence as too ambiguous to come to a firm conclusion.

It is helpful to consider the reasons for such ambiguity. First, Colossians is a relatively short letter of only 95 verses. This is an extremely narrow evidential base from which to draw conclusions about authorship. Typical arguments against Pauline authorship have been based on differences in vocabulary, style, and theology. In relation to the vocabulary it is noted that the letter uses 87 words not found among the seven letters often considered to be authentically Pauline, of which 62 are not found elsewhere in the Pauline corpus, and furthermore, of which 34 occur nowhere else in the New Testament. While the numbers are factual, it is a more subjective judgment as to whether they are significant or indicative of a different author. In a 'tongue-in-cheek' article discussing the authenticity of Ephesians (widely considered to be post-Pauline) Harold Hoehner applies the same type of arguments to Galatians that are typically used to argue against the Pauline authorship of Ephesians (Hoehner 2006). He assembles the following statistics about the vocabulary of Galatians. There are 30 words used in Galatians that occur nowhere else in the New Testament, and a further 55 words that are found nowhere else in the Pauline corpus. Hence, there are 85 words in Galatians that are unique in comparison to the rest of the Pauline letters; for Ephesians there are only 79 unique words (Hoehner 2006: 155). Therefore, by itself, consideration of the unique vocabulary of Colossians appears indecisive for determining the question of authorship.

Apart from vocabulary, there are frequently appeals to stylistic arguments. In this vein Brown notes the presence of 'long sentences in Col hooked together by participles and relative pronouns... e.g., 1:3–8, 2:8–15' (Brown 1997: 611). However, he continues by immediately noting the presence of equally long sentences elsewhere in letters whose Pauline authorship is not disputed, such as Rom. 1:1–7. Scholars who defend the Pauline authorship of Colossians do not shy away from acknowledging the observable differences in style. Commenting on stylistic differences, Moo states, 'there is some substance to the observation: the letter does, in many paragraphs, exhibit a style that is quite a bit different from that found in most other Pauline letters' (Moo 2008: 31). He notes features such as strings of genitives, such as 'the word of the truth of the gospel' (Col. 1:5), 'the kingdom of the son of his love' (Col. 1:13; for further examples, cf. 1:2, 27; 2:2, 12). In order to overcome the subjective nature of many of these judgments Mealand has undertaken a stylometric analysis of the Pauline corpus based upon a range of multivariate statistical measures, including cluster analysis and discriminant analysis (Mealand 1995). He analyzes samples of 1000 words, and for Colossians takes the material contained in Col. 1:21–4:4 as his sample. His results led him to draw the following conclusion: 'The distinctiveness of Colossians and Ephesians emerged more clearly as the tests proceeded. The results of these tests do therefore tend to confirm the views of those who have argued that these letters are deutero-Pauline' (Mealand 1995: 86). The statistical analysis conducted by Mealand presents a measure of 'distance' between samples of text from the Pauline corpus. Various sample groups cluster together, such as the major Paulines (Romans, 1 and 2 Corinthians, Galatians), a secondary group containing (1 and 2 Thessalonians and Philippians), a third group consisting of Colossians and Ephesians, and a fourth group where the Pastoral Epistles form a distinct cluster. While none of this is surprising, it does provide a numerical measure of the distance between samples and identifies which samples cluster together. What remains a subjective judgment is whether the distance between samples (based on analysis of stylistic features) is of sufficient degree to posit different authors. What Mealand's analysis demonstrates is that the distance between Colossians and the seven epistles in the first two groups which have traditionally been regarded as authentic (2 Thessalonians included, but not Philemon because of its brevity) is greater than the distance between any two of those seven epistles in his first two groups. Colossians is closer in style to Ephesians than it is to the seven epistles in the first two groups. However, it is closer in style to those seven, than it is to his sample group EphA (Eph. 1:1–3:6), but not in comparison to EphB (Eph. 3:16–6:2). This analysis provides helpful numerical data, but it remains a matter of interpretation as to whether this suggests a distinct author for Colossians from the author of the first two groups of Pauline epistles. In Mealand's judgment the distance is great enough to posit that Colossians stems from a different author.

The discussion of the theology of Colossians (in section 4) noted both the shared themes with other Pauline letters, as well as observing developments in relation to several of those themes. In common with all the letters widely regarded as genuinely Pauline, Colossians has a major interest in Christ, and expands in great detail on his significance. The author conceives of Christ in cosmic terms. This is not unprecedented in earlier letters (cf. 1 Cor. 8:6; 2 Cor. 4:4; Phil. 2:6–11). However, in Colossians the cosmic dimension of the author's christology becomes a major controlling factor for understanding the significance of Christ. According to the poetic language of Col. 1:15–20, Christ has priority over the entire cosmic order and is the creative force that brings all things to existence (Col. 1:15–16). Believers are no longer subjugated to 'the elements of the world' (Col. 2:8), since Christ is 'head of every ruler and authority' (Col. 2:10). This negates the need to offer any devotion to cosmic beings, which appears to be part of the pre-Christian spiritual experience of the addressees of the letter. Perhaps most prominently, Christ's cosmic victory is heralded in a paean that celebrates his triumph over such forces (Col. 2:15). On the negative side, it has been noted that the christology of Colossians lacks 'the characteristic Pauline evaluation of the death/resurrection of Christ as the source of justification' (Brown 1997: 611). It is debatable whether these differences and developments in christology can be accommodated by regarding them as conditioned by the situation that Paul was addressing in the Colossian community, or whether they require positing another author than Paul.

Ecclesiology is a second theological topic that has led some to suggest that the development in thought in this area requires attributing Colossians to an author different from Paul. The development is seen in a number of a ways. First, in Colossians, while there are references to the church as a local group of believers, especially with regard to the communities at Colossae or Laodicea, the author is more concerned with presenting the church as a universal organic entity, of which Christ is the head. This leads into the second difference in ecclesiology from that found in the widely accepted authentic letters. While the body metaphor is prominent in other Pauline writings, such as 1 Cor. 12:12–30 with the extended metaphor of the body being used to depict the different functions individual believers have in Christ's body, in Colossians the metaphor is reduced to a narrow purpose. It affirms both that believers form the body of Christ, but more importantly for the theology of the letter that Christ is the head of the church (Col. 1:18). Therefore, the body metaphor is not utilized as in the other Pauline letters to provide pastoral teaching about community relationships; instead, it serves the christological purpose of presenting Christ's headship over the universal body of believers. In this sense for the author of Colossians the formation of the universal church under the headship of Christ is seen as the *telos* or goal that demonstrates the exultation and priority of Christ.

The eschatology of the letter is also noticeably different from the widely accepted authentic Pauline writings at a number of points, although it needs to be emphasized that the author has not totally abandoned the future dimension of eschatological thought, such as the statement that declares that the hidden life of believers still waits to be revealed (Col. 3:4). However, this future aspect is a relatively minor strand in the eschatological outlook of the letter. Instead, the author views the Colossians as already participating in the blessings that stem from new existence in the kingdom of the son (Col. 1:13). This realized eschatology is more developed in Colossians than it appears to be in other places in the Pauline epistles widely considered to be written by the apostle. For instance, elsewhere believers are informed that they still await the transformation of their humble state into conformity with the glorious form of Christ (Phil. 3:20). Again, the question remains whether this development can be viewed as a later stage and maturation in Paul's thought, or whether it is symptomatic of a different theological perspective.

No one argument by itself, be it based on analysis of vocabulary, measureable changes in style, or different theological emphases is sufficient in itself to refute the case for Pauline authorship. However, when these factors are taken in combination their cumulative weight must be given due consideration (cf. Barclay 1997: 33–34). Nevertheless, even the accumulated force of these arguments falls well short of a decisive case against Pauline authorship, although such a case might be considered slightly stronger than the arguments for Pauline authorship. Perhaps instead of black and white categories of authorship by Paul or by another writer, it is necessary to consider 'intermediate' possibilities, which might show that such bald alternatives are not the only ways to account for the evidence.

6.3. *Mediating Solutions to the Question of Authorship*
The type of proposal that has become increasing well supported is to account for the stylistic differences and theological developments on the supposition that Paul employed a different amanuensis, or that because of his incarceration he gave Timothy greater licence in writing the letter to the Colossians in his name. Dunn is fairly typical of this line of thought:

> We may, for example, envisage Paul outlining his main concerns to a secretary (Timothy) who was familiar with the broad-pattern of Paul's letter-writing and being content to leave it to the secretary to formulate the letter with a fair degree of license, perhaps under the condition of his imprisonment at that point able only to add the briefest of personal conclusions (see on 4:18). If so, we should perhaps more accurately describe the theology of Colossians as the theology of Timothy, or, more accurately still, as the theology of Paul as understood or interpreted by Timothy. (Dunn 1996: 38)

This type of argument, with various modifications, has been reiterated by a number of commentators who seek to account for what they see as the finely balanced evidence on both sides of the authorship question. Moreover, since on this scenario Paul is still understood as being alive although incarcerated, the question of the location of imprisonment remains valid. Bird takes the introductory greeting literally, and therefore sees Colossians as being written in tandem with a co-author, Timothy (Bird 2009: 9). Obviously the use of secretaries is a writing practice that is documented in the Pauline letters themselves (Rom. 16:22). This is also the clear implication of concluding notes where Paul takes the pen from the secretary and appends his own greeting in rough script that is clearly discernible from that of his secretary (1 Cor. 16:21; Gal. 6:11; Col. 4:18; 2 Thess. 3:17; cf. Phlm. 19).

However, opting for the hypothesis of a more independent role being given to the scribe or co-author of the letter does not neatly resolve the issues of authorship in favour of the traditional claims of Pauline authorship. The type of authorship that commissions or licenses another to write on one's behalf is unquestionably different from that of simply dictating one's thoughts to a secretary, who then carries out the mechanistic physical writing of the letter. In the latter scenario, when Paul employs the services of Tertius (Rom. 16:22), or unknown scribes in other letters, there is little doubt that Paul is responsible for the contents and compositional structure of the letter. With the proposals offered as mediating positions, as the degree of compositional freedom given to a scribe increases it becomes more difficult to maintain that the person who commissioned the letter remains the author in any meaningful way. Not only is such a proposal unprovable, but as Barclay astutely notes, 'to many it appears too "convenient" by half' (Barclay 1997: 35). Yet, perhaps there is an even greater issue. If one is willing to describe the independent composition of a scribe commissioned by Paul as 'Pauline authorship', then is the same not true of letters written after Paul's death by close associates who may have been commissioned to continue proclaiming the gospel and passing on Pauline teaching? Therefore, such mediating proposals about secretarial freedom open up wider questions about the whole category of what counts as a Pauline letter, or when one may say an epistle was 'authored' by Paul. If one may class a document written by an associate during Paul's lifetime as authentically Pauline, then only a small distinction exists between that and the case of calling a letter Pauline that is written after Paul's death by his co-workers. If that is deemed legitimate, then Colossians should certainly be understood as Pauline in some sense. However, precisely what such a label might mean is different depending on whether Paul dictated the letter and a scribe acted in a mechanistic manner to write down his thoughts, or whether a scribe was given a degree of independence to compose a Pauline letter during Paul's lifetime, or whether members of the

Pauline circle composed Colossians to preserve Paul's teaching and legacy after the apostle's death. In the end, authorship becomes a far more problematic category than perhaps initially imagined.

6.4. *Scholarly Opinions on Authorship, Date, and Place of Writing*
The following table presents scholarly opinions on the authorship of Colossians, the date of its composition, and the place from where it was written. The table is not exhaustive in extent. Instead, it documents some of the key opinions, from the late eighteenth century when Edward Evanson first questioned the Pauline authorship of Colossians. Having rejected the Pauline authorship of Ephesians, Evanson continued by stating, '[t]he same insuperable objection lies against Ephesians, which is manifestly fabricated by the same opificer who composed that to the Ephesians' (Evanson 1792: 263). That 'same insuperable objection' is that both epistles presuppose a settled Christian community in both Ephesus and Colossae before Paul preached in those locations. For Evanson that is patently not the case. In relation to Colossians, he dismisses that claim on the basis of evidence drawn from Acts: '[y]et Colossae and Laodicea were both cities of Phrygia, where Luke assures us, Paul, accompanied by himself, repeatedly preached the Gospel to every city *in order*' (Evanson 1792: 264). Next to be listed in the table is Ernst Theodor Mayerhoff, who is typically presented as the first modern scholar to have questioned the Pauline authorship of Colossians. The list then continues down to recently published works. The emphasis falls on more recent works for two reasons. First, the scholarly opinions from the early period have frequently been documented in various commentaries and studies. Secondly, a survey of more recent works provides insight into the current state of scholarly opinion as reflected in commentaries and recent studies.

Scholar	Author	Date	Place
E. Evanson (1792)	Not Paul		
E. T. Mayerhoff (1838)	Not Paul (but Ephesians by Paul)	100–130 (??) Written against Cerinthus	
F. C. Bauer (1845)	Early Gnostic outlook	Middle second century, against Ebionites	

H. A. W. Meyer (1859)	Paul	60 or 61	Caesarea
H. J. Holtzmann (1872)	Shorter genuine letter expanded to form present text. Author of Ephesians		
H. von Soden (1885, 1991)	Paul, but with later glosses (nine verses 1:15–20; 2:10, 15, 18 [partly]; but only just later 1:16b–17)		
J. B. Lightfoot (1875, 1886)	Paul	63	Rome
Piconio (1890)	Paul	62	Rome
Oltramare (1891)	Paul	62	Rome
T. K. Abbott (1897)	Paul	63	Rome
G. W. Garrod (1898)	Paul	62–63	Rome
H. C. G. Moule (1898)	Paul	63	Rome
E. Lohmeyer (1930)	Paul	60 or 61	Caesarea (p. 14)
E. F. Scott (1930)	Paul	60–62 (presumably)	Rome
M. Dibelius and H. Greeven (1953)	Paul		Caesarea (p. 52)
E. Percy (1946)	Paul		
C. F. D. Moule (1957)	Paul	Around 60	Rome
F. F. Bruce (1957, 1984)	Paul	Early 60s	Rome
J. L. Houlden (1970)	Paul	Late 40s, probably before 48.	Ephesus

E. Lohse (1971)	Theologian schooled in Pauline thought	After the earthquake in Colossae (i.e. after 61, and aimed at teaching Christians in Asia Minor)	Ephesus
R. P. Martin (1972, 1973)	Paul (but with use of an amanuensis – Timothy?) Less certain in 1973	53–54 (1972) 54–57 (1973	Ephesus
B. Reicke (1973)	Paul	59	Caesarea
E. Schweizer (1976)	Not Pauline – pseudonymous. Written by Timothy during Paul's imprisonment	Not post-Pauline, during Paul's Ephesian imprisonment	Ephesus
J. Gnilka (1980)	Deutero-Pauline	c. 70	
P. T. O'Brien (1982)	Paul	60–61	Rome
M. Kiley (1986)	Pseudonymous	After 61	
N. T. Wright (1986)	Paul	52–55 (or possibly 53–56)	Ephesus
P. Pokorný (1991)	Deutero-Pauline	70 or later	Ephesus
M. J. Harris (1991, 2010)	Paul	60–61	Rome
V. P. Furnish (1992)	Pseudonymous	65–90	Southwest Asia Minor is probable
J.-N. Aletti (1993)	Open to some extent, but gives the impression that arguments against apostolic authorship are overstated and fail to account of author's rhetorical response to a given situation	If by Paul before 61–62; if not by Paul then before 70	If by Paul Rome, otherwise uncertain

A. T. Lincoln (1993, 2000)	Not Paul (but heavily influenced by Paul's thought) a Pauline disciple	After the earthquake that occurred 61–64.	Maybe Asia Minor
M. Barth and H. Blanke (1994)	Paul	No later than 61 or 62	Rome
J. D. G. Dunn (1996)	Timothy (under Paul's direction)	60–61	Rome
J. M. G. Barclay (1997)	A Pauline letter – whether by Paul, a secretary, an associate, or a pupil	Nothing rules against composition in Paul's lifetime – regardless of authorship	
R. E. Brown (1997)	Slightly in favour of the letter being deutero-Pauline	If by Paul, 54–56 or 61–63; If not by Paul, then written in the 80s	If by Paul either Ephesus or Rome; if not by Paul, written in Ephesus perhaps by a school of Pauline disciples
M. Y. MacDonald (2000)	Deutero-Pauline	At the very end of Paul's career, or shortly after his death	If Paul is still alive, then Rome (perhaps written by Timothy); if Paul is dead, then the location cannot be determined
R. McL. Wilson (2005)	A later disciple of a Pauline school	70–75	Ephesus
I. K. Smith (2006)	Paul	Second half of first century. If Ephesus, then 52–57; if Rome, then 60–61	Ephesus or Rome
O. Wischmeyer (2006)	Deutero-Pauline – an unknown author from the Pauline School	70–75	

B. Witherington III (2007)	Paul	61–62	Rome
C. H. Talbert (2007)	Deutero-Pauline	50–100 (for both Colossians and Ephesians)	
M. Trainor (2008)	Not Paul; maybe Epaphras or a Pauline writer communicating and reinterpreting the Pauline heritage for a later generation	During the third or fourth generation of Jesus followers – maybe 60s or 70s	
D. J. Moo (2008)	Paul	60–61	Rome
J. L. Sumney (2008)	An associate – pseudonymous	62–64 – after Paul's death	
M. F. Bird (2009)	Paul as 'managing editor and chief contributor', in association with especially Timothy, but also Tychicus, Epaphras, Onesimus, and Luke	55–57	Ephesus
G. Harris (2009)	Paul	Presumably around 60–61 (since Rome is taken to be the location)	Rome
J. P. Heil (2010)	Paul as primary author, but the role of co-authors and secretaries must lead to a broad understanding of authorship	59	Caesarea
D. J. Tidball (2011)	Paul, but penned by Timothy	Before 61	Rome

D. A. Hagner (2012)	Paul (probably). If not Paul, then by the same author as Ephesians	60–61	Rome
M. E. Boring (2012)	Deutero-Pauline, written in a Pauline school in Ephesus	70s or 80s.	Ephesus
R. Canavan (2012)	A Pauline disciple, probably Epaphras	60s, during Nero's reign	
D. W. Pao (2012)	Paul	60–62	Rome
L. Bormann (2012)	Paul to be understood as a literary figure. Refrains from historical questions; notes questions raised against Pauline authorship	Not discussed	Not discussed
N. K. Gupta (2013)	Paul (perhaps with the aid of Timothy)	(60–62?)	Rome

6.5. Six Scenarios for the Composition of Colossians

Drawing together the above points for Pauline authorship, in support of a mediating position with a more independent role for a secretary, or highlighting the differences in vocabulary, style and theological themes one can postulate a number of different scenarios under which the letter may have been written:[17]

1. Paul as the author in the sense of being responsible for the content, wording, and structure of the letter, but dictated to a scribe. Written during a period of imprisonment, either in Ephesus (54–57), Caesarea (59–60), or Rome (60–61).

---

[17] After writing these scenarios it came to my attention that M. E. Boring does something similar in his work, *An Introduction to the New Testament* (Boring 2012: 329–31), although with five competing scenarios.

Addressed to community of believers resident in Colossae, with which Paul had not had firsthand contact.

2. Timothy as a genuine co-author, and the letter written during Paul's lifetime. In this scenario, Timothy is guided by Paul in terms of the necessary content of the letter, but is responsible for the wording of the letter. Perhaps he consulted with Paul about what had been written before sending the letter. The letter would have been sent to the community of believers in Colossae during Paul's lifetime. From one of the prison locations mentioned above.

3. A co-worker, perhaps Timothy, commissioned by Paul to write a letter in his name in response to problems in Colossae. Paul did not have oversight of the content of the letter, but had outlined his concerns in the most general of terms.

4. Written some time after Paul's death, by a follower of Paul, to co-opt his apostolic authority in responding to a perceived misleading teaching in Colossae. Perhaps at this stage the death of Paul was not widely known. The place of writing would be unknown, but the likelihood is that it was written at a location relatively proximate to Colossae by somebody familiar with Pauline teaching and intimately acquainted with the structure and themes of his other letters. The person would also know of the situation in Colossae.

5. Written after Paul's death to address issues among the churches in the Lycus Valley region of Western Phrygia. The people responsible for composition of the letter would have been familiar with several of the letters written during Paul's lifetime. They saw themselves as guardians of the Pauline tradition and sought to propagate a christology that emphasized the cosmic role of Christ and the sufficiency of a spirituality based exclusively on mystic union with Christ.

6. Written as an encyclical letter to the universal church, as reflected in the type of ecclesiology present in the letter. Some have viewed writing a pseudonymous letter to Colossae later than the mid-60s as a clever strategy, since it is assumed that the city had been devastated and left uninhabited by an earthquake in the early 60s. In this sense Colossians may have been the first attempt to summarize key aspects of Pauline teaching. Something that was perhaps undertaken more fully with the composition of Ephesians.

6.6. *The Position Adopted in this Commentary*

Of these scenarios outlined above, the one that is adopted in this commentary is the fourth. However, this determination is made with hesitation and in the full awareness of the incomplete nature of the evidence. Furthermore, it is acknowledged that the decision is based on many finely balanced judgments. On balance, for a series of cumulative reasons it appears more likely that Colossians was written after the death of Paul. The view that Colossae had been destroyed and left uninhabited in the early 60s has little to support it (see section 2 above). The concerns of the letter appear to reflect specific circumstances, rather than being universalistic in nature. The changes in theology, when taken in combination, raise sufficient doubts to make the attribution of authorship to Paul difficult, although admittedly not impossible. The lack of references to the Spirit and the absence of any explicit citation of the Old Testament in the letter are also both striking.

Therefore, the author is most likely somebody familiar with Paul and his teaching. This person is perhaps, but not necessarily, one of the named Pauline associates mentioned in ch. 4 of the letter. The author appears to be aware of a real situation developing in Colossae and co-opts the authority of Paul and the apostle's commitment to the gospel to advocate the sufficiency of Christ without need of any further religious experience or practices. The date of the epistle is difficult to establish with any certainty, but on the basis of the reading proposed here it would have been written after the death of Paul, and before the composition of Ephesians (see section 8 below). This would suggest a date perhaps in the period 65–80 CE. The place of composition is even more uncertain. The likelihood is that if, as is suggested here, the letter is responding to a real situation in Colossae, then it was composed in a location not too distant from the city. Ephesus is not impossible, but there is no firm evidence for the hypothesis of a Pauline school based in that city after the apostle's death (Trebilco 2004: 90–94; Tellbe 2009: 29). It is equally plausible that the letter was written in one of the cities of the Lycus Valley, or perhaps elsewhere in Phrygia or Asia Minor.

However, most of what is written in the commentary section would still stand, even if Paul could be shown to be the author of the letter. While scholars continue to be interested in authorship and there remains an expectation upon a commentator to explain the position taken, the reality is that definitive answers are impossible based upon the type of material in the letter and in recognition of the fact that Colossians presents a relatively small text. Ultimately it needs to be remembered that the question of authorship, or the position one takes on it, is not the decisive issue. Rather, the significant challenge for commentators is to bring out the rich and finely crafted message of the letter.

7. Relationship to Earlier Pauline Epistles

Colossians shows few examples of extensive verbatim parallels with material drawn from Pauline letters that are generally considered to be earlier. However, perhaps the most obvious example is the opening greeting, where the initial eleven words (Col. 1:1) form an exact parallel with the opening in 2 Cor. 1:1. Furthermore, the end of the opening greeting the grace formula, 'grace to you and peace from God our father' (Col. 1:2), forms an exact parallel to an identical phrase in Rom. 1:7. What can be inferred from these parallels is less certain, especially given the fact that such phrases were fairly stock wording in Pauline greetings. At the very least, it is clear that the letter conforms to standard patterns evidenced in several of the other Pauline epistles. In the same manner, the introductory thanksgiving statement 'we give thanks to God' aligns with similar phrases in 1 Thessalonians (1 Thess. 1:2; 2:13). However, this may reflect knowledge of standard Pauline epistolary conventions rather than providing evidence of direct literary dependence.

The triad of 'faith', 'hope', and 'love', occur in reasonably close proximity in Col. 1:4–5. However, while the first two terms are closely linked (Col. 1:4), the term 'love' is more distant and more loosely related (Col. 1:5) than is the case in 1 Corinthians: 'but now remain faith, hope, love' (1 Cor. 13:13). This triad of terms is found elsewhere in the Pauline epistles (Rom. 5:1–15; Gal. 5:5–6; 1 Thess. 1:3; 5:8), sometimes in close connection and sometimes in a more dispersed arrangement. Thus the usage of the triad in Col. 1:4–5 may not be dependent on a specific Pauline text, but rather it may reflect a more general knowledge of key Pauline concepts.

There is a partial parallel between Col. 1:10 and 1 Thess. 2:12, with both epistles speaking of the author's prayer that believers might walk in a manner worthy of God. However, while the idea is similar, there is not a high level of verbal agreement in the Greek text:

περιπατῆσαι ἀξίως τοῦ κυρίου εἰς πᾶσαν ἀρεσκείαν (Col. 1:10)

εἰς τὸ περιπατεῖν ὑμᾶς ἀξίως τοῦ θεοῦ τοῦ καλοῦντος ὑμᾶς (1 Thess. 2:12)

While the same idea is clearly present, the wording is sufficiently different to prevent one suggesting that there is direct literary dependence between these two verses. Another possible example is to be found in the second half of Col. 1:10, with the sequence of words 'in every good work bearing fruit', ἐν παντὶ ἔργῳ ἀγαθῷ καρποφοροῦντες (Col. 1:10b). A similar phrase occurs elsewhere in the Pauline writings: 'you may abound to every good work', περισσεύητε εἰς πᾶν ἔργον ἀγαθόν (2 Cor. 9:8). There is obviously a conceptual affinity. However, the differences in word order, choice of preposition, different noun cases, and choice and form of verb, mean that this is not an example of direct borrowing. A further example of brief snatches of common phraseology is to be found in similar injunctions to believers to be steadfast and immovable: 'my beloved brothers, be steadfast, immovable', ἀδελφοί μου ἀγαπητοί, ἑδραῖοι γίνεσθε, ἀμετακίνητοι (1 Cor. 15:58); 'persevere in the faith being established and steadfast, and are not moved from the hope of the gospel', ἐπιμένετε τῇ πίστει τεθεμελιωμένοι καὶ ἑδραῖοι καὶ μὴ μετακινούμενοι ἀπὸ τῆς ἐλπίδος τοῦ εὐαγγελίου (Col. 1:23). While the term 'steadfast', ἑδραῖοι, is identical in both verses, the instruction to be immovable is constructed in different ways: 'immovable'. ἀμετακίνητοι (1 Cor. 15:58), and 'not moved', μὴ μετακινούμενοι (Col. 1:23). Again, Colossians reflects a familiarity with Pauline ideas, but no strong link with precise wording contained in other letters.

Examples of this type could be multiplied, and perhaps the interesting observation would be the preponderance of shared but fleeting phrases in common with wording found in Romans and the Corinthian correspondence. However, one of the more striking parallels involves the Pauline saying concerning the breaking down of various ethnic, class, gender, or religious distinctions for those who are in Christ. Perhaps the earliest form talks about believers receiving one Spirit and being baptized into one body. The train of thought continues by drawing the implication that this is the common experience of believers, 'whether Jews, whether Greeks, whether slaves, whether free' (1 Cor. 12:13). Here the four categories mentioned are given in plural form. By contrast, what is perhaps the best known formulation of this saying, gives three pairings, with each representation category given in singular form: neither Jew nor Greek, slave nor free, male or female (Gal. 3:28). Here the first four categories are the same as the four groups mentioned in 1 Cor. 12:13 and occur in the same order. The form in Colossians is perhaps the most divergent of the three. It lists eight types of people, each noun being given in the singular. In form it comprises two pairs followed by a fourfold list. The opening pairing is the same as the other two examples, however the order is reversed. The decision to place 'Greek' prior to 'Jew' may not be entirely unintentional, especially since the group of believers in Colossae was primarily (or perhaps exclusively) gentile in origin. That distinction is then reinforced with a second pairing not found in the other examples, 'circumcision and uncircumcision'. The Colossians text does not use gender categories, but concludes with the fourfold list of 'barbarian, Scythian, slave, free' (Col. 3:11). The reference to slave and free occurs in that order in all three examples. In distinction from the example in 1 Cor. 12:13, the text in Colossians does not see the common experience rooted in the shared act of being baptized in one spirit, but like Gal. 3:28 sees that distinctions are eroded because of the new life that all believers have in Christ. In this example there are points of overlapping vocabulary, and the ideas are close at a number of points. Notwithstanding these similarities, the three texts look like the careful reworking of an underlying idea to suit the situation being addressed, rather than direct borrowing from an existing literary text. While the parallels are closer here, they remain similar to the other examples that have been discussed, in that they reflect knowledge of Pauline ideas but not the facile reproduction of Pauline words.

One case that requires separate consideration is the relationship between Colossians and the brief personal letter to Philemon. There is very little similarity in the content of the two letters, or in terms of overlapping phrases. The similarity arises because of the number of named figures that occur in both letters. The following figures are mentioned in both letters.

Person	Colossians	Philemon
Paul	1:1, 23; 4:18	1, 9, 19
Timothy	1:1	1
Epaphras	1:7; 4:12	23
Onesimus	4:9	10
Aristarchus	4:10	24
Mark	4:10	24
Luke	4:14	24
Demas	4:14	24
Archippus	4:17	2

Both Philemon and Colossians assume a similar network of Pauline associates, and hence this is suggestive of a geographical link, and some kind of relationship in the perceived world that these two letters address. Most commonly it has been assumed that Philemon is to be understood as a *paterfamilias* and the slave owner of Onesimus, who is resident with his household in Colossae. While some have wished to locate the setting for Philemon and his household in another city, such as Laodicea (Knox 1959: 45–55), this suggestion has not commanded widespread assent.

The shared list of *dramatis personae* suggests that the author of Colossians intended to present the letter as addressing the believers in the same location as the destination for the letter for Philemon. In Colossians, Onesimus is described as one 'who is from you', thereby suggesting he was a fellow inhabitant of Colossae. Paul writes to the owner of Onesimus in Philemon, and that person is most plausibly Philemon – not Archippus as has been sometimes suggested (for a strong defence of Philemon as the recipient of the letter, see Moo 2008: 361–64). Therefore, although not drawing directly on the content contained in Philemon, the author of Colossians appears to have been familiar with largely the same social network of Pauline associates and community members in Colossae. Thus Colossians is addressed to the same life setting as the letter to Philemon.

There are very few places where Colossians comes close to providing parallels to other passages in earlier Pauline letters that would suggest direct literary dependence. The letter does, however, reveal at numerous points an awareness of Pauline ideas and theological concerns. These are not reproduced in a slavish manner. Instead, the author demonstrates great versatility in refashioning Pauline thought to address the concerns about developments within the community of believers at Colossae. Chiefly Colossians draws on the rich repository of Paul's christology to instruct the community about the sufficiency of faith in Christ without any need for supplement. To achieve this end, the letter presents its teaching as coming from Paul, and being validated by a significant circle of co-workers, many of whom were apparently known to the Colossians either by name or reputation.

8. *Earliest Reception in Christian Tradition*

Although not without challenge, most commentators see Ephesians as drawing upon Colossians in some way. Perhaps Mitton has provided the strongest defence of the theory of the direct literary dependence of Ephesians on Colossians (Mitton 1951: 68–74). Mitton supports the Pauline authorship of Colossians and so states his conclusion in the following manner: 'Colossians may be treated as the work of Paul, and…Ephesians may be regarded as a later amplification of Colossians, either by Paul himself or by a later writer using the name of Paul' (Mitton 1951: 74). There may also be some allusions to Colossians within the Pastoral Letters. However, such links are far less certain. In the case of the relationship between Colossians and Ephesians, the strongest example that potentially illustrates the possibility of direct literary borrowing concerns the parallel between Eph. 6:21–22//Col. 4:7–8 that describes role of Tychicus in communicating information about Paul's circumstances. Some 32 of the 34 Greek words that comprise Col. 4:7–8 are replicated in the same sequence in Eph. 6:21–22.

Col. 4:7–8	Eph. 6:21–22
Τὰ κατ᾿ ἐμὲ πάντα γνωρίσει ὑμῖν Τύχικος ὁ ἀγαπητὸς ἀδελφὸς καὶ πιστὸς διάκονος καὶ σύνδουλος ἐν κυρίῳ, ὃν ἔπεμψα πρὸς ὑμᾶς εἰς αὐτὸ τοῦτο, ἵνα γνῶτε τὰ περὶ ἡμῶν καὶ παρακαλέσῃ τὰς καρδίας ὑμῶν Everything concerning me he will make known to you Tychicus the beloved brother and faithful servant and fellow slave in the Lord, (8) whom I sent to you for this very reason, in order that you might know the things concerning us, and your hearts might be encouraged	Ἵνα δὲ εἰδῆτε καὶ ὑμεῖς τὰ κατ᾿ ἐμέ, τί πράσσω, πάντα γνωρίσει ὑμῖν Τύχικος ὁ ἀγαπητὸς ἀδελφὸς καὶ πιστὸς διάκονος ἐν κυρίῳ, ὃν ἔπεμψα πρὸς ὑμᾶς εἰς αὐτὸ τοῦτο, ἵνα γνῶτε τὰ περὶ ἡμῶν καὶ παρακαλέσῃ τὰς καρδίας ὑμῶν But that you also may know the things concerning me, what I am doing, everything he will make known to you Tychicus the beloved brother and faithful servant in the Lord, (22) whom I sent to you for this very reason, in order that you might know the things concerning us, and your hearts might be encouraged

The only difference is that the conjunction and noun 'and fellow-slave', καὶ σύνδουλος, contained in Col. 4:8 is omitted from Eph. 6:21. At least in this case one would be inclined to posit some direct literary relationship between the two epistles.

There are numerous other parallels between the two epistles. However, these are usually limited to a shared short phrase or a few common words in close connection but not in exact sequence. There are also noticeable examples of shared themes, or common literary units such as the household code. One of the stronger parallels is the shared description of the redemptive work of Christ that occurs in both epistles.

Col. 1:14	Eph. 1:7
ἐν ᾧ ἔχομεν τὴν ἀπολύτρωσιν, τὴν ἄφεσιν τῶν ἁμαρτιῶν· in whom we have the redemption, the forgiveness of sins	ἐν ᾧ ἔχομεν τὴν ἀπολύτρωσιν διὰ τοῦ αἵματος αὐτοῦ, τὴν ἄφεσιν τῶν παραπτωμάτων, in whom we have the redemption through his blood, the forgiveness of transgressions

The differences are twofold. First, instead of the term ἁμαρτιῶν, 'sins', used in Col. 1:14, the synonym παραπτωμάτων, 'transgressions', is used in Eph. 1:7. The second more substantive change is the insertion in Eph. 1:7 of the phrase 'through his blood', after the term 'redemption'. Some later manuscripts of Colossians also contain the same phrase (the minuscule manuscripts 614 630 1505 2464, the latter being the earliest and dating from the ninth century), but that is due to scribal assimilation of the text of Colossians to that of Ephesians.

It is not, however, always the case that Ephesians has the more expansive text. Describing the contrast between the former state of life and that which believers now enjoy, Colossians contains the additional phrase, 'and in the uncircumcision of your flesh'.

Col. 2:13	Eph. 2:5
καὶ ὑμᾶς νεκροὺς ὄντας [ἐν] τοῖς παραπτώμασιν καὶ τῇ ἀκροβυστίᾳ τῆς σαρκὸς ὑμῶν, συνεζωοποίησεν ὑμᾶς σὺν αὐτῷ, and you being dead in your transgressions and in the uncircumcision of your flesh, he made you alive together with him	καὶ ὄντας ἡμᾶς νεκροὺς τοῖς παραπτώμασιν συνεζωοποίησεν τῷ Χριστῷ, and we being dead in transgressions, he made us alive together with Christ

Whether omitted from the parallel in Ephesians or added to the text of Colossians, it is likely that proponents of either of those cases would argue that the additional words suited the situation of the addressees in Colossae, but not those in Ephesus. Therefore, if Ephesians were written later the phrase would have been omitted because not all those addressed by the epistle could be assumed to be uncircumcised. By contrast, in the case of Colossians being written later, then presumably the author was addressing readers who were known to have been converted from pagan religions and hence were previously uncircumcised, and thus he added the extra phrase. On a case-by-case basis such parallels between Ephesians and Colossians can perhaps be explained on the assumption that either epistle was prior. The question remains, when these cases are taken cumulatively, as to which appears to be the most convincing explanation. It may be noted that a major study of the relationship between Ephesians and Colossians detected numerous parallels. According to Mitton's enumeration, 69 of the 90 verses of Colossians are paralleled in Ephesians (Mitton 1951: 316–18). Admittedly some of these are limited in terms of the extent of verbal similarity. However, the sheer weight and range of these parallels suggests that one or other of these letters was written with a keen awareness of the other. Having identified the parallel between Col. 4:7–8 and Eph. 6:21–22 as the sole exception, in relation to the other parallels Mitton draws the sensible conclusion that 'the correspondence between the epistles is always something less than verbatim reproduction' (Mitton 1951: 59).

While the range of parallels appears to establish beyond doubt some form of relationship between the two epistles, it is still important to attempt to determine which of the two epistles is prior. It has already been noted that it is not the case that one epistle consistently or even more regularly has the shorter form of a parallel while the other has the longer or more expansive form. Therefore, even if it were accurate, one could not simply apply a dictum such as the shorter form is the earlier form. While a purely literary comparison does not assist in determining the answer, consideration of thematic and theological content may be more decisive. It has already been noted that Colossians perhaps contains only one explicit reference to the Spirit (Col. 1:8), and similarly does not cite the Jewish scriptures. By contrast, Ephesians uses the term 'spirit' on fifteen occasions of which eleven appear to denote the Holy Spirit (Eph. 1:13; 2:18, 22; 3:5, 16; 4:3, 4, 30; 5:18; 6:17, 18). A number of these eleven verses from Ephesians have parallels in Colossians. It is difficult to imagine the author of Colossians so carefully and consistently expunging all of these references. It is much easier to imagine the scenario where the author of Colossians, being aware of a form of ecstatic religion developing in Colossae, decides to downplay the pneumatological elements in early Christianity. By contrast, at a later point the author of Ephesians has no reason not to mention the Spirit, and hence when recasting material that has its origin in Colossians naturally introduces references to the Spirit.

Even more striking is the contrast between the absence of references to the Jewish scriptures in Colossians and the several explicit citations from that corpus in Ephesians. The strongest allusion to the Jewish scriptures in Colossians is the possible reference to Gen. 1:28 in Col. 3:10. Given the ubiquitous nature of the claim that humans were created in the image of God, it is not certain that the Genesis text is in view at this this point. By contrast, in Ephesians the Jewish scriptures are clearly cited on several occasions. The most obvious examples of this use of scriptural texts occurs in the second half of the epistle: Ps. 68:19 in Eph. 4:8; Zech. 8:16 in Eph. 4:25; LXX Ps. 4:5 in Eph. 4:26; LXX Gen. 2:24 in Eph. 5:21; and LXX Exod. 20:12//Deut. 5:16 in Eph. 6:2–3. Again, it is difficult to envisage the author of Colossians stripping away the use of Jewish scriptural texts either purposefully or by inadvertent omission, which would be the case if Ephesians were the earlier letter.

The theological perspectives contained in Ephesians are often considered to reflect a more developed or later period than the theological ideas expressed in Colossians. While the ecclesiology of Colossians is seen as expressing in embryonic form the idea of a universal church (Col. 1:18, 24, 25) such a perspective is more consistent and thoroughgoing in Ephesians, where all references to the church appear to be designations of a universal entity (Eph. 1:22; 3:10, 21; 5:23, 24, 25, 27, 29, 32). As has been frequently noted, in the Pauline letters the term ἐκκλησία typically denotes a gathering of believers in a local context, rather than being understood as referring to the unified mass of all believers. It is only in the three instances in Colossians, and throughout Ephesians, that one finds the term clearly used in a universal sense, although in 1 Tim. 3:15 it perhaps tends towards this sense (Lofthouse 1946: 144–49). While theological tendencies may not develop in uniformly linear patterns, it appears that in Colossians one sees the beginning of a post-Pauline understanding of the concept of church, and that this is more fully and consistently developed in Ephesians.

The same developmental pattern is likely found in regard to the eschatology of the two letters. Colossians shows a tendency towards a more realized form of eschatology (Col. 2:12–14; 3:1–3). However, alongside this the author also affirms that the fulness of blessings in Christ can only be experienced in the future when Christ is revealed in his glory (Col. 3:4). By contrast, in Ephesians, there appears to be no trace of either an explicit or implicit expectation of the parousia.

While all these arguments are suggestive rather than conclusive, they do appear to point in the direction of seeing Ephesians as a development of the thought and theology contained in Colossians, as well as offering some of its own theological perspectives. Ephesians has been described as 'the crown of Paulinism' (Dodd 1929: 1224–25) or as 'the quintessence of Paulinism' (Bruce 1977: 424). While such elevated rhetoric may be correct in viewing Ephesians as the pinnacle in expressing a developed form of Pauline thought towards the end of the first century, it needs to be noted how important a role Colossians plays in that developmental process. Many of the theological ideas that find rich development in Ephesians are already present in Colossians. In this sense, Colossians is of major significance not only for the theological perspectives it presents, but also as a major stage in the development of early Christian thought. In particular, it represents the beginning of a more theologically reflective period. This may have been the initial stage of the reformulation of Paul's thought and legacy into a form that would have continuing relevance for the nascent church, while also providing a calming influence on the exuberant ecstatic spiritual experience of the first generation of believers in Pauline communities.

9. A Prosopography of Colossians

It is perhaps useful to explain what the term prosopography means. It is derived from the Greek word for 'created-face', *prosōpoeia* (προσωποεῖα). A prosopography is not simply a list of *dramatis personae* in a literary work such as Colossians. Rather, it seeks to gain insight into a collective group of historical characters, where details about certain individuals might be minimal or non-existent. Therefore, prosopographical research has the aim of learning about group dynamics and patterns of social relationship through the study of collective biography. Typically a certain mass of data is required to undertake a prosopographical study, such as the information derived from inscriptions at a large funerary site. While Colossians does not yield this type of mass data, nonetheless it is of value to consider the characters in the letter as a whole. By so doing one is able to assemble not only their individual characteristics, but also apprehend greater detail by considering networks of relationships.

9.1. Paul
Regardless of the question of authorship, as presented in the thought-world of the letter itself, the most prominent figure is Paul, the assumed

author of the epistle. Here the purpose is not to give a comprehensive biography of Paul but to describe the way he is described, especially in relation to other figures mentioned in the letter.

The opening word of the letter is 'Paul', who is immediately identified by his role and his relationship to another figure: 'an apostle of Christ Jesus' (Col. 1:1). The designation 'apostle' was already a technical term in early Christianity for those commissioned by Jesus to lead in the propagation of the gospel. Paul claims this title for himself, and it is employed here without any concern that some in the early church contested this claim. The authorial Paul presents his relationship with the Colossians as being mediated by Epaphras (Col. 1:7). This lack of personal contact with the Colossians (and also with believers in Laodicea) is directly acknowledged in the letter (Col. 2:1). However, despite this lack of first-hand association Paul describes himself as offering thanks (Col. 1:3) and interceding tirelessly (Col. 1:9) on behalf of Colossian believers.

In a partially biographical section of the epistle Paul presents himself as a servant of the gospel (Col. 1:23), and then continues by describing his sufferings on behalf of the church (Col. 1:24). At this point he reprises the term 'servant', but instead of describing himself as a servant of the gospel, his servanthood is presented in relation to the church (Col. 1:25). In this case service to the gospel and service to the church are probably to be understood as inextricable aspects of Paul's apostolic work. Paul concludes this section by reminding the Colossians of his goal to present believers 'perfect in Christ' (Col. 1:28), and this task is something for which he strives (Col. 1:29). After this stage the *persona* of the author is no longer prominent in the letter until the final chapter.

In a section offering some generic ethical instructions following an imperative to remain constant in prayer, the author personalizes that instruction with the request that the Colossians pray also for Paul and his associates that they might have greater opportunity to announce 'the mystery of Christ' (Col. 4:3). The verse then concludes with the poignant detail that it is speaking about Christ 'because of which also I am bound' (Col. 4:3). Here Paul is presented as being imprisoned for the sake of the gospel. This is also restated at the close of the letter (Col. 4:18). Between these two references to his incarceration Paul presents a list of greetings and instructions that provide information about his social network. First he authorizes the two letter carriers, Tychicus and Onesimus, to communicate further details about the nature of his personal circumstances (Col. 4:7–9). The additional names in Col. 4:10–17 may reflect a strategy on the part of the author to create connections with the previously unknown Colossian addressees by recalling the names of mutual associates. The same 'network strategy' appears to be at play in Rom. 16:3–16, in another letter where Paul states he does not know the recipients personally. While Paul is not at the centre of the social network of people mentioned in the letter to the Colossians, he is presented as the leader and organizer of that network because of his relentless work in proclaiming the gospel. At times the figure of Paul drops from immediate view in the letter, and the instructions, especially in the ethical section, focus on the behaviour of the recipients rather than on the personality of the person providing the teaching. Nonetheless, the figure of Paul stands behind the entire letter in an overriding manner. He functions as a source of authority and as the fountainhead of the teaching contained in the epistle. In this sense the person of Paul is fundamental to the whole argument and train of thought directed to the Colossians. Thus, because the entire letter is predicated upon the status and authority of Paul, Colossians is a Pauline letter in a very fundamental sense.

9.2. Timothy

In the opening verse of the letter Timothy is presented as the co-sender along with Paul. He is described using fraternal language as 'the brother' (Col. 1:1). Such fictive kinship served two functions. First, relational language among believers may have served as a replacement for kinship bonds that had been lost by those who had aligned themselves with the Jesus movement. Second, it may have strengthened the sense of group solidarity, by attempting to create familial bonds between fellow believers. Despite the fact that the wider corpus of Pauline letters presents Timothy as Paul's closest associate, this is the only direct reference to him in the letter. The retention of the authorial plural at certain points (Col. 1:3, 9; 4:3) in the letter might suggest that he has not totally faded from consideration. However, if these plural formulations encapsulate Timothy, they do so in a subtle manner that does not press the author or the recipients to think about Timothy in any developed manner. Unlike other named characters in the letter, Timothy is not mentioned to evoke points of contact between Paul and the Colossians. Rather, describing him as 'brother' draws upon the language of familial intimacy, and draws the Colossians into a bond of fictive kinship with Paul. It is impossible to tell whether the Colossians previously knew Timothy even by reputation. While Timothy is a relatively minor figure in the letter, his function is to enlarge the scope of the social network portrayed in the letter.

9.3. *Epaphras*
The person described as bringing the Christian message to Colossae is Epaphras (Col. 1:7). He is mentioned on three occasions in the New Testament – Col. 1:7–8; 4:12–13; Phlm. 23. He is the source of Paul's information about the state of affairs within the Christian community in Colossae (Col. 1:8). Epaphras is identified as being a native Colossian. It appears to be the case that his ethnic heritage was gentile, and not Jewish. In general the Colossians are described as having received 'a circumcision made without hands' (Col. 2:11) and as being 'dead in the uncircumcision of flesh' (Col. 2:13). This implies that they had not received physical circumcision, which was an identity marker for Jews. Furthermore, in the second reference to Epaphras in the letter he is not listed along with Aristarchus, Mark, and Jesus Justus mentioned in the previous verse, where those three are described as being from 'the circumcision' (Col. 4:11). Outside of Colossians, Paul describes Epaphras as 'my fellow prisoner in Christ Jesus' (Phlm. 23). This implies a time of shared incarceration with Paul. If that description also pertained to the historical circumstances behind the letter to the Colossians, it would perhaps explain why Epaphras was not sent back to Colossae as a letter carrier.

Epaphras functions as an intermediary between the believers in Colossae along with those in the rest of the Lycus Valley and Paul. He is acknowledged as having a foundational role in establishing the Christian community in Colossae. In fact, many have taken him to be the founder of the church in Colossae (Trainor 2008: 63; Trebilco 2011: 181). While this seems to be a reasonable supposition, Huttner is correct that the statement in Col. 1:7 describes Epaphras as the primary teacher of the community, not as its founder. Thus Huttner states that '[i]t still remains unexplained who the source of the first Christian stirrings in the Lycus Valley was and whether or not Paul was actually present there' (Huttner 2013: 89). While it is correct to observe that it is an inference to see Epaphras as the founder of the Christian community in Colossae, the letter gives a strong indication that Paul had not visited the Lycus Valley. The letter describes the Colossians and Laodiceans along with 'those who have not seen my face in the flesh' (Col. 2:1). Admittedly, nothing is said about Paul's relationship to the inhabitants of Hierapolis in this context. However, given that Paul's typical strategy was to preach in urban centres, and the letter declares that Paul was unacquainted with believers in two of the three most significant population centres in the Lycus Valley (and does not say that he had visited Hierapolis), then the most plausible conclusion to be drawn from the textual evidence is that Paul is presented as not having conducted missionary work in the Lycus Valley. This would then require that another person brought the Christian message to the region. Given the way Epaphras is described, as being the one from whom the Colossians learnt the gospel, then it is not inappropriate to see him as the likeliest identifiable candidate as the originator of the Christian message in Colossae. The language that depicts Epaphras as being the Colossians' instructor in the gospel evokes the discipleship imagery of the early Jesus movement. Such a teaching role is related to the proclamation of the gospel and the moral formation of believers. As Trainor notes, '[i]t was Epaphras who proclaimed the Gospel of God at Colossae and instructed first believers in the new way of thinking and acting' (Trainor 2008: 64). All these indications are consonant with seeing Epaphras as the person who was responsible for bringing the gospel message to Colossae for the first time.

Epaphras' sphere of influence was wider than that of his indigenous home of Colossae. The author declares to the Colossians that, 'he has much toil on your behalf, and for those in Laodicea, and those in Hierapolis' (Col. 4:13). While his missionary work did not extend as widely as Paul's, it was nevertheless translocal. Such an outward, looking perspective assisted small minority Christian communities to obtain a sense of identity through connections with other geographically disparate groups of fellow believers. Therefore, such networks of communities were not just a means to standardize Christian practice and beliefs. More importantly, creating identification with a wider network of believers sustained the early movement by providing a way to overcome a potential sense of isolation. The same desire to link dispersed Christian communities can be seen in the Petrine epistles (1 Pet. 1:1) and in the letters of Ignatius (*Trall.* 13.1; *Phld.* 11.2; *Smyrn.* 12.1). Epaphras is seen as a significant broker of Pauline Christianity in the Lycus Valley. Whether he was part of the Pauline circle when he first instructed the community of believers in Colossae is uncertain. It may be the case that the author of the letter has 'co-opted' the figure of Epaphras as a means to promote the propagation of the Pauline form of belief that emphasized the exclusivity of commitment to Christ without any other supplementary religious experience. In many ways Epaphras is a 'bridge figure', both in spanning the temporal gap between the apostolic period of Paul's ministry and the period after his death, and perhaps more significantly by linking a variety of communities with divergent understandings of the Christian message by uniting them under the authority of Paul, albeit after the death of the eponymous apostle.

9.4. *Tychicus*

Unnamed until the final chapter, Tychicus is an important figure in the communication network that is described in the letter. He is presented as one authorized to communicate more detailed information concerning Paul and his companions (Col. 4:7–8), and although not explicitly stated it is highly likely that he was the bearer of the letter. Tychicus is named on five occasions in the New Testament, once in Acts (Acts 20:4) and four times in the Pastoral or deutero-Pauline letters (Eph. 6:21; Col. 4:7; 2 Tim. 4:12; Tit. 3:12). In the closing section of the letter (Col. 4:7–18) eight members of the Pauline circle are named, whom the Colossians presumably know at least by name. These people are presented as reliable transmitters of the Pauline message, and are likely to be figures entrusted with the vision of continuing Pauline teaching after the death of the apostle. It may be significant that Tychicus is named first among this group, or that may simply be functional, due to the fact that he is the first of these eight individuals whom the Colossians will meet when he arrives with the letter addressed to them.

Tychicus is described in fulsome terms as 'the beloved brother and faithful servant and fellow slave in the Lord' (Col. 4:7). This lavish and multifaceted set of descriptions speaks of a trusted individual who fulfilled multiple roles in the close circle of Pauline associates. It may be the case that these affirmations are intended to endorse Tychicus as the key figure responsible for purveying the Pauline tradition to Colossae, where it was previously relatively unknown (cf. Röhser 2009: 143). The description of Tychicus in Col. 4:7–8 is virtually identical with that in Eph. 6:21–22 (a sequence of 29 identical words). Therefore, in addressing the Ephesians Tychicus is presented again as the bearer of the Pauline tradition. Hence Huttner observes, 'Tychicus was one of the most important middlemen among the companions of Paul in the Aegean region' (Huttner 2013: 91). In the epistle addressed to Titus, Tychicus is portrayed as an envoy acting to pass on communications from Paul: 'I shall send Artemas or Tychicus to you' (Tit. 3:12). In fact, it appears that he or Artemas would be used to provide relief to Titus while providing continuity of leadership from one of Paul's trusted associates, in order that Titus might be released from his commitments to enable him to come to Paul (Marshall 1999: 341). Elsewhere, when Paul bemoans the fact that he is on his own apart from the presence of Luke, he has to acknowledge that it was his decision to send Tychicus on a mission to Ephesus (2 Tim. 4:12).

Hence Tychicus is a name that is used on multiple occasions in the later Pauline epistles. He is portrayed as a key associate who enables the Pauline mission to continue while Paul is incarcerated. He is not only likely to be one of the physical letter carriers sent to Colossae, but according to the epistle he is authorized to communicate further information about Paul's personal circumstances. It would also appear, as is also suggested in the letter to Titus (Tit. 3:12), that he is deployed to provide reliable and continuing Pauline leadership among early Christian communities.

9.5. *Onesimus*

Along with Tychicus, Onesimus is sent as the other likely courier of the letter to the Colossians. Onesimus, like Epaphras, is described as being from the city of Colossae (Col. 4:9). He is mentioned once elsewhere in the New Testament (Phlm. 10), as well as in the incipits to Colossians and Philemon, which were added to certain manuscripts of these letters at a later date. As the situation behind the letter to Philemon is most commonly understood, Onesimus was a runaway slave who was owned by the Christian *paterfamilias* Philemon. The reference to Onesimus in Col. 4:9 is one of the important links that demonstrates some kind of relationship between the two epistles. If historical circumstances are being recalled at any level in Colossians, then the decision to send Onesimus back to Colossae as a letter carrier with a personal note for his master Philemon to be read in a community context as well as with a letter to the whole church was a means of validating Onesimus' status as a 'beloved brother' (Phlm. 16). However, the personal letter may also have functioned tactically as a statement that disarmed any claim of ownership Philemon could claim over Onesimus – especially in a group where it was stated that there was no longer 'slave or free' (Col. 3:11). Therefore, recalling Onesimus in Colossians by a later author writing in Paul's name might have been a way of celebrating the inversion of slave status. This may have served as a highly valued teaching, especially if the inference is correct that a disproportionate number of group members were slaves (Col. 3:22–4:1).

9.6. *Aristarchus*

The first named of the three co-workers in Col. 4:10–11, who are identified as being 'from the circumcision' (4:11), is Aristarchus. He is described as being a fellow prisoner (4:10) along with Paul. Given that in the epistle Paul refers to his chains (4:3, 18), readers are probably to envisage Aristarchus as also being bound in a prison alongside Paul. Aristarchus' relationship to the Colossians is unclear. It appears that he is simply a person who is sending his greetings to the community, but has had no further contact. The same appears to be the case in the letter to Philemon, where along with Epaphras, Mark, Demas, and Luke he also sends his greetings (Phlm. 23–24). Aristarchus is mentioned on three further occasions in the New Testament in the book of Acts (Acts 19:29; 20:4; 27:2). These references make it clear that not only was he a Macedonian, but more specifically he came from Thessalonica (Acts 20:4; 27:2). Aristarchus was one of Paul's companions who had been present during the riot in Ephesus, where he and Gaius were dragged into the theatre by an angry mob. Moreover, according to the narrative of Acts, Aristarchus accompanied Paul on his journey to Rome. If the description of Aristarchus being a 'fellow prisoner' (Col. 4:10) is historical, this does not resolve the question of the provenance of the letter since he was a companion of Paul during his time in Ephesus and Rome. Therefore, either location would remain possible as the place from which the letter was written. Apart from being described as a fellow prisoner, in Philemon Aristarchus is also described as a 'fellow worker' (Phlm. 24). This description is also applied to him less directly in Colossians, where he is part of a group of which it is said 'these only are my fellow workers in the kingdom of God' (Col. 4:11).

Aristarchus' relationship to the Colossians seems to be understood as being as distant as Paul's. There is no indication that he had direct contact; however, as part of the wider fraternal bond of believers and as a close associate and fellow prisoner with Paul, he sends his greetings. His name might be listed to communicate to the Colossians that they were part of a larger movement, with many working (like Epaphras) for the spread of the gospel. In terms of the reception of the teaching contained in the letter, the naming of so many associates may be designed to demonstrate the size and success of the Pauline mission.

9.7. Barnabas

The prominent partner of Paul during his first missionary journey (Acts 13–14), Barnabas, is only mentioned in passing in this letter. There is no hint of the acrimonious split and other tensions that occurred between Paul and Barnabas (Acts 15:36–39; Gal. 2:13). However, a further detail contained in Colossians supplies the possible basis of the split between Paul and Barnabas. In Acts 15:36–39, Paul is unwilling to take Mark on the proposed return visit to the communities established on the first missionary journey. Barnabas insists that he should accompany them, and is not willing to compromise on this. Colossians states Barnabas and Mark were cousins (Col. 4:10). Therefore, if the relationship depicted in Colossians is historically correct, family loyalties may have been the basis of Barnabas' uncompromising commitment to his cousin Mark. However, it is possible that the reported relationship is not historical, but is due to a later author attempting to provide a basis for the split between Paul and Barnabas. If that were the case, then this is a subtle strategy, since the author makes no reference to the split. Notwithstanding the historicity or otherwise of the relationship, the author of Colossians presents a picture of an extended and harmonious Pauline circle of associates. Barnabas is mentioned only to clarify the identity of Mark, which suggests that Barnabas was a well-known figure, and that Mark was best identified by his relationship to Barnabas.

9.8. *Mark*

The Mark mentioned in Col. 4:10 appears to be identical with the figure known in Acts by the double appellative John Mark (Acts 12:12, 25; 15:37, 39). Outside of Acts, in the Pauline epistles the single name Mark is used (Col. 4:10; 2 Tim. 4:11; Phlm. 24). In contrast to the way in which Acts leaves its description of the relationship between Paul and Mark as fractious and without rapprochement, the later Pauline literary traditions do not explicitly indicate any previous rupture with Mark. Rather, he is presented as a missionary companion of Paul, and as a useful member of the Pauline circle (2 Tim. 4:11). The enigmatic parenthetical comment in Colossians recalls an instruction that the group has already received: 'if he comes to you welcome him' (Col. 4:10). This may suggest that there had been a stage when Mark was not to be received within the nascent Pauline churches. If this supposition is correct, then this period of ostracism might recall, in a veiled manner, the split between Paul and Barnabas over Mark (Acts 15:36–39). If, as is suggested here, Colossians was written after Paul's death, this may be part of a strategy to present a harmonious portrait of relationships in early Pauline Christianity by describing the relationship between Paul and Mark as having been repaired. Mark, apparently, was sufficiently well-known to the recipients of the letter that it was deemed useful to send his greetings to the believers in Colossae. Whether he was known only by reputation or in person cannot be ascertained, but the author does envisage the possibility that Mark might come to the Colossians at some stage in the future, and then he was to be welcomed.

9.9. *Jesus Justus*

A relatively unknown figure in the Pauline writings and elsewhere in the New Testament, Jesus Justus is mentioned only once in Colossians (Col. 4:11), and nowhere else in the New Testament. It has been conjectured that the name Jesus Justus was originally in the list in Phlm. 24 but was accidently omitted (Amling 1909: 261).

There is no textual basis to support this conjecture, and therefore this suggestion should be deemed unnecessary. However, two other figures have the cognomen Justus: Barsabas Justus (Acts 1:23) and Titus Justus (Acts 18:7). In wider Roman usage the cognomen Justus was relatively common, and hence there is no need to suppose that Barsabas, Titus, or Jesus Justus were not three discrete people. The cognomen Justus was a popular and common name among Jews and proselytes to the Jewish faith since it was seen as 'denoting obedience and devotion to the Law' (Lightfoot 1886: 236). Such a designation was applied in the early Jesus movement to James the brother of Jesus (not Jesus Justus), who was widely referred to as 'James the Just'. It is interesting, but perhaps unsurprising given the multicultural nature of the ancient Mediterranean world, to observe a member of the early Jesus movement who is part of the Pauline circle, who is described as being from the circumcision (Col. 4:11) – that is, having a Jewish heritage, but also possessing a Roman or Latinized name. Given the movement of people throughout the Roman Empire, the mention of an individual with a Latin name who may have been a relatively recent member of the Pauline circle does not offer any strong evidence for seeing the letter as having been written in Rome. As is the case with Aristarchus and Mark, Jesus Justus is listed as one of the three companions who have given comfort to Paul during his period of incarceration.

9.10. *Luke*

Luke is often considered to be a well-known New Testament figure. This is probably due to the association of his name with the authorship of the third Gospel and the Acts of the Apostles. Moreover, it is frequently assumed that the so-called 'we passages' of Acts reflect the first-person reminiscences of the author of that text, who is traditionally identified as Luke. All these identifications with Luke are assumptions, although that is not to say they are baseless. The hard evidence is that Luke is mentioned only three times in the New Testament. Here in Colossians Luke is described as 'the beloved physician' and is said to be sending greetings to believers in Colossae (Col. 4:14). From this description in Colossians Marshall infers that 'the way in which he is described suggests that he had given medical care to Paul, no doubt during the latter's imprisonment' (Marshall 1982: 713). However, one wonders if so much can be extracted from this description of Luke's profession. While the term 'physician', ἰατρός, is not particularly rare in the New Testament, this is the only instance when a particular individual is identified as a physician. Luke is also mentioned in the letter to Philemon. On that occasion there is no reference to his profession; instead, he is mentioned alongside Mark, Aristarchus, and Demas, who are all identified as fellow-workers (Phlm. 24). The only other explicit reference to Luke in the New Testament occurs in a somewhat desolate *cri de coeur*, where the imprisoned figure of Paul declares, 'only Luke is with me' (2 Tim. 4:11). Therefore Luke is portrayed first and foremost as a co-worker in the Pauline mission and a faithful companion during a period of incarceration. The description of him as a physician seems incidental and not integral to his role within the Pauline circle. If the tradition is correct that attributes the authorship of Acts to Luke, then through his literary work he is also instrumental in promoting the importance of Paul for the spread of early Christianity, but he does so in a way that presents a picture that is probably more irenic than is likely to have the case in reality. So perhaps rather than as a medical figure, Luke's lasting contribution to the promotion of Pauline Christianity might have be as a 'spin-doctor' who presented the Pauline mission in a sanitized and palatable form that could be appropriated as a foundational element in the story of emergent Christianity. Also Luke's medical training may align with his literate status, which would comport well with the identification of him as the author of Luke–Acts. Whether he had any role in the composition of Pauline letters cannot be determined with any degree of certainty, although some have suggested this might be the case (Strobel 1968–69).

9.11. *Demas*
Immediately after referencing Luke, the beloved physician, the author of Colossians also sends greetings from Demas. Like Luke he is mentioned three times in the Pauline Epistles and nowhere else in the New Testament. In fact, Demas is mentioned in the same three contexts as Luke (Col. 4:14; 2 Tim. 4:10; Phlm. 24). In Colossians, only the scantiest of details are provided in regard to Demas: his name, and that he sends greetings. No doubt he is to be understood as a member of the Pauline circle who is portrayed as being with Paul at the time of the writing of the letter.

The information in Philemon offers little further information – only that Demas is described as a fellow worker (Phlm. 24). It is only in 2 Timothy that a significant detail is recounted. Demas is described as having forsaken Paul during his period of imprisonment and as having gone to Thessalonica. No indication is given as to why Demas returned to Thessalonica; perhaps it was his hometown. What is characterized as an act of desertion from the perspective of the author of 2 Timothy is said to be due to Demas 'having loved the present world' (2 Tim. 4:10). There is, however, no indication of what the actual cause might be or what form love of the present world might have taken. Even on the widely held assumption that Paul was not the author of 2 Timothy, it appears unlikely that such a detail that vilifies Demas would have been invented unless it was based on some actual event. If Demas had deserted Paul during the apostle's lifetime, then the author could be recalling that historical circumstance. The difficulty is that if Colossians is post-Pauline, it seems to be unaware of such an act of desertion. That may suggest that Demas did not desert the historical Paul, but may have turned his back on the post-Pauline mission, maybe at some stage after the composition of Colossians. In that case, at the time of the writing of Colossians Demas is still part of that circle and regarded as a fellow worker. However, at a later stage when 2 Timothy is written, Demas is considered to have abandoned his association with and work on behalf of continuing Pauline Christianity. It should be noted that the sense of resentment expressed towards Demas is not as strong as that directed towards Hymenaeus and Alexander, who are described as rejecting and shipwrecking their faith and are metaphorically delivered up to Satan (1 Tim. 1:19–20), or like Hymenaeus and Philetus, whose teaching is described as gangrene, who have strayed from the truth by teaching that the resurrection (presumably of believers) has already taken place (2 Tim. 2:17–18). The form of teaching attributed to Hymenaeus and Philetus may be a further development of the type of realized eschatology that is already evident in Colossians.

9.12. *Nympha*

Despite the attempts of various manuscripts to present Nympha as a male figure, by the name of Nymphas (for a discussion of the textual variants see the commentary on Col. 4:15), there is virtually no doubt whatsoever that the author presents Nympha as a female believer who provided a meeting place in her house for fellow-believers in Laodicea. Here the author of Colossians broadens the purview of the letter and instructs the believers in Colossae to send greetings to 'the brothers in Laodicea', and then the author mentions specifically 'Nympha and the church in her house' (Col. 4:15). This is the sole reference to Nympha in the New Testament. While she is otherwise unknown, there is some significant information that can be extracted from these details, especially when they are read alongside what is known in general of the social setting and structure of the early Christian movement.

It is possible that when the letter was written the community of Christ-believers in Laodicea was sufficiently small to be accommodated in the domestic space that was provided in Nympha's house. In terms of social status, it is apparent that Nympha is represented as having access to material resources such as a sizeable dwelling place, which would indicate that she was removed from the lowest stratum of society. However, it would be wrong to portray her as belonging to extremely elevated strands of society. Presumably she was a free woman, either married to a man with significant material assets or she may have held those assets in her own right: it is simply not possible to tell from the available evidence. The household code in Colossians addresses women before their husbands (Col. 3:18). This may suggest that free women, rather than free men dispro-portionately represented the social make-up of the community. The social structure of early Christian communities was used polemically against Christians in later centuries. Therefore, as cited by Origen, Celsus attacks the intellectual abilities of believers and sees them as prone to gullibility:

> ...the following are the rules laid down by them. Let no one come to us who has been instructed, or who is wise or prudent (for such qualifications are deemed evil by us); but if there be any ignorant, or unintelligent, or uninstructed, or foolish persons, let them come with confidence. By which words, acknowledging that such individuals are worthy of their God, they manifestly show that they desire and are able to gain over only the silly, and the mean, and the stupid, with women and children. (Origen, *Contra Cel.* 3.44)

> ...only foolish and low individuals, and persons devoid of perception, and slaves, and women, and children, of whom the teachers of the divine word wish to make converts. (Origen, *Contra Cel.* 3.59)

Celsus is probably correct in representing Christian communities, even in the late second century, as disproportionately consisting of women, children, and slaves. What Celsus states pejoratively is reflected neutrally in the structure of the household code (Col. 3:18–4:1), and also the prominence of women is reflected in the reference to Nympha, who provided the space in which believers in Laodicea could come together for meetings.

9.13. *Archippus*

The geographical location of Archippus has been debated. Having discussed matters pertaining to Laodicea in the two verses that precede the reference to Archippus (Col. 4:15–16), the author simply continues by supplying an instruction concerning Archippus, who is introduced for the first time in the penultimate verse of the epistle. The lack of an explicit indication that the focus has changed from matters relating to Laodicea has led some to conclude concerning Archippus that he 'by implication is not presumed to be in Colossae' (Gillman 1992a: I, 368). However, the implication being drawn here may not be valid. First, according to the letter to Philemon, Archippus appears to be resident in the same location that is the hometown of Onesimus (Phlm. 2). In Colossians, Onesimus is best understood as being a person from Colossae (Col. 4:9). Secondly, if the Colossian recipients of the letter knew Archippus was a fellow believer in Colossae there would be no need for the author to explicitly state this. Just because the statement might cause ambiguity for modern readers, that was not necessarily the case for ancient readers who were aware of the circumstances behind the letter.

In Philemon, Archippus is described as a 'fellow soldier' (Phlm. 2), which would appear to denote that he was actively engaged in the service of the gospel. This military metaphor of 'fellow soldier' is not common in the Pauline corpus, occurring elsewhere only in the description of Epaphroditus (Phil. 2:25). This language is probably used to imply that the Christian battle required all the martial virtues of discipline, strength, resilience, and training to make one an effective worker in the Pauline mission. If Archippus was a younger relative, perhaps the son of Philemon and Apphia, as is suggested in the tradition (see Theodore of Mopsuestia), then the associations of masculinity and virility that are liked with military language may have appealed to the younger Archippus.

Understanding Colossians to be a later composition than Philemon, there appears to be a concern that the initial commitment to the work of the gospel that Archippus displayed is now waning. Consequently, the letter issues the solemn warning to tell Archippus to pay heed to or 'watch the ministry' that he received in the Lord (Col. 4:17). The nature of the ministry or service that needed attention is not specified. However, it is inferred, perhaps on the basis of the present imperative that typically denotes repeated action, that the instruction 'points to continuous service, rather than an immediate service' (Lightfoot 1886: 244). Therefore, Archippus is not one of the circle of companions around Paul. Rather he has a local ministry based in his hometown. Nonetheless, there appears to have been some diminution of commitment or enthusiasm in carrying out this role. Hence, the author calls upon the believers in Colossae collectively to encourage Archippus to return to a wholehearted commitment to his Christian work. Here individual communities of believers are seen as relatively autonomous. They are to use group pressure or encouragement to promote ongoing commitment and service. While they may be linked to the larger sphere of Pauline Christianity, and the universal church, it is at a local level that the community must regulate its corporate life.

10. *The Situation Behind the Letter*

In attempting to describe the world behind the Colossians it is important to note the limited evidence upon which such a reconstruction is based. Moreover, there is a very real danger of circularity. One interprets certain passages in light of the proposed situation that are seen as generating certain statements in the letter, then those interpretations are used to justify the reconstruction of the background to the letter as though that produced conclusive proof. While caution is necessary, the partial evidence should not lead to despair, or even a sense that the task is impossible. However, it does need to be acknowledged that while some suggestions have much to commend them, other aspects of the reconstruction of the background situation are more speculative. Despite the difficulties and pitfalls in such a task, given the attempt to read and comment upon the text in an accurate manner, it is incumbent on the commentator to attempt to present a portrait of the circumstances that may have generated the act of communication and response contained in the letter to the Colossians.

Without doubt one of the most striking features of the letter is its exclusive christology. The author rails against any attempt to supplement faith in Christ with any other type of piety or religious experience. The question remains as to whether the author's warning was directed against a real situation already unfolding in Colossae, or if the advice is a preemptive strike against a hypothetical situation that might occur in the future. Morna Hooker has strongly argued for the latter position, but in a manner that shows the evidence is open to various interpretations (Hooker 1973). Despite this case for taking the letter as anticipating a possible problem, it appears more plausible that it is reacting to a real situation. Both the vehement rebuttal against supplementing faith in Christ with other religious experiences and the specific concerns expressed in the letter are best explained not as preemptive advice against a perceived possible problem or in response to a more general 'pressure to conform to the beliefs and practices of...pagan and Jewish neighbours' (Hooker 1973: 329), but as a result of a situation that has already arisen in Colossae. The difficulty in specifying the identity of the opponents or false teachers at Colossae is well known. As many as 44 differing suggestions were catalogued by Gunther several decades ago (Gunther 1973: 3–4), and that list has continued to grow in the intervening period. However, the main concerns of the letter are expressed with sufficient clarity that it is possible to outline the broad contours of the situation to which the author was responding.

Colossians is self-evidently a highly christological letter. It asserts the centrality of Christ in the divine plan of redemption and recon-ciliation (Col. 1:13, 20, 23). There is a focus on the cross both as the instrument that removed the condemnatory charges against believers (2:14), and as the mechanism through which Christ's death has become the source of cosmic peace (1:20). The consequence for believers is that they can be viewed as already having been raised with Christ (3:1), and thus their true life is already hidden with Christ in the divine sphere (3:3). These affirmations are not made in a vacuum. They stand as the positive teaching that responds to a perceived challenge to an exclusively Christ-based faith.

The author states that in Christ one may have access to all knowledge and wisdom (Col. 2:3). Immediately following on from this statement, the author affirms that he makes this declaration in order to protect the Colossians against any individual who attempts to convince them otherwise: 'this I say that no-one may delude you with persuasive speech' (2:4). Therefore, this is the first indication that the author is responding to one or more people whose teaching is considered to be a deluding influence. A few verses later the author even more clearly issues a warning to believers against threats to their faith introduced with the 'beware' or 'watch out' formula (2:8). The warning is framed as being against 'somebody who takes you captive through philosophy and vain deceit according to the tradition of men, according to the elements of the world and not according to Christ' (2:8). These specific details describe the opposing religious system as being based upon seeing elemental forces as spiritual powers that still exercise power over Colossian believers. Instead, according to the author, the Colossians should rely exclusively on Christ as the basis of redemption and heavenly blessing. It is difficult to determine from the fleeting reference here to 'the elements of the world' (and the equally terse use of the same phrase in Col. 2:20) whether this denotes impersonal or personal forces. While the term τὰ στοιχεῖα, 'the elements', is used predominantly to denote the impersonal material that constitutes the world, the cosmogonies of early gnostic texts or of mystery religions could attribute personal force to the *archontic* powers that were constituted from primordial matter. Consequently, it is best not to create a rigid dichotomy between these options. Moreover, given the fact that 'the rulers' have already been described as deriving their existence from Christ (1:16), it seems to be the case that the author is envisaging a scenario where the Colossians are allowing themselves to become subject again to powers that have been vanquished in Christ (2:10, 15).

It may have been the case that the recipients of the letter might not have initially recognized the charge against them, that they were allowing themselves to be taken captive by forces from which they had been released in Christ. The fullest description of the problem that the author is confronting is described in Col. 2:16–19. This description would have probably made much more sense to the recipients of the letter, who were likely to be aware of the background to these statements. Whether or not the recipients accepted the author's critique of their 'defective' christology, presumably the description of angelic worship (Col. 2:18) would have been more recognizable to the Colossians than it is for those removed from the original context.

Notwithstanding the difficulty for modern readers in interpreting these verses, there are sufficient clues to provide a basic sense of the issues being confronted. Initially the author critiques a number of practices that are either ascetic in nature, or seem to reflect a commitment to differing religious systems. While the instruction not to let anybody pass judgment on believers in regard to food or drink (Col. 2:16) might be understood more as a religious scruple than as an ascetic act, when this is read in light of the comment a few verses later that some believers are living in accordance with the worldly dogmas 'do not handle, do not taste, do not touch' (Col. 2:21), it becomes apparent that restrictive ascetic practices are among the issues at stake for the author. However, the concern is not limited to ascetic practices – it also encapsulates the observance of religious ceremonies such as 'a festival or new moon or Sabbath' (Col. 2:16). There is a tendency to read the first two terms, 'festival' and 'new moon', through the lens of the last term, Sabbath. This has resulted in commentators asserting with certainty that the issue being confronted was pressure on gentiles to conform to Jewish practices (Dunn 1996: 176). While there is no doubt that Sabbath observance was a distinctively Jewish practice, the observance of festivals and new moon ceremonies was far from being exclusively Jewish. Given that the believers in Colossae apparently had not been drawn from a Jewish background, but had formerly been uncircumcised gentiles (Col. 2:11), and that in distinction to the subject matter of Galatians Jewish issues do not come to the fore in Colossians, it is not satisfactory to read these terms as exclusively reflecting a tendency towards accepting Jewish practices.

The trend of reading the problem addressed in Colossians as pressure to accept Jewish practices may reflect a tendency in New Testament studies to interpret material in light of what scholars know most about, namely first-century Judaism. Instead, the multi-cultural environment of the eastern Mediterranean was a mix of different religious practices and traditions. These various cults often used similar or shared terminology. Moreover, even at the level of practice, there was often cross-fertilization of forms of religious rites. There is no need to reject the possibility that Judaism may have been a factor in this mix, but it needs to be remembered that to date no hard evidence has been found for the existence of a Jewish community in Colossae in the first century. Excavation of the site may unearth the remains of a synagogue in Colossae or inscriptions that are demonstrably Jewish in character; however, if that does become the case this does not negate the more basic observation that pagan religion throughout Phrygia (and the rest of Asia Minor) was largely syncretistic in nature. The material remains at Aphrodisias bear testimony to the way local mystery religions were modified to accommodate imperial worship. Given that the Colossian believers were drawn from the majority Hellenistic culture of the region with syncretistic religious practices, it appears likely that some of the recent believers in Christ at Colossae saw nothing untoward in combining elements of their new faith with their earlier commitment to some of the mystery cults that perhaps offered more ecstatic rites than Christianity. This may have also entailed drawing elements from Judaism, although that remains less certain.

It is against this backdrop, and in response to a syncretistic religious pluralism that the author writes. The author adopts a number of rhetorical strategies to gain the assent of the hearers of the letter to the teaching that is being presented.

1. There is a relational strategy whereby figures known to the Colossians are presented as being faithful teachers of the belief system that is contained in the letter. Most notably Epaphras is co-opted by the author, since he is the person that established the Colossians in their faith (Col. 1:7). However, various other well-known figures from the Pauline circle are also named (4:7–14), both to create links with the Colossians and to show that the type of christology being advocated is widely held by leading Christian teachers.

2. The central teaching of the letter is first presented lyrically and doxologically (Col. 1:15–20) in a manner that gains assent in a potentially non-confrontational manner, before the author challenges the Colossians concerning the deviant teaching circulating in the community.

3. The author uses the figure of Paul to create pathos towards the apostle as a figure who strives (Col. 2:1) and suffers (1:24) on behalf of the Colossians, and endures incarceration because of fidelity to proclaiming the gospel (4:3, 18).

4. Those teaching a syncretistic form of faith are side-lined by not naming them and instead only generic references are used: 'somebody' (Col. 2:8) or 'anybody' (2:16).

5. Perhaps constituting the most intellectually based strategy, the author argues that the Colossians are already in possession of all heavenly blessings so there is no need to appease cosmic rulers and authorities. As those who exist in Christ, they have already been transferred to the heavenly realm (Col. 1:13), they have died to the elements of the world (2:20), and they have been raised with Christ in the process of becoming blessed with a new mode of existence (3:14).

Together these strategies are presented to rebut the teaching of those who call for the Colossians to engage in other cultic practices that involve the veneration of angels, and betray a concern to appease cosmic powers that are regarded as controlling the believers in Colossae.

While it is suggested that the letter is more likely not to have been written by Paul, it is Pauline in a very real sense. It appeals to the authority of Paul, and shares many of Paul's central theological affirmations, especially in terms of exclusive devotion to Christ. Pauline phraseology and thought are repackaged in ways that are both faithful to many of the apostle's key ideas, and yet mark creative developments in relation to Paul's system of thought. The epistle also self-consciously links itself with key figures in the Pauline movement, which is no doubt a strategy of legitimization. Key developments in thought are to be seen in the beginnings of the formulation of a universal ecclesiology, and in relation to an eschatology that, while containing some elements of future hope, is more fully realized in the present experience of believers than is usually the case in the earlier Pauline epistles. There are, however, a couple of areas where the perspectives of the letter stand in marked contrast to the teaching of Paul. The author's exclusive christology is so focused on believers being in Christ and Christ in believers (Col. 1:27) that there appears to be no place left in this theological system for the Spirit (cf. Col. 1:8). Moreover, the radical teaching of Paul on the flattening of social distinctions between believers is on the one hand affirmed in the letter (Col. 3:11), but is greatly softened (perhaps even undermined) with the teaching of the household code (Col. 3:18–4:1) that counsels fundamental conformity to prevailing social structures, even though internally believers may understand basic social rules as being subverted since believers are serving their heavenly Lord, not their earthly lords (Col. 3:22–23).

This may have been wise advice as a survival strategy, but it should be recognized that this teaching is an accommodation to the values of the dominant structures of the majority culture. As such it reflects part of the post-Pauline attempt to domesticate Paul's radical teaching into a form that could have enduring value.

Hence the letter is understood as being written by an author well acquainted with Pauline thought, perhaps through direct contact with Paul while he was living, and almost certainly reflecting some degree of knowledge of Paul's earlier letters. The recipients of the letter are taken to be a community of believers living in Colossae in the post-Pauline period, and who are being challenged to supplement their faith in Christ by combining it with religious practices derived from the indigenous mystery cults that were prevalent in the Lycus Valley, and Phrygia more widely. The author sees this syncretistic tendency as diminishing the significance of Christ for believers, while also subjecting themselves to cosmic forces from which they already have been freed in Christ. It is noteworthy that the ideas contained in the letter were taken up and in fact undergo even greater development in the letter to the Ephesians. In particular, Ephesians amplifies the perspectives on ecclesiology and eschatology contained in Colossians. Since the Pauline letter to the Ephesians was already known to Ignatius of Antioch by the end of the first quarter of the second century (Foster 2005: 168–75), it is likely that Ephesians was written before the end of the first century. This would imply that Colossians was written earlier still, perhaps some time between 65 and 80 CE. It was written to confront a real and present situation that the author perceived to be an example of deviant teaching present among believers in Colossae, which threatened a correct understanding of the uniqueness and supremacy of Christ.

While the details of that deviant teaching can no longer be reconstructed with certainty, the author has left a rich legacy. The soaring lyrical praise of Christ (Col. 1:15–20) is one of the high points of first-century Christian piety and theology. The moving but not over-sentimentalized portrait of an aging and imprisoned apostle battling for the faith while still in chains has functioned as an inspiration for those who suffer for their beliefs. The theological developments reflect the fact that it is incumbent on people of faith to reconsider what that faith means in different times and different places. This is a difficult negotiation between faithfulness to tradition and responsiveness to the needs of contemporary situations. While Colossians does not provide answers to all the theological questions of subsequent generations, it does present a dialectical model that reflects the necessity of meaningful fidelity to the faith handed down in the name of Paul, and yet at the same time the author seeks to apply that faith afresh with creative and new theological insights to address contemporary situations. This is no easy task, not even for those who may claim to have been raised with Christ. As the author of Colossians eloquently states, even for those with risen status, the challenge is to 'keep seeking the things above' (Col. 3:1).

Therefore, the provisionality of theological insights, especially when applied to new situations, requires a constant teasing out of the application of theological beliefs, and a willingness to think anew about what can be said about faith when it is confronted with real and challenging situations. The author of Colossians presents an approach that seeks to honour the tradition on which it is founded, but at the same time attempts to apply that faith with creative freshness to a new situation. Perhaps, rather than christological or eschatological truths, Colossians ultimately teaches more about the nature of the theological task for people who acknowledge that presently they 'see in a mirror darkly' (1 Cor. 13:12), but await to be revealed with Christ in glory (Col. 3:4).

11. *The Text of Colossians*

In most commentaries treating Colossians one of the most fundamental questions relating to the analysis of the text is regularly overlooked (cf. Bormann 2012: 1–6). That question concerns the state of preservation of the text of this first-century letter, and the reliability of the surviving witnesses to that text. During the period of the early production of the great critical editions of the New Testament text in the eighteenth and nineteenth centuries, including Mill (1707), Griesbach (1775–1777), Tischendorf's *Editio octavo critica maior* (1869–1872), Westcott and Hort's *The New Testament in the Original Greek* (1881), editors such as these were able to consult manuscripts no earlier than the fourth century at best. However, even the two great majuscule manuscripts of the fourth century vary in quality. Codex Vaticanus (typically dated to the second half of the fourth century) was seen by Westcott and Hort as representing an unadulterated state of the text. In value-laden terms, they labelled this manuscript as preserving the 'neutral text', thereby displaying great confidence that its text stood close to the 'original' text of the New Testament. Many of these judgments, which still require significant qualification, were made in regard to the texts of the gospels, and not in relation to the text of the Pauline corpus. It is commonly acknowledged that Vaticanus is in fact an inferior text for the Pauline epistles in comparison with the other great majuscule manuscript of the fourth-century Codex Sinaiticus.

However, during the twentieth century the landscape of the textual criticism of the New Testament changed with the discovery of numerous papyrus manuscripts, some of which are early, some of which are extensive, and a few of which are both early and extensive. This has led standard introductions to the topic of textual criticism to celebrate the advances in the discipline over the last century, due largely to the discovery of new manuscripts. Thus Kurt and Barbara Aland confidently wrote, '[f]or in contrast to our own generation, which possess a wealth of early witnesses dating back to the beginning of the second century, Westcott and Hort had no direct witness to the New Testament text earlier than the fourth century' (Aland and Aland 1989: 14). However, while that claim may be true in general, it does not pertain with equal force to every writing in the New Testament. Admittedly, the study of the early text of Colossians has been illumined by the discovery of one remarkable papyrus manuscript $\mathfrak{P}^{46}$, dating from the early third century (c. 200). Yet, even though this manuscript preserves a text that is approximately a century and a half earlier than that of either Sinaiticus or Vaticanus, it does not preserve the full text of Colossians. It is impressive that 81 of Colossians 95 verses are preserved, although not all of these 81 verses survive in their entirety. Therefore, for the complete text of the Epistle to the Colossians, it is still necessary to consult fourth-century manuscripts, which are the earliest witnesses to the complete text. This creates a gap of approximately three centuries between the likely date of the writing of the letter and earliest manuscript to preserve the complete text of the letter to the Colossians. The manuscript $\mathfrak{P}^{46}$, however, lends confidence to the claim that the text of the epistle was relatively stable by the beginning of the third century. Alongside this, it must be acknowledged that $\mathfrak{P}^{46}$ itself is not a highly professional manuscript. In general, the scribe had a tendency to omit portions of the text, he

113

produced a number of errors that result in nonsense readings, and he made many spelling mistakes (Royse 2008: 358).

Furthermore, it must be acknowledged that attempts to comment on the state of the text prior to the earliest surviving manuscript are precarious. Such endeavours are based on a range of assumptions, most importantly including which reading for a particular variation unit may have produced the surviving variant readings. While much energy and intellectual effort has been recently devoted to the development of a scientific method for recovering an earlier state of the text (the so-called coherence-based genealogical method, CBGM), those who have developed this method refrain from claiming that it permits access to the 'original' text. Instead they prefer to speak of their method providing access to the earliest recoverable state of the text, or to the 'initial text' (*Ausgangstext*).

It is, therefore, important to be aware that in dealing with Colossians one is typically dealing with a form of the text that is attested in only twelve manuscripts that date from the eighth century or earlier. Moreover, of these twelve manuscripts only four offer a complete text of the epistle, the two earliest being from the fourth century. Two further manuscripts prior to the ninth century preserve more than half of the epistle, the early third-century manuscript $\mathfrak{P}^{46}$ (ca. 200) that preserves at least parts of 81 of the letters 95 verses, and the fifth-century majuscule 048, where there are 58 surviving verses that survive either in full or in part.

These bare facts should at least cause some pause for thought concerning claims that the text of Colossians that is presented in major critical editions of the Greek New Testament is identical with the words that appeared in the letter penned in the second half of the first century. The earliest partial text of the epistle dates from approximately a century and a half later. The next manuscript witnesses are complete texts, both from the fourth century, which may date from three hundred years after Colossians was written. While $\mathfrak{P}^{46}$ demonstrates that the transmission of the text was relatively stable in the period from the beginning of the third century to the mid-fourth century, it is difficult to assess the stability of the text prior to this. However, where we have examples of gospel texts from the second century (although these are highly fragmentary), such texts reflect stability during a slightly earlier period. These fragmentary manuscripts provide a partial glimpse into the textual history of the gospels, during the second half of the second century and typically they reflect a stable text. Furthermore, it could be argued that the Pauline epistles were less likely to be subjected to harmonistic tendencies than was the case with the synoptic gospels – although the relationship between Colossians and Ephesian may be the principal case in the Pauline corpus where that might not be true. Against such arguments for the relative stability of the text of Colossians stands the general observation that texts are typically most unstable in the earliest phase of their transmission. However, as the 150 years of transmission is precisely the period for which there is no surviving evidence, it must be noted that there is simply no evidence available to support either the hypothesis of the stability or that of the instability of the text during this period of transmission. Therefore the analysis of the complete form of the text of the letter to the Colossians is based upon manuscript evidence that draws heavily upon the text contained in the two fourth-century codices Sinaiticus and Vaticanus. However, the extensive portions of the surviving text of Colossians available in $\mathfrak{P}^{46}$ reflect a relatively high degree of stability in the period from the beginning of the third century to the mid-fourth century, although one must take into account the inaccuracies of the scribe of this manuscript.

11.1. *Manuscript Evidence for Colossians*
The evidence for the Greek text of Colossians as preserved in manuscripts that are dated before the year 1000 is presented below. The dates follow the consensus opinions as represented by the *kurzegefasste liste* available from the Institut für Neutestamentliche Forschung in Münster (http://ntvmr.uni-muenster.de/liste).

The textual data are arranged into the traditional categories for continuous Greek New Testament manuscripts of papyrus, majuscule, minuscule, and lectionary manuscripts (although the last group is representative rather than exhaustive).

1. Papyri
$\mathfrak{P}^{46}$ (ca. 200/3rd cent) 1:1–2, 5–13, 16–24, 27–29; 2:1–19, 23–25; 3:1–11, 13–24; 4:3–12, 16–18 (14 verses entirely lost)
$\mathfrak{P}^{61}$ (ca. 700/8th cent) 1:3–7, 9–13; 4:15 (11 verses preserved)

2. Majuscules

01 ℵ	(4ᵗʰ cent)	compl.
A 02	(5ᵗʰ cent)	compl.
B 03	(4ᵗʰ cent)	compl.
C 04	(5ᵗʰ cent)	1:1–2 (2 verses)
D 06	(6ᵗʰ cent)	compl.
F 010	(9ᵗʰ cent)	missing 2:1–8 (87 verses preserved)
G 012	(9ᵗʰ cent)	missing 2:1–8 (87 verses preserved)
H 015	(6ᵗʰ cent)	1:26–29; 2:1–8, 20–25; 3:1–11 (29 verses preserved)
I 016	(5ᵗʰ cent)	1:1–4, 10–12, 20–22, 27–29; 2:7–9, 16–19; 3:5–8, 15–17, 25; 4:1–2, 11–13 (33 verses preserved)
K 018	(9ᵗʰ cent)	compl.
L 020	(9ᵗʰ cent)	compl.
P 025	(9ᵗʰ cent)	missing 3:16–4:8 (77 verses preserved)
Ψ 044	(9ᵗʰ/10ᵗʰ cent)	compl.
048	(5ᵗʰ cent)	1:20–2:8, 11–14, 22–23; 3:7–8; 3:12–4:18 (58 verses preserved)
049	(9ᵗʰ cent)	compl.
075	(10ᵗʰ cent)	compl.
0142	(10ᵗʰ cent)	compl.
0151	(9ᵗʰ cent)	compl.
0198	(6ᵗʰ cent)	3:15–16, 20–21 (4 verses preserved)
0208	(6ᵗʰ cent)	1:29–2:10, 13–14 (13 verses preserved)
0278	(9ᵗʰ cent)	1:17–3:13; 3:21–4:18 (72 verses preserved)
0319	(9ᵗʰ cent)	compl. (0319 was previously known as Dᵃᵇˢ¹)

3. Minuscules

Ninth century:

33 (9ᵗʰ cent) compl.   1424 (9ᵗʰ cent) compl.   1862 (9ᵗʰ cent) compl.
1900 (9ᵗʰ cent) compl.   2464 (9ᵗʰ cent) compl.

Tenth century:

82 (10ᵗʰ cent) compl.   93 (10ᵗʰ cent) compl.   181 (10ᵗʰ cent) compl.
221 (10ᵗʰ cent) compl.   326 (10ᵗʰ cent) compl.   398 (10ᵗʰ cent) compl.
436 (10ᵗʰ cent) compl.   454 (10ᵗʰ cent) compl.   456 (10ᵗʰ cent) compl.
457 (10ᵗʰ cent) compl.   602 (10ᵗʰ cent) compl.   619 (10ᵗʰ cent) compl.
627 (10ᵗʰ cent) compl.   920 (10ᵗʰ cent) compl.   1175 (10ᵗʰ cent) compl.
1611 (10ᵗʰ cent) compl.*   1720 (10ᵗʰ cent) compl.   1735 (10ᵗʰ cent) compl.
1739 (10ᵗʰ cent) compl.**   1836 (10ᵗʰ cent) compl.   1837 (10ᵗʰ cent) compl.
1841 (9ᵗʰ/10ᵗʰ cent) compl.   1845 (10ᵗʰ cent) compl.   1851 (10ᵗʰ cent) compl.
1871 (10ᵗʰ cent) compl.   1874 (10ᵗʰ cent) compl.   1875 (10ᵗʰ cent) compl.
1880 (10ᵗʰ cent) compl.   1891 (10ᵗʰ cent) compl.   1905 (10ᵗʰ cent) compl.
1912 (10ᵗʰ cent) compl.   1920 (10ᵗʰ cent) compl.   1927 (10ᵗʰ cent) compl.
1997 (10ᵗʰ cent) compl.   1998 (10ᵗʰ cent) compl.   2110 (10ᵗʰ cent) compl.
2125 (10ᵗʰ cent) compl.   2505 (10ᵗʰ cent) compl.   2892 (10ᵗʰ cent) compl.

* earlier dated 12ᵗʰ century.   ** likely copied from a 4ᵗʰ-century exemplar.

4. Lectionaries
*l*249 (9th cent)
*l*846 (9th cent)

Leaving aside the lectionaries, and focusing exclusively on continuous texts, it is possible to tabulate the data to show the number of available manuscripts by century. In the following table the second column gives the number of manuscripts of Colossians from each century, including fragmentary and complete manuscripts. The third column gives the number of complete manuscripts that date from the specified century. The fourth column gives the cumulative total of manuscripts of Colossians from that century or earlier – that is, it adds up the total number of manuscripts from that century or earlier. So, the 'cumulative total' until the end of the eighth century is a summation of the one third-century manuscript, the two from the fourth century, four from the fifth century, four from the sixth century and one from the eighth century, resulting in a total of twelve manuscripts. The fifth column provides the cumulative total of complete manuscripts of Colossians from that century or earlier, and involves a similar summative process as the fourth column. For the three manuscripts that are dated ninth/ tenth century in the *kurzegefasste liste* these have been grouped with the tenth-century manuscripts.

Century	Total	Complete	Cumulative Total	Cumulative Complete
1st	0	0	0	0
2nd	0	0	0	0
3rd	1	0	1	0
4th	2	2	3	2
5th	4	1	7	3
6th	4	1	11	4
7th	0	0	11	4
8th	1	0	12	4
9th	14	10	26	14
10th	42	42	68	54

It is apparent that from around the time of the introduction of the minuscule writing style in the ninth century, but especially from the tenth century when minuscule script dominates, that the number of surviving manuscripts grows significantly. This may reflect a number of factors. First, these manuscripts are more recent, so one would expect more to survive from this later period. The minuscule manuscripts may have been copied in larger numbers, thus resulting in the survival of more copies from the ninth century onwards. The copying may have taken place in organized scriptoria, which resulted in mass production facilitated by a more rapid style of writing and more highly developed facilities for the storage and retrieval of manuscripts. The development of the new minuscule script may have led to the relative neglect of older majuscule-style manuscripts. These factors, combined with the vagaries of the survival of the more ancient majuscule manuscripts and attempts to destroy Christian scriptures during the Decian and Gelarian persecutions, result in a perhaps not unsurprising distribution of surviving manuscript of Colossians from the first millennium of the common era.

Surviving Manuscripts of Colossians by Century

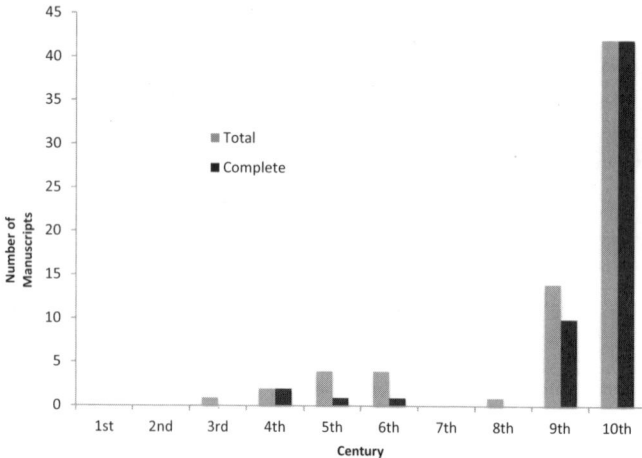

This chart displays the data from the second and third columns; that is the number of surviving manuscripts for the Epistle to the Colossians until the tenth century. It is possible to see that prior to the introduction of minuscule script in the ninth century only twelve manuscripts of Colossians survive. Of these only four are complete:

Sinaiticus (ℵ 01) fourth century
Vaticanus (B 03) fourth century
Alexandrinus (A 02) fifth century
Claromontanus (D 06) sixth century

In addition to these complete texts, 81 verses of Colossians survive to some extent in $\mathfrak{P}^{46}$ (ca. 200/third century). In the fifth-century majuscule 048, there are 58 surviving verses. Apart from these six manuscripts, it is not until the ninth century that any more manuscripts of Colossians survive that contains more than 50% of the 95 verses in the epistle. Nonetheless, some of the early fragmentary manuscripts are important for reconstructing the text of Colossians. The NA[28] lists the following manuscripts as its consistent witnesses that form the evidential basis for the reconstruction of the critical text.

The consistently cited witness for Colossians are:

Papyri:	$\mathfrak{P}^{46}$, $\mathfrak{P}^{61}$.
Majuscules:	ℵ (01), A (02), B (03), C (04), D (06), F (010), G (012), H (015), I (016), K (018), L (020), P (025), Ψ (044), 048, 075, 0198, 0208, 0278.
Minuscules:	33, 81, 104, 365, 630, 1175, 1505, 1506, 1739, 1881, 2464.
Lectionaries:	*l*249, *l*846.

That is, two papyri manuscripts, eighteen majuscules, eleven minuscules, and two lectionary manuscripts. This results in a total of 33 manuscripts.

Total and Cumulative Total of Manuscripts
of Colossians by Century

This chart also displays the data from the fourth and fifth columns; that is, it also presents the cumulative number of surviving manuscripts for the Epistle to the Colossians until the tenth century.

11.2. *Place in the Pauline Corpus*

In modern editions of the Greek New Testament, as well as in English translations, Colossians is the twelfth writing in the New Testament, and the seventh in the sequence of Pauline texts. It is placed between Philippians and 1 Thessalonians. The location of Colossians in the Pauline corpus, however, has not always been constant. In part this has been due to the inclusion of Hebrews within the collection of Pauline letters, but this is not the only factor. The arrangement of Pauline letters including Colossians in several early collections is as follows:

$\mathfrak{P}^{46}$	Rom., Heb., 1 Cor., 2 Cor., Gal., Eph., Phil., Col., 1 Thess.
Marcion	Gal., 1 Cor., 2 Cor., Rom., 1 Thess., 2 Thess., Laodiceans (= Eph.), Col., Phil., Phlm.
Muratorian	1 Cor., 2 Cor., Eph., Phil., Col., Gal., 1 Thess., 2 Thess., Rom., Phlm., Tit., 1 Tim., 2 Tim. (as well as mentioning two letters forged in Paul's name – Laodiceans and Alexandrians)

Two observations can be drawn. First, Ephesians, Philippians, and Colossians tend to stay together as a sub-group, with Ephesians at the head of that group, but with Philippians and Colossians following either in that sequence or inverted order. Second, Romans and Galatians are mobile and are placed in quite different locations in these lists. The reason for this is not entirely obvious, but at least demonstrates a lack of fixity in such lists.

12. *Structure of the Epistle*

I. Letter Opening		1:1–2:5
1.	Greeting	1:1–2
2.	Thanksgiving	1:3–8
3.	Prayer	1:9–14
4.	Poetic Reflection on Christ	1:15–20
5.	Applying Reconciliation to the Colossians	1:21–23
6.	Paul's Sufferings on Behalf of Believers	1:24–29
7.	Paul's Striving on Behalf of the Colossians	2:1–5

TRANSLATION
AND
COMMENTARY

I.
LETTER OPENING (1:1–2:5)

1. GREETING   (1:1–2)

(1) Paul an apostle of Christ Jesus through the will of God and Timothy the brother (2) to the holy and faithful brothers in Christ in Colossae, grace to you and peace from God our father.

It is often noted that Pauline epistles adopt the conventional form of Hellenistic letter openings by employing the formulaic pattern of '*name of sender* to *name of recipient*, greetings'. This observation is both correct, and yet also thoroughly inadequate. Pauline letters do not simply adopt, or even adapt, the standard pattern. Instead, conventional practice is transformed, by infusing the underlying recognizable form with theological affirmations, christological perspectives, and a description of apostolic status. Therefore, even from the opening phrase of each epistle, Paul (or a person writing in his name) takes the opportunity to place before the readers fundamental convictions that the apostle had developed from the time of his calling on Damascus Road, and which had undergone a process of reflective maturation throughout his ministry.

The perspectives presented in these theologized letter openings tend to be general in nature, rather than focusing on the context-specific concerns or problems that are discussed in the body of each letter that is addressed to a specific community or individual. By transforming formal letter openings into a theological reflection, these affirmations signal to readers what are regarded as mutual understandings or shared convictions in the Pauline churches. As an exercise in forging links with readers, the greeting presents various statements of shared beliefs, including the notion that both Paul's status and that of the recipients has been transformed through common relationship to Christ. Kinship language is also employed to attest to the relationship that Paul and his addressees now share as a result of them being drawn into this relationship with Jesus. Therefore, a sense of solidarity with the recipients permeates the opening of the letter. Furthermore, by portraying the common bond between sender and recipients that exists in Christ, as well as through injecting familial language into the expanded letter opening, the greeting announces core theological commitments and simultaneously identifies with readers, since Paul is shown to be bound to them in a shared faith, and has, like them, received a transformed status in Christ.

1 Typical of standard practice, the sender identifies himself with the opening word of the letter. The name **Paul** is the way the writer of the epistle designates himself. While the recipients have not met the implied author in person, since the author states the Colossians are known to Paul only by reputation (Col. 1:4, 7, 9), nonetheless his name is prominent enough that it may be assumed that it would be recognized. Nowhere in the surviving Pauline writings does Paul use the name Saul. This does not imply that the unexplained name-change that occurs in Acts is fictitious (Acts 13:9). Rather, the use of the name Paul was so completely accepted both by Paul himself and those who knew him, that it required no further clarification. However, while Pauline letters presented his status as **an apostle** as straightforwardly as his name, that claim may well have been far more problematic in some sections of the early Jesus movement. The term 'apostle' in wider contemporary Greek usage designated an authorized representative or envoy, and there is no doubt that this sense remains part of the word's meaning even in Paul's usage (cf. 2 Cor. 8:23; Phil. 2:25). However, it is also used as a technical term, which denotes a specific role and probably the most prominent position among early believers. Precise definitions of the role are absent in early Christian writings. However, the story of the appointment of Matthias as a replacement for the 'ministry and apostleship' of Judas (Acts 1:25) presents two criteria which must be fulfilled. First, an apostle is to be a person who accompanied Jesus during his ministry from its commencement with the baptism by John, and secondly, the person is to have been a witness to the resurrection (Acts 1:21–22). While Paul may have fulfilled the second criterion through a vision (although some of Paul's harshest critics may have disputed this, cf. Pseudo-Clement, *Hom.* 17.19.1–7), nowhere does Paul claim that he fulfilled the first criterion. It therefore appears Paul understood at least his own apostleship to be predicated on a single criterion, namely his encounter with the resurrected Jesus (1 Cor. 9:1; 15:8). Moreover, Paul understood his commission as an apostle to be a call to preach to the Gentiles (Rom. 1:5; 11:13), and his visionary experience on the journey to Damascus is also understood as being the moment when the veracity of the gospel message was revealed to him (Gal. 1:11–12).

While Paul is described here as **an apostle of Christ Jesus** as a designation of his status, the concern over challenges to that claim that occur elsewhere in the Pauline writings are not present. Hence, it may be inferred that Paul's apostolic status was not a controversial claim for the Colossians, nor had it been challenged by others in their midst. The relationship of the apostolic role to the figure named as Christ Jesus is not fully explained, and it was probably understood in a multifaceted manner, rather than having a single aspect. At its core are the ideas of origin and representation, with the latter perhaps tending towards concepts of ownership and possession. Paul's credentials are in effect presented as authorizing him to represent Christ. However, in a society where patrons often used learned slaves as commissioned envoys, the language may have evoked ideas of a close relationship between the one acting on behalf of an absent superior. It is unlikely that the reference to Christ Jesus is used here to denote the content of the message that the apostle had been entrusted to proclaim (although elsewhere Paul can use that metaphor, cf. 1 Cor. 1:23). Rather, it designates the person to whom Paul gave his allegiance. The double-barrelled referent **Christ Jesus** appears in that order in the earlier surviving manuscripts of Colossians, whereas some Byzantine manuscripts read Jesus Christ (as followed by the KJV, and some other translations). In Colossians the two terms occur alongside each other on five occasions, four times in the order Christ Jesus (Col. 1:1, 4; 2:6; 4:12) and once in the order Jesus Christ (Col. 1:3). In the wider corpus of thirteen Pauline epistles, the relative occurrence is: 'Christ Jesus' 89 times; 'Jesus Christ' 78 times.[1] While some commentators wish to emphasize the titular aspect of the term 'Christ', thereby rendering the

---

[1] Attempting to count these occurrences is not a straightforward task. Some manuscripts invert the word order, so one is unsure whether the original reading was 'Christ Jesus' or 'Jesus Christ', while others add either 'Christ' or 'Jesus' respectively to the single appellative 'Jesus' or 'Christ', either before or after what on text-critical grounds appears to be the earlier single-term referent.

expression as 'Messiah Jesus' (Bird 2009: 33), others have suggested that already by this stage the titular force of the noun Χριστός, 'Christ', had been largely lost, 'and the two words together in either order formed a single name' (Harris 2010: 129). However, a third possibility exists. The third onomastic category is that, rather than understanding the term 'Christ' as a title or a name, it may function as an honorific (see Novenson 2012: 87–97). That is, it serves as an appellative that has become closely or uniquely associated with a single person, but still conveys the connotation of the honour it describes. Examples of this category in the ancient world include the emperor Octavian designated as Augustus, Antiochus IV as Epiphanes, and the renaming of Shimon bar Kosiba as Shimon bar Kokhba, 'the son of the star', which carried messianic overtones. In the same way that Paul acknowledges that while there are many so-called lords for believers there is only one Lord (1 Cor. 8:5–6), perhaps thereby rebutting Gentile veneration of imperial figures, the unique attachment of the term 'Christ' to Jesus probably drew upon ancient Jewish messianism, but also rebutted any Jewish attempt to associate the term 'Christ' with any other messianic figure.

While Paul's apostleship finds its origin in Christ Jesus, it is also stated that his possession of that office is granted **through the will of God**. Here the author reveals an understanding of Paul's commission to the apostolic office that finds its origin in Christ, and yet simultaneously derives from the divine purpose. Such a perspective reflects Paul's own belief that his status as an apostle is not due to some self-seeking act of aggrandisement, but is a commission given by Christ and also fully aligned with the divine will. This emphasis on Christ's commission and the divine will or agency is presented more stridently in other epistles (cf. Gal. 1:1, 12). Here the same claim is made in a more dispassionate manner, but the emphasis is the same – namely, that Paul's apostleship is divinely sanctioned.

Paul often names associates in his letter openings, as, for example, in 1 Cor. 1:1, where he refers to 'Sosthenes the brother' (note that Silvanus is also mentioned in the opening verse of both 1 and 2 Thessalonians). However, the most prominent of his companions mentioned in the greetings is Timothy (2 Cor. 1:2; Phil. 1:1; Col. 1:1; Phlm. 1; 1 Thess. 1:1; 2 Thess. 1:1). A number of different formulations are used to introduce the named associates. In the opening verse of Colossians, in differentiation to Paul's own role as

an apostle, the letter refers to **Timothy the brother**. The closeness
of Paul's relationship with Timothy can be inferred through his
description of him as 'my beloved and faithful child in the Lord'
(1 Cor. 4:17), or the declaration that 'I have no one like him' (Phil.
2:20). However, Timothy is not mentioned at any other place in the
letter to the Colossians. It appears probable that, like Paul, Timothy
was personally unknown to the Colossians. Therefore, the reason for
mentioning Timothy is unclear. Perhaps it was due to his prominence
in Pauline circles and consequently he may have been known by
reputation to the believers in Colossae. Alternatively, he may have
had an active role in the composition or drafting of the letter. Another
possibility is that the author of the letter, be it Paul or a pseudonymous figure, may have conformed the opening to Paul's standard
practice – the opening words of Colossians and 2 Corinthians are
identical up to this point.

2 The opening moves from a description of the sender and his
associate, to identifying the recipients. The letter is addressed
to the holy and faithful brothers in Christ in Colossae. This
Greek syntax of this phrase causes some difficulties for translators,
although regardless of which option is chosen the central meaning
is not greatly altered. Before outlining the translational options it
is helpful to document two textual variants that do not impinge on
the grammatical problem. First, there is a variant spelling of name
of the town, as κολασσαῖς (i.e. Colassae), in some manuscripts –
(𝔓⁴⁶ A) I K P etc. Second, a number of manuscripts add the word
'Jesus' after the term 'Christ' – A D* F G etc. The latter variant is
almost certainly secondary. However, the former may be due to an
archaizing tendency, or reflect localized orthography, or it may be
the original reading, standardized to wider practice by later scribes.
Fortunately, very little hangs on this variant, and whichever choices
are made the larger syntactical problem remains the same.

This larger syntactical problem depends on whether the two Greek
words ἁγίοις and πιστοῖς are both adjectives and form a co-ordinated
pair describing the noun 'brothers', or whether the first is a noun
linked to the definite article that stands at the start of the verse and
the second Greek word is an adjective which alone qualifies the noun
'brothers'. However, there are more than two possible translations
since the second option subdivides into two possibilities depending

on whether one understands 'the holy ones' and the 'faithful brothers' as two separate groups, or if the second description is understood as a further (epexegetical) description of those called 'the holy ones'. This results in the following three possible translations:

i. to the holy and faithful brothers in Christ in Colossae
ii. to the holy ones in Colossae and to faithful brothers in Christ
iii. to the holy ones in Colossae, *who are* faithful brothers in Christ

Arguments in favour of the first alternative stress the normal syntactical structures of Greek language, whereas the latter two options emphasize the standard Pauline usage of the term ἁγίοις, 'holy', when it occurs with a definite article. The second alternative is rarely adopted, since it would appear to imply that there were two groups 'the holy ones' and 'the faithful brothers'. If this were the case it might imply some division in the community, or a hierarchy of group members (see the discussion in Lightfoot 1886: 130). There is nothing elsewhere in the epistle to suggest that this was the case. The third option is the one that has become widely accepted. The reason for this is because where the adjective occurs in introductions to other Pauline letters it functions as a substantivized noun (in particular see Phil. 1:1; Eph. 1:1). However, this observation may not be decisive for adopting the third option. First, while it is true that elsewhere in this epistle the term 'holy' is used as a noun being directly preceded by a definite article (see Col. 1:4, 26), the term is also used as an adjective on two occasions (Col. 1:22; 3:12). Secondly, regardless of the question of authorship, arguments based on comparison with use of the term elsewhere in the Pauline corpus assumes that Paul is incapable of varying his formulations. Thirdly, the construction does deviate from other Pauline introductions by using the second description 'brothers', and therefore is not directly comparable to the other occurrences. Hence it appears preferable to base a decision on typical Greek syntax, which would more naturally understand the definite article as governing the noun 'brothers', with ἁγίοις and πιστοῖς functioning as two adjectives describing the 'brothers' attributes as being 'holy and faithful'.

Therefore, the characteristics that are seen as marking out the addressees are their holiness and faithfulness. The first, being **holy**, is a term that denotes proximity to the divine, separation from profane usage, and dedication for godly purposes. The author sees the believers in Colossae as being called into a relationship with God, which thus has required them to be given a quality that makes them fit to enter the divine presence. The term has clear overtones of sacral purity and connections with temple worship. Elsewhere in the Pauline letters believers are seen as being a newly constituted holy temple (1 Cor. 3:19; Eph. 2:21). The second quality that is used to describe the addressees is that of being **faithful**. The adjective πιστός encapsulates a range of meanings. These include 'believing', 'faithful', 'reliable', and 'trustworthy'. It is unlikely that it is simply the act of 'believing' that is being highlighted here. In other Pauline letters the term is used to describe a quality of God (1 Cor. 1:9; 10:13; 2 Cor. 1:18), and in those verses the emphasis is upon divine fidelity and trustworthiness. It is also used to describe a quality required of stewards who are entrusted with a master's possessions (1 Cor. 4:2); again the emphasis is on reliability and trustworthiness. It is used to describe a range of Paul's esteemed colleagues: Timothy (1 Cor. 4:17), Tychicus (Eph. 6:21), and Epaphras (Col. 1:7). In each of these cases the attribute that is emphasized is the individual's fidelity. Likewise, with the description of the Colossians it is not so much their act of believing that is being described; rather, the second adjective depicts loyalty, or the process of continuance in their relationship with God. Hence the two qualities that are mentioned in the opening description of the addressees are the fact that the Colossians have been separated and consecrated for relationship with God – that is, they are holy – and also that they have remained steadfast in that relationship, which is how they have been faithful. The addressees are described as **brothers**. While this translation replicates the gendered language of the Greek text of the epistle, many recent English translations paraphrase this to emphasize the inclusive nature of the term 'brothers'. One common paraphrase is to render this term as 'brothers and sisters' (NIV, NLT, NET), while another option is to adopt the paraphrase 'people' (REB).

The addressees of the letter are located in two ways, one geographical, **in Colossae**, the other ontological or existential, **in Christ**. Addressing the recipients of his letters by the name of the city in which they reside is typically Pauline (Rom. 1:7; 1 Cor. 1:2; 2 Cor. 1:2; Phil. 1:1). However, while the geographical reference points towards the physical location of the community, they are also seen as 'residing' in a non-physical location. Their new existence is described as being **in Christ**. The 'in Christ' formula is a significant Pauline christological concept that denotes the union of believers with Christ (see Macaskill 2013: 219–50). The precise way in which this new ontological incorporation takes place is not explained. Elsewhere in the Pauline writings it involves some kind of trans-ference from being 'in Adam' in a state of bondage to sin, to new status of being 'in Christ' and consequently delivered from the dominion of sin (Rom. 5:12–21; 1 Cor. 15:22). While the believers in Colossae continue to reside in the same geographical location as they did prior to coming to faith, in spiritual terms they are viewed as existing in a new realm (cf. Col. 1:13). In this sense being 'in Christ' designates an entirely different ontological state and a funda-mentally new form of existence.

The opening concludes with a standard, although perhaps some-what truncated, Pauline phrase, **grace to you and peace from God our father**. Typically such opening greetings continue with the words 'and the Lord Jesus Christ' (cf. Rom. 1:7; 1 Cor. 1:3; 2 Cor. 1:2; Gal. 1:3; Eph. 1:2; Phil. 1:2; Phlm. 3). In fact, a number of early manuscripts that preserve Col. 1:2 do continue the verse with the standard phrase 'and the Lord Jesus Christ'. However, given the number of manuscripts that prefer the shorter reading, and because of the tendency to expand greetings on the basis of the more common Pauline formulations, it is highly likely that the shorter form is to be preferred (NA[28] 2012; cf. Metzger 1994: 552: 'the words, which are absent from a variety of witnesses...have no doubt been added by copyists who assimilated the text to Pauline usage').

While the salutation **grace to you and peace** is a standard element that is found in every Pauline letter opening, it would be wrong to infer that it was no more than a formulaic and insignificant element. The terms 'grace' and 'peace' are theologically rich, and it has been suggested that together they reflect a combination of Hellenistic and Hebrew greetings. However, in the Pauline letters the typical

Hellenistic greeting is not used. It was usual is Greek epistolography to conclude the opening with the term χαίρειν, 'greeting'. Paul modifies this standard and recognizable salutation. Instead here, as in other Pauline letters, the author wishes the Colossians **grace**, χάρις, thereby introducing a distinctively Christian element to the greeting. Within Greco-Roman culture of client–patron relations, the term 'grace' could designate an act of care or help, or a gift or favour bestowed by the donor upon the client. The expectation was that the materially less affluent client would be bound to the patron in a bond of subservient loyalty. More widely, however, the term denoted an act or gift freely given without an obligation being incurred. Where the term is used in Paul's letters outside the context of opening greetings it conveys the sense of a divine gift (Rom. 3:24; 4:4, 16; 5:2, 15). In Pauline vocabulary, 'grace' speaks of God's unmerited care of humanity and his freely given gift of salvation. The wish for the recipients to enjoy 'peace' points to the ultimate goal of reconciliation and the restoration of everything in the divine purpose (Rom. 5:1). The Hebrew greeting *shalom* is commonly understood to stand behind the second element in the salutation, **peace**, εἰρήνη. The Hebrew term was used in letter greetings (Nebuchadnezzar addresses the nations with the greeting 'May your peace abound', Dan. 4:1; compare also the greeting 'Mercy and peace', *2 Apoc. Bar.* 78:2; Ezra 5:7). More widely in the Hebrew Bible the term *shalom* is connected with a type of sacrifice, the peace offering (Lev. 3–4; 7). This can have multiple functions, from expressing thanksgiving (Lev. 7:11–13), to marking a vow (Lev. 7:16). Elsewhere 'peace' denotes the state that ensues when war is suspended (Josh. 9:15). Another rich strain is the concept of the 'covenant of peace' (Num. 25:12; Ezek. 34:25; 37:26) that denotes permanent security and protection from all harmful elements. Therefore, both grace and peace are divine gifts that communicate ideas of reconciliation and salvation. Paul understands the bringing of the good news, the proclamation of peace, and the announcement of salvation as virtually synonymous (Rom. 10:15). Hence the pithy greeting of 'grace to you and peace' encapsulates much of the Pauline understanding of what salvation means for those who receive it.

The salutation is concluded by explicitly stating that the source of grace and peace is **from** the one who is identified as **God our father**. There is no further explanation justifying the claim that God is both the father of the Colossians and also of Paul. However, in the following verse God is also identified as the father of our Lord Jesus Christ. In these opening verses Paul speaks of a complex web of relationships, both human and divine. He describes his own status as an apostle of Christ Jesus, but which finds its ultimate origin in the will of God. He also speaks of the Colossians as being 'holy and faithful brothers in Christ', and describes the ultimate gifts of grace and peace that likewise come from God. In this way Paul weaves together his christological understanding of the status of all believers in Christ, which originates in God and is in full accord with his divine will.

2. THANKSGIVING (1:3–8)

(3) We give thanks to God, father of our Lord Jesus Christ, always praying concerning you (4) having heard of your faith in Christ Jesus and the love which you have for all the holy ones (5) because of the hope laid up for you in the heavens, which you heard before in the word of the truth of the gospel, (6) which has come to you, just as also in all the world it is bearing fruit and increasing so [it is] also in you, from the day which you heard and knew the grace of God in truth: (7) just as you learnt from Epaphras our beloved fellow slave, who is a faithful servant of Christ on our behalf, (8) who also made clear to us your love in the spirit.

Another standard feature of Pauline letters is the thanksgiving section, which regularly follows the opening greeting. Such thanksgivings are to be found in a number of Paul's letters, although on some occasions the extent of the section is debated (for instance 1 Thessalonians). However, the beginning is marked by various phrases using slightly different forms of the Greek verb εὐχαριστῶ: 'I give thanks' (Rom. 1:8; 1 Cor. 1:4; Phil. 1:3, Phlm. 4), or 'we give thanks' (Col. 1:3; 1 Thess. 1:2), or 'we ought to give thanks' (2 Thess. 1:3). Elsewhere, the opening is followed by a eulogy, 'blessed be…' (2 Cor. 1:3; Eph. 1:3), or strikingly in Galatians Paul moves immediately from the epistolary opening to an exasperated outburst ('I am amazed that you are so quickly turning away from the one who called you...', Gal. 1:6). The purpose of these thanksgivings is, in general, to celebrate the faith and perseverance of the believers, as well as to praise God for the work of salvation he has accomplished. These are not two discrete elements, but rather in Pauline theology the grace of God proclaimed in the gospel is what leads to faith in Jesus. In turn this results in the assurance of a heavenly hope – that is, salvation.

The use of thanksgiving sections has precedent in Hellenistic letters from the mid-second century B.C. onwards (P.Hibeh 79.8; Grenfell and Hunt 1906), and in Jewish correspondence (2 Macc. 1:10–13). However, Paul does not simply follow existing conventions. He significantly modifies both the form and the purpose, so that the thanksgivings become an important vehicle for praising God for the transformation that had occurred in the lives of Gentile believers. In the Pauline letters expressions of thanks are often combined with other epistolary features, such as a prayer report or the motif of remembrance (Arzt-Grabner 2010: 131). Since the author has not visited the Colossians, the motif of remembrance is understandably absent (all three elements are present in Phil. 1:3–4; 1 Thess. 1:2–3; Phlm. 4). However, in Colossians, perhaps to compensate for the lack of prior contact, the prayer report is enlarged and recurs (Col. 1:3, 9), as does the declaration of the offering of thanks (Col. 1:3, 12).

3 The transition from the letter opening to the thanksgiving is based upon the reference to God as father. Similar to the Thessalonian letters (although a slightly different construction is used in the second epistle) the thanksgiving is issued in a plural form: **We give thanks to God**. There has been discussion concerning whether this is a genuine plural, referring to both Paul and Timothy actually giving thanks on behalf of the Colossians, or if it is a literary device or epistolary plural whereby Timothy is included by convention, since he is mentioned as one of the senders of the letter (Col. 1:1). The possibility that the author speaks of his own actions in the plural is not a convincing or consistent explanation. This is because later in this chapter when the authorial voice of Paul is employed to address the Colossians it occurs in the first person singular form (Col. 1:23–24). Thus it appears to be the case that the plural form is not simply following literary convention, but is genuinely reporting that the two named senders of the letter have shared in giving thanks since they heard the report concerning the Colossians progress in the faith. Thanks is addressed **to God**, which is not unusual in Hellenistic letters, but the basis of thanks is usually for health, prosperity, or material benefits enjoyed by the recipients of the letter (cf. 'I give thanks to the gods for your health', P.Lond. 42). As will transpire as this section continues, the reason for thanksgiving is based upon confidence in the hope laid up for the Colossians in the heavens.

One could ascribe the description of God as **father of our Lord Jesus Christ** as arising from a strict logic in Paul's thought. Since in the previous verse he has described God as both father of the Colossians and himself ('from God our father', Col. 1:2), as well as describing the Colossians as 'brothers in Christ'. The implication could be construed that since one is a brother of Christ, this would imply some level of shared parentage. However, this probably presses the logic of the familial relationship language too far, and also it would undercut the theological belief that the primary paternal–filial relationship is between God and Christ. Paul's prior conviction is that Jesus is God's Son (cf. Rom. 1:3–4), and it is because of the filial relationship of Jesus to God that believers are called into fellowship with God (1 Cor. 1:9). The phrase 'father of our Lord Jesus Christ' is placed after the word 'God' without any conjunction or linking term. This disjunction in syntax has been improved in a number of manuscripts. This has resulted in three main readings in the Greek texts. Some manuscripts add a definite article before the word father: i.e. 'God, the father of our Lord Jesus Christ'. Others supply a conjunction: i.e. 'to the God and father of our Lord Jesus Christ'. The reading followed here, which lacks both the definite article and the conjunction, has the support of fewer manuscripts than either of the other alternatives. However, the shorter reading has early support, and the insertion of either the definite article or the conjunction is such an obvious improvement to the sentence's syntax, that it is difficult to suppose that the smoother form has been intentionally changed to a more awkward formulation. Moreover, the phrase 'the God and father of our Lord Jesus Christ' occurs at various other places in the Pauline letters (Rom. 15:6; 2 Cor. 11:31; Eph. 1:3), so it is straightforward to understand why later scribes would have changed the reading followed here to the more familiar form.

The four words that conclude this verse, **always praying concerning you**, have again raised syntactical issues. In Greek the four words πάντοτε περὶ ὑμῶν προσευχόμενοι may be translated literally as 'always concerning you praying'. There is discussion over whether the 'always' refers to the act of thanksgiving, or to a description of prayer. Furthermore, there is also debate relating to the action with which the phrase 'concerning you' should be construed. This presents three major options in translation.

i. We give thanks to God, father of our Lord Jesus Christ, always praying concerning you

ii. We always give thanks to God, father of our Lord Jesus Christ, praying concerning you

iii. We always give thanks concerning you to God, father of our Lord Jesus Christ, when praying

In favour of option two, Harris offers three reasons why the adverb 'always' should be taken with the main verb 'we give thanks'. He states that this follows normal Pauline usage, that also in New Testament Greek adverbs typically follow the verb they modify, and that the purpose of the participle is to restrict the meaning of 'always', i.e. 'we always give thanks...when we pray' (Harris 2010: 14). The last point is the weakest, since it is only a corollary of the decision to take the adverb with the verb 'to give thanks'. While adverbs may follow the verb they modify this is far from being a general pattern (cf. Phil. 1:3–4). The only other use of the adverb πάντοτε, 'always', in this epistle (Col. 4:6) is inconclusive for determining the author's usage, since a main verb needs to be supplied. As for normal Pauline usage, regarding the three citations provided by Harris, one does not use the same adverb (Eph. 1:16), in one case it is more natural to take the adverb with the following participle (Phil. 1:3–4), and in the third case the adverb is syntactically much closer to the main verb (1 Thess. 1:2). In relation to the third option, few commentators who chose this translation explain why the phrase 'concerning you' should be taken with the preceding description of thanksgiving. The primary reason for this, when one is given, is that commencing a clause with the phrase 'concerning you' would make for a poor construction in Greek (Lightfoot 1886: 131). Again, requiring such polished syntax from the author seems to be an unrealistic demand. In favour of the first option, this not only more closely matches the Greek word order, but it also preserves some of the ambiguity of the placement of the term 'always', πάντοτε. Attempting to link the adverb to either the main verb 'to give thanks', or the subordinate participle 'praying', may be a case of trying to find too much precision in the author's spontaneous style, which is more about a rapid outburst of praise than the exactitude of grammatical usage. Therefore the placement of the adverb may indeed be somewhat ambiguous – so be it.

Prayer is commonly linked to thanksgiving in Paul's letters. Having described the act of thanksgiving, readers are informed that Paul prays for them regularly. These times of prayer are presumably the occasions when thanksgiving is offered up to God. Later (Col. 1:9–11), the author describes the intercessory aspect of his prayers on behalf of the Colossians. Together these descriptions provide insight into the centrality of prayers of thanksgiving and intercession as part of the author's ongoing commitment to the new Christian communities.

4 Next this section outlines the basis for rendering thanks to God. At this stage the linking term **having heard**, ἀκούσαντες, is not expanded; the source of the author's knowledge will be clarified a few verses later (Col. 1:7–8). Here two grounds for thanksgiving are identified. First, the Colossians are informed that Paul gives thanks because he has learnt **of your faith in Christ Jesus**. The English translation can give the impression that what is described by the term **faith** is an intellectual assent to a set of beliefs concerning Jesus. However, this interpretation is almost certainly incorrect. The noun 'faith', πίστις, describes a lived-out behaviour and may be better understood as denoting an attitude of 'faithfulness'. This understanding is not only closer to the range of meanings encapsulated by the Greek term, it also allows for an understanding of the following phrase **in Christ Jesus** that is more consistent with its sense in the greeting section (Col. 1:2). Rather than cognitive belief in the person of Christ, the first ground of hope is an affirmation that the Colossians' transformed lives of faithfulness, which derive from their new sphere of existence within the body of Christ, are the basis for expressing praise to God.

The second reason for giving thanks is the recognizable solidarity that the Colossians have with fellow believers. They are commended for **the love which you have for all the holy ones**. This is the positive side of the new community formed through incorporation into Christ. The converse of this can be seen with the Corinthians, where Paul chastises them for their divisions (1 Cor. 1:10–13; 11:18–19) and for boasting about status or rank in the body of Christ (1 Cor. 12:12–27). The concept of **love**, ἀγάπη, as a hallmark of Christian relationships, is an important element in Pauline theology (136 occurrences of the word group in the Pauline epistles). While love can be mentioned without further qualification (as is the case here), elsewhere it becomes clear that for Paul Christian love finds its origin in the prior act of God loving those who were undeserving of his love. Thus he writes that 'God shows his love to us…while we were still sinners' (Rom. 5:8), and that God's love is a gift freely given through the spirit (Rom. 5:5). Thus for Paul, believers who have freely received the love of God are to reflect that same quality in their relationships with fellow believers. The concept of 'love' is prominent in Colossians – there are eleven occurrences of the word group. Epaphras is described as 'beloved' (Col. 1:8), and Jesus as the 'Son of his [God's] love' (Col. 1:13). More generally, all those chosen by God are described as 'beloved' (Col. 3:12), and they are to be clothed with love (Col. 3:14). Therefore, love is seen as one of the transformative qualities that believers are to demonstrate in their new life in Christ, because of the love they have been given in the spirit (Col. 1:8).

Popular discussions often make a sharp distinction between *agapē* love and *phileō* love. The former is often seen as 'action-based' and freely given without expectation of reciprocation, whereas the latter denotes the emotion of 'liking' something or somebody and hence denotes a conditional preference. Such comments are actually nonsense. The Greek word φιλέω (*phileō*) was the far more common term during the Classical phase of the language, and gradually gave way to a preference for ἀγαπάω (*agapaō*) especially in *koinē* Greek. However, the similarity of meaning is perhaps clearly seen in Paul's use of the term 'brotherly love', φιλαδελφία (Rom. 12:10; 1 Thess. 4:9). The exhortation to 'brotherly love' using the φιλ- word group appears to call for the same quality that is commended here using the ἀγαπ- word group. While there is a preference for ἀγάπη terminology in the Pauline epistles, when φιλέω and its cognates are used the meaning overlaps with ἀγαπάω.

The love that is described here as part of the reason for offering thanks to God is recognized as being directed towards **all the holy ones**. This is not merely authorial exaggeration, but is a consequence of the letter's theology of believers being united in one body (cf. Col. 3:15). The community of those who have been made holy is transformed by the freely given love of God, which can be recognized through the mutual bond of love that exists between those who are committed to living a life of faithfulness as members of the body of Christ.

5 It is often noted that the reference to **hope**, along with the description of **faith** and **love** in the previous verse, creates another instance of that famous triad (cf. Rom. 5:1–15; 1 Cor. 13:13; Gal. 5:5–6; 1 Thess. 1:3; 5:8). However, the third element, 'hope', is not as closely tied to the previous two terms as for instance in the thanksgiving section of 1 Thessalonians where Paul says he unceasingly remembers their 'work of faith and labour of love and steadfastness of hope' (1 Thess. 1:3). In that example the three items are all illustrations of behavioural characteristics that Paul recalls. In Colossians the believers' lives of faithfulness and their love of fellow believers are the new patterns of life that are the basis for Paul giving thanks. However, the description is taken one stage further with an explanation of what causes this new pattern of life, **because of the hope laid up for you in the heavens**. The preposition that introduces this clause, διά, followed by the accusative case, presents a causal explanation, i.e. 'on account of' or 'because of'. It has been suggested that hope should be understood as the basis of the act of thanksgiving (Abbott 1897: 196). This may be ultimately true if the logic of the progression of thought is pressed, i.e. thanksgiving is caused by faithfulness and love, which in turn is caused by hope. However, it is debateable whether such a logical progression is really the author's intent. Rather, in almost doxological terms, he piles up reasons to be euphoric about the new life in Christ, of which the Colossians are now partakers. Reflection on the faithfulness and mutual love seen in the Colossian believers is the basis for thanksgiving, and conversely faith and love themselves are actions that spring forth from those who have a heavenly hope (cf. Dunn 1996: 58).

The tension between present and future realities that is often part of Christian reflection on hope is also present here. The verb 'laid up', ἀποκειμένην, occurs in the present tense, denoting that the hope is already laid up. However, the hope is not yet fully experienced; rather, it is reserved for believers in the heavens. This may be described as an anticipatory present, although the Colossian believers are already enjoying some of the benefits of that hope: namely, a transformed existence in Christ and the experience of the mutual love. The specific nature of the **hope laid up...in the heavens** is not clearly explained. The term 'hope' is used on two further occasions in Colossians. In self-referential terms, the author speaks of 'the hope of the gospel...of which I Paul was made a minister' (Col. 1:23). Again this casts little light on the content or meaning of the hope that is being described. However, a few verses later Paul outlines his ministry as making known 'the riches of the glory of this mystery among the Gentiles; which is Christ in you, the hope of glory' (Col. 1:27). Therefore, a key aspect of this hope that is laid up in the heavens appears to be that believers are drawn into even closer union with Christ. In this sense, 'hope' is a fuller Christ-centred existence. However, this is only a partial clue, since the epistle refrains from explaining the nature of the heavenly hope. The plural form **in the heavens** denotes the realm where the believers' hope resides. It has been suggested that the plural form, which is uncommon in non-biblical Greek, is drawn from the Jewish idea of a multi-layered heavenly realm (Dunn 1996: 59). In the Pauline epistles the term 'heaven', οὐρανός, is used 21 times, eleven in the singular and ten in the plural. The term is never used in the Pastoral Epistles or Philemon. The occurrences of the singular and plural forms are as follows:

	Singular	Plural
Romans	2	0
1 Corinthians	2	0
2 Corinthians	2	1
Galatians	1	0
Ephesians	0	4
Philippians	0	1
Colossians	2	3
1 Thessalonians	1	1
2 Thessalonians	1	0

What these statistics reveal is debatable; perhaps it shows a tendency towards the plural form in later Pauline writings. The exclusive use of the plural in Ephesians might possibly be considered to have implications for the question of authorship. However, Philippians only uses the plural in its single occurrence of the term. Ultimately, while this variation between singular and plural forms may be intriguing, given the small sample sizes it is unwise to conclude anything too firm on the basis of this term alone. With Colossians the first three usages are in the plural (Col. 1:5, 16, 20) and the next two are given in the singular (Col. 1:23; 4:1).

Reflection on hope continues by recalling how the Colossians came to learn of this heavenly confidence. The relative clause, **which you heard before in the word of the truth of the gospel**, clarifies the circumstance by which the Colossians came to the knowledge of heavenly hope. The verb emphasizes the prior nature of what was communicated to them. The knowledge came through the proclamation of the gospel. In an overloaded description that message is described as being 'the word', 'truth', and 'good news'. Precisely how this combination of terms is to be understood has generated debate, and rather than prejudge that question the Greek has been rendered with a literal translation. The most common option is to take the final noun as standing in apposition to the previous genitive noun, 'in the word of truth, (which is) the gospel'. Here the veracity of the gospel message is affirmed. Other proposed translations include 'when the true gospel was proclaimed' (REV), or 'when the message of the true gospel first came to you' (REB), or 'through the message heralding the truth of the gospel' (Cassirer 1989). Each of these latter suggestions seems to take the meaning further away from the Greek phraseology. While the more literal rendering adopted here is quite dense prose, its sense is not unclear although it may require unpacking. Paul speaks of the hope that the Colossians had already heard. This prepares for the reference to Epaphras' ministry, which will be described briefly in the following comments (Col. 1:7–8). The use of the term 'gospel' is not simply some arbitrary choice of terminology. It is a favourite Pauline term, with 60 of the 76 occurrences in the New Testament occurring in the letters of Paul. It is often assumed that while the term is unlikely to have originated in the Palestinian setting of the early Jesus movement, it did stem from pre-Pauline tradition. Usually this argument is based upon the observation that Paul uses the term without qualification when writing to communities he had not founded (cf. Rom. 1:1, 16), and additionally because of its use in what are considered to be pre-Pauline traditions (1 Cor. 15:1–5; 1 Thess. 9b–10). On the latter point, even if these traditions were pre-Pauline (which is far from certain), it is difficult to be certain that Paul had not rewritten them employing his own significant theological terminology. As for using the term 'gospel', εὐαγγέλιον, in letters addressed to communities he had not founded, this may not be problematic, since the term had significant resonance throughout the Roman Empire. Therefore it may be the case, given the predominance of the term in the Pauline epistles, that Paul himself took the daring step of coining this word to designate the Christian message. Even if that were not the case, the term had been previously associated with the honours attributed to Roman Emperors. By using this term, in effect Paul was subverting imperial claims that the rule of an emperor brought peace and stability to the world. Instead it was being claimed that the crucified but risen Christ was the one who reconciled the world and made peace through his cross (Col. 1:20), and that this did not stem from the *pax Romana*. Thus, instead of the message of glad tidings stemming from the reign of an emperor, the author of Colossians argues that the gospel proclaimed the primogeniture of Christ over all things (Col. 1:17–18).

Commentators have sought to find significance in the phrase **of the truth of the gospel** by relating it to the situation that might stand behind Col. 2:16–19 where certain people appear to be judging the Colossians in relation to cultic practices, or their non-participation in esoteric worship of angelic beings. Hence it has been suggested that the description of the truth of the gospel is intended to denote the message that Paul and Epaphras proclaimed, and to differentiate it from the spurious gospel of those beguiling the community (Lightfoot 1886: 132; O'Brien 1982: 12: 'a contrast with the false teaching of the Colossians heretics seems intended'). In favour of this, the expression 'the truth of the gospel' is used in Galatians in a context where Paul is asserting the veracity of his message (Gal. 2:5, 14) in comparison to other forms of the gospel proclaimed by those who opposed his message (Gal. 1:9). Nonetheless, this would be quite an obscure way to introduce a warning against false teachers.

Therefore, it is more convincing to understand the phrase simply as a fulsome way to announce that the truth of the gospel made believers aware of the hope that they now have in the heavenly realm.

6 The epistle offers another stage in the chain of regression that accounts for the reason thanks is being offered. First, the author stated that he and Timothy give thanks for the Colossians (Col. 1:3) because of their faithfulness in Christ and love of the holy ones (Col. 1:4). These in turn are behaviours that stem from knowledge of a heavenly hope (Col. 1:5a), which itself is known through proclamation of the truth of the gospel (Col. 1:5b). It is now explained how the gospel came to be preached to the Colossians. The arrival of the gospel amongst the Colossians is presented as a fact with the gospel being depicted in almost personified and self-animating terms: **the gospel, which came to you.** The opening words of this verse, 'which came to you', are more closely co-ordinated with the final words of the preceding verse, 'the gospel', than with the following explanatory clause (Wilson 2005: 91). The verb πάρειμι, translated here 'came to you', is an example of a term where the present tense can have perfect force. However, the verb also denotes presence, so another plausible translation would be 'the gospel which, is present among you'. The advantage of this alternative is that it emphasizes the ongoing presence of the gospel among the Colossian believers, and does not imply a particular moment when the message was proclaimed. Instead, it denotes the state of living in a manner that accords with the message of hope enshrined in the proclamation of the gospel. However, the translation adopted here perhaps better preserves the sense of what follows – namely, that the gospel is in the process of spreading throughout the world, and hence its initial arrival in Colossae is recalled. Thus the verb is intended to convey the movement involved with the spread of the gospel.

The way in which the gospel came to the Colossians is clarified by the first of two comparative adverbial clauses, which both use the conjunction καθώς, 'just as'/'so'. The first comparison informs those at Colossae that when the gospel came to them it was comparable to the experience of others: **just as also in all the world it is bearing fruit and increasing**. The purpose here is not to present the

Colossians' experience as normative or mundane. In fact, the aim is quite the opposite. It is intended to link the Colossians with the remarkable progress of the gospel that, according to the author, is taking place throughout the world. By connecting this instance of local success of the gospel with something that is presented as a worldwide phenomenon, there may be an underlying claim that the kingdom of God's Son (cf. Col. 1:13) is achieving universal acclaim. Two images are employed to describe this expansion. The first is horticultural, and the second, which is more general, may be informed by the first and consequently is drawing upon the image of organic growth. The first verb 'to bear fruit', καρποφορέω, occurs in the synoptic gospels only in relation to seed parables or images (Mt. 13:23//Mark 4:20// Lk. 8:15; and Mark 4:28). By contrast, in the Pauline epistles the term addresses communities that he had not visited in person (Rom. 7:4, 5; Col. 1:6, 10). In the parable of the sower the term is used figuratively, to speak of the astounding yield of the word of God when 'sown' in receptive hearts. Similarly here, the term depicts the response to 'the word of the truth of the gospel' (Col. 1:5). The second term used to depict the spread of the gospel is the more general term 'to increase', αὐξάνω. Elsewhere Paul employs the same verb to depict growth in God's garden (1 Cor. 3:7). However, in the New Testament the two verbs are linked only in Colossians (Col. 1:6, 10).

Having described the universal success of the gospel, the second καθώς, 'just as'/'so', clause brings the thanksgiving section back to the localized circumstances in Colossae: **so [it is] also in you**. The Colossians have already been described as being connected to a movement that is larger than their own community through reference to their 'love for all the holy ones' (Col. 1:4). It has been suggested by some commentators who already see statements in the thanksgiving as responding to particular opponents or false teachings operative in Colossae (Col. 2:16–19) that the worldwide reception of the same gospel message is a corrective against localized deviations (Lightfoot 1886: 132–33: 'false gospels are the outgrowths of local circumstances, of special idiosyncrasies'). However, three factors tell against this interpretation. First, Paul celebrates the universality of the gospel in other opening thanksgivings where there is no hint of deviant teaching (Rom. 1:8; 1 Thess. 1:8). Second, the phrase here, 'so it is also in you', seems to acknowledge a similar reception to the gospel in Colossae as elsewhere, not a deviant localized response. It would be too complicated to see this phrase praising initial reception, in order to criticize later deviation by withholding description of that later phase. Third, it is debatable whether the original readers would have recognized such a subtle warning. Therefore, the phrase is part of the celebration of the success of the gospel, which was flourishing in remarkable ways both in Colossae and throughout other parts of the Roman world.

Another temporal marker is provided by the phrase **from the day which**. This refers back to the time when the gospel came to the Colossians. According to the author it was at that point they accepted the message and became aware of the heavenly hope laid up for them. At this juncture they themselves became part of the universal spread of the gospel. The consequence of receiving the gospel for the believers in Colossae is stated as being that **you heard and knew the grace of God in truth**. Here a number of key concepts that have already been mentioned are brought together: hearing (Col. 1:5), grace (Col. 1:2), God (Col. 1:1, 2, 3) and truth (Col. 1:5). It is probably the case that the pair of verbs 'heard and knew' should be understood as virtual synonyms for acceptance of the gospel. Both actions denote more than passive understanding, rather active acceptance of the claims of the gospel, and participation in a transformed existence in Christ are what is being suggested by these verbs. The Colossians are told that their auditory and epistemological experience allowed them to receive **the grace of God**. In Pauline thought, the term 'grace' denotes a free or unmerited gift and it frequently functions as a feature in the apostle's introductory greetings (cf. Col. 1:2). Here the term is further clarified by adding the genitive 'of God'. It is not that God is the content of grace, but the one who supplies the gift and the one in whom grace finds its origin. The day on which the Colossians heard the gospel was not a time of a mere announcement; rather, it was the occasion when God's grace arrived among them. It is probably unnecessary to ask whether **in truth** means that the Colossians 'truly heard and knew about the grace of God', or if they 'heard and knew the truth concerning the grace of God'. The author is more concerned to assert the veracity of the whole complex of ideas. For the second time in two verses 'the truth' of what the Colossians experienced is affirmed. The key concern is that of authentication. The repetition of the term 'truth' recalls the affirmation concerning the 'truth of the gospel' that is the means by which believers know 'the grace of God in truth', and consequently receive assurance of a heavenly hope (Col. 1:5).

7 It may be wrong to describe the foregoing description as a physical or historical portrayal of the coming of the gospel to the Colossians. Rather it is better to see it as the theological understanding of the way the gospel spreads and communicates God's grace. However, in distinction to that thick theological description, the third **just as**, καθώς, clause does describe the specific or concrete events that resulted in the message concerning Christ being proclaimed to the community. They are reminded that the gospel they heard was **learnt from Epaphras our beloved fellow slave**. The idea that the Colossians 'learnt', ἐμάθετε, the gospel may provide insight into the way in which Paul and his associates sought to ensure the long-term and stable reception of the gospel message. On occasions, according to the narrative of the Acts of the Apostles, Paul spent extended periods of time with his converts. Paul is reported to have spent 'a year and six months' in Corinth (Acts 18:11) and appears to have had a more extended stay in Ephesus (Acts 19:10; 20:31). Admittedly on other occasions, sometimes due to external circumstances, the period Paul remained with his new converts was much shorter (cf. the period in Thessalonica and Berea, Acts 17:1–15). The verb 'learnt', ἐμάθετε, is related to the noun 'disciple', μαθήτης, which denotes one who is a learner, often over an extended period, following a respected teacher. While the noun 'disciple' is notably absent from the Pauline epistles, the pedagogical framework it presupposes of teaching adherents over an extended period was widespread among converts to voluntary associations such as the early Jesus movement. Hence it is perhaps not surprising to think of Epaphras as being the source from whom the Colossians learnt the gospel over an extended period.

The named associate, **Epaphras our beloved fellow slave**, is credited with instructing the Colossians in the gospel. Nothing is known of Epaphras beyond the three references in the Pauline epistles. Here the believers in Colossae are reminded that it was Epaphras who initially brought the gospel to them, that he is a representative of Paul, and that he has brought news of the Colossians to the author of the letter (Col. 1:7–8). In the closing section of this letter, Epaphras is recorded as sending his greetings, and as striving in prayer on behalf of the Colossians (Col. 4:12). Finally, in his correspondence to Philemon, Paul describes Epaphras as a 'fellow prisoner' (Phlm. 23), which would appear to suggest that he was incarcerated at the time of the writing of that letter. It has also been suggested, since Epaphras is often an abbreviated form of the name Epaphroditus, that he is also to be identified with the Epaphroditus mentioned in Philippians (Phil. 2:25–26; 4:18). This identification is to be rejected, both because of the different forms of name (although compare Silas/Silvanus) and because in Philippians Epaphroditus is apparently at liberty and able to move freely. Since some scholars have inferred Colossians, Philippians, and Philemon were all written during the same period of imprisonment this could create a tension (although this is not irresolvable). If Colossians is not written by Paul, while the portrait of Epaphras would be potentially something of a literary construct, the tension between the imprisonment of Epaphras described in Philemon and the free movement enjoyed by Epaphroditus in Philippians would remain problematic, and so it seems sensible not to equate the two figures.

Epaphras is described first as **our beloved fellow slave**. Love is a quality that has already been presented as being a hallmark of relationships between believers (Col. 1:4). The adjective 'beloved', ἀγαπητός, is frequently used to describe a special affection or relationship with a named individual, especially when it occurs in the singular form (Rom. 16:5, 8, 9, 12; 1 Cor. 4:17; Eph. 6:21; Col. 4:7, 9, 14; 2 Tim. 1:2; Phlm. 1; 2 Pet. 3:15). The term 'fellow slave', σύνδουλος, occurs only in this epistle among the writings of the Pauline corpus (Col. 1:7; 4:7). Paul often depicts himself as a 'slave', δοῦλος (cf. Rom. 1:1; Gal. 1:10), with the term denoting one who is engaged in the service of Christ. With this language of servitude Paul inverts the normal aspirations of Greco-Roman society, and uses it to denote a position of honour within the Christian community. Such an inversion is present in the Hebrew Bible where the designations 'servant of the Lord' (Josh. 1:1; Judg. 2:8) or 'My servant' (Isa. 42:1; 53:11) reflects a highly elevated status, and a position of prominence in the eyes of the deity.

The second part of the description of Epaphras is as one **who is a faithful servant of Christ on our behalf**. The language of fidelity has been employed in the greeting, where it described the Colossians as 'faithful brothers' (Col. 1:2). Here the adjective qualifies the noun 'servant', διάκονος, which overlaps in meaning with the term 'slave' (Dunn 1996: 65). Describing individuals as 'servants' is not common in the Pauline epistles, although the term is used on four occasions in this letter (Col. 1:7, 23, 25; 4:7). In the final example, employing a combination of terminology that is similar to the description of Epaphras but in a slightly different order, Tychicus is described as 'our beloved brother and faithful servant and fellow slave' (Col. 4:7). By contrast, Paul describes himself as a 'servant' twice in the opening chapter, first as a servant of the gospel (Col. 1:23) and then as a servant of Christ (Col. 1:27). Similar to the second description that the author provides of his own servanthood, here Epaphras is also described as a **servant of Christ**. Within the contemporary culture, to be a servant of a named person designated a person rendering a service to a superior either for reward or out of obligation. Whereas the term 'slave' regularly implied that the person so described was owned by another, and could only obtain freedom through an act of manumission, the description of an individual as a 'servant' did not necessarily represent such a possessive relationship and at times it could be used to describe those who held elevated public offices (cf. Plato, *Leg.* 955cd).

Interestingly, here in the letter Paul and Timothy describe Epaphras as a servant of Christ **on our behalf**. There is a significant textual variant here, with manuscripts differing in the choice of possessive pronoun between 'our', ἡμῶν ($\mathfrak{P}^{46}$ ℵ* A B D* F G 326* 1505), and 'your', ὑμῶν (ℵ² C D¹ Ψ 075 33 1881 𝔐 lat sy co). The latter option, 'your', ὑμῶν, is the reading printed in the major critical edition of the Greek New Testament (NA²⁸ 2012: 612). The primary reason that is given for preferring 'your' is on the assumption that it is later scribes who have introduced 'our' to create an agreement with of the same pronoun in the preceding phrase 'our beloved fellow slave' (Metzger 1994: 553). However, not only does the reading 'our', ἡμῶν, have the better attestation among early manuscripts, it may also be considered the more difficult reading that was rendered less problematic by later scribes. In a passage where the author is describing Epaphras' work in bringing the gospel to the Colossians it is more natural to expect him to be depicted as a servant of Christ on behalf of the Colossians, since they are the ones to whom he is rendering the service of communicating the gospel. If, however, the reading that is followed here is adopted, then the author appears to be describing the representative function of Epaphras on behalf of the Pauline mission. This would suggest that Epaphras was a member of a Pauline circle of trusted co-workers in spreading Paul's understanding of the gospel. Consequently, describing Epaphras as a **faithful servant of Christ on our behalf** may indicate his Pauline credentials and commission. However, perhaps the circumstances are not quite as transparent, and while the phrasing may communicate the claim of a previous commission from Paul, perhaps it is more an attempt to co-opt the evangelistic work of Epaphras as being part of the wider Pauline mission. By claiming this link with Epaphras, who was a well-known evangelist throughout the Lycus Valley, the Pauline author is legitimizing the decision to write to this community, which has not had prior communication from the Pauline circle. The extremely positive language in the greeting and thanksgiving, and the affirmations concerning Epaphras, may ultimately be stratagems designed to soften the blow when the author seeks to 'correct' some of their worship practices later in the epistle.

8 The role of Epaphras as a channel of communication concerning the faith of the Colossians and the circumstances in their community is elucidated here. He is portrayed as the one **who also made clear to us your love in the spirit**. The plural pronoun 'to us' still indicates that the writers of the letter are ostensibly Paul and Timothy. They acknowledge Epaphras to be the source of the positive report they have received concerning the progress of the Colossians as believers in Christ. However, the means of sending this letter back to Colossae does not appear to be via the hand of Epaphras, since he sends his greetings in this letter and the author reminds the Colossians of his constant prayers on their behalf (Col. 4:12). According to the comment here, Epaphras has 'made clear' the quality of love exemplified by the community in Colossae. The verb 'to make clear', δηλόω, has a range of related meanings.

These include 'to make known', 'to explain', 'to inform'. Here the verb carries the idea of an oral report that relates the circumstances of the Colossians' acceptance of the gospel and the changes that accompany their new mode of existence in Christ.

It is stated that Paul and Timothy have been informed by Epaphras of the **love in the spirit** that characterizes the community. It is regularly noted that this is the only explicit reference to 'the spirit' in this epistle (cf. Bruce 1984: 44). What exactly one should infer from this is less certain. The meaning of the phrase 'love in the spirit' has been debated. Some have proposed that it is just a general reference to a transformed quality of 'spiritual love', which is markedly different from human love (Moule 1957: 52). In terms of Pauline theology, this may broadly equate with the first aspect of the fruit of the spirit described in Gal. 5:22. However, others have suggested more specific references, including love of Paul, or Epaphras, or of all fellow believers (Barth and Blanke 1994: 165). Given the reference to 'the love which you have for all the holy ones' (Col. 1:4), it would appear most likely that the author is continuing with this sense. If there has been a change in meaning, the author has left no clues of this switch. However, this is probably 'charismatically enabled' love (Dunn 1996: 65; cf. Rom. 2:29; 1 Cor. 12:3, 9, 13; 14:16; 1 Thess. 1:5). It is important to remember the often ecstatic nature of early Christian experiences of the spirit (1 Cor. 14; 1 Thess. 1:5). However, here the focus is not on ecstatic expression, but rather upon the corporate love that the spirit produces in believers. Furthermore, there is no attempt to identify 'the spirit' here. It is taken as self-evident that the Colossians would understand the role of the spirit. The author adds to the participatory language already used. Having spoken of the Colossians' 'faith in Christ' (Col. 1:4), he can also speak here of their 'love in the spirit' (Col. 1:8). It seems unnecessary to ask how these two states of being in Christ or in the spirit are distinguished. The point of the thanksgiving is not to provide a discourse on systematic theology – rather, it is a euphoric and celebratory doxology, which while loaded with highly significant theological terminology, affirms the new mode of existence enjoyed by Colossian believers. Moreover, it seeks to make positive connections between the writers of the epistle and their hitherto unknown addressees.

3. PRAYER   (1:9–14)

(9) Because of this we also, from the day we heard, have not ceased praying and asking on your behalf that you might be filled with the knowledge of his will in all wisdom and spiritual insight (10) to walk worthily of the Lord in every pleasing way, in every good work bearing fruit and increasing in the knowledge of God, (11) in all power being empowered according to the might of his glory for all steadfastness and longsuffering, with joy (12) giving thanks to the father who has qualified you for a share of the inheritance of the holy ones in the light, (13) who rescued us from the dominion of darkness and transferred [us] to the kingdom of the Son of his love, (14) in whom we have the redemption, the forgiveness of sins.

The author has already described Paul and Timothy as unceasingly engaged in prayer on behalf of the believers in Colossae in the opening verse of the thanksgiving (Col. 1:3). Here, however, there is a detailed account of the content of the petitions that are being offered on behalf of the Colossians. Given this thematic link of prayer, and the fact that in this section the act of 'giving thanks to the father' continues (Col. 1:12), it may be asked whether these verses should be presented as a separate paragraph from the thanksgiving section (Col. 1:3–8), or whether it makes more sense to treat them together with the preceding section as a tightly integrating 'thanksgiving and prayer' section (Col. 1:3–14). At one level there is no correct answer to that question. The epistle is itself an organic whole, and the author is adept at using linking words and repetition of themes to tie together the progression of thought in this letter. The opening phrase of Col. 1:9, 'because of this', seeks to create a link with the previous statements by grounding the outpouring of prayer in the exuberance that is generated by the good report of Epaphras concerning the Colossians. Initially the first description of prayer (Col. 1:3) arose from the fact that Paul and Timothy had heard of the faith and love exhibited by the Colossians (Col. 1:4). Now, after informing the addressees that Epaphras had passed on news of their 'love in the spirit', this report of the spiritual well-being of the community occasions another spontaneous outburst of prayer.

However, despite this obvious link with the preceding material, there is a marked change in content. In what is labelled here as the thanksgiving (Col. 1:3–8), the author related the circumstances through which he came to know of the growth in faith demonstrated by the Colossians. By contrast, the following section (Col. 1:9–14) contains a more future looking set of intercessions, which seeks further spiritual progress. Hence while one should not overemphasize a split between these sections, it is noticeable that the concern here shifts from praise for what has taken place in the Colossian community, to that of articulating prayerful aspirations for their continuance and development in the faith. A further structural issue concerns where this section ends and the next begins. The so-called Christological Hymn (Col. 1:15–20) is taken by the vast majority of commentators to be a separate section. Yet it is integral to the flow of the whole unit of material in Col. 1:1–23. It is notable that the author has created a very smooth transition from the intercessory aspects of his prayers to the theological affirmation that God has rescued the believers by transferring them into the kingdom of his Son (Col. 1:13). This naturally leads to the christological focus that in God's Son believers are redeemed and their sins forgiven (Col. 1:14). In turn this creates the entry point into the Christ-centred poetic material of Col. 1:15–20. However, the division proposed here, taking Col. 1:9–14 as a unit, is more than a convenience. While the author skilfully links together all the material of Col. 1:3–23, there is a change of emphasis at the commencement of Col. 1:9 with the focus on prayers for future progress. Although some commentators treat Col. 1:13–14 (or 1:12–14) as a separate section from the prayer (Lohse 1971: 32), the 'with joy' at the end of v. 11 introduces a prayer of thanksgiving on behalf of the Colossians who have received a share of the inheritance (Col. 1:12), and the two following verses are tied to the preceding verses as relative clauses dependent on the foregoing statements. Therefore, without wishing to isolate Col. 1:9–14 either from what precedes or follows it, the decision to see this prayer unit as a discrete section appears to be the most helpful way of understanding the structure of this tightly integrated opening to the epistle.

9 As a consequence of the report brought by Epaphras (Col. 1:7–8), Paul and Timothy now disclose to the believers in Colossae the prayers that they offer on their behalf. Thus the opening phrase, **because of this**, διὰ τοῦτο, serves as a causal conjunction, which highlights the factor, namely the news communicated by Epaphras, which occasioned this act of intercession. Furthermore, the pronominal construction, **we also**, serves to identify those who are offering prayer: in the context of the letter they are its senders, Paul and Timothy (Col. 1:1). The action of offering prayer is linked with Epaphras, through the conjunction **also**. While Epaphras is not explicitly described as offering prayer on behalf of believers in the Lycus Valley in the preceding material, that is the implication of this opening phrase and that supposition is borne out later in the letter when the fervent prayers of Epaphras are explicitly mentioned (Col. 4:12). Next the temporal marker, **from the day we heard**, portrays the immediate effect Epaphras' report had on those writing the letter. While both the immediacy and the constancy in prayer that are mentioned here may verge on hyperbolic descriptions, the author wishes to signal to his readers both the intensity of prayer on their behalf and the jubilant response to the news concerning the Colossians. The author has a penchant for using chronological markers, with the almost identical expression 'from the day you heard', ἀφ᾽ ἧς ἡμέρας ἠκούσατε (here the final verb is 'we heard' ἠκούσαμεν), being used in Col. 1:6, where it described the Colossians' initial hearing of the gospel. Here the parallel expression describes Paul's initial hearing of the faith of the Colossians.

Having first described the basis and starting point of the as yet undisclosed action, Paul continues by outlining the prayer he offers for the Colossians: **we have not ceased praying and asking on your behalf**. The construction involves a co-ordinated pair of complimentary participles, 'praying and asking', which complete the action of the main verb, 'we have not ceased'. In wider contemporary Greek the construction is more common than in the New Testament, especially when participles are combined with a verb that suggests a consummative action, such as 'to cease'. A similar construction is used in Acts 5:42. At the beginning of Ephesians the author, writing in the first person singular (rather than the plural as here), states 'I do not cease giving thanks for you, making mention of you in my prayers' (Eph. 1:16). Along with the notion of spontaneity that occasioned the initial outpouring of prayer on the day when Paul heard of the Colossians' faith, the ceaseless nature of the intercession reveals something of the author's devotion and constancy in prayer. The combination of **praying and asking** should not be seen as denoting two actions, or even two related but not identical aspects of prayer. Such a differentiation would read too much into the fulsome language of this prayer report, where the language is lavish, rather than literal. Therefore the participle pair forms a hendiadys: that is it expresses the same idea through a linked word pair (cf. Mk 11:24 where the same pair of verbs are co-ordinated). Moreover, the author states that his addressees are the subjects of his prayers, since his intercessions are offered **on your behalf**.

The train of thought continues by revealing to the addressees one of the specific purposes for which prayer is made, namely **that you might be filled with the knowledge of his will**. The use of the subjunctive clause ἵνα πληρωθῆτε, 'that you might be filled', communicates the intended goal that the author seeks to achieve through devotion to prayer. The aim is that the Colossians 'might be filled with the knowledge of his will'. The verb used here, 'to be filled', πληρόω, is the first instance of a significant word group that occurs five times in this epistle (Col. 1:9, 19, 25; 2:9; 4:17). In relation to people, it can denote them being filled with powers or qualities. Here the quality that the author prays might fill the Colossians is knowledge of God's will. When referring to 'knowledge', the term used here is not the simple form γνῶσις, but the compound ἐπίγνωσις. This compound form of the related verb was used earlier (Col. 1:6), and might reflect the preferred vocabulary of the author. There has been debate concerning whether a specialized nuance should be attributed to the choice of the compound form over the simple form of the noun. Various options have been suggested. It is argued that ἐπίγνωσις denotes a more comprehensive form of knowledge, since this is a contrast Paul draws elsewhere (Rom. 1:21, 28; 1 Cor. 13:12) in his writings (Lightfoot 1886: 136), or, alternatively, that it is specific knowledge directed towards a particular object, here the will of God (Robinson 1928: 254). However, in Colossians there is no strong indication that the compound form, which is used on four occasions (Col. 1:9, 10; 2:2; 3:10), signifies anything more than the simple form of the verb or noun (Col. 1:27; 2:3; 4:7, 8, 9). The mixed use of these terms suggests that the author was not avoiding either word. Hence it appears unlikely that 'gnosis' had by this stage become either a catchword of a formative Gnostic movement, or that it had become tainted as a heretical term. Therefore, it appears best to understand the compound form ἐπίγνωσις as a general description of 'knowledge', and as such in this epistle it is synonymous with the simple form γνῶσις. The knowledge with which the author prays that the Colossians may be filled is that of the divine will. The concept of 'God's will' is common in Pauline thought. Specifically, it can be used to denote that the calling of Paul as an apostle was in accord with divine intention (1 Cor. 1:1; 2 Cor. 1:1; Eph. 1:1; Col. 1:1; 2 Tim. 1:1). Often the idea is simply used without clarification (cf. Rom. 12:2; 15:32; 2 Cor. 8:5), and it is particularly prominent in the letter to the Ephesians (Eph. 1:1, 5, 9, 11; 5:17; 6:6). Only occasionally is an explanation provided that clarifies the phrase: 'this is the will of God, your sanctification' (1 Thess. 4:3), or 'in everything give thanks; for this is God's will for you' (1 Thess. 5:18). However, these epexegetical comments should not be seen as determinative for the meaning of the expression in all contexts. Rather, knowing the will of God is used broadly here to designate the ability of believers to align their actions with the divine purpose, which is understood as revealing the perfect way in which believers are to live out their new life in Christ.

The concluding prepositional phrase in this verse, **in all wisdom and spiritual insight**, may be understood as linked with either the preceding phrase, 'knowledge of his will', or with the preceding verb, 'to be filled with'. Furthermore, it has been suggested that the two adjectives that frame the pair of nouns should be understood as applying equally to both, i.e. 'in all spiritual wisdom and all spiritual insight' (Lohse 1971: 27). The case for linking this phrase with the verb is based upon understanding the act of 'being filled' as first being qualified by a description of content, and then followed by an explanation of means. Hence the translation would be 'that you might be filled with the knowledge of his will, by having all spiritual wisdom and insight' (cf. Harris 2010: 27). However, it is not certain that either of these syntactical decisions is correct – either linking the prepositional phrase directly with the preceding verb, or understanding both adjectives as applying equally to the two nouns. First, there is no clear suggestion that the author is seeking to explain precisely the content and means assumed to be implicit in the verb;

rather, the link appears to be looser. Thus the phrase 'in all wisdom and spiritual insight' functions straightforwardly as a description of that with which the author prays his readers will be supplied as they apprehend the will of God. Secondly, while it would not be an impossible syntactical construction for the two adjectives to be used attributively in relation to the noun pair, it would however be somewhat unusual and unwieldy. Hence, the prepositional phrase is best understood as describing the spiritual and sapiential quality of the knowledge with which they are to be filled.

The prayer for wisdom reflects a wider concern with that characteristic in the ancient world. Here, **all wisdom** reveals the superlative and abundant nature of the aspirations that are being expressed in the prayer. In the Hebrew Bible wisdom has both didactic and ethical functions, and these aspects are sometimes closely linked. This is perhaps best seen in the book of Proverbs where instruction in wisdom directs the recipient towards a moral way of life (Prov. 4:1; 5:1–2; 10:31). Here also, although understood as an intellectual quality, wisdom is understood as having a transformative effect on the individual. Similarly, **spiritual knowledge** is not a purely cognitive apprehension, but its spiritual dimension shows that it is both given from the heavenly realm and that its purpose is to align the mind of believers with the mind of the divine. The pairing 'wisdom and insight', σοφία καὶ σύνεσις, is used frequently in the Greek translation of Hebrew Bible texts (LXX Exod. 31:3, Deut. 4:6; 1 Chron. 22:12; 2 Chron. 1:10; Isa. 11:2; 29:14 Dan. 2:20) as well as elsewhere in the Pauline writings (1 Cor. 1:19). In Ephesians the same concepts appear to be present, but the pairing is varied – 'wisdom and intelligence', σοφία καὶ φρόνησις (Eph. 1:8), with the terms σύνεσις and φρόνησις having significant overlap in their meanings. Aristotle mentions these three words wisdom/insight/ intelligence (σοφία/σύνεσις/φρόνησις) together as the intellectual virtues (Aristotle, *Nic. Eth.* 1:13). In this way the prayer envisages that as the Colossians come to know the will of God, their whole cognitive dimension will be spiritually transformed (cf. Rom. 12:2).

10 The infinitive construction that commences this verse, **to walk worthily**, announces the purpose or goal of the prayer which was offered in order that the Colossians might be filled with knowledge of God's will. Using the metaphor of 'walk' to denote the whole orientation of lifestyle, the desire to attain knowledge of God's will is not an end in itself. Rather, such knowledge produces a re-alignment of one's life, which has a key focus on acting in ways pleasing to God. The metaphor of 'walk' reflects a key Jewish theological concept, that of halakhah, which is to walk in a way that accords with God's commandments. The uses of the Greek verb 'to walk', περιπατῆσαι, as a figurative designation of one's pattern of life is a common Pauline metaphor (Rom. 6:4; 8:1, 4; 13:13; 14:15; 1 Cor. 3:3; 7:17; 2 Cor. 4:2; 5:17; Gal. 5:16; Eph. 4:1; 5:1; Col. 2:6; 4:5). The first of those references is particularly instructive, for Paul explicitly states that one 'should walk in newness of life' (Rom. 6:4). This illustrates that in Pauline terms, the metaphor of one's walk denoted a new form of life emerging from the acceptance of the gospel and union with Christ. The charge that believers are to live **worthily of the Lord** links conduct of life closely with the new existence in the Lord. Given that the previous verse speaks of gaining divine knowledge it may be questioned whether the reference here is to God or to Christ. There are two principal reasons why the latter is to be preferred. First, in terms of wider usage in Paul's letters, 'the Lord', ὁ κύριος, usually designates Christ, whereas when the term is used without the definite article, then 'Lord', κύριος, usually refers to God (Harris 2010: 28). However, given that there is dispute concerning the Pauline authorship of this letter, such an argument may not be seen as decisive. Secondly, within the context of Colossians the author uses the metaphor 'to walk' explicitly in relation to Christ, 'as therefore you received Christ Jesus the Lord, walk in him' (Col. 2:6). Furthermore, at the end of this verse 'God' is re-introduced, which suggests that there may have been a change of subject from the beginning of the verse. Therefore the exhortation is that knowledge of God should result in a life that befits the new existence believers have in Christ.

The fulsome language continues with the phrase **in every pleasing way**, which communicates very little concerning the specifics of what is pleasing to the Lord. Instead, it continues the rhetorically loaded description of the transformation that should take place in the lives of believers. The phrase is somewhat awkward to translate, and many translators and commentators prefer to supply a pronoun to clarify the phrase, i.e. 'in everything pleasing him'. However, the Greek does not state the subject of this phrase. A more literal rendering would be 'to/in all pleasingness'. The problem with this phrasing is that it is cumbersome in English. The option suggested here makes it unnecessary to resolve whether the passage is speaking of pleasing God or Christ, since it is all the believer's actions that are to be pleasing as components of that new life lived in Christ. It is commonly noted that the Greek term for 'pleasing', ἀρεσκεία, was used in Classical Greek with a negative connotation, such as 'obsequiousness' or 'ingratiation'. However, here it carries no such sense, and it describes a positive quality.

The prayer continues by describing another quality that is to exemplify the 'walk' or lifestyle of Colossian believers. Namely, they are to live worthily of the Lord, while **in every good work bearing fruit and increasing**. Again, Paul does not specify precisely what is meant by 'every good work'; it is an all-encompassing term, which embraces the totality of a moral life lived in accord with the will of God and new life in Christ. The language of **bearing fruit and increasing** has already been used (Col. 1:6). There it denoted the remarkable spread and success of the gospel. Here, however, while the metaphor still relates to growth, it describes the spiritual maturity and ethical behaviours that are to be characteristics of believers. The rigid distinction that is sometimes drawn between 'faith' and 'works' in Pauline theology is shown to be a false separation in this context. Not only here, but in a number of passages in epistles taken to be genuinely Pauline, the necessity of performing good works as a demonstration of the transformed state that results from receiving God's grace is emphasized ('God is able to make all grace abound towards you, that you…may abound in every good work', 2 Cor. 9:8; cf. Gal. 6:10; 2 Thess. 2:17). The expectation of what 'good works' may entail is uncertain, but presumably aligns with wider social expectations especially in Judaism, such as charity for the poor (Jer. 5:28), care for the sick, and abstinence from evil (1QS I, 4).

Repetition of terminology occurs again with the final clause of the verse, **in the knowledge of God**. It may be attributing too great a structural concern to the author to view this phrase as part of a heavily balanced chiasm. Instead, it appears that the opening element of the prayer is simply recalled and repeated, that the Colossians 'may be filled with knowledge of his will' (Col. 1:9). If there is an internal logic in the thought expressed here, it would suggest that the very thing for which Paul and Timothy are praying, knowledge of the divine will, produces a transformed mode of life, which in turn makes members of the Colossian community more open to growing in the knowledge of God. Hence the author may envisage a type of spiral in growth in spiritual maturity that produces deeper insight and knowledge of the will of God (1 Cor. 2:15–16).

11 The progression of thought is developed by describing the means or resources with which the Colossians are supplied to assist them in attaining the knowledge of God. The goal of the petition that the community might know God's will and walk in ways befitting their new existence is shown to be attainable, since they were provided with spiritual resources for that goal. Using an instrumental phrase, the author states that the Colossians are **in all power being empowered according to the might of his glory**. Again the language of the epistle is a celebratory affirmation, rather than a purely rational description of the transformed life of which believers partake. The letter continues piling up clauses that are introduced with the phrase 'in all'/'in every' (with the Greek using the same adjective), for the purpose of expressing the fulness of the blessings given. However, the function of this phrase appears to differ from the previous usages, for this phrase does not announce another quality that reflects a life being lived in a manner worthy of the Lord – instead, it emphasizes the means by which such a life can be attained and sustained. Therefore the Colossians are resourced with power to enable them to continue living out their lives in Christ regardless of what circumstances confront them. Paul and Timothy do not explicitly state the origin or nature of the 'power' with which believers are empowered. However, there can be no doubt that what is being described here is divine power. In wider Greek literature 'power', δύναμις, is understood to be a characteristic of God (Plato, *Cra.* 4004e; Euripides, *Alc.* 219). The same is also the case when used in a similar sense in the Greek translation of the Jewish scriptures, the Septuagint (LXX Josh. 4:24, Deut. 3:24), and on occasions it can even be used as a circumlocution for the divine name (Ps. 53:3; Jer. 16:21). Here it denotes a divine quality that is imparted to believers to enable them to live holy lives worthy of Christ. The concept of 'power' is prominent in Pauline theology. In the programmatic statement at the beginning of Romans, 'the Gospel of Christ' is declared to be 'the power of God for salvation' (Rom. 1:16), Christ is described as 'the power of God' (1 Cor. 1:24), and Paul draws a distinction preaching by word alone in contrast to a proclamation accompanied by power and the spirit (1 Thess. 1:5). It appears, according to the author, that this same power is at work amongst the Colossians, enabling them to conform their lives to the correct divine pattern. The repetition that is present in the phrase 'in all power being empowered' is seen by some as echoing Hebrew syntax, and as such there is 'sufficient indication that the thought world here is still pre-eminently Jewish' (Dunn 1996: 73). However, such repetition was also a feature in writings from Hellenistic authors of the period.

The prepositional phrase, **according to the might of his glory**, emphasizes what was implicit in the preceding expression: namely, that what is being described is divine empowerment. The 'power' with which the community is equipped is not some random event or consequence, but rather it emerges out of the might of God's glory. Here the phrase may in certain respects be equivalent to saying the Colossians are empowered according to God's will. However, the variation is probably not simply in order to avoid repetition, since the letter frequently reuses phraseology. Rather, it is conceptually important to understand that the 'power' enjoyed by the Colossians originates from God's glory, which is a demonstration of divine might. The term, 'might', κράτος, can be understood as broadly synonymous with 'power', δύναμις. However, unlike the term 'power', the noun 'might' does not occur with great frequency in the Pauline epistles (Eph. 1:19; 6:10; Col. 1:11; 1 Tim. 6:16). By contrast, the idea of 'the glory of God' is widely used and reflects the same range of meaning as the Hebrew term *kavod*, which is translated using the term δόξα in the Septuagint. The Hebrew term denotes the splendour and magnificence of God, and is often associated with the notion of God dwelling in inapproachable lightning, thunder, and cloud (Exod. 19:16; 24:16). However, whereas in the Hebrew Bible the glory of God is usually apprehended in a theophanic vision, such as the Sinai encounter, the means of experiencing God's glory is more immediate for believers according to the author of Colossians. In Col. 1:27, the phrases 'the hope of glory' and 'the riches of the glory of this mystery among the Gentiles' are both explained as being due to the indwelling of 'Christ in you'. Therefore, the transformative power of the glory of God is imparted to the Colossians through the presence of Christ.

Being endued with divine power is not an end in itself. It is intended to produce increase and growth in the 'knowledge of God' (Col. 1:10), and also it is **for all steadfastness and longsuffering**. Here the adjective 'all' is probably to be taken with both the qualities described here, and the two words are virtually equivalent in their meanings (see BDAG: 612–13, 1039–40; *EDNT*: II, 380–81). The quality of 'steadfastness' describes the patience, endurance and fortitude required of the believers in Colossae. As there is no explicit description of persecution or oppression in the epistle, it appears that the sense is that of continuing in the faith perhaps awaiting the fulfilment of the blessings of new life. However, there is little here that suggests that waiting patiently for eschatological consummation is part of what is being described. Rather, the idea might be more mundane, although no less important. The Colossians are assured that knowing they are equipped with divine power enables them to endure patiently all the challenges that confront their new-found faith in Christ in their daily lives. As such, these words are a pastoral encouragement, reassuring believers that they possess the resources to remain steadfast in faith in the here-and-now, because they have been divinely strengthened for that task.

The final two words of this verse, **with joy**, are probably best understood as connected with what follows in Col. 1:12, and it appears that the verses were not split at the most appropriate place. However, given the way the language of this letter has phrases that run into one another, allowing one idea to merge into the next, it is best not to be overly rigorous about such divisions. Nowhere else in the Pauline letters are addressees told to be steadfast and longsuffering with joy, although on a couple of occasions related ideas do emerge: 'exult in tribulations, knowing tribulation produces steadfastness' (Rom. 5:3), and 'rejoicing in hope, being steadfast in tribulation' (Rom. 12:12). The usual reason for taking 'with joy' as a description of 'giving thanks', is due to the syntactical pattern where the previous two participles have been preceded by a prepositional phrase. However, other commentators find what would then be the emphatic position of the phrase 'with joy' commencing the description of giving thanks to be syntactically difficult (Lightfoot 1886: 138). Either way, the syntactical arrangement is less than smooth. The emphasis, however, is that the new life in Christ is to be exemplified by joy, both in challenging times when resolve and resilience are required, and at moments when thanksgiving is more spontaneous (Wilson 2005: 110–11).

12 As was noted in the introductory comments to this section, a number of commentators take Col. 1:12–14 as a separate unit, or connect it more closely with the poetic section that follows it, rather than with the prayer that precedes it. There is little doubt that the emphasis moves from intercessory petition to contemplation of what the father has done for believers, and reflection upon the redemption and forgiveness provided by the Son. This in turn leads into the doxological language of Col. 1:15–20. However, the connections between prayer, theology, and doxology are not unfamiliar in the Pauline writings, and prayerful reflection often leads seamlessly into theological contemplation accompanied by an outpouring of praise. Hence it seems appropriate to treat Col. 1:12–14 as a closely linked continuation of the prayer commenced in v. 9.

The same empowering gift of God that enables steadfastness when required is also seen as generating joyful gratitude, **giving thanks to the father**. The response of 'giving thanks' suggests acknowledgment of some gift or action received by those so moved to give voice to their sense of gratitude. Here the 'giving of thanks with joy' is part of the responsive behaviour that Paul and Timothy pray might be produced in the Colossians. This is the third occasion in the letter where God has been described as father: 'God our father' (Col. 1:2) and 'God, father of our Lord Jesus Christ' (Col. 1:3). Here the term 'father' occurs is an absolute form, without any possessive pronoun. So instead of identifying the father here by relationship either to the believers in Colossae, or to Jesus, he is described in the following phrase by actions he has accomplished on behalf of those who benefit from them. Perhaps the absolute form is more appropriate here, because of the wider association between fathers and receiving an inheritance in the ancient world. Thus, in the patriarchal culture of the time it was ordinarily the father who could distribute the assets of the household. Hence here he acts on behalf of the Colossians as the one **who has qualified you for a share of the inheritance of the holy ones in the light**. The necessity of the language of 'father' is required by the discussion of inheritance: 'for the image of believers being heirs of God to have its full impact, God must be the one with authority to distribute the estate: God must be the Father' (Sumney 2008: 53). Alongside this explanation, others have seen the language of 'a share of the inheritance' as recalling the idea of inheriting what was promised to the patriarchs. Thus, in relation to this phrase, it has been suggested that 'for anyone familiar with Jewish scriptures it would immediately evoke the characteristic talk of the promised land and of Israel as God's inheritance' (Dunn 1996: 75–76). While referring to the Colossians as 'holy ones' (Col. 1:2) suggests that they are part of God's people, there is little to suggest that they are seen as being grafted into Israel's promises and inheritance (cf. Rom. 11:17), at least insofar as the author explicitly presents the argument throughout the letter.

The participial phrase, translated here as 'who has qualified', τῷ ἱκανώσαντι, is one of only two occurrences of the Greek verb ἱκανόω in the New Testament. The other instance follows on from two usages of the related noun ἱκανός, and discusses the basis of the adequacy of Paul and Timothy to be ministers of the new covenant: 'not that we are adequate in ourselves...but our adequacy is from God, who makes us adequate to be servants of the new covenant' (2 Cor. 3:5–6). Here the term conveys the idea of being 'adequate', 'sufficient', or 'qualified' for a task, or perhaps 'shading into the sense *empower, authorize*' (BDAG: 473). Given the lack of lexical data for this verb in the New Testament and other early Christian literature, greater consideration needs to be given to its use in wider Greek literature. In relation to the active forms of the verb, the primary sense is 'to make sufficient', 'to qualify' (LSJ: 825). Therefore, the father is seen as being the one who makes the believers in Colossae qualified to be partakers of the inheritance he bestows. There is a textual variant here, with a number of important manuscripts reading 'who has qualified *us*' rather than '*you*'. At one level, theologically this is not of great significance, since it is not the case that Paul and Timothy regarded themselves as being excluded from sharing in the inheritance. The significance lies in determining whether the Colossians are still being reminded of the benefits they have accrued through their acceptance of the gospel, or whether (as in Col. 1:13) the train of thought has become more generalized and is now engaged in theological reflection upon the changed status of all believers. However, on internal grounds, later copyists may have wished to make the pronouns in Col. 1:12–13 uniform, and hence changed *you* to a more inclusive *us*, agreeing with the pronoun in the following verse (Metzger 1994: 554).

There has been discussion concerning the content of the inheritance that is being described here. According to some, the language of inheritance evokes the Exodus promise of territory, since land is described as Israel's inheritance (Deut. 3:18; 19:14; Josh. 13:7). Within the Hebrew Bible, Abraham expresses concern over not having his bloodline preserved, and instead Eliezer will become heir to his possessions (Gen. 15:2). In the Community Rule, found among the Dead Sea Scrolls, there are some interesting parallels.

> To those whom God has selected he has given them an everlasting possession; until they inherit them in the lot of the holy ones. He unites their assembly to the sons of the heavens in order to form the council of the Community and a foundation of the building of holiness to be an everlasting plantation throughout all future ages (1QS XI 7–8).

In this text there is a noticeable shift away from a hope for an earth-based inheritance to one that is spiritual, eternal in nature, and located in the heavenly realm. This tendency to spiritualize inheritance hopes is even more pronounced in Col. 1:12, where there is no description of what precisely is being inherited, only that it is the common lot that is shared with the holy ones in light. Therefore, the accent is placed more on the sense of being made sufficient to become an inheritor, rather than concerned with the actual content of the inheritance.

Whereas the passage from the Community Rule sees the inheritance as a future event or an eschatological blessing, it appears that in this passage in Colossians, believers are seen as already having a share of the inheritance that is possessed by the holy ones who dwell in light. Whether this is enough to conclude that the perspective here is that of a realized eschatology, or whether it simply depicts a present status that can only be claimed when believers are united with the holy ones in light cannot be fully determined. The text does not provide a complete picture of the paradisical blessings. The identity of **the holy ones in the light** is also not spelt out clearly. If the text cited above informed the outlook of this passage, then they would be understood as heavenly or angelic beings who dwell in the nearer presence of God. That whole cosmological outlook, where the members of the community act in concert with heavenly beings, finds wider support in other Qumran texts such as the War Scroll (1QM). Elsewhere it may be possible that the Greek term for **holy ones** is used to designate heavenly beings (cf. 1 Thess. 3:13). However, such a meaning seems unlikely here. Wider usage throughout the Pauline epistles shows that the predominant use of the term 'holy ones', ὁι ἅγιοι, which occurs 39 times, with the possible exception of 1 Thess. 3:13, is to human believers. Moreover, the other five occurrences apart from this passage in Colossians (Col. 1:2, 4, 22, 26; 3:12) are either adjectives used as nouns to label believers as 'the holy ones', or adjectives that describe them as being holy. Part of the motivation for proposing a different understanding here (see Lohse 1971: 36; Pokorný 1991: 52), with 'holy ones' denoting angelic or heavenly beings, is that this then allows this verse to be read as an implicit critique of those mentioned later in the letter who are accused of luring the Colossian believers to seek after visionary experiences and to participate in 'the worship of angels' (Col. 2:18). Another possibility that has been suggested is that the term 'the holy ones' is used 'to designate the covenant people Israel' (Barth and Blanke 1994: 186). The argument is that what is being envisaged is that Gentile believers are now permitted through the work of Christ to partake of an inheritance previously reserved exclusively for the Jewish nation. This interpretation is also to be rejected, for the fundamental reason that Paul never uses the term 'holy ones' to designate the people of Israel. Also, unlike the discussions elsewhere in the Pauline writings (see Rom. 9–11; 15:8–13), there is no indication that the relationship of the gentiles *vis-à-vis* Israel is part of the author's concern in this passage. The final exegetical question is whether the expression **in the light** refers to believers now dwelling in the light, or that the inheritance of which they are now partakers is reserved for them in heaven. These two options are not necessarily mutually exclusive. In the following verse there is a reference to believers being 'rescued from the dominion of darkness' and transferred to a new kingdom. The corollary of no longer dwelling in the darkness, is that the believers now dwell in the light. This metaphor of living in an enlightened state occurs elsewhere in the Pauline epistles (Eph. 5:8), believers are described as 'sons of light (1 Thess. 5:5), and the gospel message itself is said to bring light (2 Cor. 4:4; 2 Tim. 1:10). So in Pauline thought those who have received the gospel now are described as living in the light and having left the darkness behind. However, the realm in which the deity exists is described as being a place of 'unapproachable light' (1 Tim. 6:16). Given that Colossians envisages the transference of believers from the realm of darkness into the kingdom of God's Son (Col. 1:13), it appears that both believers themselves and their inheritance are to be located in this heavenly kingdom.

13 Having assured the Colossians that they have been made fit to receive a portion of the divine inheritance along with other believers who now dwell in the light, the author describes the process that enables believers to exist in that new realm. The two actions of God mentioned here are 'rescue' and 'transference'. The first relates to leading believers out of the entrapped state in which they formerly existed. Thus in relation to believers, God is depicted as the one **who rescued us from the dominion of darkness.** The verb 'rescued' is in the past (or aorist) tense, denoting a past event or an action already completed. Here the author switches to the first person plural pronoun 'us', thereby more closely identifying with the shared experience of having been 'rescued'. The experience of 'rescue' or 'deliverance' is part of the process of salvation, which is entailed in accepting the message of the gospel. Here there is no strict sequence of events presented, such as first hearing the gospel, believing its message, experience deliverance and so on. Rather, the author presents various powerful images which resonate both with the culture in which the Colossians live, and with their spiritual experience of new life in Christ. Along with the positive benefit of having an inheritance with all the holy ones, they have also been brought out of an existence under what is characterized as an oppressive 'dominion of darkness'.

The language of 'rescue' plays a role in the story of Israel's deliverance from Egypt (Exod. 5:23; 6:6; 12:27; 14:30). A number of commentators view this story of Israel's rescue from Egypt as such an iconic story, that they propose that behind this text in Colossians one is able to detect a 'new Exodus' motif. Thus it is stated that the inheritance spoken of in the previous verse means the Colossians 'have been given a share in the new Exodus' and that Paul evokes 'a whole world of imagery relating to Israel's exodus from Egypt and her entry into the promised land'. Also using the language of rescue in Col. 1:13, Paul 'alludes to the exodus, this time referring particularly to the dramatic rescue operation in which God delivered his people from the dark power of Egypt' (Wright 1986: 64–65; cf. Beetham 2011: 81–95). However, while recollection of the Exodus may feed into the contemporary understandings of what God's rescue or deliverance entailed, to postulate a 'new Exodus' theology standing behind this passage is certainly overblown. If it is present at all, exodus imagery is only part of the religious heritage that informs the idea in this letter of believers being rescued from the dominion of darkness. Within the Hebrew Bible, the notion of rescue is particularly prominent in the Psalms. Repeatedly God is invoked to save the suppliant's soul (LXX Ps. 6:5) especially from the godless (LXX Ps. 16:13). Elsewhere God is called upon to deliver the Psalmist from death (LXX Ps. 32:19), or from persecutors (LXX Ps. 7:2), and from strong enemies (LXX Ps. 17:18). Similarly, in the book of Proverbs rescue from death is a repeated concept (Prov. 10:2; 11:4; 23:14; 24:11). In various parts of the Hebrew Bible the theme of God's deliverance is strong, but this is not necessarily related solely to the Exodus story. In Jewish literature written closer to the time of Colossians, the idea of God's rescue is often used independently from reference to the flight from Egypt. God assures his people that he will 'rescue them from all snares of the Pit' (CD XIV, 2; cf. 1QH III, 19). In Paul's writings, divine rescue is often seen as being from the coming eschatological destruction (1 Thess. 1:10), or from death itself (Rom. 7:24). Given the richness of the ways in which God could be envisaged as having rescued his people, it appears that the term draws upon a rich heritage perhaps partially informed by the foundational Exodus events. However, like so many religious images, the concept of deliverance had taken on a context-free meaning.

Here in Colossians, believers are rescued from a dominion that is the antithesis of the realm of light. The **dominion of darkness**, ἐξουσία τοῦ σκότους, carries connotations of demonic forces with the suspension of God's justice. The same phrase is used in Luke's Passion account, where Jesus tells those arresting him, 'this is your hour, and the power of darkness' (Lk. 22:53). The word translated here as 'dominion', ἐξουσία, has a large range of meanings in Greek. At its root is the notion of self-determination, so in certain contexts it can be translated as 'freedom of choice' or 'right' (cf. 2 Thess. 3:9). From this meaning the term was used to denote the ability 'to command' or 'to govern' (Mk 3:15; Rev. 13:12; *Gos. Pet.* 3:7). By extension, it came to denote the power exercised by those in authority (Lk. 7:8), or even those ruling authorities themselves Rom. 13:1). In a more abstract sense, which aligns with the usage here, it described the sphere or domain in which authority was exercised (Lk. 4:6; 23:7; Eph. 2:2). The claim that is being made is that prior to receiving the gospel, existence was within 'the dominion of darkness'. That realm stands in opposition to 'the light', and it was where evil exercised its power. There are obvious demonic overtones here, and darkness is related to a state of virtual non-existence. The shared experience of believers is that they have been rescued from this realm by God, and have been freed from the tyranny of that former marginal existence. The train of thought now turns to describing the new sphere of life into which the Colossians and all who receive the gospel have been led.

The final part of this verse relates the second already accomplished act of God, through which believers have been **transferred to the kingdom of the Son of his love**. The verb translated here as 'transferred', μεθίστημι, occurs only five times in the New Testament and denotes movement of some kind. It may refer to the act of removing a king (Acts 13:22), or a mountain (1 Cor. 13:2), or a steward removed from office (Lk. 16:4). Elsewhere it describes the effect of Paul's preaching as causing people 'to turn away' from other gods (Acts 19:26). Here the sense is of movement into a new domain. The preceding clause emphasizes the point that this move into a new sphere was dependent upon rescue from a prior state of existence; hence the sense of 'transference', or 'translation' is intended here. The sphere into which believers have been transferred is described as **the kingdom**. The image of 'kingdom' in Greek is wider than a geographical or territorial meaning, it has a functional sense designating the sphere in which royal power or sovereignty is exercised. Hence it is a conceptual space in which a new order operates, and this order is antithetical to the 'dominion of darkness'. Of the 162 occurrence of the term 'kingdom' in the New Testament, most occur in the gospels, and the vast majority speak of 'the kingdom of God', or the circumlocution 'the kingdom of heaven' in

Matthew, or 'the kingdom of the Father'. Among the 14 occurrence of the term 'kingdom' in the Pauline writings, nine explicitly use the term 'God' in a unique possessive sense to qualify the term as 'the kingdom of God'. One uses a possessive pronoun 'his' that refers to the term 'God' in the previous clause. This makes the description here, **the kingdom of the Son**, particularly striking. In one instance there is a description of dual hegemony, with the announcement that various unrighteous people will have no inheritance 'in the kingdom of Christ and God' (Eph. 5:5). Also, twice in 2 Timothy, although there is some ambiguity, the expression 'his kingdom' appears to refer to 'Christ's kingdom'. In the first reference the author exhorts his readers in the following terms: 'I charge you in the presence of God and Christ Jesus, who is about to judge the living and the dead, and by his appearing and his kingdom...' (2 Tim. 4:1). Because of the link between 'his appearing and his kingdom', commentators understand the former to refer to the *parousia* of Christ; they likewise take 'his kingdom' also to be a reference to Christ (Marshall 1999: 799; Mounce 2000: 571; Towner 2006: 596–97). Similarly, in 2 Tim. 4:18 there is a description of Paul stating that 'the Lord stood with me' during his trial (2 Tim. 4:17), and the same Lord will lead Paul 'into his heavenly kingdom' (2 Tim. 4:18). Again, in this context 'the Lord' is naturally understood as Christ, and the reference to 'his kingdom' denotes the same figure. This verse from the Pastoral Epistles stands as a striking parallel to Col. 1:13. It states, 'the Lord will rescue me from every evil work, and he will preserve me into his heavenly kingdom' (2 Tim. 4:18). Here the same notion of movement from one sphere of influence to another is envisaged; the verb 'rescue' is used to describe emancipation from the former dominion, and with that release Paul will be brought into the kingdom of Christ. However, there are two significant differences: in 2 Timothy these are future hopes that will follow the outcome of the trial, and these are actions of Christ, not God as in Col. 1:13. In Col. 1:13 the terminology of 'the kingdom of the Son', while rare in Pauline writings, may be indebted to a passage where the description is of 'the kingdom' being under God's rule. In 1 Corinthians, describing the eschatological consummation, Paul states that the end comes 'when he [Christ] delivers up the kingdom to the God and Father' (1 Cor. 15:24). Thus while the predominant usage in the New Testament and the Pauline writings in particular is to describe the kingdom as being that of God, there is a minor strand that speaks of the kingdom belonging to Christ. It is striking that the most explicit statement of this idea finds expression here, where it is described as **the kingdom of the Son.**

Further, compounding the use of unusual or slightly jarring expressions is the reference here to Christ as **the Son of his love.** What may be considered the more natural designation, 'beloved son', is never used in the Pauline writings (but compare the gospels, Mt. 3:7; Mk 9:7; Lk. 20:13; cf. 2 Pet. 1:17). However, on one occasion a Pauline expression comes close with the use of a perfect participle, literally 'the one having been loved', i.e. 'the beloved' (Eph. 1:6). The noun 'beloved', ἀγαπητός, is employed elsewhere in Colossians, but refers to esteemed co-workers (Col. 1:7; 4:7, 9, 14). Some see this designation as affirming the Davidic messiahship of Jesus. Since Col. 1:13 speaks of his kingdom, it is suggested that his royal status is being implied. Moreover, the depiction here of Jesus as God's Son is viewed as resonating with the ideology of the Royal Psalms, where the king was enthroned as God's son (Pss. 2:7; 89:27–37). In line with other kingly expectations in the Hebrew Bible, such as those contained in 2 Sam. 7, it is argued that here Jesus is being legitimized as a kingly Davidic Messiah (Barth and Blanke 1994: 190). While this is a theologically rich interpretation, it is uncertain whether the text will support it. Moreover, whether the phrase **the Son of his love** was intended to evoke recollection of the baptismal or transfiguration traditions associated with Jesus can no longer be determined. What the description does communicate is the closeness of the relationship between God and Jesus, and this will be an important theme in the lyrical passage that follows. Jesus is both God's Son and the object of his love. Already the author has announced that love is the true measure of the kinship that exists in the community of believers (Col. 1:4, 8; cf. Col. 2:2; 3:14). It is, therefore, unsurprising that the author should see the paradigmatic example of that love as finding expression in the relationship between the father and the son.

14 Having just spoken of God's Son, the author's focus moves from what God has already done for believers in rescuing them and transferring them into his kingdom, to the benefits that they are now experiencing through their union with Christ. This transition from God to Christ then leads into a fuller exploration of the identity of

God's Son and what he has achieved for believers (Col. 1:15–20). Prior to that, he describes actions of Christ that are closely linked with the concepts of 'rescue' and 'transference' contained in the previous verse.

The first declaration that is made about Christ is that he is the one **in whom we have the redemption**. The introductory phrase **in whom**, ἐν ᾧ, should not be overlooked for it signals the participatory idea of the life Colossians now lead is united with Christ's existence. The verb **we have** reveals an established state, since believers live in Christ they continue to enjoy the blessings he provides. There is a textual variant here, with a change in tense of the verb. Instead of the present tense, 'we have', ἔχομεν, one important Greek manuscript, Codex Vaticanus (and some Coptic versional manuscripts), have the past tense (Greek aorist), 'we had', ἔσχομεν. The present tense, 'we have', is almost certainly the original reading, and a later scribe has made the change to preserve the flow of past tense (aorist) verbs from the previous verse. In achieving this grammatical consistency the scribe has failed to realize the important theological point, that the benefits described here are ongoing for believers. The first thing that such believers are said to possess is **the redemption**. To modern ears 'redemption' is simply another 'churchy' term that is synonymous with being saved. This was not the case for the original recipients of this letter, where the term denoted release from slavery and gaining one's freedom. Such emancipation was often a long-held, but most frequently an unrealized hope for the majority of slaves throughout the ancient Mediterranean world and beyond. The power of the rhetoric that is used in Paul's letters where he declares the redemption or freedom of all in Christ is hard to over-estimate. What is more, in a society whose social order and economic stability were governed by slave labour, such language could be viewed as both revolutionary and inflammatory. The memory of slave revolts lived long in the memory of those who were free, and there was a fear that slaves would murder their masters while they slept in order to obtain freedom. With a sweeping and subversive declaration Pauline theology declared that all believers had been redeemed, that is, they were all emancipated in Christ. The word could also be used as a reference to those who had been ransomed from captivity, and the concept of believers being 'bought with a price' or being 'ransomed' (Mk 10:45) is another prominent metaphor in the early Jesus movement.

Within the New Testament the majority of occurrences of the term 'redemption', ἀπολύτρωσις, are found in the Pauline letters (although see Lk. 21:28; Heb. 9:15; 11:35). With similar sentiments as those expressed here, in Romans Paul speaks of 'the redemption that is in Christ Jesus' (Rom. 3:24). More directly, along with identification with other important theological terms, Christ is said to have become 'redemption' for us (1 Cor. 1:30). Elsewhere, placed in apposition to the expression 'waiting for adoption as sons', is the phrase 'the redemption of our body' (Rom. 8:23). This expansion, although presumably given for clarification is somewhat opaque. Presumably the idea is that when one receives adoption as a divine son, the corporeal body is redeemed from the state of corruption that it now undergoes (cf. Jewett 2007: 519, who sees the reference as portraying 'a socially transformed corporeality within the context of a transformed creation'). The term is particularly prominent in Ephesians, where it is used on three occasions (Eph. 1:7, 14; 4:30). The second of those references expands on the concept of a ransom, with the description of the spirit given as a pledge, which serves 'until the redemption of the property' (Eph. 1:14). The first passage from Ephesians probably accounts for a variant that is found in some late minuscule manuscripts of Col. 1:14, where the text reads 'in whom we have the redemption through his blood'. This assimilates the reading to the parallel in Eph. 1:7: 'in him we have redemption through his blood, the forgiveness of sins…'.

The final clause in this verse glosses 'redemption' as being **the forgiveness of sins**. The language of forgiveness was familiar both in Jewish and Greco-Roman religion. It is, however, the connection between 'redemption', which speaks of release of slaves or captives, and 'forgiveness of sins', which denotes divine pardon that is unexpected. Paul, citing Ps. 31:1 (LXX), calls those whose 'sins have been covered' blessed (Rom. 4:7). Yet apart from the passage in Ephesians (Eph. 1:7) that is a close parallel to Col. 1:14, there is little discussion of 'forgiveness of sins' in the Pauline writings. The idea of 'sin', without reference to forgiveness, is more common, and sin is viewed as a power that brings about death (Rom. 5:12). However, instead of 'sin' as an impersonal power, here the author speaks of 'sins' in the plural and announces forgiveness in Christ. Therefore, in a daring move, Colossians views the ongoing experience of being 'redeemed', as bringing with it the certainty of knowing one's sins are forgiven. Such a linkage is a significant development in Pauline thought, and reveals how fundamental actions of God, such as 'redemption' and 'forgiveness of sins', are easily and confidently attributed to Jesus in christological passages that reflect what being 'in Christ' means for those who accept the gospel message.

4. POETIC REFLECTION ON CHRIST (1:15–20)

(15) Who is the image of the invisible God, firstborn of all creation (16) because in him were created all things, in the heavens and on the earth, the visible things and the invisible things, whether thrones or lordships, whether rulers or authorities, all things through him and for him were created (17) and he is before all things, and all things in him hold together (18) and he is the head of the body, the church. Who is the beginning, firstborn from the dead, in order that he might be first in all things, (19) because in him all the fulness was pleased to dwell (20) and through him to reconcile all things to him, having made peace through the blood of his cross [through him], whether the things on the earth or the things in the heavens.

It is a widely held view that the material in Col. 1:15–20 is best understood as a preformed unit of tradition that the author has incorporated into this letter, making some slight adjustments in order to make it applicable to the theological outlook being espoused. Furthermore, recognition of the repetition of phrases and the apparently carefully structured balancing of clauses, coupled with content focusing on a description of the Son of God (Col. 1:13), has led to this unit being labelled as a 'Christological Hymn'. However, the arguments both for understanding Col. 1:15–20 as preformed material and for labelling it as a hymn are not always explicitly presented.

In terms of this unit being preformed prior to its incorporation into the letter, there are two major options that have been suggested. The first is that it is a pre-Christian composition, perhaps originating either in a Jewish context or within the context of one of the pagan mystery religions. On this hypothesis, the references to Christ being 'the head of the body, the church' (Col. 1:18) and the theological interpretation that he 'made peace through the blood of his cross' (Col. 1:20) are the most obvious later Christian supplements to the primitive hymn. Thus the pre-Christian hymn is understood as a paean celebrating the recovery of cosmic peace, which is brought about through the advent of a universal saviour who enters his kingdom and heralds in a new age (Käsemann 1964: 152). Connections have also been adduced with various strands of Jewish thought, such as those seen in Philo's discussion of the primal man. One of the most striking parallels, in concepts if not in form, is the following passage from the allegorical commentary on the Babel story:

> And even if there be not as yet any one who is worthy to be called a son of God, nevertheless let him labour earnestly to be adorned according to his first-born word, the eldest of his angels, as the great archangel of many names; for he is called, the authority, and the name of God, and the Word, and man according to God's image, and he who sees Israel. (*Conf.* 146)

Hence both the pagan and Jewish contexts show that many of the concepts contained in Col. 1:15–20 had antecedents in non-Christian settings. This is, however, quite different from claiming that the tradition was a pre-Christian hymn.

The other option is to see the material as originating among adherents to the early Jesus movement, but being taken over from a liturgical context, perhaps with modifications, and being placed in its present epistolary context. In fact, it has been suggested that a more primitive form of the hymn originated among the believers in Colossae, but that Paul found it theologically defective and hence corrected it (Murphy-O'Connor 1995; 2001: 1193–94). Furthermore, it is argued that the hymn represents the 'beguiling persuasive speech' (Col. 2:4) that Paul rebuts, and it had captivated the Colossians into believing 'they were articulating a mystery beyond their comprehension' (Murphy-O'Connor 2001: 1194). One is left wondering, if this were the case, why this preformed tradition would have been incorporated into the letter. On this theory it is argued that descriptions of the cosmic Christ are rooted in revelations received by the Colossians that are rejected, yet at the same time Paul did not want to repudiate their insights, presumably because he saw something of value in these mystical formulations. This is a highly ingenious proposal, but in the end it depends on assumptions about the community's situation and on proposals about the original structure of the hymn, which simply are beyond confirmation or corroboration.

In terms of the hymnic character of the material, it should first be recognized that the New Testament itself acknowledges the existence of hymns, and may well preserve some examples. Reference to 'psalms', 'hymns', or 'odes' occurs at various points in the Pauline writings, and significantly in Colossians the three terms are connected (Col. 3:16). An even more fulsome description of lyrical praise and the use of music is found in Ephesians: 'speaking to one another in psalms and hymns and spiritual odes, singing and making melody in your heart to the Lord' (Eph. 5:19). Similarly, writing to the Corinthians Paul describes the use of psalms in worship (1 Cor. 14:26). In Revelation, the four living creatures and the 24 elders sing a song of praise to the Lamb, the words of which are presented (Rev. 5:9–10); elsewhere those who triumphed over the beast sing a victory song and they are described as holding harps (Rev. 15:3–4). By contrast, the two passages in the Lukan infancy narrative typically described as canticles, the Magnificat (Lk. 1:46–55) and the Nunc Dimitis (Lk. 2:29–32), while having a poetic quality, do not provide the same indication that that they were sung in worship contexts. They are presented as spontaneous outpourings of praise in response to divine revelation. Hence there is a broad spectrum of material in the New Testament, from traditions explicitly identified as sung pieces of worship to those seen as poetic and instant responses to moments of spiritual ecstasy. None of these traditions is created in a vacuum, and their authors were aware of modes of praise current in both Judaism and pagan contexts. Thus there is nothing to suggest that the deployment in Col. 1:15–20 is a subtly subversive strategy to undermine the hoards of false teachers that scholars often posit as the basis of positive these christological affirmations. Later in the epistle, the author will tackle a problem he detects in the community, be it actual or potential (see Hooker 1973: 315–31). However, here it appears that the christological material is simply motivated by praise, rather than by polemics.

15 The elevated poetic section opens by identifying its subject obscurely with the relative pronoun, **who**, ὅς. The antecedent of this relative pronoun is to be found in Col. 1:13, where the last subject to be mentioned was 'the Son of his love'. Therefore, continuing with the change of focus commenced two verses earlier, the language of elevated praise and wonderment reflects on the role of Christ, the Son of God, in relation to his role in creation and reconciliation.

The opening clause is both paradoxical, and yet affirms the unprecedented proximity that the Son has to God, **who is the image of the invisible God.** Here Christ is declared to be the visible form of the invisible God – he allows the unseeable to be seen. However, this statement is presented as a fact, without any explanation of how or in what way the Son images 'the invisible God'. The term **image**, εἰκών, takes on a range of usages in Greek literature. However, the six occurrences in the Pauline epistles show that the concept of 'image' does not convey the sense of being a replica; rather, the image reflects certain qualities of the object being imaged. Based on this underlying 'prototype-copy' relationship, three conceptual patterns can be identified (*EDNT*: I, 389):

i.   humanity as God's image (1 Cor. 11:7; Col. 3:10);
ii.   Christ as God's image (2 Cor. 4:4; Col. 1:15);
iii. believers in their relationship to Christ's image (Rom. 8:29; 1 Cor. 15:45–49).

Although 2 Cor. 4:4 is similar to Col. 1:15 in that it speaks about Christ in almost identical terms, 'Christ, who is the image of God', the sense is markedly different. In 2 Corinthians the idea is that of Christ as an instrument of the revelation of God, who enables those who had been previously blinded to see the light of the gospel. In Col. 1:15, as the whole context of the poetic passage announces, Christ images God in regard to creation, and through being 'first born from the dead' he images God through effecting reconciliation with everything in the created order. Therefore, Christ is viewed as mirroring the cosmological relationship that God has with the entire universe.

The description of God as being invisible ἀόρατος (cf. Rom. 1:20; Col. 1:16; 1 Tim. 1:17; Heb. 11:27) draws upon the theological outlook of Jewish and ancient Israelite religion, and may stand behind the commandments against the futility of attempting to make objects in the likeness of God (Exod. 20:4). During the description of the theophany on Sinai, Moses is told 'you cannot see my face, for no man can see me and live' (Exod. 33:20). It is with dread that in the Isaianic vision the prophet declares, 'Woe is me for I am ruined... For my eyes have seen the King, the Lord of hosts' (Isa. 6:5). In first-century Judaism there was a debate concerning whether Moses had seen God (Josephus, *Ant.* 3.5.3). However, the outlook of these texts is that if one sees God death will follow, or alternatively elsewhere there are statements to the effect that nobody has seen God (1 Tim. 6:16; 1 Jn 4:12, 20). This is different from the view expressed here that God is not only incapable of being seen, but that he is actually invisible. That latter view is expressed on other occasions in the Pauline corpus. God is explicitly described as 'the King eternal, immortal, invisible' (1 Tim. 1:17), and elsewhere his attributes are described as being invisible (Rom. 1:20). Therefore, the author draws upon a strand of thinking shared with other Jewish and Christian writers, that humans cannot see God. Here the emphasis is not upon the punitive consequence that seeing God results in death, but rather it describes God as possessing the quality of invisibility. It is the actions of God in creation and reconciliation that 'the Son of his love' images in his own being, in order that there might be perception of the divine.

The connection between image and God in this verse, coupled with the wider discussion of the theme of creation in Col. 1:15–17, may evoke resonances with the creation story, where God declares that he will create man in his own image (Gen. 1:27). However, the verbal links are not particularly strong (*contra* Beale 2007: 851–55). In regard to possible imagery being evoked, Burney stated that in relation to 'the first-begotten of all creation' that this phrase 'can hardly be other than a direct reference to the O.T. passage [Prov. 8:22: "The Lord begat me at the beginning of his ways"]'. Moreover, according to Burney, since Prov. 8:22 provides the key to Gen. 1:1, then Col. 1:16–18 should be seen as 'giving an elaborate exposition of the first word in Genesis, בְּרֵאשִׁית *Berêshîth*, and interpreting *rêshîth* as referring to Christ' (Burney 1926: 173, 160). While this suggestion creates a rich theological matrix against which to read Col. 1:15–18, it has not been adopted by a significant number of scholars who have been engaged in detecting the intertextual use of the Jewish scriptures in Colossians. Burney does helpfully highlight certain texts that may have shaped the religious understanding of ideas used in Col. 1:15–18, and those concepts may have fed into the passage indirectly rather than being direct or intentional allusions.

The expression **firstborn of all creation** is ambiguous in its meaning, unclear in its relationship to the previous clause, and easily misunderstood when read through the lens of christological debates of the fourth century. Taking these problems in reverse order, if read anachronistically a superficial interpretation of this phrase may suggest that it aligns with the rejected christological affirmation attributed to Arius: 'if the Father begat the Son, he that was begotten had a beginning of existence: and from this it is evident, that there was a time when the Son was not' (Socrates of Constantinople, *Hist. Eccl.* 1.5). However, in Col. 1:15 the word **firstborn**, πρωτότοκος, is not used as a technical term, and the concerns are not those of later controversies that either sought to assert the eternal existence of the son, or portray him as a being with a fixed point of origin. Thus, the terminology is not used here to resolve matters of ontology, but to celebrate the Son's relationship both to the father and to the entire created order. Secondly, there are perhaps at least three major ways in which the two clauses could be seen as related to one another. The second clause could be taken as an explanatory gloss on the first clause: 'who is the image of the invisible God, *that is* the firstborn of creation'. This would perhaps imply that the image of God is seen through the one who is made the firstborn of creation. If this were the meaning, then the emphasis would perhaps be more on the Son as revelatory agent of God in creation. A further possibility is that rather than the second clause simply expanding or functioning as a gloss of the first, both are co-ordinated with the intention of illustrating an underlying claim, such as the Son's proximity to the father. If this were the meaning, then the Son is portrayed as being the visible manifestation of divine attributes, and being instrumental is God's creative activity. Another option is to understand these two clauses as only loosely related, the Son is the image of God and the firstborn of creation. On this reading these two descriptions are not to be seen as closely linked. Instead the author simply catalogues two of the unique aspects of the Son. The option preferred here is that the second of these possibilities comes closest to the intention of the opening lines of this poetic section. The Son is the visible manifestation of God's attributes, and the Son is also the agent of God in creation. Both of these affirmations speak of a preeminent relationship between father and son, which is unparalleled in comparison with any other being or object in the cosmos.

The term **firstborn**, πρωτότοκος, is notoriously difficult to define, and the temptation to read into it later definitions or technical theological meanings must be studiously avoided. Within the biblical text it can have a fairly straightforward meaning denoting a person or animal that is the first offspring born to a mother (Gen. 25:25; Exod. 6:14; Lk. 2:7). It can denote the special relationship between Israel and God (Exod. 4:22; LXX Jer. 31:9); it also has special significance in the sacrificial system, since certain firstborn animals were required as sacrifices to the Lord (Lev. 27:26). It is also used in the LXX version of the story of the first Passover as part of the judgment upon Egypt, where all the firstborn were killed by the Lord (Exod. 12:29; cf. Heb. 11:28). Within the Pauline writings, apart from the occurrences in this passage (Col. 1:15, 18), the term is found only on one other occasion (Rom. 8:29). It is striking in that context that the terms 'image' and 'firstborn' also occur in close connection: the holy ones or believers are 'predestined to be conformed to the image of his Son, that he might be firstborn among many brothers' (Rom. 8:29). However, it is believers who are in the image of the Son, and the Son is not the 'firstborn of creation', but 'among many brothers'. Here, however, the relationship is different and it involves priority over the entire creation, but not as more narrowly defined in Rom. 8:29 as among the holy ones. That latter perspective aligns more closely with the second use of the term in this poetic section (Col. 1:18), where the Son is 'firstborn from the dead', and this is linked to primacy in an ecclesial context. With the deployment of the term in Col. 1:15, most commentators have wanted to resist any implication that **firstborn of all creation** envisages the Son as part of the created realm, and therefore of the same order as created beings. Thus the use here is considered to be different from Rom. 8:29 and Col. 1:18, where it is argued that the term is used inclusively. In Col. 1:18 'firstborn from the dead' shows that Christ's resurrection inaugurates the possibility of resurrection for others, and in Rom. 8:29 'firstborn among many brothers' reveals a new type of fraternal bond. By contrast, here the expression is qualitatively different, in that others are not able to share in the status of 'firstborn of all creation'; so the usage here is seen as exclusive. This establishes a basis for seeing the term as denoting both temporal priority and superiority in relation to creation. This interpretation appears to be supported by the explanation that commences the following verse, 'because in him all things were created' (Col. 1:16).

The description has also been seen as having links with the role of wisdom in Jewish thought. Thus in Second Temple thought it is stated that 'wisdom has been created before all things' (Wisd. 1:4), and similarly wisdom eulogizes herself, saying, 'He created me from the beginning before the world' (Wisd. 24:9). Philo in a riddle-like passage describes wisdom as:

> the incorporeal being who in no respect differs from the divine image… For the Father of the universe has caused him to spring up as the eldest son, whom, in another passage, he calls the firstborn; and he who is thus born, imitating the ways of his father, has formed such and such species, looking to his archetypal patterns. (Philo, *Conf.* 62–63)

A little further on Philo speaks of 'the incorporeal wisdom' (*Conf.* 82), making it clear that in the former passage the reference was to wisdom. Both the personification of wisdom and its role in creation and revelation became significant in certain strands of Judaism as depicting the medium through which God created the cosmos and communicates his nature to that creation. What is striking in comparing Col. 1:15 and Philo's *Conf.* 62–63 is that not only are similar roles attributed to both wisdom and the Son, but there is significant shared terminology. Wisdom is said to differ in no respect from the *image* of the divine, and is also called the *firstborn*. The parallel is not strong enough to assert the direct dependence of Col. 1:15 on the passage from Philo. However, what this does show is that the concept of wisdom as a figure alongside God from before the creation of the cosmos and described as the *firstborn* having an active role in creation appears to have created the intellectual context in which the same system of thought could be applied to Christ as the one who is the image of God, who exists beside the deity, and who is prior to and actively involved in creation. However, noticing this link does not resolve the later christological debate. This is because the ambiguity of the term 'firstborn' is also present in its use to describe wisdom in Jewish thought, since wisdom is also understood at times as a created being, while on other occasions wisdom is seen as the agent of creation which has existed alongside God prior to creation.

16 Whereas the intended link between the two clauses in the previous verse is uncertain, the opening statement of Col. 1:16, **because in him were created all things**, is closely tied to the second part of the preceding verse. The relationship between the previous clause and the statement here is that of a dependent causal clause introduced by the conjunction **because**, ὅτι, which supplies the reason for the former assertion. Here the poetic thought is that the Son is the 'firstborn of all creation' because all things were created in him. Far more seems to be envisaged here than some kind of mechanistic process, whereby God uses the Son simply as an instrument of creation. However, a number of English bibles translate this phrase as, 'because all things were created *by* him'. This reflects the wide range of meanings that the Greek preposition ἐν can carry. In fact, it is the most common preposition in the New Testament; it has been enumerated that there are 2,698 examples of the preposition ἐν in the New Testament, and that this accounts for 26.5% of all proper prepositions in the New Testament (BDF: §218). Adopting the translation 'by him' emphasizes the role of the Son as the divine instrument of creation (BDF: §219[1]). However, not all grammarians agree that the usage is instrumental here. The most frequent sense of the preposition is spatial or denoting the sphere in which an object is found. In the immediately following clause the preposition takes on an unambiguously spatial meaning in the phrase, 'in the heavens' (Col. 1:16). Moreover, given the participatory language which is a prevalent feature of the author's christology in Colossians, with expressions such as 'in Christ' (Col. 1:4) or 'in him' (Col. 2:7, 10), and the fact that the 'in him' formula is used in this poetic section on two further occasions with a spatial sense (Col. 1:17, 19), it appears that here the Son is being described not as a mere instrument through which God caused the cosmos to be created, but as constituting the domain and locus of power in which the cosmos can be brought into existence. However, there is a danger in seeking too much precision in meaning, and the final clause shows that instead of exact distinctions the purpose is a 'catch all' description that all things were created 'in him...through him and for him'. While there is debate whether this first reference means 'creation came into existence "by means of his actions" or that it exists "within him" (i.e. envisioning the creation residing within the cosmic body of Christ)' (Sumney 2008: 66), the verse as a whole seeks to express both options, as well as affirming that in some sense Christ is the goal for creation. This description may also be informed by Jewish wisdom traditions, 'you made all things by wisdom' (LXX Ps. 103:24), which here appears to the Greek preposition ἐν in an instrumental sense to convey the meaning of the underlying Hebrew.

The action that takes place in Christ is that in him **were created all things**. Within Jewish thought creation is seen as divine action, and this is illustrated by the title 'the Creator' that is virtually synonymous with reference to God (Rom. 1:25; 1 Pet. 4:19). Once again, by associating the Son with an action usually considered to be a divine attribute, or prerogative, his proximity to God is emphasized. Earlier commentators took terms such as 'all things', and later fulness, πλήρωμα (Col. 1:19), as illustrating a 'gnostic' strand in the cosmology of this hymnic material (the latter is seen by Lightfoot as a technical term used by gnostic teachers who have influenced the Colossians; Lightfoot 1886: 100, 157; cf. Dibelius 1953: 12–19). However, this 'gnostic' interpretation is probably anachronistic, at least as a developed Christian form of Gnosticism. Instead, the language may simply draw upon the religious vocabulary of both Judaism and the Greek mystery religions, with 'all things' being a regular way of expressing the totality of the created realm. In fact, the repetition of the term 'all things' throughout this poetic section (Col. 1:16 [×2], 17, 18, 20), emphasizes the Son's precedence over the whole of creation.

With the following phrase, **in the heavens and on the earth**, the term 'all things' is glossed in such a way as to emphasize that the description 'all things' actually envisages every conceivable created object as coming into existence through the Son. Thus the creative action of the Son is both cosmic and comprehensive. The difference between prepositions *in* the heavens and *on* the earth reflects usual usages, with the heavens seen as a sphere *in* which beings exist (Mt. 5:12; 6:9; 2 Cor. 5:1; but contrast Eph. 1:10, which uses the Greek preposition ἐπί rather than the usual ἐν). Likewise, the expression 'on the earth' reflects standard expression (Mt. 6:19; Jn 17:4; Col. 3:2, 5), and the contrast between 'in heaven' and 'on earth' is also reflected in the language of the Lord's Prayer (Mt. 6:10//Lk. 11:2). The description of the all-encompassing role of the Son in creation continues by mentioning both **the visible things and the invisible things**. The term used to describe **the visible things** τὰ ὁρατά occurs only here in the New Testament. It is an intentional contrast with the following description of **the invisible things**, τὰ ἀόρατα, and like the Greek the English terms differ only by the addition of a negative prefix. Again, like the pairing of heavens and earth, here the visible and the invisible form a complementary pair that embraces the totality of creation. It is not possible to know for certain whether the pairing 'visible' and 'invisible' is to be understood as a pleonastic repetition of 'heavens' and 'earth', with visible things being earthly objects and invisible objects being heavenly, or if visible and invisible items are seen as belonging to both realms. In favour of this second option, Ignatius uses the pairing 'visible and invisible' in his letters. On the first occasion to describe heavenly things his chains now allow him to comprehend (Ignatius, *Trall.* 5.2), but on the second occasion he uses the expression apparently to describe earthly things that may prevent him from becoming a disciple (Ignatius, *Rom.* 5.3). So, if in the thought world of Col. 1:16 visible and invisible things belong to both the heavens and the earth, then the author has chosen to divide the entirety of the created order in a second different way (*contra* Moo 2008: 122), but both pairings are intended to incorporate every created object.

The fourfold list that follows specifies certain powerful though created forces or beings: **whether thrones or lordships, whether rulers or authorities**. This list appears to have a dual purpose. First, it includes things that the author may suspect the Colossians of envisaging as having an independence from the sphere of Christ's power. Secondly, it focuses on heavenly entities in a manner that further emphasizes the supremacy of the Son over the entire cosmos, not just the earth alone. Whereas the previous two pairings were comprehensive in their scope, this fourfold list does not attempt to encapsulate the entirety of creation. Instead it presents entities that the Colossians may have considered as the most powerful forces and autonomous beings in the cosmos, and the author emphasizes that these too are subservient to Christ for they are part of his creative work. Even if this poetic section is a modification of a preformed hymn, the majority of scholars who hold that view have seen these four elements as part of the editorial reworking of earlier material. Therefore, regardless of whether there is preformed material or whether this is a spontaneous outburst of poetry from the author, it appears that the decision to mention these powerful entities is the handiwork of the author of the letter, and furthermore this comment may have been written with the Colossian context directly in view. Given that 'rulers and authorities' are mentioned again in Col. 2:15, and are closely associated with the critique of the practice of worshipping angels (Col. 2:18), this suggests that the theme of powerful forces, which may potentially be considered as rivals to the unique role of the Son, is a concern of the author in this letter.

The fourfold list has occasioned considerable debate among scholars on two fronts. First, as to whether the four entities refer exclusively to heavenly beings, or to a mixture of powerful celestial and earthly forces. Secondly, whether these forces are to be understood as evil, or benevolent, or perhaps are simply a neutral description of a misunderstanding of possible rivals to the Son's status. In relation to the first debate, the theory that the four terms reflect a mix of earthly and heavenly forces is often based upon detecting a chiastic structure with the extended description of created beings that are subject to Christ (Col. 1:16). The chiasm has been presented in the following manner (Bammel 1961: 92):

A	in the heavens	B′	whether thrones
B	and on the earth	A′	or lordships
B	the visible	A′	whether rulers
A	and the invisible	B′	or authorities

The suggestion is that the A and A′ elements refer to things in the heavens which are invisible, specifically lordships and rulers, while the B and B′ elements denote entities which are both earthly and visible such as thrones and authorities. However, this highly innovative suggestion may be more brilliant than it is persuasive. Recently a larger scale chiastic structure encompassing the first stanza of the hymn (Col. 1:15–17) has been suggested that sees its element C, 'in the heavens', paired with its element C′, which is taken as the whole phrase, 'and the invisible whether thrones or

185

dominions or principalities or authorities' (Heil 2010: 65). However, the decision should not be made on the basis of one's preferred chiastic arrangement, since the competing suggestions reveal the degree of arbitrariness in formulating such structures. Rather, both issues can only be resolved by analyzing the meanings of the four terms, especially in the context of Colossians, as well as the New Testament and other relevant Greek literature more widely.

The term **thrones** (sing. θρόνος) in its literal sense refers to the seats on which figures in positions of authority sit (Herodotus, *Hist.* 1.14.3; Lk. 1:52), or metaphorically it connotes royal power or status (Aeschylus, *Ch.* 565). In the plural, as here, it can refer to twelve thrones on which the apostles will sit to judge Israel (Mt. 19:28//Lk. 22:30, cf. Rev. 20:4), to 24 lesser thrones for the elders arranged around God's throne (Rev. 4:4; 11:16). In the singular the term occurs four times in the letter to the Hebrews where it designates either the heavenly seat of God or Christ (Heb. 1:8; 4:16; 8:11; 12:2). The term does not occur in the Pauline writings in any other passage except this verse (Col. 1:16). It is, by contrast, frequently used in Revelation, where it accounts for 47 of the total of 62 occurrences in the New Testament. On the majority of occasions it is used in reference to the throne of God (e.g. Rev. 4:5; 7:10) or the throne shared by God and the lamb (Rev. 22:1, 3). However, on a few occasions the thrones of evil non-worldly powers are mentioned, such as the throne of Satan (Rev. 2:13), or the throne of the dragon (Rev. 13:2), and also the throne of the beast (Rev. 16:2). Given that much of the drama of Revelation is set in the heavenly arena it is perhaps unsurprising that the thrones it describes are also found in cosmic locations. Furthermore, even the wider New Testament usage contains a predominance of examples where reference to thrones is in relation to a heavenly context. This lends weight to the suggestion that in Col. 1:16 the idea is that of cosmic thrones, not a description of earthly powers. Some have wanted to take this observation further, and have stated that if the term 'throne' is not qualified by further description then in the New Testament it 'refers exclusively to the throne of Christ or God' (Carr 1981: 49). The problem is that for those who wish to apply this insight to Col. 1:16 they must immediately qualify it because of the plural reference to thrones, and consequently it is usually taken to denote angels in the heavenly court. This is seen as determining the meaning as 'good angels', and it is categorically stated that 'it is impossible that the term could be used of evil posers or angels' (Carr 1981: 49). However, opposing this view, it is observed when this is taken in conjunction with Col. 1:20 and 2:15 then 'these powers are understood as somehow threatening or hostile to God's cosmos' (Dunn 1996: 93). Yet, this may not be decisive, since at this stage in the epistle there has been 'no clear indication that these are hostile powers' (Wilson 2005: 140). Hence the reference to **thrones** appears to be a designation for beings that occupy cosmic thrones, and there is no clear indication in this context whether these are hostile or benevolent powers. The point is to emphasize that even the most powerful forces imaginable are actually subservient to Christ.

The next term is translated here as **lordships** (sing. κυριότης) to emphasize the connection in Greek with the term κύριος, 'lord'. Other English translations render this word as 'dominions', with further alternatives being 'kingdoms' (NLT) or 'princehoods' (Wycliffe). The term occurs on only four occasions in the New Testament. In two related, or perhaps literarily dependent passages, the term is used to describe those who reject or despise 'lordship' (2 Pet. 2:10; Jude 8), in reference to what appear to be despising the rule of Jesus as Lord. The other two usages of the term are Col. 1:16 and Eph. 1:21, with the latter passage likely to be dependent on the former in some way. The passage in Ephesians describes Christ's cosmic superiority due to his resurrection and exultation 'when he raised him [Christ] from the dead, and seated him at his right hand in the heavenly places, far above all rule and authority and power, and lordship, and every name that is named' (Eph. 1:20–21). Here the fourfold list in Ephesians – rule, authority, power, and lordship – is similar to the fourfold list in Col. 1:16 – thrones, lordships, rulers, and authorities. The main differences are that Ephesians uses 'power' in place of 'thrones', it also employs singular forms because of the grammatical construction, and furthermore the order of terms is different. However, there is a more substantial difference. In Eph. 1:21 the terms appear to denote evil powers. In Eph. 1:22 such powers are subjected under Christ's feet, with both the terms 'subjected' and 'under his feet' being common ways of referring to the defeat of enemies. However, use of the later perspective of Ephesians as the interpretative lens to determine the meaning of the fourfold list in Col. 1:16 may not be justified, since perspective in Ephesians have shifted in various parallel passages from those in Colossians, and there is a much greater emphasis on cosmic warfare (Eph. 6:12). However, while it is uncertain whether the powers listed in Col. 1:16 are benevolent or malevolent, the term 'lordships' is also best understood as denoting heavenly entities. Although the term is rare in wider Greek literature (*EDNT*: II, 331–32) on those occasions where it does it is used in association with angels or demons (Philo, *Conf.* 171; *Mut.* 59; *Mart. Pol.* 14.1; *1 En.* 61:10; *2 En.* 20:1; *Test. Sol.* 8:6).

The third term in the list is **rulers** (sing. ἀρχή). The range of meanings covered by this Greek term helps one to gain an understanding of the significance of these 'rulers' or 'powers'. In the singular the Greek term carries the sense of primacy either in relation to temporal matters, spatially as a point of origin, or in terms of status or rank. In wider Pauline thought the term 'rulers' (pl. ἀρχαί) refers to the powerful forces that are thought to control the cosmos. However, this status is over-aggrandized from the Pauline perspective, since it does not acknowledge the creaturely status of the 'rulers', who are neither temporally prior to the 'firstborn', and whose rank is less than his, since their created existence is dependent upon him. While one does not have the complex system found in certain Christian 'Gnostic' texts of a series of emanation from prior beings with each successive generative being less powerful as it moves further away from the ultimate source of being, such systems which are replete with archontic powers do share some basic similarities with the cosmology expressed in this passage (cf. the Nag Hammadi tractates, *Hypostasis of the Archons*, which quotes Col. 1:13 in its introductory discussion of the topic).

The final term in the list, **authorities** (sing. ἐξουσία), recalls a term used in Col. 1:13 where the author spoke about the Colossians having been rescued from 'the dominion/authority of darkness'. In that context the singular form was connected with the conceptual notion of spatial domain of darkness. Here the plural reference to the 'authorities' carries the same negative tones as the earlier reference, although the idea has become less spatial and refers to a set of beings opposed to the divine plan. This opposition, and the defeat of the 'rulers and authorities', becomes more fully apparent in Col. 2:15, where Christ is said to have stripped them, and to have led them captive in a triumph procession. Thus while it is unclear whether the first two terms 'thrones and lordships' should be understood negatively or just as neutral designations of high-status heavenly powers, there is more certainty that the second pairing of 'rulers and authorities' is intended to denote powers hostile to God. Elsewhere in Colossians these forces are seen as associated with darkness (Col. 1:13), and must be triumphed over by Christ (Col. 2:15). This may lend weight to the suggestion that all four terms in the list should be understood as descriptions of entities opposed to the divine plan. However, this might also be imposing more consistency on the author's thought than is actually the case. He may equally want to say that all forces, both benevolent and hostile, are inferior when compared to the status of the Son.

The verse ends with the phrase **all things through him and for him were created**, which seems to echo the opening proposition of the verse, 'because in him were created all things'. While there are obvious similarities, the author is saying something new, which further clarifies the role of the 'firstborn' in the creation process. The variation in prepositions '*in* him...*through* him...*for* him' highlights the role, agency, and purpose of the Son in relation to creation. In the thought world of Colossians, the fact that all things were created in him seems to denote some participatory aspect – namely, that the ultimate purpose for creation is that it might exist within the Son, and that it has no meaning apart from such relational existence. Next, the affirmation that all things were created through him speaks of the Son as the agent of creation. That is to say all the so-called powers are not only subordinate to the Son because he was temporally prior to them, they are subservient because their very existence depends to him. The final affirmation is that all things were created 'for him'. The Greek preposition εἰς (here translated as 'for') takes on a range of possible meanings – often in the sense of motion towards something. Thus many commentators have suggested that the author's intention is to communicate the idea that Christ is also the *telos* or eschatological goal of creation. The English translation masks the fact that two occurrences of the verb 'was created' are not identical tenses in Greek – at the beginning of the verse it is an aorist passive, while at the end it is a perfect passive. If this change is not simply due to stylistic variation, then the use of the perfect at the conclusion of the verse may support the idea that the Son is being presented as the goal of creation itself. Therefore, the use of the perfect may be employed because it is speaking of a desired state. All things have been created through Christ with the desire that they may move closer to him who is both their source and goal.

17 The notion of the Son's temporal priority, which is an element in the foregoing verse, appears to be explicitly emphasized in the declaration, **and he is before all things**. However, as already observed, it is wrong to create a false divide between priority in time and priority in rank. This same ambiguity that surrounds the term 'firstborn' (πρωτότοκος), whether it is intended to denote temporal priority, superiority of status, or perhaps more likely both. The same mix of priority in time and rank appears to be part of Jewish thinking concerning wisdom, 'wisdom was created before all things' (Wisd. 1:4; cf. Wisd. 24:9). There is an obvious temporal frame in mind here, but the elevated role of wisdom is also part of the depiction. Again, the genre of the passage must be kept in mind. The aim is not a rigorous theological disquisition on the origins of Christ – rather, it is a doxological outburst of praise that looks for multiple ways of reinforcing the conviction that he is superior to any other being in time, space, or status.

Greek grammarians have noted the unaccented text in which Colossians was originally written would have been ambiguous. It is debatable whether the words αυτος εστιν mean 'he is' (which would be accented αὐτός ἐστιν), or 'he exists' (accented as αὐτὸς ἔστιν). Taking this and other interpretative possibilities into account, Harris notes four main translational options (Harris 2010: 42):

1. 'He himself exists before all things'.
2. 'He himself exists in supremacy over all things'.
3. 'He himself is before all things'.
4. 'He himself is supreme over all things'.

These options are formed by the combination of decisions relating to whether αυτος εστιν means 'he is' or 'he exists', and the Greek preposition πρό is denoting temporal priority or superiority in rank. It has been argued that while the idea of priority in time is present, this does not exclude the meaning of priority of status. Thus options one or three appear the most plausible, and deciding between these is more complicated. Since the emphasis is on the Son's priority in comparison to other heavenly figures, there may be less concern with asserting his absolute existence. Secondly, although the accented text is a late development (eighth century onwards) the form of accenting introduced supports taking the verb as a copula which connects the pronoun 'he' with 'before all things'. Third, in the following verse the verb 'to be' is used as a copula, and it might be the case that one should expect consistency in use (although if different authors are responsible for different sections of the hymn that might weaken the force of this particular argument). Lastly, the Vulgate appears to understand the Greek in this manner, *et ipse est ante omnes*; however the Coptic appears to point in the opposite direction. On balance, the evidence favours the third of the options.

The second clause in the verse, **and all things in him hold together**, shows that Christ is not only the source but also the sustainer of all things. As at the beginning of the previous verse where the author declared that 'in him were all things created', denoting Christ himself to be the sphere of creative activity, here Christ is presented as the locus for the coherence and sustenance of all things. Whereas the earlier reference was to the original creative task, here it is to Christ's ongoing role as the one who enables the continuation of the cosmic order. The main exegetical issue is determining the sense of the verb συνίστημι, here translated 'hold together'. The basic ideas the verb covers are those of being in close relationship, i.e. 'standing together', or coherence of components, i.e. 'to consist' or 'to hold together'. In the New Testament, the closest parallel to the use here is to be found in 2 Pet. 3:5 'and the earth from water and through water *was drawn together* by the word of God'. In that context, however, the sense is more that of formation, rather than that of the maintenance of what is already established, as is the case in the passage here. In the first half of the poetic section the phrase 'all things' functions like a refrain, but its theological significance is to remind hearers that every aspect of the cosmos owes its creation and ongoing existence to Christ, since it is created in, through, and for him, and it continues to exist only within the sphere of his sustaining influence. It may be the case that the theme of Christ's cosmic role as the sustainer of the universe leads the author naturally into contemplating the way Christ also sustains the church. This would then imply the Christ is viewed as the one engaged in the continuing activity of upholding the church.

18a Many commentators have noted there is a marked shift in topic here, with the focus moving from the cosmos to the church, from creation to community. The first half of this verse is rightly regarded as the final clause of the first part of the lyrical unit. It is linked to the foregoing statement with a conjunction, stating of Christ **and he is head of the body, the church**. The transition to a statement concerning the relationship between Christ and his followers may be based upon the idea of his role as sustainer, which came to the fore in the previous clause. If this is the case, the move is, nonetheless, still quite lateral. The metaphor of the body is common in Pauline thought to describe the church. Here, however, it is presented in a very underdeveloped form, where the only 'body part' mentioned is the head, which is equated to Christ. By implication the believers form the rest of the body. By contrast, the use of the body metaphor in 1 Cor. 12:15–23 is far more developed with reference to the foot, the hand, the ear, the eye, the head, and the unseemly members. There, however, the image was used to provide instruction on relationships between group members. By contrast, in the compressed poetic language, the body metaphor has only one function, to emphasize Christ's preeminence in the church. For this reason the author does not need to draw on wider aspects of the metaphor, but only that part which demonstrates that the same priority that Christ has over the cosmos is paralleled by his relationship to believers. In this way the author shows that Christ's rightful place in the cosmos is first being established in his body, which is the church.

The language of **head**, κεφαλή, is obviously metaphorical here. The predominant use of the Greek term in the surviving literature is to refer to the physical 'head' of an animal or human. When the term is used metaphorically, as here, it can take a range of slightly different nuances. Thiselton has divided the semantic domain into three categories: (i) authority, supremacy, leadership; (ii) source, origin, temporal priority; (iii) preeminence, foremost, topmost serving (Thiselton 2000: 812–22). Perhaps it is unnecessary to split these three groups entirely when seeking the metaphorical sense of Christ's headship in this passage. If the assertions about Christ's role over the cosmos are still governing the author's thinking about Christ's relationship to the church, then the ideas of origin and preeminence may come to the fore. If the author is tapping into other Pauline references to Christ as head (cf. 1 Cor. 11:3), then perhaps there is some notion of authority or leadership. In terms of wider contemporary cosmological outlooks, the universe could be likened to an organic body, and in a frequently cited text Zeus is named as the 'head' of the cosmos (*Orphicorum Fragmenta* 168).

The reference to **the church** here takes on universal rather than local scope, which is similar to the way the term is used a few verses later, Col. 1:24 (cf. Col. 4:15, 16). The church is the locus, or perhaps the microcosm, from where the rightful recognition of Christ's role over the cosmos begins. The universal perspective on the church is already present, although perhaps not dominant in the earlier Pauline letters (1 Cor. 6:4; 12:28; Phil. 3:6). By contrast, in Ephesians the understanding of the church, ἐκκλησία, is uniformly universal (Eph. 1:22; 3:10, 21; 5:23, 24, 25, 27, 32). Sociologically the early Christian communities may have chosen to adopt terminology for their gatherings that was distinct from the name for Jewish assemblies, 'synagogue'. The term had a pedigree in Hellenistic contexts as denoting public assemblies, and the ἐκκλησία was a key institution in democratic Greek city-states, being the meeting place were eligible citizens gathered. There is no evidence that the etymology of the term ἐκ + καλέω had any influence upon its choice by early believers who had formed their own meetings in distinction from synagogues. Rather, it appears that the terminology was taken over from Greek usage to designate the open meetings of believers in Jesus.

18b The second section of this poetic unit is designed to mirror the opening of the first section. Both parts open with the two words 'who is', ὅς ἐστιν, and in common with the first strophe the second clause opens with the striking term 'firstborn', πρωτότοκος. This careful structuring of the language not only marks out the second verse or section, but shows that the author wishes to convey that the status of the Son is predicated both on his relationship to the cosmic creation and derived from his resurrection. The section opens with the statement that Christ is the one **who is the beginning**. This affirmation by itself signals no change in theme from the preceding section, and initially it appears to be a further continuation of the theme of Christ's priority over creation.

The parallel with the role of Wisdom in the creative order is often noted, 'the Lord created me the beginning of his ways' (Prov. 8:22). However, the next clause takes the reader away from contemplating creation and the beginning of the cosmos. Instead it affirms the priority of the Son in a different role – namely, he is **firstborn from the dead**. This shifts the content from the more general focus of cosmological reflections (which although in the immediate context are connected with Christ, were nonetheless more common in religious mythology of Judaism and ancient mystery cults) to the central Christian claim that Jesus had been raised from the dead. In wider Pauline theology the resurrection is seen as the way in which God publicly declared Jesus to be his Son (Rom. 1:4). Whether 'the dead' in question are only believers or all humanity may not be a question that is at the front of the author's mind. The idea that Christ is the first to be raised among faithful believers is to be found in Rom. 8:29, 'firstborn among many brothers'. Here, however, the meaning is not specified since the emphasis falls upon the priority of Christ as the first resurrected being, who, by being brought to life again, opens up the wider possibility of resurrection for humanity. The author's main point is to emphasize that the Son not only takes precedence in the creation of the cosmos, but, by becoming the 'firstborn from the dead', has priority in recreation, which is a defeat of the corrosive and corruptive forces at work in the universe (cf. Rom. 8:20–22).

The author continues by stating the purpose of Christ's status as 'firstborn from the dead'. It is in order **that he might be first in all things**. In the author's thinking, demonstration of the Son's priority in the creation of the cosmos announces that he is at its beginning, with his triumph over death regarded as a terminal point, revealing that there is no aspect of existence where Christ does not have precedence. Therefore, affirmations of the Son's fundamental role both in creation and the reconciliation of the cosmos through his cross (cf. Col. 1:13, 20) show that these are regarded as his key christological roles. While some commentators have found a tension or imbalance between the Wisdom christology in the first half of the poetic material and the christology of the cross in the second half, the insight concerning the 'inextricable complementarity of Paul's Adam christology with his Wisdom christology' (Dunn 1996: 99) helps explain why these two elements have been carefully woven together in this unit. By making these two aspects conjoint the author may seek to avoid any misunderstanding that the Son only gained preeminence through his resurrection. Rather, he occupied that role from the very beginning of creation. What the resurrection does is to re-establish or confirm that he is the one who retains such a priority of status. If these is a concern among Colossian believers concerning Christ's role and status *vis-à-vis* the elemental forces of the world (Col. 2:8), then here the author has highlighted the fact that there is no force in the cosmos that can rival the unparalleled place of the Son.

19 A further indication of this priority of status is given in this verse with the explanation **because in him all the fulness was pleased to dwell**. The meaning of the key term 'the fulness', πλήρωμα, is not obvious within this verse. However, in Col. 2:9 the author states that 'in him dwells all the fulness of the deity bodily'. Hence, the author speaks of divine fulness. Many commentators feel it is possible to identify more precisely what this divine fulness designates. Thus it is understood as 'all the nature and character of God' (Sumney 2008: 74). While this is not necessarily incorrect, it is difficult to establish what the author may have specifically understood by the references to the divine fulness in Colossians. It has been noted that the expression 'the fulness' becomes a technical term in Valentinianism, where the pleroma refers to the sphere from where emanation of the aeons come forth. These aeons are 'prototypes of the elect human seed on earth, whose return to the Pleroma is made possible through the work of the Savior' (Pearson 2007: 155; cf. *Gos. Truth* 17.4–11; 38.32–38). While there are elements throughout the poetic section that lightly resonate with aspects of the Valentinian cosmology, the developed level of complexity is lacking. It is unlikely that this unit is being used to critique a Valentinian system. Rather, some of the ideas that were taken up from the mystery religions into early Valentinianism in the second century appear to have been in circulation in the setting of certain mystery cults at the time when Colossians was written. The author attempts to subvert the claims of such groups, undercutting any alternative foundational myth by stating that the fulness already dwells in Christ, and has not been dispersed through the cosmos in a series of emanations.

Another issue in this verse is determining the subject of the verb 'was pleased', εὐδόκησεν. Three major options have been suggested among the commentators: (i) God is the subject, not being named because this is functioning as some type of divine passive; (ii) the Son is the subject, allowing the fulness to dwell in him; (iii) the fulness is personified and becomes the subject of the verb. Option two appears unlikely since the 'in him' refers to Christ, and it is difficult to see how the Son can be both the subject and the indirect object in this sentence. Most commentators, therefore, either name God as the subject in their translations of this verse, or make 'the fulness' the subject of the verb. Again, the difficulty with taking God as the subject is that he has not been named since v. 13. However, given the compressed language of this poetic material such a lack of explicit subject may be intentional. Grammatically, it is more natural to take 'the fulness' as the subject; however, this attributes the emotion of 'being pleased' to an impersonal subject, as well as creating a slight tension with the masculine form of the participle in the following verse 'having made peace' (Col. 1:20). Alternatively, the participle could be taking its masculine subject from the immediately preceding reference to the reconciliation that is achieved 'in him', which refers to the Son. If 'the fulness' is taken as the subject, it has already been seen that this is not conceived as being an independent impersonal force, since what is being designated is the divine fulness. Hence, as Moule has suggested, the expression 'all the fulness', 'may be taken as a periphrasis for "God in all his fulness"' (Moule 1957: 70). Thus God may be the ultimate subject, but designated in a removed way through the independent action of the divine fulness.

This understanding of 'all the fulness' dwelling in Christ emphasizes the author's perspective that the Son has become the centre for divine communication and activity on behalf of humanity. In the next verse those divine actions operative in the Son will be described more explicitly.

20 The key activity described here is reconciliation through the peace-making work of the cross. The statement is not only the structural finale of this poetic unit; it is also the theological climax. If the fulness of divinity dwells in the one who is before all things, then this comes to fruition through the restoration of all things, which the author describes here in the following manner, **and through him to reconcile all things to him**. It is often noted that reconciliation is an action that repairs a relationship between estranged or alienated individuals or groups. The concept of reconciliation is usually applied to humans, or to relationship between the human and the divine. However, here the author having personified the cosmos to a certain degree in the foregoing description takes this a step further by stating that 'all things' are in need of reconciliation. The cosmos itself has undergone a disruption through its failure to recognize the pre-eminent place of Christ over creation. In this verse it becomes clear that it is Christ himself who repairs the rupture between the cosmos and himself, through his death on the cross.

An interpretative issue that commentators have discussed is the question concerning the one to whom 'all things' are to be reconciled. Grammatically, it is noted that the expression 'to him', εἰς αὐτόν, when originally written in Greek would have been unaccented. Thus it is suggested that 'the sense seems to require εἰς αὐτόν, with a rough breathing... [T]he sense seems to require a reflexive... [I]t is ultimately God who is at work in Christ, reconciling all things to himself' (Wilson 2005: 154). Such arguments are dependent on wider Pauline usage, where reconciliation is usually 'to God' (Rom. 5:10; 2 Cor. 5:19; Eph. 2:16). In more explicit terms, Paul is able to write that 'God was in Christ reconciling the world to himself' (2 Cor. 5:19). There is little doubt that in that context, while Christ is the instrument of God's reconciling work, the purpose is that the world might be reconciled to God himself. This, however, may not be decisive for determining the meaning in Col. 1:20. First, throughout the poetic section the author stresses the proximity of the relationship of the Son and the father. He is 'the image of the invisible God' (Col. 1:15), he is the sphere in which all things are created (Col. 1:16), all things hold together in him (Col. 1:17), 'he is before all things' (Col. 1:18), and 'in him all the fulness dwells' (Col. 1:19). Such an identification of divine attributes and qualities belonging to the Son suggests that the author is not interested in clearly differentiated roles, but precisely the opposite – showing the commonality of purpose. The cosmic role of Christ also suggests that the redemptive and reconciling activities are focused on the Son, and moreover are accomplished in order that he might resume his correct position as the one who is over all things. Perhaps the clinching argument is to be found two verses later, where the Colossians are assured that although they were formerly alienated, 'now he has reconciled you in the body of his flesh through death' (Col. 1:22). In this verse the Son is not just an instrument, but also the active agent of reconciliation. Admittedly, such a reconciliation enables the Colossians to be presented 'holy and blameless and without reproach before him' (Col. 1:22), where the pronoun most likely refers to God. So yet again the identification of subjects of the pronouns remains ambiguous. However, the point for the author appears to be that the father and the Son work in concert, reconciling the cosmos and restoring the fractured relationship with the divine. The author's elevated christological affirmations allow for the merging of the divine actions with those of the Son, and the richness of this poetic section derives from its multivalent language, not from an analytic determination of precise processes.

While there is dispute concerning the one with whom reconciliation is made, the next clause is focused on the peace-making activity of the Son: **having made peace through the blood of his cross [through him]**. Yet it is to be noted that some commentators who take the reconciliation exclusively as being with God, continue the focus on divine action. Thus Harris describes this as 'identical, modal action: "God...was pleased...to reconcile...by making peace"' (Harris 2010: 47). While this perspective should not necessarily be rejected, it should be stressed that one of the chief points of this statement is to affirm that the Father and the Son act with common purpose. The Son is not some passive instrument, but an autonomous and active agent whose actions are so aligned with those of God precisely because 'all the fulness dwells in him', that it become virtually meaningless to separate the divine peace-making from the Son's death on the cross, which was the mechanism by which peace with the cosmos was restored. The metaphor of 'making peace' may have had particular resonances in a Greco-Roman context given the imperial propaganda associated with the claims of *pax Romana*, and claims by emperors such as Augustus to have been harbingers of divinely created peace. The subversive nature of the claim that Christ, not Caesar, was the source of universal peace, stood in stark contrast to the expectation that peace was established through military triumph and imperial conquest. Instead the author asserts that true peace is attained through the value-inverting mechanism of the 'blood of the cross'. Such a radical perspective, which opposed wider political perspectives, may have functioned as a direct challenge to imperial ideology. The expression **the blood of his cross** is unique as a unified idea, although the component parts are present elsewhere in the Pauline writings. Strictly speaking an expression such as 'blood of the cross' is an example of metonymy, a figure of speech or rhetorical strategy where one word or phrase is substituted for another with which it is closely associated. Here obviously the blood is that of Christ, not of the cross. And yet, the author uses the cross as a virtual synonym for Christ. Perhaps the important aspect is not the identification of the literary technique employed by the author, but recognition of the fact that like most early Christian writers there is a tendency to avoid graphic or gory descriptions of Christ's death. His death is presented as a fact that has soteriological effects. The actual details of the death, apart from mentioning that it was a crucifixion, are not the focus of reflection.

In Pauline thought the 'blood' of Christ is on the one hand a literal reference describing the physical substance that was shed during the crucifixion process. However, given the sacrificial system in the ancient world, and in particular the Jewish understanding of the atoning quality of blood, the term also evokes a range of cultic images. Part of the belief of the efficacy of blood sacrifices relates to the idea that the life force resided in blood (Gen. 9:4). Hence in Romans Paul can speak of the effectiveness of Christ as 'an atoning sacrifice through faith in his blood' (Rom. 3:25), and he can also expound upon the fact that believers 'have been justified by his blood' (Rom. 5:9), thereby escaping from the wrath of God. Similarly, in a later letter, redemption is seen as coming about through Christ's blood (Eph. 1:7). In various ways the shedding of Christ's blood in Pauline thought is not merely transactional, but relational. That is, it does more than simply purify believers from sin – it incorporates recipients into the body of Christ. In Colossians this is seen as the act through which universal harmony is re-established. Therefore the cosmic dimension comes to the fore.

Apart from this verse, the closest connection between the cross and blood occurs in Ephesians. There the author tells readers that although they were formerly far off, now they have 'been brought near by the blood of Christ' (Eph. 2:13). Having presented the idea that the blood of Christ undoes the experience of alienation from the covenantal promises (Eph. 2:12), the author continues by stating that enmity has been abolished so that 'he might…establish peace, and might reconcile them [Jews and Gentiles] both in one body to God through the cross' (Eph. 2:15–16). The 'cross', like 'blood', has associations with death in Paul's thought: 'being obedient to death, even death upon a cross' (Phil. 2:8). Therefore, while the sacrificial dimensions of 'blood' and the 'cross' are present here, the focus falls on reconciliatory and relational aspects of 'the blood of his cross', and upon the act of self-giving rather than on the cultic mechanics of sacrifice.

There is a textual problem with the phrase **through him**, δι' αὐτοῦ. The manuscript evidence is divided as to whether this phrase was initially present. 𝔓⁴⁶, the earliest surviving manuscript of Colossians (ca. 200), provides support for its inclusion, as do א A C Dᶜ 614 syrᵖ· ʰ copᵇᵒ goth. However, the phrase is omitted in B D* G 81 1739 it vg copˢᵃ arm eth. Probably omission is easier to explain either through accident (because a scribe inadvertently avoided repeating a phrase used also at the beginning of the verse – homoeoteleuton), or intentionally because it was superfluous and obscure. The possible later addition of the phrase is harder to explain. Perhaps it could have been introduced to make more explicit the divine role in 'making peace' through the agency of Christ. However, this would appear quite an obscure strategy (Metzger 1994: 554). On balance, the support of the earliest witness, the difficulty in explaining the phrase if it were an addition, and the obvious motivation for deleting the repeated phrase make it far more likely that it was original. The difficulty then becomes explaining its function! It is debatable whether 'through him' is completing the reflection on Christ having made peace, or if it is resumptive, taking up again the earlier occurrence of the phrase that 'through him' all things were reconciled. If the latter was the case, then that meaning is expanded in the final clause of the verse by stating the things that have been reconciled in Christ: **whether the things on the earth or the things in the heavens**. Harris prefers not to class this second function as resumptive. Instead, he argues that it is 'an emphatic repetition from v. 20a' (Harris, 2010: 47). It is questionable whether one needs to differentiate between the resumptive and emphatic functions. Given that the phrase 'through him' is used in the final clause of Col. 1:16, where its is also linked with the foregoing to 'things in the heavens and things on the earth', it appears most likely that its purpose at the end of this section is to remind readers that 'through him' the entire created order has been reconciled. The language is pleonastic and poetical, the eightfold repetition of πᾶς language ('all'/'all things'), along with forms of αὐτός ('him') being used eleven times, reveals the rhythm and repetition of central ideas in this outpouring of doxology and celebration of the role of Christ in creation and in the reconciliation of the cosmos.

Whether this poetic section was a pre-existing unit, or whether it was a modified piece, or even a fresh composition, either from a Christian or pre-Christian context, is not only beyond conclusive proof, it is in many ways irrelevant. This material derives its meaning both from its present form, and from the context in which it is now embedded. It is not so much a statement of rigorous theology, but a spontaneous outburst of praise. The author understands Christ to be both the source and the goal of creation. He is the one through whom the universe was created, and the one through whom the cosmos is reconciled. Therefore, as it now stands, this lyrical material aligns with certain central Pauline understandings of the cross as the centrepiece of the divine plan. Moreover, this section further develops a reflection on 'the blood of the cross' (Col. 1:20) as the means which brings about reparation of the ruptured relationship between the entire cosmos with God and with the one who is affirmed as both the firstborn of creation (Col. 1:15), and the first born from the dead (Col. 1:18). Thus, while this section has a lyrical quality and is an expression of spontaneous praise, it is also deeply theological. For when the author ascends to the heights of his poetic reflection on the status of Christ, it is almost inadvertently that he creates this deep theological resource. Passages such as Col. 1:15–20 would become focal points of debate in the christological controversies of later centuries. Perhaps those debates would have remained more constructive if the genre of such material had been recognized. When taken as ontological statements of the inter-relationships within the Trinity, such poetic language would be adjudged confusing and perhaps contradictory. When it is allowed to function as the author intended as a celebration of the creative and redemptive role of Christ, and the language of praise is permitted to speak to the hearer, then it is able to evoke religious affirmation of its sentiments and to move hearers to be elevated in their own feelings of praise and worship of Christ.

5. APPLYING RECONCILIATION TO THE COLOSSIANS (1:21–23)

(21) And you once were alienated and enemies in mind in evil works, (22) but now he has reconciled [you] in the body of his flesh through death in order to present you holy and blameless and without reproach before him (23) if indeed you persevere in the faith being established and steadfast, and are not moved from the hope of the gospel which you heard, which has been preached in all creation which is under heaven, of which I, Paul, became a servant.

Here the author progresses from contemplation of the universal significance of reconciliation to consideration of how it has made an impact on the specific context of the believers to whom he is writing. In this section, a classic 'before and after' perspective is given on the states in which the Colossians existed either side of hearing the gospel.

21 The opening verse in this section functions in Greek as a subordinate clause that is the object of the main verb, 'he has reconciled', in the following verse. Hence, this is why the object 'you' is not present in Col. 1:22. The reason for this slightly unusual yet permissible construction appears to be that the emphasis is to highlight the contrast between the 'before and after' states, in which the Colossians were found according to the theological perspective expressed here. Accordingly, prior to being reconciled, the author can declare that, **and you once were alienated and enemies in mind in evil works**. The author signals the former state by using the temporal marker 'once', ποτέ. This is then contrasted in the following verse with the present state being introduced by another temporal marker, 'but now', νυνὶ δέ (Col. 1:22). A similar construction is used in Rom. 11:30, where Paul states 'you *once* were disobedient to God, *but now* have been shown mercy…'. The first way the former condition is described is as being **alienated**. The verbal aspect of the perfect passive participle highlights the state in which the Colossians found themselves prior to accepting the message of the gospel. In the New Testament the verb 'to alienate, estrange, exclude', ἀπαλλοτριόω, occurs only three times, once here and twice in Ephesians (Eph. 2:12; 4:18). In these cases it is used to describe the state of existence of Gentiles prior to salvation. Therefore, for the author of Colossians the totality of the experience of the cosmos in being estranged from God and his Son is mirrored in the individual lives of the Colossians prior to their reconciliation.

The second way in which this separation is described is that of being **enemies in mind in evil works**. Whether the first term is to be understood as functioning as a noun 'enemies', or in an adjectival sense 'hostile', is not clear. This is reflected is the division in English translations between the alternatives 'hostile in mind' and 'enemies in mind'. The term ἐχθρός (noun = 'enemy'; adj. = 'hostile') occurs nine times in the Pauline writings (Rom. 5:10; 11:28; 12:20; 1 Cor. 15:25, 26; Gal. 4:16; Phil. 3:18; Col. 1:21; 2 Thess. 3:15). In all other passages the nominal sense 'enemy' seems to be intended. Moreover, the closest parallel, 'if while we were enemies, we were reconciled to God' (Rom. 5:10), seems clearly to denote people hostile to God, rather than their attitude of hostility. The same sense appears to predominate here, namely that the Colossians were, in their former state, people opposed and hostile towards God. Such enmity towards God was, according to the author, attitudinal in that the Colossians had become enemies in their 'mind', διάνοια. The idea here is that of fixed and reasoned opposition against God. Although the term is not common in the Pauline writings (cf. Eph. 2:3; 4:18), more widely it was used to denote the part of the body where reasoned and rational thought occurred. However, its lack of use in the Pauline corpus may suggest that it did not form an important part of his anthropological outlook. It appears to be a neutral, or even slightly negative, term that represents the place where thoughts opposed to God are formed.

Reason and ethics are not kept separate here. Intellectual opposition materializes in **evil works**, as the mind opposed to God carries the one alienated from him into the performance of various types of evil. Here the author presents a stereotypical Jewish perspective on the ethical behaviour of Gentiles separated from God. An intellectual disposition opposed to God is viewed as making the person more susceptible to ethical behaviour that is defective. Thus the Colossians are viewed as being in an incredibly bleak and hopeless state prior to the act of reconciliation effected by Christ.

22 Having briefly outlined the Colossians' former state of alienation from God, the author presents the experience of reconciliation as the converse to this previous experience. The affirmation **but now he has reconciled [you]** is a reasonably straightforward statement in terms of the contrast that is being set up with the former state.

However, there is a significant textual problem that revolves around the forms of the verb present in different manuscripts. The form in most printed Greek New Testaments is the third person singular aorist ἀποκατήλλαξεν, 'he reconciled'. There are several other variants:

1. ἀποκατήλλαξεν
   he reconciled   א A C D² Ψ 048 (0278) 1739 𝔐
                          aor. act. indic. third sing.
2. ἀποκατήλλαγητε
   you were reconciled   B   aor. pass. indic. second pl.
3. ἀποκαταλ[ ]γητε
   you are(?) reconciled   𝔓⁴⁶   orthographic variant?
4. ἀποκαταλλαγεντες
   having been reconciled   D* F G   aor. pass. ptc. nom. masc. pl.
5. ἀποκατήλλακται
   he has reconciled   33   perf. midd. indic. third sing.

Metzger suggests only the second variant explains the rise of the other readings, since they are attempts to correct syntactical problem of the anacoluthon between the 'you' in Col. 1:21 and the 'you were reconciled...to present you' in Col. 1:22 (Metzger 1994: 555). However, because of the widespread and relatively early support, and since the grammar of this sentence is not entirely smooth even with several of the other variants, it may be best to adopt the reading ἀποκατήλλαξεν as being the earliest recoverable stage of the textual tradition. Nonetheless, it is recognized here that the evidence is not conclusive. By contrast, Dunn's view is methodologically and logically confusing. He suggests that while variant two is original, nonetheless one should accept the first reading 'since the second person passive fits so badly we may be justified in concluding that the early correction/improvement was wholly justified' (Dunn 1996: 105 n. 1). Here, on the basis of both external attestation and internal consideration, the first option appears to have more in favour of its

1

originality than the other variants. Therefore it is adopted as the earliest recoverable stage of the textual tradition.

Here the author explains that what differentiates the Colossians' present religious state from their former experience of alienation is that Christ has reconciled them. This claim creates a thematic link with the statement in the last verse of the poetic section, where the author affirms that reconciliation has taken place on a cosmic scale through Christ (Col. 1:20). The verb used for the act of reconciling is an unusual form in that it is a doubly compounded verb with two prepositional prefixes, ἀποκαταλλάσσω, apart from the two occurrences in Colossians, elsewhere in the New Testament the only other place it is found is in Eph. 2:16. The more common form that occurs with only a single prepositional prefix, καταλλάσσω, is found six times in the Pauline writings (Rom. 5:10 [×2]; 1 Cor. 7:11; 2 Cor. 5:18, 19, 20). Most lexicographers see the two forms as synonymous, but note the form ἀποκαταλλάσσω occurs only in Christian writings. While some have posited that the double prefix is emphatic, denoting the sense 'to fully reconcile' (Abbott 1897: 220), other have suggested that it reflects a wider Hellenistic tendency to replace simpler forms with more complex ones (Barth and Blanke 1994: 214). While there may be little difference in meaning, and claims that the longer form caries a sense of the greater reach of this act of cosmic reconciliation, ultimately is beyond proof. However, this specialized language may reflect the emergence of a somewhat distinctive sociolect within early Christianity, which formed part of the insider language of this socio-linguistic community.

It is striking that the fairly generic description of reconciliation taking place 'through him' (Col. 1:20) is given much great specificity here, with the claim that such reconciliation took place **in the body of his flesh**. In Col. 1:18 the term 'body' was used figuratively to denote the church. However, here the qualification that it is the body 'of his flesh' shows that the reference is to Christ's physical body. The preposition 'in' refers to the location where reconciliation takes place. The author of Colossians makes the daring claim that the reparation of the relationship between the divine and the alienated cosmos of which the believers at Colossae were part, actually takes place in the body of Christ. Previously the cross was identified as the place where Christ's peace-making work occurred, now his body is seen as the locus where reconciliation has taken place. Although the words 'body and 'flesh' are characteristic Pauline terms, nowhere else in Paul's writings are they linked in such a close construction. The latter term 'flesh', σάρξ, often has a negative connotation in Paul's letters, here it appears as a neutral description of the physical body of Christ, and may be necessitated by the metaphorical description of the church as Christ's body just a few verses earlier. While such a claim may align with later theological concerns to affirm the reality of the incarnation, that does not appear to be the primary purpose here. Rather, as the poetic material focalized attention on Christ as the one who brought about the creation and reconciliation of the cosmos, here the Colossians are reminded of the startling claim that their own relationship with God is made possible because of what Christ undertook in his body.

If there is any doubt about the specific action being alluded to here, which Christ carried out in his enfleshed state, it is made explicit in the explanation that the reconciliation took place **through death**. Therefore, the understanding expressed here is that the reconciliation is not achieved by Christ taking a physical body, but through his death while in a bodily form.

The purpose of this act of reconciliation is now described, namely, **to present you holy and blameless and without reproach before him**. The sense of presentation may carry overtones of bringing an offering or sacrifice to the temple. What strengthens this suggestion is that terms such as 'holy' and 'blameless' (or 'spotless') reflect the terminology used to describe the description of unblemished animals being brought for sacrifice. Furthermore, the language of 'presentation' παραστῆσαι is used in the LXX to describe the bringing of a sacrifice (cf. Lev. 16:7, 'he shall take the two goats and present them before the Lord'; in this verse the preposition παρά is separated from the uncompounded verb στήσει). However, in Col. 1:22 the emphasis does not fall upon the cultic act of sacrifice, but on the notion of bringing something into the divine presence, and ensuring that it possesses the qualities required to be a fitting offering to God. In this sense, there is no specific Old Testament text or idea that is being drawn upon here. Rather, a range of Jewish concepts about sacrifice and entering into God's presence inform the images used to describe the attributes the Colossians are to possess when they are brought into the divine presence.

·

The three adjectives that are used to describe the state in which the Colossians will be presented form an alliterative sequence in Greek: **holy**, ἁγίους, **blameless**, ἀμώμους, **and without reproach**, ἀνεγκλήους. In turn these qualities speak of purity and separation, that is, holiness which is seen ultimately as a quality of God; next of being faultless – physically in relation to animal sacrifices, but also morally without blame when applied to believer; and lastly the third term, which is almost a synonym of the second term, but without the cultic overtones of the first two terms, also speaks of ethical status. Therefore, the purpose of reconciliation is to bring about preparedness for believers to be in the divine presence. The final clause, **before him**, is shorthand for entering into and existing with the divine sphere. It has been suggested that the temporal horizon for believers being 'presented…before him' is not some future of eschatological event, but denotes 'that the Christians' present lives are lived in God's presence' (Lohse 1971: 65). It is probably unnecessary to separate the present and future dimensions, although it may be the case that the future perspective is where the emphasis falls more strongly, since the following verse suggests that entering the divine presence is a consequence of 'persevering in the faith' (Col. 1:23). Admittedly, this could mean that if a believer does not remain in the faith, then that person will be removed from God's presence. However, while the meaning may not be different, the perspective is more positive. Hence, rather than seeing this as a warning concerning the necessary ongoing condition for abiding in the divine sphere, it is perhaps better viewed as a description of the prior stage that if fulfilled will have the result of a state of existence with God. Therefore, being presented before God is the eschatological climax of the reconciliation that Christ has already enacted.

23 The qualifying clause, **if indeed you persevere in the faith being established and steadfast**, outlines the challenge for believers prior to entering into the full transformative consequences of the state of reconciliation. In many ways the caveats provided here speak of the realities of the life of faith in the present, rather than remaining fixated on the cosmic and the future aspects of reconciliation that has been the focus of the discussion so far. These comments also function to exhort believers to maintain their commitment to the Christian faith. Whether such an exhortation is made in reference to

the theoretical possibility that some of the Colossians might potentially turn away from the faith, or stems from a concrete experience
within the community of having seen some who believed initially not
continue as believers, or even turn to another form Christian belief
that deviated from the Pauline understanding, is no longer possible
to determine with certainty. The verb ἐπιμένω, here translated as 'to
persevere', designates a call for persistence or continuance, with the
emphasis on active determination. The Colossians are instructed to
persist **in the faith**. In Col. 1:4, it is stated that the Colossians' faith
is in Christ. However, here the injunction to persevere in the faith
is used as a kind of shorthand for maintaining commitment to the
whole belief-system focused on Christ, which the Colossians had
been taught. Therefore, it is probably best not to render the phrase
as 'your faith' (*contra* Lightfoot 1886: 161). Given the reference to
'the gospel' later in this verse, it appears more likely that here 'the
faith' likewise denotes the objective message of belief in Christ, and
not the subjective response of the Colossians. The state in which
the Colossians are encouraged to persist, calls for firm commitment
and stability of attitude. Here there is no explicit reference to the
dangers, threats, or challenges that may have caused the Colossians
to relinquish their commitment to Christ. Instead they are presented
with the qualities of **being established and steadfast** as images of
the resilience required to persevere in the faith. The term 'being
established', τεθεμελιώμενοι, has architectural associations referring
to the act of setting a foundation or laying a firm basis. In wider
Pauline usage the related noun 'foundation' designates Paul's initial
missionary work in bringing the gospel to new communities. He can
use the term to describe his desire not to build on anybody else's
'foundation' (Rom. 15:20), or as a reference to his role in laying the
gospel's foundation (1 Cor. 3:10). The second term reinforces the
call for stability in the faith, and can be used to refer to the attitude
of one's heart (1 Cor. 7:37). The two words function together to
creature the image of firmness and permanence in the faith.

A third description of stability in the faith is added to the list, but
here instead of positive actions that are to be observed, the encouragement to persevere is expressed via a negatively defined action,
'not moved': **and are not moved from the hope of the gospel which
you heard**. Being 'moved' or 'shaken', μετακινούμενοι, is seen as the
antithesis of steadfastness. Instead of 'moving away' from the faith,

the Colossians are called upon to remain centred on 'the hope of the gospel'. Although not linked as closely as here, the terms 'hope' and 'gospel' both occur in Col. 1:5. In that context the reference was to the 'hope laid up in the heaven' and this is declared to have been 'heard before in the word of the truth of the gospel'. Here also the auditory reception of the gospel proclamation is highlighted. Thus, while using a slightly different construction, **the hope** of which the author speaks is both future and heavenly, and involves closer union with Christ (cf. Col. 1:27). However, aspects of that hope are already experienced in the present. Communication of this hope has come to the Colossians through **the gospel**, which has already become a technical term in the Christian vocabulary, yet despite being a shorthand for the entire proclamation it still retains its primary sense of an announcement of good news. The Colossians' reception of the gospel is seen as an historical event, and here as in Col. 1:5 there is a reminder of the past when the gospel was accepted. Therefore the Colossians are encouraged to persevere in accordance with the faith which they heard when the gospel was announced, and to persist in that faith until they enjoy the full hope that the gospel promises. The language of this verse recalls many of the expressions and themes contained in the opening thanksgiving. In this way the whole opening section of the epistle is given a coherence, and by returning to these themes the section is shown to have an inner logic.

The amazing claim that the gospel can be considered as something **which has been preached in all creation which is under heaven** is not to be seen simply as authorial hyperbole (*contra* Dunn 1996: 112). Also, despite the self-reference to Paul that comes after this, it is unlikely that this is a celebration of the success of the Pauline mission. Instead, the cosmic perspective contained in preceding the hymnic section (Col. 1:16–20) causes the author to announce that the impact of the gospel has already been felt throughout **all creation**. Again this reiterates a claim made earlier. In the thanksgiving it is stated that the gospel had come to the Colossians 'just as also in all the world' (Col. 1:6). Here the same idea is expressed in slightly different terms, **has been preached in all creation**. The reference to 'creation' ties this idea to the language of the so-called Christological hymn, where Christ has been described as 'the firstborn of all creation' (Col. 1:15). The reference to all creation **which is under heaven**, is not drawing a distinction between the proclamation of the gospel in the earthly realm and in the heavenly sphere. Instead, it emphatically declares the universal scope of the reconciliation, and assures the Colossians that they are caught up in a divine act that has cosmic dimensions. Again, those who are instructed that they should not be moved from the faith, are encouraged with the theological perspective that the gospel has already had an impact on the whole of creation. Hence they should not regard themselves as part of some precarious and marginal movement, but instead they have experienced the hope of the gospel that has already been preached to the whole of creation.

The final clause, like the opening word in the epistle, draws attention to Paul. Here the connection is with the gospel, concerning which the author is able to declare **of which I, Paul, became a servant**. There is a degree of mutual reinforcement occurring here, both of the Pauline ministry and of the confidence the Colossians should have in the gospel he proclaims. Unlike the opening of the letter where Paul styles himself as 'an apostle of Christ Jesus', here he describes himself as **a servant** of the gospel. The term 'servant/minister', διάκονος, was used to describe Epaphras as 'a servant of Christ'. The original hand of Codex Sinaiticus replaces the term 'servant' with the more elevated description 'herald and apostle'. While the motivation for making that change is obvious, to attribute higher recognition to Paul, it jars with the tone of what is being affirmed. Here Paul is presenting himself as subservient to the gospel. His role is to bring about recognition of and allegiance to the gospel that he sees as already having been proclaimed in all creation. Therefore, rather than reassert his apostolic status, here Paul presents his own status as a servant of the gospel as a further way of motivating the Colossians to remain resolute in the faith.

This self-reference that **Paul** makes serves to link this concluding statement in the introduction to the material that follows, where Paul first outlines his suffering for the Colossians (Col. 1:24–29), and then his struggle on their behalf (Col. 2:1–5). His self-effacing description of himself as a servant leads naturally to a description of his sufferings, concerning which he offers a theological interpretation of their relationship to the afflictions of Christ.

6. PAUL'S SUFFERINGS ON BEHALF OF BELIEVERS   (1:24–29)

(24) Now I rejoice in the sufferings on your behalf and I fill up the things lacking of the afflictions of Christ in my flesh on behalf of his body, which is the church (25) of which I became a servant according to the stewardship of God which has been given to me for you, to fulfil the word of God, (26) the mystery that has been hidden away from the ages and from the generations – but now was made manifest to his holy ones, (27) to whom God wished to make known what is the wealth of the glory of this mystery among the Gentiles, which is Christ in you the hope of glory; (28) whom we proclaim, admonishing every man and teaching every man in all wisdom, that we may present every man perfect in Christ (29) for which I labour, striving in accord to the work of him who works in me in power.

It is often noted that the transition from the previous section to this one is based upon the closing reference to Paul in Col. 1:23, and the related discussion of Paul's ministry both here and in the following paragraph (Col. 2:1–5). However, the link may be even stronger than the simple continuation of the reference to Paul. The repeated phraseology referring first to the gospel 'of which I, Paul, became a servant' and then to the church 'of which I am a servant', reveals that the link is not just based loosely on the figure of Paul, but upon presenting the nature of the way he understands himself to be engaged in the service of Christ, and of the church which is Christ's body. The other contextual observation that needs to be borne in mind is the double reference to reconciliation in the previous sections (Col. 1:20, 22). If that idea is broad enough to encompass an understanding of reconciliation as encapsulating the redemption and refashioning of the cosmic order, then the sufferings of Paul described here nay be part of that larger process (Clark 2015: 9). Notwithstanding these thematic and verbal links, the transition from the previous section still appears somewhat abrupt.

The author's train of thought may be based on providing an apostolic example of firmness in the faith after the call to the Colossians to remain steadfast. In this way the author presents Paul's own perseverance in enduring suffering on behalf of the church as an encouragement and an example to the addressees to continue in the faith which they received. Moreover, this section permits the author to present his understanding of Paul's 'labour' in the service of Christ. Currently 'mission statements' appear to be in vogue. In this section of the letter the author presents what might accurately be described as a statement of Paul's missionary goals and intentions.

24 The opening statement attributed to Paul, **now I rejoice in the sufferings on your behalf**, reveals his attitude, his experiences, and the purpose he attributes to enduring suffering. The opening word **now**, νῦν, most frequently functions as a temporal marker, introducing something that was happening in the present timeframe of the author. Here, however, it functions as a weak logical conjunction, which justifies the continuation of the author's argument. The claim made by the author, **I rejoice**, even in the face of adverse circumstances, relativizes the significance of the sufferings. Yet the reason for being able to rejoice is not explicitly stated. Unlike other Pauline passages where sufferings are deemed insignificant in comparison with coming glory (Rom. 8:18), or considered as fleeting when placed alongside future coming glory (2 Cor. 4:17), here there is the basic affirmation that Paul rejoices in the face of what he suffers. This is not a Stoic perspective on suffering, where the quest for moral perfection came by freeing oneself from the passions – such as suffering – which caused emotional rather than reasoned responses. Here sufferings are not something that one needs to be freed from, but rather they can be embraced and are a cause for rejoicing. This is indeed a bold claim. Perhaps, in part, this type of outlook helped early Christians of later generations to conceptualize an understanding of martyrdom, not simply as a fleeting trial to be endured, but as a transformative event that strengthened the church and conformed the sufferer to the likeness of Christ. The ideas here are not as developed as those of later Christian thinkers (Tertullian, *Ad Martyras*), but nonetheless here the author sees sufferings as a cause for joy, not a reason for being shaken in the faith.

The specific nature of **the sufferings** is not disclosed. In fact, while most English translations gloss this phrase as 'my sufferings', and this is supported by several later Greek manuscripts or the correctors of earlier manuscripts ($\aleph^2$ 075 81 323 326 629 1241^s 1505 2464), there is no possessive pronoun in surviving early Greek manuscripts. While some have suggested that the sufferings being described here are those of Christ and not of Paul, given the remainder of the verse that seems highly unlikely. First, since 'these suffering are "for *you*" and not "for *us*" they refer to Paul's sufferings' (Sumney 2008: 96). Second, the passage continues by describing Paul's actions as filling up what is lacking in Christ's sufferings – the most natural way to read this is as a reference to Paul's own sufferings. Lastly, elsewhere in the Pauline corpus there are references to the apostle's sufferings (2 Cor. 1:6–7; 2 Tim. 3:11). While no description of Paul's sufferings is given, it is likely that what is being alluded to here are those afflictions that Paul experienced in connection with missionary work, and perhaps in particular those endured during periods of imprisonment. The theme of imprisonment is prominent in the final chapter, where it is stated that incarceration is a consequence of Paul's declaration of the mystery of God, 'because of which I am bound' (Col. 4:3), and in the final verse of the letter, where Paul calls upon the Colossians to 'remember my chains' (Col. 4:18). Thus Paul's incarceration at the hands of imperial authorities is perhaps the most likely way in which he sees his situation paralleling that of Christ, and perhaps leads to him seeing his sufferings as supplying something analogous to Christ own sufferings. The fullest list of such sufferings in Paul's writings refers to being whipped, beaten with rods, stoned, shipwrecked, adrift at sea, danger from robbers and various other parties, opposition from false brethren, sleepless nights, hunger and thirst, freezing conditions and exposure, and mental concern for the churches (2 Cor. 11:23–28). Paul sees such sufferings as being undertaken for the sake of his fledgling communities, and the Colossians are reminded of the representative nature of Paul's sufferings when the author states that they are **on your behalf**. Perhaps the daring thing about this claim is that it is made in reference to a community Paul had never seen. This provides some insight into the wider question of the purpose of Paul's sufferings that is described more fully in the next clause.

The next part of this verse has given rise to a host of different explanations, and resulted in major exegetical debates concerning the meaning of these words. Paul states, **and I fill up the things lacking of the afflictions of Christ in my flesh on behalf of his body, which is the church**. This pivotal issue revolves around the idea that something is 'lacking' is Christ's sufferings, and the related claim that Paul is able to compensate for this lack in his own flesh. The verbal clause describes a second aspect of the apostolic ministry that is paired with 'rejoicing in the sufferings'. The verb **fill up**, ἀνταναπληρῶ, is a compound verb with two prepositions affixed to the simple verbal form πληρόω that has the meaning of 'to fill' or even 'to fill up'. The sense of the double compound form does seem to intensify the meaning, with the emphasis on filling up to completion. The compounded form occurs only here in the New Testament, and only rarely elsewhere in surviving Greek literature (BDAG: 86–87). It is doubtful whether the first preposition affixed to the verb, ἀντί, retains any of its lexical meaning, 'in place of', or some kind of reciprocity in this verbal form. Therefore, the sense of the verb is 'filling up', or perhaps in this context the idea of 'supplementing' something. The reference to **the things lacking**, τὰ ὑστερήματα, is also problematic. Generally the term is used in contexts where there is reference to supplying a need due to the lack of something. Hence, Paul can refer to co-religionists who travelled from Macedonia as those who 'fully supplied my need', τὸ γὰρ ὑστερημά μου προσανεπλήρωσαν (2 Cor. 11:9). Likewise, in Col. 1:24, the idea is that of filling up or supplying something that is needed or lacking in the 'afflictions of Christ'. The phrase **the afflictions of Christ** is most naturally understood as denoting the passion sufferings of Jesus experienced at his crucifixion. This phrase seems to be paired in some way with 'the sufferings' of Paul mentioned in the previous clause. The structure of the sentences suggests that what is lacking in Christ's afflictions is supplied through Paul's sufferings, which are on behalf of believers.

The place where 'the things lacking' is supplied is said to be **in my flesh**. Most commonly in Pauline anthropology the term 'flesh', σάρξ, frequently carries negative connotations. In its most negative Pauline sense 'flesh' denotes the physical existence that is portrayed as an active antithesis to life in the spirit. From this perspective Paul can declare 'when we were in the flesh the sinful passions were in operation' (Rom. 7:5), or that 'no good thing dwells in me, that is in my flesh' (Rom. 7:18; cf. Rom. 8:6; Gal. 5:16–17; 6:8). However, here 'flesh' is a neutral term simply referring to Paul's physical body. This is the same sense that is intended later in the epistle (Col. 2:1). While this deviates from Paul's more common negative use of the term 'flesh', in other epistles the term can also be used in a neutral sense (Rom. 11:14; 1 Cor. 6:16; 15:39; 2 Cor. 7:1). Furthermore, Flemington has argued that the close co-ordination of the words 'in my flesh' with the immediately preceding phrase is the key to understanding the sense of this verse. He argues that the emphasis in on re-enactment. Thus he states, '[t]he Christian, by his incorporation in Christ called and empowered to re-enact what Christ did, is continually striving to make that reproduction in his own person more complete' (Flemington 1981: 88). While there is a long tradition of imitating the sufferings of Christ, if that were the sense in this context then it is difficult to understand why 'the sufferings' are portrayed as distinctively belonging to Paul on behalf of the church. Moreover, if the sense is that of imitating the sufferings of Christ, then it is not clear how this would fit into the wider argument at this point. Next, creating a parallel with the opening clause where Paul tells the Colossians that the sufferings he endures are 'on your behalf', he now declares that his action is filling up what is lacking in his Christ's tribulations is **on behalf of his body**, that is, Christ's body. This is immediately glossed with the explanatory comment, **which is the church**, so the Colossians may understand that the formula 'his body' is a reference to believers as Christ's body. This aligns with the way the term 'body' is used in the christological hymn as an ecclesial reference (Col. 1:18).

While the component parts of this verse can be understood, and they can be linked together into a comprehensible sentence, the issue is whether the author actually means what it appears that the verse is saying. That is, Christ's afflictions are incomplete or defective in some sense, Paul compensates for this lack through his own sufferings (which are on behalf of the church), and Paul's suffering might be vicarious in some way. The reason that such a reading, when construed in this way, is troubling is because it seems to clash with an understanding of the absolute redemptive value of Christ's suffering. This conflict does not just occur with later church doctrine, but appears to create a tension with what Paul writes elsewhere: 'the death that he died, he died to sin, once for all' (Rom. 6:10). Hence, the difficulty arises from the way in which the verse has been taken as referring to the redemptive value of Christ's afflictions. Prior to discussing the various interpretative proposals for this verse, it should be noted that while there are no exact parallels to Col. 1:24 in Paul's writings, there is some overlap with ideas expressed elsewhere. Paul can describe the suffering of believers as participatory events whereby they suffer for Christ's sake (Phil. 1:29). Thus in the wider Pauline corpus, there is a desire to explain why believers endure afflictions and also to create a theology of suffering that is linked to Christ's own suffering. In this vein, in Col. 1:24 Paul's sufferings are presented not as a cause for giving up on the faith, but as a reason to rejoicing and as such they are linked with Christ's own afflictions which likewise were on behalf of the church. However, it is the question of the relationship between Christ's afflictions and the supplementary role of Paul's sufferings that needs to be considered. There are a number of explanations that have been proposed to explain this relationship.

(1) If the reference to Christ's afflictions is understood as denoting his redemptive work, then 'filling up what is lacking in Christ's afflictions' would suggest that Paul's sufferings are also redemptive and supplement some incomplete aspect of Christ's passion. This should not be rejected simply because it is felt to be discordant with later theological statements, or even with Pauline theology, since if the letter is not authentically Pauline a later author could have misunderstood Paul's theology or represented his own. The main reason for rejecting this suggestion is because it does not fit with the wider perspectives of the letter. In Col. 1:14, in unequivocal terms, it is stated that in Christ believers 'have redemption, the forgiveness of sins'. This is presented as something that has already been achieved, and there is no sense that this requires supplementing to make it effective. Moreover, when the author shifts to the language of recon-ciliation, it is apparent that a fully effective act of peace-making has taken place through 'the blood of the cross' (Col. 1:20).

(2) Alternatively, the Greek genitive construction that stands behind the phrase 'the afflictions of Christ' has been seen by others not as a possessive genitive (i.e. not Christ's own afflictions), but as a qualitative genitive that denotes Christian afflictions in general. On this reading Paul would be filling up afflictions that are con-nected with followers of Christ that are 'deemed a necessary step in the completion of what is required for the growth of the church'

(MacDonald 2000: 79). This interpretation has a long pedigree. The sixth-century commentator Theodore of Mopsuestia asks, 'What was it that was lacking? That by learning what are those things that have been accomplished for you, you may receive the promise of them. But this can by no means be done without toil and afflictions. Therefore, I suffer for this…so that believing with the soul's affection you may gain familial intimacy with him.' As becomes apparent in Theodore's discussion, the wider context seems to make it difficult to hold to understanding the phrase as Christian afflictions in general, but instead the qualitative sense seems to point towards something imposed uniquely upon Paul.

(3) The construction may also be taken as an objective genitive. In this sense the passage would be speaking of sufferings endured 'for the sake of Christ'. While theologically this fits with a broader way of conceptualizing Christian suffering as being a result of allegiance to Christ, within the specific context of Col. 1:24–29 it is not clear why Paul alone would be entrusted with such sufferings, or why it would be said that something was lacking in the affliction from persecution that believers endure.

(4) Given the centrality of participatory language in Pauline thought, another alternative that has been suggested is that through mystical union with Christ, Paul sees himself as supplementing and continuing Christ's suffering for the church. There is a difference of scholarly opinion as to whether Paul alone can supplement Christ's suffering through his apostolic ministry (Deissmann and Schmid), or whether all believers continued adding to Christ's afflictions through their own sufferings (Dibelius and Schneider). O'Brien rejects this interpretation since 'it seems incomprehensible how, in the light of this intimate communion of sufferings, there could be a measure of afflictions which still lacked something' (O'Brien 1982: 78).

(5) Perhaps the point of view that has become most prevalent among recent commentators is that the supplemenary activity that Paul sees himself as undertaking refers to filling up the quota of messianic afflictions. There are two major strengths of this suggestion. First, it does not diminish the wider perspective of the letter that Christ's sufferings bring about a complete redemption and reconciliation. Second, there are examples in Second Temple Jewish literature that reflect a wider understanding that the time prior to the coming of the Messiah would be a period of affliction for the faithful – these are

the 'messianic woes' that precede the Messiah's appearance. Hence in the Enochic description of the Son of Man, the Chosen One, prior to his coming, there is acknowledgment that 'that the blood of the righteous ones had been shed' and that 'endurance might not be their lot forever'. However, such things occur before 'the books of the living were opened in his presence…and the hearts of the holy ones were filled with joy' (*1 En.* 45–57; esp. 47:2–3). The Syriac *Apocalyse of Baruch* is even more fulsome, describing the duration and nature of the twelve calamities that precede the coming of the Anointed One. After enduring the sequence of commotions, slaughter, many dying, the sword, famine and drought, earthquake and terrors, appearance of ghosts and demons, falling fire, rape and violence, injustice and unchastity, then disorder and mixture of all that came before, it is only 'when all that which should come to pass in these parts has been accomplished, that the Anointed One will begin to be revealed' (*2 Apoc. Bar.* 26–30). Similarly, in the New Testament there are apocalyptic understandings of 'birthpangs' that precede the return of the Messiah (Mt. 24:1–31; Mk 13:1–27).

The major problem with applying this understanding to Col. 1:24 is that that passage itself and the rest of the letter appear to be unconcerned with apocalpytic motifs. As MacDonald observes, 'Colossians reveals virtually no interest in the imminent expectation of the end, and in fact, displays little interest even in the future' (MacDonald 2000: 79). However, despite this lack of eschatological interest, many commentators read the 'afflications of Christ' as the sufferings that Paul must endure prior to the return of the Messiah. Thus Harris states that Paul views 'his apostolic suffering as his own distinctive contribution towards reducing the "deficiency" in the divinely appointed quota of sufferings to be patiently endured by the messianic community in the last days' (Harris 2010: 60). Similarly, Dunn takes the phrase as a reference to 'the means of transition from the old age to the new' (Dunn 1996: 115). Moo states that the things lacking that required filling up 'are the tribulations that are inevitable and necessary as God's kingdom faces the opposition of the "dominion of darkness"… Paul's ministry has special apocalyptic significance' (Moo 2008: 152). Bird takes a more participatory rather than eschato-logical slant on the 'messianic woes'. He states, 'the messianic woes continue to be absorbed by the body of the Messiah, who continues the work of providing a suffering witness and so completes the role that was unfulfilled at the first advent of the Messiah' (Bird 2009: 66). Despite the strong support for this reading, the problem of a lack of interest in eschatological matters in the remainder of the letter suggests more caution is required in regard to this option than has been displayed by a number of commentators.

(6) The image combines both Jewish and Stoic reflections on noble death. Certain Jewish texts see the suffering and death of the righteous as vicarious and capable on atoning (*4 Macc.* 12:7; 17:21–22). In Stoic thought sufferings endured with dignity are exemplary. Thus Seneca can write of afflictions that 'they may teach others to endure them; they were born to be a pattern' (*Prov.* 6.6). On the basis of these influences Sumney suggests that Paul's sufferings are vicarious but not expiatory. Hence he suggests that '[b]oth understandings of vicarious suffering appear in close proximity in Colossians: Christ's expiatory suffering is the theme of 1:18–23 and Paul's mimetic (imitative) suffering appears in 1:24. Such a juxtaposition is not difficult for readers accustomed to thinking in these categories' (Sumney 2008: 101). There is little doubt that Paul portrays his ministry and suffering as exemplary. However, it is unlikely that Stoic categories inform the outlook here. First, rather than the Stoic notion of enduring suffering, Paul presents himself as rejoicing in his sufferings. This reading does not clarify what is lacking in Christ's afflictions, unless it is the ongoing example of suffering itself.

While the reasons for the attractiveness of understanding 'the sufferings' as related to filling up the messianic afflications are obvious, and while it resolves some difficult theological problems and the idea is documentable in broadly contemporary literature, the difficulty is that it appears foreign to the author's train of thought. It is probably better to seek an interpretation that has closer connection with the wider context of the letter. The double reference to reconciliation in the previous sections (Col. 1:20, 22) may reflect those ideas at the forefront at the author's thought at this point. Christ's role in the reconciliation of the entire creation (Col. 1:20) is inextricably linked to and exemplified in the reconciliation of the Colossians believers (Col. 1:22). For the author of the letter, the cosmic drama is focalized in Colossae, with the reconciling work of Christ resulting in the Colossians being presented 'holy and blameless and without reproach' (Col. 1:22). Paul is presented as being caught up in this reconciliation of the Colossians, by suffering on their behalf through his imprisonment to ensure that they 'persevere in the faith' and are not 'moved from the hope of the gospel' (Col. 1:23). Thus Paul's sufferings are unique, and are on behalf of the Colossians as they themselves become enfolded in the cosmic reconciliation established by Christ, and as that act of reconciliation made effective through 'the blood of the cross' (Col. 1:20) demonstrates Christ's preeminence over the entire created order.

25 The relative pronoun that commences this verse is connected to the preceding reference to the church, and in the context of the letter Paul defines his calling and work in relation to the ecclesial body: **of which I became a servant**. The term 'servant', διάκονος, was used two verses earlier where Paul also declares himself to have become a servant, but in that context the backward reference of the relative pronoun is to the gospel. For Paul, being a servant of the gospel and being a servant of the church were integrally related and inseparable aspects of his calling. While the self-description as a 'servant', διάκονος, is not the most common term that Paul uses to describe himself in other letters, when he does use such terminology of himself it reinforces some of the ideas being expressed here. In 1 Cor. 3:5, he tells the Corinthians that both he and Apollos are 'servants through whom you believed'. Also, in a plural reference that refers to Paul and presumably his co-worker Timothy, Paul writes that they are 'servants of a new covenant' (2 Cor. 3:6). In the same epistle, the same pair are described as 'servants of God' (2 Cor. 6:4), and also Paul differentiates himself from so-called servants of Christ stating he is more qualified to possess that title on the basis of his sufferings (2 Cor. 11:23). In a passage that probably draws directly upon the language of Col. 1:23, 25, in Ephesians Paul is described as a servant/minister of the gospel (Eph. 3:7). Therefore, the singular usage found in Col. 1:23, 25, is distinctive (apart from the Ephesians reference), but not without some antecedent in the wider Pauline writings. This role, in the present context, is defined in terms of being a servant both of the gospel and of the church, with presumably the former encapsulating the idea of service to Christ with the goal of producing new communities of believers. It is in this way that both gospel and ecclesial servanthood are bound together.

Paul moves on from defining the nature of his servant role in relation to the church, to describing its source. He states he became a servant **according to the stewardship of God which has been given to me**. The stress is upon the fact that the role Paul occupies is divinely designated, not due to self-appointment. The ministry that Paul exercises accords with God's apportioning of this work on behalf of both the gospel and the church to Paul. The Greek term that has been translated as **stewardship**, οἰκονομία, is difficult to render into English while catching the exact nuance in Greek. It is the term from which the English word 'economics' is derived. However, this technical sense would be misleading and anachronistic. Nonetheless, this more technical sense develops in patristic theology where the category of 'economy' was used to denote God's external actions directed towards creation, in distinction from discussion of the internal or ontological relationships within the Trinity. The usage here is removed from these later technical senses. In Classical Greek the term referred to the practical craft of running and maintaining a household (Plato, *Ap*. 36b; *Repub*. 498a; Xenophon, *Oec*. i.1). While this may be closer to the meaning in the New Testament, the term has become more closely connected with the role of a 'steward' as administering a household on behalf of a master. Therefore, it appears that the reference in Col. 1:25 is a way of designating the position or 'office' given to Paul, rather than simply speaking of an assigned task. Paul is speaking of a special commission given to him by God. This commission or stewardship is to be a servant of the gospel, and this understanding is brought out elsewhere is Paul's writings when he declares 'woe is me if I do not preach the gospel, for…I have a stewardship entrusted to me' (1 Cor. 9:17). When various elements of the description of this stewardship are brought together, such as the divine act of giving this stewardship and the fact that the recipient is Paul, these aspects highlight the understanding of Paul's unique role in spreading the gospel and establishing the church. This lends further weight to the suggestion in relation to the former verse that Paul is speaking of his unique role in filling up what is lacking in the afflictions of Christ, and not presenting himself as an example of a more general requirement that is placed on all believers.

Having described the nature and source of his role as a servant of the gospel and his commission as a steward of God, Paul next mentions the beneficiaries of his ministry, telling his addressees that his role as a servant of the church is **for you**. While Paul's role as a servant and steward is likely to be envisaged as something unique, his claim that he exercised this ministry for the Colossians is not a declaration that they are the exclusive recipients or beneficiaries of that role. Rather, this statement is presented for the rhetorical purpose of strengthening the connection with a community Paul had not visited. Thus it highlights the perspective that despite this lack of direct personal contact Paul's proclamation of the gospel benefits all gentile believers through the apostle's disclosure of the mystery of God (Col. 1:27). By so doing, the Colossians are linked into the divine purpose, for although God gave a unique 'stewardship' to Paul this was not an end in itself, but rather it was a means of serving nascent communities of Gentile believers.

Finally, the purpose of Paul's ministry is described in the pithy and somewhat opaque expression **to fulfil the word of God**. Precisely how the word of God is fulfilled or brought to completion is described in the next two verses (Col. 1:26–27). There the language of disclosure, which may have been part of the wider religious context of the recipients of the letter, may be informing the description of the purpose of Paul's ministry. It is to reveal a divine mystery that had been previously hidden from Gentiles. Here the phrase **the word of God** is used synonymously with 'the gospel' that was mentioned previously (Col. 1:23), and both phrases are Christian shorthand terms that encapsulate the proclamation of the work of redemption achieved in Christ that brings Gentiles into restored relationship with God. It is in Col. 1:28 that the goal of Paul's ministry in fulfilling the word of God in relation to the Colossians and other Gentile believers is more fully stated, namely that every person may be presented perfect in Christ.

Therefore, the compressed language of this verse describes Paul's role as a servant of the newly formed communities of believers; it emphasizes that Paul did not take this role upon himself but that this commission was conferred by God. While the role was unique, it was not about self-fulfilment but for the benefit of the Colossians and others, and the purpose was that the word of God should achieve its intended aim. This aim is unpacked in the following verses but climaxes with the statement that the goal is to present every person perfect in Christ (Col. 1:28). So, in this description one observes immense confidence in Paul's sense of unique vocation as a servant of the gospel and of the church. However, the goal is not presented as self-aggrandizement but the perfection of recent Gentile believers.

26 In an explanatory comment, the phrase **the mystery that has been hidden away** stands alongside the reference to 'the word of God' and serves as a reformulation of the same idea in a way that allows it to be explored from a different angle. This casts light on the magnitude of the revelatory disclosure of God's eternal purposes that is now being announced through the preaching of the gospel. While the term **mystery** may resonate with the usage of such terminology in the so-called mystery cults, in Colossians the link is not an appropriation of the theology of such cults, but more like a subversion of their claims. The author declares that it is in the message of the gospel that the true mystery of God is revealed. If the situation that caused the epistle to be written was a concern over some believers in Colossae combining their faith in Christ with elements of mystery cult belief (Arnold 1995: 271), then the language here rebuts the claim that anything needs to be combined with the message of the gospel for it is itself the full revelation of all mystery of God. In this extended section of the letter (Col. 1:24–2:5) the term 'mystery' becomes prominent, occurring three times (Col. 1:26, 27; 2:2). However, it is only in the last of those references that this 'mystery of God' is identified, where the author explicitly states that the mystery is Christ. Moreover, access to that mystery was previously impossible since it had **been hidden away**. What has changed this state of affairs is the reconciliation of all creation that Christ has brought about, and Paul's role as a servant of the gospel, whose task is proclamation of that message.

The mystery now being proclaimed has been hidden **from the ages and from the generations**. This may mean more than simply asserting that the 'mystery' made known through Paul's preaching was not capable of being known until the period in time when Christ brought about reconciliation. The author may see the 'ages' and the 'generations' as denoting cosmic forces. It is unnecessary to see this rhetoric as responding to a fully fledged gnostic system in order for the terms to be seen as denoting other worldly powers. Therefore, the terms may refer to beings who were thought to have existed throughout the span of time, in much the same way as 'thrones', 'lordships', 'rulers', and 'authorities' function in Col. 1:16. This idea may be seen as more plausible when it is recognized that in Jewish and early Christian thought of the present age as being 'dominated by Satan and his angels'. While there may be more to intended meaning of **the ages** than just a temporal sense, the more straightforward meaning of an extended period of time is certainly present in this term. Similarly, while the reference to the mystery being hidden **from the generations** might denote the generations from the beginning of the created order, again more may be intended. If the previous reference to 'the ages' denotes personal but non-earthly beings who were unable to gain insight into the hidden mystery, this reference to the generations may describe earthly beings or successive human generations who likewise have not had the divine mystery revealed to them.

The second part of the verse presents the new and contrasting situation that exists. Thus the author is able to declare that whereas the mystery was previously hidden, it is now possible to say in relation to the mystery that: that it was now **made manifest to his holy ones**. What had once been hidden and impenetrable to previous generations has been revealed to those who have been reconciled in Christ. This new state of affairs is introduced by the phrase **but now**, νῦν δέ, which unlike the use of 'now' in Col. 1:24 takes the common temporal meaning here that contrasts with the 'hiddenness' that prevailed in former ages and among previous generations. Now the previously unknowable mystery has been **made manifest**, or known through the proclamation of Christ in the message of the gospel. The scope of this revelatory act is directed to all believers – that is, **to his holy ones**. Within the newly formed community there is an equality of access to this divine unveiling of the mystery. Such a claim may be intended to contrast with those in the community who may have wanted to induct believers into fuller or deeper mysteries available only to a select few. By contrast, here there is a democratization of the revelatory experience for all believers, and a rejection of hierarchies in the new community. This is consistent with the previous use of the **holy ones** (Col. 1:4), where the reference to love of the holy ones was a characteristic that showed that the Colossians were themselves part of the wider community of believers in Christ. So here all those who are believers in Christ have both access to, and knowledge of, the mystery that was formerly inaccessible.

27 Moreover, the gaining of such knowledge of 'the mystery' was not something that had to be prised away from the deity, or was only divinely disclosed in recognition of great effort on the part of the one who gained this insight. This act of divine self-disclosure stands in contrast to some of the foundational myths of certain mystery religions. Rather, this was entirely the divine initiative, giving such knowledge to those **to whom God wished to make known** the mystery. Again, this group to whom God wished to disclose 'the mystery' is the same group referred to as the 'holy ones' at the end of the previous verse, as is made clear by the linking relative pronoun. Here God's wish is not simply some ephemeral possibility, but the determined purpose of his will – what God wishes comes about. The verb **wished**, ἠθέλησεν, is in the aorist tense, used both because the author provides commentary on God's purpose from a neutral vantage point (the perfective verbal aspect) as an almost objective description, and because the aorist indicative tense allows the author to describe a decision of God determined at some point in the past. In this context the author does not clarify how far back in the past the divine decision was made to reveal the mystery. In Ephesians, which draws upon the ideas in Colossians, there is an obvious theological reflection on the salvific events being determined by God in his eternal purposes. Thus believers were chosen in Christ 'before the foundation of the world' (Eph. 1:4), they were 'predestined...to adoption as sons' (Eph. 1:5), and the inheritance they received in Christ 'was predestined according to his [God's] purpose' (Eph. 1:11). While the temporal origin of God's decision is not explored in Colossians, the emphasis falls on the divine intention **to make known** the mystery 'to his holy ones' (Col. 1:26). The action undertaken by God in making known the mystery may be a further rebuttal of ecstatic or visionary revelations. Sumney argues that the claim that God is the source of revelation 'counters the visionaries' claims that the revelation necessary for a relationship with God comes in visionary experiences' (Sumney 2008: 105–106). While the 'opponents' at best remain shadowy, and may even be a hypothetical possibility (Hooker 1973: 315–31), the description here certainly shows the Colossians that true disclosure of the mystery was an action that God intentionally brought about.

Before proceeding to define the content of 'the mystery' in the final clause of this verse, Paul first describes its qualitative value. He states that God had made known to his holy ones **what is the wealth of the glory of this mystery among the Gentiles**. The mystery is here described in terms of wealth and glory, and its disclosure is among the Gentiles, which is yet another way of designating those described as God's 'holy ones' in the previous verse. However, in this context there is no theological explanation of the relationship between Jews and Gentiles and the respective ways in which they are included in the divine salvific privileges (cf. Rom. 1:16). The opening word in this clause, **what**, τί, is an interrogative pronoun, but can be 'used with a noun denoting quality or quantity' (Harris 2010: 63). The term πλοῦτος, translated here as **wealth**, describes the abundance supply of earthly goods or the plentiful supply of another commodity and may refer to 'wealth', 'abundance', or 'riches'. The term **glory** has already been used in the letter in reference to God who empowers the Colossians with 'the might of his glory' (Col. 1:11). In that context, the reference to 'glory' appeared to be rooted in the Hebrew idea of *kavod*, which describes the splendour of God, and is used to depict the dwelling place of God. While these wider resonances may inform the understanding here, the term 'glory', δόξα, appears to be intended in a more adjectival sense as describing the type of wealth associated with the mystery. If this is correct, then the construction in Greek is intended to communicate the surpassing value of the revealed mystery, perhaps with the intended sense of 'the glorious wealth of this mystery'. The phrase **the wealth of the glory** is found elsewhere in the Pauline letters (Rom. 9:23; Eph. 1:18; 3:16). Interestingly, in the passage from Rom. 9:23, like the usage here, Paul uses this phraseology 'to comment upon the inclusion of Gentiles among the people of God' (Sumney 2008: 105).

For the author of Colossians this mystery of surpassing value is revealed **among the Gentiles**. From a Jewish perspective the Greek term in its plural form, τὰ ἔθνη, typical translated as 'the Gentiles', denoted non-Jews. In wider Greek use the term was an inclusive way of referring to 'the nations' as a whole (this may be closer to the sense intended in Mt. 28:19). The message of the inclusion of the Gentiles among God's people was a fundamental aspect of Paul's proclamation and of his self-identity as apostle to the Gentiles. It is a common feature in Paul's thought to reflect upon the way in which gentiles have been incorporated into the people of God (cf. Rom. 9–11, esp. 11:11–24). Here, however, as well as in the rest of the letter (with the exception of Col. 3:11), there is virtually no interest in the Jews *per se*, or in the way Gentiles can be included alongside them in God's soteriological purposes. It is unclear what this reveals. Perhaps it shows that the setting in Colossians was one where Jews were not prominent, perhaps that the community to which the letter was addressed was overwhelmingly Gentile in character, or that, if the author was not Paul, while he has picked up on Paul's proclamation of the gospel to the Gentiles, he is not as attuned to his intellectual struggle to explain how Gentiles are included alongside Jews who were the recipients of God's promises. Instead of seeking to resolve this theological conundrum, the letter simply speaks of the mystery that has been unveiled among the Gentiles, and there is a celebration that what had been hidden away throughout the ages (Col. 1:26) is now revealed to the holy ones drawn from every nation.

Finally, the explanation of the nature of the mystery is stated explicitly, yet succinctly: **which is Christ in you the hope of glory**. Hence the mystery is explained as the indwelling presence of Christ among believers. Elsewhere in Paul's letters the key participatory phrase 'in Christ' frequently comes to the fore (cf. Rom. 8:1; 1 Cor. 1:30). By contrast, in this context the expression varies, and the metaphor speaks of Christ dwelling in the Colossians, rather than believers dwelling in Christ. However, in the next verse the more typical formulation surfaces, with the letter stating that Paul's goal is to present every person 'perfect in Christ' (Col. 1:28). The absence of references to the spirit in Colossians may be due in part to the way Christ himself is understood as an indwelling presence in believers. The concept of Christ dwelling in believers is not unique to Colossians. In Rom. 8:10 Paul can simultaneously affirm that 'the spirit of God dwells in you' and 'Christ dwells in you'.

Next the content, or perhaps better the consequence, of understanding the nature of the mystery is further expanded with the phrase **the hope of glory**. This is the second time 'glory' has been mentioned in this verse. Hope has also been a prominent term in the vocabulary of this chapter, with the author reminding the Colossians of 'the hope laid up for you in the heavens' (Col. 1:5), and also encouraging them not to be moved away from 'the hope of the gospel' (Col. 1:23). Here, then, the author describes two aspects of the mystery. The first is the present experience of the indwelling presence of Christ, and the second is the future hope for closer heavenly union with Christ. In this way, the letter appears to envisage a transformative process whereby believers have already begun to experience the presence of Christ in them and their lives begin to be conformed to the model of Christ-centred values. It is 'the hope of glory' which will see that process come to fulfillment, and in the next verse Paul speaks of his ongoing role in continuing that transformative process.

28 This verse illustrates the interlocking nature of theology and ethics in Pauline thought. The opening assertion, **whom we proclaim**, returns to the first person plural form of address, after a sequence of singular references, i.e. 'of which I, Paul, became a servant' (Col. 1:23); 'now I rejoice in my sufferings…I fill up' (Col. 1:24); and 'of which I became a servant' (Col. 1:25). In fact, the first person plural form of address has not been explicit since the assurance that Paul and presumably Timothy were interceding on behalf of the Colossians, 'Because of this we also…have not ceased praying' (Col. 1:9). Here the first person plural form is likely to designate Paul and Timothy, but perhaps also the other co-workers such as Epaphras already mentioned. It might also be alluding to Tychicus and Onesimus, who will be mentioned later (Col. 4:7, 9). Transmission of the Christian message with the focus falling upon Christ is perhaps the central task that author has identified as being the work that he is entrusted to carry out. Although using a different form of expression, this idea of Paul's role in communicating the Christian message is stated most clearly in Col. 1:23: 'the gospel of hope…which was proclaimed… of which I, Paul, became a servant'. The focus is on the ongoing action of describing the significance of Christ, whom Paul and his co-workers continue to **proclaim**, καταγγέλλομεν ('we proclaim'). The primary vehicle for the disclosure of the mystery, which is 'Christ in you', is none other than the apostolic proclamation of the gospel. This proclamation unveils truths that had been long hidden from those who now enjoy status as 'the holy ones' (Col. 1:26).

The purpose of the proclamation is the continuing moral formation of those who adhere to the Christian message. This enables Paul to see the proclamation of Christ as functioning for the purpose of **admonishing every man and teaching every man in all wisdom**. The male-centred terminology, **man**, reflects the patriarchal society of the author's day. For liturgical purposes, inclusive language would better capture the universal scope of thought here, and inclusive translations such as 'every person' or 'everyone' (NRSV, NIV) are common in modern English bibles. Here, however, the gendered language is preserved to reflect the author's ancient cultural perspectives. The expression **every man** appears to function almost as a refrain in this verse, being repeated on three occasions. In fact, this is a subset of the author's high frequency (perhaps even excessive) use of the term 'every'/'all' = πᾶς (thus far 19 times, cf. Col. 1:4, 6, 9, 10 [twice], 11 [twice], 15, 16 [twice], 17 [twice], 18, 19, 20, 23, 28 [three times]). Such fulsome language expresses completeness, abundance, and superlative qualities, which encapsulate the unparalleled state of affairs brought about through the proclamation of the gospel. Here Paul speaks of the goal of the universal moral reform of all humanity as every person experiences the indwelling presence of Christ. The combination of 'admonishing' and 'teaching' has precedent among Greek authors such as Plato (*Pro.* 323 D; *Leg.* 845 B), Plutarch (*Mor.* 46), Dio Chrysostom (*Or.* 33.369). Together the terms **admonishing...and teaching** speak of exhorting and instructing people to do something or to behave in a certain manner. The giving of advice may be intended to provide guidance in relation to future behaviour. The term **admonishing**, νουθετοῦντες, may suggest that advice is given as a corrective, since the Greek term does carry the connotation of a 'reprimand' or 'rebuke' that is also common in contemporary English usage. However, it is likely that the sense is more constructive, and aligns with the second action of 'teaching'. With the exception of Acts 20:32 (a speech placed on Paul's lips), the other usages of the term 'admonish' all occur in Pauline writings (Rom. 15:14; 1 Cor. 4:14; Col. 3:16; 1 Thess. 5:12, 14; 2 Thess. 3:15).[2] Similarly, **teaching** is understood to be part of Paul's apostolic task in establishing communities of believers. Elsewhere Paul reminds the Corinthians of the ways of Christ, which, he says, 'I teach everywhere in every church' (1 Cor. 4:17). Such instruction is not limited to the initial proclamation of the gospel, but the continuing instruction that Paul and his co-workers provide to the newly founded congregations. These acts of 'admonishing and

---

[2] There is a variant reading in Tit. 1:11, where the verb νουθετέω also occurs in an expanded reading in minuscule 460.

teaching' are said to be **in all wisdom** (cf. Col. 1:9). The phrase is more likely to designate the way in which Paul and his companions teach those for whom they have pastoral responsibility, rather than denoting the content of the teaching. This is because the dative construction ἐν πάσῃ σοφίᾳ refers to the mode or means by which the teaching takes place. When the content of teaching is mentioned, Greek writers use an accusative construction (Harris 2010: 66). Thus the teaching strategy is based upon a wise and reflective approach that aims to produce mature and steadfast believers, who are predisposed to morally correct behaviour.

Such an act of admonishing and teaching each individual has as its end purpose the hope **that we may present every man perfect in Christ**. Individual perfection or completion, according to Colossians, is not something attainable by only a few élite believers, but is universalized as the stated instructional goal for all the holy ones. Writing on behalf of himself and his co-workers, Paul states the aim **that we may present** all believers in a perfect state. This act of 'presentation' reveals Paul's understanding of his responsibility in ushering believers towards the fulness of their heavenly destiny. This perspective on the apostolic responsibility in presenting believers in a state of maturity and purity is described elsewhere, when Paul informs the Corinthians that 'I betrothed you to one husband, that I present you as a pure virgin to Christ' (2 Cor. 11:2). However, responsibility for being presented in an acceptable state before God is not Paul's responsibility alone, it is also incumbent on individuals to work towards this goal: 'I urge you…to present your bodies as a living and holy sacrifice, acceptable to God' (Rom. 12:1). This reference from Rom. 12:1, in combination with Greek term τέλειος – 'mature', 'complete', or 'perfect' – may be suggestive of sacrificial terminology. The same term is used in the Septuagint to describe an unblemished Passover sacrifice: 'you shall have a *perfect* sheep, a one-year old male' (LXX Exod. 12:5). Here the metaphor of presentation of offering does not refer to physical perfection, but is extended to denote being **perfect** both ethically and spiritually. Again the inclusivity of this goal is stated, with the aim being that **every man** may be presented perfect **in Christ**. Here believers' existence **in Christ** balances the author's explanation of the mystery in the previous verse, which is explained as 'Christ in you'. Thus, the author plays with slightly different metaphors to describe the way in which the Colossians have been united with Christ. It is because of this union with Christ that striving for perfection becomes an ethical imperative. To remain in any other moral state would not befit union with the one who is the image of the invisible God.

29 In explicit terms, Paul describes his commitment to bringing about the goal of presenting believers who are perfect or mature in Christ. Thus he states that it is to obtain this purpose **for which I labour**. This **labour** is not a one-off event. Paul is characterized as being engaged in intense labour and **striving** in a continuous manner. The term used here to describe this consistent 'striving', ἀγωνιζόμενος, is frequently used in wider Greek literature as a description of athletic effort. In fact, Paul draws upon this athletic metaphor when he states of those competing in a running race that 'every one that strives/competes exercises self-control in all things' (1 Cor. 9:24–27). However, here in Col. 1:29 the idea of 'striving' is not linked with athletic discipline, but functions to intensify the image of Paul's labour (cf. Phil. 2:16). Later in the letter it is Epaphras who is described as 'striving' for the Colossians in his prayers (Col. 4:12). The notion of apostolic labour on behalf of believers is a Pauline concept (cf. 1 Cor. 4:12; 15:10; Gal. 4:11; Phil. 2:16; 1 Thess. 5:12). As several of those references reveal, Paul recognizes the labours of others, as well as himself, who work tirelessly for the benefit of the various communities of believers. In this context, however, the description is of Paul's apostolic labour alone. The possibility that this could descend into a self-aggrandizing affirmation or a celebration of superior human effort is avoided. The work undertaken is not achieved through personal effort, but **according to the work of him who works in me in power**. The apostolic labour is not determined by personal design, or reflection on what needs to be done for the Colossians. Rather, it aligns with the purposes of the one who is also at work in Paul and in the believers at Colossae. However, the passage is not unambiguous in identifying the one **who works in me**. Given the previous description of the 'mystery' as 'Christ in you', perhaps the most immediate way to understand this reference is as developing the idea of Christ's indwelling presence by stating he is the one empowering Paul in his apostolic toils. Elsewhere, however, in the context of describing his apostolic toil, Paul can say 'I laboured more than all of them, yet not I, but the grace of God with me' (1 Cor. 15:10). Therefore, in this context it may be more plausible to see a reversion to speaking about the way God is at work in Paul, rather than remaining fixed upon the image of the indwelling of Christ.

Here what sustains Paul to be able to carry this burden for the churches (cf. 2 Cor. 11:28) is the inner-working or inwardly energizing divine presence. This 'work' (ἐνέργεια) describes God's activity, which operates as a supernatural force enabling Paul to bear his continuous labour. Through acknowledging the inner divine presence **of him who works in me**, Paul is able to stress that he does not undertake or accomplish these tasks in his own strength. This acknowledgment serves to shift the focus from Paul's individual efforts, and refocus attention on the labour itself, which is ultimately a divine work. The accomplishment of the task and the effectiveness of Paul in carrying out the labour are both reinforced by the declaration that God is at work in Paul **in power**. The point is that the effort required to present believers perfect in Christ is strenuous, yet it is a task underwritten and guaranteed by the powerful inner working of God. In this way the Colossians are assured that the transformative work begun in them will be brought to completion as they themselves are presented 'perfect in Christ'. This is because it is the powerful working of God who will bring this about for all believers.

7. PAUL'S STRIVING ON BEHALF OF THE COLOSSIANS (2:1–5)

(1) For I want you to know how great a struggle I have on your behalf and those in Laodicea and all those who have not seen my face in the flesh, (2) that their hearts might be encouraged, having been knit together in love and in all the wealth of the assurance of understanding, in the knowledge of the mystery of God, which is Christ (3) in whom are all the treasures of wisdom and knowledge hidden. (4) This I say that no-one may delude you with persuasive speech (5) for even if I am absent in the flesh, yet in the spirit I am with you, rejoicing and seeing your order and the firmness of your faith in Christ.

1 Commencing with a typical disclosure formula, Paul is depicted as moving from a general description of the universal nature of his apostolic suffering and labour, to an explanation of how such toil benefits the Colossians, other inhabitants of the Lycus Valley, and those in the same category as the Colossians who have not met Paul first-hand. The formulaic phrase **for I want you to know** is a familiar Pauline expression (Phil. 1:12; cf. 1 Cor. 11:3; 12:3; Gal. 1:11). Paul also often uses a form of disclosure with a double negative 'I do not want you not to know/to be unaware' (Rom. 1:13; 1 Cor. 10:1; 12:1; 2 Cor. 1:8). It has been suggested that typically Paul uses the positive form 'when he supposes that the information is already known to the addressees' and the double negative form 'to impart new information' (Collins 1999: 368). Here the usage appears to deviate from that pattern, with the positive form being used to relate information to the Colossians concerning which they were previously unaware. The Colossians who had not had previous contact with Paul were presumably previously unaware of his ministry and work on their behalf. Therefore Paul relates the specific impact his apostolic labour has upon the communities of believers in the Lycus Valley.

Building on the general discussion of the apostolic labour in the previous verse, here the matter that Paul wishes the Colossians to know is **how great a struggle I have on your behalf**. In the previous paragraph that struggle related to the instructional and formative task undertaken by Paul and his co-workers with the goal of producing mature believers in Christ. Although not in tension with that description, in this paragraph the purpose of the struggle is expressed differently, and will be unpacked in the following verse. However, Paul's initial point is to assure the Colossians that the striving or struggle that he described in the previous verse, and mentions again here, is indeed on their behalf. Paul also refers to the believers in the neighbouring town of Laodicea as the second element of his tripartite list, **and those in Laodicea**. Later in the letter he will also refer to Hierapolis (Col. 4:13) in combination with Colossae and Laodicea, thereby encompassing the three major population centres of the Lycus region.

The third element in the list of beneficiaries broadens Paul's particular focus from a specific geographic region into a claim for the universal significance of his apostolic work. Thus he claims that the same struggle that is on behalf of Colossian and Laodicean believers also impacts positively upon **all those who have not seen my face in the flesh**. While a face-to-face encounter may usually be an essential element in forging a bond, as will become evident in Col. 2:5, for Paul the deeper bond between believers is envisaged as being formed at a spiritual level. While some have extracted from this phrase the theory that the author intended the letter to have a universal scope (Schenk 1987: 3334), rather than describing the intended reach of the epistle, it is more likely that the statement provides a theological perspective on the scope of Paul's apostolic ministry.

2 Having described the apostolic strivings, and their universal scope for all believers – not just those to whom Paul had ministered directly – the author proceeds to outline the purpose of this struggle. Here the letter seeks to provide its recipients with encouragement, assurance, and knowledge. Thus having disclosed the struggle on behalf of the Colossians and all others who have not seen his face, Paul's first declared purpose in this labour for all these believers with whom he is not personally acquainted is **that their hearts might be encouraged, having been knit together in love**. The subjunctive clause introduces a condition that although not yet fulfilled is, nevertheless, expected to be accomplished through the disclosure of Paul's work on behalf of the Colossians. Paul's description of his labour is the basis of the encouragement that he expects will be produced in the recipients of the letter when they recognize how tirelessly he works for their sake. The term that describes the goal of communicating the apostolic struggle, that they **might be encouraged**, παρακληθῶσιν, covers a range of ideas in this context, the most prominent being 'to encourage' or 'to comfort'. The reference to **their heart** is often seen as aligning with Jewish anthropological understandings of this bodily organ as the seat of the emotions of spiritual feeling. The idea of hearts being encouraged occurs again in this letter (Col. 4:8), as well as twice elsewhere in the Pauline epistles (Eph. 6:22; 2 Thess. 4:18). The encouragement that Paul seeks to provide is not solely for the benefit of individual believers. Rather, as they are encouraged on an individual level this is seen as producing solidarity and corporate cohesion with their hearts **having been knit together in love**. The participle συμβιβασθέντες, 'having been knit together', creates the grammatical problem known as anacoluthon – that is, it does not follow on properly from what precedes it. If it is meant to agree with 'hearts' as the subject it should be a feminine participle; if 'their' is the antecedent subject, then it should be in the genitive case. As a nominative masculine plural participle it is neither of these things. It is somewhat futile to attempt to resolve this grammatical problem, since there is a fundamental grammatical contradiction. Then as now, writers did not always observe the niceties of grammar. However, the overall meaning is reasonably clear. There is one issue that deserves some further thought, and that is the temporal sequence and relationship between hearts that might be encouraged, and the knitting together of the believers in love. The relationship could be that the latter expresses the means by which the former happens: 'their hearts being encouraged by being knit together'. Another possibility is that the two things are simultaneous actions: 'their hearts might be encouraged as they are knit together'. A final possibility is that the unity of believers is prior to the encouragement that is being given to their hearts: 'their hearts might be encouraged having been knit together'. That last option is the one adopted here. Not only does it appear to reflect the more typical sense of an aorist passive participle, but perhaps more importantly in terms of the admittedly partial insights into communal relationships provided elsewhere in the letter, group unity appears to be established prior to the encouragement that Paul is seen as now providing. In the opening thanksgiving the Colossians already demonstrate love for all the holy ones (Col. 1:4), and such love 'is the perfect bond of unity' (Col. 3:14). Therefore, by referencing the fact the Colossians have been knit together **in love**, the epistle recalls a pre-existing condition, the loving unity of the group, which will also make Paul's apostolic labour a source of encouragement for all believers.

The bond that exists between the Colossians is not only experiential or emotional, there is also a shared cognitive understanding of the faith. Hence in addition to being united in love, they also are joined **in all the wealth of the assurance of understanding**. Again the author's fulsome writing style comes to the fore. Instead of saying the Colossians are united in love and understanding, he reflects on the superlative value and quality of the understanding they now possess. The phrase **all the wealth** recalls Col. 1:27, 'the wealth of the glory of this mystery'. Given that in parallel with Col. 1:27, this verse also speaks of God's mystery in the following clause, and then also in the same way defines the mystery as 'Christ', there is no doubt that here the author is returning to the same idea. What is considered to be of superabundant worth is the possession of **assurance of under-standing**. The term, translated here as **assurance**, πληροφορία, has two major meanings: either 'fill (completely), fulfil', or 'convince fully'. If the former were the intended sense, this clause would then emphasize the totality of the provision of 'all the wealth of all the fulness of understanding' (cf. Lohse 1971: 81). However, the entire clause appears to provide the second meaning as its emphasis. It suggests a further purpose behind Paul's apostolic labour, which is introduced by the preposition εἰς, 'in' or 'for'. The purpose is that such labour might provide the Colossians with an assurance of under-standing. Hence Paul's uncompromising struggle on behalf of the Colossians that involves both 'admonishing and teaching' (Col. 1:28), should equip them with a deeper understanding that results in a more grounded conviction or assurance in their new faith. The necessity for a stronger level of assurance may be a particular concern, especially if the author perceived that there were people in the Colossian community who taught that the full certainty of faith could only be attained when supplemented by mystical visionary experiences.

In order to correct any potential false train of thought, it is stated that Paul's striving for the Colossians is intended to encourage them since they already have full insight **in the knowledge of the mystery of God, which is Christ**. The term 'mystery', μυστήριον, recalls the reference to the mystery in Col. 1:27. Whether the language employed here is selected in direct opposition to the mystery religions of the Greco-Roman world, or whether the terminology is used simply because the author wished to make superior claims for Christ is unclear. What is certain, however, is that such terminology would have had cultic overtones for the recipients of the letter. Whereas participants in the Greco-Roman mystery cults underwent a series of rites as initiation into cultic life, here Christ is presented as the 'mystery' itself, and the participatory event and the significance of God's mystery is union with Christ: 'Christ in you, the hope of glory' (Col. 1:27). Some early Christian apologists expressed a sense of tension between such mystery cults and Christianity. In this vein, Justin refuted these cults as demonic imitations of Christian faith and Jewish traditions (Justin, *1 Apology* 62, 64). The various mystery cults – Eleusian, Dionysian, Orphic, Mithraic, and so on – had their own initiation rites and cosmological outlooks. It is not possible to detect any specific cult lying behind the rhetoric of Colossians, but the language of 'mystery' and the widespread occurrence of such cults suggest that the language is not accidental here. Therefore, the final stated purpose of Paul's apostolic work is that the Colossians might gain knowledge of God's mystery, which Paul defines in a single word, **Christ**. The Greek construction is somewhat awkward, but might be due to the author's desire to make the keyword 'Christ' the climactic term in this extended description of the purpose of Paul's work on behalf of the Colossians. The expression **knowledge of the mystery** does not designate purely intellectual knowledge, but contains a relational or personal aspect (O'Brien 1982: 94). The readers of this letter are informed that the toil in which Paul engages should be seen as a source of encouragement that is directed towards those who are united in Christ, and this apostolic labour provides the assurance that the Colossians already have complete understanding and knowledge of the only true divine mystery. Echoing the language of Col. 1:27, again believers are told that the mystery **is Christ**, the one with whom and in whom they are united.

3 As is typical in Pauline letters, the mention of Christ frequently leads to a digression, here about the benefits that accrue to believers because of faith in him. The **in whom** clause that commences this verse functions in two ways. First, it links to the immediately preceding subject – Christ – and secondly, it presents him as the central sphere of God's blessings, for in Christ **are all the treasures of wisdom and knowledge hidden**. The author's pleonastic language and theology again come to the fore with yet another occurrence of the adjective 'all'/'every', πᾶς. Here it is **all the treasures of wisdom and knowledge** that are said to exist in Christ. This statement unpacks some of the ideas present in the previous verse where 'all the wealth…of understanding' (Col. 2:2) was seen as one of the outcomes of the Paul's toil. Here, instead of 'all the wealth' the author speaks of **all the treasures**. The term **treasures** θησαυροί, like 'wealth'/'riches', πλοῦτος (Col. 2:2), is a metaphor that speaks of items of great value or worth. Here the term does not denote physical items that are luxurious or of great expense, but it is an image of the 'treasures' of divinely given understanding and insight. According to the author, Christ is the only place where such priceless **wisdom and knowledge** is to be found. In Colossians, **wisdom**, σοφία, is a recurrent theme. Paul prays that the Colossians 'may be filled with all wisdom' (Col. 1:9); declares that he teaches every man 'in all wisdom' (Col. 1:28); here, he states that in Christ are hidden 'all the treasures of wisdom' (Col. 2:3); unnecessary prohibitions are viewed as having 'the appearance of wisdom' (Col. 2:23); believers are encouraged to teach and admonish one another 'in all wisdom' (Col. 3:16); and in relation to those who are not community members the Colossians are exhorted 'to walk in wisdom' (Col. 4:5). Therefore, wisdom is understood in the letter as a cognitive quality that provides insight into the divine will, and possession of such wisdom should produce instructional insights and ethical behaviours towards those both inside and outside the community. Likewise, **knowledge**, which occurs here in the uncompounded form γνῶσις (cf. the author's more highly favoured compound form ἐπιγνῶσις Col. 1:9, 10; 2:2; 3:10), also describes an intellectual aspect of faith. Christ-centred knowledge is seen as a goal for the Colossians. Thus Paul prays that the Colossians may be filled with knowledge of the divine will (Col. 1:9); that they might 'increase in the knowledge of God'; that they may be encouraged 'in the knowledge of the mystery of God' (Col. 2:2) and see that in Christ are 'all the treasures of...knowledge' (Col. 2:3); and that they may be clothed with a new being that is renewed 'to knowledge' (Col. 3:10). Together, true 'wisdom and knowledge' originate in the divine sphere being concealed in Christ from those who have not received the insight and faith the Colossians now possess. It is for this reason that 'the treasures of wisdom and knowledge' are said to be **hidden**. Previously the letter spoke of 'the mystery that has been hidden away from the ages and from the generations – but now was made manifest to his holy ones' (Col. 1:26). Once again, it is God's revelation of the mystery, which is Christ, which makes the Colossians aware of the true resources of 'wisdom and knowledge' to which they now have access in Christ. However, to those who are not united with Christ, such things remain hidden and beyond comprehension.

4 The purpose of this encouragement and assurance becomes more explicit, being introduced with the declarative phrase, **this I say**. Thus, here Paul is offering a further explanation and the explicit nature of the declaration calls for the readers' attention at this point.

What follows expresses a genuine and real concern on the part of the author for the Colossians. Dunn suggests that '[t]hese concerns can hardly have been serious; otherwise they would have come to the fore much more quickly' (Dunn 1996: 133). This, however, is not the only explanation. As is apparent from the author's statement of lack of previous contact with the Colossians (Col. 2:1), the foregoing material has been important for building rapport with his readers, for presenting the author's understanding of the Pauline gospel and the true 'mystery of God', and for establishing Paul's own apostolic responsibility for all the churches – including those which he had not established. The problem that is said to trouble Paul is that the Colossians will be deceived by false teaching. Therefore the author states that he has written the letter in order **that no-one may delude you**. Moule suggests that the particle ἵνα that introduces this clause should be understood as imperatival in force *no-one is to delude you*, rather than having a telic or resultant sense *in order that no-one may delude you* (Moule 1953: 145). While this interpretation is not impossible, it is more likely that Paul is disclosing another aspect of his apostolic struggle on behalf of the Colossians – namely, he has told them about his toil on their behalf, so 'that no-one may delude you'. Moreover, given the emphasis on gaining insight into the 'knowledge of the mystery of God, which is Christ' (Col. 2:2), it is likely that the warning is directed against the possibility, either present or potential, that the Colossians may be deluded into thinking something else is 'the mystery of God', apart from Christ alone.

The term **may delude**, παραλογίζηται (pres. midd. subjunctive), is rare in the New Testament, and in its only other occurrence refers to an act of self-delusion (Jas 1:22). Here the potential action that is a cause for concern is described in the next phrase, where the means or instrument for such delusion is depicted as being **with persuasive speech**. While the term **persuasive speech**, πιθανογία, had a positive sense in Classical Greek (Plato, *Theaet.* 162e), undoubtedly here it is used negatively or pejoratively. In order to draw out this negative aspect a number of English translations have made this explicit with phrases such as 'beguiling speech' (RSV), 'plausible arguments' (NRSV), 'fine-sounding arguments' (NIV). Whether this is necessary is debatable, for the context makes it clear that these persuasive arguments are used to delude, not to impart truth. With this direct concern expressed about the Colossians being deceived or deluded, the tone of the letter moves away from the outright warmth of building rapport and providing encouragement to that of warning and polemics.

5 Having briefly alluded to his concerns for the Colossians, the author returns to announcing his solidarity with them and praising them for their steadfastness in the faith. The first clause, **for even if I am absent in the flesh**, acknowledges the author's physical absence. Paul's absence is mentioned at other places in his letters (1 Cor. 5:3; 2 Cor. 13:2, 10; Phil. 1:27). The closest of these parallels occurs when Paul tells the Corinthians that he will be united with them when they pass judgment on the man who has sexual relations with his father's wife. In that context he assures them that 'though absent in the body but present in the spirit, I have already judged him' (1 Cor. 5:3). For Paul, absence in the flesh is not an obstacle to unity among believers. Therefore, contrary to physical appearances, the author has Paul assure the Colossians of his spiritual presence: **yet in the spirit I am with you**. Precisely what this presence in the spirit describes has been debated. The two major options are whether this refers exclusively to Paul's own spirit – an anthropological explanation – or whether some mystic union takes place through the mutual indwelling presence of the Holy Spirit – a pneumatological explanation. Lightfoot favoured the former view, arguing for 'in my spirit' and not 'by the Spirit' (Lightfoot 1886: 241). However, it has been suggested that Paul's 'self is connected with the divine Spirit which grants strength to the apostle to unite with the community' (Lohse 1971: 83; cf. O'Brien 1982: 98). Barth and Blanke note the lack of evidence for making a decision on this question: 'We have no further indication whether the physical distance separating the apostle from the Colossian church was effectively overcome by the transmission of apostolic authority to the latter or by communion in Christ effected by the Holy Spirit' (Barth and Blanke 1994: 286). There is one piece of evidence that is usually overlooked in this discussion, the lack of references to the Holy Spirit in this letter. The only other use of the term 'spirit' is found in Col. 1:8, which refers to the Colossians' 'love in the spirit'. This earlier use may be understood as love that is produced by the Holy Spirit. However, the general replacement of typical Pauline pneumatological perspectives with christological categories in this letter, and the contrast here between Paul's physical and spiritual presence, together suggest that the author is not thinking in terms of the Holy Spirit. This leaves the problem of explaining precisely how the apostle would be present with the Colossians, maybe perhaps in Christ or through his letter, but the reality is that no explanation is provided.

This spiritual presence that is claimed means that from the author's perspective Paul can say to the Colossians that he is **rejoicing and seeing your order**. While in the previous verse there was an explicit warning about deluding and deceptive arguments, here the Colossians are characterized as being a source of rejoicing and an example of an ordered community. The pair of participles, **rejoicing and seeing**, χαίρων καὶ βλέπων, describes respectively the impact and sensory perception evoked in Paul. It has been suggested that the order of the participles is explained by understanding the latter to be the cause of the former: 'rejoicing because I see' (Sumney 2008: 120). However, given Paul's absence, the meaning of both participles should probably be given equal weight as a co-ordinated pair. Thus, the Colossians are informed that though not physically present with them, Paul is able both to see and rejoice over their steadfast faith. The letter informs the Colossians that an aspect of their corporate life that causes rejoicing is their **order**, τάξις. While the term **order** can be used to describe a physical arrangement or ordering of items – such as serving as priests in the temple in set sequence or order (Lk. 1:8), or an assigned position or post (1 Esdr. 1:15; Josephus, *Ant.* 7.36), or of military formations (Xenophon, *Anab.* 1.2.18) – by contrast here its use is metaphorical. What is being described is the perceived good ordering of the Colossian community in accordance with a proper understanding of the Pauline gospel. The term refers to the arrangement of the liturgical or worshiping life of the Corinthian community, when Paul entreats them to 'let all things be done properly and in order' (1 Cor. 14:40). The same sense may be intended here, with the author describing the corporate life of the community.

The second quality that the author claims to see in the Colossian community and concerning which he rejoices is **the firmness of your faith in Christ**. The term **firmness** στερέωμα can also be used in military contexts (see 1 Macc. 9:14) to describe the strength of fortifications. It is likely that such martial nuances have been lost.

However, the idea of firmness may carry the connotation of not being susceptible to external forces. Given the warning in the previous verse to let no-one delude you, it would appear possible that in the face of a perceived possible threat to the Colossians' acceptance of the faith as taught by Epaphras, there are forces that would change the current order and undermine the firmness that is described. The confidence the author declares to have in the Colossians is not based on some abstract qualities of 'order' and 'firmness', but because he is able to tell them that **your faith in Christ** is ordered and firm. The qualities that produce rejoicing are not an end in themselves, but are beneficial in as much as they help maintain faith in Christ. The richness of the term **faith**, πίστις, defies providing simple definitions, but encapsulates a range of ideas involving both belief and trust. It is therefore not simply intellectual response to a set of cognitive beliefs, but is also fundamentally relational, involving placing trust in the object of faith. The expression **in Christ**, εἰς Χριστόν, may be better understood as 'towards Christ', expressing the notion that Christ is the one to whom faith is directed, thereby becoming both the object and the goal of faith.

The closing verse of this section (Col. 2:1–5) returns to ideas expressed in the opening verse, namely that Paul is actively and energetically engaged with the Colossian believers. Although they have not seen him in the flesh, and even if he is physically absent from them, nonetheless his apostolic labours are no less determined or real on their behalf. Moreover, he is still able to have joy because of their maintenance of faith in Christ. That this blissful picture may not be quite as serene as the opening and closing sentiments in this section suggest is a possibility to which the author alludes in Col. 2:4, where he gives a frank statement warning the recipients of the letter not to be deluded with persuasive speech. In the remainder of this chapter (Col. 2:6–23) such concerns resurface – perhaps giving further clues as to the circumstances that may be causing anxiety for the author of the letter. However, the situation that may have occasioned these concerns and warnings is never described in a full or unambiguous manner.

II.
CHRISTOLOGICAL TEACHING
AND CORRECTIVES (2:6–23)

8. A CALL TO REMAIN ESTABLISHED IN THE FAITH (2:6–7)

(6) As therefore you received Christ Jesus the Lord, walk in him, (7) having been rooted and being built up in him, and being confirmed in the faith, just as you were taught, abounding in thanksgiving.

Having encouraged the Colossians both by describing the apostolic work on their behalf and through commending them for their order and firmness of faith, Paul now challenges the Colossians to live in a manner that befits life in Christ. At one level this is a somewhat surprising injunction, since the faith of the community has just been praised. However, as has been fleetingly described, Paul is concerned about the possibility the community could be deluded with persuasive arguments (Col. 2:4). This concern will be given fuller expression in what follows (Col. 2:8–23). Yet the description given in these verses provides only a partial insight, and leaves more questions than answers, including the central issue of whether the perceived danger was only a potential possibility or a tendency that was already a real threat.

These two verses, therefore, are a transitional unit. While they build upon the encouragement given in the material that precedes them, in many ways they are a thesis statement undergirding what follows. In the face of the concerns articulated in the following verses, the Colossians are simply to continue walking in Christ, they are called to live out the firmness of faith for which they have just been praised (Col. 2:5), and to remain steadfast in holding to the apostolic teaching as mediated through Epaphras (Col. 1:7) and by group instruction (Col. 1:28). In this way Paul presents his central appeal to the Colossians, namely that they should not deviate from the new life in Christ as they were originally taught it.

6 The opening statement recalls what is for the author a historical fact, and from that past experience he draws an implication regarding present and ongoing conduct. That past fact is described in the following way: **as therefore you received Christ Jesus the Lord**. The opening construction **as therefore** sets up a consequential argument – since X is true, do Y. This construction with the same or less frequently reverse order of these two words, is a recurrent feature in the fourth gospel (Jn 4:1, 40; 6:19; 11:6, 33; 18:6; 20:11; 21:9), although in these cases the phrase denotes a temporal connection indicating the subsequent action that is intended. Hence in the fourth gospel the phrase is best translated as 'when therefore' or 'so when'. Here, however, the nuance is slightly different, although still dependant on a past event. The connection is more logical than temporal in nature. Thus, here the more appropriate translation emphasizes the consequential nature of the argument: 'as therefore'.

The verb that follows this opening phrase, **you received**, is seen by some as denoting the handing on and reception of the Pauline version of Christian tradition (Bruce 1984: 93; Dunn 1996: 138–39). This suggestion is seen as gaining support both from the unambiguous reference to 'tradition' two verses later in the warning against following 'the traditions of men' (Col. 2:8), as well as being consonant with the wider Pauline usage of the term **you received**, παρελάβετε. Elsewhere Paul reminds the Corinthians of 'the gospel which I preached to you, which also you received' (1 Cor. 15:1), he warns the Galatians against those who 'preach to you a gospel contrary to that which you received' (Gal. 1:9), the Philippians are reminded of 'those things you learned and received and heard and saw in me' (Phil. 4:9), and the Thessalonians are told to recollect the apostolic instruction 'which you received from us as to how you ought to walk' (1 Thess. 4:1). While the last example in closest to the example in Col. 2:6, there is a notable difference since the other Pauline occurrences of the term refer to receiving the gospel or apostolic teaching. Here, by contrast, what is received is Christ. Hence what is being described is not the handing on of tradition, but the fact that the Colossian believers had received and been incorporated into Christ. The Colossians are not to recall some intellectual didactic process, but their experiential mystical union with Christ. No other rite or initiation is necessary for those who have been joined with Christ.

It is this that the author has already described as the very essence of the Christian mystery (Col. 1:27; 2:2). What the Colossians are said to have received is **Christ Jesus the Lord**. Along with the description in Col. 1:3 of God as 'the father of our Lord Jesus Christ', this is the most fulsome of christological appellatives used in Colossians. It is noteworthy that the term **Lord**, κύριος, is not particularly prominent in the first two-thirds of the letter (Col. 1:1–3:11); apart from here it occurs only in Col. 1:3, 10. There is then a sudden burst of κύριος terminology in the two sections dealing with being clothed with Christian behaviours and the household code (Col. 3:11–4:1). In these two sections there are eleven occurrences of the term κύριος, although three of these refer to earthly masters (Col. 3:22; 4:1 [×2]). There is a complexity in translating the phrase which is literally 'the Christ Jesus the Lord', with as many as six alternatives having been identified (Harris 2010: 80). The option Harris prefers is the one that takes the first term as titular, since it occurs with a definite article, and hence results in the translation 'the Christ, even Jesus the Lord'. Ultimately the difference may be fine and irresolvable, although it was noted earlier in relation to Col. 1:3 that a third onomastic category, that of an honorific, should be considered. This category denotes appellatives, such as 'Christ', which have become closely associated with a single person, yet still convey the connotation of the honour it describes. Moreover, elsewhere in the epistle the term 'Christ' can occur with a definite article in a sense that is not noticeably titular: 'when Christ is revealed' (Col. 3:4). Furthermore, the infrequent use of the term **Lord**, its occurrence with the article, and its climatic position all point to a certain emphasis falling on that term. Therefore, it may well be that both **Christ** and **Lord**, in combination, are intended to denote emphatically the unique status of Jesus. The key point for the author is that the one who is worthy of the elevated acclaim that these terms imply has already been received by the Colossians. There is no revelation more superlative than that of receiving and being united with Christ. Recognition of this should lead to action, and the necessary action is described in the final part of this verse.

The opening phrase 'as therefore' establishes the basis on which the behavioural imperative is grounded. The appeal is simple and yet all-encompassing, **walk in him**. While it has been observed that the form of verb used here, 'walk', περιπατεῖτε, is the first imperative in the epistle, it would be wrong to infer from this that the author has refrained ethical instruction till this point. The reality is that the author has provided advice about Christian behaviour already but without recourse to direct imperatival commands. In fact, the same metaphor of 'walking' has been used in Col. 1:10, where the recipients of the letter informed of prayers offered on their behalf seeking the outcome that they might 'walk worthily of the Lord' (cf. Col. 3:7; 4:5). Having received Christ, the Colossians are now commanded to conduct their lives in a manner befitting existence **in him**. As was noted in relation to Col. 1:10, the metaphor of 'walking' is likely to draw at some level on the Jewish concept of halakhah, which denotes living in a manner which accords with God's commandments. Here the matrix that shapes Christian behaviour is not Torah and its application, but the mystery of union with Christ. To be 'in him' carries spatial overtones, with believers now found in a new sphere of existence. That sphere may be understood as the mystical union with Christ (Col. 1:18), or incorporation into his body the church (Col. 1:27). For the author of Colossians, correct understanding of Christ and of believers' relationship to him results in appropriate ethical behaviour. Therefore, truly to have received Jesus as Christ and Lord, and to have understood the significance of the mystery of 'Christ in you', can have no other consequence, according to the author, than living in Christ in a manner appropriate with the mystical union that now exists. Therefore, it is understood to be the case that right behaviour and right belief cannot exist in isolation from each other.

7 After having stated the key behavioural imperative, to live in a way worthy of their new sphere of existence in Christ, the letter recalls the past act of faith using an agricultural metaphor, and the present necessity of maintaining faith using an architectural image. Thus, the Colossians are reminded that they are the ones **having been rooted and being built up in him**. The term **having been rooted** is a perfect passive participle, which communicates the idea of a divine action that brought about the new state of existence in which believers now find themselves. This participle and the following two, 'being built up' and 'being confirmed', do not function as further imperatives (*contra* Barth and Blanke 1994: 303), but describe the basis upon which the imperative to 'walk in him' is grounded. By contrast with the first participial clause, here the present participle **being built up**, still in the passive voice, indicating divine action, has a change of tense indicates a continuing action – the Colossians are being built up progressively. These two divine actions are again seen to impact upon those who live in the new sphere of existence, which for the author is created by union with Christ and therefore described simply as being **in him**.

The third divine action that is mentioned in this sequence is that of **being confirmed in the faith**. The verb used here, βεβαιούμενοι, covers a range of related meanings: 'to establish, strengthen, prove reliable, confirm'. There is debate as to whether this is a continuation of the previous building metaphor, or whether the image is drawn from commerce (Dunn 1996: 142). In relation to the latter, it is shown that the term was a commonplace in trade and business denoting a surety or bond relating to the transfer of goods or property. However, here this confirmation is a process rather than a one-off guarantee, with the Colossians having a continuous pledge of being **in the faith**, as they continue to hold fast to the gospel and live in Christ. It is perhaps the wrong question to ask how all these various statements and ideas hold together, or to enquire as to which is the basis of any other. All of these ideas reinforce the deeper idea of what life in Christ means, and what the concomitant requirements are for believers. Because they have demonstrated faith in Christ they are now able to know he is the mystery of God and they live in him. Yet equally, it is because they live in Christ that their faith is continuously confirmed and they are being built up in that faith.

In the next clause, the thought oscillates back to the temporal frame of the past, but it is inextricably linked to the key argument that there is no need to supplement or modify the form of faith initially received. Hence, the Colossians are assured that the faith in which they are now continuously confirmed does not differ from what they first heard, since it remains the same **just as you were taught**. The ideas of teaching and instruction are important in the epistle. The Colossians were reminded that they learnt the gospel from Epaphras (Col. 1:7). Moreover, it is part of the apostolic work entrusted to Paul to teach every believer in wisdom (Col. 1:28). Here the focus moves from divine actions to an apostolic act. Obviously the author sees the divine and apostolic actions as working together, for God confirms the Colossians in the faith that Epaphras taught them, and which Paul now endorses in this letter without any further addition or embellishment.

The final clause **abounding in thanksgiving** is the first use of an active verb in this verse. The response of the Colossians to this set of divine and apostolic actions on their behalf is to be the abundant outpouring of thanksgiving. This is something that has already been modelled for them in literary form in the introductory thanksgiving section of the letter, 'we give thanks…' (Col. 1:3–8). The lack of any connective conjunction makes the relationship of this final clause to the preceding statements unclear. It has been understood by some as a further antecedent circumstance related to the imperative 'walk in him'. However, it may be better to take the force as a further imperative: 'so abound in thanksgiving'. Again certainty is not possible, since the relationship of the phrase to the rest of the sentence is grammatically ambiguous. Furthermore, the injunction to thanksgiving is frequently seen as an echo of jubilant prayer in Col. 1:12 (Lohse 1971: 94). In this vein the outpouring of thanksgiving is to be understood as part of the believer's faith, and consequently praise is the sole response that can be given back to the God who planted them in that faith, and continues to build them up and thus confirms the Colossians in that same faith.

9. THE TRIUMPH OF CHRIST (2:8–15)

(8) Beware lest there will be somebody who[3] takes you captive through philosophy and vain deceit according to the tradition of men, according to the elements of the world and not according

---

[3] This is a literal translation of the Greek clause Βλέπετε μή τις ὑμᾶς ἔσται. This somewhat cumbersome Greek construction may well be intended to emphasize that a particular individual, τις, 'somebody', is in view. A smoother English translation would be 'Beware that nobody takes you captive…'. Here, however, the author is not speaking of a general case that would be expressed by the negative pronoun 'nobody'; rather, he has a specific yet intentionally unnamed 'somebody' in view.

to Christ, (9) because in him dwells all the fulness of the deity bodily, (10) and you have been fulfilled in him, who is the head of every ruler and authority. (11) In whom you also were circumcised with a circumcision made without hands in the stripping of the body of the flesh, in the circumcision of Christ, (12) having been buried together with him in baptism, in whom also you were raised from the dead, through faith in the working of God, who raised him from the dead; (13) and you being dead in your transgressions and in the uncircumcision of your flesh, he made you alive together with him having forgiven us all our transgressions, (14) having erased the handwritten debt of ordinances against us, which was against us, and he has taken it from our midst, having nailed it to the cross; (15) having stripped the rulers and authorities, he exposed them in public, having triumphed over them in him.

This section is the first part of a connected discussion that incorporates the remainder of the chapter (Col. 2:8–23). While this opening paragraph is tied to the material that follows in Col. 2:16–23, especially through the anticipatory reference to those who may try to the ensnare the Colossians by various mechanisms, such as philosophy, deceit, human traditions, or 'the elements of the world', the emphasis is placed upon Christ's triumph through the cross. Therefore, the author celebrates the victory that is achieved through the cross over rulers and authorities, over fleshly circumcision, over death, and over the debt of transgressions. It is probably correct to see Col. 2:8 as 'a heading and introductory statement' that functions 'in a chiastic form' (Dunn 1996: 144). On this reading, the lengthy opening warning sets the tone for what will follow in Col. 2:16–23, whereas the final phrase in Col. 2:8, 'according to Christ', is the theme or the entry point into the reflection that follows in Col. 2:9–15. In this section, prior to explicitly confronting the erroneous attempt to supplement the initial exclusively christocentric presentation of the gospel, the author outlines the powerful and complete triumph that Christ has achieved through the cross. This is yet another portrayal of the folly of trying to supplement the gospel. Hence the letter presents a strong warning against following those who suggest that the faith the Colossians already possess is anything less than the full provision of divine power and victory for all believers in Christ.

8 The opening warning consists of an imperative that counsels vigilance against possible future deceivers, **beware lest there will be somebody**. The verb used here, in the second person plural imperative, βλέπετε, 'see', 'consider', 'watch out', is a call for visual attentiveness. It can be employed to designate something to be avoided, as here, with a negative particle, and usually in such cases this is typically followed by the aorist subjunctive to express an unfilled condition, which may potentially either be fulfilled or avoided at some indefinite time (cf. Mt. 24:2//Mk 13:5//Lk. 21:8; Acts 13:40; 1 Cor. 8:9; Gal. 5:15). Here, however, the construction is less common, and instead of the aorist subjunctive the author uses the future indicative 'there will be', ἔσται. This is seen as making 'the danger more imminent and the warning more urgent' (Harris 2010: 83). While it is impossible for modern readers to know the details of the situation that called forth this warning, it does appear to be a real concern for the author. While this is suggested by the immediacy of the future tense, there are also much clearer indications on which to base this assumption in the more polemical section later in the chapter (Col. 2:16–19). This is further reinforced by the typical Pauline use of the indefinite pronoun for opponents whom he wishes to diminish in status (see Dunn 1996: 146; cf. Rom. 3:8; 1 Cor. 4:18; 15:12, 34; 2 Cor. 3:1; 10:2; Gal. 1:7; 2:12; Phil. 1:15).

The unnamed 'somebody' is described as one **who takes you captive**, ὑμᾶς...ὁ συλαγωγῶν. The verb συλαγωγέω is a rare term in the corpus of extant Greek literature, occurring only here in the New Testament, as well as elsewhere in Heliodorus, *Aeth.* 10.35.1, 'this is the one who took my daughter captive', and in Aristaenetus, *Ep.* 2:22, 'this is the man I seized, sir, in the act of attempting to rob my house'. These two examples illustrate the possible meaning of the term as 'to take captive' or 'to rob, despoil', with either being possible in the present context in Colossians. The term is also related semantically to the more common verb 'to strip off', συλάω, usually in reference to an opponent's weapons or armour. Although expressed using a different Greek verb, the idea of 'stripping off' is present a little later in this passage both in relation to 'stripping off the body of flesh' (Col. 2:11), or as a metaphor for Christ's conquest of cosmic powers: 'having stripped the rulers and authorities' (Col. 2:15). Since the imagery throughout this section relates to the defeat of opponents, the translation of συλαγωγῶν adopted here, 'to take captive', is selected since it is the one that best fits the overall context of this section. That is it is understood as a warning not to be taken captive oneself, but to realize that Christ, through the cross, has already despoiled and stripped the cosmic opponents of their power.

Having described the goal of the unnamed party, namely to take the Colossians captive, the means of achieving that attempted goal are now disclosed as being **through philosophy and vain deceit**. The terms 'philosophy' and 'empty deceit' are preceded by a single preposition 'through', διά. This has led most commentators to understand a single idea being expressed here rather than two different means by which the readers might be taken captive. Taken this way the second expression expands the meaning of the term 'philosophy', so the entire phrase might be better understood as 'through a philosophy which is empty deceit', or by giving the second expression a more adjectival force, 'with their empty and deceitful philosophy'. On this reading the term **philosophy** need not be understood as a general negative designation. Rather, it is the type of philosophy being promoted by those who wish to take the Colossians captive, which is here characterized as being a **vain deceit**. Many have surmised that the use of the term 'philosophy' occurs because it was the way those who wished to supplement the Pauline gospel described their own teaching. Thus O'Brien states, 'Paul no doubt adopted the term here because it was used by the false teachers themselves to refer to their own teachings in a positive way' (O'Brien 1982: 109). While this is not impossible, it may assume more insight than can actually be inferred from the text, and perhaps more importantly it may attribute a greater degree of coherence and organization to those whose teachings are considered to have erroneous tendencies. Rather than dignify this teaching with the term 'gospel' or even 'false gospel' (cf. Gal. 1:8–9), the author describes the ideas by using the neutral term 'philosophy', but then immediately shows that the variety of philosophy being taught is defective, because it consists of 'vain deceit'. The description **vain deceit** implies both that the teaching is a vanity designed to hubristically inflate those who adopt it, and that it is patently false since by supplementing the Christ-centred gospel it ends up being a denial of sufficiency of Christ as the revelation of the full mystery of God.

A dual origin is seen as standing behind this deceitful philosophy. Rather than deriving from Christ, it is first **according to the tradition of men**. The chief critique here is that it is human rather than divine in origin. The second source that is attributed to the 'philosophy' is that it is **according to the elements of the world**. While some have suggested, on the basis of Paul's familiarity with Pharisaic teaching, that the rejection of **the tradition of men** is directed against 'a form of Jewish thought' (Dunn 1996: 148; cf. Wright 1986 [2008]: 106), there is in fact little in the context that allows for the 'tradition' to be identified in this or any other specific manner. Rather, the critique is more general – what is being criticized is defective because of the human origin of such traditions. This rebuttal could be applied to either received Hellenistic or Jewish ideas that are seen as contrary to the core theological conviction that Christ is Lord (Col. 2:6), and the failure to understand him as the full revelation of the divine mystery (Col. 2:2). The meaning of the second origin, which rejects the philosophy because it is **according to the elements of the world**, is more difficult to determine. The phrase **the elements of the world**, τὰ στοιχεῖα τοῦ κοσμοῦ, has been understood in various ways:

1. The physical elements of which the universe is composed.
2. Elemental spiritual forces of the cosmos (perhaps with reference to celestial bodies).
3. The elementary teachings of the world.
4. The elemental spirits of the world/universe.

The second and fourth options are close in their respective interpretation, with the key difference being whether the oppositional elements are impersonal forces (as in the second option) or personal spiritual beings (as in the fourth option). The first option adopts a more physical interpretation, thereby understanding that trust in the constituent components of the universe rather than in their ultimate source as being the vain philosophy that is rejected here. The pre-Socratic philosopher Empedocles (ca. 490–430 B.C.) conceptualized a system whereby all physical structures were composed of the four basic elements, earth, air, fire, and water. However, he called these elements 'roots', and did not use the term 'elements', which may have first been used by Plato. The third option places this expression in a closer, if not synonymous, relationship with the phrase 'the traditions of men'. It is doubtful, however, whether the term 'elements', στοιχεῖα, in this context can be equated with 'teachings'. That use can be found in the writings of Xenophon, describing education as starting with 'the elementary principles' (*Mem.* 2.1.1), and in Plato where it refers to a 'fundamental assumption' (*Leg.* 7.790C). This sense does not appear dominant in the first century, although it may be reflected in Heb. 5:12, which is perhaps influenced by Platonic, or at least extra-biblical, ideas. Thus, while not being persuaded by the third option, the other three options capture the more common range of meaning encapsulated in the Greek term as used in first-century sources. Although this multiplicity of nuances may appear to create ambiguity especially for modern readers, it in fact reflects a strand in Hellenistic cosmology whereby the building-blocks of the universe were not neutral entities, but could be thought of as powerful forces that could act with independent volition. However, attempts to link the term with specific spiritual beings, or with the angels described in Col. 2:18, faces the problem that in the surviving first-century usage of this term it is not found as a referent for such beings. The phrase 'the elements of the world' occurs again in Col. 2:20, but this does not add any further clarity to its meaning, and also in Gal. 4:3 (cf. Gal. 4:9, 'the weak and beggarly elements'). In Galatians, Paul first tells his readers that 'we were enslaved under the elements of the world' (Gal. 4:3). This is later expanded upon when he picks up the same idea a few verses later. First he tells the Galatians that 'you were slaves of beings not gods by nature' (Gal. 4:8), then in mocking questioning he asks 'how is it that you turn back again to the weak and beggarly elements, to which you wish to be enslaved again?' (Gal. 4:9). Therefore, the things that are 'not gods by nature' are equated with 'the weak and beggarly elements'. Given the regular Jewish polemic against pagan gods as being inanimate objects hewn from stone or crafted from wood, it may be the case that in Galatians the warning is against attributing divine powers to the basic elements of the universe (cf. de Boer 2011: 252–56). In Pauline thought such gods could simultaneously be thought of as being of no consequence, and yet by being treated as gods they become objects of great power (1 Cor. 8:4–5). Hence, in Colossians it may be the case that the readers are warned not to trust the philosophy that attempts to take them captive, because it is based on their pre-Christian outlook that attributed power and veneration to the elements. However, it is probably the case that the author has not hermetically delimited these options. It is likely that an impersonal elemental cosmology could easily be combined with the view that basic components of the universe also were manifest as personal cosmic powers, such as the *archons* known in later Nag Hammadi texts. For instance, in *The Hypostasis of the Archons*, a figure called Eleleth, the great angel, teaches Norea a daughter of Adam and 'his female counterpart Eve' concerning the protology of the archons: 'I have taught you about the pattern of the rulers, and the matter in which it was expressed' (*Hyp. Arch.* 96.15–16). The angelic revelation dialogue reflects the close interplay between the origin of the archons and their composition from the fundamental matter of the universe. Therefore, while the phrase 'elements of the world' can be understood as denoting impersonal matter, from a latter period it is possible to see that the distinction between the impersonal nature of matter and the primordial personal rulers who came forth from such matter was not necessarily maintained.

The fundamental problem with the philosophy that is seen as being a threat to the Colossians is that it is **not according to Christ**. The danger of the philosophy according to the author of Colossians is not just its faulty dual origin, based on human traditions and the veneration of the elements, more fundamentally it removes Christ from the centre of their religious understanding. It is this challenge to the ultimate and unrivalled significance of Christ that makes the philosophy 'empty' and a 'vain deceit'. It is for this reason, according to the train of thought expressed here, that any attempt to supplement the gospel is not simply an addition, but a total negation of the significance of Christ.

9 As is frequent in the Pauline writings, mention of Christ leads into a christological affirmation. At times these are mere digressions triggered by a spontaneous outpouring of praise. Here, however, the christological claim that is made is fundamental to the argument that is being advanced. The philosophy mentioned in the previous verse is deemed to be unnecessary in light of the Christ event, **because in him dwells all the fulness of the deity bodily**. The affirmation made here is a close reformulation of the statement in the christo-logical hymn, 'because in him all the fulness was pleased to dwell' (Col. 1:19). The key differences between the two statements are the removal of the reference to the fulness being 'pleased' to reside in Christ, and the addition of the clarifying expansion that the fulness is that 'of the deity', and also supplying the adverb 'bodily' in Col. 2:9. The reason for this internal echo is to recall what hopefully is a shared christological belief, and using it as leverage against the tendency towards the 'philosophy' that presents a form of Christian belief that is supplemented by further cosmological speculations that results in, at least from the author's perspective, a form of faith that does not maintain the ultimate centrality of Christ. This verse and the following statement in Col. 2:10 introduce two reasons why the Colossians should resist a possible tendency towards accepting the philosophy against which the author writes. Both these reasons are centred on Christ. The first, presented in this verse, is because it is impossible to supplement the fulness of the divine activity, presence, and purpose that has taken place through Christ. Secondly, in the following verse, the Colossians are corporately linked with Christ – they now exist in him and no longer need to have any concern about any other 'ruler and authority' (Col. 2:10), since Christ is pre-eminent over such forces.

This verse opens with a conjunction, **because**, ὅτι, which here functions in a causal manner to introduce the two reasons that show the folly of the philosophy that has been mentioned in the previous verse. While the conjunction introduces a dependent clause that supplies the reason for following the behaviour being advocated – rejection of the philosophy – its precise grammatical antecedent is not clear. At one level it is most natural to read this clause as dependent upon the immediately foregoing reference to Christ, especially since it develops a christological response. However, the fundamental purpose of the causal clause is to show why the Colossians should not allow themselves to be taken captive by the false philosophy. In this sense it provides the basis for which the alternative teaching should be resisted. There is perhaps a step missing in this argument, which was unnecessary for the original readers since they presumably knew the content of the philosophy. However, this remains obscure for those reading the letter without the knowledge of the initial recipients. Given what is asserted in this verse it would appear that others perhaps were not rejecting Christ, but had failed to recognize him as the full expression of the mystery of God and the location of divine presence.

The key phrase **in him** appears here again, last being used in Col. 2:7, where believers were reminded about being rooted and built up 'in him'. There the change in their status and orientation of behaviour was based upon union with Christ. Here, the 'in him' phrase is a spatial expression, denoting the location where divine fulness is now found. The 'in him' language functions as a repeated refrain in the following section, with the Colossians reminded that 'you have been fulfilled in him' (Col. 2:10). Related phrases are also used to describe the union of believers with Christ. He is the one 'in whom you were circumcised' (Col. 2:11), they were buried 'with him' (Col. 2:12), and he is the one 'in whom' they were raised with him (Col. 2:12). They have been made alive together 'with him' (Col. 2:13), and the triumph over all rulers and authorities has been achieved 'in him' (Col. 2:15). This first occurrence of the phrase in this section (Col. 2:8–15) is the sole example where it does not denote the union of believers with Christ, but designates Christ as the sphere in which divine presence dwells.

Much has been made of the change of tense in the verb **dwell**, which here occurs in the present κατοικεῖ, but in the christological hymn was employed as an aorist infinitive κατοικῆσαι (Col. 1:19). Thus it is suggested that 'here the action is kept in mind, which was carried out through the divine will cited in 1:19: only in the Messiah does God allow himself to be "recognized"' (Barth and Blanke 1994: 311). Classically, for Lightfoot, here the verb denoted that the fulness of the deity 'has its fixed abode' in Christ (Lightfoot 1886: 179). It has been observed that while this places too much weight on the meaning of the verb, nonetheless it does insist that the fulness resides uniquely in Christ. This may imply the permanence of that indwelling, although that theme is not explicitly developed.

What is said to dwell in Christ is **all the fulness of the deity**. The author employs one of his favourite catchwords, **all**, to express the totality of the quality that resided in Christ. As was the case in Col. 1:19, the precise meaning of **the fulness**, πλήρωμα, is not given detailed explanation, although here it occurs with the explanatory genitive **of the deity**. This genitive of content communicates the quality or item that the fulness carries. The term for **deity**, θεότης, has been compared with the related and more common term θειότης, 'divine nature'/'divinity' (cf. Rom. 1:20). The distinction is often presented as follows: 'The term "divine nature" (θειότης) describes the character of God, divinity. The term "deity" (θεότης) describes the quality of divine being' (Lohse 1971: 100). It is dubious whether such debates about the author's selection of certain terms in distinction from others actually reflect an intentional and highly differentiated choice of meaning. Such arguments then allow for the claim that it is the essence of divine being, rather than the characteristics and qualities of God that are being described here. This appears to align too neatly with fourth-century christological debates, but does not reflect the concerns of the author. The claim the author makes is elevated, and focuses on the unique position of Christ, without loading the term 'deity' with a precise and technical sense. Regardless of whether the author is referring to God's ontological essence or qualitative characteristics, or even some blurred overlap of the two, what is apparent is that the author rejects attempts to add any other requirement to the gospel apart from understanding Christ as the superlative expression of divine activity and presence. Furthermore, what speaks strongly against the imposition of this modern dichotomy of the terms 'divinity' and 'deity' is the comment made by Theodore of Mopsuestia in the fourth century, where after citing the verse he observes in relation to the key phrase:

> *quoniam in ipso inhabitat omnis plenitude diuinitatis corporaliter.*
> *omnen plentitudinem deitatis* hoc in loco iterum dicit uniuersam creaturam repletam ab eo.

> 'For in him the entire fulness of divinity dwells bodily'.
> By 'the entire fulness of deity' in this place he means the entire creation filled by him.
> (Theodore of Mopsuestia, *ad Colossenses* 2.9)

Here the terms 'divinity' (*diuinitatis*) and 'deity' (*deitatis*) are used interchangeably for the underlying Greek term θεότης.

The second addition that is made to this statement in comparison with the form in Col. 1:19 is that the fulness dwells in Christ **bodily**, σωματικῶς. Numerous proposals have been advanced to explain the meaning of the adverb 'bodily' in relation to the rest of this verse. At least nine major suggestions have been put forward:

1. 'In bodily form': it may be too much to read a theology of incarnation from this. However, it does speak of the embodied state of deity dwelling in Christ (Dunn 1996: 145, 152).
2. Related to the first solution is the idea that the emphasis is upon the placement on the elevated Christ in a human body. This is seen to give more weight to the present tense of the verb 'to dwell' (Meyer 1859: 314).
3. Also related to and perhaps overlapping with solution two is the idea that the emphasis is on the reality of the bodily presence of deity. Schweizer argues that the word 'bodily' is used 'in the sense of "actual, real," and hence is set in contrast with all that is merely apparent' (Schweizer 1982: 138).
4. The term has been seen as directed specifically against false teachers who claimed that some other mechanism was required to apprehend the fulness of God, other than appreciating that it was revealed within the body of Christ (Haupt 1902: 31–33).
5. Drawing upon the reference to 'shadow' in Col. 2:17, it is suggested 'bodily' implies that the divine presence is real in Christ, whereas all other manifestations had been partial (cf. Dibelius and Greeven 1953: 29).
6. 'Corporately': referring to the manifestation of deity in the body of Christ, which is the church (Col. 1:18). This interpretation is supported by Lohse: 'the body of his is the church… over which he already in the present exercises his universal rule' (Lohse 1971: 101).
7. 'In one person': thereby placing the emphasis on the unique role of Christ as the embodied representation of deity, and perhaps challenging the view that deity was mediated through a series of intermediate beings or emanations (Horsley 1983: 3:86).
8. 'Something of substance': this depends on late antique renderings of the term as part of ongoing christological debates (cf. Oecumenius of Trkka, sixth century: PG 119, 32; John Damascenus, eighth century: PG 95, 893).
9. 'A sign of fulness': this argues that as the reconciler of the entire universe, the totality of divine purpose resides in Christ (Lohmeyer 1953: 106).

A number of these proposals are more creative than persuasive, and the degree of specificity they suggest may load too great an interpretative weight on a single word. Solutions that relate to christological debates (number eight) or those that are related to some kind of proto-gnostic idea appear anachronistic. While the whole statement is responding to the claims of the philosophy mentioned in Col. 2:8, seeing the term 'bodily' as specifically directed against false teachers to subvert their ideas (solution four) does not gain sufficient support from the text. Ecclesiastical interpretations, that understand the term as a communal or corporate reference, fail to appreciate that the emphasis is on christology at these point, rather than the ecclesial body. Similarly, the 'universal' reading (solution nine) overplays an aspect of the text that is not dominant in this section. Recognition of the reality of the indwelling fulness (option three) may be implied, but it is not the key point of the term, and the contrast with the shadow mentioned later in the chapter (solution 5) would require an implausible reading strategy on the part of the audience. This leaves the first two related proposals. The second runs into the danger of placing too much weight on the present tense of the verb 'to dwell'. It seems preferable to adopt the most usual and straightforward interpretation of the Greek word σωματικῶς. It designates the embodiment of the fulness of deity in Christ, and identifies that divine presence with the corporeal form of Christ. Thus the text affirms the mystery of the divine fulness dwelling in Christ, and this act of revelation in bodily form requires no additional or supplementary act of disclosure. The text, therefore, assumes the enfleshment of the fulness of deity in Christ, but it 'does not point directly to the act of incarnation' (Harris 2010: 89).

10 The conjunction that introduces this verse, co-ordinates the second reason for resisting the false philosophy with the first reason: **and you have been fulfilled in him**. Moreover, key terminology links the two verses, both through the repetition of the **in him** clause, and the use of the word group that includes the noun 'fulness' (Col. 2:9) and the participle **have been fulfilled**. The construction here is a Greek periphrastic form, combining the present tense of the verb 'to be' with a perfect participle forming a periphrastic perfect **you have been fulfilled**. In the Greek syntax of this verse the phrase **in him** is placed towards the beginning of the phrase, literally 'and you in him have been fulfilled'. This has two effects. First it places greater emphasis on this expression, and secondly it creates greater parallelism with the previous version where the 'in him' phrase also occupies an emphatic position. The meaning of the **in him** expression is, however, different here from Col. 2:9, where it denoted the location of the indwelling fulness of deity in Christ. Here the use returns to the sense of the two occurrences of the expression in Col. 2:6–7, where it describes the sphere of existence for believers, and the consequences of their union with Christ. The periphrastic perfect **you have been fulfilled** is stative, recalling a benefit that the Colossians continue to enjoy, but which was established at some point in the past – presumably at the moment they came to believe in Christ. The verse does not make clear with what the Colossians 'have been fulfilled'. Some have understood this as an assertion 'that the "fullness" of forgiveness and relationship with God are "in him"' (Sumney 2008: 134). While this is an intriguing possibility, the verse does not explicitly support this, and it may be better to connect the 'fulfilling' in this verse with the previous verse, which speaks of the fulness of deity resides in Christ (although cf. O'Brien 1982: 113, who believes that on theological grounds this would be 'asserting too much'). Therefore, the unique divine fulness enjoyed by Christ is mediated and transmitted to those who are in union with him. By existing 'in him' believers now have greater access to divine fulness than that promised by the false philosophy. Some have seen this nebulous declaration concerning believers having been filled as responding to a claim made by those promoting the philosophy that is being opposed. Namely, that the expanded form of teaching promised a more complete experience of the divine. Regardless of whether this expression is a parody of the language used in support of the rejected philosophy, the author claims that Christ is the unique location of divine fulness, and that through union with him believers share in that fulness.

The second half of the verse takes the argument in a slightly different although related direction. Drawing upon language found in the christological hymn, here the letter asserts that Christ is the one **who is the head of every ruler and authority**. This may be responding to another aspect of the philosophy, which may have advocated some form of devotion to other cosmic beings (cf. Col. 2:18). In Col. 1:18 Christ was declared to be '*the head* of the body, the church', and at the end of the list in Col. 1:16 the terms 'rulers' and 'authorities' in the plural were paired together. This same pairing is mentioned again in this section in Col. 2:15. While 'the rulers and the authorities' may be thought of as negative rather than neutral or positive forces, the key point is to remind the Colossians that such entities are subservient to Christ. They are subservient to him because they were created in him and through him (Col. 1:16), they are subservient to his authority because he exercises headship over them (Col. 2:10), and they are subservient to him because he has defeated them and stripped them of all power (Col. 2:15). The repeated emphasis illustrating that 'the rulers and the authorities' are inconsequential and powerless in comparison to Christ suggests that there may have been a strand in the thinking of the Colossians that regarded them as otherwise, and this needed to be decisively corrected. The sense of the term **the head** may differ slightly from its use in Col. 1:18. In that context, Christ being head of the church emphasized his role as the source and originator of this corporate entity of believers. Here, the emphasis is placed more strongly on 'authority, supremacy, leadership', especially over cosmic forces.

11 The train of thought progresses by continuing to emphasize that the Colossians are in union with Christ. The phrase **in whom**, ἐν ᾧ, differs from the more frequent 'in him' construction that has been prominent in the epistle; however, the core meaning is much the same (the NASB translates this as 'in Him'). The author moves from the fairly universal metaphor of receiving the divine fulness as a benefit of incorporation into Christ, to the ethnically religious specific metaphor of circumcision. The question arises as to whether the metaphor is an abstract image of participation and divesting bodily passions (so Wilson 2005: 201–204; Sumney 2008: 136–38), or whether it is responding to some external pressure to accept physical circumcision (Dunn 1996: 155, 'circumcision was indeed a factor in the threatening situation at Colossae'). Circumcision was not actually a uniquely Jewish custom, although the popular perception was to equate circumcision with Judaism. Hadrian's proscription of the custom on the grounds that it was a form of genital mutilation appears to have been specifically directed against Jews, and was a cause of the Bar Kochba revolt (*Hist. Augusta Hadr.* 14.2). By itself this description need not suggest that there was pressure on the Colossians from some quarter to accept physical circumcision. The description here metaphorically speaks of a circumcision made without hands. More weight may be added to the case that physical circumcision was a factor at Colossae, when it is combined with the warning not to let anybody pass judgment in relation to food, drink, festivals, new moons, or sabbaths (Col. 2:16). Here the reference to sabbaths appears to be a more concrete warning, and one that would arise out of a tendency to accept Jewish practices. Whether this provides sufficient cumulative evidence to understand the situation in Colossae as somewhat parallel to the one in Galatia, where Paul describes external pressure on Gentile believers to accept circumcision (Gal. 5:2–4), is debatable. It may simply be the case the metaphor had wider applicability in the Jesus movement, which found its origins in Judaism. Alternatively, the author of the epistle may have been Jewish and perhaps by default reverted to imagery from that religious background (Sumney 2008: 136: 'a non-Jew would probably not select circumcision as a favorable metaphor through which to express the idea of incorporation into Christ'). In light of the lack of explicit statements, like those in Gal. 5:2–4, which reveal external pressure on the Galatians to accept physical circumcision, the more likely explanation is that here the image of non-physical circumcision is used as a metaphor of incorporation into the body of Christ.

The further way in which the Colossians have been set apart from needing to follow any act of human piety is described as being through a further change of status through union with Christ in which, according to the letter, **you also were circumcised with a circumcision made without hands**. The Greek is a much more compressed formulation than can be expressed in English, with just three words after the conjunction 'also', περιετήθητε περιτομῇ ἀχειροποιήτῳ. The first statement is indeed a daring one, whether penned by Paul or somebody writing in the Pauline tradition. The perspective of Pauline theology entailed the rejection of circumcision as a necessary requirement for males as a rite of incorporation into the people of God. The declaration **you were circumcised** must have been jarring to the ears of Gentile believers in Colossae, especially as they knew that physically they had not been circumcised. The claim that the Colossians had been circumcised **with a circumcision** would be unremarkable and in fact a mere tautology if the reference was to physical circumcision. However, since this is a circumcision **made without hands**, even labelling it as 'circumcision' involves a radical shift in the way the term was commonly understood. Admittedly, even in the Hebrew Scriptures one finds the precedent to speak of a metaphorical circumcision, when the author of Deuteronomy calls for a 'circumcision of the heart' (Deut. 10:16; 30:6; and also in the Deuteronomistic tradition, Jer. 4:4). However, such sentiments in Judaism were pleas for one's inner attitude to live up to what the physical mark on the flesh symbolized. This was no radical call to dispense with the outward sign, and to live out only the ideological ideals of circumcision. Thus it was this willingness to dispense with the physical act of circumcision, while claiming to enshrine the spiritual values to which the physical act pointed, that was a key division between Pauline Christianity and Judaism. The terms 'made with hands' and 'made without hands' are loaded expressions in the New Testament. During his trial Jesus declares that he 'will destroy this temple made with hands, and in three days I will build another made without hands' (Mk 14:58). Similarly in Acts, God is described as one who 'does not dwell in temples made with hands' (Acts 7:48; 17:24), whereas Paul can state that if the earthly body is destroyed then believers have 'a house not made with hands, eternal in the heavens' (2 Cor. 5:1). These entities that are said to exist without the artifice of human hands thus point to divine agency. In effect the author of Colossians is stating that believers have been divinely circumcised through their union with Christ. From this perspective physical circumcision is emptied of value, and the image is redefined from being a concrete and physical action, instead being transformed into a metaphorical and spiritual state.

Continuing to play with the image of circumcision, this circumcision made without hands still results **in the stripping of the body of the flesh**. However, in line with Pauline theology, it is not the removal of the penile foreskin that is being described, but the suppression of human or sinful actions, which can be characterized as life in the flesh (Rom. 7:5, 8, 25; 8:3–9, 12; see esp. Rom. 8:13, 'if you are living according to the flesh, you must die'). The reference to **the stripping**, ἀπέκδυσις, of the flesh is an image that will be taken up later in this section to describe the defeat of the rulers and the authorities (Col. 2:15). Here it describes the removal of a negative force, **the flesh**. Later in this chapter, those who trust in visionary experiences are accused of 'being puffed up by the mind of the flesh' (Col. 2:18). The complete expression **the body of the flesh** is found nowhere else in the Pauline writings. It may, however, express the same idea as the phrase 'the body of sin' (Rom. 6:6). That phrase, 'the body of sin', is also a unique Pauline expression, which refers 'to the life of the Christian prior to baptism' (Hultgren 2011: 249). As baptismal imagery is used in the following verse (Col. 2:12), there is a highly compressed and overlapping chain of ideas that connects the 'circumcision made without hands' with putting off the flesh, and union with Christ through being buried together with him in baptism. This removal of a sinful nature and the consequent experience of resurrection with Christ (Col. 2:12) is the complex of events which is the basis of the moral imperatives that follow later in the letter (Col. 3:1–17).

This verse concludes with yet another phrase that describes believers participating in Christ-centred events. It describes 'circumcision without hands' and the 'stripping of the body of the flesh' being accomplished through believers sharing **in the circumcision of Christ**. This is not a reference to the story of the physical circumcision of Jesus as narrated in Luke's Gospel (Lk. 2:21–24, 39), but is an alternate way of describing the circumcision not made with hands. However, some have seen the circumcision described here as denoting an act undergone by Christ, in which believers participate. Typically the event is understood to be the crucifixion, when Christ's physical body was stripped off and he was clothed with a resurrection body (O'Brien 1982: 117). This interpretation may find support in the imagery that follows describing participation in the death and resurrection of Christ (Col. 2:12). However, the sequence reads more like a rapidly shifting chain of images, rather than a single idea replayed through synonymous parallels. If the genitive is not subjective, then it could be an objective genitive describing an activity that Christ performs on believers, as he strips away their former sinful nature using non-physical means. The other major option is that it is a possessive (or even mystical) genitive, referring to a type of circumcision that is experienced by those who now live in the new sphere that is existence in Christ. In this sense it is a circumcision performed by divine agency, that is possessed but not performed by Christ, and is the transformation of the sinful nature into a Christ-like nature through mystic union. This interpretation may align with the wider perspective of the letter, where believers are told 'to strip off the old man' (Col. 3:9). Therefore, in this verse the metaphor of circumcision speaks of the transformation of human nature, and this can only take place through divine agency when believers live in union with Christ.

12 The next participatory act that is described, which union with Christ brings about, is that believers are those **having been buried together with him in baptism**. The portrayal of baptism as an image of being buried with Christ is an understanding of ritual washings or baptism that could have only been formulated in the period after Jesus' death, and as such is a uniquely Christian theological development. The same image is also found in the letter to the Romans (Rom. 6:3–4). As such this may suggest that it was a product of Paul's thinking and reflection on the participation of believers in the death of Christ. The ideas expressed in Romans are virtually identical, although in that context baptism is mentioned before burial, with Paul asking in his rhetorical question 'do you not know that all who have been baptized into Christ Jesus have been baptized into his death?' (Rom. 6:3). Thus baptism is viewed as a participation in the death of Christ. In the following verse Paul utilizes the metaphor of burial: 'therefore we have been buried with him through baptism into death' (Rom. 6:4a). Both in Rom. 6:4 and here in Col. 2:12 a compound verb is used, **buried together**, συνθάπτω, which when used literally refers to either 'being buried in a shared grave or to participants joining together in burying the deceased' (Jewett 2007: 398). Here the language of co-burial is metaphorical, drawing on the reality of Christ's burial, the notion that baptism is a participatory act whereby believers are baptized into Christ, and the daring equation of baptism with burial. The theological pay-off in Pauline thought is that both the burial of Christ and the baptism of believers are seen as transformative events, entailing a raising up from either the grave or the water, after which both Christ and believers are said to exist in a new state. In relation to Christ the new state is a resurrection body, for believers it is a new life resulting in a different manner of existence that is spiritually regenerated through the death of the sinful nature that typified the former mode of being.

There is a textual variant involving the phrase **in baptism**. The more common Greek word used by New Testament writers to refer to Christian baptism is the feminine noun βάπτισμα, and occurs 19 times. By contrast the masculine noun βαπτισμός occurs only four times (if one accepts it is the correct reading in Col. 2:12). The manuscript evidence is divided over whether the masculine or feminine is to be read here, although in both cases the word is in the dative following the preposition 'in', ἐν. The manuscript support is as follows:

βαπτισμός	𝔓⁴⁶ ℵ² B D* F G 075 0278 6 365 1939 1881
βάπτισμα	ℵ* A C D² Ψ 33 𝔐

The masculine form is to be preferred not only because it has stronger and wider manuscript support, but also since it is more likely to have been replaced by the more common feminine form that became the standard signifier for Christian baptism. The masculine form that appears to have been the original reading here is used elsewhere to denote rites of lustration in Judaism (cf. Mk 7:4; Heb. 6:2; 9:10).

Given that the author has just stated that the true act of circumcision is found in union with Christ, the same claim may be advanced about acts of ritual washing. The only meaningful 'baptism' is the one that takes place when believers are buried with Christ, not those offered through the mediation of Jewish ceremonies or any other religious rite.

Communal death is not the end point of the union of believers with Christ, for the Colossians are reminded that through their participation in Christ he becomes the one **in whom also you were raised from the dead**. The sequence again follows wider Pauline thought found in Romans, where it was declared that the purpose of baptism into Christ's death was 'in order that as Christ was raised from the dead through the glory of the Father, so we might walk in newness of life' (Rom. 6:4b). While both Rom. 6:3–4 and Col. 2:12 describe believers as having been co-buried with Christ, the precise language of being resurrected in Christ does not occur in the passage from Romans. There Christ's transformative resurrection enables believers to walk in 'newness of life', although the following verse continues by stating that if 'we have been made partakers in the likeness of his death, then too we shall be of his resurrection' (Rom. 6:5). Again, this idea is consonant with wider Pauline theology, although there appears to be a distinction between the future aspect of the hope of Rom. 6:5, and what is seen as the realized eschatology of Col. 2:12. The introduction to this phrase **in whom**, ἐν ᾧ, has two possible antecedents, either referring to Christ as the one in whom they have been raised, or to baptism as the act 'in which' they were raised. In favour of taking 'baptism' as the antecedent is the argument that it is the immediately preceding term. However, the range and repetition of participation language suggests that the focus remains upon Christ as the locus in which the resurrection of believers takes place. Moreover, the parallel phrase at the beginning of Col. 2:11, where the antecedent can be none other than Christ, supports taking this as a further example of speaking of union with Christ. However, at one level little is changed in terms of interpretation. If Christ is the antecedent, then this phrase is stating that believers are raised in their new sphere of existence, which is life in Christ. If baptism is the antecedent, then believers are raised through the act of baptism, which itself is a participatory act that unites believers with Christ's death.

The manner in which believers are raised from the dead is said to have taken place is **through faith in the working of God**. The **faith** that is described here is that of believers who place their trust in the message of the gospel that it was God who was at work in Christ. It has been suggested that drawing on the wider semantic domain of the Greek term πίστις, it is better understood here as a reference to 'faithfulness', and hence the phrase should be translated as 'through the faithful working of God' (Sumney 2008: 140). While Paul can at times use the Greek term in this way, the use elsewhere in Colossians does not lend support to this suggestion (Col. 1:4, 23; 2:5, 7). Therefore participation in Christ by undergoing the physical act of baptism must also be accompanied by the cognitive acknowledgment that God is the one at work in all the events that centre on Christ, his own baptism, death, burial and resurrection. The word translated as **working**, ἐνέργεια, has already been used in this epistle to describe the effective and energizing work of God within Paul, that enables him to carry out his apostolic ministry (Col. 1:29). Here the **working of God** is focused on Christ. The object of faith in the working of God is recognition that he is the one **who raised him from the dead**. Hence the central work of God in which the

Colossians must have faith is his Christ-centred act of raising Christ from the dead. Dunn has noted that the expression 'God who raised him from the dead' had become a credal or confession formula (see Rom. 4:24; 8:11; 10:9, 1 Cor. 6:14; 15:15; 2 Cor. 4:14; Gal. 1:1, 1 Thess. 1:10; Dunn 1996: 162). The implication is that believers, who are raised from the dead in Christ, are also subject to the same eschatological and transformative power of God that raised Christ from the dead.

13 The final word of the previous verse, 'dead', functions as a catchword that enables the author to progress his train of thought. This occurs through a declaration concerning the state in which the Colossians found themselves prior to receiving their transformed mode of existence in Christ: **and you being dead in your transgressions and in the uncircumcision of your flesh.** In the previous verse the pairing that was used to portray existence prior to and after regeneration was less polarized, because the moment of being 'buried together with him' already speaks of union with Christ, and the reference to Christ being raised depicts the commencement of the transformative process. Here, however, the temporal gap between life prior to faith and that afterwards is widened. Thus the description of **you being dead** conveys the idea of an ongoing condition in the past, and hence the phrase could be rendered as 'when you were dead' (so the NRSV), or concessive 'though you were dead' (Dunn 1996: 145). The image of 'death' here is different from that at the end of the previous verse. There it spoke of Christ's physical death through crucifixion. Here it is a metaphor for spiritual death: the alienation from God caused by sin. That 'sin' is the implied cause is shown by the remedy to this condition at the end of the verse, which is forgiveness. Prior to being united with Christ the state of believers is represented as mortification. In essence, their realm of existence was the opposite of life itself.

Prior to their regeneration, in contrast to now being in Christ, the individuals who are directly addressed are first characterized as being trapped **in your transgressions**. The term παράπτωμα is commonly translated as 'transgression, trespass' and can probably be regarded as a near synonym for the Greek word that is usually translated as 'sin', ἁμαρτία. This similarity in meaning is reinforced by the fact that in Col. 2:11 the 'circumcision made without hands' is described as 'the stripping of the body of sin'; and it is to that idea of circumcision that the author returns in the following clause. Etymologically, the Greek term παράπτωμα is a compound of words that mean 'false step', hence the metaphorical sense of not walking properly, or of crossing some ethical boundary. The second state that characterizes the former necrotic existence is that of being dead **in the uncircumcision of your flesh**. This is a metaphorical image that returns to the idea expressed in Col. 2:11, that the Colossians in their new life in Christ had been 'circumcised with a circumcision not made with hands'. Since the Colossians could be described in the period before they received the gospel as being in a state of **uncircumcision**, this strongly suggests that they were Gentiles, or at least a significant proportion of this community came from a Gentile, rather than from a Jewish background. However, while the reference denotes the non-circumcision of these Gentiles, 'it was not the absence of the physical act of circumcision itself that imposed death, as the connection with trespasses demonstrates' (Sumney 2008: 142). Therefore, there is no call for Gentiles to receive circumcision in the flesh. The image of uncircumcision speaks of exclusion and alienation from God. The remedy to this former condition is to be found in Christ, and one way the author adopts to characterize this event of reconciliation is via the metaphor of non-physical circumcision.

Having vividly described the previous state of being dead due to existing in transgressions and uncircumcision, the focus now falls on the transformed reality that results from the revivifying work of God, **he made you alive together with him**. That God is the subject of the verb **he made you alive** is suggested by the fact that God is the last subject mentioned in the previous verse, 'the working of God, who raised him from the dead' (Col. 2:12). What God has done for Christ when 'he raised him from the dead', he now does for believers, making them alive in the face of the state of death in which they formerly existed. There are variant readings for this phrase. The reading here 'he made you alive' is supported by ℵ* A C K L 6 81 326 1739 1881 D² Ψ 33 𝔐. Some manuscripts read 'he made *us* alive' (𝔓⁴⁶ B 33 323); and others omit the pronoun altogether, 'be made alive' (ℵ² D F G Ψ 075 0208 0278 𝔐). While the combination of the manuscripts 𝔓⁴⁶ B is impressive in support of the pronoun 'us', here the motivation for changing to 'us' or dropping the pronoun altogether is to avoid the clash created with the pronoun in the next phrase 'having forgiven *us*'. In fact, in some manuscripts the harmonization between pronouns is achieved by changing the second pronoun to 'you'. Either way, the reading 'he made you alive' is to be preferred, although some have argued the clash between pronouns is due to a later scribe failing to hear the difference (see Comfort 2008: 628). The basic theological point remains clear regardless of which variant is adopted. The Colossians were formerly stranded in the state of spiritual death, but God has intervened decisively by raising Christ, and God through this act has also made the Colossian believers alive **with him**. Thus through Christ, who was dead but raised to life, the Colossians are restored to life. This image of being raised with Christ aligns with Rom. 6:5, where it is through being united with Christ that believers share in his resurrected life. This also lends weight to the argument in the previous verse that with the phrase ἐν ᾧ, either 'in whom'/'in which', the first translational option referring to Christ is to be preferred. While being buried with Christ in baptism is a Pauline metaphor (Rom. 6:3–4; Col. 2:12), there is no description in Pauline letters of being raised through baptism. Instead one is raised in union with Christ through the power of his resurrection (Rom. 6:5; Col. 2:12–13).

God's action of making the Colossians alive is closely bound up with that of **having forgiven us all our transgressions**. It seems artificial to understand the participle **having forgiven** as standing in a causal relationship with the verb 'he made alive': i.e. 'he made you alive *because* he has forgiven us all our sins' (so O'Brien 1982: 123). The tense of the particle χαρισάμενος (aorist), 'having forgiven', has caused commentators problems in accounting for the correct sequence of events. It has been understood as contempora-neous with the divine act of 'making alive' (Dunn 1996: 146), or as 'logically antecedent' (Abbott 1897: 254). While a strict temporal sequence of events should not be constructed, it does suggest that the forgiveness of sins is a condition that must occur in order that a believer can be made alive. This act of forgiveness is God's way of dealing with the 'transgressions' mentioned earlier in the verse, and referred to again here. The verb χαρίζομαι can denote either the action of giving something freely (Rom. 8:32; 1 Cor. 2:12; Phil. 1:29; 2:9; Phlm. 22), or the act of pardoning or forgiving an offence or offender (2 Cor. 2:7, 10; 12:13). Here it is the second sense that is intended. One of the prominent words in Colossians, 'all', occurs here to declare emphatically the totality of God's pardon of sins, in that he has forgiven **all our transgressions**. This verse not only describes the state of the Colossians prior to belief 'being dead', and afterward 'being made alive'. It also describes the cause of the former state – dwelling in transgressions and uncircumcision – and the remedy to that state – God has forgiven all our transgressions. Thus, 'every impediment to relationship and life with God has been removed' (Sumney 2008: 143). Later in Colossians the action of forgiveness is to be exercised between community members, and is to be based upon the fact that the Lord has forgiven them (Col. 3:13). Here the reference to the forgiveness of transgressions leads into the description of the process by which the 'handwritten debt' of sin is removed by the cross.

14 At this point the author deploys the last image in a series that represents a sequence of metaphors that portrays the change that the Colossians underwent from the state they existed in prior to belief, and that in which they find themselves now they are united with Christ:

> The body of flesh was removed through a circumcision not made with hands. (Col. 2:11)

> By being buried with Christ in baptism, they have been raised in him to life. (Col. 2:12)

> Formerly being dead in transgressions and uncircumcision, they have been made alive through God's forgiveness (Col. 2:13)

> The debt against has been erased by it being nailed to the cross. (Col. 2:14)

In the face of the possibility that the Colossians were susceptible to 'being taken captive through philosophy and vain deceit' (Col. 2:8a), and the failure to recognize that all the blessings of the mystery of God were 'according to Christ' (Col. 2:8b), this set of striking images emphasizes the complete and effective transformation believers have already undergone in union with Christ.

This verse commences the final image used to depict the trans-formative process by declaring what from the perspective of the recipients of this letter is now viewed as a past event: **having**

erased the handwritten debt of ordinances against us. Again the subject of the action is not explicit here. Is the one who expunged the debt 'God' or 'Christ'? Given that God was the last previously named subject (Col. 2:12), and that God is most likely to be the one envisaged as forgiving transgressions in the previous verse (Col. 2:13), and moreover that in the following verse it appears to be God who 'stripped the rulers and authorities', since the subject is said to have 'triumphed over them through him' (Col. 2:15) where the 'him' is Christ and is different from the one doing the 'stripping' and the 'triumphing', this is strongly suggestive that it is God who is seen as the agent in all of these actions. However, the actions and purposes of God and Christ overlap to a significant degree and there is not necessarily always a clear division in understanding as to which action should be attributed to God or to Christ. In some ways such a strict division would be false in the mind of the author since together they reconcile humanity, and partake in disclosing the fulness of the divine mystery.

The verb **having erased**, ἐξαλείψας, is not a common word in the New Testament (ἐξαλείφω: elsewhere Acts 3:19; Rev. 3:5; 7:7; 21:4). In Acts it describes the 'wiping away' of sins (Acts 3:19), while in Revelation it is used to promise that the one who overcomes will not have his name 'erased' from the book or life (Rev. 3:5), or that all tears will be 'wiped away' (Rev. 7:17; 21:4). Therefore the term speaks of the permanent removal of some object so as to leave no trace. As the term is employed in early Christian usage it is frequently used to describe the removal of sin, 'let us wipe away the former sins from ourselves' (*2 Clem.* 13:1). Hence it appears that the erasure of **the handwritten debt of ordinances against us** is a metaphor for the removal of sins. The term for **handwritten** occurs only here in the New Testament, but its sense is fairly straightforward, being a compound of two common words (as in English). The term can be used to designate a ledger in which outstanding debts are recorded (Polybius, *Hist.* 30.8.4; Tob. 5:3; 9:5). The *Apocalypse of Zephaniah* uses the term (a Greek loanword in the Coptic text) where in contrast to the book of the living kept at heaven's gateway by the angels of the Lord, there is a handwritten record kept by the angels of the accuser, in which are written 'all the sins of men' (*Apoc. Zeph.* 3:7–8). Similarly, in the *Apocalypse of Paul* when a soul comes before the Lord for judgment and protests that it had not sinned, an angel brings forward a handwritten document, which contains a catalogue of sins committed (*Apoc. Paul.* 17). Thus while in secular contexts the term designated a legal or business document recording debt to be repaid, in Jewish or Christian contexts it takes on the technical designation for a list of sins used at the heavenly assize.

Both the opening words of this clause in Greek, literally 'the against us' handwritten debt, and the clause that immediately follows, **which was against us**, together emphatically state the oppositional nature of the metaphorical document that was a source of accusation against people prior to coming to faith. What is stated as standing in an accusatorial role against the Colossians is **the handwritten debt of ordinances**. In Greek this expression is constructed from a noun pair with the first term being in the accusative case and the second noun occurring in the dative χειρόγραφον τοῖς δόγμασιν. Literally, the expression could be rendered as 'handwritten debt with/in the ordinances'. This is an instrumental use of the dative where the second noun specifies the content or material of which the head noun comprises. The idea is better expressed in idiomatic English by using the preposition 'of' to describe the material of which the head noun consists. Some have understood the 'ordinances', or 'decrees', or 'dogmas' as denoting the regulations of the Mosaic law, which Gentiles had failed to observe. However, it is possible to understand this more generally as a list of sins, without reference to the Mosaic law. Rather than taking the phrase as an instrumental dative, others have described this as an epexegetical dative, translating the expression along the lines of 'the certificate of debt consisting of decrees' (NASB; TDNT: II, 231). However, Harris understands it slightly differently as an 'associative dat. or dat. of accompanying circumstances' (Harris 2010: 97), and thus translates it as 'the bond, along with its decrees'. The nuance between these two major options is slight, but it appears more likely that the author is describing the items that comprised the handwritten debt, rather than seeing these elements as attendant circumstances.

The way in which this accusatory certificate of debt has been dealt with is a two-stage process. First it was removed from the sight of those whose guilt was catalogued in the document. The verbal expression **and he has taken it** portrays of conscious act of physical removing or carrying away an item. The verb occurs in the perfect and shows that the result is a state that prevails in the present on the basis of an act carried out in the past. The description that the handwritten debt was removed **from our midst** shows that the concern was that it should no longer be present to accuse those who follow the earlier injunction 'to walk in him' (Col. 2:6; cf. Rom. 8:1–4). The pastoral aspect of this divine act is noteworthy, and the image is a vivid one with God portrayed as physically carrying away the handwritten document that accused those united in Christ, and he removed this certificate of debt from the midst of those who had incurred the debt. The second stage refers to the destruction of the document. In another startling image, God is seen as destroying the force of this debt by **having nailed it to the cross**. Without wishing to enter into anachronistic debates about theories of atonement that were formulated in a much later period than when this epistle was written, there is a clear sense that the cross is either the tool which is used in the eradication of the document that contained ordinances that were listed as debts, or it is the location where this erasure of the debt takes place. Numerous metaphors coalesce in this verse, and it would be foolhardy to attempt to construct a theory of atonement (if one wanted to do such a thing anyway) on the basis of this swirl of images. Yet, more than being foolish, it would negate the almost poetic impact of this rapid and vivid expression of the effective work of God in dealing with the former human condition, which brings about reconciliation through union with Christ. The verb **having nailed**, προσηλώσας (lexical form: προσηλόω), is another term that occurs only here in the New Testament writings. In fact, the New Testament is remarkably restrained in commenting upon the means by which Jesus was affixed to the cross. Only in the fourth gospel is there a reference to 'the print of the nails' (Jn 20:25). In later Christian texts there are implied references to the means of crucifixion:

> Truly in the time of Pontius Pilate and Herod the Tetrach, he was nailed on our behalf in the flesh. (Ignatius, *Smyrn.* 1.2)

> For the one who prophesied about him said, 'Spare my life from the sword' and 'Nail my flesh, because an assembly of evildoers has risen up against me'. (*Barn.* 5:13)

Here, however, taken literally, it is the handwritten document that is being nailed to the cross, not Jesus himself. Yet it is questionable whether such a literal reading is intended. Behind this conflation of images is the reality that it was Jesus, and not some handwritten document, who was 'nailed' to the cross. In this way the death of Christ is seen as expunging the condemnation of sin. Such ideas are explored in different ways elsewhere in the Pauline writings: 'God made him who had no sin to be sin for us, so that in him we might become the righteousness of God' (2 Cor. 5:21; cf. Rom. 8:3). Therefore, the death of Christ can be alluded to metaphorically as an act whereby a catalogue of the transgressions of the Colossians is nailed to the cross, and the condemnatory power that it had held over them was destroyed. Again, this represents the transformative process they had undergone in terms of having their existence transferred from an uncircumcised, mortified and condemned state to one where they had been made alive and freed from sin as they participate in new life in Christ.

15 The destruction of the metaphorical certificate of debt achieved through the cross was characterized as a divine action. It is God whose activity is described here also. However, there is a shift in the focus in the way this metaphor is employed. The four previous metaphors (Col. 2:11–14) depicted the changed sphere of existence of the Colossians before and after coming to faith in Christ. Here the focus returns to the spiritual forces that are opposed to the divine purposes. Employing terminology that has been used earlier in the letter, the author describes God's past action of **having stripped the rulers and authorities**. The nominal form from the same word group as 'having stripped', ἀπεκδυσάμενος, was used in Col. 2:11 in reference to the stripping away of the flesh, in the circumcision made without hands. In Col. 3:9 the verbal form is used again, and like Col. 2:11 it is used to call upon the Colossians to lay aside their previous state of existence and the past practices that accompanied that mode of being. Here, however, the act of 'stripping' is not experienced by believers, but is the action that divests the **rulers and authorities** of their power. Some commentators have argued for an unannounced change of subject at some point during this section, with the principal actor changing from God to Christ. Based on this theory, the verb **having stripped** is understood to be in the middle voice, and consequently self-referential to the subject of the verb, that is Christ. This results in a translation such as 'having divested himself of the rulers and authorities' or 'having divested himself (in death), he put the rulers and the authorities to open shame' (Wilson 2005: 191). This does not appear to be the most natural reading of the syntax, and moreover the requirement of an unsignalled change of subject is unnecessary and unconvincing.

Instead, the militaristic metaphor that occurs here would have resonated with the contemporary readers. Defeated enemies were commonly stripped of armour and sometimes of clothing, and paraded as captives before the victorious force. Plutarch describes the surrender of the Gallic military leader Vercingetorix in the following terms:

> And the leader of the whole war, Vercingetorix, after putting on his most beautiful armour and decorating his horse, rode out through the gate. He made a circuit around Caesar, who remained seated, and then leaped down from his horse, stripped off his suit of armour, and seating himself at Caesar's feet remained motionless, until he was delivered up to be kept in custody for the triumph. (Plutarch, *Caesar* 27.9–10)

After being imprisoned in the Tullianum in Rome for five years, Vercingetorix was publically displayed in the triumphal procession of Caesar in 46 B.C. Then, according to custom, he was executed after the triumph, probably by strangulation. In Colossians, there is an irony in that the cross is portrayed as a symbol of triumph. In wider first-century Mediterranean culture the cross was the implement of defeat, public shame, and physically for Christ it displayed him as stripped and executed. However, from the stance of the world-inverting theology of the early Christians, it was during this event of apparent defeat that Christ actually triumphed over the 'rulers and authority', and in fact he was the one who stripped them of their power. These **rulers and authorities** were first mentioned in the epistle in the christological hymn, where they were the final two elements in the list of the things created in Christ (Col. 1:16). They recur again in the singular, when Christ is said to be 'the head of every ruler and authority' (Col. 2:10). Here they are mentioned again as the archetypal opponents, whose defeat and public shame has already taken place.

The language of military conquest continues. For having stripped the opposing forces, it is said of God that **he exposed them in public**. Most commentators take this exposure as the emotional experience of ridicule. Thus Lohse argues that God 'has divested them of their usurped majesty by putting them on public display and exposing them to ridicule' (Lohse 1971: 112). The verb 'he exposed', ἐδειγμάτισεν, can be used of various forms of disgrace. However, given the military metaphors in the rest of the verse, and the fact that it was used of adulteresses being physically disgraced by shaving of hair (Dio Chrys. 47 [64] 3) and even of the exposure of others (Vettius Valens, *Astr.* 43.26; Hephaesto, *Astr.* 2.32, 34; P.Ryl. 1.28.70), it is more likely here that it is an image of defeated powers being stripped naked **in public** and thus exposed to physical humiliation.

The final aspect of the overwhelming shock and awe directed towards the opponents is based upon the explanation that God was able to expose the 'rulers and authorities' since God had defeated them, **having triumphed over them in him**. Here there is another rare term in the New Testament, **having triumphed**, θριαμβεύσας (cf. 2 Cor. 2:14). This appears to be used here in a technical sense of leading a defeated person or a captor in a triumphal procession. Such Roman victory processions were part of the imperial display of power. The intertwining of the purposes of God and the role of Christ is emphasized by the key phrase that God triumphed over the rulers and authorities **in him**. There is a close identification between the agent of God's defeat of the powerful forces, which is Christ, and the instrument of that victory, which is the cross. The paradox, which is expressed elsewhere in Pauline writings (1 Cor. 1:18–25), is that the cross, an implement of death and defeat, is in fact the divine means of achieving life and victory.

In this section the letter has presented an exposition of its own thesis, expressed in Col. 2:8b, that the Colossians should live according to Christ and not according to the elements of the world. The argument has been based on a series of daring and vivid metaphors. However, that was only half of the thesis statement. The other half was the imperative that the Colossians should be on their guard lest anybody attempt to take them captive using human philosophy or vain deceit (Col. 2:8a). It is to that subject that the letter now returns.

10. RESIST FALSE RELIGIOUS PRACTICES
(2:16–19)

(16) Therefore do not let anyone judge you in food and in drink, or in respect of a festival or new moon or Sabbaths (17) which are a shadow of the coming things, but the body is Christ. (18) Let no one abuse you delighting in humility and the worship of angels, which he has seen while being initiated, being vainly puffed up by the mind of his flesh, (19) and not holding to the head, from whom all the body through the joints and the ligaments, being supplied and held together, increases with the increase of God.

This paragraph takes up the concern expressed in the opening part of Col. 2:8 that there was a danger, potential or real, that the Colossians might fall prey to the idea that the message of Christ needed to be supplemented with 'philosophy' or 'human tradition'. Here is perhaps the best indication that the author is dealing with a specific situation that was confronting believers in Colossae. Notwithstanding the importance of these verses for supporting the idea of a specific problem confronting the community, it is the case that what may have been obvious to the recipients of the letter from these verses is unfortunately now obscure to modern readers. The result has been the expenditure of much scholarly energy on these verses. Some of these investigations have been very valuable, suggesting important ways to read this material with the illumination of texts that describe various cultic practices either from Jewish writings or those descriptions of mystery religions.

16 Paralleling the imperative in Col. 2:8a, 'beware lest there will be somebody who takes you captive', here the letter returns to the same theme with another negative prohibition: **therefore do not let anyone judge you**. The agreement is more obvious in Greek with the phrase μὴ οὖν τις ὑμᾶς here, differing from Col. 2:8a only by the interruption of the conjunction οὖν, which cannot stand in first position in Greek. This repeated phraseology may act as a signal to those who heard this letter being read to recall the earlier prohibition, and to read these more specific injunctions in light of the more general warning against 'philosophy and vain deceit' (Col. 2:8a).

The connecting conjunction **therefore** can indicate either temporal or logical sequence. Here it is the latter that is intended. The consequence of the defeat of the 'rulers and the authorities' should be that the Colossians do not allow themselves to be defeated or judged by any others. Hence resistance of false religious practices is to be based on the new state of existence that believers now have, and which has been elucidated in the series of metaphors in Col. 2:10–15. If the indefinite pronoun **anybody** is referring to an actual person rather than a hypothetical antagonist, then the stratagem of not dignifying opponents by naming them appears to be adopted here. The prohibition **do not let anyone judge you** is of course a near impossibility, since if taken literally the act of judging is an internal attitude on the part of those who regard the faith of the Colossians as inadequate. This imperative is a shorthand way of instructing the recipients of the letter not to accept the judgment that their faith is not fully valid. The injunction is a rhetorical device intended to empower the Colossians to reject the 'program of spiritual development that does not have Christ at its heart' (Moo 2008: 218). The verb **judge**, κρίνω, has a spectrum of nuances from being a positive act of discernment to that of forming a negative and inaccurate assessment, as is the case here. In non-eschatological contexts God's judgment on believers is a call to moral rectitude, 'but being judged by the Lord we are corrected' (1 Cor. 11:32). While the exercise of judgment is primarily a divine prerogative, elsewhere Paul can proclaim that 'the holy ones will judge the world' (1 Cor. 6:2). However, here, since the act of judgment is not exercised by God, or by those aligned with the correct understanding of the gospel, this act of judgment is seen as defective, and thus its validity is to be rejected by the Colossians (cf. Rom. 2:1, 3; 14:3, 10, 13).

The content of the judgment is then identified, and it covers two major areas relating to dietary matters and the observance of religious festivals. The co-ordinated pair of actions that instructs the Colossians not to allow themselves to be judged **in food and in drink** describes dietary scruples. While these issues are known to be an aspect of Jewish cultic practice, they are not exclusive to Judaism. Asceticism was also a feature in certain pagan religions. The ingestion of dead flesh was seen as inhibiting the soul's return to the higher spiritual realm since it encumbered the soul with physical matter. Moreover, bloody flesh was connected with demonic energy, and activated the negative powers, thereby threatening to enslave the soul in the body of flesh (Porphyry, *Abst.* 1.56–57). Within Judaism dietary prohibitions centred primarily on a binary classification system of clean and unclean foods. While the origins of Jewish food laws are to be found in the Hebrew Scriptures (Lev. 11:1–47; note especially 'make a distinction between the unclean and the clean', Lev. 11:47a), dietary regulations pertaining both to food and drink were live issues in the late Second Temple period and beyond. For instance, Josephus reports that some Essenes expelled from the community chose to starve because they would not partake of food that was deemed impure by the standards set by the group (*B.J.* 2.143–44). Similarly, a Mishnaic debate is recorded concerning whether a fowl and cheese could be served on the same table if not eaten together – so the House of Shammai – or whether they could neither be eaten nor served together – so the House of Hillel (*m. Hullin* 8.1; *m. Eduyoth* 5.2). In relation to drink, the Dead Sea Scrolls community attests a debate about the purity of liquids, where flowing or poured liquids are seen as capable of transmitting impurity between containers (4QMMT). Concerns over the regulation of consumption of food for religious reasons would have made sense and been familiar both in a pagan and in a Jewish context.

The second area in which the Colossians are warned against allowing themselves to be judged is **in respect of a festival or new moon or Sabbaths**. While the two elements pertaining to diet were linked by the connective conjunction 'and', καί, here a different conjunction 'or', ἤ, is used, which is usually taken to have some disjunctive force, denoting separable alternatives. While the majority of manuscripts (א A C D F G I Ψ 075 0278 33 𝔐) harmonize the first conjunction, changing it to 'or' to make it agree with the three following conjunctions, such a move is unnecessary and simply reflects a desire for stylistic uniformity. The sequence of conjunctions reveals a connected sequence with the final three items not presented as discrete alternatives, but as correlated possibilities. Here this triad of terms designates calendric concerns of a religious nature. Again such issues were of concern in both Hellenistic and Jewish settings. In relation to the term **festival**, in the pagan setting there was substantial overlap concerning the calendar for both civic and religious reasons. While there was variety between the religious calendars of each

10. RESIST FALSE RELIGIOUS PRACTICES (2:16–19)

city or Roman colony, the ordering of religious celebrations was a fundamental concern. The types of festivals encompassed various areas of life, such as agriculture (*Cerealia*, 19 April), civic celebration (*Saturnalia*, 17 December), military life (*Equirria*, 27 February, 14 March), or the structure of the year (*Diualia*, or winter solstice, 21 December). This linkage between civic and religious obligations, which were regulated by a series of annual festivals as designated by regional calendars, pervaded life in the Mediterranean world. Judaism observed a series of major annual festivals. These included the celebration of Passover and Unleavened Bread, Festival of Weeks, Day of Atonement, Tabernacles, Hanukkah, and Purim. Thus, the observance of festivals was the common experience of Jews and pagans in the first-century world. The reference to the term **new moon** is general and somewhat imprecise in nature. Again, the term is found across all strands for first-century society. In pagan contexts the term can occur with an overtly religious sense, as evidenced in the phrase contained in one of the magical papyri, 'the new moon according to God' (P.Mag. Par. 1.787.2389). Within the Jewish tradition the new moon is connected with a reference to the Sabbath and is considered a propitious day to consult a prophet (2 Kgs 4:23); elsewhere, like the reference here, it is connected with 'offerings for Sabbaths, for new moons, and for festivals' (2 Chron. 31:3). The connection of the same three terms in 2 Chron. 31:3 that occurs here in Col. 2:16 forms an interesting parallel, though it is not necessary to suggest direct literary dependence, especially given the widespread use of all these terms.

The final element, **Sabbaths**, is the distinctive Jewish weekly seventh-day festival of rest, which marked the completion of the seven-day cycle. The requirement of Sabbath observance was a dividing issue between Judaism and certain sectors of the early Christian movement. In the *Epistle of Barnabas*, in connection with new moons, the Lord prophetically declares 'your new moons and Sabbaths I cannot stand' (*Barn.* 2:5; cf. 15:8; Isa. 1:13). From this reference to the Jewish weekly festival, some have wished to infer that the target of this verse with its prohibitions against being judged in relation to food, drink, festivals, new moons, and Sabbaths reflected a problem that was exclusively a tendency towards accepting Judaizing practices. Thus with great certainty Dunn declares:

281

> But if sabbath is so clearly a distinctively Jewish festival, then the probability is that the "festival" and "new moon" also refer to the Jewish versions of these celebrations. The point is put beyond dispute when we note that the three terms together, "sabbaths, new moons, and feasts," was in fact a regular way of speaking of the main festivals of Jewish religion… We must conclude, therefore, that all the elements in this verse bear a characteristically and distinctively Jewish color, that those who cherished them so critically must have been the (or some) Jews of Colossae, and that their criticism arose from Jewish suspicion of Gentiles making what they would regard as unacceptable claims to the distinctive Jewish heritage without taking on all that was most distinctive of that heritage. (Dunn 1996: 175)

Apart from the observation that the Sabbath was 'a distinctively Jewish festival', every one of the other claims Dunn makes is open to challenge, and none is beyond dispute. The discussion above has shown that, with the exception of the term 'Sabbath', each one of the terms was important in both Greco-Roman and Jewish religious systems. As to the presence of Jews in Colossae, this may have been the case, but so far no positive archaeological evidence has been unearthed to establish that claim. Even if a Jewish presence were to be discovered it would not prove the claim that Dunn asserts. One thing that is certain is that the majority religious culture was paganism, probably incorporating civic religion and the existence of mystery cults – and it was from that pluralistic religious culture that the Colossian believers had been drawn. The scenario for an exclusively Jewish challenge fails to recognize the mixed language of both Judaism and the mystery religions that pervades the letter, and it appears to force the discussion into some Procrustean bed of a theological problem that seems to have been derived from Paul's letter to the Galatians, rather than from the actual contents contained in the Epistle to the Colossians. Instead, the language here would make sense to any person familiar with the religious landscape of the first-century Mediterranean world, whether pagan or Jewish. Such a person would have recognized the religious nature of the ascetic call for restraint in issues of 'food and drink', and of the public piety expressed through observance of festival or new moons, or even the distinctively Jewish Sabbath. For the author of this letter, however, such things were at best extraneous, and worse still they were potentially fatal distractions because they removed attention from Christ and placed trust in vacuous religious practices.

17 The author's assessment of these areas where the Colossians are being judged, namely dietary concerns and observance of festivals, is that they are of an insubstantial nature: **which are a shadow of the coming things**. The term **shadows**, σκία, can be used in a literal sense in the New Testament to describe the area of darkness of partial illumination formed when an object obscures light rays (Acts 5:15). However, here its metaphorical use relates both to the partial illumination and perhaps even more so to the insubstantial aspect and lack of matter that constitute a shadow. The term occurs nowhere else in the Pauline writings, but a similar metaphorical sense is employed by the writer of Hebrews (Heb. 8:5; 10:1). The main critique of those who would pass judgment on the Colossians is that they were pressuring the recipients of the letter to adopt religious practices that are in fact inferior not just to what has already been received in Christ, but also to **the coming things**. These 'coming things', τὰ μελλόντα, have been seen by some as not having a future aspect from the stance of the author. Instead, taking the elements in the previous verse as uniformly Jewish in character it is argued that the coming things are 'to be interpreted from the period when the legal restrictions of verse 16 were enjoined; it is future from the standpoint of the OT' (O'Brien 1982: 140). There has been a reticence to give the natural future force to the reference to 'the coming things', primarily to shore-up the exclusively Jewish interpretation of the elements in that verse (Col. 2:16). However, once that unnecessary linkage is broken, it becomes possible to read this verse more naturally as part of the sustained critique of false religious practices. Things that are being pressed upon the Colossians now are to be resisted because the mystery of God has already been experienced by believers and at some point in the future the coming things will reveal even more fully the shadowy nature of the religious practice that the Colossians are urged to follow. There should be no hesitancy to see an eschatological dimension in this description, even if an explicit reference to the *parousia* is not present in the letter. While the author emphasizes the present experience of receiving divine blessings, there is also a future dimension to the new life that is still to be revealed. Only a few verses later the Colossians are promised that 'when Christ, your life, is revealed, then you also will be revealed in glory with him' (Col. 3:4). Likewise, here the author refers to the future blessings, and argues that the final rebuttal of those who attempt to promote ascetic and pietistic practices will occur when Christ is revealed in his glory (cf. Barth and Blanke 1994: 'in Col. 2:17 *skia* is interpreted eschatologically through the addition of *tōn mellontōn*', 340).

Instead of being lured to place trust in insubstantial things the recipients of the letter are told **but the body is Christ**. Taking the conjunction as adversative, δέ, **but**, shows that here the correct source of true spiritual substance and confidence is Christ. While the basic meaning of this phrase is fully apparent, exactly what the expression **the body is Christ** denotes has been the source of various suggestions. Grammatically, the phrase is fairly straightforward; however, the interpretative choices arise because of the range of meanings encompassed by the term **body**, σῶμα. At least four major alternatives have been suggested:

1.   'the substance', 'the reality'.
2.   the physical body of Christ.
3.   the church.
4.   the eschatological body of the exalted Christ.

Given that there is an explicit contrast with the term 'shadow', instead of such insubstantial and dark penumbras of reality, the term 'body' is a metaphorical way of speaking of something that is solid and substantial. While Wilson agrees with this primary understanding, he draws attention to the fact that the term 'body' is used elsewhere in the letter. Noting that twice it is used in reference to Christ's physical body (Col. 1:22; 2:11), and twice in reference to the church (Col. 1:18, 24), he concludes that '[i]t is difficult to avoid the conclusion that these associations were somehow present to the mind of our author as he wrote' (Wilson 2005: 220). In contrast, Sumney argues for an ecclesiological understanding of the term 'body', not just on the basis of previous usages in the epistle, but also because later in this paragraph 'body' is used in a clearly ecclesiological sense (Col. 2:19). This second argument is the stronger argument, but as Sumney astutely comments, 'no translation of this part of v. 17 is certain' (Sumney 2008: 152). However, the understanding of 'body' in this passage in the first sense, that is as denoting something substantial in contrast to a shadow without substance, has a long pedigree in the history of interpretation. Theodore of Mopsuestia commented that:

> Those things are as much weaker than what has to do with Christ as a shadow is weaker than the body. In fact, a body is a substance, but a shadow ordinarily merely appears. Moreover, the shadow could by no means appear by itself, if there were not a body, for the body ordinarily supplies the possibility for the shadow to come into being or be seen. (Theodore of Mopsuestia, *ad Colossenses* 2.17)

Given the natural contrast that is drawn with 'shadow', and also the history of interpretation, it appears best to take the primary meaning as denoting something real and substantial. However, given that the term is used in different ways throughout the letter, including in an ecclesial sense two verses later, it is also important to affirm the dexterity of the author in selecting terminology that evokes various images within the letter itself. The ambiguity of this multivalent term therefore appears intentional, and it is probably best to translate the term a 'body' in English to capture that sense of ambiguity.

Hence the thing of substance, contrasting with the shadowy things, **is Christ**. The intention is obvious. In stark contrast to those who would desire to lure the Colossians into observing certain dietary practices or religious festivals, the author again reminds readers that the centre, substance, and totality of their faith is Christ. In fact, he will be disclosed to be the fulness and mystery of God in the eschatological age, but they are to know him as that already without supplement or replacement in their own experience of being in him.

18 This verse is perhaps simultaneously one of the most intriguing and most difficult in the letter. It appears to provide some specific details concerning the pressure being brought to bear on the Colossians to engage in certain religious practices. However, determining what the descriptions actually mean is difficult both because of the rarity of some of the terminology and also because the grammatical constructions and syntax are cumbersome and allow various interpretations.

A second negative prohibition in this section (Col. 2:16–19), in the form an imperative command, commences with this verse, **let no one abuse you**. The first exegetical challenge concerns the verb that has been translated here as **abuse**, καταβραβευέτω (pres. act. imperative 3rd singular). Harris offers three translational options – none of which is adopted here, although the last one comes closest to the sense of 'abuse'. Harris' three possibilities, with some of the supporting authorities replicated here, are (Harris 2010: 106).

1. 'disqualify' (NAB², ESV); 'declare disqualified' (Moule 1957: 104).
2. 'rob of a (rightful) prize' (RV, NAB¹, NASB², Zerwick 1966: 451).
3. 'condemn' (GNB, O'Brien 1982: 141).

The first option is preferred by Harris and the majority of commentators. While the compound Greek verb καταβραβεύω occurs nowhere else in the New Testament and is in fact rare in all extant Greek literature, the simple form βραβεύω while also occurring only once in the New Testament, in Col. 3:15, is a more common term and has a range of meanings such as 'judge', 'award prizes', 'rule' (BDAG: 183). Consequently, with the rare compound verb καταβραβεύω the meaning has usually been determined by giving the prefix κατα- its full force of 'against', and hence the phrase is commonly translated as 'let no one rule against you/disqualify you'. The problem with this is that, as in English, while compound verbs can retain the meaning of their component parts they often change meaning in unexpected ways. In a much-overlooked article (Yinger 2003: 138–45), Yinger sets out five discrete understandings of the verb:

1. 'rob of a prize'.
2. 'award a prize unjustly'.
3. 'disqualify', either in an athletic or non-athletic sense.
4. 'condemn', where a forensic background is assumed.
5. 'injure, mistreat, victimize'.

The only surviving pre-Christian usage of this term is in the fourth century BCE oration of Demosthenes, *Against Meidas*: 'For this reason we know that Straton was condemned (καταβραβευθέντα) by Meidas and disenfranchised contrary to all justice' (*Oration* 21). The translation 'rule against/disqualify' tends to emerge only in the context of Christian commentators discussing Col. 2:18. However, when Christian writers used this term in other contexts, although the evidence is sparse, they tend to offer a sense closer to options four or five. For instance, in a third-century CE letter cited by Eusebius that describes the ill-gotten gains of Paul of Samosata, his actions are described in the following terms: 'For he deprives the injured of their rights (καταβραβεύων τοὺς ἀδικουμένους), and promises to help them for money' (Eusebius, *H.E.* 7.30.7). The athletic metaphor that is associated with the simplex verb βραβεύω in the earlier period of the Greek language, and which is often associated with the compound verb as used in Col. 2:18, appears to have been largely lost. This leads Yinger to conclude:

> To translate καταβραβευέτω in Col 2:18 with 'mistreat, victimize, take advantage of' or even 'bring under accusation' also makes good sense contextually…rather than continuing the lexically questionable route of preferring 'rob of a prize' or 'disqualify [from athletic games].' (Yinger 2003: 144–45)

Therefore, following Yinger's careful analysis, the translation adopted here avoids athletic imagery, and instead is a warning to avoid mistreatment or abuse from those who would subject the Colossians to unnecessary religious practices.

The abuse that is to be avoided is expanded upon by reference to two practices in which those who are influencing the Colossians engage. The first characteristic of those who would abuse the Colossians is that they are people **delighting in humility**. This is a modal clause, which expresses the circumstances that are required or enable the possible abuse against which the Colossians are to protect themselves. Here those who would lead the Colossians into error are described as having misplaced emphases in their outlook, since their goal is that of **delighting** in religious experiences. The sense 'delighting' is not the primary or most common meaning of the Greek verb θέλω. However, that meaning does appear in the Septuagint, where the verb expresses 'a liking for something' or 'a delighting in something' (cf. LXX Pss. 21:9; 39:7; Hos. 6:6). This meaning occurs here, and elsewhere in the New Testament (cf. Lk. 20:46).

The term **humility**, ταπεινοφροσύνη, is regularly a positive virtue in the New Testament and early Christian writings (esp. Col. 3:12; cf. Acts 2:19; Phil. 2:3; 1 Pet. 5:5; *1 Clem.* 21:8; Origen, *Contra Cel.* 6, 15, 23). However, here the humility is misdirected since it appears to be focused on heightening one's own spiritual experience and religiosity, rather than for the sake of living a life worthy of Christ (cf. Col. 2:23). The implication appears to be that those who wish to impose certain religious practices, do so in order to delight in their experiences and self-perceived spiritual progress. Given that the Colossians may have been experiencing pressure to conform to certain dietary regulations and observance of religious festivals, it is possible that this humility is some kind of self-denying asceticism.

The second practice of the self-inflated religious experientialists is described as being **the worship of angels**. The flexibility of the genitive construction in Greek often creates major interpretative debates, and this specific example is an extremely contested case. Alongside grammatical considerations are also to be found theological factors – especially for those who see the practices that are being imposed on the Colossians as essentially Jewish. If that were the case, then worship directed towards angels would, it is argued, contravene the strict monotheism of first-century Judaism. In effect, a prior decision concerning the identity of the putative opponents or errorists is used to exclude one of the grammatical possibilities for this phrase. With the Greek phrase θρησκείᾳ τῶν ἀγγελῶν the first noun stands in the dative case because it is governed by the preposition ἐν. This grammatical construction reveals a second area in which those who would judge the Colossians see their own religious practices as superior to those of the recipients of the letter, who are encouraged to maintain faith in the Pauline form of the gospel without the addition of any supplementary practices. The non-repetition of the preposition points to the close co-ordination of the two actions described here, but it is unnecessary to see this as a hendiadys with a resultant translation, such as 'by insisting on servility in the worship of angels' (NAB[1]). The two major options are either:

1. subjective genitive = 'angelic worship', 'worshipping with angels'.
2. objective genitive = 'the worship of angels', 'worship directed towards angels'.

In favour of the first option, commentators have drawn on evidence from late Second Temple Judaism, such as the belief of the Qumran community that 'the Angels of Holiness are [with] their [congregation]' (1QSa 2.8–9). From this and similar references it is clear that there is 'evidence of a desire particularly within apocalyptic and mystical circles of first-century Judaism to join in with the worship of angels in heaven' (Dunn 1996: 180–81). Those who support this option express the case against the second possibility in the following terms: 'characteristic of Judaism, however, was warning against worship of the host of heaven... Were the Colossian "philosophy" Jewish in character, on this hypothesis, we would have to envisage a very syncretistic form of Judaism, unlike anything else we know of' (Dunn 1996: 180). As is apparent, the rejection of the second alternative is based on assessments of what was and what was not possible within first-century Judaism. However, having rejected such an exclusively Jewish background as the basis of the critique in Col. 2:16, and instead seeing a more all-encompassing critique of supplementary religious practices whether from Judaism or paganism, this leaves open the second possibility (Wilson 2005: 222–23). Lightfoot cited a ruling from the Council of Laodicea, geographically proximate but temporally much later (c. 363 C.E.), which legislated against the invocation of angels (Lightfoot 1886: 68; citing canon 35). Moreover, and in far greater detail, Arnold shows that angelic beings were not unique to Judaism, and the veneration of angels is attested in pagan contexts. Apart from magical texts where angels are invoked to protect the suppliant, or to deliver a curse, there are other pagan angel texts that reveal the existence of angel cults in Asia Minor. One of Arnold's collected examples will suffice to illustrate the veneration of angels (Arnold 1995: 71):

1. To Zeus Most High and the Good Angel, Claudius Achilles and Galatia, with all their household, made a thank offering for deliverance.
2. To Zeus Most High and the Divine Angel, Neon and Euphrosune [give thanks] on behalf of their household.
3. We give thanks to the Angelic Divinity for deliverance.
4. We give thanks to the Angelic Divinity.

In combination with Zeus in the first two lines, and named separately in the final two lines, an angelic being is given an elevated title and venerated and praised for the blessings that have been granted. Given this contextual evidence from the wider area of Phrygia and surrounding regions, it is possible to see evidence for the practice of worship directed towards angelic beings. Therefore, it is plausible that those whom the Colossians were told to resist saw one of their superior religious practices being that of the veneration of angels. Precisely what this denoted is not recoverable, and it may even be the case that the author of the letter has described the practice in this way for polemical purposes. However, what appears to be envisaged is a worship or veneration directed towards angels as the objects or recipients of cultic worship.

In relation to the next part of the verse, **which he has seen while being initiated**, Arnold has stated that 'the phrase ἃ ἑόρακεν ἐμβατεύων in Colossians 2:18 has proven to be the single most perplexing exegetical problem of the letter' (Arnold 1995: 104, 252). This assessment appears to be justified. Some manuscripts emend the text in one of two ways with the addition of a negative: 'which he has not seen while entering'. The negative particle μή is added by manuscripts ℵ² C D¹ Ψ 075 0278 𝔐, while οὐκ is added in the reading of F and G, both meaning 'which he has not seen'. Some modern commentators have proposed that all extant forms are corrupt and that 'the original reading is lost' (Lightfoot 1886: 195, 252). However, such a drastic conclusion may be unwarranted. The textual variants that insert a negative particle are motivated by a desire to deny in an unambiguous manner the reality of the visionary experience in which those who judged the Colossians were boasting, and the ingenuity of the various conjectural emendations does not demonstrate their necessity. The text attested by the earliest and most weighty manuscripts (𝔓⁴⁶ ℵ* A B D* I 33 1739), difficult as it is, should be allowed to stand.

Syntactically the phrase presents certain difficulties. The plural relative pronoun **which** (literally: 'which things') appears to refer back to the dual reference to the acts of humility and the worship of angels, which constitute the basis of 'delight'. These things are to be part of the visionary experience of the one enwrapped in such mystical acts, since the text states these are the things **he has seen**. The meaning and the intended reference of the participle ἐμβατεύων (here translated as **while being initiated**) is the key issue in determining the meaning of the entire clause. The term occurs only here in the New Testament, so one must look at the wider corpus of Greek literature to gain insight into the meaning of this verb. In general, the verb communicates the idea of 'entering' into a place, or putting one's foot on something. However, the sense seems to demand reference to something seen after entering. Four principal areas of meaning have been set out in lexical studies:

1. 'set foot upon', 'enter, visit' (Josephus, *Ant.* 2.265; 1 Macc. 12:25; 13:20)
2. 'come into possession of', 'acquire'; Eur., Demosth., papyri.
3. 'investigate closely', 'go into detail' (2 Macc. 2:30; Philo, *Plant.* 80)
4. 'entry into a sanctuary', technical term for 'initiation' (OGI 530.15)

Only the second of these possibilities does not naturally fit the context. The first would indicate that these possessors of visions saw these ocular experiences as providing the basis for faith: 'taking his stand on what he has seen'. The third would describe the boastful speech of those who wish to conform the Colossians to their own understanding of spirituality: 'going on in detail about what he has seen'. The fourth would recount the experience of those who had been initiated into some spiritual entrance ritual: 'which he has seen while entering'. Opinion is divided among scholars as to which of these interpretations is correct. In favour of the fourth option, which is the interpretation adopted here, is the fact that inscriptions discovered in the wider region of Asia Minor attest to its use as a technical term for initiatory rites in certain mystery religions. Arnold documents inscriptions from the temple of Apollo at Claros first published in 1894 (Arnold 1995: 110). The relevant line reads: '*Theopropoi* came [to enquire of the oracle], namely Crispus Tryphonus and Poplius Poupius Kallikes. These men were initiated and then they entered (ἐμβάτευσαν).' Other examples of similar inscriptions exist originating from the same temple setting. It would then appear that the term denotes some stage in the initiatory rites of the mystery religions. Having been inducted into the cult, those initiated then enter into the inner sanctum or sacred space. In this space the devotees of the mystery cults claimed to have visionary experiences, probably understood to incorporate release from the cosmic powers that governed the physical world. Heavenly ascent journeys or visions may have constituted part of these cultic entrance rites.

If this is the correct understanding of the terminology used in this clause, then the Colossians may have been subjected to persuasive rhetoric to embrace some type of syncretistic religion that combined their faith in Christ with the ecstatic visions of the heavenly sphere that were part of the mystery cults. Those who were passing judgment on the Colossians viewed their form of religion as inferior. They claimed heightened spiritual experiences, which involved ascetic practices of humility and engaging in the worship of angels. These were the things that the self-declared visionaries claimed to have seen through the induction process into the cultic mystery they embraced and promoted to the Colossian believers as offering a superior encounter with the divine sphere.

This attitude is mocked as not being truly spiritual, but is rather an act of the 'flesh'. Thus any individual who promotes this type of spirituality is accused of **being vainly puffed up by the mind of his flesh**. The word **vainly** typically stands before the word it qualifies. It shows the indulgent and baseless nature of the self-inflated attitude being adopted by those who consider that the gospel requires some supplementary religious rites. The participle **being puffed up** describes those concerning whom at the beginning of the verse the Colossians have been counselled 'let no one mistreat you'. The term occurs elsewhere in the Pauline writings (1 Cor. 4:6, 18; 5:2; 8:1; 13:4), where it also acts as a metaphor to describe conceited or pride-filled attitudes. According to the author's assessment, what has caused this conceited or 'puffed up' attitude is that such an individual is governed **by the mind of his flesh**. This assessment may be redolent with sarcasm. For, while from their perspective they boast of a higher form of spirituality free from the controls of the flesh, the assessment is that contrary to their claims it is their enslavement to the flesh that has caused this arrogant and incorrect attitude. Such a perspective, according to the author, has failed to recognize that the fulness of spiritual experience is found in Christ alone. Therefore, in contrast to their purported delight in 'humility', those being described here are depicted as having exaggerated opinions about themselves. This phrase has been seen as the most cutting part of the rebuke, since the spiritual benefit of participating in mystery religions or certain Hellenistic philosophies was seen as providing the capacity to escape the realm of earth-bounded existence (see Dunn 1996: 184–85). By declaring those who claimed to have a heightened spiritual experience as ruled 'by the mind of his flesh', this in essence undercut any qualification to enter into a higher visionary realm, or of being able to engage in the worship of angels (O'Brien 1982: 146).

19 Having explained what those who disdain the Colossian believers do that is wrong in the eyes of the author, he now describes what they do not do, which would be correct behaviour. While they continue in their self-aggrandizing assessment of their heightened spirituality, this is coupled with the omission of what they should be doing, which is described in the following terms: **and not holding to the head**. The act of **holding** speaks of connection and firmness. Those who denigrate the religious practices of the Colossians have in effect broken their link with the one who is the source of true spirituality. This may suggest that those advocating additional spiritual practices and understandings had been or continued to be members of the community, and claimed to be followers of Christ. However, because they have failed to recognize the full sufficiency of the Pauline gospel, they are seen as being disconnected from the true origin and source of spirituality. Within Colossians, when the term **the head** is used it is a reference to Christ (Col. 1:18; 2:10). He is declared to be 'the head of the body, the church' (Col. 1:18). In that context the metaphor of the body is prominent as a way of describing the community of believers; that same metaphor is used in this verse. By contrast, in Col. 2:10 the metaphor of headship is used to describe Christ's authority over 'every ruler and authority'.

Having described Christ as 'the head', the author uses this image to expand on the body metaphor as a description of the relationship between the church and Christ as its head, **from whom all the body through the joints and the ligaments, being supplied and held together**. As has been noted, the word **body**, σῶμα, is a polyvalent term in the letter. It describes Christ as the head of the church, which is called the body (Col. 1:18, 24; 2:19; 3:15); it describes the physical body of Christ that was crucified (Col. 1:22); it describes the fleshy nature of the Colossians prior to union with Christ or the physical body possessed by humans (Col. 2:11, 23); and it can denote things of substance, in contrast with insubstantial shadowy things (Col. 2:17). The most frequent use of the term is as a metaphor for the community of believers, which is linked to Christ, who in line with the body metaphor is described as the head. Whereas those who are causing unrest among the Colossians were seen as not holding to Christ, by contrast the recipients of the letter are seen as a having a close linkage. Anatomical images describe the linkage from the head to the body being achieved **through the joints and the ligaments**. No allegorical explanation of these physical connection devices is given. Thus the author does not exploit the anatomical language; instead, the terms given to describe the linking material in a physical body are simply used to advance the proposition that the body is joined to the head, as the parts of the body themselves are interconnected. In the New Testament the first term **joints**, ἁφῶν, occurs only here and in the parallel passage in Eph. 4:16. It is best translated 'either physiologically as a medical t.t. for *ligaments* or *muscles* or as a general term for *joints* or *connections*' (*EDNT*: I, 181). The second term **ligaments**, συνδέσμῶν, occurs slightly more frequently in the New Testament (Acts 8:23; Eph. 4:3; Col. 2:19; 3:14). This term takes on a wider range of meanings, with four related senses being identified: 'fastener', 'uniting bond', 'fetter', and 'bundle' (BDAG: 966). While in Col. 3:14 (and Eph. 4:3) the second sense appears to be intended, denoting the connecting force that results in separate entities becoming a unity, here in line with the anatomical imagery it refers to the internal physiological connections and fasteners is the body, hence the translation ligaments. Moo suggests that 'sinew' more accurately captures the sense, stating that the reference is to 'the tissue that connects muscles to bones (also "tendons")' (Moo 2008: 231). However, it is uncertain if the anatomical feature being denoted was unambiguous, and whether it is possible to be so certain about the precision of the translation. The terms 'ligament', 'sinew', and 'tendon' are all legitimate and it is questionable whether ancient physiology differentiated consistently between these bodily elements. The important point is theological, not anatomical: the body of believers at Colossae is firmly connected to Christ who is their head. This differentiates them from their critics who have lost a grip on Christ, since they no longer regard him as the full and superlative expression of spiritual experience.

The next clause describes the purpose of these 'joints and ligaments' that connect the body to its head. It is through these elements that the body is **being supplied and held together**. The twin functions of these connectors are that of sustenance ἐπιχορηγούμενον and linkage συμβιβαζόμενον. It is unnecessary to probe the supply and structural functions of 'joints and ligaments'. The point is that the recipients of the letter are the ones who enjoy the benefits of Christ's sustenance and support. By contrast, the one who is 'puffed up' is disconnected from Christ, and despite the boastful claims being made, the alternative spirituality being presented is devoid of true spiritual nourishment, since that comes only from being connected to Christ.

This point is emphasized in the final clause in this section, where the Colossians are promised that through connection with Christ the body **increases with the increase of God**. The increase envisaged here is not entirely clear. It is the 'increase' or 'growth' of the body that is being supplied. This is unlikely to be a reference to numerical growth. Rather, given the stated aim of Paul's proclamation and teaching 'that we may present every man perfect in Christ' (Col. 1:28), it is more likely that what is envisaged here is an increase in spiritual wisdom and maturity. It is interesting that the **increase** is said to be **of God**, and not to come from 'the head', that is Christ. Part of the reason for this might be to highlight the divine empowerment that the Colossians enjoy, as well as showing that Christ's sustenance of the body is consonant with God's purposes. Another reason for the reference to **God** is probably to identify the ultimate source of the growth. Thus, as is common throughout the letter, there is a close association between what God and Christ provide in concert in order to produce spiritual growth in the Colossians. It is, however, possible that this is a further attempt to undermine the claims of those who were inflated by their own spiritual experience. If what they claimed was heavenly ascent, and heightened experience of the divine, then it may well be the case that as a corrective both to the individualism of personal spiritual experience and the claim of superior access to the divine that the author instructs the Colossians to remain connected to Christ through the ecclesial body, for it is the corporate relationship to Christ that actually supplies the spiritual growth which those who denigrate the Colossians so desperately crave.

11. THE EMPTINESS OF HUMAN RELIGION
(2:20–23)

**(20) If you died with Christ from the elements of the world, why
do you submit to dogmas as if living in the world? (21) 'Do not
handle, do not taste, do not touch', (22) which refer to things that
all perish in being used, according to the precepts and teachings
of men, (23) which are a matter having wisdom in self-delighting
worship, and humility by severe treatment of the body, [but are]
of no value [in guarding] against the gratification of the flesh.**

In Col. 2:18–19 the letter has first described the actions performed
by those who seek heightened experiences of self-centred spirituality (Col. 2:18), before continuing to explain the key behaviour
they should carry out, but fail to do so. The required behaviour that
has been overlooked is 'holding to the head' – that is, cleaving to
Christ and being joined to him within the body of believers (Col.
2:19). Now turning attention to the believers in Colossae, rather
than describing the religious practices of those who pass judgment
upon them, the author gives a similar two-part structure: explaining
first behaviours they should not continue to practise (Col. 2:20–23),
before turning attention to the attitudes that should now characterize
their existence (Col. 3:1–4). The contrast between these two sections
is intentional. The first section opens with the conditional phrase,
'if you have died with Christ' (Col. 2:20). The second commences
with the structurally and verbally similar expression 'if therefore'
you were raised with Christ' (Col. 3:1). Thus the author sees that
dying with Christ should put to death certain tendencies to trust in
earthly dogmas and religious practices, and being raised with Christ
should enliven the Colossians to embrace a transformed outlook that
seeks 'the things above', since despite appearances they now live
with Christ in the divine sphere. Therefore, the rejoinder to those
who promise heavenly ascent and ecstatic moments of heavenly
vision through ascetic practice is that the Colossians do not need
such fleeting experiences because their whole mode of existence is
already with Christ in the heavenly sphere. Before the author can
complete this argument, he must first warn the Colossians against
the tendency to embrace human spirituality.

20 The opening proposition **if you died with Christ** is a challenge to the Colossians to accept the reality of the existential transformation they underwent when they accepted the gospel. Although using different word groups in Greek, the verb **you died**, ἀπεθάνετε, picks up the imagery in Col. 2:12–13 where the Colossians are said to have been 'buried with Christ in baptism' (Col. 2:12a), they are reminded that God raised Christ from the dead (Col. 2:12b), and that they were 'dead in trespasses' (Col. 2:13a). Here the author continues to exploit the image of death, with this clause being closest to the statement in Col. 2:12a, which described union with Christ through the burial-baptism image. Here the concept of participating **with Christ** in death is redeployed, as a corrective to the possibility of being captivated by the philosophy of those who promote heightened spiritual experiences.

From the perspective of the letter, what this process of Christ-centred mortification involves is dying **from the elements of the world**. The choice of preposition is probably significant in that it reveals that the death the Colossians experienced resulted in them being drawn away **from** the sphere of influence of **the elements of the world**. Because of this there can be no basis for the Colossians to submit themselves to the authority of these elements. Earlier in the letter the phrase 'the elements of the world' was used in the warning not to be taken captive by a philosophy that was 'according to the tradition of men, according to the elements of the world' (Col. 2:8). When discussed previously the four major suggestions for the interpretation of this phrase were examined. It was suggested that it functions as a reference to the physical elements that constitute the universe personified as cosmic powers. There is, therefore, a call issued to the Colossians to be freed from their pre-Christian understanding, which attributed power to these elements. In this passage, the reference to the elements is placed first, before the author critiques the tendency to live 'according to the precepts and teachings of men' (Col. 2:22). Therefore this section returns to what was almost a thematic statement in Col. 2:8, which announced the topic and the substance of the argument in Col. 2:8–23.

Wrapped up with this failure to break fully from the religious practices of the past, the Colossians are characterized as enslaving themselves to unnecessary regulations that no longer have any currency or relevance for them. Consequently, the author asks the stinging rhetorical question **why do you submit to dogmas as if living in the world?** The implication is that the Colossians have failed to realize that they have been 'rescued from the authority of darkness' (Col. 1:13). It is incongruous that the Colossians should continue **living** a pattern of existence that is described as being **in the world**. The interrogative pronoun that introduces this clause is both 'a rhetorical question and a rebuke' (O'Brien 1982: 149). The adverbial particle **as** functions to introduce the characteristic quality of the type of 'life' that the Colossians are following. The term 'world' has already been given negative connotations in this verse through its use in the phrase 'the elements of the world'. Here 'living in the world' incorporates a type of existence that does not demonstrate freedom from the supposed controlling influence of these elements, but it also entails more than this. Living **in the world** depicts a life that is antithetical to life in Christ. In the next section the letter will declare that the true life for believers is hidden with Christ (Col. 3:3), and in fact it is Christ who is their life (Col. 3:4). However, life in the world is synonymous with remaining in a state of death, to which the remedy was God's act of forgiveness (Col. 2:13). The way the Colossians are at risk of continuing to live in the world is if they **submit to dogmas** imposed on them by those claiming to have accesses to heightened spiritual experiences. In direct reference to the pressure some are wishing to exert on the Colossians, the author describes the Colossians as subjecting themselves to the dogmatic rules taught by others. While many commentators have taken the verbal form δογματίζεσθε as being in the passive mood – hence 'why do you let yourselves be dictated to?' (Zerwick 1993: 608) – it is probably better understood as a reflexive or direct middle – 'why do you subject yourselves to ordinances'. Examples of these 'dogmas' or rules that characterize living in the world are provided in the next verse.

21 The three prohibitions that are stated here are intended to provide examples of the type of rules to which the Colossians are either in danger of submitting, or perhaps to which they have in some way already begun submitting (Harris 2010: 113). The view of certain Patristic authors (Hilary, Pelagius, Ambrose, *de Noe et Arca* 25; *de Abr.* 1.6) that these prohibitions were Paul's own, and contrasted with the restrictions being promoted by those he writes against, is a total misunderstanding of the meaning of the passage ('a complete shipwreck of the sense', so Lightfoot 1886: 201). However, not all early Christian authors take this line of interpretation. Theodore of Mopsuestia paraphrases the sense as 'for what reason do you put up with those who set up laws for you as though you were living in the present life and who say: eat this, do not touch this, and other things of this kind?' (Theodore of Mopsuestia, *ad Colossenses* 2.20–21).

The series of three prohibitions, **do not handle, do not taste, do not touch**, contains in the first and third elements two near synonyms. The distinction between the two Greek terms ἅψῃ and θίγῃς has been understood as relating to the duration and degree of the tactile experience. The first term, here translated as **handle**, in the middle voice, means 'touch, take hold of, hold'. It can denote a tactile experience of extended duration, as appears to be the case in Jesus' command to Mary Magdalene, 'do not *cling* to me' (Jn 20:17). The second element **do not taste**, μηδὲ γεύσῃ, prohibits certain experiences of gustation. While Aristotle had examined the physical experience of taste, and had developed a taxonomy of basic tastes (Aristotle, *De anima* 422b 10–16), the concern here appears to be with the ritual regulation of ingesting certain substances. The intention is to impose certain ascetic practices upon the Colossians, and the emphasis here is that such practices are not only of no value to the Colossians, but actually detract from the faith they have received, which is not regulated by such rules. Perhaps as a slight contrast to the first term 'handle', the third term **touch** may represent a more fleeting tactile encounter (cf. Heb. 11:28; 12:20). However, the quest to distinguish between these two terms (cf. Harris 2010: 113) is perhaps due to the desire for stylistic variation in English translations. The reality is that there is 'little basis in Greek for any difference at all between the verbs: both simply mean "touch"' (Moo 2008: 235). Those who have seen the 'philosophy' that is being urged upon the Colossians as exclusively Jewish in origin have argued that these three prohibitions arise from Jewish purity laws, especially those that pertain to maintaining the distinction between 'clean' and 'unclean' foods, corpse impurity, contact with a discharge of blood, or with lepers (cf. Dunn 1996: 190–92). However, since no object is expressed for each of these general prohibitions it is unlikely that the concerns are either purely dietary, or that they relate exclusively to the Jewish cult. The major point is that as people who have been joined with Christ in his death, it is self-destructive folly to subject oneself to such human rules.

22 The letter mocks the efficacy of these acts of ascetic abasement. Contrary to the claim that they result in heightened spiritual experience, the letter parodies them as being practices **which refer to things that all perish** (lit. 'which are all for corruption'). Precisely what the author intends to communicate by this statement is uncertain. However, there have been numerous suggestions. Some have seen this statement as announcing a corrective to the false understanding being propagated by those who would impose prohibitions. Thus all the things that are forbidden by the 'philosophy' are items concerning which 'God has decreed that all of them without exception...be consumed through man's use' (Lohse 1971: 124). Such a reading may align with the Markan authorial declaration, 'thus he declared all foods clean' (Mk 7:19c). On this basis some have seen Isaiah's critique of human precepts as standing behind Col. 2:20–23, since it is cited in Mk 7:7. The Septuagintal version of the text states, 'in vain do they worship me teaching the commandments and doctrines of men' (LXX Isa. 29:13). While there are some conceptual affinities and items of shared vocabulary, the ideas expressed in Col. 2:20–23 were common enough that one need not posit any direct literary link. Also seeing the objects destined for destruction as speaking 'especially, but not exclusively, of food', O'Brien understands their corruption not due to believers using them inappropriately, but because of their materiality, they are by nature perishable. Thus he states, since 'these objects are transient and perishable then the proponents of the "philosophy" lack a true sense of proportion by making them central to their teaching' (O'Brien 1982: 150). The basis for understanding this as relating primarily to the consumption of food is due to the phrase **in being used**, τῇ ἀποχρήσει. Some commentators see use of the rare composite noun as having perfective force because of the addition of the prefix, thus it is taken to mean 'using up' or 'consumption' with food being a natural reference (Dunn 1996: 193). However, as Barth and Blanke note, in the admittedly infrequent extant use of the term while it can be intensificative in function, 'it can also have the same meaning of the simplex' (Barth and Blanke 1994: 356–57). In that case it could be referring back more generally to the decrees mentioned at the end of Col. 2:20, rather than to the specific prohibitions in Col. 2:21. In this sense the whole practice of using regulations to determine religious practice is total stupidity. This is because in light of the Christ event such dogmas are outmoded and have become corrosive influences on those who practise them, and such decrees themselves are destined for corruption.

In addition to the ultimate perishability of such dogmas, the immediate problem with them is that they are **according to the precepts and teachings of men**. Whereas the gospel is the revelation of the divine mystery, the dogmas that the Colossians are being asked to follow are insubstantial 'shadows' (Col. 2:17), and they originate through human design rather than coming from the revelation of God. This second problem with such decrees may be the more fundamental problem according to the letter – the first criticism being a somewhat parenthetical comment introduced by a relative clause, whereas the latter appears to be the major issue. Again, from the author's perspective, the Colossians are in danger of exchanging direct access to the divine mystery through their union with Christ for mediated human rules, which will perish, and are not fit for purpose in providing spiritual enrichment. The terms 'precepts', ἐντάλματα, and 'teachings', διδασκαλίας, also occur in combination in the synoptic tradition and are seen as human in origin: 'teaching as doctrines the precepts of man' (Mt. 15:9//Mk 7:7). The second term 'teachings', διδασκαλίας, does not always have a negative connotation in the Pauline writings (Rom. 12:7; 15:4; 1 Tim. 1:10; 4:6; 2 Tim. 3:10, 16) or early Christianity, where an important instructional text was entitled *The Didascalia*. Here, however, because of the association with human origin, and its antithetical contrast with the message preached by Paul that emphasized the completeness of reconciliation in Christ, such reliance on human teaching is denigrated and despised.

23 The assault on the spirituality being promoted by those who judge the Colossians' form of religion as inadequate continues here with rhetorical flourishes that verge towards parody. While the sense of this verse is clear in general terms, the exact translation is difficult. The relative clause that commences this verse, **which are a matter having wisdom**, is at first appearance concessive since the author states that human 'teachings and precepts' have wisdom. This will quickly be shown to be a false assessment. The decision to describe such human instruction and regulation as **a matter** using the Greek term λόγος may reflect a careful word choice. Given that the teaching that is being referred to here has been described as a 'philosophy' (Col. 2:8), and since the term λόγος played such an important function in Hellenistic philosophy especially in the formulations of Plato and Aristotle, the choice of terminology may be far from coincidental. According to Plato, the idea of *logos* encapsulates the whole rational enterprise (cf. Plato, *Theaetetus*), while for Aristotle, *logos*, as argument from reason, is one of the three basic modes of persuasion (Aristotle, *Rhetoric*). The concept of *logos* retained currency and importance down to the time of the Middle Platonists such as Plotinus (ca. 205–270) and Porphyry (ca. 235–ca. 305), and beyond into late antique period and Medieval scholasticism. The semblance that might be attributed to the 'philosophy' is the notion that the teaching is something **having wisdom**. The concept of 'wisdom' is important in the letter, being a positive attribute. In this vein Paul is portrayed as praying for the Colossians that 'they might be filled with all spiritual wisdom' (Col. 1:9). Elsewhere in relation to the key activity of instruction, it is stated that Paul teaches 'with all wisdom' (Col. 1:28). Moreover, as part of the christological perspective of the letter, the author says in Christ 'all the treasures of wisdom are hidden' (Col. 2:3). Wisdom is also a fundamental quality that should characterise the recipients of the letter. Therefore, the word of Christ is to dwell in believers 'with all wisdom' (Col. 3:16), and the Colossians are to behave 'with wisdom' to those outside the community (Col. 4:5). Thus wisdom is a positive quality that the author seeks to promote among believers, and which they should strive to nurture within themselves. Even here in Col. 2:23 wisdom is not a negative idea. Rather, the problem arises from attributing wisdom to activities that cannot result in acquiring that quality. The language is highly compressed in this verse and many English translations have tried to unpack the sense of these statements by glossing the Greek:

Which things have indeed a shew of wisdom... (KJV)

These are matters which have, to be sure, the appearance of wisdom... (NASB)

Such regulations indeed have an appearance of wisdom... (NIV)

These rules may seem wise... (NLT)

Such conduct may have an air of wisdom... (REB)

Most English translations take a similar approach in understanding the text to imply that the regulations being promoted have an 'appearance' or 'showing' of wisdom. This may well capture the sense of the author, although it is not exactly what is stated in the text. The prescriptive dogmas are said to have wisdom in regard to the type of religion that is being promoted by those who teach the philosophy the author opposes. However, the problem is that such wisdom is deemed to be of no value since it derives from a pattern of spirituality that is worthless in comparison with the wisdom that is produced in those who are united with Christ both in his death and his transforming risen life (Col. 2:12–13).

What the wisdom offered by those who are imposing their spirituality on the Colossians do is sustain their own religious system. Here there are two characteristics that are listed (some manuscripts take the phrase 'by severe treatment of the body' as a third clause by inserting the word 'and'; see below). These characteristics are described as **self-delighting worship and humility**. The shared terminology with Col. 2:18 is often overlooked. It is helpful to set out the parallels between that verse and Col. 2:23:

θέλων ἐν ταπεινοφροσύνῃ καὶ θρησκείᾳ τῶν ἀγγελῶν
delighting in humility and the worship of angels (Col. 2:18)

ἐν ἐθελοθρησκίᾳ καὶ ταπεινοφροσύνῃ
self-delighting worship and humility (Col. 2:23)

The most significant difference is that Col. 2:23 has no reference to 'the angels'. However, the unusual construction in Col. 2:18 that describes 'delighting in…worship' is not replicated. Instead, this statement utilizes the even less common compound noun ἐθελοθρησκία (only here in the New Testament). This term is often translated rather meaninglessly as 'will-worship'. However, the translation adopted here aligns it with the sense given in Col. 2:18: thus it is rendered as **self-delighting worship**. This appears to reflect the same criticism that was inherent in the second half of Col. 2:18. That is the accusation that the promoters of the philosophy are self-indulgent individuals 'puffed up' by their own quest for heightened spiritual encounters, which they seek through their own religious mysteries. The second term that parallels the wording of Col. 2:18 is the reference to **humility**. Picking up on the same sentiments as expressed previously, the generally positive quality of 'humility' is here portrayed as one of the negative features of the spirituality practised by those who judge the Colossians. While it was unclear what might have constituted such humility in Col. 2:18, the next clause may cast more light on that issue.

Here the term 'humility' is expanded, and that behaviour of the errorists is said to involve the **severe treatment of the body**. There is a textual problem here. The majority of manuscripts create a list of three behaviours, while others see the third element as describing what produced the attitude of humility.

Variant 1:	self-delighting worship and humility and severe treatment of the body
	ℵ A C D H Ψ 075 𝔐
Variant 2:	self-delighting worship and humility of the mind and severe treatment of the body
	F G
Variant 3:	self-delighting worship and humility by severe treatment of the body
	𝔓⁴⁶ B 1739

The second reading appears due to an expansionist clarification of the first variant. By contrast, while the first reading has wider attestation it also resolves the more problematic syntax of the third variant.

The final variant is probably the most difficult, hence inviting scribal emendation, and is supported by the earliest extant manuscript and also surviving in Codex Vaticanus and 1739, which show that it is not simply an aberrant singular reading. For this reason variant three most likely represents the earliest recoverable state of the text.

Therefore, given that dietary practices are an area in which proponents of the philosophy judge the Colossians, 'in regard to food and drink' (Col. 2:16), and given that one of their regulations appears to involve not tasting certain items (Col. 2:21), at the very least this severe treatment appears to involve certain proscrip tions concerning edible items. It may also encapsulate other ways of treating the body harshly, but that would be speculative since there are no further specific clues in the text about other potential areas of severe treatment that have featured in certain religions, such as sexual abstinence, or self-flagellation. It is not possible to attribute such practices to those interacting with the Colossian believers, since there is no supporting evidence. The term **severe treatment**, ἀφειδία, is another word that is found only here in the New Testament. It denotes 'unsparing treatment' **of the body** and 'suggests a rigorous asceticism' (Wilson 2005: 230).

The final clause is another element that is difficult to translate. The prior question concerns the relationship of this phrase to the rest of the sentence. It does not expand on the three practices just described, 'but is the contrast answering the earlier μέν clause (see BDF: §447[2] for the omission of the adversative δέ after μέν)' (Harris 2010: 116). This contrast between the first part and the final part of the verse makes the following type of argument: the regulations 'are things which have [a type of] wisdom…but that is not of any honour…'. The phrase **[but are] of no value [in guarding] against** supplies the adversative **but**, which is omitted in the Greek construction. It declares the self-made human regulations to be without 'honour' or 'value'. The key problem involves the final clause **the gratification of the flesh**. As it stands, the sense appears to say that the practices and rules of those who hold to the philosophy 'are of no value for the gratification of the body'. This would appear to imply that the body should rightly be gratified or indulged. One would expect some kind of negative construction, such as 'are of no value *against* the gratification of the body'. This is indeed the translational strategy adopted by the majority of English versions. The word **gratification**, πλησμονή, is another term that is unique in the New Testament. In other Jewish and early Christian literature (*Ps.Sol.* 5:17; Josephus, *Ant.* 11.34; Justin, *Dial.* 126.6) it denotes the 'process of securing complete satisfaction, *satiety* esp w. food and drink, but also with other types of enjoyment, *satisfaction, gratification*' (BDAG: 830). In the context of providing a discussion about the futility of dietary regulations and ascetic practices it is a contrasting term that makes sense in discussion of the purpose of food and other physical activities that satisfy the body. This clause speaks about the gratification **of the flesh**. It has already been seen that the term 'flesh' can be used either in a negative sense in the letter (Col. 2:11, 13, 18), or in a neutral sense describing the matter that constitutes humans (Col. 1:22, 24; 2:1, 5; 3:22). If the term is being used in a neutral sense here, then the sense might be that contrary to the ascetic practices and severe treatment imposed by restrictive practices the Colossians should not engage in this abuse of their bodies. However, if the term 'flesh' retains its negative connotation, then one is forced to supply some kind of negative force to the clause, and understand what is being said to be that even if one adopts the regulations imposed by those who practise such severe treatment of the body, those practices are 'of no value in guarding against the gratification of the flesh'.

Despite the difficulty in understanding the specific details of this verse, its overall assessment of the pattern of religion practised by adherents of the philosophy is apparent. That belief system is seen to be based upon self-delighting indulgence, it fails to deliver what it promises, and the areas in which it does possess wisdom are of no consequence for those whose lives are now united with Christ.

III.
ETHICAL INSTRUCTION FOR RENEWED EXISTENCE (3:1–4:6)

12. LIVING TRANSFORMED LIVES (3:1–4)

(1) If therefore you have been raised with Christ, seek the things above where Christ is – seated at the right hand of God. (2) Consider the things above, not the things on earth. (3) For you died and your life has been hidden with Christ in God. (4) When Christ is revealed, who is your life, then you also will be revealed with him in glory.

This paragraph is a pivotal point in the letter. It concludes the train of thought begun as far back as Col. 2:6, and is thematically related to the imperative contained there: 'as therefore you received Christ Jesus the Lord, walk in him'. While making no further reference to the opinions of the individuals who were harassing the Colossians, it draws an obvious contrast with Col. 2:20–23. That section opened with the declaration 'if you have died with Christ', and then questioned what benefit the Colossians could possibly derive from living according to human regulations. Here the section opens with the affirmation 'if therefore you have been raised with Christ', and consequently asks the Colossians how they could fail to live lives that are transformed, that now exist in a different sphere, that are Christ-centred, and are awaiting the future revelation of the fulness of life. Here the present change in the lives of the Colossians is held alongside an expectation of a future manifestation of the glorious nature of the life that they have already received.

This section also links forward to the remainder of the letter, where specific ethical imperatives for living as believers in their own contemporary setting are presented. In the rest of the letter certain attitudes and behaviours are deemed unacceptable (Col. 3:5–11), while others are to be embraced – stemming from union with Christ (Col. 3:12–17). Relationships for believers are to be transformed, primarily because of relationship with Christ (Col. 3:18–4:1), and a life of piety is described that is lived in contact with those inside and outside the community of faith (Col. 4:2–6). The letter closes with a series of greetings that encapsulates the uniting bond of a shared faith lived in union with Christ.

1 The opening phrase in this paragraph draws an intentional contrast with Col. 2:20, which describes union with Christ in death: 'if you have died with Christ'. However, here it is union with Christ in resurrection that is announced. Both of these conditional clauses are given for rhetorical impact, rather than genuinely questioning whether the Colossians have truly died and been raised with Christ. The fact that the Colossians are believers, means that from the author's perspective both of these events are spiritual realities. In effect what is being said is *since* the Colossians have died and been raised with Christ, they should not contemplate living according to a belief system that is not Christ-centred; instead, they should live the type of lives that reflect their transformed state of existence.

The phrase **if therefore you have been raised with Christ**, focuses attention on the new existence that the Colossians experience through union with Christ. The conjunction **therefore**, οὖν, is logical in emphasis, stating that if the condition of being raised with Christ holds, then the implication is that believers should have their minds fixed on heavenly things and not on matters such a prohibitions and regulations (Col. 2:20–21). The idea of being raised with Christ has already been mentioned in the letter (Col. 2:12), where after describing the participatory experience of burial with Christ in baptism it is stated that believers have also been 'raised up with him through faith'. The sentiment expressed here and in Col. 2:12 has been seen as depicting a realized eschatology that is not characteristic of Paul's regular theological formulations. Moo provides a helpful summary of the nature of the perceived problem:

> The controversy arises because many interpreters allege that the claim of a past "being raised" with Christ contradicts the theology of the "authentic" Paul, who always taught that the believer would be raised with Christ only in the future. Transferring this resurrection with Christ from the future to the present, it is argued, is the most evident symptom of the "overrealized" eschatology of Colossians... The author of Colossians has turned Paul's temporal orientation into

a spatial one, according to which Christians no longer have to wait to be identified with Christ's resurrection in the future, but can even now join Christ "above" in the heavenly realm. (Moo 2008: 245)

The observation is correct that among the seven letters that are commonly seen as authentically Pauline there is no account of believers having already experienced resurrection with Christ, although they are able to partake in the power of Christ's resurrection (Rom. 6:4, 12; Phil. 3:10). However, it should also be observed that in Col. 3:1–4 the author does not present a fully realized eschatology, since the full disclosure and experience of transformed existence will only be realized when in the future 'Christ is revealed' (Col. 3:4). The questions concerning whether this theological development – and it certainly is a development – of seeing believers as already having experienced being raised with Christ is possible within Paul's own theological framework, or whether it reflects another mind building upon Paul's thought, cannot be answered conclusively. Yet, in many ways this 'authorship issue' is not the most important aspect of this passage. What is more significant is appreciating the theological resource that this creative reformulation offers. The ethical imperatives that are drawn from this theological perspective are based upon the fact that believers are not only empowered by Christ's resurrection, but in some proleptic sense they have already been transformed by partaking in the experience of having been raised with him. That understanding creates a much stronger link between the theological reflections contained in the letter and the ethical teaching that is based upon those reflections.

The consequence of having been raised with Christ is to be demonstrated in a changed mode of thinking. From now on those who have been raised are to **seek the things above where Christ is**. Like the thematic present imperative 'walk in him' (Col. 2:6), the command to **seek the things above** calls for an ongoing attitude. The description of **the things above**, τὰ ἄνω, is a rare expression in the New Testament, occurring only here. Resurrection with Christ is intended to bring about a radical reorientation in outlook. Here a spatial metaphor is used to denote the spiritual realm that is now seen as the place **where Christ is**. Associating the divine realm or 'the heavens' (Col. 1:5, 16, 20, 23) with the physical space above the earth is a common feature in many religious traditions. However, here the image is used not simply to separate a divine ineffable being from the material world; instead, the addressees are to see this divine space as the place to which they should direct their thoughts and which they should regard as the location of their true existence. It is the place where Christ now exists, and consequently through union with him that is where the real life of believers is to be found. The notion of a heavenly home is found elsewhere in the New Testament (cf. Heb. 11:16; Rev. 21:1–3), and this is seen as the genuine abode of those who believe in Christ.

Here the translation is rearranged to follow the word order of the Greek: **at the right hand of God seated**. This is done in order to avoid both mistranslation and misreading of this verse that can arise by connecting the word 'seated' with the wrong clause. Some translations run the final two clauses together, while others simply use a comma to separate the phrases (and this can be too easily missed).

> seek those things which are above, where Christ sitteth on the right hand of God (KJV)

> keep seeking the things above, where Christ is, seated at the right hand of God (NASB)

> the things above seek, where Christ is, at the right of God seated (Greek word order)

The first translation places the emphasis on Christ 'being seated' above, instead of the twin affirmations that Christ is now above, and that he is also now seated at the right hand of God. Most commentators agree that the participle should not be connected with the form of the verb 'to be' (i.e 'is') to create the periphrastic tense 'is seated' (O'Brien 1982: 161; Harris 2010: 120). Therefore, having first affirmed that Christ now dwells in a realm that can being described spatially as being 'above', a second affirmation is made concerning his enthronement at the position of power next to God. The wording here resonates with the statement in Ps. 110:1 (LXX Ps. 109:1).

LXX Ps. 109:1   κάθου ἐκ δεξιῶν μου
                sit at my right
Col. 3:1   ἐν δεξιᾷ τοῦ θεοῦ καθήμενος
                at the right of God seated

While the ideas are certainly related, given both the divergence in syntax and terminology, and the prominence of Ps. 110:1, 4 in the New Testament (perhaps over thirty citations or allusions; Hay 1973: 15), it is unlikely that this is a direct allusion to or echo of the Psalm. Rather, it appears that this affirmation had embedded itself in early Christian thought to such an extent that here it can be used without intentional reference to the original context. Being seated at God's right hand is an image that showed the occupant of the prestigious position exercised the power on behalf of the potentate or deity who held supreme power. Here Christ is portrayed as God's viceroy, and as the one entrusted with representative power on behalf of God as well as occupying the position of highest honour alongside God (cf. Ps. 80:18; Isa. 41:40; 48:13; Jer. 22:24). Hence Christ's position and status are affirmed in this verse using two spatial metaphors – he is both above in the heavenly realm, and at the right hand of God in the position of power and honour. This is the true heavenly mystery to which the Colossians now have access. Hence they have no need of the initiation of entrance rituals (Col. 2:18) that those who promote the alternative 'philosophy' claim as furnishing heightened access to the divine mysteries.

2 Continuing the train of thought commenced in Col. 3:1, the author repeats the instruction to contemplate heavenly things. However, this is now set antithetically against prohibition not to think about earthly things. While the general sense remains the same, the imperative verb changes from the command to 'seek the things above' to the form here **consider the things above**. The meaning of the verb φρονεῖτε centres on the idea concentrated thought, or focused intellectual endeavour. Lexically, the verb can describe formation of opinions or attitudes, or as here a decision 'to give careful consideration to someth., *set one's mind upon, be intent on*' (BDAG: 1065). The purpose of such careful consideration is not solely as a protection against the ideas of others, although that is certainly in the mind of the author. There is also the positive benefit of having a mindset that is aligned with what is seen as the true heavenly existence of believers with Christ. In one sense the Colossians are encouraged to adopt an attitude that aligns with the reality of their heavenly existence.

The negative contrast that is presented is **not** to fix thoughts upon **the things on earth**. Here the logic undercuts and inverts the claims of those who are puffed up by their visions. Contemplation of Christ and his exaltation through the humiliation of the cross is presented as the authentic way to access the mystery of God. This is at odds with those engaged in a self-delighting religion that seeks experience for its own sake, and engages in ascetic acts of humiliation, yet in the process fails to see that because of the death and cross of Christ (Col. 2:12, 15), the 'body of the flesh' (Col. 2:11) that belongs to this world should no longer occupy the thoughts of believers. However, this should not be thought of as some kind of 'super-asceticism' that rejects the material world. Instead, it may entail 'a rejection of the visionaries' regulations that involve food and drink, among other things' (Sumney 2008: 179). Fundamentally the concern is with a change of attitude. Believers are not to be fixated on the 'rulers and authorities', which might be perceived as dominating this world. Rather, they are to know that the Christ, who is seated at the right hand of God, is the only source of divine power.

3 The next affirmation if presented in isolation would not be particularly uplifting, **for you died**. However, this death is seen as a transition to a different kind of life. Themes announced previously in the letter are picked up once again, with the author returning to the idea that the Colossians have been 'buried' with Christ 'in baptism' (Col. 2:12). The type of death that is described here is a death liberating them from the former forces that governed existence while they were part of the world. This contrasts with the spiritual necrosis experienced by the Colossians when they were 'dead in transgressions' (Col. 2:13). The death spoken of here is an experience that is part of the union with Christ in his death. Moreover, this union with Christ in death is a death that takes the Colossians out of the sphere of influence of the 'elements of the world' (Col. 2:20), and importantly for the prevailing argument they are dead to the necessity of being governed by human regulations and prohibitions (Col. 2:20–21). The author uses the metaphor of death in a complex way throughout the letter and it is that multifaceted use of the metaphor that allows the construction of new ways of thinking about life and death as existential categories. The Colossians are told that when they previously thought they were alive they were actually 'dead in transgressions' (Col. 2:13). When they were joined with Christ as symbolically depicted in baptism they both died with him and in him they were raised by the God who raised Christ (Col. 2:13). The affirmation here that believers have died picks up the idea that the elemental forces have no power over those united with Christ (Col. 2:20). The post-death experience of being raised with Christ (Col. 3:1) is the basis for a transformed way of living, and a renewed mindset that is now focused on 'the things that are above' (Col. 3:1–2).

The consequence of having died is not that the Colossians now cease to exist, but paradoxically that they now have a new life that is more secure and enduring. Having participated in Christ's death, the author can also inform the Colossians that through sharing in his resurrection **your life has been hidden with Christ in God**. If death is a multifaceted metaphor, the concepts of 'life' and 'living', although not employed to the same extent, present the same dual use. According to the letter, the Colossians are said to have lived previously according to certain vices (Col. 3:7), and they are again being persuaded to live in a way governed by human regulations: 'why as if living in the world do you submit to dogmas?' (Col. 2:20). By contrast, here their life is hidden with Christ, and the nature of that life will be disclosed when Christ himself is revealed (Col. 3:4). The fact that the Colossians' mode of existence **has been hidden** communicates the liminal state in which believers now exist. Although they are people who have been raised with Christ, they are not recognized as such, since their new mode of existence is still to be revealed. There are other references to hiddenness in the letter that may be part of the strategy of subverting the claims of those who advocate a philosophy based on gaining insight into hidden mysteries. The 'mystery' described in Col. 1:26, which was once hidden away, is now revealed – but only to the holy ones. Likewise, in Christ all the treasures of wisdom and knowledge are hidden (Col. 2:3). Thus for the author it is **with Christ**, who is understood as a secure repository and guardian, that the treasure of insight and true life are held. The author can say to believers that their life is hidden with Christ, because in one sense they are united with Christ. However, here the image has changed. The Colossians have died and no longer exist in the apparent earthly reality. Instead, they are to look upwards to where Christ is, and to where their life now exists. Thus in their earthly existence they are separated from their true life, which is hidden with Christ. This separation appears counterintuitive, but the tension is explained in the next verse where it is explained that Christ is the one 'who is your life' (Col. 3:4). So although mystically united with Christ, they are not yet with him, but their life is secure in heaven because Christ is in fact their life. What this reasoning demonstrates is that according to the author all meaningful categories of spiritual existence are subsumed into Christ, who is not only the guardian of believers' risen life, but is in fact their life.

Finally, Christ is linked to the divine by stating that he is **in God**. Being 'in God' is an uncommon expression in the Pauline corpus (1 Thess. 1:1; 2 Thess. 1:1; Eph. 3:9), however it aligns with the wider theology of this letter. While Christ is 'the mystery of God' (Col. 2:3) and the one in whom 'the fulness of deity dwells bodily' (Col. 2:9), he now exists 'above' (Col. 3:1), sitting at his right hand, and thus so linked with God that his actions and being are 'in God'. In this way, according to the logic of the letter, the Colossians are more firmly linked to the divine realm than they, or their detractors, may have realized. Therefore, there is a need to perceive a reality that can only be seen from a thoroughly Christ-centred vantage point.

4 The opening statement shows the future aspect of the author's eschatological outlook, since it looks forward to a moment **when Christ is revealed**. This perspective is in common with wider Pauline understanding of a future *parousia*, even though Paul's own perspective appears to have undergone development. Colossians envisages Christ as being the goal of creation since 'all things were created...for him' (Col. 1:16), and the consummation of all things, 'Christ is all in all' (Col. 3:11). Yet alongside these developments, the author shows that these telic conceptions of a universal Christ-centred cosmos have not entirely subsumed the more primitive Pauline perspective on the *parousia*. However, although the basic affirmation of Christ's future return is present here, as it is in other Pauline writings (1 Thess. 1:10; 2 Thess. 2:1), the detailed descriptions that elsewhere accompany statements about Christ's return (1 Thess. 5:1–11; 2 Thess. 2:3–12) are absent here. Instead, the reference to the future manifestation in this context is employed to reinforce the idea that the Colossians are united with Christ. The semi-technical term for Christ's return, *parousia*, is not used in Colossians. Instead, the future appearance of Christ is said to be the time when he is to be **revealed**, φανερωθῇ.

The verb is used four times in Colossians (twice in this verse), and elsewhere it describes the disclosure of the divine mystery (Col. 1:26), or Paul's public announcement of 'the mystery of Christ' (Col. 4:3–4). The use of revelatory language is probably not due to a desire to avoid the term *parousia*. Rather, it better reflects the understanding in Colossians of the unveiling of the divine mystery, and Christ's future return is seen as the final stage of the revelation.

In the next clause the author makes the link between the thought of the previous verse, 'your life is hidden in Christ' (Col. 3:3), and the ideas in this verse even more clear. The leap from speaking about the hidden heavenly life of believers to the future manifestation of Christ, and believers with him, is justified in the author's mind since not only is their life kept safe with Christ, but more fundamentally because the Colossians are informed that it is Christ **who is your life**. There is a common textual problem here with certain manuscripts reading the pronoun 'your', ὑμῶν ($\mathfrak{P}^{46}$ ℵ C D* F G P Ψ 075 33), while others read 'our', ἡμῶν (B D¹ H 0278 1739 𝔐). The choice between these variant readings is not entirely obvious. Copyists could have been motivated to alter 'our' to 'your', 'to agree with the second person pronoun before and after' (Metzger 1994: 557). However, given stronger manuscript attestation for 'your', that reading is adopted here and by NA[28].

The concluding statement in this verse, **then you also will be revealed with him in glory**, has an important pastoral function. It assures the Colossians that contrary to what their detractors may be saying, believers already have a new existence, the quality of which cannot be matched by any other system of religion. Believers are so closely united with Christ for the author of Colossians that his future is their future. The Colossians are informed that union with Christ, which in their contemporary situations is real but hidden, will become real and public. The future transformation of believers at the *parousia* is an idea that is present in a number of Paul's letters. Believers who are alive at his return, according to Paul, 'will be caught up together with them in the clouds to meet the Lord in the air, and thus we shall always be with him' (1 Thess. 4:17). Transformation is a key hope of *parousia* expectations: 'the dead will be raised imperishable, and we shall be changed' (1 Cor. 15:52). Here, however, the hope is not on transformation, for that is viewed as already having happened through union with Christ. Instead, the emphasis is on revelation and manifestation. The eschatological hopes are not future in Colossians in a classic Pauline sense. Instead, they are seen as being mystically present for God's holy ones through the revealed, but hidden, divine mystery (Col. 1:26). For those who are not believers such mysteries are beyond perception until Christ is revealed, and in a certain sense even for believers they will be actualized and appropriated in the future when they **will be revealed with him**. The state in which this revelation will take place is described as being **in glory**. This description of existence in the future heavenly state as being 'in glory' is not a common formulation in the New Testament. Perhaps the closest parallels are to be found in three other letters in the Pauline corpus. The Philippians are told that God will supply their needs 'according to his riches *in glory*' (Phil. 4:19). Here the phrase 'in glory' is locative, denoting the place of divine dwelling. In the second example the phrase is not identical, but the conceptual parallel may be closer, with the Thessalonians being encouraged to behave in a manner 'worthy of the God who calls you into his kingdom and glory' (1 Thess. 2:12). This example describes the divine realm into which the Thessalonians are invited to participate. Other examples of this idea include the promise that in comparison to present affliction, 'an eternal weight of glory' awaits believers (2 Cor. 4:17), and that the future expectation that humble bodies will be remade in the likeness of 'the body of his glory' (Phil. 3:21) The first example from Philippians (Phil. 4:19) is closely aligned with the description of 'the riches of the glory of this mystery' in Col. 1:27. Given that Col. 3:4 has strong conceptual links with material in Col. 1:26–27, it may be the case that here the author has expanded upon ideas relating to the revelation that comes through the gospel (Aletti 1993: 220). If this is the case, then the message here is that the 'fullness of that revelation comes only at the second coming' (Sumney 2008: 182). Therefore the letter sees the disclosure of the divine mystery as realized in the present for believers, while the fulness of the life that brings it is appropriated in the future.

This transitional section in Colossians has effectively summarized much of the theology of the letter, especially the ideas pertaining to union and life with and in Christ. It has implicitly critiqued the claims of those who dispute the validity of the belief system of the Colossians, and instead declare that their own mystical experiences provide superior access to the divine. Here the author announces that the very existence of believers 'is hidden with Christ in God'. Consequently, there is by implication no need to seek visionary experiences. Also the author provides pastoral reassurance to his readers. They are informed that although their heavenly existence is currently a secret truth, it will be fully revealed when Christ himself is made manifest. The ethical imperatives that follow in the next sections are thus grounded in these theological statements, which have been so strongly reasserted in the face of a challenge from various detractors.

13. PUT AWAY PAST PRACTICES (3:5–11)

(5) Put to death therefore the members that are on earth: fornication, impurity, passion, evil desire, and greed, which is idolatry. (6) Because of which things the wrath of God is coming. (7) In which you also once walked, when you were living in them. (8) But now you also, put away all these things: wrath, rage, malice, slander, obscene speech from your mouth. (9) Do not lie to one another, having stripped off the old man with his practices, (10) and having put on the new one, who is being renewed in knowledge according to the image of the one who created him. (11) Where there is not Greek and Jew, circumcision and uncircumcision, barbarian, Scythian, slave, free, but Christ is all and in all.

The author continues to develop the metaphors of 'death' and 'life' in the material that follows Col. 3:1–4. Living new transformed lives through the power of God that raised Christ from the dead (Col. 2:12), and participating in that resurrection (Col. 3:1), means that the Colossians are to adopt a form of life that conforms to the pattern of a risen life that is hidden with Christ in glory (Col. 3:4). Death and resurrection are two aspects of union with Christ, both symbolized in baptism (Col. 2:12). Having died and being raised with Christ, having been dead in transgressions yet made alive in him (Col. 2:13), the Colossians must actively put to death behaviours characteristic of their former earthly mode of existence, and in their stead put on a pattern of life that is consonant with the life they now have in Christ (Col. 3:12–17).

There is also a community focus in the ethical teaching that is given in Colossians, both in terms of avoiding certain practices that are destructive among fellow group members (Col. 3:9), and in relation to the encouragement that is given to engage in worship practices that are corporately uplifting. Thus there is a balance between individual and corporate ethics, and this contrasts with the self-indulgent quest for individual exultation and self-gratifying religious experiences that exemplify the form of religion practised by those who pass judgment on the Colossians (Col. 2:16). While many of the behaviours that are proscribed are general in nature in Col. 3:5, 8, the motivation for not conforming to such practices stems from the unity that believers experience in Christ. They have been renewed in his image (Col. 3:10), and Christ has become the unifying focus of the cosmos (Col. 3:11).

5 Although readers have already been told that they have been buried with Christ (Col. 2:12), and they were previously dead in transgressions (Col. 2:13), there is still a need to mortify aspects of their existence that do not reflect their transformed status as those whose lives are hidden in the heavenly sphere. This section opens with an imperative and a logical conjunction, **put to death therefore**. Having declared that the Colossians are the recipients of a new heavenly life, the inference that is drawn is that they are to kill off anything that does not align with Christ-centred existence. The relationship between these two sections can be seen as an example of a Pauline technique of moving from doctrinal indicatives (Col. 3:1–4) to ethical imperatives (Col. 3:5, 8–10). Dunn highlights various occurrences of introducing the doctrinal indicative with a 'since'/'if' construction, and then presenting the ethical imperative with a 'therefore' clause (cf. Rom. 6:4a–b; 1 Cor. 5:7a–b; Gal. 5:1a–b, 13a–b; Phil. 2:12–13; Dunn 1998: 627). Here the moral instruction is tightly linked with the theological indicatives that have been presented in the letter, although it may be a mistake to read Pauline ethical teaching exclusively in light of this paradigm. The assurance of Christ being their life (Col. 3:4) means that the believers' lives should be Christ-like. What the

Colossians are told to put to death are **the members that are on earth**. Most commentators have found this to be an unacceptable translation, or lacking a clear referent. Consequently most supply a second person pronoun: 'what is earthly in you' (Schweizer 1982: 181; Pokorný 1991: 158); 'what belongs to your earthly nature' (O'Brien 1982: 173); 'the parts of you which are "on the earth"' (Dunn 1996: 210). Dunn also notes that his 'of you' was 'not part of the original text, but is implied, and was added in the latter textual tradition' (Dunn 1996: 210 n. 2). It is possible to agree with two of Dunn's statements: the second person pronoun was not part of the earliest stage of the textual tradition, and the word ὑμῶν, 'your', is added in the following manuscripts: א² A C³ D F G H Ψ 075 0278 1881 𝔐. However, there may be reason to pause before accepting the third statement that the second person pronoun is implied. The perspective that permeates the letter is that the Colossians have been transferred into the kingdom of the Son (Col. 1:13). It may jar with that outlook to declare that believers have not been fully transferred to the divine realm, and that might be implied if the author had spoken of 'your earthly members'. Rather than saying that there are parts of the Colossians that still require regeneration, the author seems to say there are 'members' that do not belong to the Colossians, but are earthly in nature, and hence those things which are not part of them, nor belong to their heavenly existence, must be put to death. This is not a renunciation of the material world *per se*, or the physical body in particular. Instead, as becomes clear in the list that follows, 'the members that are on earth' is a phrase that is used as a metaphor for certain unacceptable forms of behaviour.

A representative list of five practices that are no longer acceptable for people who live in union with Christ is presented. These practices are **fornication, impurity, passion, evil lust, and greed, which is idolatry**, with the fourth noun being accompanied by an attributive adjective, and the final noun being expanded by a relative clause that highlights the fundamental issue at stake with 'greed'. This list, and the five-membered list in Col. 3:8, may be seen as examples of the known pattern of the 'vice list'. While the form might have been widespread in the ancient world the content appears to depend more on traditional Jewish concerns in regard to perceived immoral Gentile activities. The first noun, **fornication**, πορνεία, embraces a range of sexual practices, which within a Jewish ethical framework were deemed irregular and sinful. The term πορνεία is used in the Septuagint in a variety of ways: to refer to prostitution (Gen. 38:24); incestuous relationships (Tob. 8:7); a man or a woman engaged in promiscuous activity (Wisd. 23:16–23; 26:26); and, most prominently, especially in the prophetic tradition, as a metaphor for idolatry (Mic. 1:7; Nah. 3:4; Isa. 47:10; Jer. 2:20; Ezek. 16:25). The use of the term as a metaphor for idolatry may stem from the use of sexual activities in certain fertility rites or cultic practices. Within the Pauline writings, the concern of irregular sexual practices is a recurrent problem. The case of the man who has his father's wife is described as πορνεία in 1 Cor. 5:1, and there denotes sexual activity within a prohibited degree of relationship, or incest. In a less transparent example in the same letter Paul argues that because of πορνεία every man should have his own wife (1 Cor. 7:2), and the term may denote sexual relations outside of marriage in this context. Despite numerous suggestions, the meaning of the charge to 'abstain from sexual immorality (πορνεία)' (1 Thess. 4:3) is not made clear by the advice in the following verse that 'each of you should know how to possess his vessel in sanctification and honour' (1 Thess. 4:4). Then as now social taboos surround precise descriptions of which sexual activities were being envisaged. It is likely that here the term is a broad designation of sexual activity that was not in line with traditional Jewish laws. The term certainly covered 'fornication', but was almost certainly wider than pre-marital intercourse. However, translations such as 'any sexual irregularity' or 'sexual impurity' are perhaps too non-descript and too clinical to capture the harshness of the Greek term and the value judgment that the word carries.

The second behaviour that is described is **impurity**, ἀκαθαρσία. This word is the antonym of 'cleanness', καθαρός. However, in religious contexts it is not a term that refers to the lack of physical hygiene, but rather denotes ritual impurity. In Pauline thought 'impurity' is presented as the state that is opposite to 'holiness' (1 Thess. 4:17), and he is able to declare that his message does not come 'from error, or from impurity, or by guile' (1 Thess. 2:3). Writing to the Corinthians, he informs them that many who sinned in the past 'have not repented of the fornication and impurity and sensuality which they have practised' (2 Cor. 2:12). Given the way 'impurity' is linked with the terms 'fornication' and 'sensuality', in certain Pauline contexts it appears to be a way of further designating sexual sins.

The same pairing that opens this vice list, 'fornication, impurity', is found at the head of the list in Galatians where Paul writes, 'now the works of the flesh are evident, which are fornication, impurity, sensuality...' (Gal. 5:19). Therefore, the fact that these two nouns stand at the head of both lists of vices, and that these are both addressed to Gentiles, suggests that they are seen as paradigmatic from a Jewish perspective of a fundamental Gentile tendency towards sexual sins that were proscribed in Jewish tradition. Such activities, according to the author, are incompatible with the new existence that has been given to believers, and hence these things are to be put to death in order that they might walk worthily (cf. Col. 1:10; 2:6) of Christ, since they now live in union with him.

The third negative quality listed here is **passion**, πάθος. While in Stoic thought it was used to designate a lack of emotional self-control, in Pauline usage (it occurs in no other part of the New Testament) the term takes on a different sense. In Rom. 1:26 it is used to describe 'shameful passions' of a sexual nature practised by women, and in another passage where the sexual practices of Gentiles are being rejected, the Thessalonians are told that each one of them should know 'how to possess his own vessel in sanctification and honour, not in lustful passion, like the Gentiles who do not know God' (1 Thess. 4:5). Again the term in used in the Pauline writings to denote Gentile sexual practices, which in Jewish thought were seen as common to non-Jews, and hence on this basis Jews stigmatized such people as sinful. The practices of 'promiscuity and love of money' are seen as the 'two passions contrary to God' in the *Test. Jud.* 18:6. Again, in the Judeo-Christian tradition 'passion' is not a broad philosophical description of a life governed by emotions, but a designation of unrestrained and promiscuous sexual behaviour.

The fourth element in the list is described as **evil desire**, ἐπιθυμία κακή. By itself 'desire' can be seen as a positive quality. In the passion narrative, Jesus declares 'I have earnestly desired to eat this Passover with you' (Lk. 22:15). In the Pauline writings the term can be used positively to designate Paul's 'desire to depart and be with Christ' (Phil. 1:23), or to tell the Thessalonians of his 'great desire to see your face' (1 Thess. 2:17). However, despite these occurrences it is used more frequently as a negative term. Paul can speak of the 'desires of their hearts' in a context referring to Gentile sexual practice (Rom. 1:24); sin is not to reign in one's body 'that you should obey its desires' (Rom. 6:12). In Rom. 7:7–8 it is used as a technical term for 'coveting'. Again in relation to lust, believers are not 'to make provision for the flesh in regard to desire' (Rom. 13:14). The Galatians are not to 'fulfil the desire of the flesh' (Gal. 5:16), and 'passions and desires' are to be crucified (Gal. 5:24). The last example is particularly instructive because it combines the same two elements as the third and fourth terms in the list in Col. 3:5. Moreover, these are things that are to be 'crucified', which is another metaphor of mortification, paralleling the opening imperative in Col. 3:5, 'put to death'. Therefore the author makes clear that the **desire** in Col. 3:5 is negative, since it is accompanied by the attributive adjective **evil**. Given the wider Pauline use of the term with its frequent occurrence in the context of Gentile sexual sins (Rom. 1:24; 6:24; Gal. 5:16, 24; 1 Thess. 4:5), and because of its connection in the context of Col. 3:5 with three terms that unambiguously refer to irregular sexual practices, this rejection of 'evil desire' is primarily a renunciation of these practices. The author is concerned that his addressees are liable to revert to such practices, since these behaviours were viewed as a stereotypical Gentile tendency to engage in sexual sin.

The final item in the vice list is **greed**, πλεονεξία. This represents the tendency to desire more for oneself in an unstrained and selfish manner. The range of meaning this term covers is defined as 'the state of desiring to have more than one's due, *greediness, insatiableness, avarice, covetousness*' (BDAG: 824). While the term may on occasion be connected with sexual greed. Some have seen the verbal form in 1 Thess. 4:6: 'that no man transgress and *defraud* his brother', as referring to sexual practices. However, it is not obviously the case that the term is designating sexual irregularity. In general, the actions described by the term 'greed' are not sexual in nature. Therefore, it is best to resist attempts to force it into line with the four previous terms and insist that it is also a sexual referent, thereby describing it as 'the ruthless insatiableness evident when sexual appetite is unrestrained in a man with power to gratify it' (Dunn 1996: 215). The term is used in the vice list in Rom. 1:29–31, where only one term, 'fornication', is sexual in nature, but the other 22 items are not. In 2 Cor. 9:5, it is used in a traditional sense to describe 'covetousness' in relation to a gift of monetary value. Instructively, Paul describes 'flattering speech' as 'a pretext for greed' (1 Thess. 2:5). Thus, it is better to see a change of direction in the chain of thought at this juncture from sexual vices to a warning against the tendency to acquire material possessions in an unrestrained manner. As has been seen when discussing the third item in the list, 'passion', the *Testament of Judah* describes the two passions contrary to God as 'promiscuity and love of money' (*Test. Jud.* 18:6). Here also one sees the connection between sexual sins and material greed. The term 'greed' is glossed with the relative clause, **which is idolatry.** Whereas the detrimental aspect of the sexual vices could be assumed as self-evident to the audience of the letter, here the problem with greed is made explicit. The basis for this rejection of greed is apparent through its connection with 'idolatry', which again is a stereotypically regarded as a marker of Gentile ethical failing. The author of Colossians is not the first writer to identify greed with idolatry. Again in the *Testament of Judah* it is stated that 'the love of money leads to idolatry; because, when led astray through money, men name as gods those who are not gods' (*Test. Jud.* 19:1; cf. Philo, *Spec.* 1.23–27; 1QpHab. 6.1; 8.11–12). The incompatibility between seeking wealth and worship of God is set out in the Sermon on the Mount (Mt. 6:4). The significance of the link between 'greed' and 'idolatry' means that it cannot be dismissed as a lesser offence: 'by tying avarice to idolatry, Colossians makes it one of the deep causes of human sin' (Sumney 2008: 191).

The practices contained in this list represent forms of behaviour that are now at odds with the new mode of existence in which the Colossians partake. They exist in union with Christ, their lives are with him, and they have been transferred into the kingdom of the Son of his love (Col. 1:13). As renewed beings, actions such as **fornication, impurity, passion, evil lust, and greed, which is idolatry** no longer belong to their nature. These vices are to be mortified. This idea aligns with wider Pauline theology: 'for if you are living according to the flesh, you must die; but if by the Spirit you are putting to death the deeds of the body, you will live' (Rom. 8:13). Although reference to the Spirit is absent in Colossians, the fundamental idea is very similar. Believers are actively to put to death either 'the members on earth' (Col. 3:5) or 'the deeds of the body' (Rom. 8:13). Such an action is what befits the life above (Col. 3:3), or it results in life rather than death (Rom. 8:13). Both the thought expressed in Rom. 8:13 and the views that emerge in Col. 3:5 show that these are not individual actions designed to heighten one's own spirituality, but that 'the community through its discernment and ethical choices is to kill the actions of the old age as they crop up' (Jewett 2007: 495).

6 Next the consequence of such actions is described, albeit in impersonal terms. In relation to the continuing practice of the vices listed the author of Colossians declares, **because of which things the wrath of God is coming**. The majority of manuscripts append to the end of this verse the variant reading 'upon the sons of disobedience'. It has been suggested by some that this is indeed the original reading because the following verse implies a reference to people (Dunn 1996: 210 n. 4). Others have chosen to retain it because of the sheer weight of manuscript support (Wilson 2005: 246, 248). The first observation in fact provides a reason why a later scribe may have wished to modify the text. The second fact concerning the wide and diverse manuscript attestation is correct in its description of the data, but not necessarily so in its assessment of the significance of the manuscript evidence. The phrase is absent in two of the earliest and most important manuscripts ($\mathfrak{P}^{46}$ B); it is also omitted in some of the early versions (cop^{sa} eth^{ro}), and also lacking in the writings of various early Christian authors (Clement, Cyprian, Macrobius, Abrosiaster, Ephraem, and Jerome). Moreover, given the parallel in Eph. 5:6, which supplies these words to produce a smoother text, it is likely later scribes harmonized the text of Col. 3:6 to that of Eph. 5:6 to clarify the transition to Col. 3:7. Lohse goes as far as to state that the shorter reading 'certainly offers the original text' (Lohse 1971: 139). There are very few things that are 'certain' in adjudicating between variant readings, and in this case the weight of manuscripts in favour of the longer reading means the extended text cannot be dismissed lightly. However, on balance, the shorter text, followed here, has a higher degree of probability in being the earliest recoverable form of the text.

This verse commences with the preposition **because of**, διά, which indicates that the listed vices are the causal factor that results in the circumstances described in this verse. The neuter plural relative pronoun, **which**, that follows the preposition refers to the five practices described in the previous verse. Four of the nouns were feminine and one was neuter in gender, but it is not uncommon for a neuter relative pronoun to be used to encompass a list of multiple entities. In the Greek syntax the next element in the verse is the verb **is coming**. Most likely this is a futuristic present 'depicting the certainty of future divine action' (Harris 2010: 128). While the verb is sometimes understood as 'gnomic present', which refers to continuous and permanent action, 'the wrath of God always comes on such things', this is not the most plausible interpretation here. That is both because in wider Pauline usage the wrath of God is typically a future activity (Rom. 2:5, 8; 3:5; 5:9; 9:22; 1 Thess. 5:9) and also since the author has just been describing the eschatological future in Col. 3:4. What is said to be coming in reaction to such vices is **the wrath of God**. The anger of God is certainly something to be avoided, and knowledge that it is directed against the vices listed in the previous verse provides a further motivation for 'putting to death' those practices. In wider Pauline theology the idea of the 'wrath of God' is most prominent in Romans, but elsewhere Paul describes Jesus as the one 'who rescues us from the coming wrath' (1 Thess. 1:10), and he promises the Thessalonians that 'God has not destined us for wrath' (1 Thess. 5:9). Displaying much the same perspective as Col. 3:6, in Romans Paul writes that 'the wrath of God is revealed from heaven' (Rom. 1:18) against various vices and the practitioners of those sins, and it is stated that individuals can 'treasure up wrath for themselves in the day of wrath' (Rom. 2:5) by not putting off evil practices. Divine wrath in Pauline theology is, therefore, directed against certain evil practices, it is a consequence of not accepting the act of rescue that the gospel brings, and escape from it requires putting to death vices that do not align with life in Christ.

7 Here the antecedent of the relative pronoun, **in which**, remains the five vices listed in Col. 3:5. The change in status of the Colossians in relation to sins that were typically associated with Gentiles, at least from a Jewish perspective, is described here. The metaphor of 'walking' is employed again in the letter. However, previously it has been a positive image of the new way in which the Colossians conduct their lives in Christ (cf. Col. 1:10; 2:6). Here the metaphor of 'walking' that describes their former lifestyle, reminds the Colossians that it was in such practices **you also once walked**. Once again, the author places distance between the Colossians and their former ethical behaviour. The distance is temporal in nature, since what is described is a prior mode of conduct when they **once** behaved in a manner typified by sexual vice and self-indulgent greed.

The second clause in the verse, **when you were living in them**, forms an expression that is almost synonymous with the idea expressed in the first half of the verse. Perhaps the key difference relates to the different tenses used for the two verbs 'walked' and 'were living'. While both designate action in the past, in contrast to the aorist (or simple past) used with the first verb, the imperfect tense, **were living**, reveals a habitual and perhaps a habituated attitude to engaging in the standard Gentile vices. Thus the second clause may suggest that the Colossians 'characteristically participated in the vices of v. 5' (Sumney 2008: 193).

The purpose of this verse is to remind the Colossians that they were once in a state that made them potential recipients of the coming wrath of God. The author commences the first half of a statement that contrasts the former mode of life ('once', Col. 3:7) with the current prevailing state of existence ('now', Col. 3:8). Such a contrast between the former and present life has been described previously in the letter with the antithesis between 'being dead in transgressions' and being 'alive together with him' (Col. 2:13), as well as the description of the former alienation and the present reconciliation (Col. 1:21–22). Pauline theology offers a stark dichotomy between the former life characterized by immoral practices, and the present life that is lived in union with Christ, and transformed through him.

8 The second half of the contrast set up in the previous verse is now completed here. The opening to this verse aligns with the imperatival command at the beginning of this section, 'put to death therefore the members that are on earth' (Col. 3:5). In the same vein the author opens with the imperatival clause, **but now you also, put away all these things**. The command is a consequence of the fact that believers now partake of a transformed state of existence; their lives are hidden with Christ in God (Col. 3:3). The actions of 'putting to death' or 'putting away' practices that are not consistent with that transformed existent are not the mechanism for obtaining new life, but the ethical necessities of living in that new state.

The command is in the contemporary period for the audience
of the letter, but the **now** also has an eschatological aspect since
believers are already accruing the benefits of transfer into a different
realm (Col. 1:13), and have their lives safeguarded with Christ (Col.
3:3). The pronoun **you** emphasizes the fact that the recipients of
this instruction are called to produce behaviour that is suitable for
their new eschatological status, and with their union with Christ.
Hence the imperative **put away** stresses that the result of having
been reconciled to God in Christ is actively to pursue a way of life
that reflects that new ontological state. Passivity is not appropriate;
instead, what is required is an active 'putting away', ἀπόθεσθε, of
behaviour inconsistent with their new status. The verb 'put away'
can describe the physical stripping off of clothing (Acts 7:58), but
elsewhere in the New Testament tends to be used in a figurative
manner. Thus the author of Hebrews can call upon addressees to
'put aside every weight and sin' (Heb. 12:1). In Romans the term is
used as a hortatory subjunctive, 'let us therefore cast off the works
of darkness' (Rom. 13:12). In these contexts, as in Col. 3:8 (cf. Eph.
4:22), the term is both active and figurative, describing a negative
activity or attitude of which those being addressed are implored to
divest themselves. In this context the Colossians are called upon to
put away **all these things**. If one read no further, then the obvious
referent of 'all these things' would be the five vices mentioned in
Col. 3:5, which have been the focus of the discussion to this point.
However, 'all these things' is also placed in apposition to a new list
of five vices in the second half of this verse. Given that in Col. 3:5
the syntactical construction shows that the things that are to be 'put
to death' are the following five vices, here it is also most likely that
what are to be 'put away' are the five vices that follow in this verse.
However, such syntactical exactitude and parallelism would perhaps
create too rigid a divide between the putting to death of the first
five items, and the putting aside of the second five. Both together
are to be put to death and to be put to death. The calls to 'put to
death' and to 'put away' are figurative ways of referring to the action
necessary in order that believers might rid themselves of practices
not commensurate with their new existence. The repetition in calling
for these twin actions is dramatic and replete with rhetorical effect.
To create some qualitative or theological distinction misses the point
of the author's ethical injunctions.

This second vice list contains five elements that are more general in terms of the activities they cover, and less focussed than the first list where the first four elements all appeared to relate to sexual misdemeanours. Here it has been suggested that the catalogue of five inappropriate behaviours, **wrath, rage, malice, slander, obscene speech from your mouth**, may have been dependent upon a traditional vice list. Even if this were the case, they may have been selected because they were particularly relevant to the concerns and situation of the letter. If one were to look for a unifying feature in this fivefold list, it might be that they are all actions that can be verbal in nature. However, this might be a false attempt to find a unifying principle where one does not exist. The other interesting feature of the two fivefold lists is that in both the final item is supplied with further explanatory qualification.

The first item in the list, ὀργή, is frequently and not incorrectly translated as 'anger'. Here, however, it has been rendered as **wrath**, which is a perfectly acceptable translation, in order to maintain a consistent translation of the term ὀργή in Col. 3:6, where it is used in the expression 'the wrath of God'. It would be possible to render that phrase as 'the anger of God', but that choice may have been jarring, and perhaps evoked ideas of uncontrolled anger. Hence, the consistent translation of ὀργή as 'wrath' seemed to be the preferable choice. However, when the term is used in the New Testament to refer to human anger it depicts an uncontrolled and emotional outburst that is fundamentally an inferior characteristic. Elsewhere, the warning against 'wrath' is given because such behaviour is seen as contrary to the divine qualities that should exemplify the conduct of believers: 'the wrath of a man does not achieve the righteousness of God' (Jas 1:20). Hence in various New Testament writings 'wrath' is seen as being antithetical to the life of righteousness (*EDNT*: II, 529).

Some commentators have sought to highlight a distinction between the first vice, **wrath**, and the second element in the list, **rage**, θυμός. Thus Harris notes that if the two terms are to be distinguished then 'the former denotes chronic anger, the latter a passionate outburst of anger' (Harris 2010: 130). However, as Harris hints, it is questionable whether such a distinction is permissible. The lack of material difference between these two terms has been regularly noted (see Wilson 2005: 249). Moreover, 'wrath' and 'rage' frequently occur together as a type of emphatic and synonymous pairing (LXX Num. 14:34; 32:14; Deut. 9:19; Ps. 77:38; Job 20:23).

The third term is perhaps the most general in the list, and the choice of **malice** as a translation is an attempt to capture that broad sense. The Greek term κακία is given a wide range of meanings in the lexica, such as: '1. the state or quality of wickedness, *baseness, depravity, wickedness, vice…* 2. A mean spirited or vicious disposition, *malice, ill-will, malignity*' (BDAG: 500). A reference to Col. 3:8 is listed under the second field of meaning, hence the choice of malice as the best translational equivalent in this context.

The fourth term, βλασφημία, is often translated as 'blasphemy' in relation to ridiculing speech addressed to a divine being or heavenly entity. Hence the related verb is translated as 'to blaspheme' when God or some divine entity is the object: 'the name of God is blasphemed among the Gentiles' (Rom. 2:24); 'that the word of God may not be blasphemed' (Tit. 2:5). However, when the object is human the meaning is more generic and 'can have the simple meaning *disparage, slander, defame*' (*EDNT*: I, 220). Since the noun is used in a generic sense here, the translation **slander** is adopted. This stands in contrast to the use in Revelation, where the dragon utters blasphemy against God and against his name (Rev. 13:5–6). If the intention is to describe 'slander' directed against fellow human beings, then the term designates any form of vilification, 'either by lies or gossip' (O'Brien 1982: 188).

The fifth and final element in the list is translated as **obscene speech**, αἰσχρολογία. The Greek word occurs only here in the New Testament. The term is also relatively rare in wider Greek literature (cf. Polybius, *Hist.* 8.11.8; 31.6.4). While in general the meaning of words cannot necessarily be derived from their component part, here the two compounded terms appear to give a fairly unambiguous sense of the meaning of the word: αἰσχρός meaning 'shameful' or 'repulsive' (1 Cor. 11:6; 14:35; Eph. 5:12; Tit. 1:11), + λόγια, in the sense of utterances (cf. 1 Pet. 4:11). Hence the sense here is that of 'shameful utterances' or **obscene speech**.

Following on from this final item in the list is the prepositional phrase **from your mouth**. The syntactical relationship of this clause to the remainder of the verse is disputed. Harris lists four options. The first and third are similar, the key difference being whether the phrase 'from your mouth' is linked to the opening imperative, or whether the opening imperative and the phrase 'from your mouth' are separated by the list of five vices (see Harris 2010: 130).

1. Construing the phrase with the opening imperative: 'Put away out of your mouth all these things' (Moule 1957: 117–18).
2. Applying only to the last two elements in the list: 'abusive and filthy language from your mouth' (cf. GNB).
3. Relating to all five vices: 'have done with...banish them all from your lips' (cf. REB).
4. Qualifying the final element alone: 'obscene speech from your mouth' (cf. KJV, NASB, RSV, etc).

Against the first option is the factor of the distance of the prepositional phrase from the imperative. With option two, it is unclear why the first three terms should be separated from the final two, presumably because the last two are verbal forms of utterance. The third option does not signal the connection of the prepositional clause to all of the preceding elements; rather, this is supplied in English translations that suggest the translation 'banish *them all* from your lips'. By contrast, the fourth option is not only the most straightforward in terms of syntax, but forms an obvious parallel to the vice in Col. 3:5 where only the final term is qualified by supplying additional information.

Unlike the list of five practices that the Colossians were urged to 'put to death' in Col. 3:5, which were commonly perceived by Jewish critics to be symptomatic of Gentile behaviour, this list is more generic. The list is not 'again typically Jewish' (*contra* Lohmeyer 1964: 139; Dunn 1996: 218), but reflects the wider ethical teaching of the Greco-Roman world (cf. Seneca, *Ira.* 2.36). The reason for the author highlighting these verbal vices is unclear. One may speculate that such sins of speech were a prominent problem among the Colossian community, but they may also be a generalized and non-specific list with no direct application to a particular situation in

Colossae. Rather, these vices may be representative of the types of behaviour that are no longer appropriate for those who live in union with Christ to practise. Therefore the changed mode of believers' existence, as those who now have their true life with Christ, means that their actions in the present earthly state should conform to what, although future, is their authentic existence.

9 The imperative that commences this verse emphasizes the communal orientation of the ethical instructions that are given here. Focussing on group interactions, the author commands the Colossians **do not lie to one another**. This directive follows on naturally from the preceding fivefold vice list with its focus on inappropriate verbal practices. In the Pauline letters there are repeated declarations from the apostle where he states 'I am not lying' (Rom. 9:1; 2 Cor. 11:31; Gal. 1:20; 1 Tim. 2:7). In those cases the author offers a personal indicative declaration. In Col. 3:9 the author continues the train of thought with a generalized imperative instruction. Perhaps the closest parallel to this command is to be found in the Epistle of James: 'do not be arrogant and so lie against the truth' (Jas 3:14). Thus lying in general terms is a verbal statement contrary to the truth. In Colossians one of the characteristics of the gospel is that it is the 'word of truth' (Col. 1:5). Therefore falsehood is the antithesis of a life shaped by the gospel, and opposes the 'grace of God' that came to the Colossians 'in truth' (Col. 1:6). Here the incongruity of carrying out such behaviour at the expense of fellow believers is presented as a self-evidently wrong action. Hence the author provides no explanation of why such action is deemed as being inappropriate. The concern appears to be that it is not only wrong in itself, but is destabilizing and destructive if practised among this new fledgling community of believers. It is probably too much of a stretch to see the prohibition as being directed against the 'philosophy' of those who are passing judgment on the Colossians. The concern appears to have a more internal focus, directed towards those who are integrally part of the community. It is lying **to one another** that has the potential to undermine the fraternal relationships that have been created in the community because of the mutual experience of life in Christ.

While the author does not explain what is intrinsically wrong with lying, the reason he offers for determining that it is no longer appropriate within the community of believers is due to their changed status. He describes this change of being as **having stripped off the old man with his practices**. The verb used here, **having stripped off**, like the imperative in the previous verse, 'put away', speaks of divesting oneself of past practices. Here the verb is more explicitly related to the removal of clothing (see Canavan 2012: 134–78), and is employed to create a contrast with the description in the following verse of 'having put on' (Col. 3:10). The double compound form is favoured by the author of Colossians, either as a noun ἀπέκδυσις (Col. 2:11), or as a verb ἀπεκδύομαι (Col. 2:15; 3:9), but is used nowhere else in the New Testament. Various translations and commentaries have glossed what is admittedly a potentially androcentric expression τὸν παλαιὸν ἄνθρωπον, **the old man**. Translations include the following options: 'your old self' (NIV); 'the old self' (ESV, NASB); 'the old nature' (ISB); 'the old human nature' (REB); 'your old sinful nature' (NLT). The translation adopted here is both literal and traditional: 'the old man' (KJV, RV, Douay-Rheims). The advantage of retaining the literal translation is that it does not communicate the idea that the author is speaking in metaphysical categories of 'nature' or 'self', but is using the earthly description of stripping off 'the old man'. This anthropocentric description of people as humans reveals a conception of the necessity of treating the Colossians as whole people, and the need for people to be transformed in light of new life in Christ. Admittedly the problem with this translation is that the gendered nature of the author's language may be problematic, especially when the text is used in liturgical or worship settings. Here, however, the purpose is to understand what the author wrote in the original cultural context, which reflected patriarchal values and androcentric perspectives. Such an outlook does not need to be replicated in a modern setting. Linking this act of stripping off the old man to the two vice lists just mentioned (Col. 3:5, 8), the author drives the main point of this section home, by telling the Colossians that what needs to be stripped off is the old man **with his practices**. The recipients of the letter are left in no doubt that their new life requires a change in lifestyle, with a suspension of engaging in the deeds that characterized that former mode of existence. The change is therefore personal in nature – it employs the concrete imagery of stripping off or divesting oneself of the previous self and the practices associated with that humanity. However, this change has communal implications since inner-group ethics also are to be transformed, and the relationships established between members are not to be exemplified by the vices that have been prohibited. Therefore, the theological basis for the ethical change that is being demanded is that the Colossians have become the recipients of a new life in Christ. Hence, the implication is that their behaviour must now align with that transformed status.

10 Recognition that the Colossians have 'stripped off the old man and his practices' (Col. 3:9b) is only half of the theological reason for no longer continuing with the practices enumerated in the two vice lists (Col. 3:5 8), as well as only part of the explanation for why practising deception towards fellow community members is inappropriate (Col. 3:9a). The letter envisages a transfer and change in status. Believers not only were buried with Christ, they were raised with him (Col. 2:12). Constructing a similar bipartite image, the clothing metaphor is not restricted to the act of having divested oneself of the previous way of life. Therefore, the metaphor is extended, with the image being inextricably linked to the notion of re-clothing oneself with a new form of existence that is divinely fashioned. The change that has taken place is seen as involving two stages. Having stated that the old man has been removed, the author can declare, that **having put on the new one**, former practices are no longer appropriate for the new form of existence possessed by the Colossian believers.

Many commentators have seen an allusion to baptism in this metaphor of stripping off, and then being dressed in a new mode of being. This two-stage transformation has been described earlier in the letter in direct connection with baptism (Col. 2:12), and elsewhere in the Pauline writings the verb 'put on', ἐνδύω, is used in relation to baptism: 'for as many of you who were baptized into Christ, have *put on* Christ' (Gal. 3:27). The link may be strengthened by the fact that the next verse in Colossians (Col. 3:11) forms a close parallel to Gal. 3:28, with the Gal. 3:28 text following the baptism reference in the preceding verse. However, against this possibility, if Col. 3:9–10 is read on its own in the context of Col. 3:5–11, there is little in the passage that would evoke baptismal imagery. There is no evidence at this stage concerning a baptismal liturgy that required the divesture of clothing. The practice, attested from the mid-second century, of 'nude baptism and the accompanying change into different clothes afterwards' (Sumney 2008: 199), is not supported by the earlier baptismal accounts in Acts. Moreover, the verb 'put on' is used 14 times in the Pauline writings, and only in Gal. 3:27 is it used unambiguously of baptism, whereas there is debate concerning whether Col. 3:10 (and the parallel in Eph. 4:24) carries baptismal imagery. In the other eleven cases the term 'put on', ἐνδύω, is used without the idea of baptism being present. While it is of course impossible to prove that baptism was not in the mind of the author when the passage was penned, it is certain that an image of changed status and renewal is certainly being communicated through the language of 'stripping off' the old and 'putting on' the new.

According to the author, the new mode of existence is in a constant process of being reshaped according to the divine image. Therefore, the Colossians are informed that the new person they have become is the one **who is being renewed in knowledge**. Here the present tense suggests an ongoing activity being carried out by God, since believers are **being renewed**. Grammatically, the participle τὸν ἀνακαινούμενον has durative force, which 'makes clear that the "new self," the new reality ruled by Christ, is not in its final state: it is in a state of becoming' (Moo 2008: 269). This creates a tension in the author's thought, which is in fact found in many strands of early Christianity. The author can declare that the Colossians have already been transferred into the divine realm (Col. 1:13), that their new life already exists with Christ (Col. 3:3–4), and yet alongside of this they are in a constant process of becoming what they really are. This process takes place through 'putting to death the members on earth' (Col. 3:5), setting aside inappropriate forms of speech (Col. 3:8), and above all by continuously being renewed (Col. 3:10). The verb 'to renew', ἀνακαινόω, occurs only here and at 2 Cor. 4:16. It denotes the action of renewal, and in these two passages is 'figurative of the spiritual rebirth of the Christian' (BDAG: 64). The related noun, 'the renewing', is found twice in the New Testament, with both occurrences in the Pauline writings (Rom. 12:2; Tit. 3:5). Transference language is particularly prominent in Romans, where Paul calls upon his audience not to be 'conformed to this world', but to be 'transformed by the renewing of your mind' (Rom. 12:2). The language in the second example is more compressed, but describes 'the renewing of the Holy Spirit' (Tit. 3:5). In each of these cases the one who is being renewed is translated from one sphere of influence (e.g. 'the world') and is ethically refashioned in order to live in a manner where the transformative ethics of Christ have been imprinted on the individual being renewed. Here this continuous transformative process is described as being renewed **in knowledge**. There is much uncertainty concerning both the meaning of the prepositional clause, and its relationship to the rest of the sentence. It is uncertain whether this is intended as a response to those who tried to persuade the Colossians to adopt the 'philosophy' they promoted. For that reason, it is probably best not to read this as a subtle attempt to undercut the type of knowledge being offered by those promoting a different philosophy. The term 'knowledge', ἐπίγνωσις, has been used three times previously in the letter, on the first two occasions in the context of a prayer where Paul asks that the Colossians might be filled 'with the knowledge of his will' and that they may 'increase in the knowledge of God' (Col. 1:9, 10). Likewise, on the third occasion it describes insight into the divine revelation, with the apostolic ministry resulting in the Colossians attaining 'the knowledge of the mystery of God, which is Christ' (Col. 2:2). Assuming that the term is used fairly consistently, then the knowledge that is described here is a deep apprehension of the divine will and the mystery that results in the process of believers being renewed in God's image through that understanding of the divine purpose.

The force of the preposition **in**, εἰς, is more difficult to ascertain. Harris provides five differentiated ways of understanding the expression, each of which speaks in some way of being renewed in relationship to knowledge, where that knowledge is of God, or of his will and purposes.

1. expressing direction: 'towards true knowledge', 'unto knowledge'
2. equivalent to the locative ἐν: 'in the sphere of knowledge', 'in knowledge'
3. telic: 'for full knowledge'
4. consecutive: 'leading to knowledge'
5. temporal: 'until it reaches fullness of knowledge'

The reality is that there is little clue in the text to determine which of these senses best captures the author's meaning. Harris prefers a temporal understanding (Harris 2010: 132). However, given that believers have been transferred into the divine realm (Col. 1:13) and it is in that location where they obtain the knowledge of his will, which in turn produces renewal, it may be preferable to take the locative interpretation as the most likely since it coheres with the wider thought in the epistle (cf. BDAG: 369; Barth and Blanke 1994: 4; O'Brien 1982: 173, 191–92).

Divine orientation in this renewal in knowledge is shown to be the author's key concern since that regenerative process within each believer is **according to the image of the one who created him**. Many have detected here an echo of the creation story: 'let us make man in our own image' (Gen. 1:26). Building upon this insight some commentators have wanted to evoke wider ideas contained in the 'Adam story', and because of the language of 'putting off' and 'putting on' in this chapter, have read into the subtext Paul's theology of the old Adam and the new Adam (cf. Rom. 5:12–21). In this vein Beale argues:

> The creation in God's image in order to rule and subdue and to be fruitful and multiply (Gen. 1:26–28) is now applicable not only to Christ, but also to his people, since he and they have entered into the sphere of new creation and have begun to do what Adam failed to do... On this basis, Paul exhorts them to stop being identified with the traits of the former life in the "old Adam" (cf. 3:5–9a) and be characterized by those of the new life in the last Adam. (Beale and Carson 2007: 865)

It is important not to deny that in some way language of 'the image of the one who created him' is indebted to the Genesis story. However, given the foundational nature and widespread knowledge of this story in Jewish thought, while the creation story may ultimately stand behind the phrasing here, it is unnecessary to suggest a direct or intentional allusion or echo. Moreover, nowhere in the letter does the author make reference to Adam, so both to read Adam into the exegesis of this passage and to evoke Paul's second Adam theology appears at best tenuous. It is better to interpret the wording that the author actually wrote, rather than importing the wider story and theology of Gen. 1:26–28 or Rom. 5:12–21. The primary point is that those who have been united with Christ undergo the continuous process of renewal. Consequently, the ethical orientation of life should be lived in conformity with the image and will of the creator. In this new life, true knowledge is now possessed by those renewed in the image of the creator. According to the perspective of the epistle, divine knowledge is received through participation in the life of the risen Christ. Perhaps the more important textual link is the one that is internal to this letter. The Colossians have already been told that Christ, the subject of the poetic section, is the one 'who is the image of the invisible God' (Col. 1:15). Therefore, as believers are united with him and in him, and as they are renewed through that union, they are conformed in knowledge to the divine image.

11 The transformative power of the gospel is not limited solely to the renewal of individuals in isolation from one another. The Colossians have already been told that their communal ethics must undergo a radical re-orientation: 'do not lie to one another' (Col. 3:9). The corporate aspect of renewal comes to the fore again here, as the author boldly proclaims that previous marks of distinction are dispensed. Categories previously seen as being polar opposites are no longer appropriate, neither are other ways of distinguishing between groups. Christ is seen as the over-arching basis of relationship both with the divine and among humanity.

The opening word, **where**, has occasioned some confusion since it is not entirely clear what its referent might be. The Greek term ὅπου, 'where', typically refers to place or location, being classified grammatically as an adverb of place (BDF: §106). Some have taken its use to be metaphorical in Col. 3:11: 'in the figurative sense, ὅπου indicates 1) (temporal) circumstance or condition...in Col 3:11' (*EDNT*: II, 524). However, given the author's spatial perspective in relation to the divine realm, this adverb of place may not be figurative, but serve as a reflection of the cosmology that is part of the letter. That is, believers now live in a new sphere of existence, described variously as 'a share in the inheritance of the holy ones in light' (Col. 1:12), 'the kingdom of the Son of his love' (Col. 1:13), or they live in a new existential realm as those who 'have put on the new man' (Col. 3:10). The 'where' that the author describes is the place in which believers have their renewed lives safeguarded with Christ. It is in this new sphere where union with Christ is everything, that previous forms of differentiation have lost meaning and significance (cf. Sumney 2008: 204).

The negation of previous categories that divided rather than united humanity is announced emphatically with the assertion **there is not**. Here the author marks the cessation of former boundary-marking distinctions, which is articulated in a type of tribalism that is divisive and serves only to alienate fellow members of humanity from one another. As the author reaches the climax of his progression of thought at the end of the verse, it will become apparent that Christ not only is the primary basis of identity for believers, but that he eradicates human distinctions; he is the source of unity and solidarity in all things, thus echoing the thought of the lyrical material that occurred earlier in the letter (Col. 1:15–20); and he is the final and climactic goal not only for humanity, but the entire cosmos.

Prior to reaching the end of the verse there is a list of categories or classes of humanity that, from the author's perspective, no longer form a meaningful basis for distinction for those who have now been renewed in Christ and whose lives already authentically exist in the eschatological heavenly sphere with Christ in God (Col. 3:4). With the following list of categories there are differing viewpoints among commentators as to how to best understand the structure of the eightfold list. Some see the list as 'four contrasting pairs' (Sumney 2008: 204). However, one may question whether the structure is that of four pairs, and furthermore it is also possible to enquire whether an antithesis or contrast is the intention with each pairing, if that is indeed the correct way to divide the list. In part the tendency to read this list as a series of four contrasting pairs is due to the two parallel lists that occur elsewhere in the Pauline writings. Thus presenting the three parallels in canonical order highlights both the similarities and differences:

1 Cor. 12:13   For also in one spirit we all were baptized into one body, whether Jews, whether Greeks, whether slaves, whether free men, and all were given one spirit to drink.

Gal. 3:28   There is neither Jew nor Greek, there is neither slave nor free, there is neither male nor female; for you are all one in Christ Jesus.

Col. 3:11   Where there is not Greek and Jew, circumcision and uncir-
              cumcision, barbarian, Scythian, slave, free, but Christ is all
              and in all.

All three lists have as their two opening terms a reference to 'Jew' and 'Greek', although 1 Cor. 12:13 pluralizes these terms, and Col. 3:11 reverses the order in comparison with the other two catalogues. Also, all three lists use the terms 'slave' and 'free', although again the use of plural forms is maintained in 1 Cor. 12:13. Only in Gal. 3:28 do the terms 'male' and 'female' occur as part of that list. However, the differences in structure are perhaps more significant. With the fourfold list in 1 Cor. 12:13, each item is introduced by the co-ordinating conjunction εἴτε, 'whether'. The sixfold list in Gal. 3:28 has similarity of structure in the first two pairs using the repeated construction οὐκ ἔνι...οὐδὲ..., 'there is neither...nor...'; however, the construction with the final pairing differs slightly. By contrast, in Col. 3:11 a uniform pattern is not maintained. The first pair is introduced by a phrase which serves as a wider opening to the whole sequence, 'where there is not', and then the initial pairing **Greek and Jew** is co-ordinated by the conjunction καί, 'and'. The second pair, **circumcised and uncircumcised**, while not having an introductory phrase, is linked by the same conjunction as the previous phrase. Finally, this eight-membered catalogue concludes with a simple list of the last four elements that are not prefixed by any introductory formula or co-ordinating conjunctions: **barbarian, Scythian, slave, free**. Therefore the form of the catalogue in Col. 3:11 is, in terms of structure, the least consistent of the three examples. It is also the most extensive list. The structural change between the first four elements which are linked as pairs, and the final four items which occur as a straightforward list, raise the possibility that one should not think of four pairs, perhaps with the tendency to structure the list as four pairs being influenced both by 1 Cor. 12:13 and Gal. 3:28. Rather, the structure appears to be two pairs followed by a fourfold list. Thus, the author's purpose may not be solely to list binary contrasts. Those who have attempted to read the structure as four contrasting pairs have always struggled to explain the supposed appositional nature of a barbarian–Scythian pairing. While the initial two pairs almost certainly have a contrasting aspect, the emphasis may fall on the complementarity of the elements. Together they express the totality of humanity, in all its forms, and this ultimately is now subject to Christ's cosmic rule, without previous differentiations or distinctions.

The first pair, **Greek and Jew**, is interesting because of its reversal of the order of these terms when compared with the other two examples from similar lists in Paul's writings. The choice to place 'Greek' before 'Jew' and to make it the headword in the list may reflect the non-Jewish character of the recipients of this letter. The use of the term 'Greek' as an all-encompassing expression to denote non-Jews is a commonplace among Jewish writings (Acts 17:4; Rom. 1:16; Josephus, *B.J.* 7.45). Given the salvation-history perspective of Rom. 1:16, 'to the Jew first and also to the Greek', the order in Col. 3:11 has been seen as a significant change in outlook from that of Romans. On this basis it has been argued that 'it seems less likely that Paul would have written the words in the order found in Col 3:11' (Sumney 2008: 205). While this is an interesting observation that needs to be combined with other features of the letter that deviate from regular Pauline style and theology, by itself it illustrates the variability in the form and content or the three catalogues found in the Pauline writings. The fact that all three lists commence with reference to Jews and Greeks may reflect not only the traditional nature of this formulation, but that the tensions between Jewish and Gentile sections of the early Jesus movement had not fully abated at the time of the writing of this letter.

The second pair, **circumcision and uncircumcision**, appears to represent the same division as the first, namely between Jew and Greek, although this time the ordering is reversed, with the reference to the circumcised Jew prior to the description of the uncircumcised Gentile. While this pair is unique among the three lists, here in Col. 3:11 its purpose appears to be a simple reiteration of the first pair of terms, but expressed through a physical mark of identity rather than by an abstract formulation of ethnicity. Furthermore, unlike Galatians, where one of the pressures on that nascent Pauline community is to accept the Jewish practice of circumcision, this does not seem to be an issue in Colossians, since the author does not elaborate any concerns about the group accepting circumcision. Hence it is unwarranted to read this issue into the letter at this point or elsewhere (cf. Dunn 1996: 224). Rather, the author presents a traditional way of distinguishing among humanity, especially from a Jewish perspective, and states that such a mode of differentiation no longer has meaning. Moreover, the recipients of this letter have already been instructed that while they had formerly been uncircumcised, they had received a true spiritual circumcision, since they 'were circumcised with a circumcision made without hands' (2:11). Therefore, circumcision is used symbolically on the two occasions it is mentioned in the letter, to denote 'the removal of the body of the flesh' (2:11), and to illustrate the fact that ethnic distinctions are no longer appropriate within the body of Christ (3:11).

The concluding list of four elements, **barbarian, Scythian, slave, free**, illustrates the completeness of the removal of boundaries and distinctions. The first term in this list, **barbarian**, often held a derogatory nuance in wider use. After the Persian War the term gradually ceased being used to designate a specific national group, and was used to denote non-Hellenized people who were seen as lacking in education and culture. Whereas the first two pairs showed that distinctions between Jews and Greeks are no longer appropriate, here the inclusion of 'barbarian' in the list reveals that from the author's perspective the renewal of life in Christ also removes the traditional Hellenistic distinction, which asserted Greek superiority and separateness in comparison to those regarded as uncivilized and barbarous. Within Greek thought the expression 'Greeks and barbarians', which is found in Paul's writings (Rom. 1:14a), may have upheld the traditional Hellenistic outlook through the following synonymous pair 'both to the wise and to the foolish' (Rom. 1:14b). Here the Greeks are perhaps equated with the wise, whereas the barbarians are equivalent to the foolish. Elsewhere the combined reference to Greeks and barbarians was seen as a way of encompassing all people (Plato, *Theaetetus* 175a). The term **barbarian** occurs six times in the New Testament (Acts 28:2, 4; Rom. 1:14; 1 Cor. 14:11 [×2]; Col. 3:11). In the Pauline writings it is used in combination with reference to Greeks to designate the totality of humanity (Rom. 1:14), or in 1 Cor. 14:11 in line with its original meaning referring to a person 'who speaks a strange, unintelligible language' (*EDNT*: I, 198). Here in Col. 3:11 it is used in its standard contemporary sense to designate non-Greeks. However, from the perspective of the letter the wider connotation of the term as emphasizing derision and distinction is now negated, since those who are renewed in the image of the one who created them (Col. 3:10) share an equality of status in the body of Christ. The second term in the list, **Scythian**, refers to a nationalistic group of non-Greeks living beyond the northern frontiers of the Roman Empire. Those who insist on reading the eightfold list as a series of four opposing contrasts, assume that in opposition to the Scythians as the northern people the term 'barbarian' here is designating those non-Greek people who live to the far south, namely the inhabitants of Ethiopia and Somalia. The basis for understanding 'barbarian' in this restrictive and highly specialized manner appears to be forced for the sake of forming a contrast. It is better, in this context, to understand the terms 'barbarian' and 'Scythian' as representative of the totality of non-Greek humanity, which when renewed in the image of the creator has no less status in the body of Christ than Jews or Greeks.

The final two terms in the list, **slave, free**, represent the social reality of servitude and freeborn status. It is difficult for modern readers to appreciate how the social fabric of the Mediterranean world was predicated on maintenance of the distinctions between the freeborn and those entrapped in slavery. While it is true that certain slaves owned property or slaves of their own, and in some cases obtained manumission, the lot of the majority of slaves was extremely poor. Admittedly, there were some humanitarian laws regulating treatment of slaves. However, especially in light of the third servile war led by Spartacus (73–71 BCE), the freeborn had an almost pathological fear of the possibility that slaves would turn against them. Thus, in 10 C.E. the Silanian *senatusconsultium* legislated for the torture of all slaves present in a household when the master was murdered (Treggiari 1996: *CAH* X, 886). It is difficult to over-emphasize the radically destabilizing nature on Roman society of Christian teaching concerning the equality of all believers in Christ. It may be the case that, while asserting the principle of equality, Christian writers did not fully apprehend the ultimate implications of this egalitarian perspective. Thus in Colossians while the author can assert the general idea that such distinctions have been removed in Christ, only a few verses later and at some length the author provides detailed instructions concerning how slaves should behave in a manner that upholds the prevailing social structure and the institution of slavery (Col. 3:22–4:1). This might not be a 'blind-spot' in the author's thought. Rather, it might be a pragmatic realization that while the gospel dismantles such social distinctions, nonetheless within the first-century setting Christians were powerless to introduce such radical social changes.

In order to underscore this fundamental equality and its basis in Christ this section concludes with the assertion, **but Christ is all and in all**. Here one of the most prominent terms in Colossians is reprised, with the double use of **all**, πᾶς. The point being made here remains consistent with what has already been expressed in this verse, that all divisions that characterize existence in the present age are negated in the eschatological realm where Christ now dwells, and it is in that realm that the renewed lives of believers are hidden away (Col. 3:3). What comes to the fore, from the perspective of the author, is that this radical equality has a christological focus. The one in whom 'all the fulness of the deity dwells' is the one who unifies the whole cosmic order under his headship, and who subdues all the rulers and authorities (Col. 1:16; 2:10, 15), since 'all things have been created by him and for him' (Col. 1:16). Given that the tradition in Gal. 3:27–28 resonates with so much of the thought in Col. 3:10–11, the final phrase of Gal. 3:28, 'you are all one in Christ Jesus', may provide a clue to the way the enigmatic declaration that 'Christ is all and in all' is to be understood. If this is the case, Christ is the basis of cosmic unification, and as 'head of the body' has become 'first in all things' (Col. 1:18). Thus, as head of the new cosmic order, which is finding eschatological prefigurement in the ecclesial body, all renewed life finds its existence in connection with him.

14. PUT ON CHRIST-LIKE PRACTICES
(3:12–17)

(12) Put on therefore, as the elect of God, holy and beloved, hearts of compassion, goodness, humility, gentleness, longsuffering, (13) bearing with one another and forgiving each other if any one has a complaint against any other: just as also the Lord forgave you, so also should you. (14) And in all these things – love, which

**is the bond of perfection. (15) And let the peace of Christ rule
in your hearts, in which also you were called in one body, and
be thankful. (16) Let the word of Christ dwell in you richly, in
all wisdom teaching and admonishing each other, with psalms,
hymns, spiritual songs singing in gratitude in your hearts to God,
(17) and all that you do in word or in deed, do all things in the
name of the Lord Jesus, giving thanks to God the Father through
him.**

Whereas the previous section focused on the need for believers to
divest themselves of certain practices associated with their former
mode of life prior to receiving the gospel, here the emphasis falls
upon living in a manner that is commensurate with the new life that
is received through union with Christ.

12 In the previous section the two fivefold vice lists (Col. 3:5, 8) were
introduced respectively with the imperatives 'put to death therefore'
(Col. 3:5) and 'put away' (Col. 3:8). Here the fivefold list of virtues
is introduced with the imperative **put on therefore**. While an obvious
contrast is formed with the two imperatives that introduce the two sets
of vices, the verb **put on**, ἐνδύσασθε (ἐνδύω), is the direct antonym
of verb 'strip off', ἀπεκδυσάμενος (ἀπεκδύομαι), used in the participial construction in Col. 3:9. The contrast introduced here with the
material in Col. 3:5–11 is formed at a number of levels, but perhaps
the strongest revolves around the 'clothing' metaphor of removing
former behaviours and being re-clothed with actions that befit life
in Christ. The logical conjunction, **therefore**, likewise creates a link
with the preceding material. The imperative to engage in the actions
listed in the second half of the verse is thus predicated on what the
author has stated in the foregoing section. Here the basis for aligning
actions with the virtues is most likely found in Col. 3:9b–10, and not
in Col. 3:11, which although a climactic consequence that speaks
of the removal of human distinctions in light of spiritual renewal,
nonetheless does interrupt the overall flow of the argument. Rather,
the train of thought is that the Colossians, who are those who have
'stripped off' the previous mode of life (Col. 3:9b), and have put on a
new form of existence in which they are renewed in the image of the
creator (Col. 3:10), are also to 'put on' behaviours that align with that
new existential reality. The use of the verb **put on**, ἐνδύω, both in Col.

3:10 and here again in Col. 3:12. suggests that the second occurrence is a resumption of the train of thought that was discussed in Col. 3:10, but interrupted by the material that follows the conclusion drawn in Col. 3:10. Hence there is a return to the major point of these linked sections. Since believers have received a new life hidden in Christ there are certain behaviours that must cease, while others must be actively embraced.

Status, which is defined in relationship to God, is given as a further motivation for pursuing a virtuous way of life. This relationship is described by reminding the Colossians of their status **as the elect of God**. Being described as the **elect** or 'chosen ones' not only signifies selection, but the terminology is used in the Jewish scriptures to describe the covenantal relationship between God and his people (LXX Isa. 65:9, 23). Thus it has been suggested that there is a transference of descriptive terminology used to depict the relationship between God and the Jewish people, which is here applied to the status that the Colossians and other believers now enjoy through acceptance of the message of the Gospel (Lightfoot 1886: 219). The language of choice or election reflects the action of God, rather than human merit. Moreover, the fact that the Colossians can now be described as the elect **of God** shows, by use the possessive genitive, that have been selected by God and brought into relationship with him, and belong to him as his chosen people. This newfound status is described further. Not only are the Colossians the chosen ones of God, they now are described as **holy and beloved**, using the nominative masculine plural adjective ἅγιοι and the perfect passive participle ἠγαπημένοι, with the latter functioning as a verbal adjective. The first quality that is seen as an attribute of the Colossians is that of being holy. The term **holy** is a recurrent lexical item in the letter, being used either nominally or adjectivally to describe those who have become believers in Christ (Col. 1:2, 4, 12, 22, 26; 3:12). While the use of the term is concentrated in the opening chapter, here the author returns to this terminology. The purpose of this description is to use the status that believers now possess, according to the theology of the letter, to motivate them to conduct their lives according to ethical behaviours that align with such holiness. Ultimately, in the Jewish tradition, holiness is seen as a fundamental quality of God, and it is to be emulated by his people: 'you shall be holy, for I the Lord your God am holy' (Lev. 11:44; 19:2; 20:7; cf. 1 Pet. 1:16).

The second attribute, **beloved**, is another important concept used in the Pauline writings. The conceptual origin of this description is not certain. It may be indirectly dependent on Hosea (Hos. 1:10) as a description of the people of God, which is used in a tradition cited by Paul: 'I will call those who were not my people, "my people", and her who was not beloved, "beloved"' (Rom. 9:25). However, Paul also uses the description 'beloved' in his earlier writings. Thus, in the Thessalonian correspondence he addresses the 'brothers, beloved by God' (1 Thess. 1:4), and as 'brothers, beloved by the Lord' (2 Thess. 2:13). The first passage is important in relation to Col. 3:12, since it too connects election with those who are beloved by God: 'knowing brothers, beloved by God, his choice of you' (1 Thess. 1:4). The author appeals to the Colossians as those chosen by God, as those imprinted with his holiness, and as those who are recipients of new life, to live in a manner that reflects this renewed existence and relationship with God.

There follows a fivefold list of virtues that are presented as commensurate with believers' new mode of life. This balances the two fivefold lists of vices that exemplified behaviours, in which it was no longer fitting for the Colossians to participate (Col. 3:5, 8). In contrast, the first quality listed that is to exemplify the new life in Christ and their calling as God's people is showing that they have **hearts of compassion**. The expression σπάγχνα οἰκτιρμοῦ has been traditionally and literally translated as 'bowels of mercy' (KJV). In Greek physiological thought the intestines or bowels were seen as being the seat of emotion. This is a common metaphor in Paul's writings as the place in a human from which positive affections or feelings of emotion originate (2 Cor. 7:5; Phil. 2:1; Phlm. 7, 12, 20). As such, the expression is equivalent to 'heartfelt compassion', or perhaps just 'compassion' without any anatomical referent. However, to stay close to the Greek without replicating the archaic reference to 'bowels', but preserving the plural form, the translation adopted is 'hearts of compassion'.

The second quality that befits those who have 'put on the new man' (Col. 3:10) is **goodness**. The Greek term χρηστότης incorporates both the sense of being morally upright, as well as being benevolent. Hence the lexical meaning is given as '1. Upright in one's relations with others, *uprightness*... 2. The quality of being helpful or beneficial, *goodness, kindness, generosity*' (BDAG: 1090). There is a significant degree of separation between the terms 'goodness' and 'kindness' in English, with the former describing ethical behaviour that might be adjudged as right on a more objective scale, and with 'kindness' speaking of actions which perhaps carry less of an objective evaluation, but describe generous acts which while not incumbent on the one performing them are reflective of a gracious and generous disposition. However, the Greek term embraces both aspects, and it is difficult to find an English word that encapsulates both senses. In the Pauline writings the emphasis can fall more heavily on one or other of these aspects. When used to describe divine actions translators have typically rendered the term as 'kindness' (Rom. 2:4 [with difference in translations]; 11:12; Eph. 2:7; Tit. 3:4). In reference to humans it can depict moral goodness (Rom. 3:12), or acts of mutual kindness (Eph. 4:32). The implied sense of the term is most difficult to determine in virtue lists (2 Cor. 6:6; Gal. 5:22; Col. 3:12), where there is little guidance from context, and a rapid shift from one virtue to the next. However since the emphasis is on the imperative to live appropriately it may be the case that ethical 'goodness' is the concern, rather than promoting an abundance of acts of kindness. The distinction, however, is a fine one, and perhaps cannot be resolved with any certainty. This virtue is prominent in wider Hellenistic society, especially in funerary inscriptions where it is the most frequent virtue to be praised (Spicq 1994: III, 513), and when used of rulers 'it means that they are magnanimous' (Sumney 2008: 213).

The third virtue is that of **humility**, ταπεινοφροσύνη. In comparison with Greco-Roman virtue lists, the inclusion of 'humility' as an aspirational quality is unexpected and somewhat discordant. This is because this quality or virtue was typically associated with a servile demeanour, characteristic of slaves. Within the wider context of this epistle, the term 'humility' is also viewed negatively when being encouraged by those who teach the 'philosophy'. Those who promote this teaching are described as delighting in the imposition of acts of abasement on others (Col. 2:18), or take self-delight in forms of humility based upon the harsh treatment of the body (Col. 2:23). However, elsewhere in Paul's writings humility is viewed as a positive quality, standing in opposition to selfishness and conceit.

Primarily, it is the quality that guards against seeking prominence over others in the community (Phil. 2:3). Similarly, in this context humility is a positive virtue. While rejecting the self-seeking humility of those that chase after visions and religious experiences, the type of humility that is advocated here is not individualistic, but occurs in a communal context where the well-being of another takes precedence over one's own prominence.

Next, the fourth quality listed is **gentleness**, πραΰτης. In the New Testament it is a term used primarily in Pauline writings (eight times; elsewhere, Jas 1:21; 3:13; 1 Pet. 3:15). It occurs elsewhere in a list of positive virtues (Gal. 5:23; and as a variant reading in 1 Tim. 6:11, 𝔐). Within the synoptic tradition the adjectival form 'gentle', in combination with 'humble', is used by Jesus to describe himself: 'for I am gentle and humble in heart' (Mt. 11:29; cf. Mt. 21:5). This tradition may be a Matthean redactional creation since it is unparalleled in the other gospels, although others think it is a pre-Matthean unit (so Davies and Allison 1991: II, 238), or perhaps a lost saying from a Jewish wisdom text placed on the lips of the historical Jesus (Bultmann 1963: 160). Regardless of whether it pre-dates or post-dates Colossians, it is interesting to observe that two qualities that at some stage are associated with Jesus should also characterize his followers. In the wider contemporary Hellenistic society, the term tended to be found in literary texts rather than in inscriptions or papyri. Although some viewed 'gentleness' as a weakness, others continued to see it as a positive quality that contrasted with outbursts of rage and anger. As with humility, there may be a communal aspect to this virtue in the mind of the author. The quality of 'gentleness' reflects an attitude that is not overbearing, but reflects a non-threatening disposition in dealing with others.

The fifth and final virtue in the list is **long-suffering** or 'patience', μακροθυμία. It describes steadfastness in the face of adversity, and on the one other occasion when it is used in this letter it is linked with 'steadfastness' (Col. 1:11). When used in Romans it denotes a divine quality whereby God delays his wrath to provide an opportunity for repentance (Rom. 2:4; 9:22). It occurs in the ninefold list of the fruit of the Spirit (Gal. 5:22–23). In the Pastoral Epistles, the authorial voice of Paul declares that he is the perfect example of Christ's long-suffering, and as such he becomes an example to all who would believe (1 Tim. 1:16). Again, a quality that is a divine attribute, and exemplified in Christ, is to be a characteristic of the new Christ-like existence of those have been given a renewed life. Together these virtues do not simply define a new pattern of life, but call for a new pattern of life that reflects divine attributes and Christ-like qualities. Living 'in him', means living like him, in terms of the virtues that characterize the new mode of existence.

13 While there have been indications in some of the five virtues listed in the previous verse that the author of Colossians was con cerned with the corporate nature of Christian ethics, in this verse the communal aspect becomes explicit. As God's chosen people, the recipients of the letter are reminded that inner-group relations should be transformed because of their renewed lives. Thus, as those united with Christ, the Colossians are told that an indication of that renewal is to be seen through **bearing with one another and forgiving each other**. These twin instructions provide concrete examples of how the general virtues listed in Col. 3:12 are to shape behaviour in the concrete setting of the community of believers. The two actions described here, 'bearing with' and 'forgiving', are more likely to function as further ethical imperatives (cf. 'put on' in Col. 3:12), than simply being the means by which the five virtues are expressed (Sumney 2008: 215–16). Whether there was any specific problem in the community that stood behind this call for forbearance and forgiveness, or whether this was a piece of general and somewhat formulaic moral instruction, cannot be determined with certainty. The parallel passage in Ephesians suggests that the instruction to forbear with one another was generalizable in other contexts: 'with long suffering, bearing with one another in love' (Eph. 4:2).

The first action that is required of the Colossians is **bearing with one another**. The Greek verb **bear with**, ἀνέχομαι, occurs 15 times in the New Testament, and while it can be used in an ironic sense (see the five occurrences 2 Cor. 11:1 [×2], 4, 19, 20), or even to express exasperation ('how long am I to bear with you?', Mt. 17:17//Mk 9:19//Lk. 9:41), here it expresses a genuine call for mutual tolerance. The attitude being encouraged is that of patience in the face of mild irritation between group members. While still expressing the same train of thought, the instruction that the Colossians demeanour should also be characterized by **forgiving each other** might envisage a more serious offence between individuals in the community. The circumstances that may necessitate such acts of forgiveness might occur **if any one has a complaint against any other**. This conditional clause recognizes the very real possibility that in certain group situations there will be justifiable causes of complaint even among fellow believers. Therefore, in order to maintain the community and to exemplify the virtues listed in the previous verse, generous acts of forgiveness must be forthcoming. The use of the indefinite pronoun 'any one...against any other' reveals the general nature of this instruction, and thus (unless the author is being extremely subtle) it appears that no specific situation is being envisaged. The term **complaint**, μομφή, should be understood as 'cause for complaint', 'ground for blame', 'grievance' and not as a 'quarrel' or 'wrangle' (see Harris 2010: 141). The term is rare, occurring only here in the New Testament, and not occurring in the Septuagint. While originally a poetic form in Classical Greek, by the Hellenistic period it became more common. A close parallel to the expression here is to be found in Pindar's *Isthmian Odes* (fifth century B.C.E.), 'to have a cause of complaint with someone' (Pindar, *Isth. Odes* 4[3].36; for further details LSJ: 1143).

The basis for adopting an attitude of forgiveness is given with the statement, **just as also the Lord forgave you**. Here the Colossians are reminded that they themselves are recipients of forgiveness. The christological basis of the ethical imperatives that are being given once again comes to the fore. The majority of commentators understand **the Lord**, in line with typical Pauline usage, apart from its use in Old Testament citations, to be a reference to Christ and not to the Father (O'Brien 1982: 202; Aletti 1993: 238). This has been seen to cause a theological tension with wider Pauline ideas. Dunn states that this statement 'adds to the untypically Pauline character of thought, since the idea of Christ forgiving sins is even more unusual than the talk of forgiveness itself' (Dunn 1996: 231). The unease over Paul attributing forgiveness to Christ rather than to God is not only a modern concern. The author of Ephesians in the parallel passage based on Col. 3:13 modifies the source text and transforms it into the more comfortable statement 'Forgiving each other, just as God in Christ also has forgiven you' (Eph. 4:32). Later scribes of Colossians also demonstrate their concern through various variant forms of the text:

1.	ὁ κύριος	'the Lord'	𝔓⁴⁶ A B D* F G
2	ὁ Χριστός	'the Christ;	א² C D¹ Ψ 1739 𝔐
3.	ὁ θεός	'God'	א*
4.	ὁ θεός ἐν Χριστῷ	'God in Christ'	33

Metzger notes that the final variant is 'due to scribal assimilation...
to Eph 4:32' (Metzger 1994: 558). Whether the second or third
readings are introduced under the direct, but partial, influence of
Eph. 4:32, or whether in the third alternative the scribe independently
identified 'God' as the source of forgiveness, cannot be determined.
Given that there are a series of textual variants in the next few verses
that read either 'Christ' or 'God', and that in the majority of cases
'Christ' appears to be the earlier reading, it is interesting to note
that the author has little difficulty in attributing divine attributes or
activities to Christ. The examples will be discussed in more detail
below, but with the two examples that immediately follow the better
attested reading is given first: 'the peace of Christ'/'the peace of
God' (Col. 3:15); 'the word of Christ'/'the word of God'/'the word
of the Lord' (Col. 3:16a). These two cases, and the one here in Col.
3:13, emphasize the author's elevated understanding of Christ as the
basis and model of community life and ethics.

Having reminded the Colossians that they are all recipients of the
Lord's forgiveness, he forcefully restates the imperative 'forgiving
each other', with the succinct conclusion, **so also should you**.
As those who now live in union with Christ, their lives are to be
patterned on the model of his life. Christ's act of forgiveness is seen
as a key attribute. Therefore the Colossians, as the body of Christ
of which he is the head (Col. 1:18), are to demonstrate the same
pattern of forgiveness in their community relationships as they have
received from the one described as 'the Lord' in this verse.

14 In this verbless and almost fragmentary clause the author articulates the overarching virtue that the Colossians are to 'put on': **and
in all these things – love**. While the train of thought had been interrupted by the related digression concerning the need for Christ-like
forgiveness in the community, it now returns to the major idea of
the virtues that are required of believers. Some press the clothing
metaphor of the command 'put on' and thus understand **love** as a

kind of over-garment that subsumes all the other virtues (Moo 2008: 280). However, if this image is intended it certainly is not explicit. Without straining the metaphor of clothing, the imperative 'put on' still governs this clause, but in a more general manner, and while 'the metaphor itself is not pursued further…it is the importance of love as such that determines the second clause' (Dunn 1996: 232). While Harris also rejects the interpretation of the preposition ἐπί as 'over' in the sense of 'on top of', thus developing the clothing metaphor, he notes two further possibilities (Harris 2010: 141). These possibilities are either taking the preposition in the sense of 'in addition to' (BDF: §235[3]; O'Brien 1982: 203; Wilson 2005: 262), or as 'above all' or 'to crown all' (Zerwick and Grosvenor 1993: 610; Dunn 1996: 210, 232–33). It may not be necessary to separate these two senses. While O'Brien understands the preposition as meaning 'in addition to the other virtues, he also states that love 'is the crowning virtue which the new man has to put on' (O'Brien 1982: 203). In wider Pauline thought, ἀγάπη, **love**, is presented as the superlative quality that marks out Christian life. This is nowhere more obvious than the classic formulation 'now remain faith, hope, love, these three; but the greatest of these is love' (1 Cor. 13:13). As used in Colossians, 'love' is mentioned five times, this being the last. It refers to a quality that the Colossians are said to 'have for all the holy ones' (Col. 1:4); in Epaphras' report, Paul states that he has described 'your love in the spirit' (Col. 1:8); in a unique phrase Jesus is said to be 'the Son of his love' (Col. 1:13), depicting his relationship with the father; and Paul prays for all who have not seen his face that they may be 'knit together in love' (Col. 2:2). Apart from Col. 1:13, with each of these instances there is an obvious communal focus to love, and that is drawn out here in the second half of the verse.

Having instructed the Colossians to put on love as the quality that permeates and surpasses the other virtues mentioned in Col. 3:12, the author now explains why love is such a potent force among believers. The relative clause, **which is the bond of perfection**, provides the explanation for the preceding charge to put on love. Those who extend the clothing metaphor to see love as an over-garment, frequently claim that the reference to a **bond** here is also drawing on the language of clothing. Thus Sumney observes, '[b]y calling love a bond, v. 14 may continue to develop the clothing metaphor…, because *syndesmos* sometimes stands for the band (or belt) that holds together one's clothes' (Sumney 2008: 218). Not only has it been argued that the clothing metaphor does not extend to this verse, more significantly the only other occurrence of σύνδεσμος **bond**, in this letter does not refer to haberdashery, but to anatomy: 'ligaments' (Col. 2:19). Therefore, without reference to any specific type of bond in this context, love is seen as the binding force that brings about **perfection**. It is not entirely clear whether it is the bond itself that is 'perfect', or if the bond produces 'perfection'. The other issue concerns whether such a bond of perfection occurs within the individual, or as part of the communal life of believers. Adopting an individual interpretation, Sumney argues that love 'binds together Christian virtues and thus leads to "perfection" or maturity' (Sumney 2008: 219). Hence, he sees love as linking the five virtues of Col. 3:12 together, with the result that the one who is putting on a new mode of being will be led into maturity. Against this reading, the parallel passage in Ephesians that speaks of 'the unity of the Spirit and the bond of peace' (Eph. 4:3). This in turn leads into a description of corporate Christian life: 'there is one body, and one Spirit…' (Eph. 4:4). While this is not determinative for establishing the meaning here, it is also significant to note that several manuscripts preserve the variant reading 'the bond of unity' (D* F G). While this is unlikely to be the earlier form of the text, and may be influenced by Eph. 4:3, it does suggest that the language could be understood in a corporate, rather than an individual, manner. Moreover, given that the list of five virtues led to further communal imperatives to 'bear with' and to 'forgive' one another, it seems more likely that the superlative virtue, love, has a group focus. The **bond of perfection** that occurs when believers put on love is better understood as resulting in the formation of a mature community in which the virtues that reflect new existence in Christ are lived out in an exemplary fashion, which anticipates the full realization of the eschatological life that is now 'hidden with Christ in God' (Col. 3:3), but will be made public 'when Christ is revealed' (Col. 3:4).

15 A transition is made from speaking about love as a 'bond of perfection', to a further imperative that is directed towards the Colossians collectively, **and let the peace of Christ rule in your hearts**. This image again speaks of the Colossians being governed and controlled by Christ-like qualities and attributes. In the letter **peace** is a divine gift mediated either through God or Christ. In formulaic terms it is coupled with 'grace' in the greeting, where the author expresses his desire that the Colossians should receive the 'grace and peace' that come from God (Col. 1:2). The peace-making activity of Christ is also described in the compound participle 'having made peace' (Col. 1:20), which in that context is said to have been achieved 'through the blood of his cross'. While there is no direct reference to Christ's peace-making activity here, the fact that peace is to reign in the hearts of the Colossians shows that for the author Christ's peace is one of the defining characteristics of the cosmic order established by the Son. Against the widespread imperial propaganda that the *Pax Romana* was due to the beneficence of the semi-divine Emperor, the assertion that Christ conveyed true peace was a subversive claim. However, Colossians goes further than just countermanding Roman imperial ideology. The scope of Christ's peace is cosmic, having rescued the Colossians from the power of darkness (Col. 1:13). Christ has now established peace with all things, 'whether the things on earth, or the things in heaven' (Col. 1:20). While those references to **the peace of Christ** indicate the new cosmic order, here it seems to speak of the internal manifestation of that peace. On the macro-level the whole cosmos is now under the sovereignty of Christ's rule, yet here the author focuses on the fact that for believers the peace Christ brings is for them an interior experience, which they are told to **let rule in your hearts**. However, what is being conceived here is not some type of religious individualism. Hence Colossian believers are being appealed to collectively. The imperative **let rule**, βραβευέτω, speaks of a prevailing and authoritative state that is to govern the new lives that the Colossians now experience. The Greek verb is lexically related to the compound form καταβραβεύω that occurs in Col. 2:18. However, it was argued that the compound form was not just antithetical in meaning, i.e. 'let nobody rule against you', but had taken on a more independent and intensive meaning, i.e. 'let nobody abuse you'. Notwithstanding that, it is likely that the recipients of the letter would have heard the resonance in vocabulary. Instead of being abused by the regulations and demands of those who promoted a philosophy based on self-abasement and visions, the Colossians are informed that the governing force in their lives is to be the peace of Christ. The author tells the Colossians to let peace rule **in your hearts**. Again, the focus is on the collectivity of the Colossian community having a life together that is typified by a harmonious and peaceful co-existence.

There should be no doubt that what is being advocated here stands in contrast to the individualism of those who encouraged the Colossians to pursue ecstatic experiences. In this vein mutual love is the bond that unites believers, and the peace that is to be the inner experience is not to be sought for self-fulfilment. Rather, peace is the hallmark of group unity. Hence the Colossians are reminded that it was through the peace of Christ **in which also you were called in one body**. Thus, **body** terminology is a signal to readers that their calling is a collective one, not an individualistic self-gratifying spirituality. Recollection of the fact the Colossians **were called** provides a historicized dimension to their status as believers, which might be aimed at undercutting the continuous pursuit of spiritual experiences. Hence corporate identity is stressed over individual experiences. The calling results in a dual participation, with believers being called into 'the peace of Christ' and also being brought into that sphere of existence **in one body**. The complexity of the author's thought is revealed through the inter-relatedness of being in Christ and being in one body. Elsewhere in this letter Christ is declared to be the head of the body, which is the church (Col. 1:18; cf. 1:24). As such, the corporate nature of the calling has a particularly Pauline understanding. The Colossian believers are not simply a 'body' by virtue of simply being a gathered community. Rather, their oneness finds its coherence through being called into Christ and being reconciled in 'the body of his flesh' (Col. 1:22). Therefore, this calling produces the bond of peace and results in the ecclesial unity of believers.

The final clause at the end of this verse, **and be thankful**, καὶ εὐχάριστοι γίνεσθε, makes logical sense but breaks the train of thought. The term 'thankful ones', εὐχάριστοι, is unique in the New Testament in this context. It is attested more widely in Greek literature, papyri, and inscriptions (Xenophon, *Cynegeticus* 8.3.49; *Inscr. Prien.* 103.8). There has been no indication that the Colossians were people who failed to give thanks. That being the case, it is unlikely that the imperative is functioning as a corrective to some behavioural deficiency. Rather, it is an exhortation to continue producing the type of behaviour that reflects their identity as people called into the sphere of Christ's peace, and formed as his body. Furthermore, elsewhere in the epistle, the correct response of believers to the life they have received in Christ is thankfulness or thanksgiving (Col. 2:7; 3:17; 4:2). Here the adjectival form reflects the exhortation that the Colossians should live as thankful people. This suggests that for the author consideration of the new status enjoyed by believers should generate an attitude of joyous thanksgiving, and that the Colossians should be recognized as people characterized by unalloyed thankfulness. Such thankfulness in regard to one's own sense of identity and status in the body of Christ should result in the recognition that the same calling of God is effective in other group members. In this way, living as thankful people is likely to be seen as another way of reinforcing group solidarity and mutual love. The basis for thankfulness is the experience of having been freed from oppressive elemental forces (Col. 2:8) and being transferred in a new sphere of existence in Christ (Col. 1:13). This focus on 'thanksgiving' becomes more prominent at the conclusion of this section, where all actions are to be done in the name of the Lord Jesus while 'giving thanks to God' (Col. 3:17).

16 The basic sense of this verse is clear: the indwelling presence of Christ's word is to produce constructive behaviour towards fellow-believers and a worshipful attitude towards God. While the overall sense of the verse might be straightforward, there have been various understandings of the syntax and the relationship of the various clauses to one another. The choice made between these options does have implications for understanding the author's thought. This is especially the case in relation to how he sees the relationship of a believer to Christ, fellow group members, and to God. The diversity of opinion can perhaps be best seen by looking at the translations offered by various English versions of this text:

GENEVA BIBLE (1560)
Let the word of Christ dwell in you plenteously in all wisdom, teaching and admonishing your own selves, in Psalms, and hymns, and spiritual songs, singing with a grace in your hearts to the Lord.

BISHOPS' BIBLE (1568)
Let the worde of God dwell in you richly in all wisdome, teachyng and admonisshyng your owne selues, in psalmes, and hymmes, and spirituall songes, singyng with grace in your heartes to the Lorde.

KING JAMES VERSION (1611)
Let the word of Christ dwell in you richly in all wisdom; teaching and
admonishing one another in psalms and hymns and spiritual songs,
singing with grace in your hearts to the Lord.

J. N. DARBY TRANSLATION (1867–90)
Let the word of the Christ dwell in you richly, in all wisdom teaching
and admonishing one another, in psalms, hymns, spiritual songs,
singing with grace in your hearts to God.

REVISED STANDARD VERSION (1952)
Let the word of Christ dwell in you richly, teach and admonish one
another in all wisdom, and sing psalms and hymns and spiritual songs
with thankfulness in your hearts to God.

J. B. Phillip, *Letters to Young Churches* (1966)
Let Christ's teaching live in your hearts, making you rich in the true
wisdom. Teach and help one another along the right road with your
psalms and hymns and Christian songs, singing God's praises with
joyful hearts.

NEW AMERICAN STANDARD BIBLE (1977)
Let the word of Christ richly dwell within you, with all wisdom
teaching and admonishing one another with psalms *and* hymns *and*
spiritual songs, singing with thankfulness in your hearts to God.

REVISED ENGLISH BIBLE (1989)
Let the gospel of Christ dwell among you in all its richness; teach and
instruct one another with all the wisdom it gives you. With psalms and
hymns and spiritual songs, sing from the hearts in gratitude to God.

NEW LIVING TRANSLATION (2007)
Let the message about Christ, in all its richness, fill your lives. Teach
and counsel each other with all the wisdom he gives. Sing psalms and
hymns and spiritual songs to God with thankful hearts.

Two major issues arise. The first is whether the phrase ἐν πάσῃ
σοφίᾳ, 'in all wisdom', belongs with the first clause in the verse or
with what follows. The second issue, and the more difficult question
to resolve, is whether the verse should be divided into a two- or
three-part structure.

In relation to the first issue, while the earlier translations (and
also the Phillips translation) tended to link 'in all wisdom' with the
opening clause, the majority of translations and the punctuation in
recent editions of the Greek New Testament take this as connected

with what follows. There are three main reasons for this decision. The imperative ἐνοικείτω, 'let dwell', has already been qualified by one adverbial clause ἐν ὑμῖν πλουσίως, 'in you richly'. It is felt that the construction would be overloaded if it were further qualified by the clause 'in all wisdom' as well. The second reason is because the sense of ἐν πάσῃ σοφία, 'in all wisdom', 'accords better with "teaching" than "indwelling"' (Harris 2010: 145). The third reason is perhaps the strongest. The author has already connected the phrase 'in all wisdom' with the activities of teaching and admonishing earlier in the letter when describing the ministry of Paul: 'admonishing every man and teaching every man in all wisdom', νουθετοῦντες πάντα ἄνθρωπον καὶ διδάσκοντες πάντα ἄνθρωπον ἐν πάσῃ σοφίᾳ (Col. 1:28).

This leaves the larger question concerning whether the material after the initial clause should be understood as two separate statements concerning behaviour to fellow believers and worship of God, or whether it is a single statement explaining how fellow believers are to be instructed through the singing of spiritual songs to God. In favour of understanding this material as two separate statements, the reference to wisdom could be taken as aligning with the acts of teaching and admonishing one another. By contrast, the three types of melodic utterance – 'psalms, hymns, spiritual songs' – appear to be linked to the separate worshipful act of singing to God out of a sense of gratitude. Obviously the syntax of the verse is open to interpretation, hence the range of translations with their differing divisions and linkages of clauses. Short of asking the author his intention, absolute certainty is impossible. However, there are two neglected pieces of evidence that further suggest that the whole verse should be read as three clauses and not two.

While the majuscule Greek New Testament manuscripts are largely written in a continuous script and without punctuation, several of the bilingual (Greek and Latin) manuscripts, or those related to them, are written in sense units or show sense units by other means. In Codex Claromontanus (D 06) folio 343 *verso*, the opening phrase concludes with the word πλουσίως, 'richly'. This is the only word on the line on which it occurs. Although there is plenty of remaining white space, the phrase 'in all wisdom' commences a new clause on a separate line. The word ψαλμοῖς, 'with psalms', also occurs at the start of a new line. However, here the evidence is not as decisive since there is no

white space on the preceding line. On the following line the following
words occur: πνευματικαῖς ἐν [τῇ] χάριτι, lit. 'spiritual in the grace'.
This suggests that the 'spiritual hymns' are closely linked to the act
of rendering thanks to God. The evidence of Codex Boernerianus
(G 012) is even more decisive. This manuscript is closely related to
the form of the text in Claromontanus, and it is likely that these two
manuscripts share a common ancestor. While not written in sense lines,
the sense units are preserved by the use of an enlarged letter. There are
three oversized letters in this manuscript: Ὁ λόγος... Ἐν πάσῃ σοφίᾳ...
Ψαλμοῖς... ('The word... In all wisdom... With psalms...'). The scribe
of this manuscript, almost certainly following his exemplar, divided the
text into a threefold structure.

Apart from manuscript evidence, some of the earliest commentaries
also offer support for a tripartite reading. Theodore of Mopsuestia's
commentary on the Minor Pauline Epistles survives only in a Latin
translation, although it was originally written in Greek. Theodore
breaks the text into various units, and under each section of biblical
text he offers comments of varying length. His division breaks Col.
3:16 into three clauses, with the phrase 'in all wisdom' standing at
the beginning of the second clause (Theodore of Mopsuestia, *ad
Colossenses* 3:16). Given the combination of linguistic arguments,
the sense unit divisions in those early manuscripts that preserve such
paratextual features, and the sectional breaks in early commentaries,
there is a strong case for understanding the syntax of the sentence as
comprised of three clauses. These can be arranged in the following
manner, which helps to offer a more accurate understanding of the
meaning of this verse:

> Let the word of Christ dwell in you richly,
> in all wisdom teaching and admonishing each other,
> with psalms, hymns, spiritual songs in gratitude singing in your hearts
> to God.

Therefore the verse opens with a Christ-centred imperative, from
which should flow two types of behaviour that are reflective of the
rich indwelling of Christ's word.

The verse opens with the command to **let the word of Christ
dwell in you richly**. This metaphor, similar to the expression 'the
peace of Christ' in the previous verse, reveals that all the positive
aspects of believers' new mode of existence are seen as being

ultimately derived from Christ. Elsewhere when the author refers to the 'word' it functions as a short-hand way of denoting the Christian message. Thus Paul can declare 'I became a servant…to fulfill the word of God' (Col. 1:24). Prior to this it is even more apparent that the 'word' is a Christian term that refers to the message proclaimed by believers: 'the word of the truth of the gospel' (Col. 1:5). The call to **let the word of Christ…**, is a plea directed to the recipients of the letter to allow what should be the experience of all believers to have its full impact on the way they conduct themselves towards fellow group members and to God. That the word should **dwell in you richly** makes the Colossians aware of the potential for their existence to be permeated with Christ-like qualities. This should occur to the extent that all their activities and relationships are transformed by their newfound reality of the peace and word of Christ residing within them both individually and corporately as the body of believers.

The first outcome that should result from the indwelling presence of Christ concerns relationships with others in the community. Members of the group are to instruct and encourage one another in the faith. The manner by which this is to be achieved is **in all wisdom teaching and admonishing each other**. The importance of **wisdom** is seen elsewhere in the letter. In Col. 1:9 the same phrase 'in all wisdom' is used as part of the prayer request made by Paul that the Colossians might fully know the divine will. However, the closer link occurs in Col. 1:28, where Paul describes his preaching of Christ: 'whom we proclaim admonishing every man and teaching every man in all wisdom'. The goal that Paul sets for himself, when describing his ministry earlier in the letter, is the same one that he now sets before the Colossians. If there is a concern that the Colossians are being confronted with some aberrant teaching, the positive emphasis on correct instruction combined with concomitant negative admonition if necessary is perhaps more understandable (Moo 2008: 289). Therefore, the logic is that if the word of Christ is truly dwelling in the Colossians richly, then they should be providing wise teaching and corrective admonitions that prevent members of the community being lured into the false teaching that may be captivating some of the group.

This verse is perhaps one of the most important in the Pauline corpus, if not the whole New Testament, for providing a glimpse into the pattern of earliest Christian worship. The place of **teaching** is a central activity in group-gatherings. In Col. 1:28 'teaching' is part of Paul's apostolic ministry, whereby the gospel message concerning Christ is introduced to those to whom it is being proclaimed. Here it is a continuing task of all believers to instruct one another. It is apparent that the letter is advocating maintenance of Christ-centred instruction in the face of different teachings and promises of mystical experiences. The responsibility for this teaching ministry is laid upon all believers in Colossae equally. Hence the corporate task is not entrusted to designated teachers or leaders of the group, but is seen as being the duty of every member to ensure that the provision of sound instruction is taking place. Similarly, with the negative task of **admonishing each other**, this too is not entrusted to a select few, but is presented as a responsibility incumbent to each individual in the group. The goal of admonition is to reform or reshape a person's beliefs or actions with the desired outcome of producing behaviour that aligns with the beliefs and ethics of the group. In this sense correction and warning is part of the task set before each person in the community. This mutuality in teaching and admonishing within the community will be reflected in the ethics of relationship that will be laid out shortly in the letter (Col. 3:18–4:1). In that context reciprocity and mutuality are the key values that undergird the regulation of household relationships for believers.

The final extended clause in this verse presents the second consequence that arises from the indwelling of the word of Christ as being the worship of God. Again the text gives a further insight into the pattern of early Christian worship. Music, especially of a vocal type, is seen as a fundamental way of rendering praise to God. Therefore, union with Christ should result in the following response from the Colossians: **with psalms, hymns, spiritual songs singing in gratitude in your hearts to God**. As has been argued above, the various forms of lyrical praise should not be understood as the mode for teaching and admonishing one another as mentioned in the previous clause, any more than Paul's acts of teaching and admonishing in Col. 1:28 should be thought of as being sung! Rather, these offerings of musical praise are directed to God in gratitude for the new mode of existence of being in

Christ, as is now experienced by the Colossians. Most commentators correctly note that attempts to differentiate separate forms of melodic worship being denoted by the three terms **psalms, hymns, spiritual songs** are misguided. While there has been a tendency to see **psalms** as denoting the singing of the Old Testament Psalms, and **hymns** as newly coined Christian songs (Lightfoot 1886: 222–23), the terms were at times used interchangeably and without precise distinctions. For instance, Josephus describes the 22 books of Jewish scripture as consisting of the five books of Moses, thirteen of the prophets, and the 'remaining four books contain hymns to God' (Josephus, *Ap.* 1.8). These four books included the Psalms. The reference to **spiritual songs** or odes is the only item in the list qualified by an adjective, 'spiritual'. In Greco-Roman culture more widely an 'ode' was a lyrical or poetic piece of writing frequently performed with musical accompaniment. The main types of odes were modelled on the form or style of Pindar or Horace, although others were freer in form. The use of the adjective **spiritual** may have been a means of distinguishing early Christian songs from secular compositions. The other possibility is that the reference to spiritual songs is intended to denote spontaneous spirit-led outbursts of song. This possibility might align with the description of the meetings in Corinth, 'when you assemble, each one has a psalm, has a teaching, has a revelation, has tongue, has an interpretation' (1 Cor. 14:26). Whichever is the correct understanding of these spiritual odes, they are not significantly distinguished from the other two categories of Christian song. Thus the three terms are to be taken as being synonymous.

The purpose of such songs is to express thankfulness to God. Hence the Colossians are told that their hymnody should be expressed **singing in gratitude in your hearts to God**. The term χάρις, translated as **gratitude**, is the same Greek word used in the introduction to express the wish for 'grace' to be bestowed on the Colossians. The term χάρις covers a range of meaning, including the sense of being grateful or expressing gratitude (1 Tim. 1:12; 2 Tim. 1:3; see BDAG: 1080). Therefore the manner in which the Colossians are to sing to God is with a deep sense of gratitude. The Colossians are instructed that such gratitude should by manifest by **singing in your hearts to God**. Since singing in your hearts might imply silent hymnody (Standhartinger 1999: 244–45), a number of commentators have reconfigured the Greek word order in their English translations, thereby rendering the entire clause along the lines of 'with gratitude in your hearts singing to God' (Campbell 2013: 60). However, it is unlikely that the expression **in your hearts** implies internal silent singing. The same expression was used a verse earlier, in the command to 'let the peace of Christ rule in your hearts' (Col. 3:15). There, as here, the metonymic expression referred to the heart to denote the entire being. Consequently the Colossians are told that if the word of Christ dwells in them, then gratitude to God should be expressed by singing to him with their whole being. The exhortation to thanksgiving directed towards God permeates the whole of Col. 3:15–17. Because of their new existence in the one body they are told to 'be thankful' (Col. 3:15). Here, because the word dwells in them richly, they are to sing to God with gratitude or thankfulness (Col. 3:16). In the following verse all actions are done so one might give thanks through Christ to God (Col. 3:17).

17 The train of thought broadens out in this verse. The ethics that are to govern communal meetings through the wise teaching and admonition of fellow believers, and the thankful worship of God through song, are to be applied to all actions. Those actions were seen as the outcome of the peace of Christ and his word being present in believers in such a way that their behaviour was realigned in accordance with what was honouring to God. At this point in the letter a christological motivation for behaviour is also explicitly stated. All behaviour should be suitable to be done in the name of Christ, and in that same name one should render thanks to God.

In the previous verse, maybe standing as a corrective to the worship of angels (Col. 2:18), the Colossians were encouraged to worship God through song with the totality of their beings. Here the horizon is enlarged to incorporate **all that you do in word or in deed**. When writing to the Romans, Paul declares that his goal is to bring about 'the obedience of the Gentiles by word and deed' (Rom. 15:18). In that context where Paul wishes to declare that the totality of his actions in relation to his Gentile mission, he employs the combination of speech and works. Also, when addressing the Thessalonians, Paul declares that he will comfort them and 'establish them in every good deed and word' (2 Thess. 2:17). The same terms are found in various Jewish writings written in Greek, 'in deed and word honour your father' (Sir. 3:8). Also turning to Hellenistic writings, the first-century philosopher Cebes describes a person who came to study ancient wisdom as 'a sensible man and outstanding in wisdom, who in word and deed was emulating a Pythagorean and Parmenidean way of life' (Cebes, *Tab.* 2.2). Thus, the pairing of word and deed in either order was a widespread expression that denoted to totality of one's actions. The function of this introductory clause is to intensify the main clause that follows.

Therefore, reiterating that this injunction covers all actions, the Colossians are instructed to **do all things in the name of the Lord Jesus**. The command to carry out all actions **in the name** shows that all they do must be under the control or influence **of the Lord Jesus**. This is the main clause of the verse, but Greek does not replicate the verb ποιῆτε, 'do', from the intensive clause at the beginning of the sentence and hence it has to be supplied in the English translation. Having presented a rich theology of the Colossians' participation in Christ, the author now calls upon those believers to ensure that they live according to that new mode of being, by ensuring that everything they do is consistent with being in Christ (O'Brien 1982: 211–12). This command to ensure that all things are done in alignment with life in Christ is a logical consequence for the author, who has stated that 'all things have been created for him' (Col. 1:16), that 'in him all things hold together' (Col. 1:17), and that it was the divine purpose 'through him to reconcile all things to himself' (Col. 1:20). Hence believers who have been brought into union with Christ must conduct their entire life in accordance with his name.

This section concludes with a final appeal that informs the Colossians that they should be **giving thanks to God the Father**. The repeated refrain in Col. 3:15–17 declares that people existing in union with Christ should direct all acts of thanksgiving to God because they have been rescued and transferred into the kingdom of the Son (Col. 1:13), and it is in that state that they enjoy a new mode of existence. This positive directive to offer thanks to God may also undercut a possible practice whereby the worship of angels involved offering up gifts to these intermediary heavily beings, perhaps in a cultic context. Sumney (2008: 228) notes 'the important role expressions of gratitude play in Greco-Roman religions'. Perhaps even more significantly he observes that society was underpinned by notions of gift-giving and the reciprocal duty of deference and giving of thanks. He states that 'religion mirrored this understanding of social relations, those granted a gift by a god saw themselves under obligation to give appropriate thanks to that god' (Sumney 2008: 228). The recipients of the letter are addressed in a way that reflects their awareness of such Hellenistic conventions. The author is calling upon the Colossians to re-centre the act of **giving thanks**, by directing it exclusively **to God the Father**.

The final phrase, **through him**, shows the means by which the giving of thanks is to be mediated to the Father. In the same way that this verse has declared that everything should be done in the name of Jesus, here also even the act of thanksgiving directed to the Father is to be channelled back to God through his Son. What this exactly entailed is not developed. Whereas in Greco-Roman religions animal sacrifices, libations, or the offering of material gifts were often the means of expressing thanks to the gods, such physical items did not constitute the early Christian practice of rendering thanks to God. Rather, through acts of worship, such as the songs described in Col. 3:17 perhaps along the lines of the poetic praise in Col. 1:15–20, the Colossians expressed their devotion both to Christ and to the Father. Essentially the acts of recognizing Christ and glorifying him are inextricably tied to the act of giving thanks to God the Father. This may reflect the definition of 'binitarianism' given by Hurtado: '[the] concern to define and reverence Jesus with reference to the one God' (Hurtado 2003: 151). The corollary of this statement, which also reflects such binitarianism, may be more evident here. That is the concern to define and reference God with reference to Jesus.

The sentiments in this section commenced with an intentional contrast to Col. 3:5–11, where believers were instructed to 'put off' certain former practices. Here the author opens this section with the command to 'put on' various virtues (Col. 3:12). However, what is presented to the Colossians quickly moves beyond a typical Hellenistic virtue–vice catalogue. The author continues to emphasize the Christ-centred nature of the belief system he calls upon the Colossians to adopt totally. He instructs them to forgive one another for no other reason than the fact that they were forgiven by Christ (Col. 3:13). The peace of Christ is to govern their existence because through Christ they were formed into one body (Col. 3:15). Finally, the indwelling word of Christ is to reform their attitudes to fellow group members, is to direct their worship towards God, is to be the basis of all speech and action, and is the mechanism through which thanks can be offered to God.

The Christ-focused nature of the Pauline religious system governs the ethical basis of the letter, the motivation for rendering thanks to God, and the regulation of relationships. The way believers are to teach and admonish each other in wisdom has already been described. The author now turns to describing the way believers are to regulate their conduct away from group meetings, in the place where they live and work – the household.

15. LIVING AS BELIEVERS WITHIN HOUSEHOLDS (3:18–4:1)

(18) Wives, be subject to husbands as is proper in the Lord. (19) Husbands, love [your] wives and be not embittered toward them.

(20) Children, obey [your] parents in all things, for this is pleasing in the Lord. (21) Fathers, do not provoke your children lest they become discouraged.

(22) Slaves, obey in all things your masters according to the flesh, not with eye-service, as pleasing men, but in singleness of heart, fearing the Lord. (23) Whatever you do, work from the soul, as for the Lord and not for men, (24) knowing that from the Lord you will receive the reward of the inheritance. It is the Lord Christ you are serving. (25) For the wrongdoer will receive back the wrong he has done, and there is no partiality. (1) Masters, grant justice and equality to slaves, knowing that you also have a master in heaven.

According to Aristotle, the 'household' formed the fundamental building block of civil society in the Greco-Roman world. Thus he could write, as an apparently self-evident truth, 'seeing then that the state is made up of households, before speaking of the state we must speak of the management of household' (Aristotle, *Pol.* 3.1). These ancient households differed considerable from modern Western society nuclear families. Apart from immediate blood relatives, in larger wealthy households those present could include more distant relatives, retainers, and slaves. The household was typically headed by the *paterfamilias* ('father of the family'), a Latin term denoting the leading male member of the household. In Colossians this person is referred to by the more generic term κύριος, 'master'/'lord'. Aristotle typically uses a different Greek word for the designation of the 'master' or 'lord' of a house, δεσποτικός. Elsewhere in the New Testament, in material that regulates the household relationships, the related term δεσπότης is used to denote the senior figure in a household (1 Tim. 6:1–2; Tit. 2:9; 1 Pet. 2:18).

Patronage was part of the fabric of society. Households frequently functioned not only as places of residence, but locations of commerce, business, or enterprise. Rural households could be the centre of a large agricultural industry, while in urban households many other types of business were conducted from artisan crafts to financial activities. The *paterfamilias* was often simultaneously the patron for his own household members and perhaps as well for a wider network of clients. However, frequently he was also the client of wealthier patrons. Thus society was governed by a complex network of social relations, and within that social web giving due deference to patrons, or supplying goods or social advancement to one's clients was a key part of existing successfully within the larger society. Moreover, knowing one's place in the household was in many ways simply a part of recognizing one's role in wider society. Therefore, members of a household who failed to show deference to their social superiors not only dishonoured themselves, but threatened to bring shame on the whole household, and in particular upon the head of that social unit, the *paterfamilias*.

Given these attitudes towards social heirarchy, and concerns over the lower eschalons of society seeking to assert their freedom or rebelling against masters, a key feature of such descriptions of households was to regularize prevailing social roles through the maintenance of the traditional order. The statement declaring the equality of all believers in Christ a few verses earlier in the letter, 'there is not…slave, free, but Christ is all and in all' (Col. 3:11), could be seen as a destabilizing mandate that challenged the prevailing social order. However, in the context of Col. 3:18–4:1 the author provides more explicit support for the household structure. This may reflect a greater degree

367

of cultural convergence toward the prevailing structures of society than is the case with the charter for equality in Col. 3:11. Barclay has discussed this cultural convergence between diaspora Jewish groups and wider Greco-Roman society in Mediterranean settings, by considering the three scales of social contact: assimilation (social integration); acculturation (language/education); and accommodation (use of acculturation) (Barclay 1996: 92–102). There are some key differences between the cases of diaspora Judaism and the Colossian group. First, and most significantly, the Colossian believers appear to be largely gentiles, and hence their cultural heritage is that of Greco-Roman society. Secondly, in becoming believers they have, to some extent, broken with their parent culture rather than having a commitment to a cultural background that is alien to the geographical location. Notwithstanding these key differences, given that their conversion to a new set of religious beliefs involved some denial of the validity of the wider socio-religious system, they were now in a position of having to re-negotiate their own identity as believers in Christ in relation to the prevailing cultural context. The household code is perhaps the strongest evidence that the process of accommodation was beginning to take place in early Christian communities. Unsurprisingly, given the gentile background of the majority of the addressees, the author is able to take for granted his audience's familiarity with the social structure of the household and the power-relations typically operative within that social unit. The author counsels a strategy of accommodation – wives subject to husbands, children obedient to parents, slaves subservient to masters. However, the group is definitely not encouraged to assimilate fully to the cultural values that underpin such power structures. In fact, the author provides a different rationale for maintaining the social structure to that articulated by pagan thinkers. From their perspective, a hierarchical and regulated state provides stability and a better quality of life for all members, even if some are subjected by an inferior nature to serve another (Aristotle, *Pol.* 4.1). By contrast, the epistle undercuts this prevailing narrative with the claim that the Colossian believers should adhere to the social *status quo* not for its own sake, but because of their newfound existence 'in the Lord', and since such behaviour is pleasing to Christ. In this way the societal norms are both upheld at a surface level, but at a deeper level there is a subversive counter-narrative being created within the community, that informs believers of their equality in Christ (Col. 3:11) and their obedience to the prevailing power systems is actually a strategy of resistance, since they do not accept the fundamental basis of the prevailing social narrative. As a result of the tension created between the household code and other theological perspectives in the letter (cf. Col. 1:13), a number of scholars have understood the material in Col. 3:18–4:1 as a preformed unit that has been dropped into its current location. Two supporting arguments have been marshalled in support of this hypothesis. First, that the thought of the letter flows naturally from Col. 3:17 to 4:2, being connected by the topics of prayer and thanksgiving (Crouch 1972: 10). Furthermore, it has been noted that there is a high concentration of *hapax legomena* (words that occur only once in the thirteen Pauline letters) to be found in the household code. For these reasons, in his major study of the household code in Colossians, Crouch suggests that 'both its composition and loose relationship to context indicate that it is an independent unit most probably of pre-Colossian origin' (Crouch 1972: 11).

Such arguments can be challenged. The argument concerning *hapax legomena* is fallacious. Out of the 117 Greek words that form the NA[28] text of Col. 3:18–4:1 there are are only three words used (πικραίνεσθε, 'to be embittered', Col. 3:19; ἀθυμῶσιν, 'to be discouraged', Col. 3:21; ἀνταπόδοσιν, 'to reward', Col. 3:24) that are unique within the wider Paul corpus, and a further two words (ὀφθαλμοδουλία, 'eye-service'; and ἀνθρωπάρεσκοι, 'pleasing men', Col. 3:22) that are unique to this section and the parallel household code in Eph. 5:21–6:9. The sample size is too small to draw any significant conclusions concerning authorship, and the presence of *hapax legomena* is probably more a reflection of the change of subject matter than any other factor. The observation that the themes in Col. 3:16–17 are related to those of Col. 4:2–6 does not negate the fact that Col. 3:18–4:1 sits comfortably within the flow of the ethical teaching that is being presented. Having first instructed individuals concerning the types of moral behaviour they should 'put on' (Col. 3:12–15), the author next turns to the ethics that should be practised within the corporate context of group meetings (Col. 3:16). In turn, this results in the general maxim of Col. 3:17 that everything should be done in the name of the Lord Jesus. The epistle then provides instructions concerning the most common context in which believers will have to apply that general principle in their daily lives, namely within the setting of the household. Even if the unit were 'preformed' in some sense, it is admirably suited to the flow of the argument. The schema of the household code is known to have existed more widely prior to the composition of Colossians. It may even have been the case that the author had used a similar pattern of ethical instruction in other pedagogical contexts prior to deploying the same instructions in this letter. In fact, it is perhaps likely that this Christianized household code had been used as a form of teaching during meetings of believers. The application of it to the Colossian context was an authorial decision, for there is nothing to suggest that this material was inserted after the composition of the letter. Therefore, such questions about the unit being preformed are somewhat otiose. The author chose to incorporate this material into his own composition, and may have modified it to some unknown extent to address the specific situation of the Colossian believers. As such, it is an integral component of the letter, deployed by the author as a key part of his teaching on ethics and part of his overall argument.

Another issue that has troubled scholars is whether the author derived the household code, or his knowledge of such patterns of instruction, from Hellenistic or Jewish diaspora culture. In support of the former Dibelius suggested that some of the terminology, such as ἀνήκω, 'fitting', and εὐάρεστος, 'well-pleasing', was reflective of Hellenistic ethical teaching, rather than being distinctively Christian (Dibelius 1953: 46). Following this line of thought, others have adduced Stoic parallels. Weidinger viewed the household codes that emerged during the Roman period as Stoic in nature. While those that occurred in the Pauline epistles had been lightly infused with Christian phrases, they remained basically Stoic in form and content (Weidinger 1928: 50). Lohmeyer challenged this theory, arguing that the Colossian household code was Jewish in origin, arising particularly from Pharisaic ethics (Lohmeyer 1930: 152). Expressions such as φοβούμενοι τὸν κύριον, 'the fear of the Lord' (Col. 3:22), and 'the Lord', seen as denoting the Father rather than Christ, were taken as signs of Jewish origin. Rather than seeing it as Stoic or Pharisaic in origin, Crouch argued that the source of the Colossian code arises from 'the propaganda of Hellenistic Judaism' (Crouch 1972: 119). His main argument is that Stoic codes do not consist of the reciprocal pairings of duties found in the Colossian code. He argues that such reciprocity is a hallmark of oriental origin, and that it bears greatest resemblance to Hellenistic Jewish ideas, rather than to related texts from Hellenistic or Palestinian Jewish contexts. Finally, others have seen the form of the household code as being so thoroughly reworked in Colossians that the form preserved both here and in Ephesians is in fact a new form that is specifically Christian (Schroeder 1959: 151–52). Such distinctions between Hellenistic and Jewish culture create a false dichotomy. Both Jews and gentiles lived within the wider social matrix of Mediterranean culture. While there was variety, and differing degrees of cultural contact, people did not live in hermetically sealed isolation from other strands of society. The household code finds its origin in Hellenistic philosophical texts that discuss the correct relationships within an ordered society. These forms of instruction were taken up by diaspora Jews, and grounded in the beliefs and stories of the Jewish religion. Philo employs a number of Hellenistic ethical tropes in the service of the entreaties he makes to Jewish readers, while drawing upon Jewish texts and moral commitments. In the end, in the Colossian household code one finds a series of ethical imperatives that would garner consent from both Hellenistic and Jewish members of Greco-Roman society. That is precisely the author's aim: to instruct the Colossians to conform to the prevailing social norms. The unique aspect to his teaching is that he sees that conformity to this standard is not based upon upholding the established social order. Rather, for those in the Lord, such behaviours are pleasing and fitting to the Lord, and yet stem from a radical obedience to Christ, rather than being an affirmation of existing power structures.

By contrast with the household instructions in Colossians, where in each pair of instructions the group in the position of lesser power is addressed first, the Greco-Roman examples speak to those in dominant positions, or list the party in the position of power in first place in such discussions. Several examples will illustrate this point:

> [The] parts of a family are master and slave, husband and wife, father and children. We have therefore to consider what each of these three relations is and ought to be: I mean the relation of master and servant, the marriage relation (the conjunction of man and wife has no name of its own), and thirdly, the procreative relation (this also has no proper name). (Aristotle, *Pol.* 1.3.1)

[Philosophy]...for instance, advises how a husband should conduct himself towards his wife, or how a father should bring up his children, or how a master should rule his slaves. (Seneca, *Epistles* 94.1)

For through philosophy...it is possible to attain knowledge of...how a man must bear himself in his relations with the gods, with his parents, with his elders, with the laws, with strangers, with those in authority, with friends, with women, with children, with servants; that one ought to reverence the gods, to honour one's parents, to respect one's elders, to be obedient to the laws, to yield to those in authority, to love one's friends, to be chaste with women, to be affectionate with children, and not to be overbearing with slaves. (Plutarch, *Lib. ed.* 10)

In Col. 3:18–4:1 the author lays down the pattern for Christian behaviour within this basic unit of Greco-Roman society, the household. Three types of relationship are mentioned, those between wives and husbands, children and parents, and slaves and masters. Two things are immediately striking. First, in each case the first party to be addressed is the group that would naturally be considered the more marginalized and disenfranchised in the larger society. Second, there is a disproportionate treatment of the relationship between slaves and masters. If it is not extracting too much from the text, this may suggest that the group of believers at Colossae may have included a large proportion of slaves. This supposition may gain further support if it is correct that the epistle to Philemon is addressed to a figure who is a master of a household based in Colossae.

18 For those familiar with the form of the household code from Greco-Roman Roman writings, the address to **wives** would have been a striking departure from the standard pattern. Uniformly the dominant party was addressed, the husband, the parent, or the *paterfamilias*. This deviation from the normal pattern probably is due to two factors operative in the early Christian movement: the radical theological teaching concerning equality, and the social reality of the classes of society from which group members were drawn. In wider society, admittedly with some well-known but infrequent exceptions, women occupied a subordinate position to men. Aristotle, citing previous authorities, advocates male dominant status:

> Clearly, then, moral virtue belongs to all of them; but the temperance
> of a man and of a woman, or the courage and justice of a man and of
> a woman, are not, as Socrates maintained, the same; the courage of a
> man is shown in commanding, of a woman in obeying. And this holds
> of all other virtues, as will be more clearly seen if we look at them
> in detail, for those who say generally that virtue consists in a good
> disposition of the soul, or in doing rightly, or the like, only deceive
> themselves. Far better than such definitions is their mode of speaking,
> who, like Gorgias, enumerate the virtues. All classes must be deemed
> to have their special attributes; as the poet says of women, 'Silence is
> a woman's glory', but this is not equally the glory of man. (Aristotle,
> *Pol.* 1.13)

It would be wrong to suggest that in early Christian writings one sees a charter for the emancipation of women. In fact, in many ways the household codes are a form of accommodation to the wider societal norms. However, it needs to be recognized that such an accommodation is deemed necessary since in certain sectors of the early Jesus movement there was a social challenge arising from women who were able to exercise considerable leadership and freedom within early Christian groups. The author of Colossians may be aligning Paul's more radical perspective on the role of women in his communities with the prevailing social structures. Whereas Paul could write to the Galatians that 'there is neither male or female' (Gal. 3:28), that statement of gender parity is dropped in Col. 3:11, where only the distinctions between ethnic groups and between slaves and masters are quashed. Nonetheless, while at one level upholding wider social values, the household code also lightly subverts the prevailing structure by addressing the powerless first, and by undermining the basis for the maintenance of such relationships. Within Greco-Roman society, the preservation of 'order' through the rigorous commitment to prevailing social hierarchies was seen as the cornerstone of a stable society. By contrast, here the reason given relates not to enjoying the benefits of a stable society, but arises because of the new life one has in the Lord.

The address to 'the wives' uses the articular nominative plural form for the plural vocative, since there is no separate vocative form. There is also a convention in Attic Greek in place of vocatives to use 'simple substantives only in addressing inferiors, who were, so to speak, thereby addressed in the 3rd person' (BDF: §147[3]).

However, in Col. 3:18–4:1 the purpose does not appear to be to mark out inferiors, since 'husbands', 'fathers', and 'masters' are addressed in a similar manner. Therefore, the Attic usage appears to have broken down in later *koinē* Greek. The wives are told to **be subject to husbands**. A number of manuscripts gloss this by adding the second person plural pronoun, ὑμῶν, 'your' (D* F G 075 it vg^{mss} sy$^{p.h**}$), while others add ἰδίοις, 'your own' (L 6 365 614 630 1175 1881 2464 𝔐 lat sy^h; Cl Ambst). While neither of these readings has a strong claim to be original, both variants make explicit the intended meaning. The advice given is not to be subject to *any* man, but for a wife to be subject to her own husband. Here then, in line with wider values, family relationships within the household context are seen as fundamental to the correct ordering of society. The command for wives to **be subject** utilizes the Greek verb ὑποτάσσω. However, attempts to create a distinction between 'submission' and 'inferiority' are simply modern explanations that seek to make the statement more palatable for contemporary audiences (in support of this distinction see Moule 1957: 128; cf. O'Brien 1982: 221–22, who suggests that the middle voice 'denotes subjection of oneself'). Reading such statements as directly applicable to contemporary circumstances is a failure to take the text seriously as an ancient writing, both reflecting and at times critical of its own social context. This instruction calling upon wives to 'be subject' or under the command of their husbands undeniably creates a gendered power hierarchy wherein males are given precedence over females. This is unsurprising given the patriarchal structure of both Greco-Roman and Jewish society in the first-century, and throughout the antique period. The chief duty for wives within the household setting that is outlined here is to be subordinate **to husbands**. As has been pointed out, a number of manuscripts make clear the intended sense of the verse, that the reference is for wives to be subject to their own husbands. In general, the leading male, the *paterfamilias*, wielded power in the household and all other members were expected to accede to his authority. In exceptional cases a widow or a wealthy Patrician woman may have been able to exercise a greater degree of freedom. However, this was certainly not the lot of the majority of women in society. It may have been the case that within the patriarchal society, of which early Christians were part, that membership of the new movement afforded women a greater degree of autonomy and leadership than they experienced in their other roles. The household code in Colossians appears to reflect the first stage towards moderating the greater degree of freedom enjoyed by women in the early Jesus movement. The verse concludes with the grounds for justifying the submission of wives to husbands. The comparative clause declares this is to be **as is proper in the Lord**. The verb employed, **is proper** or 'is fitting' (Greek ἀνήκω), occurs here in the imperfect tense: literally, 'as was fitting', ἀνῆκεν. The use of the imperfect here may express a state of being rather than a process (Campbell 2013: 62). However, the more traditional explanations of the use of the imperfect in this context appear to provide greater help. The imperfect tense is typically regarded as idiomatic usage (Moule 1957: 129; BDF: §358). This idiomatic usage may have arisen through a description of an action that was based upon a determination in the past, but required being carried out in the present (Lightfoot 1886: 225; Harris 2010: 154). Elsewhere in the New Testament, the verb 'to be fitting/proper', ἀνήκω, is also linked with a compound of –τασσω: 'I have confidence to command you to do what is proper', παρρησίαν ἔχων ἐπιτάσσειν σοι τὸ ἀνῆκον (Phlm. 8). The imperfect form is used elsewhere in the Pauline epistles with a present sense: ἃ οὐκ ἀνῆκεν, 'which are not fitting' (Eph. 5:4). On the basis of this evidence, it appears that the imperfect form ἀνῆκεν is used idiomatically to denote behaviour that needs to be practised in the present, though inaugurated in the past.

The choice of the ἀνήκω terminology, relating to proper behaviour in household conduct, is frequently viewed as deriving from Stoic thought. The related term καθήκω is part of the title of Zeno's treatise of ethical conduct, 'Concerning what is fitting', Περὶ τοῦ καθήκοντος. The term καθήκω is also part of Pauline ethical vocabulary: 'to do those things which are not proper', ποιεῖν τὰ μὴ καθήκοντα (Rom. 1:28). Therefore, the principle of acting properly or fittingly in relation to ethical conduct was deeply rooted in Greco-Roman culture. However, for the author of Colossians, the motivation did not stem from some form of social contract or a sense of civic responsibility. Instead, for believers, this sense of propriety is to arise from being **in the Lord**. Sumney notes that the addition of the qualifier 'in the Lord' is not simply some 'light-touch' Christianization of the prevailing ethical outlook, but that it redefines the command to be subject 'in a radical way' (Sumney 2008: 242). Instead of being no more than an expression of duty, such acts of submission are the outworking of the new life in Christ. In this way the author is able to counsel conformity to prevailing social norms, while presenting an entirely different basis for practising such behaviour. In fact, while there is the appearance of support for the dominant social practices, at a more fundamental level the whole basis of the societal system of ethics is undermined. In this way the author's theology subverts the prevailing social conventions. Dunn sees the phrase 'as is fitting in the Lord' being intended to supply some limitation upon the basis of submission that is required of wives. He argues that the Christian moral code was intended to limit compliance with social values by following them only insofar as they could be judged to be 'fitting in the Lord' (Dunn 1996: 248). While this at one level appears to be an attractive proposal, the expression **in the Lord** and similar phrases in the letter denote the new sphere in which believers now exist, not simply as a measure for assessing ethical practices (*contra* Lightfoot 1886: 225; Harris 2010: 155). Rather, the author is reminding his readers that it is because they now exist in a new realm where they participate in the Lord that it is only proper they should submit to the prevailing social relationships. The purpose appears to be to counsel a quietistic attitude among wives, children, and slaves towards those who occupy positions of power.

19 Set in parallel to the command for wives to be subject to husbands in the previous verse, here one finds instructions directed towards the male partners in the marriage relationship. Structurally, the two verses are not balanced. The instructions to wives comprises a command to 'be subject' coupled with as accompanying explanatory clause, 'as is fitting in the Lord'. By contrast, the instructions to husbands consist of two imperatives, one positive and one negative. The first command is formulated simply as, **husbands, love [your] wives**. Again, the address to **husbands** is an example of articular nominative plural form being employed for the plural vocative. The content of the commanded action is expressed by the single word **love**. The meaning of this term is not expanded in this context. Presumably it was felt that it would be self-evident, perhaps because of the wider use of the term among believers, and also because of the other usages of *agapē* terminology in the letter. Both nominal and verbal forms of ἀγαπ- and the cognate adjective ἀγαπητός occur eleven times in the letter (see Col. 1:4, 7, 8, 13; 2:2; 3:12, 14, 19; 4:7, 9, 14). Perhaps the most theologically significant is the immediately preceding occurrence of such terminology, where the Colossians are instructed to put on 'love, which is the bond of perfection' (Col. 3:14). In that context, the distinctive quality of Christian life, which is the overriding ethical imperative, is love. It is likely that having heard just a few verses earlier that love was the capstone of the virtues that were listed – compassion, goodness, humility, gentleness, longsuffering, forbearance, forgiveness (Col. 3:12–13) – that here the command given to love one's wife encapsulates those same actions. Colossians does not go as far as Ephesians (at least not explicitly) in commanding mutual submission ('be subject to one another', Eph. 5:21). However, as a counterpart to the command to wives to be subject to husbands it places upon husbands the injunction to show love towards their wives, and that concept of love is based both upon the example of Christ's love and the ethical virtues that should be practised by believers who now have their lives united with his. The concept of love that is called for here entails sacrifice and service, and is based upon placing the needs of the other before one's own desires. This is a typically Pauline understanding of marriage (cf. 1 Cor. 7:3–5). The love that husbands are called upon to display is to be directed to **wives**. As in the previous verses the implication is that this love should be directed to one's own wife, and again a range of manuscripts insert the second person pronoun 'your' to make explicit this intended meaning (ὑμῶν, D* F G it vg^cl sy; Amst Spec).

If there were any uncertainty concerning what the command to 'love' is intended to entail, then its meaning is spelled out through the negative example of a prohibited type of behaviour that is the opposite of love. Whereas in the previous verse the second clause had an explanatory function that was introduced by use of the comparative particle ὡς, 'as', here the second clause is another imperative presented through the more straightforward connective conjunction καί, 'and'. Using this grammatical form, husbands are given a further instruction concerning behaviour towards their wives: **and be not embittered toward them**. The negative prohibition **be not embittered** is expressed in Greek using a negative particle and a verbal form which has occasioned some division of opinion as to whether it is in the middle or passive voice, μὴ πικραίνεσθε. The distinction then depends upon the volition of the subjects, 'the husbands'. If the voice is middle, then one may view husbands as allowing themselves to become embittered towards wives. By contrast, if the voice is passive, then the subjects might be seen as less conscious of their actions. Campbell classifies the verbal form as a present middle imperative (Campbell 2013: 63). This classification of voice as being middle is presumably due to the fact that Campbell sees the form calling attention to the subject (the husbands), and the subject is acting in relation to itself. In this case one might over-translate this as 'do not allow yourselves to have bitter feelings towards your wives'. Most grammarians and commentators, however, understand the form as passive in meaning, without an agent expressed (Dunn 1996: 249; Harris 2010: 155). In such a case there is no volition or meaningful awareness on the part of the subject. This may explain why the author has to call attention to the possibility that husbands may unwittingly become embittered towards their wives by not loving them fully. In classical usages of this form the context suggests that the passive voice is intended (Plato, *Leg.* 731d; Theocritus 5.120).

The force of the injunction is to describe an action that is the antithesis of love, and which must always be avoided. The verb πικραίνω when used literally carries the sense of the physical property of making something taste bitter or sharp (cf. Rev. 8:11; 10:9–10). However, just as the term 'bitter' may function in English, here it is used metaphorically to describe an attitude that is harsh or poisonous in relation to others. Hence a possible translation is 'do not be harsh with them' (so REB). In the New Testament the closest parallel example does not involve the verbal form, but the related noun 'bitter' is also found in the Pauline writings: 'the mouth is full of curses and bitter words' (Rom. 3:14; see also Jas 3:14). In wider Greek literature Plutarch uses a compound form of the verb to instruct husbands concerning behaviour towards women. He tells them not to 'be bitter towards women', πρὸς γυναῖκα διαπικραίνονται (*Mor.* 6.457). Here in Colossians the author expresses the same sentiment, warning males against developing harsh attitude **towards them**, that is, against their own wives, whom they should love in the fullest way possible. Without attempting to turn the values surrounding marriage into modern understandings of equality, there is nonetheless a genuine expression of a sacrificial attitude of love that husbands are called upon to exhibit towards their wives. For the author of Colossians, it is a new mode of existence in Christ that is to transform the basic fabric of the marriage relationship from one of dominance and power-brokering, into a fitting partnership that reflects the love of Christ and his submission to the cross as an act of self-giving.

20 Having outlined the way in which both parties are to behave in regard to one set of relationships in the nuclear family, that of wives and husbands, the author now turns to another familial relationship. Hence, after addressing the gender-based family relationship between wife and husband, the focus now falls upon the generationally based relationship between children and parents. Structurally, this verse and the following verse follow the pattern established in Col. 3:18–19. Initially there is a positive command addressed to the group that would be considered as being in the inferior position in the power hierarchy. This is followed by an accompanying reason for adopting the recommended course of behaviour, based on life 'in the Lord'. In the second verse of each pair, the party in the position of natural social authority is addressed. Here the structure of Col. 3:19 and Col. 3:21 do not correspond as closely. The former (Col. 3:19) gives a positive command followed by a prohibition, whereas Col. 3:21 states a prohibition with an accompanying reason. The internal parallelism between Col. 3:20 and 3:21 is actually stronger than was the case in Col. 3:18–19. This is because with Col. 3:20–21 both verses commence with the articular nominative plural form functioning as the plural vocative, followed by a command – either positive or negation, and in Col. 3:20–21 (unlike Col. 3:18–19) the final element in each verse is an explanatory clause that forms the basis of the command articulated in the immediately preceding clause.

The address to **children** follows the pattern established in the two preceding verses, employing the nominative plural with definite article used for the direct address. It remains uncertain, however, whether the term **children** is specifying this group by their relational status, or by their age. Pao makes a strong cumulative case for an age designation (see Pao 2012: 268–69). This is based upon Aristotle's reference to children being subject because of their age and stage of maturity (*Pol.* 1.1260b), and also because the parallel code in Ephesians instructs fathers to bring up children 'in the training and instruction of the Lord' (Eph. 6:4). These points lend weight to the suggestion that those being addressed have not reached the age of majority. However, there is not a clear indication within the text of Colossians itself whether age of relationship defines the way the author understands the child–parent instructions, so while these points are suggestive, they are far from being decisive. It may be the case that this appeal is a somewhat stylized piece of advice that follows the general pattern of the household code without the author reflecting in detail on the age of the children in question. This suggestion is reinforced by the observation that in his letters Paul appears to have little concern for the role of children in his communities (cf. Gaventa 2008: 234). Perhaps even more telling was the strain of thought in Greco-Roman writing that placed children in a subordinate position to parents throughout their lives. Describing the laws given by Romulus, Dionysius of Halicarnassus notes that his regulations were more stringent than those known in his own society, and thus he comments:

> the lawgiver of the Romans gave virtually full power to the father over his son, even during his whole life, whether he thought proper to imprison him, to scourge him, to put him in chains and keep him at work in the fields, or to put him to death, and this even though the son were already engaged in public affairs, though he were numbered among the highest magistrates, and though he were celebrated for his zeal for the commonwealth. (Dionysius, *Ant. Rom.* 2.26.4)

Hence children, regardless of the specifics of their identity, are stereotypically instructed to **obey [your] parents in all things**. Such an instruction resonates widely with societal values across the ancient Mediterranean world. As has been seen, Plutarch instructs children 'to honour one's parents, to respect one's elders' (Plutarch, *Lib. ed.*, 10). Moving from the Greco-Roman context, embedded in the central commandments of Judaism is the instruction, 'honour your father and mother' (Exod. 20:12; Deut. 5:16). The book of Proverbs is replete with sayings concerning the instruction and upbringing of children, and the required disposition towards parents (Prov. 22:6, 15; 23:13; 29:15, 21; 31:28). Thus, there is an unwavering assumption that the duty of children is to exhibit obedience to parents, that parents should instruct and discipline children, and that together these qualities exemplify a well-run household.

The command to **obey** is both traditional *and* subordinates children to parents. Whereas wives are called upon to be submissive (Col. 3:18), both children (Col. 3:20) and slaves (Col. 3:22) are instructed to obey those in authority over them. The similarity of status for children and slaves was enshrined in Roman law, with both seen as the property of the *paterfamilias*. Paul uses the image of the child who has not reached maturity as a metaphor for those living under the law (Gal. 4:1–7), and states that 'as long as the heir is a child, he does not differ at all from a slave' (Gal. 4:1). In this servile position, the duty of children was to display obedience. Here the household code calls for such obedience to be rendered to both **parents**. While it becomes further apparent in the next verse that the father was the figure wielding authority within the home, the child was to exhibit deference to both the mother and the father. The all-encompassing nature of the instruction is emphasized in the phrase **in all things**. No exceptions are entertained or suggested. The command is given as an absolute instruction. While in the following verse fathers are told to be moderate in the treatment of their children, lack of moderation is not the basis for non-obedience. This is strikingly different from some of the traditions in the gospels where Jesus himself rejects parental authority (Mk 3:31–35), questions parental oversight (Lk. 2:48–49), calls into question his filial relationship (Jn 2:3), or in the non-canonical gospels rebukes his father when he tries to discipline him (*Inf. Gos. Thom.* 5). The blanket instruction given here aligns more closely with the prevailing status of children in ancient Mediterranean society, rather than reflecting Jesus' own attitude concerning the need to transcend that standard because of loyalty to God (cf. also Lk. 9:59–60). Hence this instruction reflects a high degree of acculturation and acceptance of wider Greco-Roman social values.

However, the reason given for children accepting this traditional subservient role has been thoroughly Christianized. The basis for obedience is not the maintenance of the societal structure, but, according to the author, **for this is pleasing in the Lord**. Obedience is seen as justifiable because of its **pleasing** nature. The Greek term εὐάρεστος encapsulates the idea of something being 'pleasing', 'pleasant' or 'acceptable' (*EDNT*: II, 74). The term is used five times in the Pauline letters, and is used to instruct slaves to be pleasing to their masters (Tit. 2:9). This further illustrates the similarity with which children and slaves were regarded in Greco-Roman house-holds. The explanatory clause does not simply state in an unqualified manner that obedience is 'pleasing', but rather it emphasizes that the obedience of children to their parents is pleasing **in the Lord**. This same phrase was employed when instructing wives to be submissive to their husbands because such action was fitting 'in the Lord' (Col. 3:18). Again, this is not intended as a limiting phrase, but as an overarching justification. Given the new mode of existence that the Colossians now possess in Christ, all their actions are to be commensurate with that transformed existence. The phrase is not simply a way of saying the submission of wives to husbands or the obedience of children to parents is fitting or pleasing to the Lord (*contra* Pao 2012: 270), but that such uncontentious behaviour that upholds societal norms befits those who are now in Christ, and who know that their true mode of existence is not earthly, but heavenly (Col. 1:3; 3:2–3). In this way the advice to conform to typical social practices is not an affirmation of those practices. Rather, from the author's perspective, they are so radically undermined for believers who now are in Christ that they are not even worthy of opposition since their life is now in a heavenly sphere.

21 The most striking feature of the group addressed, **fathers**, is that it does not correspond to the group named in the previous verse, 'parents'. In Col. 3:18–19 the careful symmetry was maintained, with wives instructed to be subject to their husbands, and then husbands exhorted to love their wives. In Col. 3:20–21, while children are commanded to obey parents, the reciprocal responsibility is addressed to fathers alone. This is a reflection of the power hierarchy in a typical Greco-Roman household, rather than desig-nating that the Greek term πατέρες in the plural is being employed in a gender-inclusive manner (*contra* Barth and Blanke 1994: 443).

The fathers are given a negative commandment, or a prohibition, **do not provoke your children**. The Greek term ἐρεθίζετε is used here negatively, hence the translation 'provoke', which carries the sense of causing irritation (*EDNT*: II, 51), and hence the phrase is glossed as 'provoke not your children *to anger*' in the KJV. However, the term does not have an intrinsically negative sense. The only other use in the New Testament typically renders the verb ἐρεθίζω as 'arouse' in a positive sense. Addressing the Corinthians, Paul writes, 'your zeal (ἠρέθισεν) has stirred up most of them' (2 Cor. 9:2). Here in Col. 3:21, however, the term is clearly negative. This is indicated both by the fact that it is an action that is prohibited, and the reason given in the second half of the verse that sees that failure to desist from provoking children will result in their discouragement. The use of the verb in 2 Macc. 14:27 describes a royal figure 'being provoked (ἐρεθισθεὶς) by false accusations'. The sense of the term in that context stands in close parallel to its use in Col. 3:21 (cf. 1 Macc. 15:40). With the expression **your children**, the text for the first time in the household code makes the relationship more explicit through the use of the genitive pronoun ὑμῶν, 'your'. While it has been suggested that this might be an explicit attempt to remind fathers that these children belong to them (O'Brien 1982: 226), it is perhaps more likely to be a stylistic device that brings out what was implicit in each of the other relationship pairings that have been discussed.

An explanation is provided as to why fathers should avoid provoking their children: **lest they become discouraged**. In the Greek construction the conjunction ἵνα introduces a negative purpose clause – literally, 'in order that they may not lose heart'. Thus the consequence of exasperating one's children is not viewed as leading to active rebellion or disobedience on the part of children, but a deeper and more resigned sense that the child is unable to please the father. The verb ἀθυμέω that describes this passive despondency conveys the idea of being discouraged, losing heart, or becoming dispirited. The verb occurs nowhere else in the New Testament, although it is used on several occasions in the LXX (Deut. 28:65; 1 Kgs 1:6, 7; 15:11; 2 Kgs 6:8; 1 Chron. 13:11; Judg. 7:22; Isa. 25:4; Jer. 30:12; 1 Macc. 4:27). It is interesting that the consequence is understood in terms of the potential psychological damage that may be caused to children by a father who constantly provokes his offspring. This is seen as resulting in a loss of motivation on the part of children trying to please their parents. As a counter-balance to this eventuality the injunction in Col. 3:21 does not call upon fathers to exercise their authority, but to behave responsibly toward their children (Dunn 1996: 251). This verse is frequently compared with its counterpart in Ephesians: 'And, fathers, do not provoke your children to anger; but bring them up in the discipline and instruction of the Lord' (Eph. 6:4). In that context after the prohibition against provocation, fathers are directed towards their positive duty to provide Christian instruction.

In Col. 3:21 no positive actions are laid out. Instead, the text prohibits provocation, and sets out the consequences of not refraining from such behaviour.

22 Slaves are the next group to be addressed. Following the pattern that was used with the instructions given to wives and children, here also the group in the position of powerlessness is addressed prior to speaking to those who hold power over them. However, whereas the two previous relationship pairings were formulated in a compressed manner, wives and husbands (Col. 3:18–19), children and parents or fathers (Col. 3:20–21), the advice given to slaves and their masters is greatly expanded (Col. 3:22–4:1). This leads to the supposition that the primary concern in relation to household behaviour to be addressed among the Colossian believers was the conduct of believing slaves in their daily life in positions of subservience in typical Greco-Roman households. The ubiquitous role of slaves in first-century Mediterranean society had resulted in much being written in relation to the handling of slaves and reflection on their position in society. Moreover, there were perennial fears of slave uprisings, and such fears were not unfounded. The slave revolt led by Spartacus had left a graphic imprint on the collective mind of the Patrician classes, and harsh laws were implemented that further eroded the status of slaves in society.

The command given to household slaves is that they are to **obey in all things your masters according to the flesh**. The parallels to the instruction given to children in Col. 3:20 are obvious. Both children and slaves are called upon to **obey** and there is no limit put on the type of obedience expected since obedience is to be rendered **in all things**. The phrase 'in all things', κατὰ πάντα, is omitted in a number of manuscripts. While decrying the institution of slavery, it is still too easy to sanitize and domesticate it by comparing slaves with household servants of more recent times. The difference was not simply a matter of lack of financial remuneration, but revolved around a fundamental loss of freedom and having no right to self-determination. As the property of their masters, slaves could be sold, separated from their loved ones, beaten, maimed or killed with impunity from the law, and could be made to engage in sexual acts for their owners. Therefore, slaves were physically, socially and sexually vulnerable (Joshel 2010: 40). If slaves formed a significant component of the community of believers in Jesus at Colossae, the command to be obedient to masters in all things would not sound like good news in their ears. While the early Christian movement was itself marginal, and not in a place to challenge overtly the existing social structures, there is a covert challenge to the institution of slavery. The instruction given demonstrates both subservience and subversion. Slaves are indeed to obey their owners, but at a deeper level they are to recognize them for what they truly are – only **your masters according to the flesh**. In Greek the term for master is κύριος. This is precisely the same term as the title used to describe Jesus as 'Lord', κύριος. There is therefore not simply a play on words occurring here, but a radical relativization of the power that earthly lords or masters possess. The one whom all believers ultimately serve, be they freeborn or slaves, is the Lord Jesus. On the surface, slaves are commanded to continue in their obedience and thereby to maintain social conformity. At a deeper level, those who exercise power over slaves in their current situation have that power only **according to the flesh**, κατὰ σάρκα. This description of the masters not only reminds slaves of their higher allegiance, but also stresses the impermanence and lack of spiritual authority of these earthly masters (*contra* Schweizer 1982: 224). This limited authority stands in stark contrast to that of their true Lord, who is preeminent over all creation (Col. 1:18), and is the one from who all lordships derive their existence and authority (Col. 1:16). In this way the powerless, such as wives, children, or slaves, are able to redefine their obedience and subservience as actually being acts of subversion and resistance. In a similar value-inverting manner, early Christian reflections on martyrdom redefined being but to death as a death-negating act, since through death they entered into true life. Here the household code redefines earthly obedience both as an act of resistance and as a means of serving the true Lord. This aligns with the wider phenomenon identified by sociologists of religion whereby members of marginal new religious movements can develop 'hidden transcripts' and counter-ideologies that call into question the legitimacy of prevailing power structures (Scott 1990: 18–119; Sumney 2008: 237).

While the instructions may have an undertone of resistance against the prevailing power structure, this is not to be read as grounds for rendering incomplete obedience, or only partial service. To make this clear two negative examples are presented of the type of obedience that is not to be practised towards earthly masters. Believing slaves must not practise sham obedience; their behaviour is to be genuine, being performed **not with eye-service, as pleasing men**. The type of obedience that is not to be countenanced is described as **eye-service**, ὀφθαλμοδουλίᾳ. There is a textual variant here, with a number of manuscripts replacing the dative singular form with the dative plural ὀφθαλμοδουλείαις (א C Ψ 0278 33ᵛⁱᵈ 1739 1881 𝔐 syʰ). While there is no difference in the English translation, there might be a slight shift in nuance. The singular could potentially denote the state of being one who obeys only with eye-service, whereas the plural may refer to a series of repeated acts, 'eye-services' or 'acts of eye-service'. However, such a distinction may in fact be creating a difference where the change is simply due to scribal preference. The singular form has the stronger earlier attestation, being found in 𝔓⁴⁶ A B D F G 075 81n 104 365 1241ˢ co. The problem that is identified with 'eye-service' is that it is reflective of the type of obedience that is characteristic of those who live **as pleasing men**, ἀνθρωπάρεσκοι. Such calculating obedience cannot, according to the author, be the hallmark of those who strive to please a non-earthly master. The two compound nouns 'eye-service', ὀφθαλμοδουλίᾳ, and 'man-pleasing', ἀνθρωπάρεσκοι, occur only in the household codes here and in Eph. 6:22. While the author may have coined these neologisms, their meaning is self-evident, simply being the combined meaning of their constituent parts.

Standing in contrast to such negative examples of obedience and fidelity in service, slaves are instructed to obey their earthly masters in a manner that contrasts with the superficial and calculating attitude that has just been described. Thus slaves are commanded that their obedience should not be simply outward man-pleasing obedience, **but** should arise **in singleness of heart, fearing the Lord**. The term ἁπλότης denotes 'simplicity, sincerity, uprightness' (*EDNT*: I, 123), but also refers to a 'singleness' of purpose or an undivided attitude. This sense of 'singleness' or 'unity' is seen most clearly in Mt. 6:22, where the cognate phrase ὁ ὀφθαλμός σου ἁπλοῦς refers to the 'single', or clearly focused eye (cf. Moo 2008: 310). Here, this sincerity or **singleness of heart** is presented as reflecting an unfeigned and proper motivation.

The final participial clause in the verse, **fearing the Lord**, parallels the instructions given to wives (Col. 3:18) and children (Col. 3:20) that the behaviours enjoined upon them are to be performed 'in the Lord'. Whereas it was suggested that the expression 'in the Lord' denoted the new sphere in which believers now exist, and hence wives and children were being encouraged to behave in a manner consistent with their new ontological state, here the metaphor is slightly different. While the metaphor remains relational, here the emphasis is on slaves recognizing the one who is their true master. The phrase **fearing the Lord** has been understood mainly in one of two different ways. It may be taken circumstantially, 'as you fear the Lord'. In this case it denotes the manner in which obedience to masters and an attitude of singleness of heart are to be brought about. Alternatively, the phrase may be understood causally, 'because you fear the Lord' (Harris 2010: 158). In this case it would refer to the pre-existing motivation that is the basis for correct obedience. Both the context of the argument and the Old Testament background to the concept of 'the fear of the Lord' suggest that the causal sense is intended. The closest parallel to the final clause is found in Jewish intertestamental literature: 'in singleness of heart in fear of the Lord' (*Test. Reub.* 4.1). However, given the widespread nature of the concept of 'the fear of the Lord' direct dependence on the *Testament of Reuben* is unlikely. Typically 'fear of the Lord' is linked with wisdom, where 'the fear of the Lord is the beginning of wisdom' (Prov. 1:7; cf. Ps. 111:10; Sir. 1:14, 16, 18, 20, 27). The link with wisdom is not necessarily present here. However, that link with wisdom illustrates that 'fear' is different from 'an emotional fear' (Dunn 1996: 254). Therefore, the sense here should not be understood or reduced to a constant state of worrying for safety and well-being. Instead, it reflects a fundamental reverence and awe for the Lord, which produces sincerity of behaviour and the correct motivation for obeying masters.

Here, as in Col. 3:18, 20, **the Lord** is Christ. This use of a Jewish scriptural expression originally having God as its object, and applying it without explanation to Christ, shows the relative ease with which certain earlier believers could apply the language of the deity to their descriptions of Jesus in his exalted state. In fact, a number of manuscripts preserve the variant reading 'fearing God' ($\mathfrak{P}^{46}$ $\aleph^2$ D^2 K 104 630 $\mathfrak{M}$). Apart from $\mathfrak{P}^{46}$, the majority of these are later manuscripts, or later corrections to earlier manuscripts, and probably do not reflect the earliest recoverable state of the text. The motivation for the change may have been theological, since it may have been felt that 'fear of the Lord' is to be directed to the Father rather than to Christ. However, here the text almost certainly read 'fearing the Lord', with Christ being designated by the term 'lord' in this context (cf. Col. 3:24b). Therefore, believing slaves who have come to reverence Christ as their true master should see Christ's status as the true Lord as the basis of their motivation for obeying their 'masters according to the flesh' in an unalloyed and wholehearted manner.

23 The address to slaves continues in this verse with the author reinforcing the point made in the previous verse, although reformulating to emphasize the all-encompassing nature of the obedience that is to be rendered to earthly masters by believing slaves. The scope of sincere service is presented in the opening phrase **whatever you do**, ὃ ἐὰν ποιῆτε. The subjunctive construction is used to envisage any potential service that the slave must perform for the earthly master. Sincere motivation is commanded through the imperatival phrase **work from the soul**. Again, inner attitudes are privileged above outward performance or showy displays. The term 'soul', ψυχή, is used to denote the inward motivation in much the same manner as the word 'heart', καρδία, functioned in the previous verse (Col. 3:22). These terms are virtually synonymous. It has been suggested that the close proximity of the terms 'heart' and 'soul' is intended to recall the *Shema* (Dunn 1996: 257–58), 'you shall love the Lord your God with all your heart, and with all your soul, and with all your strength' (Deut. 6:4–5). However, the language of 'heart' and 'soul' is stereotypical for denoting the inner being, so at best the proposed connection is suggestive rather than conclusive. There is often a lack of precision in Greek anthropology between terms such as 'heart', 'soul', 'mind', and other designations of the centre of being or intellect. For this reason, no significant difference should be drawn from the singleness of purpose that is seen as arising from the 'heart', and the work which issues from the 'soul'. These are simply stylistic variants that both denote the correct inner attitude to be displayed by slaves. While the emphasis is on the inner motivation, the command to 'work' demonstrates that correct motivation must produce appropriate actions. There can be no doubt that the household code envisages slaves continuing in their service to masters, what is paramount is that the inner attitude is not one of resentment or begrudging action.

Again mirroring the instruction given in the previous verse where obedience to masters was to arise from 'fear of the Lord', here the work done is to be done **as for the Lord and not for men**. The expression **as for the Lord** does not represent some pretence or denote a literary simile. Rather, the work carried out ostensibly for earthly masters is actually performed by believing slaves to the honour and glory of the Lord. This point is made even more explicitly in the following verse with the direct statement, 'it is the Lord Christ you serve' (Col. 3:24b). The contrast between the prevailing earthly state of affairs and the ultimate heavenly reality is emphasized by the declaration that the slaves' work is for their true Lord, **and not for men**. This rejection of perceiving one's service as for the benefit of human masters was also present in the previous verse with the instruction not to obey in a 'man-pleasing' manner (Col. 3:22), but that the required obedience is in reality an act of service given by those who are 'fearing the Lord'. Here also the human–divine contrast is drawn once more. The required pure and inwardly motivated work is for the Lord himself, and not for human overlords who enslave those who have been made free in Christ. These slaves now serve Christ in all that they do. In this way the commandments to engage in faithful and wholehearted service of earthly masters remains a subversive strategy, for it stems from a belief that it is not earthly masters who are being served and that their lordship is nothing, since only Christ can be called Lord.

24 The first half of this verse provided a further reason for slaves to understand that in actuality they are working for the Lord. This is because their true recompense comes from the Lord: **knowing that from the Lord you will receive the reward of the inheritance**. The perfect participle **knowing**, εἰδότες, is from the verb οἶδα. The verb οἶδα denotes the possession of knowledge (*EDNT*: II, 494). Hence new knowledge is not being disclosed to the addressees. Instead, they are being reminded to recall a previously or well-known fact. In this regard the participle has a causal sense, 'since you know' (Harris 2010: 159). Therefore, as a further motivation for slaves to work with a sincere attitude, the author recalls the widely acknowledged expectation among believers **that from the Lord you will receive the reward**. The eschatology of Colossians is often seen as being already fulfilled or at least more 'realized' than is the case with many of the other Pauline epistles. There is definitely a basis for that conclusion. The letter can speak of believers having been already 'rescued from the authority of darkness and transferred into the kingdom' (Col. 1:13), it envisages them as having been raised with Christ (Col. 3:1). However, this verse clearly shows that alongside those ideas there is also a future aspect to the eschatology presented in the epistle. Here the letter speaks of a future reward that will be given by the Lord. Moreover, as is the case with most early Christian writings, the eschatological perspective is neither 'fully realized' nor 'totally future'; rather, it is a mixture of both elements. In Colossians there is a noticeable emphasis on the heavenly benefits already experienced and enjoyed by believers, but not to the extent that future hope and a fully transformed mode of existence have been removed.

The syntax of the clause is structured in such a way as to emphasize **the Lord** as the source of what is to be received. The noun 'Lord' in the prepositional phrase ἀπὸ κυρίου, **from the Lord**, is anarthrous. This is not uncommon in prepositional phrases. Harris suggests that it might function 'to stress the exalted status of the One who will reward his slaves' (Harris 2010: 159–60). The 'Lord', who is Christ as the second half of the verse makes clear, is characterized as the judge who recompenses his servants in the age to come. The portrayal of Christ in this role of final arbiter is found elsewhere in the Pauline writings (2 Cor. 5:10), and again attributes a divine role (Rom. 14:10) to Christ without any sharp distinction (Dunn 1996: 256).

Thus the letter declares to the slaves that it is 'from the Lord', that benefits accrue: **you will receive the reward of the inheritance**. The compound verb ἀπολήμψεσθε occurs in a construction with the preposition ἀπό, which is present before 'the Lord' is a common Greek construction. In Classical Greek the compound form ἀπολαμβάνω differs in meaning from the simple form λαμβάνω. In the wider linguistic context this for is typically found in commercial usage, denoting a repayment or receiving something back. However, it appears to have lost such meaning in the New Testament, and

instead it designates the act of receiving something, without signi-
fying the giver was indebted to the receiver. However, it can be used
by Jewish or Christian writers in eschatological contexts for the
receiving of future rewards (*4 Macc.* 18:23). Therefore the choice
of the verb in this context may reflect its eschatological overtones.
Furthermore, **the reward**, τὴν ἀνταπόδοσιν, has the sense of a gift
being given freely on the part of the giver, rather than something
earned or obligated to be repaid. What will be received is described
here as **the reward of the inheritance**, which is a somewhat cumbersome phrase. Here slaves are promised that, as a reward for their
obedience and sincere service, which is really to the honour of the
Lord and not for human masters, they will receive their inheritance
from the Lord. In a system where slaves were dispossessed and not
part of the inheritance structure of households, this is a further subversive counterclaim upholding their spiritually privileged status.
Not only did Roman law legislate against slave becoming inheritors,
such attitudes against slave inheritance were typical in contemporary Judaism. Paul takes this for granted when he writes, 'But
what does scripture say, "Drive out the slave and her child, for the
child of the slave will not share the inheritance with the child of the
free woman"' (Gal. 4:30). Inheritance has been mentioned earlier
in the letter, where all the Colossians were declared to be partakers
of this future reward: 'giving thanks to the father who has qualified
you for a share of the inheritance of the holy ones in the light' (Col.
1:12). Here slaves, presumably because of their marginal status and
perhaps due to their numerical prominence in the community, are
especially mentioned and affirmed as those who will receive this
inheritance. They have already been reminded that in Christ they
are no longer slaves (Col. 3:11). So, in the new reality that they now
inhabit, they will receive the inheritance from the Lord.

The final clause in this verse stands apart from what precedes
it as a separate statement. However, it is unclear whether the verb
δουλεύετε should be taken as an indicative, **it is the Lord Christ
you are serving**, or an imperative, 'serve the Lord Christ'. As Moo
has noted, most of the English versions take 'the last clause of v. 24
as a statement...and, somewhat surprisingly, the commentators are
generally out of step with the translations, favoring the imperative by
a large margin' (Moo 2008: 313). In favour of the indicative it can be
argued that the phrase is an explanatory conclusion to the statement

made in Col. 3:24a. On this logic the slaves are told they will receive a reward from the Lord, because it is the Lord Christ they serve and not earthly masters. By contrast, in favour of understanding the verb δουλεύετε, 'serve', imperativally Harris offers four supporting reasons. The first is perhaps the strongest, that if the verb is read as an imperative here then it resumes the imperative ἐργάζεσθε of Col. 3:23. Second, he argues that the γάρ of Col. 3:25a 'is more easily understood by a preceding impv. than a preceding indic.'. Third, the imperative accords with Col. 3:24a as well as the indicative. Fourth, Rom. 12:11 has a similar construction, τῷ κυρίῳ δουλεύοντες, but uses an imperatival participle (Harris 2010: 161). The third reason is false: as will be suggested below, the imperative does not accord with Col. 3:24a as well as the indicative. The fourth reason given is perhaps a distraction. The inescapable fact is that in Rom. 12:11 a participle is used (perhaps with imperatival force), but not the verbal form that causes the ambiguity here. With the second reason, the logical force of the conjunction γάρ, is preserved whether the preceding clause is an indicative or an imperative. In the end, one is left to make the decision based on the better fit with context, and perhaps as a default based upon the knowledge of the far greater prevalence of indicative forms over imperative forms. While admitting that the case is indeed ambiguous, it does appear that the case for the indicative is slightly stronger (see Campbell 2013: 66). This assessment is based on fit with the wider context. The clause reasserts the central claim of the argument in Col. 3:22–24, that those addressed are slaves of Christ not of earthly masters. Therefore, the author makes the strong declarative statement: **it is the Lord Christ you are serving**. This reminds the slaves of the fundamental reason that they are to carry out their acts of service in a whole-hearted and unbegrudging manner. Regardless of harsh treatment from earthly masters, their work is not being done for them. Instead, it is done for the one who is truly Lord, Christ. He is the one who will reward them with a heavenly inheritance, and instead of being dispossessed non-entities, they have become heirs in the coming kingdom (Col. 1:13).

25 The tone here appears to change from one of encouragement to one of chastisement. The opening clause sounds like a proverbial saying or a familiar maxim: **for the wrongdoer will receive back the wrong he has done**. The key issue concerns the identity of those being warned. Is it slaves who do not perform their duties in a sincere manner, or masters inclined to mistreat their slave, or are both groups simultaneously being warned? While a double referent is ingenious (for this possibility see Schweizer 1982: 226–27), such a meaning is not signalled in what is written. Similarly, although 'masters according to the flesh' were mentioned in Col. 3:22, the material in Col. 3:22–24 has been uniformly addressed to slaves and there has been no indication of a change of subject at this point. Consequently, it appears more probable that the address is still directed to slaves.

Primarily, the verse describes the negative consequence for slaves who do not work in a genuine manner. Whereas the one who carries out work in the knowledge that such service is for the Lord will receive the reward of heavenly inheritance, the person who renders only 'eye-service' (Col. 3:22) will be repaid in like measure according to the type of work he has performed. This concept of differentiated rewards in the eschatological age is seen more widely in the Pauline writings, and is applied to all believers and their work rather than narrowly to slaves as is the case here (Rom. 2:6–11; 1 Cor. 3:13–15; 2 Cor. 5:10). In contrast to a slave working faithfully in the knowledge that his Lord is Christ, the person presented here as an exemplar is described as ὁ ἀδικῶν, 'the wrongdoer' – that is, a person who acts in an unjust manner, or does wrong. What will happen to such a **wrongdoer** is described by the verb κομίζω, which may have the sense of getting back something that one is owed, or to come into possession of something or to receive something. Here the future middle form κομίσεται denotes an eschatological recompense, and that repayment will be directed against the one described as the wrongdoer. In the Pauline writings more widely, the term is used of receiving the appropriate recompense (2 Cor. 5:10; Col. 3:25; Eph. 6:8). In each of these cases it refers to a future recompense or **receiving back** for actions carried out in the present life. The recompense that will be meted out to wrongdoers is commensurate with their action, for such an individual will be recompensed according to **the wrong he has done.** For the second time in this verse a form of the verb ἀδικέω is used. The term ἠδίκησεν is not simply re-used to create a stylistically balanced saying, but more importantly to illustrate that the divine recompense is fair. While this statement might strike readers as a stark threat in comparison to the more encouraging exhortations given to slaves in the previous verses, there is at least implicitly the encouragement that God will likewise repay the one who works well according to that standard of work. In fact, that was the message of Col. 3:23–24.

The final statement is an explicit articulation of divine fairness, **and there is no partiality**. The Greek term προσωπολημψία uses the metaphor of 'receiving face' to describe partial or differentiated treatment of people. It occurs four times in the New Testament (Rom. 2:11; Eph. 6:8; Col. 3:25; Jas 2:1), and is a compound form derived from the Septuagintal phrase λαμβάνω πρόσωπον (LXX Ps. 81:2; Sir. 4:22; 35:13; Mal. 1:8). However, the word προσωπολημψία occurs only in Christian writings and in the *Test. Job* 43:13. The practice of 'showing face', or acting with partiality, is uniformly depicted as not representing the way God passes judgment, and hence is regarded negatively when practised by humans. Here, the negative formulation may serve not only to remind slaves of the equity of the way in which the Lord will recompense everyone, it may also seek to contrast the divine impartiality with the partiality that slaves were experiencing at the hands of earthly masters. This comment on the impartial treatment practised in the heavenly realm leads naturally into the instructions given to masters in the following verse.

1 Following the longest address to a single group in the household code (Col. 3:22–25), the pattern is resumed of speaking to pairs of addressees who are connected by power relationships. Again, the author speaks in second place to the group that would be considered the socially superior in each pairing. Such an ordering may be due to two factors. First, there may be a desire to invert or even subvert perceptions about social hierarchies. Second, it may reflect the reality that the majority of the author's addressees were numbered among the socially powerless (cf. 1 Cor. 1:26). However, having dealt at length with the responsibilities of slaves within the basic social structure of the household, now the author addresses the masters or overlords of slaves, with two brief statements. It may be worth remembering that the three groups addressed in second position in each pairing – husbands, fathers, and masters – were in all likelihood not three separate groups, but three roles carried out by a single person who was head of the household. Thus it is probably the case that the *paterfamilias* is addressed on three occasions within the household code, with the overriding advice in each case being to behave moderately and fairly, in an encouraging and just manner. Hence the household code expects such figures to set the tone of concord and equity within the small community units of which they were head.

The opening injunction, **masters, grant justice and equality to slaves**, is probably an indication that slaves did not regularly enjoy equality and justice, since they were deemed to have no rights. If slave-owners were part of the community being addressed, then the fact that some of their slaves may have been part of the same community of believers must have challenged the attitude of believing masters, at least towards believing slaves. The reason for this might well be that '[t]hese masters have, after all, just heard the author identify slaves as heirs' (Sumney 2008: 254).

Following the pattern established earlier in Col. 3:18–4:1 the articular nominative plural form, κύριοι, is used for the plural vocative. Next, following the Greek syntax the two qualities **justice and equality** that are required of masters are listed. The term here translated as 'justice', δίκαιος, had a wide semantic range, with the neuter denoting 'that which is obligatory in view of certain requirements of justice' (BDAG: 247). The second term 'equality', ἰσότης, is infrequent in the New Testament (2 Cor. 8:13, 14; Col. 4:1), and denotes a sense of balance or fairness that produces common treatment without favouritism. Following on from the claim in the previous clause that 'there is no partiality', these two qualities are best understood as the means by which masters are to ensure the impartial treatment of their slaves. As Holtz notes, the justice and equality spoken of here are 'obviously not a reference to social equality' (*EDNT*: II, 202). Masters are not being commanded to make slaves their social equals, but not to discriminate in the way they treat different slaves. Their actions towards slaves are to be reasonable, and to be carried out with equity. These qualities are to be directed **to slaves**. Here the relational responsibilities of masters to their slaves are articulated. In a society that saw slaves as chattels without any rights, the radical nature of this command needs to be underscored. From the perspective of the household code it is incumbent on masters to 'grant' or to 'provide' some basic human rights to those for whom they have responsibility. The verb παρέχεσθε is 'one of those loosely used, imprecise terms…but here the middle form clearly means to "grant" something to someone' (Dunn 1996: 259).

Thus, here the reciprocity of the relationship is stressed, but from the perspective of the author what is instructed makes sense because all people are in a subordinate relationship to Christ, who is the Lord of all things (Col. 1:16–17).

The second clause in this verse parallels the opening clause in Col. 3:24. Slaves were commanded to work as for the Lord 'knowing that from the Lord you will receive the reward of the inheritance' (Col. 3:24a). Here masters are to grant justice and equality, **knowing that you also have a master in heaven**. Addressing believing slave owners, the household code reminds such individuals that they are not autonomous oligarchs, but they are servants of a heavenly master. Thus, whereas slaves were reassured that if they performed their duties with sincerity they would become heavenly heirs, by contrast masters are instructed to carry out their duties in a just and equitable manner because they are slaves of a heavenly master. The strategy is to invert the present power relations – masters are slaves in heaven and slaves are heirs of a heavenly inheritance. In this sense the final clause presents an eschatological sanction for earthly masters. In the realm where there is no partiality they will be treated according to the standard by which they have treated their slaves in the present life.

Is the household code subversive? Taken at face value the answer is 'no'. It commands wives to be submissive to husbands, children to obey parents, and slaves to work willingly for masters. There appears to be no overt challenge to the prevailing social fabric. However, at many levels this code flattens the societal distinctions, and goes so far as to invert the structure of those who are privileged and those who are without rights. Written from a position of the powerless, the subversion of the dominant and oppressive structure of society through belief in an inverted eschatological order was perhaps the only plausible way to confront the prevailing power structures. As such the household code need not be read as antithetical to the general principle of equality stated in Col. 3:11. Rather, the instructions given in Col. 3:18–4:11 were seen as interim measures, legislating for a present that was passing away prior to the arrival of the future inheritance that promised equality under the lordship of a heavenly master in whom there was no partiality.

16. FINAL INSTRUCTIONS FOR THE PRESENT LIFE   (4:2–6)

(2) Hold fast to prayer, being watchful in it with thanksgiving. (3) Pray, at the same time, also for us, that God might open for us a door for the word, to speak the mystery of Christ, because of which also I am bound, (4) that I might reveal it as it is necessary for me to speak. (5) Walk in wisdom to those outside, redeeming the time. (6) Let your speech, always with grace, be seasoned with salt, to know how it is necessary for you to answer to each one.

This section concludes the major topic commenced in Col. 3:1, concerning how believers who have already been raised with Christ are to live out their current existence, which, however, they are not to see as their ultimate reality. Within this larger section (Col. 3:1–4:6) readers have been provided with ethical instructions in forms that draw upon existing Greco-Roman tropes. This includes lists of vices (Col. 3:5, 8), and virtues (Col. 3:10), as well as drawing on the form of the household code (Col. 3:18–4:1). The patterns of behaviour required of believers in specific settings have been described, such as communal worship where mutual teaching and admonition should take place alongside rendering praise to God in musical form (Col. 3:16). Similarly, the extended instructions to slaves, living in typical domestic situations, reveal that from the author's perspective they are to render wholehearted service, since their work is in reality for the Lord, and not for their human masters (Col. 3:22–25).

The final instructions, unlike the preceding household code, are not addressed to specific groups but are directed to every member of the community in Colossae. The two emphases in Col. 4:2–6 are prayer and mission. These are not discrete themes, but are fundamentally intertwined since prayers are specifically requested for the spread of the gospel message and also in order that Paul might have the opportunity to speak of 'the mystery of Christ' (Col. 4:3b). The generalized appeal to 'walk in wisdom' (Col. 4:5a) summarizes many of the specific appeals and instructions given in Col. 3:1–4:6, and it follows on from the household code as a particularly appropriate way of encapsulating the overall principle operative in that section (see Lincoln 2000: 661). Furthermore, there is a sense of eschatological urgency present here with the command to be 'watchful' (Col. 4:2), and through the more enigmatic instruction to redeem the time (Col. 4:5). In this way these final ethical instructions do more than simply summarize the discussion of Col. 3:1–4:6 (or even the entire letter to this point). This section also extends the author's appeal to the Colossians to continue walking in Christ (Col. 2:6) by informing them that through their prayers, they are integral to the Pauline mission, and through their upright behaviour and gracious speech they too are able to respond to those outside (Col. 4:5). Perhaps also the injunction for measured speech is intended to offer counsel on how to respond to those pressurizing the Colossians to adopt a hybrid form of the Pauline gospel mixed with elements drawn from the local mystery cults. It is for this reason that the figure of Paul once again declares that his purpose is to announce 'the mystery of Christ' (Col. 4:3b), and simultaneously co-opts the Colossians as his co-workers through their prayers on behalf of the proclamation of the Christ-only gospel preached by Paul.

2 Constancy in prayer forms the opening appeal of this section, issued with the command **hold fast to prayer**. The Greek syntax places the imperative verb after the dative definite article and noun, τῇ προσευχῇ, **to prayer**. In this way prayer is emphasized. Previously in the letter it is the prayers of Paul and his companions on behalf of the Colossians that have been described (Col. 1:3, 9). Now the focus falls on the duty of the Colossians to be actively engaged in prayer. The command is given using the present imperative, **hold fast**, which communicates a general and continuous command. The Greek verb προσκαρτερεῖτε denotes an attitude of persistence, and means to 'be busily engaged in, be devoted to' something, or 'hold fast to, continue in, persevere in something' (BDAG: 881). The plural form of the imperative suggests that the prayer envisaged here is a communal activity, and it may be part of the mutual 'teaching and admonition' that was mentioned earlier (Col. 3:16). Thus, '[t]his directive enjoins the church to call on God constantly in prayer' (Sumney 2008: 256). This emphasis on the importance of prayer may have a dominical origin (Mt. 6:9–13//Lk. 11:2b–4; Mt. 17:21//Mk 9:29; Mt. 26:36–46//Mk 14:32–42//Lk. 22:40–46). Whether or not such a link existed, it is clear that the notion of constant prayer is a prominent Pauline theme (Rom. 1:9–10; Eph. 6:18;

1 Thess. 5:17). In the Pauline communities, prayer was a spontaneous and often spirit-led utterance (Rom. 8:26; 1 Cor. 14:15; Eph. 6:18; cf. Jude 20).

Not only are the Colossians commanded to persist in prayer, they are also told to maintain an attitude of alertness: **being watchful in it with thanksgiving**. The verb **being watchful** γρηγορέω is a neologism in Hellenistic Greek, and it refers to one who is wakeful or watchful and 'is drawn from the imagery of guard duty (Neh. 7:3; 1 Macc. 2:27; Mark 14:34, 37)' (Dunn 1996: 262). It is used in Christian literature to refer to watchfulness prior to the *parousia*. Lohse rejects any eschatological emphasis in this context, stating that the command 'is not motivated here by a reference to the day of the Lord which will occur suddenly and unexpectedly' (Lohse 1971: 165). However, given the instruction later in this section to redeem the time (Col. 4:5) and the fact that this term γρηγορεῖτε is also used in the Gethsemane scene (Mk 14:38//Mt. 26:41) where there is a link with prayer and an overtone of imminent crisis, it appears that an eschatological aspect is present, and that this urges believers to conduct themselves correctly prior to the return of Christ.

The pronoun in the command **being watchful in it** is a reference back to prayer, in the opening clause. The participle is given imperative force here, forming a typical Greek construction where a following participle takes on the force of the preceding verb. Hence a second command is given in relation to prayer. Not only is constancy commended, but also alertness. Therefore, watchfulness in community prayer is perhaps seen as a remedy to a self-serving focus on one's own visionary experiences. The alertness that the Colossians are to practise is not to be burdensome, but should be accompanied **with thanksgiving**. The reason for such 'thanksgiving' is not explained in the present context. However, more widely in the letter, the injunction to give thanks is seen as part of the response believers offer to God in consideration of the new life they now freely experience in Christ. Hence, they have already been commanded to give thanks joyfully to the father 'who has qualified you for a share of the inheritance' (Col. 1:12). They are also to be 'abounding in thanksgiving' (Col. 2:7) knowing that they have been established in Christ. Moreover, just prior to the household code the Colossians have been instructed that the totality of their actions are to be done 'in the name of the Lord Jesus, giving thanks to God the father through him' (Col.

3:17). Therefore, once again the emphasis on thanksgiving comes to the fore here. The perseverance and alertness in prayer is not to be characterized by trepidation, but by joyful thanksgiving. Presumably this is because prayer is itself another divine gift that allows access to God, and reflects their new status of being in Christ. Thus, as has already been stated, since the peace of Christ now reigns in believers' hearts the only response is to 'be thankful' (Col. 3:15).

3 The theme of prayer continues in the verse, but here the thought moves from the general topic of prayer to that of requesting a specific supplication from the Colossians on behalf of the wider Pauline mission. The participle that commences this verse, **pray**, προσευχόμενοι, still derives imperatival force from the opening imperative verb in Col. 4:2 (Sumney 2008: 257). The particle ἅμα signals temporal simultaneity and is also used in this sense in Acts 24:26; 27:40; Phlm. 22; 1 Tim. 5:13. The temporally overlapping actions envisaged here that are to take place **at the same time** are both acts of supplication. Therefore, during general community prayer, the believers are encouraged to pray **also concerning us**. In this way the letter calls upon the Colossians to offer up prayer for Paul and his companions. Various prayer requests are made in the Pauline epistles. The use of the plural pronoun **us** occurs only in letters that identify a co-sender in the opening greeting. In the Thessalonian correspondence the letters are sent from Paul, Silas, and Timothy. These two letters have prayer requests with a plural pronoun: 'brothers, pray [also] concerning us' (1 Thess. 5:25); 'finally pray, brothers, concerning us' (2 Thess. 3:1). By contrast, in Romans, sent in the name of Paul alone, the prayer request occurs in the following form: 'strive together with me in prayers concerning me to God' (Rom. 15:30; also 2 Cor. 1:11; Phil. 1:19; see Moo 2008: 321). Hence, in Colossians, which is sent in the names of Paul and Timothy (Col. 1:1), one finds a plural prayer request. This conforms to the general pattern in the other Pauline epistles as described above. Thus, the request, **pray, at the same time, also for us**, envisages prayer being offered at least both for Paul and Timothy, and perhaps even for a wider circle of associates.

The request for prayer is explicitly linked to the Pauline mission, **that God might open for us a door for the word**. The understanding of prayer that is present in this clause is that it is a supplication for

God to act in way that facilitates the spread of the gospel. Such supplicatory prayer does not reflect the full understanding of early Christian prayer practice as reflected either in this epistle, or the wider Pauline corpus. In the previous verse (Col. 4:2), and more prominently elsewhere in the letter, prayer is seen as a means of rendering thanks to God: 'we give thanks to God…always praying concerning you' (Col. 1:3). The specific request is that God **might open for us a door for the word**. The metaphor of 'opening a door' describes entrance and access, and is used elsewhere in Pauline writings (1 Cor. 16:9; 2 Cor. 2:12). Barth and Blanke argue that the image is not one of removing hindrances, but that God would make effective the proclamation of the previously hidden mysteries (Barth and Blanke 1994: 453). It is not obvious that such a sharp distinction is intended. Given the reference to Paul's imprisonment at the end of this verse, it is more natural to read this request both as a plea for God to make the proclamation effective, and to remove those obstacles that impede the spread of the gospel. Describing the gospel message as **the word** is a recurrent expression in this epistle (Col. 1:5, 25; 3:16), and prominent elsewhere in the Pauline writings (cf. 1 Cor. 1:18; 2:4; 2 Cor. 1:18; Phil. 1:14). In this way 'the word' is a Pauline technical term for the message that Paul and his followers proclaim, and it functions metonymically for the salvific work of Christ that results in people becoming members of the community of faith.

Such shorthand terminology is glossed here as praying that Paul and his associates might have an opportunity **to speak the mystery of Christ**. Although elsewhere in the Pauline corpus it can be stated that Paul's message was not in words alone, but that it came with power (1 Thess. 1:5), the primary way in which the gospel is communicated is through oral proclamation (Rom. 10:14–15). Therefore the term **speak**, λαλέω, describes the principal way in which the early Jesus movement transmitted its claims through speech-acts. If hearers assented to the spoken message and were initiated into the community, then they were viewed as having received salvation and entering into a new mode of existence. In essence this is **the mystery of Christ** that Paul strives to proclaim effectively. In this letter **the mystery** has been described earlier: 'the mystery that has been hidden away' (Col. 1:26); 'the wealth of the glory of this mystery' (Col. 1:27); and 'the mystery of God' (Col. 2:7). Two things are striking. First, that this theme is resumed at this point, and second, whereas as it had been described as 'the mystery of God' it is now called 'the mystery of Christ'. The language of **mystery** may well be used here again to counter claims that Colossian believers needed to supplement their faith with some of the rites of local mystery cults (Col. 2:16–18). Instead, the author claims that the entire mystery required for salvation is made known through proclamation **of Christ**. Hence speaking of 'the mystery of Christ' is in essence a proclamation of the author's christological beliefs and their salvific ramifications. The link between divine action and the glorification of Christ is prominent. As Moo states, 'God is therefore here once more defined in christological terms: God opens the door for the mystery of Christ to be proclaimed' (Moo 2008: 323).

This verse concludes with one of the clearest descriptions in this letter of Paul's circumstances, **because of which also I am bound**. The Greek construction emphasizes both the cause, **because of which**, and the consequence that results in Paul's present state. The perfect verb δέδεμαι is stative, reflecting an action begun in past but having enduring force in the present, **I am bound** (Harris 2010: 168). It is not until this stage in the letter that readers learn that Paul is portrayed as writing to the Colossians while being incarcerated. Scholars have long debated which period of imprisonment is being referred to here. Drawing on the description in the book of Acts, either a Caesarean (Acts 23:31–26:31) or a Roman (Acts 28:16, 30–31) imprisonment are suggested, or an Ephesian imprisonment is inferred on the basis of the length of the stay in that location (Acts 19:10). The latter is more geographically proximate to Colossae and hence lends weight to the idea that Paul can receive information of the progress of the gospel in Asia Minor, and oversee his mission even while in prison. Against an Ephesian setting is the fact that such an imprisonment is a hypothesis. Those who argue for a Roman imprisonment see Colossians stemming from a later period in Paul's life and hence Rome is seen as the likely location. The argument is obviously somewhat circular here. The possibility of Caesarea has few supporters. Moreover, if Colossians is written in the name of Paul and not by the apostle himself, then the reference to a period of imprisonment is perhaps a way of adding an air of authenticity to the letter without necessarily having any specific location in mind.

More significant than the place of imprisonment is the fact that Paul's state of being imprisoned is said to be **because of** proclaiming 'the mystery of Christ'. Hence it appears that the unrelenting and uncompromising proclamation of the gospel is seen as what has led to Paul being placed in prison. Thus, '[i]t was this preaching which had incited the opposition to him and resulted in his imprisonment' (Dunn 1996: 264).

4 The foregoing reference to Paul's imprisonment is in many ways a parenthetical comment describing the purpose of the imprisonment being endured. However, in this verse the main train of thought is resumed. The Colossians have been urged to pray on behalf of the Pauline mission that God would make effective Paul's proclamation of 'the mystery of Christ'. That thought continues with two clauses. The first reveals a further purpose **that I might reveal it**, while the second, **as it is necessary for me to speak**, describes the means. The verb φανερώσω, **I might reveal**, is particularly appropriate to describing the unveiling or revelation of a mystery, especially in relation to a religious mystery that was not accessible to the uninitiated, and which had been declared to have 'been hidden away' (Col. 1:26). Therefore the term conveys an apocalyptic meaning in terms of the disclosure of divine knowledge. The antecedent of **it** is to be understood grammatically as 'the mystery of Christ', rather than the word – although the two are closely connected in Col. 4:3. The pronoun αὐτό, 'it', is neuter agreeing with the neuter μυστήριον, and not the masculine λόγος.

The second clause describes the manner in which the mystery is to be revealed, namely, **as it is necessary for me to speak**. The third person impersonal verb δεῖ probably does not describe compulsion here (Moo notes that δεῖ does not have the sense of divine determination as frequently in Paul's writings as elsewhere in the New Testament – Moo 2008: 326). Instead, it is focused upon the appropriate mode of speech to produce the maximum effect of the proclamation of the mystery. The main purpose of these three verses (Col. 4:2–4) has been actively to involve the Colossians as partners in the Pauline mission through requesting their prayers for its success. The strategic reference to 'the mystery of Christ', and the description that it is being revealed by Paul's proclamation of the gospel, requires their intellectual assent that the Pauline proclamation has a divine origin. Furthermore, the apocalyptic language places Paul in the role of a revelatory figure, and thereby ascribes to him a special role in the divine plan.

The generalized opening injunction to 'hold fast to prayer' (Col. 4:2a) quickly moved to a specific request to become partners with Paul in his proclamation of the gospel through prayer. Acceptance of the view that the message announced by Paul is the act of revealing the full divine mystery undercuts any tendency to subscribe to other supplementary religious rites in order to heighten one's spiritual experiences. Previously this syncretistic tendency had been confronted directly in the letter (Col. 2:6–19). Here the strategy is more subtle. The Colossians are invited to support and subscribe to the Pauline message in its entirety (Lohse 1971: 165). In this way, by being engaged in prayer for the success of Paul's mission, the Colossians are being reshaped as more centrist Pauline believers.

5 The focus shifts from prayer for the Pauline mission to the conduct of believers in Colossae towards those who are not part of their believing community. In this way the theme of 'mission' continues, but it is related to way the Colossians present the message about Christ to those who, although living in the same location, are not believers. The final instructions concerning the conduct of those who 'have been raised with Christ' (Col. 3:1) continue with a further behavioural imperative: **walk in wisdom**. Here the imperative **walk** is used in a moral sense (Harris 2010: 169), denoting the mode of conduct to be adopted. The term περιπατέω is used four times in the letter (Col. 1:10; 2:6; 3:7; 4:5), and on each occasion it is used metaphorically as a description of conduct. In the context of the vice list, the reference in Col. 3:7 is used to depict the former immoral lifestyle of the Colossians (at least from the author's perspective). In the other three examples it is used to exhort believers to behave in a manner that aligns with their new life in Christ: 'to walk worthily of the Lord' (Col. 1:10); 'walk in him' (Col. 2:6). In the present context the metaphor is not tied as explicitly to the new mode of existence in Christ, but describes the mode of behaviour as conducting oneself **in wisdom**. The concept of 'wisdom', σοφία, is a prominent theme in the author's thought (Col. 1:9, 28; 2:3, 23; 3:16; 4:5), and in the first example has already been linked with the verb 'to walk', περιπατέω, 'that you might be filled with the knowledge of his will in all *wisdom* and spiritual insight *to walk* worthily of the Lord' (Col. 1:9b–10a). The recollection here of a central theme with which the body of the letter commenced, after the opening greeting and thanksgiving (Col. 1:1–8), as part of the final ethical exhortation in the body of the letter here in Col. 4:5, is probably an intended *inclusio* (Dunn 1996: 265). Therefore, the author emphasizes that there is to be an intentionality in the mode of life believers adopt in consideration of their new-found life in Christ.

The type of **wisdom** that is required is not described here. Rather, the term is taken to be self-evident. It has been suggested that wisdom themes stand behind the hymnic material of Col. 1:15–20, although the term σοφία is notably absent in that context. However, elsewhere in the epistle 'wisdom' is seen to originate in Christ 'in whom are all the treasures of wisdom' (Col. 2:3), and it signifies the mode in which the 'teaching and admonishing' of fellow believers is to be undertaken (Col. 3:16). In this context, the exhortation to 'walk in wisdom' appears to have a more practical or pragmatic nuance. It relates to a form of behaviour that is both effective and sensitive **to those outside**.

This reference to 'outsiders', τοὺς ἔξω, is formed by use of a substantivized adverb (cf. the similar construction in Col. 3:1, τὰ ἄνω, 'the things above'). It functions as a generalized reference to non-believers who are not part of the community in Colossae that had come to faith in Christ. It is unlikely that this functions as a specific reference to the 'false teachers' who were promoting the philosophy that is opposed in the letter (*contra* Gnilka 1980: 230–31). Instead, and in somewhat stereotypical terms for new religious movements, the community adherents are defined over and against those who are seen as being beyond its boundaries. Here the language of 'outsiders' reflects a common way of defining those who do not share the beliefs of the in-group, although other designations for outsiders are also used in the New Testament and Jewish literature of the period. Those beyond the insider community can be described as those of the night (1 Thess. 5:5, 7), or 'sons of darkness' (1QM I.1). Here, while there is a distinction between community members and 'those outside', the reference to outsiders is not pejorative. Instead, the Colossian believers are to conduct themselves in a manner that is attuned to the impact upon those who are not part of their community. However, the need to behave in a manner that is prudent towards non-believers may reflect some level of perceived antagonism among the addressees of the letter from those living in the same locale who do not share their beliefs.

The final clause in the verse is somewhat enigmatic. Coupled with the command to behave wisely towards non-group members is the participial phrase, **redeeming the time**, τὸν καιρὸν ἐξαγοραζόμενοι. Two issues arise. First, how does this clause relate to the preceding command, and second what is the intended meaning? Considering the first question, there are several ways of understanding the link between Col. 4:5a and Col. 4:5b:

1. means or mode   'by redeeming the time'
2. temporal   'as you redeem the time'
3. purpose   'so that you may redeem the time'
4. resultant   'thus you redeem the time'
5. resumptive imperative 'redeem the time'
6. attendant circumstances 'while you redeem the time'

A decision is not straightforward due to the ambiguous nature of this construction and the fact that there is no further explanation of this brief clause. The parallel expression in LXX Dan. 2:8 is often discussed in connection with this verse (Pao 2012: 296; Bormann 2012: 187). In that context Nebuchadnezzar sees through the ruse of his astrologers, when he orders them to tell him the content and the interpretation of his dream. He accuses them of playing for time, or perhaps more literally, trying to buy themselves time: ὅτι καιρὸν ὑμεῖς ἐξαγοράζετε (LXX Dan. 2:8). The sense is negative, with Nebuchadnezzar accusing his magicians and astrologers of stalling for time; by contrast, in Col. 4:5, buying or redeeming the time is a positive act. More importantly for determining the form of the construction, in LXX Dan. 2:8 the conjunction ὅτι, 'that', introduces a purpose clause, 'that you buy time'. Here the lack of a conjunction leaves the connection more ambiguous. However, one would perhaps expect to find a conjunction or connecting particle if means, purpose, or result were intended. While it is possible that the mood of the participle ἐξαγοραζόμενοι might derive imperative force from the preceding imperative, 'walk', περιπατεῖτε (cf. the opening participle in Col. 4:3), this is perhaps not the most natural way to understand the construction. There is little to split the second and sixth options, since the attendant circumstances would occur temporally at the same time. While either of these options is the most likely link with the preceding clause, the syntax of the construction is ambiguous, meaning that it is probably better to preserve the ambiguity in the translation.

The meaning of the phrase is also open to a number of possible interpretations. The nominal phrase 'the time', τὸν καιρόν, is one of the frequent temporal nouns used in *koinē* Greek. Another frequent temporal term, *chronos* (χρόνος), is typically seen as denoting chronological temporal references. In philosophical thought this term reflects 'time' that comes about due to the movement and measurement of change in celestial bodies (Plato, *Tim.* 37–41; Aristotle, *Phys.* IV.11.219b). In distinction, the wider use of καιρός is seen as referring to 'a point or period of time, a season, or an opportunity' (see BDAG: 497–98). However, such distinctions between the two terms are not always particularly sharp, and in the Pauline epistles they become virtually synonymous and can be used to form a *hendiadys*. Despite this flattening of the distinction, the term used here, καιρός, 'refers to eschatologically filled time, time for decision' (*EDNT*: II, 232).

The verb ἐξαγοράζω is used four times in the New Testament, with all occurrences being in Pauline writings (Gal. 3:13; 4:5; Eph. 5:16; Col. 4:5), with the final two examples probably being literarily dependent. The two examples in Galatians pick up the language of the manumission of slaves and apply this as a metaphor to the redeeming work of Christ where people are bought out of their slavery to sin. By contrast, the usage in Col. 4:5 and Eph. 5:16 does not have Christ's salvific redemption directly in view. The example in Col. 4:5 has the missionary or evangelistic endeavours of the Colossians in view. They are to 'buy back' or to 'buy up' the time available for the activity of proclaiming the gospel to those who are not members of the community of faith. In this sense the phrase **redeeming the time** not only looks back to the preceding phrase with its ethical imperative to 'walk in wisdom', it also links with what follows. Therefore, the 'buying back' of the time describes seeking an opportunity to speak in a gracious manner to those outside the community of faith. Hence, although the type of link with Col. 4:5a is ambiguous, a temporal relationship may be slightly preferred. This is because the καιρός language of the clause appears to describe finding a fitting opportunity to behave prudently to those outside and to speak to them in a gracious manner that gains a positive hearing for the message of Christ. Given the eschatological sense of the term καιρός elsewhere in the Pauline corpus, there may be a redemptive aspect to the meaning here. The Colossian believers are to seek to redeem (or perhaps to 'extend', or 'buy back') the time before the *parousia* in order that they might have greater opportunity for their own mission to the non-believers around them.

6 The Greek construction ὁ λόγος ὑμῶν πάντοτε ἐν χάριτι, which is translated here as **let your speech, always with grace, be...** is formed without a verb. As Harris notes, 'a vb. such as ἔστω ("let it be"; 3 sg. impv. of εἰμί) is to be supplied' (Harris 2010: 170). The words **with grace**, ἐν χάριτι, can be taken, as here, as expressing the manner in which the speech is to be offered, or it can be translated adjectivally 'let your speech always be gracious'. While the latter makes for the smoother English translation (cf. RSV, NEB, NAB), given the wider usage of χάρις terminology in the epistle it appears less likely that the author is describing 'pleasant' or 'gracious' speech, but is instead describing a proclamation that is empowered with divine grace (*contra* Moo 2008: 329–30). The three other occurrences of 'grace' describe the author's desire for the Colossians to receive the 'grace and peace' which come from God (Col. 1:2); or denotes the knowledge of 'the grace of God' that the Colossians received when they became believers (Col. 1:6); and occurs in the final prayer, where the author declares 'grace be with you' (Col. 4:18), which calls for divine blessing upon the Colossians. Therefore, given the usage elsewhere in the letter, and that the dative construction expressing instrumentality rather than an adverbial expression is most likely employed here, it appears best to understand this imperatival clause as reflecting the grace which they have received themselves.

The further aspect of the Colossians' speech is that it is to **be seasoned with salt**. The metaphor is not obvious, although being seasoned with salt is seen as something positive. Metaphors derive their force from links with literal meaning. This literal sense is drawn out in a question focusing on the physical property of salt: 'can that which is unsavoury be eaten without salt?' (Job 6:6). The physical use of salt in cultic practice may also inform the metaphor in this context, 'and make an incense as blended by the perfumer, seasoned with salt, pure and holy' (Exod. 30:35). Thus salt is regarded as a substance with a distinctive taste, and one that has sacrificial connections related to purity and holiness. Alongside the speech of believers being characterized by the grace of God, also it is not to be bland and insipid (cf. Mt. 5:13). Instead, in the same manner that salt carries a distinctive and unique savour, the proclamation made by believers is to have a markedly characteristic essence of its own.

The verse ends with a purpose clause that provides the reason why the Colossians should strive to speak in a manner that is characterized by grace and by its distinctiveness. The reason is in order **to know how it is necessary for you to answer to each one**. Harris understands the perfect infinitive **to know**, εἰδέναι, as 'telic', that is, it expresses an event or action as being complete in some sense, and hence he translates it as 'so that you may know' (Harris 2010: 171). Hence the final clause expresses purpose, which has a completed outcome resulting in appropriate speech. The purpose expressed again reveals the continuation of the focus upon mission-oriented perspectives being at the centre of the community's conduct. They are to be aware of **how it is necessary for you to answer to each one**. This construction is introduced in Greek by the interrogative pronoun πῶς, 'how', followed by the impersonal third person verb δεῖ, 'it is necessary', and the second person accusative pronoun ὑμᾶς, 'you', forming the phrase **how it is necessary for you**, or 'how one must'. This impersonal and generalized introduction shows that the instruction applies to every believer within the collective setting of the Colossian community. Sumney notes that the obligation of being ready to provide an **answer to each one** is stated with the household code still ringing in the ears of the recipients of the epistle. Therefore, the **each one** 'includes unbelieving husbands, parents, and masters, perhaps also unbelieving wives, children and slaves' (Sumney 2008: 263). Again the author does not offer abstract and platitudinous advice, but specific instructions that perhaps would have created tensions and difficulties for the powerless wives, children, and slaves in their concrete life situations.

What is required of these believers is to know how **to answer** ἀποκρίνεσθαι. The verb used here, ἀποκρίνομαι, is the common Greek term for a responsive speech or an answer. That such conversation is possible reflects permeable boundaries between the social worlds of insiders and outsiders. While believers may view themselves as already transferred to another realm due to their new life in Christ, their present reality was different. The Colossian believers were for the large part not socially autonomous, and were not protected by the power structures of society since many of them may have been drawn from various of the underclasses. As adherents to a new and socially deviant belief system, they may have been all too aware of their vulnerability. The advice given here is not to withdraw and hence to become a ghettoized community; instead, they are to follow the apostolic model of Paul. As one who was not socially bound but physically chained, he continued to seek God-given opportunities for proclaiming 'the mystery of Christ'. Similarly, the Colossians are to follow that same pattern of behaviour. Rather than being rebarbative in their response, they are to rely on the grace of God to speak a distinctive message to those around them.

At this point the body of the letter comes to its conclusion. The primary purpose of the letter has been to show that a correct understanding of the unique and cosmic significance of Christ leads to the moral formation of the Colossians in the image of Christ, in whom they now exist. This robust christology also sought to rebut the counterclaims of those who argued that the Pauline message required supplementation with teaching about heavenly mysteries. The author now turns to his concluding greetings. Although Col. 4:7–18 forms the letter's conclusion, it divides into a number of subsections. In Col. 4:7–9 the epistle authorizes Tychicus and Onesimus to pass on further information about Paul's situation. It is likely that these individuals were the letter bearers, although that is not explicitly stated. Next, Col. 4:10–15 contains a series of greetings along with authorial comments on the named individuals. The epistle then offers two specific instructions. The first is for the wider circulation of this letter and also for the exchange with the one addressed to the Laodiceans (Col. 4:16). Next follows a personal instruction to Archippus (Col. 4:17). The epistolary postscript is declared to be added by Paul in his own hand (Col. 4:18). This functions as an authorizing signature. He then makes a final reference to his imprisonment, before a final prayer for grace to be with the Colossians, which mirrors the opening greeting.

IV.
LETTER CONCLUSION (4:7–18)

17. AUTHORIZED REPRESENTATIVES
(4:7–9)

(7) Tychicus, the beloved brother and faithful servant and fellow slave in the Lord, will make known to you everything concerning me, (8) whom I sent to you for this very reason, in order that you might know the things concerning us, and your hearts might be encouraged, (9) with Onesimus the faithful and beloved brother, who is one of you: they will make known to you everything happening here.

7 This section commences by informing the Colossians that they might obtain further information about Paul through Tychicus, a figure who has not been mentioned previously in the epistle. There is a need to rearrange the Greek syntax here in order to produce a smooth English translation. Literally, the sequence in the Greek states, 'Everything concerning me he will make known to you, Tychicus the beloved brother and faithful servant and fellow slave in the Lord'. This reveals that the emphasis is first placed upon the mechanism for acquiring further knowledge about Paul's state of affairs, rather than the identity of the messenger. Moreover, each verse in this section contains a reference to the circumstances of Paul and his companions in their current location: 'everything concerning me' (Col. 4:7); 'the things concerning us' (Col. 4:8); 'everything happening here' (Col. 4:9). The introductory clause **everything concerning me**, τὰ κατ᾽ ἐμὲ πάντα, uses the preposition κατά in a referential sense 'denoting relationship to someth.' (BDAG: 513) to describe events that are currently occurring with respect to Paul.

Following the Greek word order, the next phrase offers the pithy statement, **he will make known to you**. This functions as a disclosure or communication formula. The author continues to focus upon the means put in place for the Colossians to learn about the current circumstances of the author and his associates. Still, the name of the authorized agent of communication is not stated at this point. The verb **he will make known**, γνωρίσει, 'is not a technical concept' (Barth and Blanke 1994: 477) either for declaring the gospel (although cf. 1 Cor. 12:3; 15:1), or for disclosing divine revelation. While it may be used in the latter sense in this epistle to describe God's divine communication of 'the mystery' (Col. 1:27), here it describes a simple act of communication, or information transference. There is a strong literary parallel between Col. 4:7–8 and Eph. 6:21–22. With the exception of the two Greek words καὶ σύνδουλος, 'and fellow-servant', in Col. 4:7, which are omitted in Eph. 6:21, there is a string of 29 identical words. This is the strongest evidence for the direct literary dependence between Colossians and Ephesians.

After emphasizing the communication process, the person entrusted with passing on the information about Paul is finally identified as **Tychicus**. The name **Tychicus**, Τύχικος, occurs five times in the New Testament – once in Acts as a companion of Paul on his third missionary journey (Acts 20:4), here in Colossians and in the parallel passage in Ephesians (Col. 4:7//Eph. 6:21), and twice in the Pastoral Epistles (2 Tim. 4:12; Tit. 3:12). The association with Paul, or Pauline circles, in each of these references suggests that the same figure is intended in these five cases. If the information in Acts is reliable at this point, then in the aftermath of the riot in Ephesus (Acts 19:38–40), and following a three-month period in Macedonia and Greece, Paul's intention was to return by sea to Syria. However, fearing an attack by 'the Jews' (Acts 20:3), the plans were changed in preference of an overland journey with travelling companions. Among those accompanying Paul are 'Tychicus and Trophimus from the province of Asia' (Acts 20:4). Here Tychicus is described as coming from the province of Asia. However, unlike Onesimus of whom it is stated that he 'is from you' (Col. 4:9), since there is no comparable note in relation to Tychicus being from Colossae 'one concludes that Tychicus was probably not from that city' (Gillman 1992b). In the Pastoral Epistles, Tychicus is portrayed as one of Paul's 'trouble-shooters'. In 2 Tim. 4:12 Tychicus is dispatched to Ephesus to deal with issues there, and he is possibly sent to Crete, apparently as a replacement for Titus who is to journey to meet Paul in Nicopolis (Tit. 3:12).

The information in Col. 4:7 is more descriptive of Tychicus' character and standing as a believer. The letter first describes him as **the beloved brother**. The term **beloved**, ἀγαπητός, is used four times in the letter, and on each occasion this adjective is used in reference to an individual who is a close and trusted associate of Paul. In one instance it is used to describe Luke as 'the beloved physician' (Col. 4:14). The adjective describes Epaphras as 'your beloved fellow slave' (Col. 1:7). Twice it is used as part of the stock phrase **the beloved brother**, in reference Tychicus (Col. 4:7), and Onesimus (Col. 4:9). As Sumney notes, while this description as 'beloved brother' does not attribute a unique position to Tychicus it does indicate that those described in this way 'are more than just fellow believers...they are especially close to him [Paul] and his mission' (Sumney 2008: 267).

The second descriptor states that Tychicus is not only regarded as 'the beloved brother', but also as being **a faithful servant**. The adjective **faithful**, πιστός, is used in the epistle to describe both individuals and groups. The Colossians are collectively described as 'faithful brothers in Christ' (Col. 1:2). In relation to Onesimus the adjectives 'beloved' and 'faithful' form a co-ordinated pair: 'the faithful and beloved brother' (Col. 4:9). However, the adjective 'faithful' is used in close connection with the noun 'servant', διάκονος, on one other occasion when it is employed in relation to an individual. Thus, Epaphras is depicted as one 'who is faithful on your behalf, a servant of Christ' (Col. 1:7). This connection between fidelity and the role of a servant may reflect the wider societal understanding of what constituted the prime quality of one engaged in service of another. In fact, Paul elsewhere explicitly lists faithfulness as the chief quality to be displayed by a person entrusted with a stewardship: 'it is required of stewards that they should be found faithful' (1 Cor. 4:2). Thus, leadership in the Pauline churches is conceived in terms of faithful service, and this conception of leadership is also embedded in the synoptic tradition (see Mk 10:45).

The final element in the description of Tychicus is that alongside being 'the beloved brother and faithful servant', he is seen also as **a fellow slave in the Lord**. Among the Pauline epistles the term **fellow slave**, σύνδουλος, occurs twice, both times in this letter (Col. 1:7; 4:7), first in relation to Epaphras and then here describing Tychicus. It is unlikely that it is intended as a technical term for one who had endured imprisonment for the gospel (O'Brien 1982: 247). This is not because it is applied to both Epaphras and Tychicus in this letter, since elsewhere the former is called a 'fellow prisoner' (Phlm. 23). Rather, it is because a few verses later the term 'fellow prisoner', συναιχμάλωτος, is used to designate Aristarchus (Col. 4:10), and to single out his status as one incarcerated alongside Paul. Therefore, the term is more likely to refer to those engaged in the work of the gospel. The use of the term **fellow** raises the question whether Tychicus is a 'fellow' slave with Paul, Epaphras, or with the Colossians. Paul's describes himself as a slave of Christ (Rom. 1:1; Gal. 1:10) referring to his work for the gospel. Therefore, it appears likely that both Tychicus and Epaphras are given this appellation because they share in Paul's missionary endeavours.

In the Lord could describe the work being done for Christ – thus, Tychicus is commended as 'a fellow slave in the work of Christ' (cf. O'Brien 1982: 247). However, given the wider use of 'in Christ' language throughout the epistle, it is more likely that here the phrase 'in the Lord' functions to signal that Tychicus is one of those who share a new status as a result of the existence that believers now enjoy because of the transformative work of Christ. In this way such service occurs in a different realm, one created and sustained by Christ himself. However, that status as a **fellow slave in the Lord** confers an authority derived from Christ, and it is mediated through association with the Pauline ministry (Sumney 2008: 269).

8 The description of Tychicus continues. However, there is a shift from the portrayal of his character and status, to an explanation of his purpose in relation to the Colossians. This resumes the statement in Col. 4:7a that he is the one who is to make known the current affairs and circumstances of Paul. Therefore, Tychicus is described, referring back to Col. 4:7a, as the one **whom I sent to you for this very reason**. The aorist verb **I sent**, ἔπεμψα, is an epistolary aorist, whereby the act of sending is an accomplished fact from the perspective of the recipients of the letter at the time when they read the correspondence. This raises the widely accepted idea that Tychicus and Onesimus were the letter carriers. Although this is not explicitly stated, there are good reasons to consider this possibility. First, there are no greetings sent from either Tychicus or Onesimus, they are simply commended. Secondly, the epistolary aorist assumes that these two co-workers will have been sent by the time that the Colossians received the letter, and hence it is perhaps natural to consider that they arrived with the letter. Thirdly, the wider infrastructure of the day used couriers to convey information, and there are examples of such people being not only passive carriers, but also authorized envoys. While it must be acknowledged that there is no explicit statement to the effect that Tychicus functioned as the carrier for this letter, it does appear that details in the way he is depicted are consonant with understanding him as fulfilling such a role. If that were the case, then it is likely he was also involved in the delivery of the letter to the Laodiceans (Col. 4:14). The expression **for this very reason** draws attention back to the previous verse where Tychicus' role is to communicate news of Paul's personal circumstances. If the detail in Acts 20:4 is correct in describing Tychicus' origin in the province of Asia, then while not apparently originating from Colossae he had local knowledge of the area more broadly, and this made him suited to the task at hand.

The phrase 'for this very reason' looks back to what was stated in Col. 4:7a, but also forward to the reiteration of the same idea in the next clause. Here the author reasserts that Tychicus is commissioned to supply additional information about Paul and his companions: **in order that you might know the things concerning us**. The move from the singular 'the things concerning me' (Col. 4:7a), to the plural **the things concerning us**, reveals that Paul wishes to communicate information not only about himself but also about his circle of associates. This suggests that certain members of Paul's inner circle may have had connections with Colossae specifically, or perhaps Asia Minor more broadly. If these statements have connections with reliable details of the Pauline mission, then one may see some corroboration for the idea that during the lengthy stay in Ephesus, Paul and his associates had actively engaged in spreading the gospel to the inland areas of the province. The Colossians are informed here that Tychicus is instructed to pass on further information about the Pauline group in their current location. It is **in order that you might know** about things not contained in the letter (cf. Col. 4:7a where the same verb is used) that the trusty lieutenant Tychicus has been sent to them. There is a significant textual variant here. Instead of **you might**

know the things concerning us, γνῶτε τὰ περὶ ἡμῶν, supported by (א* 1241ˢ: ὑμ-) A B D*.ᶜ F G P 048 075 0278 33 81 365 1175 *al* it saᵐˢˢ, a number of manuscripts read γνῷ τὰ περὶ ὑμῶν 'that he might know the things concerning you', 𝔓⁴⁶ א⁽²⁾.ᶜ C D¹ Ψ 1739 1881 𝔐 f vg sy saᵐˢˢ bo. While the external evidence is not compelling for one reading in preference to another, the reading given here, 'you might know the things concerning us', better fits the context of informing the Colossians that Tychicus will communicate details about Paul's circumstance. If the alternative reading is accepted, then the statement 'that he might know the things concerning you' is not a source of encouragement, as is claimed in the final clause of the verse, but a declaration that Tychicus has been sent on a surveillance mission. This appears to be out of line with what is stated elsewhere in Col. 4:7–9; as Metzger states, 'the reading adopted for the text is congruent with the writer's declared purpose of Tychicus's visit' (Metzger 1994: 626). In contrast to this view, Head provides a strong defence for the reading γνῷ τὰ περὶ ὑμῶν being the oldest form of the text (Head 2014: 303–15).

However, as the final clause of the verse makes clear, this is not the communication of knowledge for its own sake. The letter states that the Colossians are to have access to this further information not only so they can know further details of Paul's work. Such news is both for information **and** so **your hearts might be encouraged**. The encouragement of the hearts of the Colossians was central to Paul's prayer earlier in the epistle (Col. 2:2), and here his circumstances, which on the surface are a cause for concern, are seen rather as a sense of encouragement to the Colossians. In this context the specific cause of encouragement is not described. It is likely to be related to the continuing work of Paul's mission even while he is imprisoned. The connection is not as explicit as is the case in other letters written from prison ('my bonds have become known throughout the whole Praetorium', Phil. 1:13). The verb 'might be encouraged', παρακαλέσῃ, conveys the idea of 'exhorting, admonishing, encouraging' (BDAG: 764–65; *EDNT*: III, 23–27). It is a prominent term in the Pauline corpus, and is used to inform recipients of his letters that Paul wishes to instil a positive and cheerful sense in his readers (Rom. 12:8; 2 Cor. 1:4b; 7:6a; Eph. 6:22; 1 Thess. 3:2, 7; 2 Thess. 2:17). This act of sending Tychicus is, the Colossians are told, to encourage **your hearts**. Here the heart is understood as the seat of emotion, especially of positive emotion that results in courage and good cheer. Thus, the Colossians are to be informed of Paul's circumstances as a way of encouraging them in their own faith and commitment to the Pauline mission through the proclamation of the gospel message.

9 A second figure is introduced here through the prepositional phrase **with Onesimus**. Elsewhere in the Pauline corpus the name **Onesimus** occurs only in the brief letter to Philemon (Phlm. 10). Despite this sole reference in the letter to Philemon, Onesimus is the subject of the entire epistle, although Paul refrains from mentioning him by name with any frequency. Despite the occasional denial that these two figures are identical (see O'Brien 1982: 248), the case that the same person is intended is strong, regardless of the authorship of Colossians. The name is not particularly common in early Christian literature, and the Onesimus in both references is associated with Paul and has connections with people mentioned in both the letter to Colossians and that to Philemon, such as Epaphras (Col. 1:9; 4:12; Phlm. 23), Mark (Col. 4:10; Phlm. 24), Demas (Col. 4:14; Phlm. 24), Luke (Col. 4:14; Phlm. 24), and Archippus (Col. 4:17, Phlm. 2). Based upon this identity of the figure named in both epistles, then it is possible to infer that the Onesimus named in Col. 4:9 had been a fugitive slave who had fled to Paul. Onesimus had been sent back to his master, Philemon, by Paul, with a request for clemency since the slave was now a fellow believer who had rendered comfort to Paul (Phlm. 11). Since there is no reference to Onesimus' slave status in Col. 4:9, it may be the case that 'the master indeed released Onesimus for temporary service to Paul's mission' (Lampe 1992: V, 22). If that is the correct scenario, then here ostensibly Onesimus is being returned to Philemon, and along with Tychicus he is entrusted with the responsibility for delivering the letter to the Colossians. Alternatively, it has been suggested that the pair of delegates are carrying simultaneously both the letter to the community at Colossae and the personal note to Philemon. If Colossians is not written by Paul, then the author has read Philemon and wishes to create an air of harmony by presenting Onesimus without reference to slave status, leaving readers to infer that Paul's request to Philemon had been granted and that this former slave had become instrumental in the Pauline mission. This could be a powerful message to a community constituted largely of slaves (Col. 3:22–25).

The description of Onesimus is not as fulsome as the preceding comments concerning Tychicus. He is described as being **the faithful and beloved brother**. Whereas Tychicus was portrayed as 'the beloved brother and faithful servant' (Col. 4:7), here the same two adjectives are coordinated to qualify the noun of fraternal relationship. As already noted, the adjective **faithful** is particularly apt as a description of loyal service (Col. 4:7). It is possible that this is a reference to service Onesimus rendered to Paul during his imprisonment (Phlm. 13). Alternatively, it may be a generic description of his character. The expression **beloved brother** was the first element in the characterization of Tychicus (Col. 4:7). It was suggested that the term **brother** in Pauline vocabulary denoted somebody who was regarded as a fellow believer, while the adjective **beloved** might indicate a closer degree of association with the Pauline mission when applied to individuals. The decision not to label Onesimus as either a 'servant' or a 'slave' (cf. Col. 4:7) may reflect sensitivity concerning his former status. However, Sumney suggests that the author refrains from using those titles not because of concerns about Onesimus' former status, but because he 'does not have the same kinds of connections with the Pauline mission that Tychicus does' (Sumney 2008: 269). There is not sufficient evidence in the text to favour either of these explanations.

However, unlike Tychicus, Onesimus is explicitly identified as being a person **who is one of you**. Thus the letter understands Onesimus to be a member of the Colossian community. Such a connection would explain the choice of him to accompany Tychicus as an authorized communicator on behalf of Paul. If Philemon had not yet agreed to the release of Onesimus, then linking him with the Pauline mission could be part of the strategic plan to get Philemon to view his slave in a different light. Commentators have understood the reference to Onesimus here 'almost as an afterthought' (Dunn 1996: 273). However, it is possible that the decision to delay mentioning Onesimus is intentional to create a certain shock-value. If Tychicus and Onesimus were also the letter carriers, the community after hearing of Tychicus' elevated role in the Pauline mission may be amazed to hear that the fugitive slave returned to them was also a key figure in Paul's work. For the third time the task of Tychicus and Onesimus is reiterated, **they will make known to you everything happening here**. Unlike the description of the role of Tychicus in Col. 4:7, 'he [sing.] will make known to you' everything about me, here that role is shared, since **they** [Tychicus and Onesimus] **will make known**, γνωρίσουσιν details of Paul's circumstances and about the progress of his mission. Again, rather than being an afterthought, Onesimus is seen to have an equal role with the trusty co-worker Tychicus in communicating details about Paul and his mission to his fellow believers in Colossae. Thus Onesimus receives a clear and unequivocal commission as a key person in the Pauline circle.

18. GREETINGS FROM PAUL'S ASSOCIATES (4:10–14)

(10) Aristarchus my fellow prisoner greets you, and Mark the cousin of Barnabas (concerning whom you received instructions – if he comes to you receive him), (11) and Jesus, the one called Justus, those from the circumcision, these only are my fellow workers in the kingdom of God, these have been a comfort to me. (12) Epaphras, who is one of you, greets you – a slave of Christ, always striving on your behalf in prayers, that you may be established perfect and fully convinced in all the will of God. (13) For I testify about him that he has much toil on your behalf, and those in Laodicea, and those in Hierapolis. (14) Luke, the beloved physician, greets you, and Demas.

Lists of personal greetings are common in Paul's letters (Rom. 16:21–23; 1 Cor. 16:19–21; 2 Cor. 13:12; Phil. 4:21–22; Col. 4:10–14; 2 Thess. 3:17; 2 Tim. 4:21; Tit. 3:15; Phlm 23–24). Typically such greetings are sent from a wider group than the putative authors of the epistle, and only in 2 Thess. 3:17 is the greeting sent from Paul alone.

In Colossians one finds the longest list of greetings communicated to the recipients of an epistle. However, in Romans, apart from the list of greetings sent to the believers in Rome, there is an extensive list of people whom those in Rome are to greet. It is striking that the longest lists of named associates occur in the two letters that Paul is portrayed as sending to communities he had not visited. Such a practice may function strategically to establish rapport and commonality with the recipients to these letters by drawing attention to the common network of associates.

10 The list of greetings commences with reference to **Aristarchus my fellow prisoner** who **greets you**. The name **Aristarchus** occurs twice in the Pauline letters (Col. 4:10; Phlm. 24) and three times in Acts (Acts 19:29; 20:4; 27:2). Acts identifies Aristarchus both generally as a Macedonian (Acts 19:29; 27:4), and more specifically as coming from the city of Thessalonica (Acts 20:4; 27:2). Moreover, he was present during the riot in Ephesus (Acts 19:29). Therefore, Aristarchus is portrayed as a long-term associate of Paul, and he may have accompanied him on his trip to Rome. In Phlm. 24, along with Mark, Demas, and Luke, Paul identifies Aristarchus as 'my fellow worker'.

The description **fellow prisoner** has been understood as metaphorical by some commentators. In this vein, Sumney suggests that it is possible that the reference to Aristarchus in Acts 19:29 may stand behind this epithet. Hence the term 'fellow prisoner of war' would stress 'his more general willingness to stand for the faith in the midst of opposition' (Sumney 2008: 271). Furthermore, it is felt that the more complex and unusual term used here – συναιχμάλωτος, 'fellow prisoner of war' – is more likely to be metaphorical than would be the case had the author used the more familiar term σύνδεσμιος (see Hübner 1997: 118–19). However the Greek term σύνδεσμιος is not attested in Classical or *koinē* Greek (see LSJ: 1701), although the term συνδεσμώτης does occur (Thucydides, *Hist.* 6.60; Plato, *Rep.* 516c) with the sense 'fellow prisoner'. With the usage of the term συναιχμάλωτος in the Pauline corpus there is no indication that anything but a literal meaning is intended. Also, as Moo observes, when a metaphorical sense of being 'taken captive' is intended (2 Tim. 3:6; cf. Rom. 7:23; 2 Cor. 10:5) a cognate but different verb is used αἰχμαλωτίζω (Moo 2008: 338). Finally, the fact this term is reserved for only four individuals mentioned in the Pauline corpus may suggest that it describes a particular and infrequent situation, and is not describing all those battling for and imprisoned through their proclamation of the gospel.

The fact that here Aristarchus is described as **my fellow prisoner** may also be an indication that Colossians is written at a later stage than Philemon, and that by the time of the composition of Colossians, Aristarchus was imprisoned along with Paul. If that inference is correct, then it might also be the case that Onesimus had been released by Philemon and was sent back to Colossae after being a participant in the Pauline mission (see Col. 4:9). The designation **fellow prisoner** συναιχμάλωτος is used to describe four of Paul's associates: Andronicus and Junia (Rom. 16:7), Aristarchus (Col. 4:10), and Epaphras (Phlm. 23). It appears that Andronicus and Junia had been in prison with Paul (although the details concerning location and duration are unknown), and by inference most likely they had released by the time of the writing of Romans. There is, however, no indication that Epaphras had been released by the time Colossians was written, and the fact that he was not sent with Tychicus and Onesimus to Colossae may suggest that was due to his incarceration. The letter declares that Aristarchus is now captive in prison. It is from that location, as a fellow prisoner of Paul, that the letter states Aristarchus **greets you**. The term **greets you**, ἀσπάζεται, is 'the normal term used of greeting in the NT; forty-seven of its sixty occurrences are as an epistolary formula' (O'Brien 1982: 249). The term conveys the idea of the 'hospitable recognition of another (w. varying degrees of intimacy), greet, welcome' (BDAG: 144). Within the circles of early believers who constructed their identity through the fictive familial language of sibling relationships, such greetings are best understood as being on the level of intimacy shared within the family setting.

Governed by the head verb ἀσπάζεται, the Colossians are informed that **also Mark the cousin of Barnabas** greets you. There are perhaps three main reasons for the reference to **Barnabas**. The name **Mark** was a common Hellenistic and Latin name. Also, this **Mark** might have been less well known than his relative **Barnabas**. Thirdly, there may have been more than one Mark known to the Colossians. There are eight references to a figure called Mark in the New Testament (Acts 12:12, 25; 15:37, 39; Col. 4:10; 2 Tim. 4:11; Phlm. 24;

1 Pet. 5:13). Given the limited size of the early Jesus movement, it is likely that these all refer to the same person. Moreover, taken together they create a coherent composite picture that supports the identity of a single character. The second reference in Acts tells of Mark's role alongside Barnabas and Paul on their first missionary journey to Cyprus (Acts 12:25). It is not until the aftermath of the Jerusalem Council that the painful split between Barnabas and Paul took place. This revolved around Barnabas' desire to take Mark on their next journey. However, Paul's refusal stemmed from Mark's abandonment of the pair at Pamphylia during the first journey (Acts 15:37–38). Furthermore, the tension between Paul and Barnabas mentioned in Galatians may have been a contributing factor to the split. Dunn suggests differing attitudes to Mark may also be part of that dispute: 'there are dark hints in Gal. 2:11–14 that the breach between Barnabas and Paul had other, much more serious causes' (Dunn 1996: 276). Colossians adds one further piece to this jigsaw of details that explain the rupture between Paul and Barnabas, namely Barnabas' loyalty to Mark was based on family ties, for Mark was **the cousin of Barnabas**. The initial structure of the Jesus movement may have been based on family groupings, with Jesus' brothers having a prominent role in Jerusalem, and here Barnabas showing loyalty to his cousin Mark, whose mother Mary had a house in Jerusalem which was a meeting place for early believers including Peter (Acts 12:12; this may also explain Mark's link with the Petrine circle, 1 Pet. 5:13).

Given this composite portrayal of Mark, the parenthetical comment that follows the greeting from Mark to the Colossians is more readily understandable. The reason for understanding the concluding part of Col. 4:10 as parenthetical is due to the apparent resumption of the greetings at the beginning of Col. 4:11 with the reference to 'Jesus, who is called Justus' still governed by the verb at the beginning of Col. 4:10 (see Moo 2008: 339). The letter only alludes to the circumstances that have led the author to comment further about Mark. The parenthetical remark falls into two parts. First there is a recollection formula, **concerning whom you received instructions**. Here the comment calls upon the Colossians to remember previous directions given in regard to Mark. The term ἐντολάς, here translated as **instructions**, can have a stronger sense denoting 'commandments', either of human or divine origin (BDAG: 341). In the New Testament the predominant use is in reference to divine commands, and it can function as a virtual synonym for the Torah, or to describe specific ordinances that are part of the law (cf. Mt. 5:19; 22:34–40; Mk 12:28–34; Lk. 1:6; 18:20; 23:56). In fact, of the 67 instances of the term ἐντολή in the New Testament, only four, or perhaps five, refer to human commands or instructions (Lk. 15:29; Jn 11:57; Acts 17:15; Col. 4:10; and perhaps also Tit. 1:14, 'Jewish myths or commandments'). In these cases the lighter sense of 'order' or 'instruction' is more appropriate, than the more overtly divine sense of a commandment or ordinance.

The second part of the parenthetical comment is a brief summary of the gist of the instructions, namely **if he comes to you receive him**. Here the letter is silent about the background that led to this instruction. Given the split with Barnabas in relation to Mark, it is possible to speculate that Mark had become *persona non grata*, 'an unwelcomed person', in Pauline circles in the aftermath of the rift. The instructions received by the Colossians previously, and which are reiterated in the letter, may have effectively lifted a ban on receiving Mark. Moo suggests that the instructions about Mark may not have originated with Paul, since the construction is not direct, 'I have given you instructions about him' (Moo 2008: 339). Postulating a non-Pauline origin for these instructions seems unlikely, especially as Paul was unlikely to be bound by the orders of others. Even if Paul is not the author of the letter, it would appear that the purpose of this elusive comment is to portray an air of harmony in the early Christian movement. This would not necessitate the author of Colossians to have read Acts, for it appears the rift with Mark and Barnabas had left its imprint upon early believers. Presumably, Luke chose to minimize the split by only mentioning it fleetingly. By contrast, in Colossians the rupture is repaired with Paul requiring the Colossians to receive Mark. Such a rapprochement may have a basis in historical reality, given that elsewhere Paul describes Mark as 'my fellow worker' (Phlm. 24).

11 The list of greeting is resumed at this point: **and Jesus, the one called Justus**. Here the three names of Aristarchus, Mark, and Jesus are the nominative subject of the verb at the head of Col. 4:10, ἀσπάζεται, 'greets you' (Campbell 2013: 72). This is the only reference in the New Testament to an early believer named **Jesus**, known as Justus. However, the name 'Jesus' was common in the period, being the Greek form of the name Joshua. Perhaps it was natural for those who shared the name Jesus with the movement's foundational figure to be distinguished from Jesus of Nazareth. The complement, **the one called Justus,** supplies a second appellative, or a nickname for this figure. That name **Justus** presumably marked somebody out as being 'just'. Such a designation was not uncommon in the New Testament, and it was frequently taken by Jewish proselytes (Lightfoot 1886: 236). The unsuccessful potential replacement for Judas was known by multiple names 'Joseph, called Barsabbas, who was also known as Justus' (Acts 1:23). Similarly, James the brother of Jesus, was known as James the Just (*Gos. Thom.* 12), presumably both as an indication of his character, and to distinguish him from other members of the community called James (cf. James the brother of John, Acts 12:2). In this verse we learn only three things about this Jesus – his name, that he was known as Justus, and that along with Aristarchus, and Mark, 'he was from the circumcision'. This last detail suggests either that he was born a Jew, or that he was a gentile convert to Judaism who later converted to Christianity. Only in Mark's case, given his mother's home in Jerusalem (Acts 12:12), can a strong case be made that he was born Jewish, and not a proselyte to Judaism. It may be the case that Jesus, especially given his Jewish name, was also born a Jew. By contrast with Aristarchus, it might be more likely that he was first a gentile convert to Judaism. This is based upon his Thessalonian origin, and that Paul declares that the Thessalonians 'turned to God from idols to serve a true and living God' (1 Thess. 1:9). These last two suggestions are made on a slender evidential basis, and little hangs upon such possibilities.

The next two clauses cause significant exegetical problems. This is because they are co-ordinated with the material that precedes them in an unclear manner. It may be worth noting that there are no textual variants here, so ancient readers may not have felt the difficulty that has been identified by modern commentators. If taken at face value, then Aristarchus, Mark, and Jesus called Just are almost incidentally said to be Jews ('from the circumcision'), and then more wistfully Paul declares them to be his only fellow workers. Having declared these three alone to be his fellow workers, Paul then sends greetings from Epaphras, Luke, and Demas. This would suggest that Paul had more than three fellow workers after all. Depending on the punctuation of these clauses, there are at least three possibilities for understanding the sense (see Harris 2010: 178). The first option presents Aristarchus, Mark, and Jesus Justus as Paul's only co-workers, and incidentally mentions that they are Jewish. The other two options read the text as stating that they are the only co-workers from among 'the circumcision'. However, the two final options differ as to whether περιτομή denotes Jewish Christians (i.e. circumcised believers of Jewish origin who maintained Torah observance), or if it designates ethnic Jewish believers in Jesus, without implying anything about their commitment to Torah.:

1. Ἰησοῦς ὁ λεγόμενος Ἰοῦστος, οἱ ὄντες ἐκ περιτομῆς. οὗτοι μόνοι: 'Aristarchus…Mark… Jesus, the one called Justus, who are of the circumcision. These alone are my fellow workers…' (Barth and Blanke 1994: 5, 480–81; Dunn 1996: 274, 278; Wilson 2005: 295; NAB²).

2. Ἰησοῦς ὁ λεγόμενος Ἰοῦστος. οἱ ὄντες ἐκ περιτομῆς, οὗτοι μόνοι: 'Aristarchus… Mark… Jesus, the one called Justus. Of the Jewish Christians, these are the only ones who are my fellow workers…' (REB; NJB; NET).

3. Ἰησοῦς ὁ λεγόμενος Ἰοῦστος, οἱ ὄντες ἐκ περιτομῆς, οὗτοι μόνοι (NA²⁸; UBS⁴): 'Aristarchus… Mark… Jesus, the one called Justus. These are the only Jews among my fellow workers…' (O'Brien 1982: 245, 251; Moo 2008: 332, 341–43; Sumney 2008: 265, 272; Harris 2010: 178; NIV).

There is little doubt that either of the last two options resolves an exegetical difficulty. This might raise suspicions that these two options are preferred for that reason, whereas the first option preserves the apposition of the Greek clauses: 'these are from the circumcision, these alone are my fellow workers'. However, between options two and three the chief distinction is whether the phrase **who are of the circumcision** is best understood as designating the Jewish nation as a whole, or whether it refers to a subset – those Torah-observant Jews (or converts) who are believers in Jesus. The term περιτομή, **circumcision**, can be used in either sense in early Christian writings, but in general tends to be a designation for ethnic Jews (Skarsauna 2007: 12, 161). While some commentators devote space to attempting to resolve this issue (Moo 2008: 342–43), in many ways it is immaterial. If the trio of Aristarchus, Mark, and Jesus are the only co-workers of

Paul who are circumcised (although Dunn suggests that Aristarchus might not be included because of the statement of his origin in Acts 20:4, and presumably because he is mentioned before the other two – Dunn 1996: 278), then they are simultaneously ethnic Jews, and are also believers who are part of the Pauline circle. It seems inconceivable that these three associates of the Pauline mission could be portrayed as 'Jewish Christian' in the sense the term περιτομή occurs in Gal. 2:12 and Tit. 1:10, where it denotes an ultra-conservative group of Jewish believers in Jesus – the circumcision group, who are actively opposed to the Pauline mission. Thus, the second option does not appear possible, at least in that sense. Therefore, it seems most compelling to read this verse as designating Aristarchus, Mark, and Jesus as being ethnically Jewish. This is further confirmed when one considers the terminology employed here.

The term **circumcision**, περιτομή, occurs 34 times in the New Testament, and only five of these do not occur in the Pauline writings (see Jn 7:22, 23; Acts 7:7; 10:45; 11:2). In Pauline contexts, when used of physical circumcision rather than metaphorically of circumcision not made with hands (Col. 2:11) or of the heart (Rom. 2:29), it appears to denote a marker of Jewish identity. Circumcision is for those who keep the law (Rom. 2:25); it can be placed in synonymous parallelism with being a 'Jew' (Rom. 3:1); Abraham is 'father of the circumcised' (Rom. 4:12); Peter is the apostle to the circumcision in distinction to Paul's ministry to Gentiles (Gal. 2:7, 8, 9, 12); and Paul is circumcised on the eighth day as a member of the race of Israel (Phil. 3:5). These examples have a strong ethnic understanding of the term **circumcision**. While some cases may be ambiguous – such as Tit. 1:10, where it is unclear whether the 'rebellious people, … especially of the circumcision' are Jews or Jewish Christians – overwhelmingly the Pauline use of the term designates those males who were born or became Jews prior to becoming believers in Jesus. Therefore, taking the term in line with wider Pauline usage, then the statement appears to refer to Aristarchus, Mark, and Jesus as Jews. This would appear to exclude option two, which glosses **circumcision** as 'Jewish Christian'. Therefore, it appears that Paul identifies the trio named in Col. 4:10–11 as being Jews in origin, and at the time he writes he identified them as his only fellow workers who are with him offering support during his imprisonment.

Thus Aristarchus, Mark, and Jesus, at the time when the letter is written, are singled out – **these only are my fellow workers in the kingdom of God**. The description of **only** them has a slightly mournful note, although solace is derived from their support. They are described as **fellow workers**. Apart from 3 Jn 8, the other twelve occurrences of the term **fellow worker**, συνεργός, are to be found in Paul's epistles (Rom. 16:3, 9, 21; 1 Cor. 3:9; 2 Cor. 1:24; 8:23; Phil. 2:25; 4:3; Col. 4:11; 1 Thess. 3:1; Phlm. 1, 24). Some of the usages are generic, such as 'we are God's fellow workers' (1 Cor. 3:9). Specific people who are explicitly named as **fellow workers** in the Pauline epistles include, Prisca and Aquila (Rom. 16:3), Urbanus (Rom. 16:9), Timothy (Rom. 16:21; 1 Thess. 3:2), Titus (2 Cor. 8:23), Epaphroditus (Phil. 2:25), Clement (Phil. 4:3), Aristarchus, Mark, and Jesus (Col. 4:11, for the first two see also Phlm. 24), Philemon (Phlm. 2), and Mark, Aristarchus, Demas, and Luke (Phlm. 24). Among these thirteen individual, four are named twice (Timothy, Titus, Aristarchus, and Mark). It appears that the term **fellow worker**, συνεργός, was not a fixed title, with Luke being described by this term in Phlm. 24, but in the present epistles he is described as 'the beloved physician' (Col. 4:14). These co-workers are described as labouring **in the kingdom of God**. While the language of 'the kingdom of God' is not as prominent in Paul's writings as in the synoptic tradition, the phrase does occur nine times: Rom. 14:17; 1 Cor. 4:20; 6:9, 10; 15:24, 50; Gal. 5:21; Col. 4:11; 2 Thess. 1:5; see also 'his/his own kingdom', 1 Thess. 2:12; 2 Tim. 4:1; and 'the kingdom of Christ and of God', Eph. 5:5). Sometimes in Pauline writings the phrase occurs without the definite article – θεοῦ βασιλείαν or βασιλείαν θεοῦ ('kingdom of God') – but here the full form is given. Elsewhere in Colossians the only other explicit use of 'kingdom' language occurs in the phrase 'the kingdom of the Son of his love' (Col. 1:13). In that context it denotes the realm into which believers have been transferred as a result of their new existence in Christ. Here in Col. 4:11 the force of the preposition εἰς may be either that of purpose 'for the kingdom of God', or a spatial or locative use 'in the kingdom of God'. The earlier use of kingdom terminology (Col. 1:13) favours a spatial meaning here. The co-workers, like Paul, are those who now ultimately exist in the sphere of God's rule. This expression has probably not lost its full eschatological force (*contra* Lohse 1971: 172). Rather, as

427

Sumney suggests '[w]hile Colossians does not stress the imminence of the end, its interpretation of the place of believers in the world is fully eschatological and apocalyptic' (Sumney 2008: 273). Thus the current circumstances of Paul and his fellow workers are not to be seen as their ultimate reality – they labour in God's realm and not in earthly kingdoms.

There is a doleful tone to the comment that this trio of individuals are Paul's only co-workers at the point when the letter was written. However, this is immediately turned into a positive fact, **these have been a comfort to me**. Given Paul's focus on his mission, it is most likely that the comfort they bring is through the continuance of his work while he is incarcerated. The term **comfort**, παρηγορία, is a New Testament *hapax legomenon*. It does occur more widely in Greek literature, and can refer to an 'exhortation' or 'persuasion', but more commonly in the sense of a 'consolation' or something that is 'soothing' (Plutarch, *Cim.* 4; IG 7.2544 [Thebes]; Secundus, *Sent.* 6; Hippocrates, *Acut.* 53; Justin, *1 Apol.* 71). Therefore, despite his own imprisonment, Paul is portrayed as finding consolation in those who continue the work of his mission, and he affirms their status as those who now live under the rule of God.

12 The greetings resume again at this point, but because of the distance from the governing verb and the distraction of other phrases and comments, the verb **greets you**, ἀσπάζεται, is repeated here. The fourth personal greeting in this list is sent from **Epaphras**, who is described as being **one of you**. He is mentioned by name only in this letter (Col. 1:7; 4:12), and in the personal note to Philemon (Phlm. 23). Not only is he described as the one from whom the Colossians learnt about the new faith (Col. 1:7), he is also described as being **one of you**. Whether this means he was a native of Colossae (O'Brien 1982: 252), or that he was an important member of the community of believers he had established in the city (Moo 2008: 343) is not entirely certain. In another context Epaphras also sent his greetings to Philemon (Phlm. 23), and this reinforces the sense of the close connection that he had with the Colossian community (Morgan-Gillman 1992: II, 533).

A second aspect of Epaphras' identity is now described. Not only is he a person who is from Colossae is some sense, in terms of Christian identity he can also be called **a slave of Christ**. This servitude to Christ is a recurrent feature in the description of Epaphras. When he is first mentioned in the letter, he is described as 'our beloved fellow slave' (Col. 1:7). While Paul not infrequently describes himself as a slave of Christ (Rom. 1:1; Gal. 1:10; Phil. 1:1; Tit. 1:1), it is not common for him to depict others in this way (cf. Timothy, but in connection with Paul, Phil. 1:1). Designating Epaphras in this manner within the Pauline circle reveals the high regard in which he was held. Designating Epaphras' slave status may also hold another important resonance for Colossian readers. Labelling him as 'our fellow slave' (Col. 1:7) follows on from the description of him being 'one from you'. Not only does he share a Colossian connection, but he is also linked with many Colossian believers who appear to have been slaves (cf. the lengthy instructions to slaves Col. 3:22–25). Even those among their number who might be free have been reminded that they are slaves of a master in heaven (Col. 4:1). In this way identity as a slave is transformed, and celebrated as the peak status in the group. This is part of the author's value-inverting strategy, which not only reverses the positions of masters and slaves, but more radically negates all earthly levels of identity subsuming them under the ultimate relationship of union with Christ (see Trainor 2008: 82).

There is a textual variant here, with some manuscripts expanding the reference to Christ:

Χριστοῦ	Christ	$\mathfrak{P}^{46}$ D F G K Ψ 075 630 1505 1739 1881 $\mathfrak{M}$ it vg^{mss} sy; Ambst Hier
Ἰησοῦ Χριστοῦ	Jesus Christ	P 1241^{s} vg^{mss}
Χριστοῦ Ἰησοῦ	Christ Jesus	ℵ A B C I L 0278 33 81 104 365 629 1175 2464 lat

The weight of manuscripts that supports the shorter reading is indeed impressive, and the variant readings do appear to reflect 'a growing text', which has developed in two independent ways from the shorter reading Χριστοῦ.

The description moves from an overview of the identity of Epaphras to a description of his work. The first thing the Colossians are told concerning Epaphras' labour is that he is **always striving on your behalf in prayers**. The emphasis on this intercessory role stresses the pastoral concern that Epaphras has for the believers in Colossae. This work of prayer links Epaphras with Paul, who has already informed the Colossians that he himself is 'always praying concerning you' (Col. 1:3; cf. Col. 1:9). Furthermore, Paul has described his ministry using the same verb ἀγωνιζόμενος, **striving**, in order to present every believer 'perfect in Christ' (Col. 1:28–29). The term ἀγωνίζομαι denotes an active and strenuous struggle, often in connection with athletic or sporting contexts, with the athletic metaphor particularly prominent in 1 Cor. 9:24–27 (*EDNT*: I, 25–27). Thus, although Epaphras is absent, he is denoted as actively engaged in the well-being of the believers in Colossae through his struggle **on your behalf in prayers**. Here the plural προσευχαῖς, **prayers**, may be significant. In Col. 4:2, when elucidating a general principle, the Colossians were instructed to 'hold fast to prayer' (Col. 4:2), with 'prayer', προσευχή, being a singular term. Here the plural signals both constancy and repeated acts of intercession on behalf of the believers in Colossae.

Having described the intensity of Epaphras' continuing labour of prayer for the Colossians, the purpose of such intercession is now mentioned. The purpose given is twofold. First, the Colossians are told, it is so **that you may be established perfect**. Again there is a clear link with Paul's missionary goals. He, and those who work with him, strive in order that 'we might present every man perfect in Christ' (Col. 1:29). The same Greek term, τέλειος, **perfect**, is used both for Epaphras' purpose in prayer specifically for the Colossians, and for Paul's entire missionary work for all the Gentiles. Again a sense of commonality and solidarity is present between the work and goals of Paul and Epaphras. This may be part of the strategy of more comprehensively claiming the missionary work of Epaphras as an extension and representative of the wider Pauline mission. The verb σταθῆτε, here translated as **you may be established**, has the sense of 'causing to stand' as opposed to allowing something to fall down. It describes 'firmness' or 'stability', and conveys the sense of having a secure base or foundation. There is a textual variant here with the more widely attested aorist passive subjunctive form σταθῆτε, being replaced with the aorist active subjunctive στῆτε in the following manuscripts: ℵ² A C D F G Ψ. The change perhaps reflects grammatical norms at a later stage of *koinē* Greek, but there is little difference in meaning (Harris 2010: 179).

The term **perfect** is being used in a developmental sense in reference to believers' faith. Thus the first goal of Epaphras' prayer is that the believers in Colossae may develop towards a firmly grounded mature faith (see Harris 2010: 179). This has less to do with moral perfection, and is focused on a developed faith – although the former would be seen as a consequence of the latter (Col. 3:12–15).

The second and related goal of Epaphras' prayers on behalf of the Colossians is that they might also be **fully convinced in all the will of God**. The verb πληροφορέω, **fully convinced**, is not common in the New Testament, occurring only six times (Lk. 1:1; Rom. 4:21; 14:5; Col. 4:12; 2 Tim. 4:5, 17), although five of these are in the Pauline corpus. This probably explains why this somewhat uncommon term πεπληροφορημένοι, **fully convinced**, is replaced with πεπληρωμένοι, 'to be filled', in some manuscripts:

πεπληροφορημένοι, 'fully convinced'	ℵ A B C D*.c F G 33 81 104 365 1241s 1939 (1881) 2464 *pc* sy^{hmg}
πεπληρωμένοι, 'to be filled'	𝔓⁴⁶ D² Ψ 075 0278 𝔐 sy

Not only is the manuscript attestation stronger for πεπληροφορημένοι, **fully convinced**, but that term also better suits the point being made. Epaphras strives in his prayers in order that the Colossian might have full conviction about their faith. This may be a further attempt to portray the solidarity between Paul and Epaphras in refuting the claim that some were making that the Colossians needed to supplement their faith with another philosophy (Col. 2:6), and that they were lacking the mystical visionary experiences that others claimed to enjoy (Col. 2:18). As a corrective to this perceived tendency, Epaphras prays that the Colossians may have a solid conviction **in all the will of God**. It is not that the Colossians require instruction in **the will of God**; rather, the author asserts that what is necessary is for them to be fully convinced of it. Here **the will of God** overlaps with similar expressions, such as 'the mystery of God' (Col. 1:27). Therefore, Epaphras' prayers are presented as being fully aligned with the purposes of Paul as communicated in this letter. Paul by his writing and Epaphras by his prayers are both striving to see the Colossians established perfect and fully convinced of God's plan of salvation, in order that they might recognize Christ as the head of all things and realize that faith in Christ requires no further addition.

13 The assessment of Epaphras given here provides both attestation and authorization of his labour, while co-opting him as part of the wider Pauline mission. The declaration **for I testify about him** legitimizes and confirms 'his status as authorized bearer of Paul's teaching' (Trainor 2008, 84). In this way he is given an *imprimatur* as an agent of the Pauline mission. In many ways what is affirmed concerning Epaphras, **that he has much toil on your behalf**, may be a restatement of what was said in the previous verse, that he is 'always striving on your behalf in prayers' (Col. 4:12). It is, however, probable that with the statement **he has much toil**, more is intended than a simple repetition of describing his prayers. While prayer may well be part of the **toil** described here, the description here perhaps is broader and encapsulates the totality of his work on behalf of believers at Colossae. The term **toil**, πόνος, describes 'work that involves much exertion or trouble, *(hard) labour, toil*' (BDAG: 852). It is a relatively uncommon term in Greek literature. In the Pauline corpus it occurs only here, and elsewhere in the New Testament only additionally in Rev. 16:10, 11; 21:4. Unfamiliarity with this term almost certainly led to a number of fairly weakly attested variant readings. The two best supported are κόπον (D* F G 629) which has some overlap in its meaning 'activity that is burdensome, *work, labour, toil* (BDAG: 558), and ζῆλον 'zeal' (D¹ Ψ 075 33 𝔐 sy). In relation to the first of these variants a verbal cognate of κοπιῶ is used to describe Paul's work on behalf of believers: 'for which I labour' (Col. 1:29). However, the reading **toil**, πόνος, is almost certainly to be preferred. Thus, although not using the same terminology, both Paul and Epaphras are depicted as engaged in hard toil on behalf of their converts. This may be a further reason why some manuscripts bring the term in Col. 4:13 into alignment with Col. 1:29. Epaphras' labours are again given a narrower focus than Paul's. While Paul strives for 'every man', Epaphras is working **on your behalf** with direct reference to the Colossians.

However, the letter immediately widens Epaphras' sphere of activity. It is not solely on behalf of the Colossians, but also for **those in Laodicea, and those in Hierapolis**. During the first-century these two cities were much larger than Colossae, which had diminished in size and importance in comparison to its more affluent neighbours. Together these three Lycus Valley cities formed a wider network for commerce, and for social and religious interactions. The city of

Laodicea, which was situated 11 miles (18 km) to the northwest of Colossae, appears to have had a community of believers that was closely linked with the group in Colossae. The epistle describes Paul's work on behalf of the Colossians 'and those in Laodicea' (Col. 2:1). Perhaps more significantly, there is an instruction for a letter exchange, with the Colossians and the Laodiceans to read the correspondence sent to both communities (Col. 4:16). The Colossians are also instructed to greet the 'brothers in Laodicea' on Paul's behalf (Col. 4:15). Evidence for a Christian community at Laodicea is found also in Rev. 3:14–22.

By contrast, apart from this reference, the city of Hierapolis is not mentioned elsewhere in the New Testament. The reference to **those in Hierapolis** suggests the presence of a community of believers in that city. However, beyond that little can be said with any certainty concerning Christians in Hierapolis during the first century. The city of Hierapolis was more distant from Colossae than Laodicea, being located some 15 miles (24 km) north-north-west from Colossae, and thus there may not have been as close relations with the believers in that city in comparison to the closer location of Laodicea.

The reference to these three cities of the Lycus Valley may provide some partial insights into the social networks of early believers in Jesus, and perhaps also into the wider society itself. Epaphras, while closely connected with Colossae, also had links with believers in the wider geographical region. He may have been a key 'linking' figure between these fledgling communities of believers, perhaps sharing news and encouraging stories about the success and reception of the gospel message. It is clear that the letter to Colossians wishes to present Epaphras as the key promoter and propagator of the Pauline mission in the Lycus Valley.

14 This list concludes by briefly mentioning two people who also send their greetings to the Colossians, **Luke, the beloved physician, greets you, and Demas**. As was the case in Col. 4:12, where intervening comments made it necessary to repeat the governing verb **greets you**, here too after the extensive comments about Epaphras (Col. 4:12–13) the verb has to be repeated once more. The connection that **Luke** may have had with the Colossians is uncertain, but he was presumably sufficiently well known in Colossae for his greeting to be recorded in this letter, as well as in the more personal piece of correspondence to Philemon, where Luke is described as a 'fellow worker' (Phlm. 24). Although it is often inferred that Luke was a travelling companion of Paul, due to the narrative of Acts breaking into the first person plural form on several occasions, Luke is never mentioned by name in the text of Acts. In the New Testament he is named three times. He is described as a 'fellow worker' (Phlm. 24), as the only one with Paul during a period of imprisonment (2 Tim. 4:11), and here as **the beloved physician** (Col. 4:14). The term **beloved** was used in reference to Epaphras (Col. 1:7), Tychicus (Col. 4:7), and Onesimus (Col. 4:9). It describes a person who is highly valued by Paul. Although the term **physician**, ἰατρός, occurs seven times in the New Testament (Mt. 9:12; Mk 2:27; 5:26; Lk. 4:23; 5:31; 8:43; Col. 4:14), this is the only occasion where a specific person is named as a physician. Sumney notes that this profession 'either locates Luke among persons of some wealth or as a slave who had been educated to be someone's personal physician' (Sumney 2008: 276). Given Luke's apparent freedom to travel, he was presumably a free person at least by the time he is described in the Pauline letters. Despite suggestions that Luke acted as a physician to Paul (Abbott 1897: 332), or that he attended to Paul during his illness in Galatia (Lightfoot 1886: 241), there is no textual evidence to support these suppositions. Luke, by inference, is also seen by some as being a Gentile, since he is described as a co-worker in Phlm. 24, and more importantly since in Col. 4:11 he is not listed among the co-workers who are 'from the circumcision' (Moo 2008: 347). The language in Col. 4:11 is somewhat obscure, and hence it may be best not to draw such strong conclusions from such an uncertain piece of text.

Almost as an afterthought, after the third person singular verb ἀσπάζεται, **greets you**, was used to communicate Luke's greeting, the author adds another name, **and Demas**. The name Demas occurs three times in the New Testament, and on each occasion it occurs in close association with the name of Luke (Col. 4:14; Phlm. 24; 2 Tim. 4:9–10). While nothing beyond his name is stated about Demas in this context, in Phlm. 24 he is described as a 'fellow worker' along with Mark, Aristarchus, and Luke. The information concerning Demas in 2 Tim. 4:10 is tinged with sorrow and disappointment: 'for Demas has deserted me, loving the present age, and has gone to Thessalonica'. It is best not to read the terse reference in Col. 4:10

as an anticipation of the defection by Demas (Moo 2008: 348). Here he is simply a figure who passes his greetings on to the believers in Colossae. As such, he is viewed as part of the inner Pauline circle.

19. FINAL INSTRUCTIONS (4:15–17)

(15) Greet the brothers in Laodicea, and Nympha and the church in her house, (16) and when the letter is read among you, make sure that it is also read in the church of the Laodiceans, and that also you read the one from Laodicea. (17) And tell Archippus, 'Watch the ministry which you received in the Lord, that you fulfil it'.

A number of commentators (Moo 2008: 332) and English translations place Col. 4:15 as the final verse in the section Col. 4:10–15. The connection is based upon the continued use of the verb 'to greet', ἀσπάζομαι, in Col. 4:15, which is also used in Col. 4:10, 12, 14. However, there is a key difference. Whereas the three previous indicative forms of the verb were all used to send greetings to the Colossians, here the imperatival form ἀσπάσασθε commands the Colossians to send a greeting themselves. Commencing a new section at Col. 4:15 is the more common pattern among commentators (cf. Dunn 1996: 274; Sumney 2008: 265).

15 The Colossians are commanded to make two greetings in this verse. Presumably these are on Paul's behalf, and are not because they have been negligent in relations with the Laodicean community. However, it is possible that the author sees a close relationship with another Pauline community as a further way to resist a tendency to accept non-Pauline teaching. A more general instruction is given first: **greet the brothers in Laodicea**. The relationship between believers in Colossae and Laodicea appears to be based on more than geographical proximity. The letter speaks of Paul's 'struggle' on behalf of both communities (Col. 2:1), and it appears that Epaphras was a peripatetic teacher, well known to believers in both locations (Col. 4:13). The call for the Colossians to greet the Laodiceans has been seen as redundant, especially in light of the following verse where it is stated that a separate letter had been sent to Laodicea from Paul. This has perplexed some commentators, and led Lightfoot to suggest that since the greeting was not directed to a church in Laodicea, but to 'the brothers in Laodicea', that the Colossians were being encouraged to greet a family that had relocated from the city of Colossae to its near neighbour Laodicea (Lightfoot 1886: 243). This somewhat brilliant suggestion outstrips the evidence. Other possibilities exist. Given the concerns over syncretistic practices, the author may be commanding the Colossians to greet the Laodiceans for strategic reasons. If the Laodiceans had not succumbed to the tendency to supplement belief in Christ with mystical visionary practices from the local cults, perhaps by getting the Colossians to engage with the Laodiceans, the author is seeing that believers in that city can correct the Colossians' religious tendencies. Alternatively, others have suggested that the letter to the Colossians was actually a cipher, and that the intended recipients were the Laodiceans (see Lindemann 1983). From this perspective, both the greeting and the letter exchange mentioned in the next verse are ways of engaging with believers in Laodicea. The theory of an intended Laodicean destination is intriguing, but unnecessary. The absence of Hierapolis after linking it with Colossae and Laodicea two verse earlier (Col. 4:13; cf. Col. 2:1) is also puzzling. Perhaps the Colossians already had an existing relationship with the nearer neighbour Laodicea, but no mutual ties with Hierapolis. Moo suggests that Hierapolis is probably omitted in this context because 'the false teaching had not spread to Hierapolis and so Paul did not need to establish his apostolic authority there' (Moo 2008: 349). All of these suggestions reveal the gaps in the knowledge of commentators about a 'back story' that may have been entirely obvious to the letter's recipients. All that can be stated with certainty is that the Colossians are instructed to greet the community in Laodicea. The believers in Laodicea, like the Colossians, had not been visited by Paul (Col. 2:1), but had benefitted from the work of Epaphras (Col. 4:13), and further the epistle states there was a separate letter sent to that city (Col. 4:16).

After this general instruction, the Colossians are commanded also to greet **Nympha and the church in her house**. There is a significant textual issue here that affects how one understands the gender of **Nympha** (female) or 'Nymphas' (male). Both names in

Greek, in the accusative case in which they occur here, have the same spelling. They are, however, accented differently: Νύμφαν (female) or Νυμφᾶν (male). Consistent use of Greek accents is a relatively late phenomenon, and they typically begin to be found in a more consistent manner in minuscule (written with lower case letters) manuscripts dating from the ninth century onwards. Early manuscripts tend to be devoid of accentation. Rather, in earlier manuscripts, the gender of the person Nympha/Nymphas is signalled by the pronoun that occurs in the following phrase **and the church in her house**. Instead of **her**, a number of manuscripts read 'his' or even 'their' house. In later minuscule manuscripts the accentation of the name is made to agree with the choice of the pronoun. It is also worth noting that the early papyrus manuscript of Colossians $\mathfrak{P}^{46}$ (ca. 200) is lacunose (the text is not preserved due to damage) at this point. This means that the earliest Greek manuscript evidence available dates from the fourth century and that the manuscript tradition is already split into male and female renderings of the name by the fourth to sixth centuries, or else they are ambiguous because of the plural pronoun 'their'. The textual evidence may be set out as follows:

αὐτῆς
Nympha and the church in her house

B 0278 6 424ˢ 1739(*) 1877 1881 *pc* syʰᐟ ᵖᵃˡ ᵐˢ sa Origen

αὐτοῦ
Nymphas and the church in his house

D (F G) Ψ 𝔐 syᵖᐟʰᵐᵍ

αὐτῶν
Nympha/Nymphas and the church in their house

א A C P 075 33 81 104 326 1175 2464 *pc* bo

The third option, 'the church in their house', arises by combining both **brothers** and Nympha(s) in the reference to **the church**. The earliest attestation to this reading, Codex Sinaiticus, contains no accentation of the name. Both the weight of manuscripts (Metzger 1994: 560), and the wider tendency to change feminine names associated with leadership roles in the early church to masculine forms, such as the case with Junia to Junias in Rom. 16:7 (see Epp 2005: 23–31), supports the name being taken as a feminine form here.

In that case, **Nympha**, is to be understood as a wealthy patroness who hosts meetings of believers. It is most natural to see Nympha as a leading figure among the believers at Laodicea. The greeting to her is given in the wider context of instructions concerning the Laodicean community. The believers residing there are to be greeted (Col. 4:15a), and then there are instructions about reciprocal letter reading (Col. 4:16). Sandwiched between this is the command to greet Nympha and those who meet in her home. This strongly suggests that the **church** in question is based in Laodicea. Despite this evidence it has been suggested that Nympha and her household meeting are based in Hierapolis (Gnilka 1980: 244). This is based upon a desire to see the three locations mentioned in Col. 4:13 replicated here. However, there is nothing to suggest a change of location under discussion, and hence to understand Nympha as based in Hierapolis rather than Laodicea is not compelling. The expression **the church in her house**, τὴν κατ᾽ οἶκον αὐτῆς ἐκκλησίαν, takes the Greek preposition κατά in a locative sense. When employed in constructions with the accusative case, as here, the preposition functions as a 'marker of spatial aspect' (BDAG: 511; Harris 2010: 182). The expression is not a reference to a church group constituted solely from members of Nympha's household (since the parallel expression concerning the missionaries Prisca and Aquila in Rom. 16:5 does not refer to wealthy patrons with slaves and a circle of retainers). Instead, the expression 'indicates the use of a believer's home as a gathering site' (Adams 2013: 19). The widespread consensus that believers met exclusively in the large houses, the 'atrium house' (Latin *Domus*) of wealthy patrons during the first two to three centuries of the Christian movement is increasingly being challenged, and a number of studies have illustrated the variability in the choice of spaces for Christian meetings. However, in this context Nympha's own home is designated as the meeting space, and this might be an indication of her wealth and elevated social status.

It may be the case that the community of believers in Laodicea was small enough to meet in a single house. Meeting in the home of a wealthy patron was a common pattern in the Pauline churches, and would have been recognizable to the Colossians who met in the home of Philemon (Phlm. 2). Moo tentatively suggests, presumably because of Nympha's leadership role and apparent independence, that she 'was perhaps a wealthy widow who used her home and resources to support the church' (Moo 2008: 349; cf. Sumney 2008: 278, who also suggests Nympha was a widow). This is obviously one possibility that may explain the data, but there is no clear indication of the marital status of **Nympha**. Her financial prosperity may be assumed to be above average, since she possessed a dwelling large enough to host a meeting of believers in a relatively prosperous town. Whether she was a slave-owner is uncertain, but the greater her wealth the more likely this would become. Her position of wealth, her role as a host of meetings of believers, and the fact that she alone among those based in Laodicea is greeted by name suggests that she may have been the leader of the believers who met in her house. The leadership of women in Pauline communities accords with other evidence both in the epistles and Acts (Witherington 1988: 24–127).

16 A second more complex instruction is given to the Colossians that also involves the Laodicean community. Here the author discloses that a letter has also been written to believers in Laodicea, and that there is to be a mutual letter exchange. This would suggest that the contents of the two letters were sufficiently different from each other that both communities would gain further encouragement by reading the contents of the other letter. Unfortunately, since we do not possess that letter to the Laodiceans, it is not possible to gauge the similarities and differences.

The instruction about the letter is introduced by a construction that envisages a future action having already taken place, **and when the letter has been read among you**. The term **when**, ὅταν, introduces a future temporal clause, which because it is an unfulfilled condition, is described using the subjunctive mood ἀναγνωσθῇ, **has been read**, or even 'is read'. The description of **the letter** is self-referential, meaning 'this letter' (Harris 2010: 182). The phrase παρ' ὑμῖν, **among you**, marks out the Colossians as the first recipients or hearers of the letter prior to its exchange with the Laodiceans. No information is supplied about how the letter is to be read among the Colossians. Perhaps one may imagine it being read in a meeting of the believers, perhaps by Tychicus (Col. 4:7–8), or even Onesimus (Col. 4:9) if he was literate. It is possible that the prepositional phrase **among you** may refer to more than one act of reading, especially if there were several meetings of believers in different houses (Dunn 1996: 286). However, it is equally possible that there was just one household meeting, and that the phrase refers to a collective gathering of all believers in Colossae.

Having imagined the circumstance when the letter has been read, the author now gives the first part of his instruction, **make sure that it is also read in the church of the Laodiceans**. Once again a close relationship between the believers in Colossae and Laodicea is reflected here (cf. Col. 2:1; 4:13, 15). The reading of letters and other texts was a key means of communication in antiquity, and it was a medium of communication that early Christian leaders utilized to great advantage to sustain fledgling communities both in the New Testament period and beyond (cf. the letters of Ignatius, *First Clement*, and into the third century the letters of Novatian). While the statements in this verse are far too weak to support theories about the collection (let alone the canonization) of Paul's letters, it does attest the early circulation of Pauline writings. Within the literary culture of early Pauline churches '[t]he author of Colossians did not think that such an exchange would be considered extraordinary' (Gamble 1995: 97).

The imperative verb **make sure** introduces the action being commanded with the Greek term ποιήσατε, denoting a very general reference to an unspecified action, 'make, do' (*EDNT*: III, 123–26), here with the force of 'cause' or 'bring about' (Harris 2010: 182). The following subjunctive construction, **that it is also read**, denotes an aspiration on the part of the author, albeit an aspiration that has been commanded with the expectation that it will be fulfilled. The location where the letter to Colossians is to gain a second reading is among their near neighbours **in the church of the Laodiceans**. The typical way Paul refers to his churches is by the formula 'the church in X', where X specifies a location such as a city (with variations see 1 Cor. 1:2; 2 Cor. 1:1) or to churches in a geographical region (Gal. 1:2). However, the formulation here, 'the church of Y', where Y specifies the people or inhabitants of a location, is also attested (1 Thess. 1:1; 2 Thess. 1:1). The singular form **church** is probably not decisive by itself for determining whether or not there was more than one household where believers met, or if the expression simply designates the church in Nympha's house. However, given the greeting in the previous verse only to 'Nympha and the church in her house', one might feel that the scant evidence is slightly in favour of a single meeting in Laodicea.

The instructions in relation to the Laodiceans conclude by informing the Colossians that the Laodiceans possess a letter that the Colossians should also read, **and that also you read the one from Laodicea**. Once again, there are tantalizing details concerning both letter circulation and the reading culture of early Christian communities. However, many of the specific details, which would have required no explanation for the original recipients of these letters, are no longer recoverable. It is likely that these letters were read publicly in group-meetings, by one of the literate believers, although there is nothing to suggest that the office of *lector* had become a fixed position at this stage. The exchange of letters would have presumably taken place when a member from one of the communities travelled to the other location with the letter from the town where that person was based. Maybe the same person returned with the other letter. It is unknown if copies were made by either the Colossians or the Laodiceans at this early stage, which would have allowed them to be in possession of both letters. Professional scribes were available in most urban settings, and they could have made a professional copy for a set fee. Alternatively, if the expertise was available, then perhaps a member of one of the churches could have made copies. The Colossians are commanded, **that also you read** the letter that the believers in Laodicea possess. The triple reference to reading, through the threefold repetition of the verb ἀναγινώσκω emphasizes that the medium of reading was a primary mode of communication.

The phrase **the one from Laodicea**, τὴν ἐκ Λαοδικείας, is also imprecise and may suggest alternatives. Concerning this letter, Dunn, although he rejects it as being less likely, notes '[p]ossibly it was not *to* Laodicea but *from* Laodicea (τὴν ἐκ Λαοδικείας), that is, had been written in Laodicea by someone else' (Dunn 1996: 286). The obvious difficulty with such a theory is explaining how the author of the letter to the Colossians would have known about this letter that he did not write. The suggestion that it was written by Epaphras only raises the further complication of why it would not have been designated in that way. It seems more likely that the preposition **from**, ἐχ, designates the location where the letter is to be found, and from where it is to be collected. In other words, the author is saying, 'get the letter from Laodicea which I wrote to them, and make sure you read it'. If that is the correct interpretation, then it raises the question of the fate of this letter to the Laodiceans. There exists an apocryphal letter to the Laodiceans (see the edition of Tite 2012), however the composition of this letter post-dates Colossians, so this cannot be the document that is intended. Others have attempted to reconstruct this letter, seeing it as a source behind both Colossians and Ephesians (Muddiman 2001: 24–31, 302–305). It has also been identified with Philemon (Knox 1959: 45–55). Drawing on more ancient evidence, Marcion, around the middle of the second century, made use of a collection of ten Pauline letters – his *Apostolikon*, including one to the Laodiceans. However, citations from this letter make it clear that this was Marcion's title for the letter known as Ephesians in the New Testament. In sum, if Colossians had indeed been written by Paul, then the letter to Laodiceans is likely to have been an epistle sent to believers in that city. If the letter to the Colossians is not by Paul, then Laodiceans could be a pseudonymous letter by the same author as Colossians, but now lost. Alternatively, the letter to the Laodiceans could be a literary fiction – to which New Testament scholars have devoted far too much attention!

Despite all the unknowns in this verse, the author describes a situation where two letters are in circulation. For the mutual encouragement and benefit of the Colossians and Laodiceans he instructs them to exchange letters. In a situation where Christians were in the minority and often felt beleaguered, the sense of connectedness with a larger movement of believers could have helped to sustain these small marginal groups.

17 The last in the sequence of three final instructions is linked to the preceding two commands by the conjunction **and**, χαί. However, while the first two directives concern matters regarding believers at Laodicea, there is reason to believe that here the focus has moved back to issues in the community at Colossae. The final instruction is introduced through the imperative issued to the Colossian believers to **tell Archippus**. Their role is to verbalize Paul's written instruction, probably with the command to **tell**, εἴπατε, being achieved in a group setting through the public reading and reiteration of this instruction. Collectively, therefore, the group is to become the spokesperson for the commandment that is issued under the auspices of apostolic authority.

The name of **Archippus** occurs only here and as one of the co-recipients of the letter to Philemon (Phlm. 2). In that context, he is described as 'our fellow soldier'. The term 'fellow soldier', συστρα-τιώτης, is used on only one other occasion in the New Testament, as part of the lavish description of Epaphroditus as, among other plaudits, 'my brother and fellow-worker and fellow-soldier' (Phil. 2:25). The term 'presupposes the metaphor of the struggle of faith on behalf of the gospel in a world hostile to God' (*EDNT*: III, 314). It is used to denote a fellow-combatant in Greek literature (Polyaenus, *Stratagems* viii.23.22), and the related Latin term *commilitones* is placed on the lips of Julius Caesar as a way of showing solidarity with his troops (Seutonius, *Divus Iulius* 67).

Some have assumed that **Archippus** is part of the Laodicean community by implication of the preceding two instructions (Lightfoot 1886: 244; Gillman 1992a: I, 368), which might then imply that the letter to Philemon was sent to Laodicea (Knox 1959: 45–55), because Archippus appears to be part of Philemon's household (Phlm. 2). However, given that the original readers of Colossians are charged with verbally reinforcing the instruction that Archippus would have heard, and because they are assumed to know of his whereabouts, it would have been unnecessary to signal a change in the geographical focus between the three instructions in Col. 4:15–17. Beyond the description of Archippus as a 'our fellow-soldier', his likely location in Colossae and his connection with Philemon and Apphia (Phlm. 2), and the instruction here to complete his ministry (Col. 4:17), nothing further is known of him with any certainty. However, as Moo wryly notes, this has not stemmed speculation: '[a]lmost as much scholarly ingenuity has been devoted to this verse as to the "Letter to the Laodiceans," and with equally inconclusive results' (Moo 2008: 352). Perhaps the major speculative proposal, put forward by Knox, was that Archippus was the owner of the slave Onesimus, and the work he is being asked publicly to fulfil in Col. 4:17 is what has been put to him more privately and fulsomely in the letter to Philemon, namely, that he should free Onesimus so he might continue to minister to Paul

(Knox 1959: 49–51). One must admit that the syntax of Phlm. 2 is somewhat ambiguous at this point, and it is not impossible that the reference at the end of that verse to 'the church in your house' could take as its antecedent the immediately preceding figure of Archippus. However, against this, Philemon is clearly the principal recipient of the letter that bears his name, and it is more natural to understand the phrase 'the church in your house' as taking the main addressee as its antecedent. If this is correct, it must still be noted that Archippus is given prominence in the opening greetings, which suggests he was a person of significance among the believing community at Colossae, and may have enjoyed a special position or rank in Philemon's household. It has been proposed that he was 'perhaps a close relative of Philemon and Apphia, such as a son or brother' (Gillman 1992a: I, 368). However, again, there is no firm evidence for such a precise proposal.

The information that the Colossians are to communicate collectively to Archippus is summarized by two verbal clauses. The first is that they are to tell Archippus to **watch the ministry you received in the Lord**. The opening verb **watch**, βλέπε, is a second person singular present imperative, which directs the instruction to Archippus and may also suggest that the necessary watchfulness is an on-going task. If the present imperative signals continuity of the action commanded, then this might speak against the suggestion that what was required of Archippus was the one-off action of releasing Onesimus, or any other specific task that had been neglected. The word **ministry**, διακονία, in general Greek usage can refer to discharging some specific act of service, aid, or support (LSJ: 398; BDAG: 230). In Christian usage the term tends to denote service or **ministry**, which is more permanent in nature and relates to 'gospel ministry' (Pao 2012: 321). The related noun 'minister/servant', διάκονος, is used on four occasions in Colossians to designate those engaged in Christian service: Epaphras is a 'servant of Christ' (Col. 1:7); Paul describes himself in absolute terms as a 'servant' (Col. 1:23); and also as being 'a servant according to the stewardship of God' (Col. 1:25); and Tychicus is called 'a faithful servant...in the Lord' (Col. 4:7). The last example is closest to the language addressed to Archippus, here told to pay attention to **the ministry which you received in the Lord**. The verb **received**, παραλαμβάνω, in Col. 2:6 'is employed for the receiving of a tradition' (O'Brien 1982: 259). The sense is somewhat different here, referring to a calling that was imparted **in the Lord**. Whether the prepositional phrase refers to Archippus as its subject – 'the task you received as a believer in the Lord' (cf. Col. 4:7, where Tychicus is called 'a faithful servant...in the Lord') – or whether it qualifies the act of service – 'the ministry for the Lord' – is perhaps creating too fine a distinction. However, while it may have been a precondition for Archippus receiving this ministry because he was a believer, it must be noted that it appears not all believers have this specific ministry given to Archippus. Therefore, without knowing the specific details of the nature of scope of the task, it seems more likely that Archippus was given an on-going **ministry** that was divinely imparted in some way and most likely involved working for the gospel, perhaps in some kind of leadership capacity. The description of him as a 'fellow-soldier' (Phlm. 2) may suggest he had endured hardship for the gospel in a way that was comparable to some degree with Paul's own sufferings.

The second verbal clause is tightly linked to the first, and suggests that encouragement is required in order that Archippus might persist with his task, or perhaps even that he had become deficient in carrying out the ministry and needed to re-engage with it. Thus Archippus is told to pay attention to his ministry, so **that you fulfil it**. It is perhaps important to preserve the syntax of the Greek at this point in order to given this phrase its climactic or final impact. Without knowing the circumstances behind the epistle it is not possible to determine with certainty whether the phrase is offered as an encouragement, or if it is intended to be more chiding in tone. On the basis of its position, and unlike milder translations such as 'see that you complete your work that you received in the Lord' (NIV; cf. RSV; O'Brien 1982: 245; Pao 2012: 321), the tone appears more rebarbative, 'take heed to the ministry that thou received in the Lord, that thou fulfil it' (KJV; cf. Sumney 2008: 265). Therefore, Archippus may be viewed as having neglected the ministry to which he had been called, or perhaps showing signs of waning in enthusiasm for this continuing work. Ostensibly, Paul's knowledge of this negligence can be assumed to have come from Colossae, possibly through Epaphras, or maybe from the household slave Onesimus. Perhaps as a strategy of public shaming, the community are enlisted with the task of drawing Archippus back to his task.

20. PAUL'S PERSONAL GREETING (4:18)

(18) The greeting of Paul in my hand. Remember my bonds. Grace be with you.

The closing verse consists of three elements, a hand-written greeting from Paul, a call for the Colossians to recollect his situation in prison, and the expression of a final wish for grace to be upon believers in Colossae.

Explicit references to Paul taking up the pen to write in place of his amanuensis occur in five places in his letters (1 Cor. 16:21; Gal. 6:11; Col. 4:18; 2 Thess. 3:17; Phlm. 19). The note in Phlm. 19 does not come at the conclusion of the letter, and also appears to serve a rhetorical function 'I, Paul, am writing this with my own hand: I will repay you myself – not to mention that you owe me in addition your very self' (Phlm. 19). Here Paul mimics the practice of signing debt sureties. The following note about 'not mentioning'(!) the greater debt owed to him by Philemon reveals that Paul did not expect this guarantee to be cashed. By contrast, the other four examples do occur in letter closings. The example in Galatians draws attention to Paul's unprofessional handwriting – 'see with what large letters I write to you in my hand' (Gal. 6:11). The remaining three examples (1 Cor. 16:21; Col. 4:18; 2 Thess. 3:17) all employ exactly the same formulation, ὁ ἀσπασμὸς τῇ ἐμῇ χειρὶ Παύλου, **the greeting of Paul in my hand**, although the example in the Thessalonian correspondence continues in a much more fulsome manner: 'the greeting of Paul in my hand, which is a sign in every letter, thus I write' (2 Thess. 3:17). Given that nowhere else in Colossians can a parallel to 2 Thessalonians be found, whereas there are parallels with 1 Corinthians (e.g. the triad of 'faith, hope, and love', 1 Cor. 13:13 and Col. 1:4–5), if Colossians is not written by Paul, then it would appear that this exact sequence of six parallel words is most likely derived from 1 Cor. 16:21. Unlike the example in 2 Thess. 3:17, here the Pauline signature is less concerned with self-authentication, and more to do with communicating identity and presence with believers in Colossae although Paul is physically absent. If Paul did not write Colossians, then one wonders at the way in which this ruse of a Pauline signature was carried out. Did the

scribe have another person pen these final words, or did he modify
his own writing style at this point, or was there no attempt to do these
things? Also, one wonders about the way in which signed documents
were used by fledgling Pauline communities? Was it enough to hear
a lector read out that Paul had picked up the pen, or was the visual
impact of his 'large letters' (Gal. 6:11) shown to those who heard
the original letter read? Ultimately none of these questions can be
answered. However, they are useful in that they help modern readers
to think more concretely about the impact of the arrival of a letter
from Paul, and how it might have functioned as a substitute for the
absence of the apostle. Thus, whether Paul was alive but imprisoned
when the letter was composed, or dead and hence more permanently
absent when the epistle was written in his name, the handwritten
greeting has much the same function – to bring Paul closer to early
communities of believers.

Unlike the earlier greetings which were written using the verbal
form ἀσπάζεται – for example 'Aristarchus greets you' (Col. 4:10) –
here the nominal form is employed, **the greeting**, ὁ ἀσπασμός. With
the two qualifying expressions that follow Harris offers four possible
ways in which the expression might be construed, with much of the
variation stemming from the way in which the genitival phrase **of
Paul** is to be understood.

1. Subjective genitive, dependent on ὁ ἀσπασμός: 'This greeting,
   in my own hand, is from Paul' (GNB, Harris 2010: 184).
2. Possessive genitive, dependent on ὁ ἀσπασμός: 'This greeting
   of Paul, in my own hand' (Wilson 2005: 296).
3. Possessive genitive, dependent on a second χειρί that is to be
   supplied: 'The greeting is in my own hand, Paul's' (NAB²).
4. In apposition to the genitive idea in the possessive adjective
   ἐμῇ: 'The greeting of me, Paul, with my own hand' (NJB,
   REB).

While Harris argues that the definite article at the beginning of
the phrase has demonstrative force, it appears more likely that
the expression is a typical Greek sandwich construction, with the
nominal expression ὁ ἀσπασμός separated from the genitive Παύλου
that is dependent upon it by additional detail τῇ ἐμῇ χειρί. Thus, the

second option that refers to **the greeting of Paul** and then supplies the details that this greeting is **in my hand** appears to be the most likely sense.

With the next element of this verse, for the second time Paul briefly draws attention to his imprisonment (cf. 'because of which also I am bound', Col. 4:3). Here the second brief but self-contained statement brings Paul's incarceration even more to the fore, **remember my bonds**. What precisely the Colossians are to **remember** is unclear. It appears to envisage more than evoking empathetic sentiments for the sufferings of Paul. Perhaps recollection of his noble suffering is intended to generate a positive reception for the teachings and perspectives communicated in the letter. Sumney suggests that recalling Paul's bonds 'reemphasizes this element of Paul's ethos and thereby encourages readers to trust him and to grant him authority' (Sumney 2008: 282; cf. Dunn 1996: 289). Moo sees this phrase as a poignant prayer request (Moo 2008: 353). He notes the connection between remembrance language and prayer elsewhere in the Pauline epistles (Rom. 1:9; Eph. 1:16; Phil. 1:3; 1 Thess. 1:2; 2 Tim. 1:3; Phlm. 4). While there may be an element of a prayerful request in this reference to Paul's imprisonment, when Paul previously mentioned his bonds he asked for prayers for the effectiveness of his mission: 'pray…that God might open for us a door for the word' (Col. 4:3). So, if this brief phrase is intended as a prayer request it is more likely to be that the Colossians should intercede for the continued effectiveness of the Pauline mission, not for relief for personal sufferings that supplement those of Christ (Col. 1:24).

The final phrase of the epistle, **grace be with you**, turns the attention from Paul back to the Colossians. At the heart of apostolic concern for this nascent community of believers is the wish to see them flourish in God's grace. The letter is 'bookended' with the desire that the Colossians should be recipients of divine grace (Col. 1:2; 4:18). As such, this replicates the way in which Paul frequently communicates with communities to which he writes (1 Cor. 1:3; 16:23; 2 Cor. 1:2; 13:13; Gal. 1:3; 6:18; Eph. 1:2; 6:24; Phil. 1:2; 4:23; 1 Thess. 1:1; 5:28; 2 Thess. 1:1; 3:18; 1 Tim. 1:2; 6:21; 2 Tim. 1:2; 4:22; Tit. 1:4; 3:15; Phlm. 3, 25). The phrase **grace be with you**, ἡ χάρις μεθ᾽ ὑμῶν, finds exact parallel only in 1 Tim. 6:21 and 2 Tim. 4:22. Other final grace benedictions typically contain a christological referent, such as 'the grace of the Lord be with you' or 'the grace of the Lord Jesus Christ be with you'. It is perhaps striking that in Colossians, where christological issues are so much to the fore of the author's thought, that this christological element is omitted. However, the form appears to assume a divine subject. Hence, **grace be** emphasizes the fact that all the blessings and benefits enjoyed by the Colossians in their new existence (Col. 1:13) have a divine origin. As such, the author's decision implicitly to recall the divine work that has been done among the believers in Colossae is a fitting conclusion to a letter that strives to teach its recipients of the totality of the work of God in Christ that has resulted in their reconciliation.

The concluding 'Amen', Ἀμήν, added in a number of manuscripts, is almost certainly a secondary element, typically added by later scribes in many early Christian documents. The word is found in the following manuscripts ℵ² D Ψ 075 0278 1739ᶜ 𝔐 lat sy boᵖᵗ, but absent in ℵ* A B C F G 048 6 33 81 1739* 1881 *pc* vgᵐˢˢ sa boᵖᵗ Ambst.

V.
TITLE

21. SUBSCRIPTS

To the Colossians

The subscription, or the title added at the end of a work, was almost certainly not part of the earliest recoverable text of Colossians, and one finds great variability along with increasing expansiveness in such subscriptions. However, this information provides important early evidence about the perceived destination, authorship, place of writing, and means of sending the letter. The earliest surviving witness to the text of Colossians, $\mathfrak{P}^{46}$, does not contain a subscription at the end of the letter, but an inscription at the head of the epistle. The surviving evidence is as follows (Comfort 2008: 639):

1. No subscription, but 'To the Colossians', Προς Κολοσσαεις, at the head of the epistle
    $\mathfrak{P}^{46}$

2. No subscription
    323 365 629 630 1505 2464

3. 'To the Colossians', Προς Κολοσσαεις
    ℵ B* C (D F G) Ψ 048 33

4. 'To the Colossians written from Rome', Προς Κολοσσαεις εγραφη απο Ρωμης
    (A) B¹ P

5. 'To the Colossians written from Rome through Tychicus and Onesimus', Προς Κολοσσαεις εγραφη απο Ρωμης δια Τυχικου και Ομησιμου
    075 1739 1881 𝔐

6. 'An epistle of Paul the apostle to the Colossians written from Rome through Tychicus', Παυλου αποστολου επιστολη προς Κολοσσαεις εγραφη απο Ρωμης δια Τυχικου
    0278

Apart from the detail that the letter was written from Rome, all of the other details can be gleaned from within the letter itself. The information contained in these subscriptions had a powerful influence on the formulation of the traditional understanding of the background circumstances to the letter.

BIBLIOGRAPHY

1. Commentaries on Colossians

Abbott, T. K. 1897. *A Critical and Exegetical Commentary on the Epistles to the Ephesians and to the Colossians*, ICC (Edinburgh: T. & T. Clark).

Aletti, J.-N. 1993. *Saint Paul Épître aux Colossiens*, ÉB (Paris: Gabalda).

Barth, M., and H. Blanke. 1994. *Colossians: A New Translation with Introduction and Commentary*, AB 34B (New York: Doubleday).

Beare, F. W. 1955. 'The Epistle to the Colossians', *IB*, vol. 11 (Nashville, TN: Abingdon).

Bengel, J. A. 1994. *Gnomon Novi Testament*, repr. (Edinburgh: T. & T. Clark).

Bieder, W. 1943. *Der Kolosserbrief* (Zurich: Zwingli).

Bird, M. F. 2009. *Colossians and Philemon*, A New Covenant Commentary (Eugene, OR: Cascade Books/Wipf & Stock).

Bormann, L. 2012. *Der Brief des Paulus an die Kolosser*, THKNT 10/I (Leipzig: Evangelische Verlagsanstal).

Bruce, F. F. 1957. In E. K. Simpson and F. F. Bruce, *Commentary on the Epistles to the Ephesians and the Colossians*, NICNT (Grand Rapids, MI: Eerdmans).

———. 1984. *The Epistles to the Colossians, to Philemon, and to the Ephesians*, NICNT (Grand Rapids, MI: Eerdmans).

Caird, G. B. 1976. *Paul's Letters from Prison*, NCB (Oxford: Oxford University Press).

Calvin, J. 1965. *The Epistles of Paul the Apostle to the Galatians, Ephesians, Philippians and Colossians* (Grand Rapids, MI: Eerdmans).

Campbell, C. R. 2013. *Colossians and Philemon: A Handbook on the Greek Text*, BHGNT (Waco: Baylor University Press).

Carson, H. M. 1960. *The Epistles of Paul to the Colossians and to Philemon*, TNTC (Grand Rapids, MI: Eerdmans).

Conzelmann, G. 1976. *Die Briefe an die Galater, Epheser, Philipper, Kolosser, Thessalonicher und Philemon*, NTD 8, 14th ed. (Göttingen: Vandenhoeck & Ruprecht).

Dibelius, M. 1953. *An die Kolosser, Epheser, an Philemon*, HNT 12, 3rd ed., rev. H. Greeven (Tübingen: Mohr Siebeck).

Dunn, J. D. G. 1996. *The Epistles to the Colossians and to Philemon*, NIGTC (Grand Rapids, MI: Eerdmans).

Eadie, J. 1957. *Commentary on the Epistle of Paul to the Colossians*, repr. (Grand Rapids, MI: Zondervan).

Ernst, J. 1974. *Die Briefe an die Philipper, an Philemon, an die Kolosser, an die Epheser*, RNT (Regensburg: Pustet).

Ewald, P. 1905. *Die Briefe des Paulus an die Epheser, Kolosser und Philemon*, KNT 10 (Leipzig: Deichert).

Furter, D. 1988. *Les Épîtres de Paul aux Colossiens et à Philémon*, Commentaire Évangelique de la Bible 8 (Vaux-sur-Seine: Faculté libre de théologie évangélique).

Garland, D. E. 1998. *Colossians and Philemon*, NIVAC (Grand Rapids, MI: Zondervan).

Garrod, G. W. 1898. *The Epistle to the Colossians: Analysis and Examination Notes* (New York: Macmillan).

Gnilka, J. 1980. *Der Kolosserbrief*, HTKNT 10.1 (Freiburg: Herder).

Gorday, P. (ed.). 2000. *Colossians, 1–2 Thessalonians, 1–2 Timothy, Titus, Philemon*, ACCS (Downers Grove, Ill.: Inter-Varsity).

Greer, R. A. (trans.). 2010. *Theodore of Mopsuestia: Commentary on the Minor Pauline Epistles*, Writings from the Greco-Roman World 26 (Atlanta, GA: SBL).

Gupta, N. K. 2013. *Colossians*, Smyth & Helwys Commentary (Macon, GA: Smyth & Helwys).

Harris, M. J. 1991. *Colossians and Philemon*, Exegetical Guide to the Greek New Testament (Grand Rapids, MI: Eerdmans).

―――. 2010. *Colossians and Philemon*, Exegetical Guide to the Greek New Testament, new ed. (Nashville, TN: B&H Publishing).

Haupt, E. 1992. *Die Gefangenschaftsbriefe*, KEK 8–9 (Göttingen: Vandenhoeck & Ruprecht).

Hay, D. M. 2000. *Colossians*, ANTC (Nashville, TN: Abingdon).

Heil, J. P. 2010. *Colossians: Encouragement to Walk in All Wisdom as Holy Ones in Christ* (Atlanta, GA: SBL).

Houlden, J. L. 1977. *Paul's Letters from Prison*, PNTC (London: SCM).

Hübner, H. 1997. *An Philemon, an die Kolosser, an die Epheser* (Tübingen: Mohr Siebeck).

Huby, J. 1947. *Les Épîtres de la captivité: Colossiens, Philémon, Ephésiens, Philippiens, aux Colossiens*, Verbum Salutis (Paris: Beauchesne).

Hugedé, N. 1988. *Commentaire de l'Épître aux Colossiens* (Geneva: Labor et Fides).

Lightfoot, J. B. 1875. *Saint Paul's Epistles to the Colossians and to Philemon*, 1st ed. (London: Macmillan).

———. 1886. *Saint Paul's Epistles to the Colossians and to Philemon*, 8th ed. (London: Macmillan).

Lincoln, A. T. 1993. In A. T. Lincoln and A. J. M. Wedderburn, *The Theology of the Later Pauline Epistles* (Cambridge: Cambridge University Press).

———. 2000. 'The Letter to the Colossians', in L. E. Keck (ed.), *The New Interpreter's Bible*, vol. 11 (Nashville, TN: Abingdon) 553–669.

Lindemann, A. 1983. *Der Kolosserbrief*, ZBK 10 (Zurich: Theologischer Verlag).

Loane, M. L. 1972. *Three Letters from Prison* (Waco, TX: Word).

Lohmeyer, E. 1930. *Die Briefe an die Kolosser und an Philemon*, KEK 9 (Göttingen: Vandenhoeck & Ruprecht).

———. 1964. *Die Briefe an die Philipper, an die Kolosser und an Philemon*, KEK 9, rev. by W. Schmauch (Göttingen: Vandenhoeck & Ruprecht).

Lohse, E. 1971. *Colossians and Philemon*, Hermeneia (Philadelphia: Fortress).

Lucas, R. C. 1980. *The Message of Colossians and Philemon: Fullness and Freedom*, The Bible Speaks Today (Downers Grove, IL: Inter-Varsity).

Luz, U. 1998. 'Der Brief an die Kolosser', in J. Becker and U. Luz (eds), *Die Briefe an die Galater, Epheser und Kolosser*, NTD 8.1 (Göttingen: Vandenhoeck & Ruprecht).

MacDonald, M. Y. 2000. *Colossians and Ephesians*, Sacra Pagina 17 (Collegeville, MN: Liturgical).

Martin, E. D. 1993. *Colossians, Philemon*, Believers Church Bible Commentary (Scottdale, PA: Herald).

Martin, R. P. 1972. *Colossians: The Church's Lord and the Christian's Liberty: An Exposition Commentary with a Present-Day Application* (Grand Rapids, MI: Zondervan).

———. 1973. *Colossians and Philemon*, NCBC (Grand Rapids, MI: Eerdmans).

———. 1991. *Ephesians, Colossians, and Philemon*, IBC (Atlanta: John Knox).

Masson, C. 1950. *L'Épître de Saint Paul aux Colossiens*, CNT 10 (Neuchâtel: Delachaux).

Melick, R. R. 1991. *Philippians, Colossians, Philemon*, NAC 32 (Nashville, TN: Broadman).

Meyer, H. A. W. 1859. *Kritisch-exegetisches Handbuch über die Briefe an die Philipper Kolosser und an Philemon*, KEK 9 (Göttingen: Vandenhoeck & Ruprecht).

Moo, D. J. 2008. *The Letter to the Colossians and to Philemon*, PNTC (Grand Rapids, MI: Eerdmans; Nottingham: Apollos).

Moule, C. F. D. 1957. *The Epistles to the Colossians and to Philemon*, The Cambridge Greek Testament Commentary (Cambridge: Cambridge University Press).

Murphy-O'Connor, J. 2001. 'Colossians', in J. Barton and J. Muddiman (eds), *The Oxford Bible Commentary* (Oxford: Oxford University Press) 1191–99.

Mußner, F. 1971. *Der Brief an die Kolosser*, Geistliche Schriftauslegung 12/1 (Düsseldorf: Patmos).

O'Brien, P. T. 1982. *Colossians, Philemon*, WBC 44 (Waco, TX: Word).

Pao, D. W. 2012. *Colossians and Philemon*, Zondervan Exegetical Commentary on the New Testament (Grand Rapids, MI: Zondervan).

Pokorný, P. 1991. *Colossians: A Commentary* (Peabody, MA: Hendrickson).

Schlatter, A. 1963. *Die Briefe an die Galater, Epheser, Kolosser und Philemon*, EzNT (Zurich: Benziger).

Schweizer, E. 1976. *Der Brief an die Kolosser*, EKKNT 7 (Stuttgart: Calwer).

———. 1982. *The Letter to the Colossians: A Commentary* (London: SPCK; Minneapolis: Augsburg).

Scott, E. F. 1930. *The Epistles of Paul to the Colossians, to Philemon and to the Ephesians*, MNTC (London: Hodder & Stoughton).

Seitz, C. R. 2014. *Colossians*, Brazos Theological Commentary on the Bible (Grand Rapids, MI: Brazos).

Soden, H. von. 1885. 'Der Kolosserbrief', *JPTh* 11: 320–68.

———. 1891. *Die Briefe an die Kolosser, Epheser, Philemon. Die Pastoralbriefe*, HKNT 3 (Freiburg i.B.: Mohr).

Sumney, J. L. 2008. *Colossians: A Commentary*, NTL (Louisville, KY: Westminster John Knox).

Talbert, C. H. 2007. *Ephesians and Colossians*, Paideia Commentaries on the New Testament (Grand Rapids, MI: Baker).

Thompson, M. M. 2005. *Colossians and Philemon*, The Two Horizons New Testament Commentary (Grand Rapids, MI: Eerdmans).

Wall, R. W. 1993. *Colossians and Philemon*, IVPNTC (Downers Grove, IL: IVP).

Wilson, R. McL. 2005. *A Critical and Exegetical Commentary on Colossians and Philemon*, ICC (Edinburgh: T. & T. Clark).

Witherington III, B. 2007. *The Letters to Philemon, the Colossians, and the Ephesians: A Socio-Rhetorical Commentary on the Captivity Epistles* (Grand Rapids, MI: Eerdmans).

Wolter, M. 1993. *Der Brief an die Kolosser. Der Brief an Philemon*, ÖTK 12 (Gütersloh: Gerd Mohn).

Wright, N. T. 1986. *The Epistles of Paul to the Colossians and to Philemon*, TNTC (Leicester: IVP).

2. *Other Secondary Literature*

Aageson, J. 2012. 'Genesis in the Deutero-Pauline Epistles', in M. J. J. Menken and S. Moyise (eds), *Genesis in the New Testament*, LNTS 466 (London: Bloomsbury T&T Clark) 117–29.

Aasgaard, R. 2004. *'My Beloved Brothers and Sisters!' Christian Siblingship in Paul*, JSNTSup 265 (London: T&T Clark International).

Adams, E. 2013. *The Earliest Christian Meeting Places: Almost Exclusively Houses?* LNTS 450 (London: Bloomsbury T&T Clark).

Aland, K., and B. Aland. 1989. *The Text of the New Testament*, trans. E. F. Rhodes, rev. and enlarged ed. (Grand Rapids, MI: Eerdmans).

Aletti, J.-N. 1976. 'Créés dans le Christ, Col. 1,15–20', *Christus* 23: 343–56.

———. 1981. *Colossiens 1,15–20: Genre et exégèse du texte: function de la thématique sapientielle*, AnBib 91 (Rome: Pontifical Biblical Institute).

———. 1999. 'Colossiens: un Tournant dans da christologie Neotestamentaire: problemes et propositions', *LASBF* 49: 211–36.

Allen, W. 1990. 'The English for *Agona* at Colossians 2.1', *Reformation Biblical Studies Bulletin* 1: 10–12.

Amling, E. 1909. 'Eine Konjektur in Philemonbrief', *ZNW* 10: 261–62.

Anderson, C. P. 1966. 'Who Wrote the Epistle from Laodicea?', *JBL* 85: 436–40.

Argall, R. A. 1987. 'The Source of a Religious Error in Colossae', *CTJ* 22: 6–20.

Argyle, A. W. 1954. *'Prōtotokos Pasēs Ktiseōs* (Colossians 1.15)', *ExpTim* 66: 61–62.

———. 1955. 'Colossians 1.15', *ExpTim* 66: 318–19.

Arnold, C. E. 1992a. 'Colossae', in *ABD* I, 1089–90.

———. 1992b. *Powers of Darkness: Principalities and Powers in Paul's Letters* (Downers Grove, IL: IVP).

————. 1994. 'Jesus Christ: "Head" of the Church (Colossians and Ephesians)', in J. B. Green and M. Turner (eds), *Jesus of Nazareth, Lord and Christ: Essays on the Historical Jesus and New Testament Christology* (Grand Rapids, MI: Eerdmans) 346–66.

————. 1995. *The Colossian Syncretism: The Interface between Christianity and Folk Belief in Colossae*, WUNT 77 (Tübingen: Mohr Siebeck).

Arzt-Grabner. P. 2010. 'Paul's Letter Thanksgiving', in S. E. Porter and S. E. Adams (eds), *Paul and the Ancient Letter Form*, PS 6 (Leiden: Brill) 129–58.

Attridge, H. W. 1994. 'On Becoming an Angel: Rival Baptismal Theologies at Colossae', in L. Bormann, K. Del Tredici, and A. Standhartinger (eds), *Religious Propaganda and Missionary Competition in the New Testament World* (Leiden: Brill) 481–98.

Aune, D. 1997. *Revelation 1–5*, WBC 52A (Dallas: Word).

Balchin, J. F. 1985. 'Colossians 1:15–20: An Early Christian Hymn? The Arguments from Style', *VE* 15: 65–94.

Bammel, E. 1961. 'Versuch Col 1:15–20', *ZNW* 52: 88–95.

Bandstra, A. J. 1974. 'Did the Colossian Errorists Need a Mediator?, in R. N. Longenecker and M. C. Tenney (eds), *New Dimensions in New Testament Study* (Grand Rapids, MI: Zondervan) 329–43.

Barclay, J. M. G. 1996. *Jews in the Mediterranean Diaspora: From Alexander to Trajan (323 BCE–117 CE)* (Edinburgh: T. & T. Clark).

————. 1997. *Colossians and Philemon* (Sheffield: Sheffield Academic).

————. 2001. 'Ordinary but Different: Colossians and Hidden Moral Identity', *ABR* 49: 34–52.

————. 2011. *Pauline Churches and the Diaspora Jews*, WUNT 275 (Tübingen: Mohr Siebeck).

Barclay, W. 1978. *The All-Sufficient Christ: Studies in Paul's Letter to the Colossians* (Edinburgh: Saint Andrew).

Bauckham, R. 1975. 'Colossians 1:24 Again: The Apocalyptic Motif', *EvQ* 47: 168–70.

————. 1983. *Jude, 2 Peter*, WBC 50 (Waco, Texas: Word).

————. 2003. 'Where Is Wisdom to Be Found? Colossians 1.15–20 (2)', in D. F. Ford and G. Stanton (eds), *Reading Texts, Seeking Wisdom: Scripture and Theology* (Grand Rapids, MI: Eerdmans) 129–38.

Baugh, S. M. 1985. 'The Poetic Form of Col 1:15–20', *WTJ* 47: 227–44.

Bauer, F. C. 1845. *Paulus, der Apostel Jesu Christi: Sein Leben und Wirken, seine Briefe und seine Lehre* (Stuttgart: Becher & Müller).

Beale, G. K. 2007. 'Colossians', in G. K. Beale and D. A. Carson (eds), *Commentary on the New Testament Use of the Old Testament* (Grand Rapids, MI: Baker; Nottingham: Apollos) 841–70.

Beale, G. K., and D. A. Carson (eds). 2007. *Commentary on the New Testament Use of the Old Testament* (Grand Rapids, MI: Baker; Nottingham: Apollos).

Beasley-Murray, G. R. 1973. 'Second Chapter of Colossians', *RevExp* 70: 469–79.

Beasley-Murray, P. 1980. 'Colossians 1:15–20: An Early Christian Hymn Celebrating the Lordship of Christ', in D. A. Hagner and M. J. Harris (eds), *Pauline Studies* (Grand Rapids, MI: Eerdmans) 169–83.

Beetham, C. A. 2008. *Echoes of Scripture in the Letter of Paul to the Colossians* (Leiden: Brill).

Behr, J. 1996. 'Colossians 1.13–20: A Chiastic Reading', *SVTQ* 40: 247–64.

Bellai, Z. 1986. 'Traces of the Ancient Church's Liturgy of Baptism in the New Testament (Col.1.15–20)', *Theologiai Szemle* 28: 6–9.

Benoit, P. 1983. 'Pauline Angelology and Demonology: Reflections on Designations of Heavenly Powers and on the Origin of Angelic Evil according to Paul', *Religious Studies Bulletin* 3: 1–18.

———. 1984. 'The "Plērōma" in the Epistles to the Colossians and the Ephesians', *SEÅ* 49: 136–58.

Berkhof, H. 1979. 'The Holy Spirit and the World: Some Reflections on Paul's Letter to the Colossians', *JTSA* 29: 56–61.

Best, E. 1997. 'Who Used Whom? The Relationship of Ephesians and Colossians', *NTS* 43: 72–96.

———. 1998. *A Critical and Exegetical Commentary on Ephesians*, ICC (Edinburgh: T. & T. Clark).

Beuttler, U. 1999. 'Christus, das Heil der Natur', *Glaube und Denken* 12: 81–88.

Bevere, A. R. 2003. *Sharing in the Inheritance: Identity and the Moral Life in Colossians*, JSNTSup 226 (Sheffield: Sheffield Academic).

Blanchette, O. A. 1961. 'Does the Cheirographon of Col 2:14 Represent Christ Himself?', *CBQ* 23: 306–12.

Bockmuehl, M. 1988. 'A Note on the Text of Colossians 4:3', *JTS* 39: 489–94.

Boring, M. E. 2012. *An Introduction to the New Testament: History, Literature, Theology* (Louisville: WJK).

Bornkamm, G. 1961. 'Die Hoffnung im Kolosserbrief: Zugleich ein Beitrag zur Frage der Echtheit des Briefes', in O. Eissfeldt (ed.), *Studien zum Neuen Testament und zur Patristik: Erich Klostermann zum 90 Geburtstag dargebracht*, TU 77 (Berlin: Akademie Verlag) 56–64.

Botha, J. 1997. 'A Stylistic Analysis of the Christ Hymn (Col 1.15–20)', in J. H. Petzer and P. J. Hartin (eds), *A South African Perspective on the New Testament Scholars Presented to Bruce Manning Metzger During His Visit in South Africa in 1985* (Leiden: Brill) 238–51.

Bouttier, M. 1976. 'Complexio Oppositorum: sur les formules de I Cor 12.13; Gal 3.26–8, Col 3.10, 11', *NTS* 23: 1–19.

Bowen, C. R. 1924. 'The Original Form of Paul's Letter to the Colossians', *JBL* 43: 177–206.

Bowers, W. P. 1975. 'A Note on Colossians 1:27a', in G. F. Hawthorne (ed.), *Current Issues in Biblical and Patristic Interpretation* (Grand Rapids, MI: Eerdmans) 110–14.

Bradley, J. 1972. 'The Religious Life-Setting of the Epistle to the Colossians', *Studia Biblica et Theologica* 2: 17–36.

Bratcher, R. G., and E. A. Nida. 1977. *A Translator's Handbook on Paul's Letters to the Colossians and to Philemon* (Stuttgart: United Bible Societies).

Brixhe, C. 2008. 'Phrygian', in R. D. Woodard, *The Ancient Languages of Asia Minor* (Cambridge: Cambridge University Press) 69–80.

Brown, R. E. 1997. *An Introduction to the New Testament*, ABRL (New York: Doubleday).

Bruce, F. F. 1977. *Paul: Apostle of the Free Spirit*, rev. ed. (Exeter: Paternoster).

———. 1984a. 'Colossian Problems I: Jews and Christians in the Lycus Valley', *BSac* 141: 3–15.

———. 1984b. 'Colossian Problems II: The "Christ Hymn" of Colossians 1:15–20', *BSac* 141: 99–111.

———. 1984c. 'Colossian Problems III: The Colossian Heresy', *BSac* 141: 195–208.

———. 1984d. 'Colossian Problems IV: Christ as Conqueror and Reconciler', *BSac* 141: 291–302.

Bujard, W. 1973. *Stilanalytische Untersuchungen zum Kolosserbrief als Beitrag zur Methodik von Sprachvergleichen*, SUNT 11 (Göttingen: Vandenhoeck & Ruprecht).

Bultmann, R. 1963. *History of the Synoptic Tradition* (London: SCM).

Burger, C. 1975. *Schopfung und Versohnung: Studien zum Liturgischen Gut im Kolosser-und Epheserbrief*, WMANT 46 (Neukirchener: Neukirchener Verlag).

Burney, C. F. 1926. 'Christ as the APXH of Creation (Prov. 8:22, Col. 1:15–18, Rev. 3.14)', *JTS* 27: 160–77.

Cadwallader, A. H. 2007. 'A New Inscription [=Two New Inscriptions], A Correction and a Confirmed Siting from Colossae', *EA* 40: 109–18.

———. 2011. 'Refuting an Axiom of Scholarship on Colossae: Fresh Insights from New and Old Inscription', in A. H. Cadwallader and M. Trainor (eds), *Colossae in Space and Time: Linking to an Ancient City*, NTOA 94 (Göttingen: Vandenhoeck & Ruprecht) 151–79.

———. 2012a. 'Honouring the Repairer of the Baths at Colossae', in S. R. Llewelyn and J. R. Harrison (eds), *New Documents Illustrating Early Christianity*, vol. 10 (Grand Rapids, MI: Eerdmans) 110–13.

———. 2012b. 'Honouring the Repairer of the Baths: A New Inscription from Kolossai', *Antichthon* 46: 150–83.

———. 2015. *Fragments of Colossae: Sifting Through the Traces* (Hindmarsh, South Australia: ATF).

Cadwallader, A. H., and M. Trainor (eds). 2011. *Colossae in Space and Time: Linking to an Ancient City*, NTOA 94 (Göttingen: Vandenhoeck & Ruprecht).

Cahill, M. 1992. 'The Neglected Parallelism in Colossians 1:24–25', *ETL* 68: 142–47.

Callow, J. 2002. *A Semantic and Structural Analysis of Colossians*, 2nd ed. (Dallas: SIL International).

Campbell, D. A. 1996. 'Unravelling Colossians 3.11b', *NTS* 42: 120–32.

———. 1997. 'The Scythian Perspective in Col 3:11: A Response to Troy Martin', *NovT* 39: 81–84.

Canavan, R. 2012. *Clothing the Body of Christ at Colossae: A Visual Construction of Identity*, WUNT 2/334 (Tübingen: Mohr Siebeck).

Cannon, G. E. 1983. *The Use of Traditional Material in Colossians* (Macon, GA: Mercer University Press).

Carlos Reyes, L. 1999. 'The Structure and Rhetoric of Colossians 1:15–20', *Filologia Neotestamentaria* 12: 139–54.

Carr, W. 1973. 'Two Notes on Colossians', *JTS* 24: 492–500.

———. 1981. *Angels and Principalities: The Background, Meaning and Development of the Pauline Phrase* hai Archai kai hai Exousiai, SNTSMS 42 (Cambridge: Cambridge University Press).

Carrez, M. 1951. 'Souffrance et Gloire dans les épîtres Pauliniennes (contribution à l'exégèse de Col 1:24–27)', *RHPR* 31: 343–53.

Cassirer, H. W. (trans.). 1989. *God's New Covenant: A New Testament Translation* (Grand Rapids, MI: Eerdmans).

Chadwick, H. 1955. '"All Things to All Men"', *NTS* 1: 261–75.

Charles, R. H. 1913. *Eschatology: A Critical History of the Doctrine of a Future Life in Israel, Judaism and Christianity*, 2nd ed., rev. and enlarged (London: Black).

Chiricat, É. 2013. 'The "crypto-Christian" Inscriptions of Phrygia', in P. Thonemann (ed.), *Roman Phrygia: Culture and Society*, Greek Culture in the Roman World (Cambridge: Cambridge University Press) 198–214.

Christopher, G. T. 1990. 'A Discourse Analysis of Colossians 2:16–3:17', *Grace Theological Journal* 11: 205–20.

Clark, B. T. 2015. *Completing Christ's Afflictions*, WUNT 2/383 (Tübingen: Mohr Siebeck).

Cole, H. R. 2001. 'The Christian and Time-Keeping in Colossians 2.16 and Galatians 4.10', *AUSS* 39: 273–82.

Collins, R. F. 1988. *Letters That Paul Did Not Write: The Epistle to the Hebrews and the Pauline Pseudepigrapha*, GNS 28 (Wilmington, DE: Michael Glazier).

———. 1999. *First Corinthians*, Sacra Pagina (Collegeville, MN: Liturgical).

Comfort, P. W. 2008. *New Testament Text and Translation Commentary: Commentary on the Variant Readings of the Ancient New Testament Manuscripts and How They Relate to Major English Translations* (Carol Stream, IL: Tyndale House Publishers).

Constantelos, D. J. 1998. 'Religious Cultural Diversity and Christian Unity in the Church of Colossae: An Exegesis of Colossians 2:16 to 3:4', in G. Papadopolous and P. A. Chamberas (eds), *Agape and Diakonia: Essays in Memory of Bishop Gerasimos of Abydos* (Brookline: Holy Cross Orthodox) 53–61.

Cope, L. 1985. 'On Rethinking the Philemon-Colossians Connection', *BR* 30: 45–50.

Copenhaver, A. 2012. '"Watch Out for Whom?": Reconstructing the Historical Background of Paul's Rhetoric in the Letter to the Colossians' (unpublished dissertation; Aberdeen: Highland Theological College).

Cosby, M. R. 2008. *Apostle on the Edge: An Inductive Approach to Paul* (Louisville: WJK).

Coutts, J. 1958. 'Relationship of Ephesians and Colossians', *NTS* 4: 201–207.

Craddock, F. B. 1965. '"All Things in Him" – A Critical Note on Col 1:15–20', *NTS* 12: 78–80.

Crouch, J. E. 1972. *The Origin and Intention of the Colossian Haustafel*, FRLANT 109 (Göttingen: Vandenhoeck & Ruprecht).

Davies, W. D., and D. C. Allison (eds). 1988–97. *A Critical and Exegetical Commentary on the Gospel according to Saint Matthew*, ICC, 3 vols. (Edinburgh: T. & T. Clark).

de Boer, M. C. 2011. *Galatians: A Commentary*, NTL (Westminster: John Knox).

DeMaris, R. E. 1994. *The Colossian Controversy: Wisdom in Dispute at Colossae*, JSNTSup 96 (Sheffield: JSOT).

Dettwiler, A. 2013. 'La lettre aux Colossiens: une théologie de la mémoire', *NTS* 59: 109–28.

Dodd, C. H. 1929. 'Ephesians', in F. C. Eiselen, E. Lewis, and D. G. Downey (eds), *The Abingdon Bible Commentary* (New York: Abingdon).

Drake, A. E. 1995. 'The Riddle of Colossians: Quaerendo Invenietis', *NTS* 41: 123–44.

Dubbers, M. 2005. *Christologie und Existenz im Kolosserbrief: Exegetische und Semantische Untersuchungen zur Intention des Kolosserfriefes*, WUNT 191 (Tübingen: Mohr Siebeck).

Dunn, J. D. G. 1994. 'The "Body" in Colossians', in T. E. Schmidt and M. Silva (eds), *To Tell the Mystery* (Sheffield: JSOT) 163–81.

———. 1995. 'The Colossian Philosophy: A Confident Jewish Apologia', *Bib* 75: 153–81.

———. 1998. *The Theology of Paul the Apostle* (Grand Rapids, MI: Eerdmans).

Edsall, B., and J. R. Strawbridge. 2015. 'The Songs We Used to Sing? Hymn "Traditions" and Reception in the Pauline Letters', *JSNT* 37: 290–311.

Edwards, D. R. 1994. 'Defining the Web of Power in Asia Minor: The Novelist Chariton and His City Aphrodisias', *Journal of the American Academy of Religion* 62: 699–718.

Efird, J. M. 1980. *Christ, the Church, and the End: Studies in Colossians and Ephesians* (Valley Forge, PA: Judson).

Eitrem, S. 1949. '*Embateuo:* note sur Col 2:18', *ST* 2: 90–94.

Ellingworth, P. 1962. 'Colossians I.15–20 and Its Context', *ExpTim* 73: 252–53.

Ellis, E. E. 2006. 'Colossians 1:12–20: Christus Creator, Christus Salvator', in D. L. Bock and B. M. Fanning (eds), *Interpreting the New Testament Text: Introduction to the Art and Science of Exegesis* (Wheaton, IL: Crossway) 415–28.

Epp, E. J. 2005. *Junia: The First Woman Apostle* (Minneapolis: Fortress).

Evans, C. A. 1982. 'The Colossian Mystics', *Bib* 63: 188–205.

————. 1984. 'The Meaning of *Plērōma* in Nag Hammadi', *Bib* 65: 259–65.

Evanson, E. 1792. *The Dissonance of the Four Generally Received Evangelists, and the Evidence of Their Respective Authenticity Examined* (Ipswich: G. Jermyn).

Fee, G. D. 2006. 'Old Testament Intertextuality in Colossians: Reflections on Pauline Christology and Gentile Inclusion in God's Story', in Sang-Won (Aaron) Son (ed.), *History and Exegesis: New Testament Essays in Honor of Dr. E. Earle Ellis for His 80ᵗʰ Birthday* (London: T&T Clark International) 201–21.

————. 2007. *Pauline Christology: An Exegetical-Theological Study* (Peabody, MA: Hendrickson).

Feuillet, A. 1965. 'La creation de l'univers dans le Christ d'après l'épître aux Colossiens (1:16a)', *NTS* 12: 1–9.

Flemington, W. F. 1981. 'On the Interpretation of Colossians 1:24', in H. Merklein (ed.), *Suffering and Martyrdom in the New Testament* (London: Cambridge University Press) 84–90.

Fossum, J. 1989. 'Colossians 1:15–18a in the Light of Jewish Mysticism and Gnosticism', *NTS* 35: 183–201.

————. 1995. 'The Image of the Invisible God: Colossians 1.15–18a in the Light of Jewish Mysticism and Gnosticism', in *The Image of the Invisible God: Essays on the Influence of Jewish Mysticism on Early Christology* (Göttingen: Vandenhoeck & Ruprecht) 13–39.

Foster, P. 'The Epistles of Ignatius of Antioch and the Writings that Later Formed the New Testament', in A. F. Gregory and C. M. Tuckett (eds), *The Reception of the New Testament in the Apostolic Fathers*, The New Testament and the Apostolic Fathers 1 (Oxford: Oxford University Press) 159–86.

————. 2011. 'The Eschatology of the Thessalonian Correspondence: An Exercise in Pastoral Pedagogy and Constructive Theology', *JSPL* 1: 57–81.

————. 2012. 'Who Wrote 2 Thessalonians? A Fresh Look at an Old Problem', *JSNT* 35: 150–75.

Fowl, S. E. 1990. *The Story of Christ in the Ethics of Paul: An Analysis of the Function of the Hymnic Material in the Pauline Corpus*, JSNTSup 36 (Sheffield: JSOT).

Francis, F. O. 1962. 'Humility and Angelic Worship in Col 2:18', *ST* 16: 109–34.

———. 1967. 'Visionary Discipline and Scriptural Tradition at Colossae', *LTQ* 2: 71–81.

———. 1977. 'Christological Argument of Colossians', in J. Jervell and W. A. Meeks (eds), *God's Christ and His People* (Oslo: Universitetsforlaget) 192–208.

Francis, F. O., and W. A. Meeks (eds). 1973. *Conflict at Colossae: A Problem in the Interpretation of Early Christianity Illustrated by Selected Modern Studies*, Sources for Biblical Study 4 (Missoula, MT: Scholars Press).

Furnish, V. P. 1992. 'Colossians, Epistle to the', in *ABD* I, 1090–96.

Gamble, H. Y. 1995. *Books and Readers in the Early Church: A History of Early Christian Texts* (New Haven/London: Yale University Press).

Gardner, P. D. 1983. '"Circumcised in Baptism – Raised through Faith": A Note on Col 2:11–12', *WTJ* 45: 172–77.

Gatuma, K. wa. 2008. *The Pauline Concept of Supernatural Powers: A Reading from the African Worldview*, Paternoster Biblical Monographs (Milton Keynes: Paternoster).

Gaventa, B. R. 2008. 'Finding a Place for Children in the Letters of Paul', in M. Bunge, T. Fretheim, and B. R. Gaventa (eds), *The Child in the Bible* (Grand Rapids, MI: Eerdmans) 233–48.

Giem, P. 1981. '*Sabbaton* in Col 2:16', *AUSS* 19: 195–210.

Gillman, J. 1992a. 'Archippus', in *ABD* I, 368–69.

———. 1992b. 'Tychicus', in *ABD* VI, 682.

Glasson, T. F. 1967. 'Colossians 1:18, 15 and Sirach 24', *JBL* 86: 214–16.

———. 1969. 'Col. 1,18.15 and Sir 24', *NovT* 11: 154–56.

Goulder, M. D. 1995. 'Colossians and Barbelo', *NTS* 41: 601–19.

Grasser, E. 1967. 'Kol 3,1–4 als Beispiel einer Interpretation Secundum Homines Recipientes', *ZTK* 64: 139–68.

Green, G. L. 2008. *Jude & 2 Peter*, BECNT (Grand Rapids, MI: Baker).

Grenfell, B. P. and A. S. Hunt. 1906. *The Hibeh Papyri*, Part I (London: Egypt Exploration Fund).

Gunther, J. J. 1973. *St. Paul's Opponents and Their Background: A Study of Apocalyptic and Jewish Sectarian Teachings* (Leiden: Brill).

Gunton, C. 1996. 'Atonement and the Project of Creation: An Interpretation of Colossians 1:15–23', *Dialog* 35: 35–41.

Gupta, N. 2010. 'New Commentaries on Colossians: Survey of Approaches, Analysis of Trends, and the State of Research', *Themelios* 35.1: 7–14.

———. 2013a. 'Beholding the Word of Christ: A Theological Reading of Colossians', *Canadian Theological Review* 2.1: 21–43.

———. 2013b. 'What Is in a Name? The Hermeneutics of Authorship Analysis Concerning Colossians', *Currents in Biblical Research* 11: 196–217.

Hagner, D. A. 2012. *The New Testament: A Historical and Theological Introduction* (Grand Rapids, MI: Baker).

Hagnes, J. C. 2012. *Paul, Founder of Churches: A Study in Light of the Evidence for the Role of 'Founder-Figures' in the Hellenistic-Roman Period*, WUNT 292 (Tübingen: Mohr Siebeck).

Halter, H. 1977a. 'Kol 1,12–14: Errettet aus dem Machtbereich der Finsternis, Erlost im Lichreich des Sohnes', *FTS* 106: 183–90.

———. 1977b. 'Kol 2,6–23: Begraben und Ausferweckt mit Christus, Befreit von Sundentod und kosmichen Machten', *FTS* 106: 190–204.

Hamilton, W. J. 1837. 'Extracts from Notes Made on a Journey in Asia Minor in 1836', *JRGS* 7: 34–61.

Hanson, S. 1946. *The Unity of the Church in the New Testament: Colossians and Ephesians*, ASNU 14 (Uppsala: Almqvist & Wiksell).

Hanssler, B. 1973. 'Zu Satzkonstruktion und Aussage in Kol 2,23', in H. Felt and J. Nolte (eds), *Wort Gottes in der Zeit* (Düsseldorf: Patmos) 143–48.

Harrington, D. J. 1992. 'Christians and Jews in Colossians', in J. A. Overman and R. S. MacLennan (eds), *Diaspora Jews and Judaism* (Atlanta: Scholars Press) 153–61.

Harris, G. 2009. *Paul*, SCM Core Text (London: SCM).

Harrisville, R. A. 1977. 'God's Mercy – Tested, Promised, Done (An Exposition of Genesis 18:20–32; Luke 11:1–13; Colossians 2:6–15)', *Int* 31: 165–78.

Hartman, L. 1985. 'Universal Reconciliation (Col 1,20)', *SNTSU* 10: 109–21.

———. 1987. 'Code and Context: A Few Reflections on the Parenesis of Col 3:6–4:1', in G. F. Hawthorne (ed.), *Tradition and Interpretation in the New Testament* (Grand Rapids, MI: Eerdmans) 237–47.

———. 1995. 'Humble and Confident: On the So-Called Philosophers in Colossae', in D. Hellholm, H. Moxnes, and T. Karlsen (eds), *Mighty Minorities* (Oslo: Scandinavian University Press) 25–39.

————. 1997. 'Doing Things with the Words of Colossians', in *Text-Centered New Testament Studies: Text-Theoretical Essays on Early Jewish and Early Christian Literature* (Tübingen: Mohr Siebeck) 195–210.

Hatina, T. R. 1999. 'The Perfect Tense-Form in Colossians: Verbal Aspect, Temporality and the Challenge of Translation', in S. E. Porter and R. S. Hess (eds), *Translating the Bible: Problems and Prospects* (Sheffield: Sheffield Academic) 224–52.

Hay, D. M. 1973. *Glory at the Right Hand: Psalm 110 in Early Christianity*, SBLMS 18 (Nashville, TN: Abingdon).

Hayes, H. D. 1995. 'Colossians 2:6–19', *Int* 49: 285–88.

Hays, R. B. 1989. *Echoes of Scripture in the Letters of Paul* (New Haven/London: Yale University Press).

————. 2005. *The Conversion of the Imagination: Paul as Interpreter of Israel's Scriptures* (Grand Rapids, MI: Eerdmans).

Head, P. M. 2014. 'Tychicus and the Colossian Christians: A Reconsideration of the Text of Colossians 4:8', in P. Doble and J. Kloha (eds), *Texts and Traditions: Essays in Honour of J.K. Elliott* (Leiden: Brill) 303–15.

Helyer, L. R. 1983. 'Colossians 1:15–20: Pre-Pauline or Pauline?', *JETS* 26: 167–79.

————. 1988. 'Arius Revisited: The Firstborn over All Creation (Col 1:15)', *JETS* 31: 59–67.

————. 1994. 'Cosmic Christology and Col 1:15–20', *JETS* 37: 235–46.

Hengel, M. 1993. *Die johanneische Frage: Ein Lösungsversuch*, Mit einam Beitrag zur Apokalypse von Jörg Frey, WUNT 67 (Tübingen: Mohr Siebeck).

Hill, C. E. 2004. *The Johannine Corpus in the Early Church* (Oxford: Oxford University Press).

————. 2007. 'Papias of Hierapolis', in P. Foster (ed.), *The Writings of the Apostolic Fathers* (London/New York: T&T Clark International) 42–51.

————. 2010. '"The Orthodox Gospel": The Reception of John in the Great Church Prior to Irenaeus', in T. Rasimus (ed.), *The Legacy of John: Second Century Reception of the Fourth Gospel*, NovTSup 132 (Leiden: Brill) 582–629.

Hinson, E. G. 1973. 'Christian Household in Colossians 3:18–4:1', *RevExp* 70: 495–506.

Hockel, A. 1965. *Christus der Erstgeborene: Zur Geschichte der Exegese von Kol 1,15* (Düsseldorf: Patmos).

Hoehner, H. W. 2002. *Ephesians: An Exegetical Commentary* (Grand Rapids, MI: Baker).

———. 2006. 'Did Paul Write Galatians?', in Sang-Won (Aaron) Son (ed.), *History and Exegesis: New Testament Essays in Honor of Dr. E. Earle Ellis for His 80ᵗʰ Birthday* (London: T&T Clark International) 150–69.

Hofius, O. 2001. '"Erstgeborener voraller Schopfung" – "Erstegeborener aus den Toten": Erwagungen zu Struktur und Aussage des Christushymnus Kol 1,15–20', in F. Avemarie and H. Lichtenberger (eds), *Auferstehung-Resurrection: The Fourth Durham-Tübingen Research Symposium* (Tübingen: Mohr Siebeck) 185–203.

Hollenbach, B. 1979. 'Col 2:23: Which Things Lead to the Fulfilment of the Flesh', *NTS* 25: 254–61.

Holscher, A. 1998. 'Christus als Bild Cottes: Zum Hymnus des Kolosserbriefes', in A. Holscher and R. Kampling (eds), *Religiose Sprache und ihre Binder: Von der Bibel bis zur modernen Lyrik* (Berlin: Morus) 114–33.

Holtzmann, H. J. 1872. *Kritik der Epheser- und Kolosserbriefe auf Grund einer Analyse ihres Verwandtschaftsverhältnisse* (Leipzig: Wilhelm Engelmann).

Hooker, M. D. 1973. 'Were There False Teachers in Colossae?', in B. Lindars and S. S. Smalley (eds), *Christ and Spirit in the New Testament: Studies in Honour of Charles Francis Digby Moule* (Cambridge: Cambridge University Press) 315–31.

———. 2003. 'Where Is Wisdom to Be Found? Colossians 1.15–20 (1)', in D. F. Ford and G. Stanton (eds), *Reading Texts, Seeking Wisdom: Scripture and Theology* (Grand Rapids, MI: Eerdmans) 116–28.

Horsley, G. H. R. (ed.). 1983. *New Documents Illustrating Early Christianity: A Review of the Greek Inscriptions and Papyri published in 1978*, vol. 3 (Sydney: Macquarie University Press).

Hultgren, A. J. 2011. *Paul's Letter to the Romans: A Commentary* (Grand Rapids, MI: Eerdmans).

Hurtado, L. W. 2003. *Lord Jesus Christ: Devotion to Jesus in Earliest Christianity* (Grand Rapids, MI: Eerdmans).

Huttner, U. 2013. *Early Christians in the Lycus Valley*, Ancient Judaism and Early Christianity 85/Early Christianity in Asia Minor (Leiden: Brill).

Jewett, R. 2007. *Romans*, Hermeneia (Minneapolis: Fortress).

Jones, P. 1999. 'L'évangile pour l'âge du verseau: Colossiens 1:15–20', *RRef* 50: 13–23.

Joshel, S. R. 2010. *Slavery in the Roman World* (New York: Cambridge University Press).

Käsemann, E. 1933. *Leib und leib Christi: eine untersuchung zur paulinischen begrifflichkeit* (Tübingen: Mohr).

———. 1964. *Essays on New Testament Themes* (London: SCM).

Kennedy, H. A. A. 1904. *St. Paul's Conception of the Last Things* (London: Hodder & Stoughton).

———. 1913. *St. Paul and the Mystery-Religions* (London: Hodder & Stoughton).

Kiley, M. C. 1986. *Colossians as Pseudepigraphy*, The Biblical Seminar (Sheffield: JSOT).

Knight, G. W. 1991. 'Husbands and Wives as Analogues of Christ and the Church: Ephesians 5:21–33 and Colossians 3:18–19', in J. Piper and W. Grudem (eds), *Recovering Biblical Manhood and Womanhood: A Response to Evangelical Feminism* (Wheaton: Crossway) 165–78.

Knowles, M. P. 1996. '"Christ in You, the Hope of Glory": Discipleship in Colossians', in R. N. Longenecker (ed.), *Patterns of Discipleship in the New Testament* (Grand Rapids, MI: Eerdmans) 180–202.

Knox, J. 1959. *Philemon among the Letters of Paul: A New View of Its Place and Importance*, rev. ed. (Nashville, TN: Abingdon).

Kremer, J. 2001. 'Was an den Bedrangnissen des Christus Mangelt: Versucht einer Bibeltheologischen Neuinterpretation von Kol 1,24', *Bib* 83: 130–46.

Kümmel, W. G. 1966. *Introduction to the New Testament* (London: SCM).

Ladd, G. E. 1973. 'Paul's Friends in Colossians 4:7–16', *RevExp* 70: 507–14.

Lahnemann, J. 1971. *Der Kolosserbrief: Komposition, Situation und Argumentation*, SNT 3 (Gütersloh: Mohn).

Lamarche, P. 1975. 'Structure de l'epitre aux Colossiens', *Bib* 56: 453–63.

Lamp, J. S. 1998. 'Wisdom in Col 1:15–20: Contribution and Significance', *JETS* 41: 45–53.

Lampe, P. 1992. 'Onesimus', in *ABD* V, 21–22.

Lane, W. L. 1978. 'Creed and Theology: Reflections on Colossians', *JETS* 21: 213–20.

Langkammer, H. 1968. 'Die Einwohnung der "Absoluten Seinsfülle" in Christus Bemerkungen zu Kol 1,19', *BZ* 12: 258–63.

Leaney, R. 1952. 'Colossians 2:21–23 (the Use of *Pros*)', *ExpTim* 64: 92.

Legaré, C. 1993. 'La dimension pathémique dans l'épître aux Colossiens', in L. Panier (ed.), *Temps de la lecture: exègése biblique et semiotique: recueil d'hommages pour Jean Delorme*, LD 155 (Paris: Cerf) 215–27.

Leppä, O. 2003. *The Making of Colossians: A Study on the Formation and Purpose of a Deutero-Pauline Letter*, Publications of the Finnish Exegetical Society 86 (Göttingen: Vandenhoeck & Ruprecht).

Levick, B. 2013. 'In the Phrygian Mode: A Region Seen from Without', in P. Thonemann (ed.), *Roman Phrygia: Culture and Society*, Greek Culture in the Roman World (Cambridge: Cambridge University Press) 41–54.

Levison, J. R. 1989. '2 Apoc Bar 48:42–52:7 and the Apocalyptic Dimension of Colossians 3:1–6', *JBL* 108: 93–108.

Lewis, E. 1948. 'Paul and the Perverters of Christianity: Revelation through the Epistle to the Colossians', *Int* 2: 143–17.

Lincoln, A. T. 1990. *Ephesians*, WBC 42 (Dallas, TX: Word).

———. 1999. 'The Household Code and Wisdom Mode of Colossians', *JSNT* 74: 93–112.

Lincoln, A. T., and A. J. M. Wedderburn, 1993. *The Theology of the Later Pauline Letters*, New Testament Theology (Cambridge: Cambridge University Press).

Lindemann, A. 1981. 'Die Gemeinde von "Kolossä", Erwägungen zum "Sitz in Leben" eines psWederburneudopaulinischen Briefs', *WD* 16: 111–34.

Lofthouse, W. F. 1946. 'The Church Which Is His Body', *ExpTim* 57: 144–49.

Lohse, E. 1964. 'Christologie und Ethik im Kolosserbrief', *BZNW* 30: 156–68.

———. 1965. 'Christusherrschaft und Kirche im Kolosserbrief', *NTS* 11: 203–16.

———. 1970a. 'Die Mitarbeiter des Apostles Paulus im Kolosserbrief', in *Verborum Veritas: Festschrift für Gustav Stählin zum 70. Geburtstag* (Wuppertal: Theologischer Verlag Rolf Brockhaus) 189–94.

———. 1970b. 'Ein Hymnisches Bekenntnis in Kol 2,13–15', in *Melanges bibliques en homage au R. P. Beda Rigaux* (Gembloux: Duculot) 427–35.

Lona, H. E. 1984. *Die Eschatologie im Kolosser- und Epheserbreif*, FB 48 (Würzburg: Echter).

Lyonnet, S. 1962. 'L'épître aux Colossiens (Col 2:18) et les mystères d'apollon clarien', *Bib* 43: 417–35.

Macaskill, G. 2013. *Union with Christ in the New Testament* (Oxford: Oxford University Press).

MacDonald, M. Y. 1999. 'Citizens of Heaven and Earth: Asceticism and Social Integration in Colossians and Ephesians', in L. E. Vaage (ed.), *Asceticism and the New Testament* (New York: Routledge) 269–98.

———. 2007. 'Slavery, Sexuality and House Churches: A Reassessment of Col. 3.18–4.1 in Light of New Research on the Roman Family', *NTS* 53: 94–113.

———. 2008. 'A Place of Belonging: Perspectives on Children from Colossians and Ephesians', in M. Bunge, T. Fretheim, and B. R. Gaventa (eds), *The Child in the Bible* (Grand Rapids, MI: Eerdmans) 278–305.

Maier, H. O. 2011. 'Reading Colossians in the Ruins: Roman Imperial Iconography, Moral Transformation, and the Construction of Christian Identity in the Lycus Valley', in A. H. Cadwallader and M. Trainor (eds), *Colossae in Space and Time: Linking to an Ancient City*, NTOA 94 (Göttingen: Vandenhoeck & Ruprecht) 212–31.

———. 2013. *Picturing Paul in Empire: Imperial Image, Text and Persuasion in Colossians, Ephesians and the Pastoral Epistles* (London: Bloomsbury T&T Clark).

Malina, B. 1972. 'Does *Porneia* Mean Fornication?', *NovT* 14: 10–17.

Manns, F. 1979. 'Col 1:15–20: Midrash chrétien de Gen 1:1', *RevScRel* 53: 100–110.

Marshall, I. H. 1982. 'Luke', in J. D. Douglas (ed.), *New Bible Dictionary*, 2nd ed. (Leicester: IVP) 713–14.

———. 1999. *A Critical and Exegetical Commentary on the Pastoral Epistles*, ICC (Edinburgh: T. & T. Clark).

Martin, M. W., and B. A. Nash. 2015. 'Philippians 2:6–11 as Subversive *Hymnos*: A Study in the Light of Ancient Rhetorical Theory', *JTS* 66: 90–138.

Martin, R. P. 1964. 'An Early Christian Hymn (Col 1:15–20)', *EvQ* 36: 195–205.

———. 1974. 'Reconciliation and Forgiveness in Colossians', in R. Banks (ed.), *Reconciliation and Hope: New Testament Essays on Atonement and Eschatology* (Grand Rapids, MI: Eerdmans) 104–24.

———. 1981. *Reconciliation: A Study of Paul's Theology* (Atlanta: John Knox).

Martin, T. W. 1995. 'But Let Everyone Discern the Body of Christ (Colossians 2:17)', *JBL* 114: 249–55.

———. 1995. 'The Scythian Perspective in Col 3:11', *NovT* 37: 249–61.

———. 1996a. *By Philosophy and Empty Deceit: Colossians as Response to a Cynic Critique*, JSNTSup 118 (Sheffield: Sheffield Academic).

———. 1996b. 'Pagan and Judeo-Christian Time-Keeping Schemes in Gal 4.10 and Col 2.16', *NTS* 42: 105–19.

———. 1999. 'Scythian Perspective or Elusive Chiasm? A Reply to Douglas A. Campbell', *NovT* 41: 256–64.

Mayerhoff, E. T. 1838. *Der Brief an die Colosser, mit vornehmlicher Berücksictigung der drei Pastoralbriefe kritisch geprüft* (Berlin: Hermann Schultze).

McCown, W. 1979. 'The Hymnic Structure of Colossians 1:15–20', *EvQ* 51: 156–62.

Mealand, D. L. 1995. 'The Extent of the Pauline Corpus: A Multivariate Approach', *JSNT* 59: 61–92.

Meecham, H. G. 1955. 'Colossians 1:15', *ExpTim* 66: 124–25.

Meeks, W. A. 1977. 'In One Body: The Unity of Humankind in Colossians and Ephesians', in J. Jervell and W. A. Meeks (eds), *God's Christ and His People* (Oslo: Universitetsforlaget) 209–21.

———. 1993. '"To Walk Worthily of the Lord": Moral Formation in the Pauline School Exemplified by the Letter to Colossians', in E. Stump and T. P. Flint (eds), *Hermes and Athena: Biblical Exegesis and Philosophical Theology* (Notre Dame: University of Notre Dame Press) 37–58.

Merk, O. 1989. 'Erwägungen zu Kol 2,6f.', in H. Frankemölle and K. Kertelge (eds), *Vom Urchristentum zu Jesus: Fur Joachim Gnilka* (Freiburg: Herder) 407–16.

Merklein, H. 1981. 'Eph 4,1–5,20 als Rezeption von Kol 3,1–17: Zugleich ein Beitrag zur Problematik des Epheserbriefes', in P.-G. Muller and W. Stenger (eds), *Kontinuitat und Einheit: Festschrift für Franz Mussner* (Freiburg: Herder) 194–210.

———. 1981. 'Paulinische Theologie in der Rezeption des Kolosser und Epheserbriefes', in K. Kertelge (ed.), *Paulus in den neutestamentlichen Spatschriften* (Freiburg: Herder) 25–69.

———. 1997. 'Im Spannungsfeld von Protologie und Eschatologie: Zur kurzen Geschichte der aktiven Beteiligung von Frauen in paulinischen Gemeinden', in M. Evang, H. Merklein, and M. Wolter (eds), *Eschatologie und Schöpfung: Festschrift für Erich Gräßer zum siebzigsten Geburtstag* (Berlin: de Gruyter) 231–59.

Metzger, B. M. 1994. *A Textual Commentary on the Greek New Testament*, 2nd ed. (Stuttgart: Deutsche Bibelgesellschaft).

Mitchell, S. 1993. *Anatolia: Land, Men, and Gods in Asia Minor*, Vol. I, *The Celts and the Impact of Roman Rule*; Vol. II, *The Rise of the Church* (Oxford: Clarendon).

Mitton, C. L. 1951. *The Epistle to the Ephesians: Its Authorship, Origin and Purpose* (Oxford: Clarendon).

Morgan-Gillmann, F. 1992. 'Epaphras', in *ABD* II, 533.

Moir, I. A. 1979. 'Some Thoughts on Col. 2.17–18', *TZ* 35: 363.

Moritz, T. 2004. 'The Psalms in Ephesians and Colossians', in S. Moyise and M. J. J. Menken (eds.), *The Psalms in the New Testament* (London: T&T Clark International) 181–95.

Motyer, S. 1989. 'The Relationship between Paul's Gospel of "All One in Christ Jesus" (Galatians 3:28) and The "Household Codes"', *VE* 19: 33–48.

Moule, C. F. D. 1953. *An Idiom Book of New Testament Greek* (Cambridge: Cambridge University Press).

———. 1973. 'The New Life in Colossians 3:1–17', *RevExp* 70: 481–93.

Moule, H. C. G. 1898. *Colossian Studies: Lessons in Faith and Holiness from St. Paul's Epistles to the Colossians and Philemon* (New York: A. C. Armstrong & Son).

Mounce, W. D. 2000. *Pastoral Epistles*, WBC 46 (Nashville, TN: Nelson).

Muddiman, J. 2001. *The Epistle to the Ephesians*, BNTC (London: Continuum).

Mullins, T. Y. 1984. 'The Thanksgivings of Philemon and Colossians', *NTS* 30: 288–93.

Munderlein, G. 1962. 'Die Erwählung durch das *Plērōma* – Kol 1:19', *NTS* 8: 264–76.

Munro, W. 1972. 'Col 3:18–4:1 and Eph 5:21–6:9: Evidences of a Late Literary Stratum?', *NTS* 18: 434–47.

Murphy-O'Connor, J. 1995. 'Tradition and Redaction in Col 1:15–20', *RB* 102: 231–41.

Nash, H. S. 1899. '*Theiotes – Theotes*, Rom. i.20: Col. ii.9', *JBL* 18: 1–34.

Novenson, M. V. 2012. *Christ among the Messiahs: Christ Language in Paul and Messiah Language in Ancient Judaism* (New York: Oxford University Press).

O'Brien, P. T. 1974. 'Col 1:20 and the Reconciliation of All Things', *RTR* 33: 45–53.

———. 1987. 'The Church as a Heavenly and Eschatological Entity', in D. A. Carson (ed.), *The Church in the Bible and the World* (Exeter: Paternoster) 88–119.

———. 1992. 'Principalities and Powers: Opponents of the Church', *Evangelical Review of Theology* 16: 353–84.

Oke, C. C. 1952. 'A Hebraistic Construction in Colossians I.19–22', *ExpTim* 63: 155–56.

Olbricht, T. H. 1971. 'Colossians and Gnostic Theology', *ResQ* 14: 65–79.

———. 1996. 'The *Stoicheia* and the Rhetoric of Colossians: Then and Now', in S. E. Porter (ed.), *Rhetoric, Scripture and Theology: Essays from the 1994 Pretoria Conference* (Sheffield: Sheffield Academic) 308–28.

O'Neill, J. C. 1979. 'The Sources of the Christology in Colossians', *NTS* 26: 87–100.

Overfield, P. D. 1978. '*Plērōma*: A Study in Content and Context', *NTS* 25: 384–96.

Pearson, B. A. 2007. *Ancient Gnosticism: Traditions and Literature* (Minneapolis: Fortress).

Percy, E. 1946. *Die Probleme der Kolosser – und Epheserbriefe* (Lund: Gleerup).

———. 1951. 'Zu den Problemen des Kolosser-und Epheserbriefes', *ZNW* 43: 178–94.

Perriman, A. C. 1991. 'The Pattern of Christ's Sufferings: Colossians 1:24 and Philippians 3:10–11', *TynBul* 42: 62–79.

Peterson, J. 2001. '"The Circumcision of Christ": The Significance of Baptism in Colossians and the Churches of the Restoration', *RevQ* 43: 65–77.

Piper, O. A. 1949. 'Savior's Eternal Work: An Exegesis of Colossians 1.9–29', *Int* 3: 286–98.

Pöhlmann, W. 1973. 'Die hymnischen All-Prädikationen in Kol 1.15–20', *ZNW* 64: 439–50.

Polhill, J. B. 1973. 'Relationship between Ephesians and Colossians', *RevExp* 70: 439–50.

Pollard, T. E. 1981. 'Colossians 1.12–20, a Reconsideration', *NTS* 27: 572–75.

Porter, S. E. 1992. 'P.Oxy. 744.4 and Colossians 3.9', *Bib* 73: 565–67.

Porter, S. E., and K. D. Clark. 1997. 'Canonical-Critical Perspective and the Relationship of Colossians and Ephesians', *Bib* 78: 57–86.

Price, S. R. F. 1984. *Rituals and Power: The Roman Imperial Cult in Asia Minor* (New York: Cambridge University Press).

Punt, J. 2011. 'Eschatology in Colossians – "At Home in the World"', in J. G. van der Watt (ed.), *Eschatology of the New Testament and Some Related Documents*, WUNT 2/315 (Tübingen: Mohr Siebeck) 283–301.

Ramsay, W. M. 1883. 'The Cities and Bishoprics of Phrygia', *JHS* 4: 370–436.

———. 1890. *The Historical Geography of Asia Minor* (London: John Murray).

————. 1895–97. *Cities and Bishoprics of Phrygia*. Part I, *The Lycos Valley and South-Western Phrygia*; Part II, *West and West-Central Phrygia* (Oxford: Clarendon).

Reicke, B. I. 1952. 'Zum sprachlichen Verständnis von Kol 2.23', *ST* 6: 39–53.

————. 1973. 'Historical Setting of Colossians', *RevExp* 70: 429–38.

Reumann, J. H. P. 1990. 'Colossians 1.24 ("What Is Lacking in the Afflictions of Christ?"), History of Exegesis and Ecumenical Advance', *CurTM* 17: 454–61.

————. 1998. 'Jewish Mystical Experience in the Early Christian Era as Background to Understanding Colossians', *Neot* 32: 161–98.

Robertson, A. T. 1934. *A Grammar of the Greek New Testament in the Light of Historical Research*, 4th ed. (New York: Hodder & Stoughton).

Robinson, J. A. 1928. *St Paul's Epistle to the Ephesians*, 2nd ed. (London: Macmillan).

Robinson, J. M. 1957. 'A Formal Analysis of Colossians 1.15–20', *JBL* 76: 270–87.

Röhser, G. 2009. 'Der Schluss als Schlüssel: zu den Epistolaria des Kolosserbriefes', in P. Müller (ed.), *Kolosser-Studien*, Biblisch-Theologischer Studien 103 (Neukirchen-Vluyn: Neukirchener) 129–50.

Rollins, W. G. 1982. 'Christological *Tendenz* in Colossians 1.15–20: A *Theologia Crucis*', in R. F. Berkley and S. A. Edwards (eds), *Christological Perspectives: Essays in Honor of Harvey K. McArthur* (New York: Pilgrim) 123–38.

Ross, A. 1958. 'The Epistle to the Colossians and Its Message for Today', *EvQ* 30: 43–48.

Rowland, C. 1983. 'Apocalyptic Visions and the Exaltation of Christ in the Letter to the Colossians', *JSNT* 19: 73–83.

Royalty, R. M. 2002. 'Dwelling on Visions: On the Nature of the So-Called Colossians Heresy', *Bib* 83: 329–57.

Royse, J. R. 2008. *Scribal Habits in Early Greek New Testament Papyri*, NTTSD 36 (Leiden: Brill).

Rusam, D. 1992. 'Neue Belge zu den *stoiceia tou kosmou* (Gal 4,3.9, Kol 2,8.20)', *ZNW* 83: 119–25.

Sanders, E. P. 1966. 'Literary Dependence in Colossians', *JBL* 85: 28–45.

Sappington, T. J. 1991. *Revelation and Redemption at Colossae*, JSNTSup 53 (Sheffield: JSOT).

Scharlemann, M. H. 1965. 'The Scope of the Redemptive Task (Colossians 1.15–20)', *CTM* 36: 291–300.

Scheid, J. 2003. *An Introduction to Roman Religion* (Edinburgh: Edinburgh University Press).

Schenk, W. 1983. 'Christus, das Geheimnis der Welt, als dogmatisches und ethisches Grundprinzep des Kolosserbriefes', *EvT* 43: 138–55.

———. 1987. 'Der Kolosserbrief in der neueren Forschung (1945–1985)', in *ANRW* II 25,4: 3327–64.

Schottroff, L. 1997. 'Ist Allein in Christus Heil? Das Bekenntnis zu Christus und der Erlosung (Kol 1,15–120)', in D. Henze (ed.), *Antijudaismus in Neues Testament? Grundlagen für die Arbeit mit biblishen Texten* (Gütersloh: Kaiser) 79–89.

Schroeder, D. 1959. 'Die Haustafeln des neuen Testaments (ihre Herkunft und theologischer Sinn)' (unpublished dissertation; Hamburg: Mikrokopie).

Schweitzer, A. 1931. *The Mysticism of Paul the Apostle* (London: A. & C. Black).

Schweizer, E. 1961. 'Church as the Missionary Body of Christ', *NTS* 8: 1–11.

———. 1976a. 'Zur neueren Forschung am Kolosserbrief (seit 1970)', in J. Pfammatter and F. Furger (eds), *Theologische Berichte* V (Zurich: Benzinger) 163–91.

———. 1988. 'Slaves of the Elements and Worshipers of the Angels: Gal 4.3, 9 and Col 2.8, 18, 20', *JBL* 107: 455–68.

———. 1989. 'Askese nach Kol 1,24 oder 2,20f.', in H. Merklein (ed.), *Neues Testament und Ethik* (Freiburg: Herder) 340–48.

———. 1989. 'Altes und neues zu den "Elementen der Welt" in Kol 2,20; Gal 4,3–9', in K. Aland (ed.), *Wissenschaft und Kirche* (Bielefeld: Luther-Verlag) 111–18.

———. 1990. 'Colossians 1.15–20', *RevExp* 87: 97–104.

Scott, J. C. 1990. *Domination and the Arts of Resistance: Hidden Transcripts* (New Haven: Yale University Press).

Shogren, G. S. 1988. 'Presently Entering the Kingdom of Christ: The Background and Purpose of Col 1.12–14', *JETS* 31: 173–80.

Skarsauna, O. (2007). 'Jewish Believers in Jesus in Antiquity – Problems of Definition, Method, and Sources', in O. Skarsauna and R. Hvalvik (eds), *Jewish Believers in Jesus: The Early Centuries* (Peabody, MA: Hendrickson) 3–21.

Smith, I. K. 2006. *Heavenly Perspective: A Study of the Apostle Paul's Response to a Jewish Mystical Movement at Colossae*, LNTS 346 (London: T&T Clark International).

Spicq, C. 1994. *Theological Lexicon of the New Testament*, trans. and ed. J. D. Ernest, 3 vols. (Peabody, MA: Hendrickson).

Standhartinger, A. 1999. *Studien zur Entstehungsgeschichte und Intention des Kolosserbriefs*, NovTSup 94 (Leiden: Brill).

————. 2004. 'Colossians and the Pauline School', *NTS* 50: 572–93.

Standhartinger, A., and B. McNeil. 2000. 'The Origin and the Intention of the Household Code in the Letter to the Colossians', *JSNT* 79: 117–30.

Stanton, G. N. 2004. *Jesus and Gospel* (Cambridge: Cambridge University Press).

Stettler, C. 2000. *Der Koloosserhymnus: Untersuchungen zu Form, Traditionsgeschichtlichem Hintergrund und Aussage von Kol 1,15–20*, WUNT 131 (Tübingen: Mohr Siebeck).

Stettler, H. 2000. 'An Interpretation of Colossians 1.24 in the Framework of Paul's Mission Theology', in J. Ådna and H. Kvalbein (eds), *The Mission of the Early Church to Jews and Gentiles*, WUNT 127 (Tübingen: Mohr Siebeck) 185–208.

Still, T. 2004. 'Eschatology in Colossians: How Realized Is It?', *NTS* 50: 125–38.

Strecker, G. 1989. 'Die neutestamentlichen Haustafeln (Kol 3,18–4,1 und Eph 5,22–6,9)', in H. Merklein (ed.), *Neues Testament und Ethik* (Freiburg: Herder) 349–75.

Strelan, R. 2011. 'The Languages of the Lycus Valley', in A. H. Cadwallader and M. Trainor (eds), *Colossae in Space and Time: Linking to an Ancient City*, NTOA 94 (Göttingen: Vandenhoeck & Ruprecht) 77–103.

Strobel, A. 1968–69. 'Schreiben des Lukas? Zum sprachlichen Problem der Pastoralbriefe', *NTS* 15: 191–210.

Sumney, J. L. 1993. 'Those Who "Pass Judgment": The Identity of the Opponents in Colossians', *Bib* 74: 366–88.

Swart, G. J. 1999. 'Eschatological Vision or Exhortation to Visible Christian Conduct? Notes on the Interpretation of Colossians 3.4', *Neot* 33: 169–77.

Tellbe, M. 2009. *Christ-Believers in Ephesus: A Textual Analysis of Early Christin Identity Formation in a Local Perspective*, WUNT 242 (Tübingen: Mohr Siebeck).

Thiselton, A. C. 2000. *The First Epistle to the Corinthians*, NIGTC (Grand Rapids, MI: Eerdmans).

Thompson, G. H. P. 1960. 'Ephesians 3.13 and 2.10 in the Light of Colossians 1.24', *ExpTim* 71: 187–89.

Thompson, J. W. 2011. *Moral Formation according to Paul: The Context and Coherence of Pauline Ethics* (Grand Rapids, MI: Baker).

Thonemann, P. 2011. *The Maeander Valley: A Historical Geography from Antiquity to Byzantium*, Greek Culture in the Roman World (Cambridge: Cambridge University Press).

———. 2013. 'Phrygia: An Anarchist History, 950 BC–AD 100', in P. Thonemann (ed.), *Roman Phrygia: Culture and Society*, Greek Culture in the Roman World (Cambridge: Cambridge University Press) 1–40.

Thonemann, P. (ed.). 2013. *Roman Phrygia: Culture and Society*, Greek Culture in the Roman World (Cambridge: Cambridge University Press).

Thornton, T. G. C. 1989. 'Jewish New Moon Festivals Galatians 4.3–11 and Colossians 2.16', *JTS* 40: 97–100.

Tidball, D. J. 2011. *In Christ, In Colossae: Sociological Perspectives on Colossians* (Milton Keynes: Paternoster).

Tite, P. L. 2012. *The Apocryphal Epistle to the Laodiceans: An Epistolary and Rhetorical Analysis*, TENT 7 (Leiden: Brill).

Towner, P. H. 2006. *The Letters to Timothy and Titus*, NICNT (Grand Rapids, MI: Eerdmans).

Trainor, M., 2008. *Epaphras: Paul's Educator at Colossae*, Paul's Social Network: Brothers and Sisters in Faith (Collegeville, MN: Michael Glazier – Liturgical).

———. 2011. 'Excavating Epaphras of Colossae', in A. H. Cadwallader and M. Trainor (eds), *Colossae in Space and Time: Linking to an Ancient City*, NTOA 94 (Göttingen: Vandenhoeck & Ruprecht) 232–46.

Trebilco, P. 1991. *Jewish Communities in Asia Minor*, SNTSMS 69 (Cambridge: Cambridge University Press).

———. 2004. *The Early Christians in Ephesus from Paul to Ignatius*, WUNT 166 (Tübingen: Mohr Siebeck).

———. 2011. 'Christians in the Lycus Valley: The View from Ephesus and Western Asia Minor', in A. H. Cadwallader and M. Trainor (eds), *Colossae in Space and Time: Linking to an Ancient City*, NTOA 94 (Göttingen: Vandenhoeck & Ruprecht) 180–211.

Treggiari, S. 1996. 'Social Status and Social Legislation', in A. K. Bowman, E. Champlin, and A. Lintott (eds), *The Cambridge Ancient History*. Vol. X, *The Augustan Empire 43 B.C.–A.D. 69*, 2nd ed. (Cambridge: Cambridge University Press) 873–904.

Trudinger, L. P. 1973. 'Further Brief Note on Colossians 1:24', *EvQ* 45: 36–38.

Van Broeckhoven, H. 1997. 'The Social Profiles in the Colossian Debate', *JSNT* 66: 73–90.

van der Watt, J. G. (ed.). 2011. *Eschatology of the New Testament and Some Related Documents*, WUNT 2/315 (Tübingen: Mohr Siebeck).

Vawter, B. 1971. 'Colossians Hymn and the Principal of Redaction', *CBQ* 33: 62–81.

Wallace, D. B. 1996. *Greek Grammar: Beyond the Basics – An Exegetical Syntax of the New Testament* (Grand Rapids, MI: Zondervan).

Walsh, B. J., and S. C. Keesmaat. 2004. *Colossians Remixed: Subverting the Empire* (Downers Grove, IL: IVP).

Wansink, C. S. 1996. *Chained in Christ: The Experience and Rhetoric of Paul's Imprisonments*, JSNTSup 130 (Sheffield: Sheffield Academic).

Weidinger, K. (1928). *Die Haustafeln: Ein Stuck urchristlicher Paränese*, UNT 14 (Leipzig: Hinrichs).

Wessels, G. F. 1987. 'The Eschatology of Colossians and Ephesians', *Neot* 21: 183–202.

Williams, M. H. 2013. *Jews in a Graeco-Roman Environment*, WUNT 312 (Tübingen: Mohr Siebeck).

Wilson, S. G. 1979. *Luke and the Pastoral Epistle* (London: SPCK).

Wilson, W. T. 1997. *The Hope of Glory: Education and Exhortation in the Epistle to the Colossians*, NovTSup 88 (Leiden: Brill).

Wink, W. 1984. *Naming the Powers: The Language of Power in the New Testament* (Philadelphia: Fortress).

Wischmeyer, O. 2012. *Paul: Life, Setting, Work, Letters*, trans. Helen S. Heron with revisions by Dieter T. Roth (London: T&T Clark International; German orig., 2006).

Witherington, B., III. 1988. *Women in the Earliest Churches*, SNTSMS 59 (Cambridge: Cambridge University Press).

Woyke, J. 2008. 'Nochmals zu den "schwachen und unfähigen Elementen" (Gal 4:9): Paulus, Philo und die στοιχεῖα τοῦ κόσμου', *NTS* 54: 221–34.

Wright, N. T. 1990. 'Poetry and Theology in Colossians 1:15–20', *NTS* 36: 444–68.

Yamauchi, E. M. 1964. 'Qumran and Colossae', *BSac* 121: 141–52.

———. 1970. 'Note on Colossians 1:24', *EvQ* 42: 88–92.

———. 1985. '"The Worship of Angels" (Col 2.18)', *ExpTim* 97: 12–15.

———. 1986. 'Colossians and Gnosis', *JSNT* 27: 49–68.

———. 1990. 'Colossians 2:14: Metaphor of Forgiveness', *Bib* 71: 248–59.

———. 1991a. 'The Christian Way of Life: The Paraenetic Material in Colossians 3:1–4:6', *EvQ* 63: 241–51.

————. 1991b. 'Colossians '2:15: Christ Triumphant', *NTS* 37: 444–68.

————. 1996. 'From Christology to Soteriology', *ExpTim* 107: 268–70.

Yinger, K. 2003. 'Translating *Katabrabeueto* ["Disqualify", NRSV] in Colossians 2.18', *Bible Translator* 54: 138–45.

Zerwick, M., and M. Grosvenor (eds). 1993. *A Grammatical Analysis of the Greek New Testament*, 4th ed. (Rome: Pontifical Biblical Institute).

INDEX OF REFERENCES

INDEX OF REFERENCES

Colossians (cont.)

1:2 — 25, 27, 34, 38, 68, 81, 129, 132, 136, 138, 146, 149, 163, 164, 166, 345, 354, 408, 413, 448
1:3–27 — 58
1:3–23 — 153
1:3–14 — 152
1:3–8 — 68, 120, 134, 152, 153, 248
1:3–7 — 115
1:3 — 25, 27, 29, 30, 61, 91, 92, 127, 134, 135, 144, 146, 152, 163, 245, 382, 398, 401, 430
1:4–5 — 81, 446
1:4 — 29, 34, 81, 126, 127, 130, 138, 144, 145, 148, 151, 152, 166, 171, 182, 208, 224, 229, 235, 267, 346, 352, 377
1:5–13 — 115
1:5 — 27, 49, 50, 68, 81, 140, 142, 144–47, 209, 227, 309, 331, 360, 401

1:6 — 27, 54, 144, 145, 155, 159, 209, 229, 331, 408
1:7–8 — 62, 93, 138, 142, 148, 154
1:7 — 18, 49, 64, 84, 91, 93, 109, 126, 131, 147–49, 171, 243, 247, 377, 413, 428, 429, 434, 444
1:8 — 36, 88, 93, 110, 139, 150, 151, 171, 240, 352, 377
1:9–14 — 120, 152, 153
1:9–13 — 115
1:9–11 — 138
1:9–10 — 405
1:9 — 91, 92, 126, 135, 152–55, 159, 163, 228–30, 238, 302, 335, 360, 398, 404, 417, 430
1:10–12 — 116, 229
1:10 — 27, 31, 54, 82, 145, 155, 157, 162, 238, 245, 246, 321, 325, 335, 404

1:11 — 160, 161, 226, 229, 348
1:12–14 — 54, 153, 163
1:12–13 — 165
1:12 — 25, 27, 135, 152, 153, 162, 163, 165, 248, 337, 391, 399
1:13–14 — 153
1:13 — 24, 28, 34, 47, 54, 58, 68, 70, 106, 110, 132, 139, 145, 153, 164, 167, 168, 170, 171, 174, 177, 188, 189, 194, 196, 298, 319, 323, 327, 334, 336, 337, 352, 354, 356, 364, 369, 377, 390, 392, 427, 449
1:14 — 86, 87, 153, 171, 173, 216
1:15–20 — 31–33, 54, 69, 74, 109, 111, 120, 153, 163, 172, 174–76, 201, 338, 365, 405
1:15–18 — 179

488

INDEX OF AUTHORS

INDEX OF SUBJECTS

INDEX OF SUBJECTS